T0345080

THE COLLECTED WORKS OF

F. A. Hayek

VOLUME XVIII

ESSAYS ON LIBERALISM
AND THE ECONOMY

PLAN OF THE COLLECTED WORKS
Edited by Bruce Caldwell

THE COLLECTED WORKS OF

F. A. Hayek

VOLUME XVIII

ESSAYS ON LIBERALISM
AND THE ECONOMY

EDITED BY

PAUL LEWIS

The University of Chicago Press

The University of Chicago Press, Chicago 60637
The University of Chicago Press, Ltd., London
© 2022 by The Estate of F. A. Hayek
Published 2022
Printed in the United States of America

31 30 29 28 27 26 25 24 23 22   1 2 3 4 5

ISBN-13: 978-0-226-78133-4 (cloth)
ISBN-13: 978-0-226-78147-1 (e-book)
DOI: https://doi.org/10.7208/chicago/9780226781471.001.0001

Library of Congress Cataloging-in-Publication Data

Names: Hayek, Friedrich A. von (Friedrich August), 1899–1992, author. |
    Lewis, Paul, 1971– editor. | Hayek, Friedrich A. von (Friedrich
    August), 1899–1992. Works. 1989 ; v. 18.
Title: Essays on liberalism and the economy / by F.A. Hayek ; edited by
    Paul Lewis.
Description: Chicago : University of Chicago Press, 2022. | Series:
    Collected works of F. A. Hayek ; volume XVIII | Includes index.
Identifiers: LCCN 2021037138 | ISBN 9780226781334 (cloth) |
    ISBN 9780226781471 (ebook)
Subjects: LCSH: Economics. | Economic policy. | Liberalism.
Classification: LCC HB171 .H438 2022 | DDC 330—dc23
LC record available at https://lccn.loc.gov/2021037138

♾ This paper meets the requirements of ANSI/NISO Z39.48-1992
(Permanence of Paper).

THE COLLECTED WORKS OF F. A. HAYEK

Founding Editor: W. W. Bartley III
General Editor: Bruce Caldwell

Published with the support of

The Hoover Institution on War, Revolution and Peace
Stanford University

The Cato Institute

The Earhart Foundation

The Pierre F. and Enid Goodrich Foundation

The Heritage Foundation

The Morris Foundation, Little Rock

CONTENTS

EDITORIAL FOREWORD

This is the eighteenth volume of *The Collected Works of F. A. Hayek*. It assembles essays drawn from almost the entirety of Hayek's long career, the earliest appearing in 1931, the last in 1984. Many, though by no means all, of the chapters are taken from three earlier collections: *Individualism and Economic Order* (1948); *Studies in Philosophy, Politics and Economics* (1967); and *New Studies in Philosophy, Politics, Economics and the History of Ideas* (1978). However, while most of the chapters are already in the public domain, two have never been published before, whilst two others have not previously been published in English.

British spellings have been used throughout the volume. Typographical and minor grammatical errors have been silently corrected, as have minor inaccuracies in Hayek's quoting and referencing of others. Corrections to more significant errors are indicated by their being placed within square brackets. Each of the chapters is intended to stand alone, so the usual practice of providing a full reference to sources the first time they appear and abbreviated ones thereafter holds only within each chapter.

I have incurred many debts during the long period of time over which I worked on this volume. The greatest is to Bruce Caldwell, the General Editor of *The Collected Works of F. A. Hayek*, upon whose considerable reserves of knowledge, wisdom, and patience I have drawn liberally. Bruce's guidance on all aspects of the task of editing the material contained herein has been invaluable, as too were his comments on a draft of my Introduction. Jochen Runde also provided helpful comments on that Introduction, as did two anonymous referees. Ted Burczak read part of the Introduction and provided useful advice. I am grateful to all of the aforementioned for their help. I also gratefully acknowledge with thanks advice and assistance in dealing with particular queries received from Andrew Farrant, Pierre Garello, Christine Henderson, Karen Horn, Iain Hampsher-Monk, Ed McPhail, David Mitch, and Larry White. I am indebted to Karen Horn, Sheila Watts, and, in particular, Hansjoerg Klausinger for significant assistance with certain German passages. I am grateful also to Christine Henderson for assistance in checking some of the French passages that appear below. Needless to say, responsibility for any remaining errors and infelicities is mine alone.

It has been a pleasure to work with Alicia Sparrow, Chad Zimmerman, and Jenni Fry at the University of Chicago Press on the task of bringing the manuscript to press. Susan Tarcov was a meticulous copy-editor. I am grateful to them all for their assistance and professionalism.

The work involved in preparing this volume involved the use of several libraries and archives: the British Library; the British Library of Political and Economic Science; the Cambridge University Library; the Hoover Institution Library and Archives; the Marshall Library of Economics, Cambridge University; the David M. Rubenstein Rare Book and Manuscript Library, Duke University; the Library of Nuffield College, Oxford University; and the Ward Library, Peterhouse, Cambridge. I am thankful for the courtesy, expertise, and patience displayed by the librarians and archivists who work in all those institutions.

The organisations whose financial support has made possible the publication of *The Collected Works of F. A. Hayek* are listed at the beginning of this volume. On a more personal note, I should like to acknowledge that some of the early work for this project was done whilst I held a Visiting Fellowship at Peterhouse, Cambridge (fittingly, the College in one of whose buildings the London School of Economics was housed in its period of evacuation from London during World War II). I am very grateful to the Master and Fellows of Peterhouse for their support and hospitality. I was also fortunate enough to be awarded a place at the Third Annual Workshop on Political Economy, organised by the Hoover Institution Library and Archives, which afforded me an invaluable opportunity to consult the Hayek papers housed therein.

I would also like to thank the following institutions for permission to reproduce various essays and letters included in this volume: *Il Politico*; the Institute of Economic Affairs; the Institute of Public Affairs; J. P. Morgan Chase; the National Association of Manufacturers; the New Commonwealth Foundation; News UK, for *The Times*; the *University of Chicago Law Review* and the University of Chicago Law School; the University of Virginia Press; John Wily and Sons, for *Economica*; Routledge; and the Wincott Foundation. I gratefully acknowledge the permission of *The Times* to quote in footnote 28 of chapter 25 and footnote 47 of chapter 31 excerpts from articles that first appeared in its pages. Sincere thanks are also due to the Estates of Wynne Godley, Nicholas Kaldor, and Arthur Seldon for permission to quote from letters written by those individuals. I am grateful to Lord Tebbit for permission to quote from one of his letters to Hayek. Passages from letters written to Hayek by the then Prime Minister of the United Kingdom Margaret Thatcher are reproduced with permission from the estate of Lady Thatcher.

Last, but most certainly not least, I am grateful almost beyond words to my wife, Nadine, whose steadfast support was instrumental in work on this volume being brought to a successful conclusion.

Paul Lewis
London, May 2021

EDITOR'S INTRODUCTION
Paul Lewis

This volume of *The Collected Works of F. A. Hayek* contains material from almost the entire span of Hayek's career: the earliest piece was published in 1931; the last dates from 1984. The works were written for a wide variety of purposes and audiences, and include—in addition to conventional academic papers—encyclopaedia entries, after-dinner addresses, a lecture for graduate students, a book review, newspaper articles, and letters to the editors of national newspapers. While most are already in the public domain, two have never before appeared in print, while two others have not previously been published in English. The number of topics is large, encompassing the nature of, and prospects for, liberalism; the economic analysis of rent controls, planning and inflation; methodological issues in the social sciences; and a classical liberal perspective on key concepts in political philosophy (including justice, law and democracy).

The material is presented in roughly chronological order, with four notable exceptions. First, some essays in which Hayek reminisces about the history of the classical liberal movement come earlier in the volume than their date of publication might otherwise suggest, the better to fit with the narrative developed in this Introduction. Second, Hayek's early essay on rent controls is placed later in the volume than its original publication date of 1931 might indicate, so that it sits alongside other contributions where Hayek addresses questions of economic policy. Third, a series of letters to the editors of national newspapers spanning the years 1931–81, which Hayek hoped would be collected and published as a single volume, are brought together here as the final chapter of the book. Fourth, the collection opens with an essay on "Liberalism" from the mid-1970s, which provides a convenient summary of Hayek's views at that time on many important topics discussed in this volume. As such, it provides a useful guide to many of the essays that follow.

"Liberalism"

The essay on "Liberalism" was drafted by Hayek in 1973 and published in 1978, both in the Italian encyclopaedia for which it was commissioned and also in Hayek's *New Studies in Philosophy, Politics, Economics and the History of Ideas*.[1] Hayek's entry is divided into two main parts: the first provides a history of liberalism; the second offers a systematic account of the liberal conception of key ideas in political philosophy, including the notions of freedom, law, justice and equality.

For Hayek, what one might call 'true' liberalism took its modern form in the late seventeenth and early eighteenth centuries. Its chief value was individual freedom "in the sense of a protection by law against all arbitrary coercion" (p. 5).[2] A classic early formulation, oft-mentioned by Hayek, was provided by Locke in his *Second Treatise of Civil Government*. Locke argued that if government activity was limited by rules that were general, certain and equally applied to all, then the rule of law thus established would protect people from coercion and thereby create a realm of individual freedom in which they could act independent of the arbitrary will of others.[3] This liberal conception of freedom was further developed by Immanuel Kant who, as summarised by Hayek, argued that if a free person is one not subject to arbitrary coercion, then "for man living in society protection against such coercion required a restraint on all men, depriving them of the possibility of coercing others". On this view, which for Hayek expressed the fundamental principle of classical liberalism, the coercive activities of government should be limited to the enforcement of general rules, equally applicable to everyone. For Hayek, therefore, liberal constitutionalism required that the state be granted a monopoly over the power of coercion but then limited constitutionally in its use of that power to "that minimum which is necessary to prevent individuals or groups from arbitrarily coercing others" (p. 22).

While this liberal doctrine of limited government was first introduced in seventeenth-century Britain because of "sheer distrust of all arbitrary power", especially that exercised by the monarchy, the work of Adam Smith in particular subsequently "made people understand that those restrictions on the powers of government . . . had become the chief cause of Britain's economic prosperity" (p. 11). This was because where people act in accordance with a set of rules—in particular the laws of property, tort and contract—possessing the attributes of generality, certainty and impartiality, there will arise a self-generating or spontaneous market order in which their plans are mutually adjusted so as to maximise the chances of their being brought to a success-

---

[1] F. A. Hayek, "Liberalismo", in *Enciclopedia del Novecento*, vol. 3 (Rome: Istituto dell'Enciclopedia Italiana, 1978), pp. 982–93, and chapter 9 of F. A. Hayek, *New Studies in Philosophy, Politics, Economics and the History of Ideas* (London and Henley: Routledge & Kegan Paul, 1978).

[2] All otherwise unattributed page references refer to the essays found in the current volume.

[3] J. Locke, *Two Treatises of Government*, ed. P. Laslett (Cambridge: Cambridge University Press, 1960).

ful conclusion. And by affording people the opportunity to make effective use of their local knowledge—of people's desires, the availability of resources, and the available technologies—a regime of liberty under the law made possible the "utilisation of more knowledge of particular facts than would be possible under any system of central direction", thereby bringing about "as large an aggregate product of society as can be brought about by any known means" (pp. 25–26).[4]

In Hayek's opinion, the European country that came closest to realising the liberal vision during the long nineteenth century that ended with the advent of the First World War was Great Britain. As A. J. P. Taylor famously observed, "Until August 1914 a sensible, law-abiding Englishman could pass through life and hardly notice the existence of the state, beyond the post office and the policeman. He could live where he liked and as he liked".[5] Liberalism reached its zenith in the 1880s and 1890s, when it was the main governing principle of both the Liberal Party under Gladstone and the Conservative Party under Disraeli. Gladstone in particular "came to be widely regarded as the living embodiment of liberal principles" (p. 17). Towards the end of the nineteenth century, however, 'collectivist' ideas began to make inroads on the liberal state, first in piecemeal fashion as policies related to factory reform and public health were implemented to deal with the pressing social problems created by rapid industrialisation and urbanisation, then more systematically, as anti-liberal or—as Hayek would ultimately term them—constructivist rationalist ideas rose to prominence. In stark contrast to the liberal view that many of the institutions underpinning peaceful social cooperation and growing prosperity developed and operate spontaneously—that is, in the absence of a designing and directing mind—constructivist rationalism claims that all useful institutions are and should be the deliberate creation of conscious human reason.

Hayek attributed the rise of this tradition of thought to several factors. One was the work of John Stuart Mill. Whilst acknowledging the importance of Mill's "celebrated book *On Liberty*", Hayek argued that Mill "directed his criticism chiefly against the tyranny of opinion rather than the actions of government", going on to claim that Mill "by his advocacy of distributive justice and a general sympathetic attitude towards socialist aspirations in some

---

[4] Indeed, Hayek values freedom primarily on such instrumental or consequentialist grounds, arguing that "the case for individual freedom rests chiefly on the recognition of the inevitable ignorance of all of us concerning a great many of the factors on which the achievement of our ends and welfare depends". See F. A. Hayek, *The Constitution of Liberty*, ed. R. Hamowy, vol. 17 (2011) of *The Collected Works of F. A. Hayek* (Chicago: University of Chicago Press; London: Routledge), p. 80.

[5] A. J. P. Taylor, *English History: 1914–1945* (Oxford: Clarendon Press, 1965), p. 1.

of his other works, prepared the gradual transition of a large part of the liberal intellectuals to a moderate socialism" (p. 18).[6] A further impetus was provided by the work of the idealist philosopher Thomas Hill Green, who argued that genuine liberty required people to possess the power or capacity actually to carry out some worthwhile course of action, and also that the state had a role to play in affording people the means required to exercise such positive freedom. Significantly for what follows, Hayek observes that Green "stressed the positive functions of the state against the predominantly negative conception of liberty of the older liberals" (p. 18). Green's views helped to shape the thinking of the so-called 'new' liberals such as English sociologist and journalist Lionel Hobhouse, whose *Liberalism* was an attempt to synthesise the ideas of Green and Mill in support of government intervention designed to enhance people's positive freedom.[7]

The new liberals—along with Fabian socialists, who were also influenced by Mill's support for economic reform[8]—were devoted to providing intellectual justification for the extension of state power. At least partly under their influence, in the early twentieth century the Liberal government under Herbert Asquith introduced measures such as old-age pensions and unemployment and health insurance that "were only doubtfully compatible with the older liberal principles" (p. 19). This helped to usher in an age of 'New Liberalism' where the state accepted the responsibility to tax its citizens in order to pursue the collectivist goal of improving 'social welfare'. The tendency towards greater state intervention was further encouraged by that "grim harbinger" of collectivism, namely the First World War.[9] The success of Britain's war effort seemed to many to confirm the view that 'collectivism' was a more effective approach to the organisation of society than 'individualism'. The

---

[6] For more on Hayek's views on Mill, see B. Caldwell, "Hayek on Mill", *History of Political Economy*, vol. 40, 2008, pp. 689–704, and S. Peart, "Editor's Introduction", in F. A. Hayek, *Hayek on Mill: The Mill-Taylor Friendship and Related Writings*, ed. S. Peart, vol. 16 (2015) of *The Collected Works of F. A. Hayek*.

[7] T. H. Green, "Liberal Legislation and Freedom of Contract", in T. H. Green, *Works of Thomas Hill Green*, ed. R. L. Nettleship (London: Longmans, Green & Co., 1888), vol. 3, and L. T. Hobhouse, *Liberalism* (London: Williams and Norgate, 1911).

[8] As Hayek wrote elsewhere, Mill "probably led more intellectuals into socialism than any other single person: fabianism was in its beginnings essentially formed by a group of his followers". See F. A. Hayek, *The Fatal Conceit: The Errors of Socialism*, ed. W. W. Bartley III, vol. 1 (1988) of *The Collected Works of F. A. Hayek*, p. 149.

[9] The phrase is taken from C. Bouglé's "Preface to the Original Edition" of E. Halévy, *The Era of Tyrannies: Essays on Socialism and War* [1938], trans. R. K. Webb (London: Allen Lane, 1967), p. xix. The gradual rise of collectivism in Britain has been chronicled by several historians, notably A. V. Dicey, whose *Lectures on the Relationship between Law and Public Opinion in England during the Nineteenth Century*, 2nd edn. (London: Macmillan and Co., 1917) Hayek elsewhere describes as "[t]he classical description of the manner in which ideas at a long interval affect policy." See Hayek, *The Constitution of Liberty*, p. 179 n. 16.

upshot was that, as Hayek put it in another of the essays reproduced below, "At the end of the First World War the spiritual tradition of liberalism was all but dead . . . [T]he intellectual forces then at work had begun to point in quite a different direction . . . There was no longer, at that time, a living world of liberal thought which could have fired the imagination of the young" (pp. 42–43). The economic difficulties of the 1920s, culminating in the Great Depression, and the advent of Keynesian economics, only encouraged a shift towards collectivism that was already well under way.

Hayek argued that both the classical economists and, in particular, their nineteenth-century liberal successors had inadvertently contributed to this outcome. The key insight of the classical economists was that many of the institutions that had facilitated the development and preservation of modern industrial society had arisen, not through deliberate design, but rather as the unintended consequence of actions directed at quite different goals. Their main practical conclusion was a negative one, namely that there should be a presumption against government interference in the market. For the problem with all too many policies designed to alleviate the less appealing features of the free enterprise system was that they paid insufficient heed to the role played by those features in sustaining that system. As a result, such policies were likely to disrupt its operation so badly that they would in fact impede, rather than promote, the attainment of the goals their advocates sought to achieve.[10]

Valuable though that lesson was, Hayek believed that the classical economists—and, perhaps more significantly, their later nineteenth-century followers such as Spencer, Cobden and Bright—had over-emphasised it, leading to their adopting "a somewhat more extreme *laissez faire* position than would have been required by the liberal principles of Adam Smith and the classical economists following him" (p. 17).[11] In this way, over the course of the nineteenth century, British liberalism in particular became closely—and unnecessarily—identified with the view that government activity should be limited to the protection of life and property, the prosecution of fraud and the enforcement of contracts. As Hayek explained in his 1933 inaugural lecture as Tooke Professor of Economic Science and Statistics at the London School of Economics (LSE), nineteenth-century liberals paid insufficient attention to "the positive part of the economist's task, the delimitation of the field within which collective action is not only unobjectionable but actually a useful means

[10] See Hayek, "The Trend of Economic Thinking" [1933], reprinted as chapter 1 of F. A. Hayek, *The Trend of Economic Thinking: Essays on Political Economists and Economic History*, ed. W. W. Bartley III and S. Kresge, vol. 3 (1991) of *The Collected Works of F. A. Hayek*, pp. 19–20, 23–28, 31.

[11] For similar points, see L. Robbins, *The Theory of Economic Policy in English Classical Political Economy* (London: Macmillan & Co., 1952), pp. 55–61, 188–90.

of obtaining the desired ends . . . To remedy this deficiency must be one of the main tasks of the future".[12] What we see here are two related themes that will recur in several of the essays to follow: a belief in the power of ideas to shape public opinion, in particular about the appropriate boundaries of state intervention; and a concern that the supporters of liberalism had allowed themselves to be portrayed as advocates of a laissez-faire approach that confined itself to the negative task of criticising misguided forms of intervention and so left no scope for articulating a positive vision of legitimate collective action. The conclusion Hayek drew was that a revival of liberalism would require it to be rethought, with much more attention being devoted "to the positive task of delimiting the field of useful State activity".[13]

"The Transmission of the Ideals of Economic Freedom"

In "The Transmission of the Ideals of Economic Freedom", Hayek describes the scholars who in the 1920s and 1930s bore the burden of reviving the fortunes of liberalism. The essay was written in 1951 in honour of Ludwig von Mises, who had "been working since the early 'twenties on the reconstruction of a solid edifice of liberal thought in a more determined, systematic and successful way than anyone else" (p. 46). Mises had acquired a reputation as an uncompromising critic of socialism, not least owing to his seminal article on the impossibility of rational economic calculation under a socialist regime.[14] He was also Hayek's mentor; Hayek worked under his direction in an Austrian government office shortly after World War I and attended his private seminar in the 1920s and early 1930s. Hayek was part of the small group,

---

[12] Hayek, "The Trend of Economic Thinking", p. 31. Hayek continued to expound such views almost half a century later, for example in F. A. Hayek, "Liberalism" [1978], republished as chapter 1 of this volume, pp. 33–34.

[13] Hayek, "The Trend of Economic Thinking", p. 31. On the same page, Hayek refers to Jeremy Bentham's distinction between the 'agenda' and the 'non-agenda' of government, which had also been mentioned seven years earlier by Keynes in his widely-read essay on "The End of Laissez-Faire". In arguing that economists should pay greater heed to the 'agenda' or positive role of government, therefore, Hayek was indicating that—notwithstanding their many differences of opinion—he agreed with Keynes that "the chief task of economists at this hour is to distinguish afresh the *Agenda* of government from the *Non-Agenda*". See J. M. Keynes, "The End of Laissez-Faire" [1926], reprinted as chapter 2 of part IV of J. M. Keynes, *Essays in Persuasion*, vol. 9 (1972) of *The Collected Writings of John Maynard Keynes* (London: Macmillan for the Royal Economic Society), p. 288.

[14] L. von Mises, "Economic Calculation in the Socialist Commonwealth" [1920], in *Collectivist Economic Planning: Critical Studies on the Possibility of Socialism*, ed. F. A. Hayek (London: Routledge and Kegan Paul, 1935).

also including Fritz Machlup and Gottfried von Haberler, surrounding Mises who dedicated themselves to defending the liberal tradition upon which they believed Western civilisation depended.[15]

A second important bastion of liberalism was to be found at the LSE. In Hayek's opinion, it was the university's first professor of economics, Edwin Cannan, who "created the tradition which, more than anything else, determined the intellectual climate in the central department of the School".[16] Cannan was a notable student of classical liberalism and an applied economist whose support for the market is encapsulated by his remark that "Modern civilisation . . . is based on the principle of making things pleasant for those who please the market, and unpleasant for those who fail to do so, and whatever defects this principle may have, it is better than none".[17] Cannan's liberal approach carried over to his students who "later formed what probably became the most important centre of the new liberalism" (p. 43). The most significant was Lionel Robbins, who had graduated from the LSE in the early 1920s before returning in 1929 as Professor of Economics and Head of Department. Robbins, whose conversion to liberalism began under the influence of Cannan's teaching and received considerable impetus from his reading of Mises,[18] played an especially significant role in the continued development of the classical liberal tradition at the School. He not only brought the work of the Austrian School of Economics to the LSE but was also instrumental in Hayek's being invited to deliver a series of four lectures there early in 1931. The lectures were so well received that Hayek was offered a one-year visiting position, which subsequently become permanent with his appointment to the Tooke Chair in 1932.[19]

---

[15] For more detailed recollections, see F. A. Hayek, "The Economics of the 1920s as Seen from Vienna" [1963], pp. 23–32, and F. A. Hayek, "The Rediscovery of Freedom: Personal Recollections" [1983], pp. 185–86, published as the prologues to part 1 and part 2 respectively of F. A. Hayek, *The Fortunes of Liberalism: Essays on Austrian Economics and the Ideal of Freedom*, ed. P. Klein, vol. 4 (1992) of *The Collected Works of F. A. Hayek*. The importance of the Viennese context for understanding the sense in which Austrian economists saw themselves as seeking to analyse, and defend, the foundations of civilisation is discussed by E. Dekker, *The Viennese Students of Civilization* (Cambridge: Cambridge University Press, 2016).

[16] F. A. Hayek, "The London School of Economics 1895–1945", *Economica*, n.s., vol.13, 1946, pp. 1–31 at p. 6.

[17] The quotation is taken from E. Cannan, *An Economist's Protest* (London: P. S. King, 1927), pp. vi–vii. Hayek discusses Cannan at greater length on pp. 51–54 of F. A. Hayek, "The Economics of the 1930s as Seen from London" [1963], published as chapter 1 of F. A. Hayek, *Contra Keynes and Cambridge: Essays, Correspondence*, ed. B. Caldwell, vol. 9 (1995) of *The Collected Works of F. A. Hayek*.

[18] See L. Robbins, *Autobiography of an Economist* (London and Basingstoke: Macmillan, 1971), pp. 56–58, 83–85, 93–94, 106–9.

[19] The lectures were published as *Prices and Production* (1st edn., 1931; 2nd edn., 1935), now republished as pp. 167–283 of F. A. Hayek, *Business Cycles, Part I*, ed. H. Klausinger, vol. 7 (2012)

As Cannan's students—such as Robbins and Arnold Plant[20]—embarked upon their own academic careers, and especially after Hayek's arrival, the economists at the School acquired a reputation for offering a liberal alternative to the more interventionist doctrines being developed in the Cambridge of Pigou and Keynes. As Ronald Coase, who was a student at the LSE from 1929 until 1931, observed, "the effect of the teaching of Robbins, Hayek, and Plant was to make students look to private enterprise for solutions to economic problems".[21] It was for this reason that Hayek held Cannan to be one of the small handful of people through whose efforts "the main body of liberal thought has been safeguarded through that eclipse in the intellectual history of liberalism which lasted throughout the fifteen or twenty years following the First World War" (p. 43).

The third centre for liberal thought was located at the University of Chicago. The key figure was Frank Knight, whose courses afforded graduate students an acute appreciation of the importance of the price mechanism and spontaneous market order. As Hayek observed, "Knight's personal influence, through his teaching, exceeds even the influence of his writings. It is hardly an exaggeration to state that nearly all the younger American economists who really understand and advocate a competitive economic system have at one time been Knight's students" (pp. 48–49). The most important was Henry Calvert Simons, who in 1934 wrote a pamphlet defending liberalism entitled "A Positive Program for Laissez Faire". Simons argued, against the view that all government needed to do was remove impediments to free contracting, that the restoration of a liberal system required the state to play an active role in creating and enforcing a legal framework that would lead to the "[e]limination of private monopoly in all its forms". This reflected what Simons held to be "[t]he essence of . . . liberalism", namely a "distrust of all concentrations of power".[22] Simons' pamphlet was just the kind of work Hayek had called

---

of *The Collected Works of F. A. Hayek*. For more on Hayek's appointment, see B. Caldwell, "Introduction", in Hayek, *Contra Keynes and Cambridge*, pp. 19–21, and H. Klausinger, "Introduction", in Hayek, *Business Cycles, Part I*, pp. 11–12.

[20] Plant (1898–1978) graduated from the LSE with degrees both in Commerce (1922) and in Economics (1923), becoming Professor of Commerce and Head of the Department of Social Administration in 1930. He was an applied economist with an interest in industrial organisation, especially the significance of property rights.

[21] R. Coase, "Economics at the LSE in the 1930s: A Personal View" [1982], reprinted as chapter 15 of R. Coase, *Essays on Economics and Economists* (Chicago: University of Chicago Press, 1994), p. 214. For more detailed accounts of LSE economics in the 1930s, see Hayek, "The Economics of 1930s as Seen from London", and A. W. Coats, "The Distinctive LSE Ethos in the Interwar Years", *Atlantic Economic Journal*, vol. 10, 1982, pp. 18–30.

[22] H. Simons, "A Positive Program for Laissez Faire: Some Proposals for a Liberal Economic Policy" [1934], reprinted as chapter 2 of H. Simons, *Economic Policy for a Free Society* (Chicago:

for in his inaugural lecture, and Hayek wrote a warmly enthusiastic letter of appreciation after its publication in 1934.[23]

Similar views were held by the members of the fourth contingent upon whom Hayek believed the future of liberalism rested, namely the ordo-liberals. This group "came into being through the association of a number of younger men whose common interest in a liberal economic order brought them together during the years preceding Hitler's seizure of power" (p. 52). Its leading figures included economists Walter Eucken and Wilhelm Röpke, economist and politician Alfred Müller-Armack, sociologist and economist Alexander Rüstow, and jurists Hans Großmann-Doerth and Franz Böhm. They were united by their belief that a satisfactory understanding of a free society required an analysis of the system of rules governing economic activity, informed both by the discipline of law and also by economics. Like Simons, but in contrast to Mises, the ordo-liberals departed from nineteenth-century laissez-faire by arguing that the state needed to be strong enough to establish and enforce a legal framework that would promote competition, even in the face of the efforts of interest groups keen to secure special privileges—such as barriers to entry—that would enhance their market power. Underlying this divergence of opinion was the ordo-liberals' belief that spontaneous market activity could give rise to monopolies and cartels, endogenously as it were, whereas Mises contended that such temporary concentrations of power could persist only as a result of misguided government policies that limited competition.[24] It is because of such differences with classical liberalism that Hayek later described the ordo-liberals as adopting "a restrained liberalism" and as a "neo-liberal" movement or group.[25]

University of Chicago Press, 1948), p. 57, and H. Simons, "Some Reflections on Syndicalism" [1944], reprinted as chapter 6 of the same volume, p. 124.

[23] See F. A. Hayek to H. Simons, December 1, 1934, Henry Simons Papers, box 3, folder 40, University of Chicago.

[24] Eucken reportedly clashed with Mises over such issues at the 1949 meeting of the Mont Pèlerin Society, and those who, like Mises, remained committed to the principle of laissez-faire were said—by Alexander Rüstow—to be "paleo-liberals". See pp. 219–20 of V. Vanberg, "Markets and Regulation: On the Contrast between Free-Market Liberalism and Constitutional Liberalism", *Constitutional Political Economy*, vol. 10, 1999, pp. 219–43, and pp. 131–32 of H. M. Oliver, Jr., "German Neoliberalism", *Quarterly Journal of Economics*, vol. 74, 1960, pp. 117–49.

[25] F. A. Hayek, "The Rediscovery of Freedom", p. 190; F. A. Hayek, "The Transmission of the Ideals of Economic Freedom" [1951], reprinted as chapter 2 of this volume, p. 53; and Hayek, "Liberalism", p. 34. Hayek rarely used the term 'neo-liberal', and when he did so, it was often—as here—to refer specifically to the ordo-liberals. Also see F. A. Hayek, *The Political Order of a Free People*, vol. 3 (1979) of *Law, Legislation and Liberty* (Chicago: University of Chicago Press; London: Routledge, 1973–79), p. 83. He did, however, use the term in a broader sense, to denote a "new school of liberalism" that encompassed the advocates of liberal ideas at the LSE and Chicago as well as the ordo-liberals, in a short article published in the early 1950s, where

There were, then, a few remaining bastions of liberal thought in the 1930s.[26] But their members had only limited opportunities to interact with each other, so that "the few remaining liberals each went his own way in solitude and derision" (p. 53). In the mid-to-late 1930s, however, efforts began to bring them together with a view to reviving liberalism, an initiative that—as we shall see—culminated after the end of the Second World War with the foundation of the Mont Pèlerin Society. An important landmark in this process was the publication in 1937 by the influential American journalist, author and social commentator Walter Lippmann of his *Inquiry into the Principles of the Good Society*. Lippmann had been an early supporter of Roosevelt's New Deal, but by the mid-1930s his views had begun to shift. In particular, at least in part owing to his reading of Mises's and Hayek's work, Lippmann had become sceptical about claims that relief from poverty and economic disorder could be achieved through more state intervention. But he was also highly critical of the idea that freedom of contract alone was a sufficient foundation for liberalism. As he saw it, liberals needed to recognise that all economic activity is sustained by laws created by the state, after which they could "interest themselves in the question of whether this law was a good law, or of how it could be reformed or improved".[27] For Lippmann, therefore, liberalism was more than a negative and reactionary doctrine; it also had a positive aspect, centering on the actions of a state that would establish a legal framework that would eliminate monopoly and other types of power arising from the granting of legal privileges and then be strong enough to enforce those rules so as to ensure free competition.

---

he referred to those groups as "proponents of neo-liberalism" and as constituting "a neo-liberal movement". See F. A. Hayek, "A Rebirth of Liberalism". *The Freeman*, vol. 2, July 1952, 729–31, at pp. 729, 731.

[26] Hayek might also have added to his list the Graduate Institute for International Studies at the University of Geneva, where a group of liberals led by French economic historian Paul Mantoux (1877–1956) and Swiss economic historian and diplomat William Rappard (1883–1958) was gathered. It included Ludwig von Mises, who held a Chair of International Economic Relations at the Institute from 1934 until 1940, and Wilhelm Röpke, who joined the Institute in 1937. The Institute was also visited by several other liberals, with Robbins delivering a series of lectures there in 1935 and Hayek in 1937.

[27] W. Lippmann, *An Inquiry into the Principles of the Good Society* (London: George Allen & Unwin, 1937), p. 191. Lippmann's positive proposals are set out on pp. 203–40 and 265–81 of that work. Lippmann wrote at the outset of the book that he wanted to "acknowledge particularly the influence of . . . Professor Ludwig von Mises and Professor F. von Hayek, whose critique of planned economy has brought a new understanding of the whole problem of collectivism". See Lippmann, *The Good Society*, p. vii, and also pp. 94, 168–76. The current of influence ran in the other direction as well, with Hayek drawing on Lippmann's ideas about the importance of the rule of law in developing his own political philosophy. See B. Jackson, "Freedom, the Common Good, and the Rule of Law: Lippmann and Hayek on Economic Planning," *Journal of the History of Ideas*, vol. 73, 2012, pp. 47–68.

The Good Society was warmly, if not entirely uncritically, received by several of the beleaguered champions of liberal thought. Hayek wrote to Lippmann in 1937 expressing his enthusiasm for the book, remarking that he had "always regarded it as the fatal error of classical liberalism that it interpreted the rule that the state should only provide a semi-permanent framework most conducive to the efficient working of private institutions as meaning that the existing legal framework must be regarded as unalterable".[28] It seemed to both men that the generally favourable reception accorded *The Good Society* was indicative of a widespread willingness amongst the remaining liberals to re-examine the philosophical foundations of a free society. The book's publication therefore provided them with a pretext for encouraging the members of that small group to collaborate in their efforts to rethink the liberal approach. In the course of his correspondence with Lippmann, Hayek identified people who might contribute to this endeavour. His list included many of those mentioned in "The Transmission of the Ideals of Economic Freedom", including colleagues from London (such as Robbins and Plant), old friends from Vienna (in particular, Mises, Haberler and Machlup), Henry Simons from the USA, and groups centring on Luigi Einaudi in Italy, Walter Eucken in Germany, and William Rappard in Geneva. What Hayek was seeking to do was to bring together people who, although not agreeing about all the major issues, had enough in common to engage in fruitful discussion about how liberalism could be revitalised so as to provide a reasonably coherent opposition to collectivism.[29]

Hayek also put Lippmann in touch with the French liberal philosopher Louis Rougier, who had just been given the opportunity by La Librairie de Médicis, a new French publishing house, to edit a series of works in the liberal tradition. Rougier soon persuaded Lippmann to allow him to publish a French translation of *The Good Society*.[30] Upon learning that Lippmann would be visiting Paris, Rougier took the opportunity to organise a conference at which Lippmann's ideas would be discussed. The Colloque Lippmann, as it became known, was held in August 1938 and attended by twenty-six people, including academics, civil servants and industrialists. In addition to Rougier and Lippmann, participants included Hayek, Mises, Michael Polanyi, Wilhelm Röpke and Alexander Rüstow. Discussion focused on how to renew the foundations of liberal thought so as to win over the intellectual elites who governed the conduct of economic policy.[31] With the notable exception of Mises,

---

[28] F. A. Hayek to Walter Lippmann, August 11, 1937, Walter Lippmann Papers, box 66, folder 1011, Yale University.

[29] F. A. Hayek to Walter Lippmann, June 11, 1937, Walter Lippmann Papers, box 66, folder 1011.

[30] W. Lippmann, *La Cité libre*, trans. G. Blumberg (Paris: Librairie de Médicis, 1938).

[31] The proceedings of the colloquium were published as *Compte-rendu des séances du Colloque Walter Lippmann* (Paris: Librairie de Médicis, 1939). An English translation can be found in J. Rein-

who remained committed to laissez-faire, a majority of attendees agreed that liberalism should be differentiated from nineteenth-century Manchesterism. But there was much less agreement on where the line between warranted and unwarranted intervention should be drawn, and what the new version of liberalism ought to be called.[32]

After the colloquium, Rougier sought to create a forum where those unresolved issues might be considered further. Accordingly, in 1939 he established in Paris the Centre International d'Études pour la Rénovation du Libéralisme, in order to provide an institutional basis for further discussion. Though a conference was scheduled for 1939, the advent of the Second World War led to the suspension of work on the project. Nevertheless, the Colloque Lippmann had the important long-term consequence of enabling Hayek to make "many of the personal contacts which after the war were to form the basis of a renewed effort on an international scale" to promote liberal ideas, thereby providing "a very important foundation" for the creation of the Mont Pèlerin Society (p. 51 n. 15, p. 82).

"The Prospects of Freedom"

The background to the foundation of that Society is provided by Hayek's departure in April 1945 for the United States, where a five-week lecture tour had been arranged so that he could promote the recently published *Road to Serfdom*.[33] During his voyage across the Atlantic, an abridged version of the

---

houdt and S. Audier, *The Walter Lippmann Colloquium: The Birth of Neo-Liberalism* (Basingstoke: Palgrave Macmillan, 2018), pp. 93–188. A complete list of participants, along with biographical sketches, can be found on pp. 53–78 of that volume. The stenographers who were present at the colloquium recorded only those contributions made in French and German, not those made—as by Hayek—in English. Unfortunately, therefore, few of Hayek's remarks can be found in the published proceedings.

[32] It was suggested during the colloquium that the term 'neo-liberalism' should be used in order to distinguish the revised form of liberal thought sought by the participants from older forms of liberalism. There was not, however, agreement about its use. Others preferred phrases such as "neo-capitalism" or "positive liberalism", while Mises wished to retain the word 'liberalism' unmodified in any way. See *The Walter Lippmann Colloquium*, pp. 93, 101, 110–15, 121–25, 170. The Colloque Lippmann is often held to be the start of the 'neo-liberal' movement. For discussions, see A. Burgin, *The Great Persuasion: Reinventing Free Markets since the Depression* (Cambridge, MA: Harvard University Press, 2012), pp. 72–73; S. Kolev, "Paleo- and Neoliberals: Ludwig von Mises and the 'Ordo-interventionists'", in *Wilhelm Röepke (1899–1966): A Liberal Political Economist and Conservative Social Philosopher*, ed. P. Commun and S. Kolev (Cham: Springer, 2018), pp. 66–68; and J. Reinhoudt and S. Audier, "Introduction", in *The Walter Lippmann Colloquium*, pp. 3–5, 25–37.

[33] F. A. Hayek, *The Road to Serfdom: Text and Documents*, ed. B. Caldwell, vol. 2 (2007) of *The Collected Works of F. A. Hayek*.

book was published by *The Reader's Digest*. This led to considerable public interest, and Hayek's itinerary was changed to include an array of public lectures.[34] After one such event, Hayek was approached by Harold Luhnow, a Kansas City businessman and the President of the William Volker Charities Fund. After some discussion, Luhnow and Hayek agreed that the Fund would support a three-year, American-based study of the conditions necessary for a competitive economy.[35] In the course of planning this venture, Hayek sought—and received—funding for another journey to the United States, as part of which he would visit the University of Chicago, which was thought to be the most likely institutional home for the proposed study, and also Stanford University. Whilst at Stanford, he delivered a lecture on "The Prospects of Freedom". The text of that lecture, which has never before been published, is the third paper in this volume.[36]

Hayek began by observing that while the ascendency of collectivist ideas threatened to take society down the path to a totalitarian state, there was nothing inevitable about that development. Invoking Keynes's famous dictum about the power of ideas, Hayek argued that because people could be persuaded to revise their beliefs about the scope for planning, the trend towards collectivism could be reversed and the road to serfdom avoided.[37] As he stated in a clarion call addressed to his fellow liberals, "If we do not flinch at this task, if we do not throw up our hands in the face of overwhelming public opinion but work to shape and guide that opinion, our cause is by no means

[34] For details, see B. Caldwell, "Introduction", in Hayek, *The Road to Serfdom*, pp. 18–23, and Burgin, *The Great Persuasion*, pp. 87–94.

[35] Hayek arranged for the project, which would come to be known as the 'Free Market Study', to be based at the Law School at the University of Chicago and ultimately recruited American economist Aaron Director to lead it. See R. Van Horn and P. Mirowski, "The Rise of the Chicago School of Economics and the Birth of Neoliberalism", and R. Van Horn, "Reinventing Monopoly and the Role of Corporations: The Roots of Chicago Law and Economics", published as chapters 4 and 6 respectively of *The Road from Mont Pèlerin: The Making of the Neoliberal Thought Collective*, ed. P. Mirowski and D. Plehwe (Cambridge: Harvard University Press, 2009). Also see B. Caldwell, "The Chicago School, Hayek, and Neoliberalism", published as chapter 11 of *Building Chicago Economics: New Perspectives on the History of America's Most Powerful Economics Program*, ed. R. Van Horn, P. Mirowski, and T. Stapleford (Cambridge: Cambridge University Press, 2011).

[36] See, for example, F. A. Hayek to H. Luhnow, August 15, 1945, and January 23, 1946, and H. Luhnow to F. A. Hayek, September 7, 1945, and January 28, 1946, Hayek Papers, box 58, folder 16, Hoover Institution Archives (hereafter FAHP 58.16, and similar). Hayek recorded the words "Prospects of Freedom" as his diary entry for Tuesday 2nd July 1946, suggesting that was the date on which he delivered the lecture. See FAHP 122.4. The same phrase was used by Lippmann at the opening of chapter 13 of *The Good Society*.

[37] See J. M. Keynes, *The General Theory of Employment Interest and Money* [1936], reprinted as vol. 7 (1973) of *The Collected Writings of John Maynard Keynes* (London: Macmillan for the Royal Economic Society), pp. 383–84.

hopeless" (p. 73). For Hayek, therefore, it was imperative that a concerted attempt be made to re-examine the basic tenets of liberalism. The new philosophy of freedom had to afford liberals a vision of the future society at which they were aiming and a set of general principles to guide decisions on particular issues, thereby enabling them to offer a genuine alternative to collectivism. This would help to ensure that liberalism was once again a "living and developing philosophy which will enlist the sympathy and support of the young and enthusiastic" (p. 59).

Hayek believed that the revival of liberalism would be catalysed by the creation of an organisation that would enable committed liberals to come together to debate key issues, learn from one another and coordinate their efforts. "The organisation which seems to be needed is something half-way between a scholarly association and a political society":

> It would differ from a purely scientific group in that its members would be held together by a basic agreement on the aims for which they are seeking the means. And it would differ from any political organisation in that it would not be concerned with short run policies . . . but with the general principles of a liberal order. And it would have a double task: it would not only have to study and discuss the many questions of what would be the best framework in which a free system would work efficiently and beneficially; it would also have to interpret and apply these general principles by the discussion of recent history and contemporary events. (pp. 63–64)

The tradition that this group would seek to revive had, in Hayek's view, received its most satisfactory statement hitherto in the writings of British historian and moralist Lord Acton and French historian and political scientist Alexis de Tocqueville. Accordingly, Hayek suggested that the organisation be named "the Acton-de Tocqueville Society" (p. 72).[38]

"The Webbs and Their Work"

In his Stanford lecture, Hayek acknowledged that changing the climate of opinion would take a good deal of time, probably at least a generation. Those striving to revive liberalism should therefore focus on the long-term rather than the short-run effects of their efforts. In particular, they needed to display the "courage to be 'utopian'" (p. 57). The reason, as Hayek explained else-

---

[38] Hayek had first made a public case for such a society in a paper read to the Political Society at King's College, Cambridge, in February 1944. See F. A. Hayek, "Historians and the Future of Europe" [1944], reprinted as chapter 8 of Hayek, *The Fortunes of Liberalism*.

where, was that the willingness of socialists to describe their ideal society lent their programme an appeal denied the more grounded, detail-oriented liberal offerings of the first half of the twentieth century. Only if liberals also engaged in similar long-run speculation would they too be able to inspire the support and loyalty of the public and thereby shift the climate of opinion in favour of a free society.[39] Such an approach had hitherto been the preserve of socialist thinkers, whose willingness to play the long game was in Hayek's eyes one of the principal reasons for their success in shaping people's views. The socialists' approach was exemplified for Hayek by Beatrice and Sidney Webb.

In 1948, Hayek reviewed the second volume of Beatrice Webb's memoirs.[40] The most vivid impression left upon Hayek was of the Webbs' appreciation of "the decisive position which the intellectuals occupy in shaping public opinion" (p. 74). Hayek defined 'intellectuals' as "professional secondhand dealers in ideas".[41] Their ranks included journalists, writers, government ministers, lecturers and scientists, in short—Hayek contended—a majority of those from whom ordinary people learn about what is politically feasible and desirable. Hayek portrays the Webbs as past masters at the art of exercising behind-the-scenes intellectual leadership in order to persuade such individuals of the merits of collectivism, with a view to exploiting their pivotal role in the shaping of public opinion so as to advance the cause of progressive politics. Their strategy afforded liberals a "unique lesson" (p. 74), centring on the importance of developing a general philosophy of freedom that would convert the intellectuals and ultimately the public at large to an individualistic worldview, from which policy applications would follow only later. In advocating such a strategy, Hayek adopted what might be described as a Fabian approach to the production of ideological change.

"Closing Speech to the 1984 Mont Pèlerin Society Meeting"

Hayek recounts how he gave practical effect to his plan for an international society devoted to the revival of liberalism in a text originally delivered as the closing speech at a regional meeting of the Mont Pèlerin Society, held in Paris in 1984. Hayek explains in particular how he obtained the funding that facilitated the initial meeting. In 1945, as the Second World War drew to a close, Wilhelm Röpke sought to create a journal that would promote liberal

---

[39] F. A. Hayek, "The Intellectuals and Socialism" [1949], reprinted as chapter 11 of F. A. Hayek, *Socialism and War: Essays, Documents, Reviews*, ed. B. Caldwell, vol. 10 (1997) of *The Collected Works of F. A. Hayek*, pp. 232–37.

[40] B. Webb, *Our Partnership*, ed. B. Drake and M. Cole (London: Longmans, Green, and Co. 1948).

[41] Hayek, "The Intellectuals and Socialism," p. 221.

ideas. By the summer of 1946, he had secured financial support from a consortium of industrialists led by Swiss businessman Albert Hunold. However, Röpke and Hunold disagreed over who would control the journal, so that by that summer their project had faltered and was abandoned. But the money raised remained available and, following a chance meeting with Hunold, Hayek was able by autumn of the same year to secure the funds for the purpose of supporting an international gathering of those committed to restoring the fortunes of liberalism.

Hayek arranged for a meeting to be held April 1–10, 1947, at the Hotel du Parc on Mont Pèlerin sur Vevey in Switzerland. Of those invited, thirty-nine were able to attend. A majority were academics, most of them economists.[42] What united them was a conviction that Western civilisation was under threat from growing state power and increasing intervention. They believed that the root cause of this crisis lay in mistaken ideas about society—it was ideas, they thought, that ultimately determined how society was understood and organised—so that a concerted effort to revive liberal thought was required in order to turn the tide of opinion and safeguard the foundations of a free society. As Hayek put it in "The Prospects of Freedom", the defeat of collectivism required not only "destructive criticism" of socialist ideas but also the provision of "a real alternative to the current beliefs" (p. 61).

Hayek delivered his opening address to the conference on April 1, 1947. Re-iterating the need to differentiate liberalism from laissez-faire, he argued that it was imperative that liberals "re-examine their own convictions" and avoid the mistake of taking the "accidental historical form of a liberal society which they have known as the ultimate standard". He then considered the topics to be discussed, the "most important" of which was "the relation between what is called 'free enterprise' and a really competitive order". Hayek proposed that the whole of the first afternoon and evening of the conference should be devoted to that topic, opening the discussion himself.[43]

---

[42] A full list of attendees can be found on pp. 45–46 of R. Hartwell, *A History of the Mont Pelerin Society* (Indianapolis: Liberty Fund, 1995). The presence of a small number of academics from the disciplines of law, history, political science and philosophy reflected Hayek's belief that the task of reviving liberalism required input from several disciplines, of which economics was but one. As Hayek put it in 1983, "The intention was—and remains my goal even today, although it has not been entirely fulfilled—to have a group consisting not only of pure economists but also social philosophers, jurists, and especially historians". See Hayek, "The Rediscovery of Freedom", p. 192. One person who was conspicuous by his absence from this initial meeting was Walter Lippmann who, perhaps surprisingly given his earlier involvement in efforts to revive the liberal tradition, appeared to distance himself from Hayek after World War Two. See Burgin, *The Great Persuasion*, pp. 85–86.

[43] The quotations in this paragraph are taken from pp. 238 and 242 of F. A. Hayek, "Opening Address to a Conference at Mont Pèlerin" [1947], reprinted as chapter 12 of *The Fortunes of Liberalism*. A complete list of the sessions for this first meeting can be found on pp. 47–49 of Hartwell, *A History of the Mont Pelerin Society*.

"'Free' Enterprise and Competitive Order"

The title of the paper Hayek read that afternoon, "'Free' Enterprise and Competitive Order", was intended to highlight one of the main questions liberals needed to address, namely whether "competition can be made more effective and more beneficent by certain activities of government than it would be without them" (p. 93). Hayek answered in the affirmative, arguing that "the most fatal tactical mistake" of nineteenth-century liberals was to have portrayed the fundamental principle of liberalism "as absence of state activity rather than as a policy which deliberately adopts competition, the market, and prices as its ordering principle and uses the legal framework enforced by the state in order to make competition as effective and beneficial as possible" (pp. 92–93). More specifically, he contended that "[w]e cannot regard 'freedom of contract' as a real answer to our problems if we know that not all contracts ought to be made enforceable and in fact are bound to argue that contracts 'in restraint of trade' ought not to be enforced" (p. 97). He also suggested that there was a pressing need to reform corporate law and the law of patents, both of which in their current form had he believed fostered monopoly power.[44] The need for government action to ensure effective competition also applied to trade unions. Hayek lamented how from the early twentieth century liberals had been complicit in granting unions exemptions from many laws, as for example in Britain where the 1906 Trades Disputes Act had afforded them immunity from liability for damages arising from strike action. The result had been "to all intents and purposes, to legalise violence, coercion, and intimidation" (p. 99).[45]

The meeting at Mont Pèlerin included an opportunity for conferees to consider whether a permanent organisation should be established.[46] This session took place on the afternoon of April 4, when it was decided that a society should indeed be created. Its principal goal was to "contribute to the preservation and improvement of the free society", which it would do by reasserting and exploring through further study certain "valid ideals" concerning the functions of the state in the liberal order, ways of re-establishing the rule of law, and the possibility of sustaining a minimum standard of living without hampering the working of the market.[47] Hayek's view that the organisation should be called the Acton-Tocqueville Society was rejected in favour of nam-

---

[44] Also see Hayek, *The Road to Serfdom*, pp. 71–73, 85–90.

[45] Also see Dicey, *Lectures on the Relation between Law and Public Opinion in England during the Nineteenth Century*, pp. xliv–xlviii, and Hayek, *The Constitution of Liberty*, pp. 384–86.

[46] On what follows, see Hartwell, *A History of the Mont Pèlerin Society*, pp. 40–45, and R. Cockett, *Thinking the Unthinkable: Think-tanks and the Economic Counter-revolution, 1931–1983* (London: Fontana Press, 1994), pp. 115–17.

[47] See the "Statement of Aims of the Mont Pèlerin Society", reproduced on pp. 41–42 of Hartwell, *A History of the Mont Pèlerin Society*.

ing it after the location at which they were meeting. 'The Mont Pèlerin Society' was born.[48]

"The Economic Conditions of Inter-state Federalism"

While in his opening address to the 1947 conference Hayek stated that the relation between 'free enterprise' and a competitive order was the most important topic to be considered, he also suggested two further subjects for discussion. These involved "questions of the practical application of our principles to the problems of our time rather than questions of the principles themselves" and centred in particular on "the problem of the future of Germany, and that of the possibilities and prospects of a European federation".[49] Both were topics on which Hayek had written for some years. In chapter 15 of *The Road to Serfdom*, where Hayek considered the prospects for the emergence of an international order after the end of the Second World War, he argued in favour of the creation of an inter-state federation, defined as "[t]he form of international government under which certain strictly defined powers are transferred to an international authority, while in all other respects the individual countries remain responsible for their internal affairs". The organisation would enforce a set of rules governing states' actions, designed to reduce conflict by preventing a country from pursuing policies that would advance its own immediate interests but only by harming other nations.[50]

In the course of his account, Hayek refers the reader to one of his earlier papers as a source of additional details about why federalism would restrict the scope for government intervention and thereby advance the cause of peace.[51] The paper was entitled "The Economic Conditions of Inter-state Federalism". It was originally published in September 1939 as part of an issue of the journal *The New Commonwealth Quarterly* dedicated to the topic of 'Federalism and World Order'.[52] Hayek argues that a sustainable federal system required

[48] Critics of Hayek's preferred name variously argued that neither Acton nor Tocqueville took a stance on economic issues; that it was inappropriate for a liberal society to be named after two Catholics; and that the organisation should be named after principles rather than people. See "Proceedings of the 1947 Mont Pelerin Conference", Mont Pèlerin Society Records, Hoover Institution Archives, box 140, folder 6, pp. 243–45.

[49] Hayek, "Opening Address", p. 244.

[50] Hayek, *The Road to Serfdom*, p. 232. Hayek made similar claims about the importance of federalism for securing peace in the post-war world both in his 1944 essay on "Historians and the Future of Europe", pp. 213–14, and also in a 1945 essay on "A Plan for the Future of Germany", reprinted as chapter 11 of *The Fortunes of Liberalism*, pp. 224–27.

[51] Hayek, *The Road to Serfdom*, p. 233 n. 11.

[52] This was an extremely topical issue in the late 1930s, and both Hayek and Robbins were amongst those arguing for the creation of a European federation as the basis for interna-

both political union (in the form of common foreign and defence policies) and economic union (involving the adoption of liberal policies). For Hayek, maintaining the internal coherence of the political union would require free movement of goods, labour and capital, because trade barriers would produce a solidarity of interests amongst the inhabitants of any one state, and a conflict between their interests and those of the citizens of other countries, that would soon undermine the union's stability.

The free movement of goods, labour and capital would also make it difficult for member nations to implement many kinds of interventionist policy. It would impede the efforts of any one state to assist particular industries through policies designed to raise the prices received by domestic firms, while the scope for one nation to pursue a distinctive tax policy would be circumscribed by the prospect of mobile factors of production going elsewhere in the union. Hayek argued, moreover, that the interventionist policies rendered infeasible for individual member states would not necessarily be re-introduced at the federal level. He advances two reasons for this conclusion, taking the case of a tariff on imports into the federation as an example. First, it might well be the case that most of the competitors against whom protection was sought were themselves located in member states, in which case there would be little reason for producers to demand an external tariff. Second, the inhabitants of any single member nation would be reluctant to sacrifice their welfare to benefit industries located elsewhere in the federation. "Is it likely that the French peasant will be willing to pay more for his fertilizer to help the British chemical industry?", Hayek (p. 108) asked. "Will the Swedish workman be ready to pay more for his oranges to assist the Californian grower?" Hayek answered in the negative, concluding that because the policy-makers would be denied the opportunity to appeal either to a strong nationalist ideology or to people's sympathy with their fellow countrymen, "[i]t is difficult to visualise how, in a federation, agreement could be reached on the use of tariffs for the protection of particular industries" (p. 108).

For Hayek, therefore, federation inhibits the formation of interest groups that would favour interventionism in general and protectionism in partic-

tional order. See, for example, F. A. Hayek, "An Anglo-French Federation" [1939], reprinted as pp. 162–64 of Hayek, *Socialism and War*, and L. Robbins, *Economic Planning and International Order* (London: Macmillan and Co., 1937). Robbins and Hayek were members of Federal Union, an organisation advocating federalism established in November 1938 that had 12,000 members and 225 branches by June 1940. They also joined the organising committee of the short-lived 'Federal Union Research Institute' that had been established in the aftermath of a conference convened in Oxford in 1939 by Sir William Beveridge. See S. Howson, *Lionel Robbins* (Cambridge: Cambridge University Press, 2011), pp. 345–52, and O. Rosenboim, *The Emergence of Globalism: Visions of World Order in Britain and the United States, 1939–1950* (Princeton: Princeton University Press, 2017), pp. 100–107, 157–65.

ular. The upshot is that "certain economic powers, which are now generally wielded by the national states, could be exercised neither by the federation nor by the individual states" so that "there would have to be less government all round" (p. 111). Interstate federation is therefore "the consistent development of the liberal point of view", with "the abrogation of national sovereignties and the creation of an effective international order of law" it entails being "the logical consummation of the liberal programme". Recognising this should make it possible to disentangle true liberalism from the nationalism with which nineteenth-century liberals had mistakenly joined forces, thereby leading to a "rebirth of real liberalism, true to its ideal of freedom and internationalism" (pp. 114–15).[53]

"The Meaning of Government Interference"

Hayek elaborated on another of the issues raised in "'Free' Enterprise and Competitive Order", namely the appropriate role of the state in economic life, in a later, hitherto unpublished essay on "The Meaning of Government Interference". The essay, which dates from 1950, addresses the oft-heard complaint made after the publication of *The Road to Serfdom* that Hayek had failed to provide a clear set of principles for identifying legitimate forms of government action. For example, while Keynes wrote that it was a "grand book" with which "morally and philosophically I find myself in agreement", he also criticised Hayek for failing to offer a criterion for differentiating acceptable from unacceptable kinds of government activity: "You admit here and there that it is a question of knowing where to draw the line. You agree that the line has to be drawn somewhere, and that the logical extreme is not possible. But you give us no guidance whatever as to where to draw it".[54] Hayek responded by setting out in this essay what he thought was a clear criterion by reference to which such judgements could be made.

The criterion was provided by "the old principle of *equality before the law*",

---

[53] Hayek discusses the relation between liberalism and nationalism in several works written in the 1940s, including "Historians and the Future of Europe," pp. 213–14, *The Road to Serfdom*, pp. 233–34, and F. A. Hayek, "The Prospects of Freedom", [1946], published as chapter 3 of this volume, pp. 67–68. His emphasis on the intimate connections between liberalism and internationalism is, along with his focus on the epistemic role of institutions, one of the distinguishing features of his version of liberal political philosophy. See C. Kukathas, "Hayek and Liberalism", in *The Cambridge Companion to Hayek*, ed. E. Feser (Cambridge: Cambridge University Press, 2006).

[54] John Maynard Keynes to F. A. Hayek, June 28, 1944, published in J. M. Keynes, *Activities 1940–1946: Shaping the Postwar World, Employment and Commodities*, vol. 27 (1980) of *The Collected Writings of John Maynard Keynes* (London: Macmillan for the Royal Economic Society), pp. 385–88, at pp. 385, 386.

which required that government activities should take place in accordance with rules possessing particular attributes: they should be *certain* in the sense of being "fixed rules announced in advance" of the activities they are to govern; they should be "abstract" in that the conditions in which they apply should be expressed in terms of the typical features of situations rather than in terms of particular, concrete circumstances; and they should be *equal*, which is to say that they "must be observed irrespective of whether in the particular instance their infringement is harmful or not". The enforcement of rules satisfying those criteria would "eliminate a great deal of those activities which the believer in a free economy thinks objectionable" (pp. 119–21). In particular, centralised state direction of economic activity would be prohibited, because it would require the government to discriminate between people—in terms of what they were allowed or obliged to do—in ways ruled out by such rules.[55]

A regime of this kind would promote liberty by securing for individuals a sphere of autonomous decision-making, free from arbitrary government interference, within which they could pursue their own goals.[56] Furthermore, by requiring both private citizens and the state to observe known rules, it would also help to ensure that people could predict the behaviour of other actors well enough to be able to formulate plans with a decent chance of coming to fruition. Hence submission to such rules "is the main condition for the possibility of order in a free society" (p. 121). Moreover, if the state must be involved in creating and enforcing the rules that facilitate orderly market activity, then it is misleading to conceptualise it as standing completely outside the market. Rather, when the state acts in accordance with the rule of law, it helps to *constitute* markets.[57] The question of whether it should 'act' or 'interfere' in the economy is misleading, posing an altogether false alternative: "The question is not really whether government should ever concern itself with economic matters at all, but what kind of government action is legitimate, what should be its range and how it should be limited" (p. 118). It is only when the policies implemented are not in conformity with abstract rules applying equally to all that government can be said to be interfering in markets. Hence "we should

[55] Also see Hayek, *The Constitution of Liberty*, pp. 340–41, and Hayek, "Liberalism", pp. 21–22, 29–30. For critiques of Hayek's claim that the formal requirements of generality, equality and certainty are sufficient to ensure that coercion is minimised, see R. Hamowy, "Hayek's Concept of Freedom: A Critique", *New Individualist Review*, vol. 1, 1961, pp. 28–31, and J. Raz, "The Rule of Law and Its Virtue", in J. Raz, *The Authority of Law: Essays on Law and Morality* (Oxford: Clarendon Press, 1979), especially pp. 226–29. For a spirited defence of Hayek's position, see J. Gray, *Hayek on Liberty*, 3rd edn. (London and New York: Routledge, 1998), pp. 61–71.

[56] For Hayek, people are free when they are equal before the law: "The great aim of the struggle for liberty has been equality before the law". *The Constitution of Liberty*, p. 148.

[57] For similar points, see Hayek, *The Constitution of Liberty*, pp. 329–41; F. A. Hayek, *Rules and Order*, vol. 1 (1973) of *Law, Legislation and Liberty*, p. 62; and F. A. Hayek, *The Mirage of Social Justice*, vol. 2 (1976) of *Law, Legislation and Liberty*, pp. 128–29, 188 n. 21.

regard the infringement of equality before the law as the best *definition* of 'government interference'" (p. 120).[58]

At around the same time as he wrote this essay, Hayek also organised two seminar series, on the topics of "Equality and Justice" and "The Liberal Tradition". Evidently, the notion of equality before the law, and its role in liberal thought, was occupying much of his thought in the early 1950s. The essay discussed above is an early product of his labours in this regard, which bore additional fruit first in his 1955 Cairo lectures on "The Political Ideal of the Rule of Law", where he developed a fuller treatment of many of the issues discussed in "The Meaning of Government Interference", and finally and most fully in 1960 with the publication of *The Constitution of Liberty*.[59]

"The Economics of Development Charges"

One of the examples of government interference briefly mentioned in Hayek's 1950 paper is British government policy towards the use of land, something he explores in more detail in "The Economics of Development Charges". The essay's origins lie in three articles published in *The Times* on April 26, 27 and 28, 1949, assessing the impact of the 1947 Town and Country Planning Act. The Act established that ownership of land no longer conferred the right to develop it; planning permission from government—in the guise of a body called the Central Land Board—was also required. The notion of 'development' was defined very broadly, so as to encompass—with only a small handful of exceptions—any material change in use. The Act therefore gave the state something close to a monopoly in development rights, "entirely suspending the operation of the price mechanism with regard to land" (p. 136).

Where permission was granted, a 'development' charge would be levied. Its level would be fixed by ministerial order. Thus, the Act "placed in the power of a minister unlimited discretion to lay down even the 'general principle' on which its most important provision was to be administered" (p. 137). That the Central Land Board was able to exercise discretion in this way implied that the energies of the private citizen "will have to be bent, not so much to discovering the real facts of the situation, as to finding arguments which will appear plausible to those who have to fix the terms on which he will be allowed to

---

[58] Hayek expresses similar points both earlier in his career and much later. See Hayek, *The Road to Serfdom*, p. 118, and Hayek, *The Mirage of Social Justice*, pp. 128–29.

[59] F. A. Hayek, "The Political Ideal of the Rule of Law" [1955], reprinted as chapter 5 of F. A. Hayek, *The Market and Other Orders*, ed. B. Caldwell, vol. 15 (2014) of *The Collected Works of F. A. Hayek*, and *The Constitution of Liberty*, pp. 329–41. Some material from Hayek's seminar on "The Liberal Tradition" is reproduced on pp. 69–71 of J. Raybould, *Hayek: A Commemorative Album* (London: Adam Smith Institute, 1998).

go ahead with his plans". In consequence, the citizen's "opportunity to plan wisely and the likelihood of his serving the best social interest will be greatly decreased" (p. 134). Moreover, the fact that the development charge would typically be set equal to any increase in value of the land due to the change in its use implied that "no private person or corporation will have any incentive to improve economic efficiency, where this involves a change in the use of land" (p. 136). Hence the original title of the series of articles in *The Times*, namely "A levy on increasing efficiency". As Hayek noted in a later work, the central features of the Act "were found unworkable and had to be repealed after seven years".[60]

"The Economics of Development Charges" is the first of a number of papers in this volume where Hayek applies to concrete problems of social and economic policy what he had come to view as one of the fundamental principles of liberalism, namely the notion of equality before the law (or, as he also terms it, the rule of law). He does so both to criticise initiatives that are inconsistent with a regime of liberty and also to identify policies that enhance freedom. Hayek subsequently used material contained in several such papers—including not only "The Economics of Development Charges" but also "Full Employment, Planning and Inflation", "Inflation Resulting from the Downward Inflexibility of Wages", and "Unions, Inflation, and Profits"—in Part III of *The Constitution of Liberty*, where he explored systematically and in detail the type of policies sustained by a liberal point of view.[61] Before turning to those essays, however, we shall consider another, very early example of Hayekian policy analysis as well as three more theoretical pieces, in which Hayek surveys the state of the discipline of economics; examines the relationship between theory and history; and considers the implications of his views on the nature of theoretical and applied work for the educational needs of graduate students.

"Effects of Rent Control"

"The Economics of Development Charges" was not the first time Hayek had analysed the impact of government intervention on the use of land. In an earlier essay, first published in German in 1931, Hayek considered how a policy of rent control could cause widespread disruption in the economy and fall short of achieving its own goals. Hayek's objective in the paper was "to give a systematic review of the consequences of rent control" (p. 155), with particular reference to the case of Vienna in the 1920s. In doing so, he used eco-

---

[60] Hayek, *The Constitution of Liberty*, p. 479.
[61] Hayek, *The Constitution of Liberty*, pp. 367–516.

nomic analysis, arguing that while the immediate effects of rent controls on existing tenants and landlords were obvious to anybody, "the unintended consequences of any intervention of this sort can be clarified only with the help of theory" (p. 155).[62]

The reduction in rents below market-clearing levels will cause an increase in the demand for housing not just because of greater affordability but also because the resulting shortage of accommodation "converts possession of an apartment into an economic asset and reinforces the tenant's urge to hold on to his apartment, even . . . were he assured of finding a new apartment when the need arose" (p. 146). The reluctance of the occupants of rent-controlled apartments to move means that the allocation of rental space will gradually become 'calcified' in the sense of "correspond[ing] less and less to changing needs the longer tenant protection remains in effect" (p. 148). Rent control thus leads to an inefficient allocation of the existing housing stock and, as Hayek later stated, "perpetuates the housing shortage" with which it was meant to deal, thereby "worsen[ing] in the long run the evil it was meant to cure".[63] Similar problems arise in the case of new housing. Foreshadowing his later work on the informational role of market prices, Hayek argues that rent controls deprive construction firms of the information required to know what quantity, and kind, of new housing to build. "[D]eprived of the guidance of freely determined prices . . . we have no idea for what size and what quality apartments there exists a real need", leading to a failure to make good use of whatever resources are devoted to building new houses (p. 154). Further damaging unintended consequences arise from the public housing projects with which policy-makers often respond to the problems created by rent controls, which—in Hayek's view—restrict the amount of capital available for investment elsewhere in the economy, reducing labour productivity and wages below what they would otherwise have been.

"Economics"

Hayek's entry on "Economics" for the *Chambers's Encyclopaedia* was published in 1950. At the outset, he states that economics seeks to explain those features of society "which are not the result of deliberate design but the produce of the interplay of the separate decisions of individuals and groups" (p. 158). To do so, economists strive to identify and explain the causal mecha-

---

[62] Hayek also emphasised the use of economic theory to identify the unintended consequences of government policy in his inaugural lecture at the LSE. See Hayek, "The Trend of Economic Thinking", pp. 21–23, 31.

[63] Hayek, *The Constitution of Liberty*, p. 469.

nisms through which the actions that people take on the basis of their sub-jective beliefs are unintentionally transformed into particular kinds of out-come, including the creation of the more elaborate structures that constitute the social world. Hayek underlines the importance of adopting this subjectiv-ist approach—which he describes elsewhere as the compositive method—by arguing that economic problems arise not because of the physical attributes of goods and services but rather because of how the latter fit into people's plans. "[T]he distinguishing characteristic of the problems of economics", Hayek (p. 174) writes, is that they are concerned with issues such as "whether a good or service is regarded as useful for many different purposes or for only a few, whether it can be easily replaced by other goods or not, whether in view of the whole situation more or less important needs depend on the availability of the whole quantity of it, etc.".[64]

Hayek refers to the techniques that economists have developed for analys-ing how people deal with such problems as the "economic calculus" (p. 175). This encompasses the analytical tools—such as indifference curve anal-ysis and producer theory—used to describe the problems faced by decision-makers when all the relevant facts are known to a single mind. However, the economic calculus is no more than a "preliminary to . . . [the] main task" of analysing "a complex economic system in which the separate plans of indi-viduals and groups must be adjusted to one another if their aims are to be achieved" (p. 175).[65] Whilst Hayek alludes to the possibility that "mental mod-els can be constructed which will show how attempts to carry out . . . sepa-rate plans will interact", and also mentions the "'tendency' towards equilib-rium" (p. 175), he does not give an account of how people learn enough about one another's intentions to bring their plans into alignment. He does so, however, in his 1945 essay on "The Use of Knowledge in Society", where he explains how variations in market prices provide a publicly available indica-tion of changes in the scarcity of various resources, thereby helping people to adjust their plans so as to make them more compatible.[66]

Hayek ultimately came to argue that the dissemination of knowledge required for plan coordination is facilitated not only by relative price signals but also by systems of shared social rules (including both the formal rules of property, tort and contract law and also informal norms of trustworthiness

---

[64] For details, see F. A. Hayek, *Studies on the Abuse and Decline of Reason: Text and Documents*, ed. B. Caldwell, vol. 13 (2010) of *The Collected Works of F. A. Hayek*, pp. 88–107, 142–48.

[65] Hayek discusses these issues at greater length in his seminal paper on "Economics and Knowledge" [1937], reprinted as chapter 1 of *The Market and Other Orders*, especially pp. 57–62, 69–70. For more on the economic calculus, see B. Caldwell, "F. A. Hayek and the Economic Calculus", *History of Political Economy*, vol. 48, 2016, pp. 151–80.

[66] F. A. Hayek, "The Use of Knowledge in Society" [1945], reprinted as chapter 3 of *The Mar-ket and Other Orders*.

and promise-keeping). By facilitating enforceable contracts, those rules help to reassure people that the contributions they need others to make for their plans to come to fruition will be forthcoming. The rules can thus be seen to be an important source of the knowledge that helps people to devise mutually compatible plans. While there are gestures towards this argument in some of Hayek's earlier writings,[67] he made the point most fully in his post-1960 writings on political philosophy and the law, where his most complete account of the possibility of social order in decentralised market economies can be found. Those later writings can thus be seen to contain what one commentator has felicitously referred to as "Hayek's Implicit Economics".[68]

"The Uses of 'Gresham's Law' as an Illustration of 'Historical Theory'"

Hayek provides an example of the advantages of using the compositive method in "The Uses of 'Gresham's Law' as an Illustration of 'Historical Theory'", published in 1962 in *History and Theory*. The paper is a brief commentary on a longer article published in that journal by Arthur Lee Burns, a political scientist at the Australian National University. Burns explores the extent to which historical explanation can proceed without explicit reference to theoretical concepts and laws, illustrating his argument using the example of Gresham's Law (that is, the tendency for 'bad' or debased money to drive out 'good', full-value currency). According to Burns, the historian who wishes to explain some concrete instance of the disappearance from circulation of full-value metal coins can do so without knowing about, or making use of, Gresham's Law.[69]

Hayek defends the role of theory, arguing that it performs an indispensable service. He contends that Gresham's Law should be viewed not, as he thinks Burns has done, simply as an empirical generalisation—"as a mere empirical rule it is practically valueless" (p. 183)—but rather as an example of compositive social theory: "If Gresham's Law is properly stated with the conditions in which it applies, it will appear that as a proposition of compositive social

---

[67] See Hayek, *The Road to Serfdom*, p. 113, and Hayek, "The Use of Knowledge in Society", pp. 101–2.

[68] See F. A. Hayek, "Kinds of Rationalism" [1965], reprinted as the Prologue to *The Market and Other Orders*, pp. 49–50, and Hayek, *The Mirage of Social Justice*, pp. 107–32. Also see K. Vaughn, "Hayek's Implicit Economics: Rules and the Problem of Order", *Review of Austrian Economics*, vol. 11, 1999, pp. 129–44, and P. Lewis, "Hayek: From Economics as Equilibrium Analysis to Economics as Social Theory", in the *Elgar Companion to Hayekian Economics*, ed. R. Garrison and N. Barry (Cheltenham: Edward Elgar, 2014).

[69] A. L. Burns, "International Theory and Historical Explanation", *History and Theory*, vol. 1, 1960, pp. 55–74, especially pp. 62–66.

theory it can indeed provide a useful tool of historical explanation" (p. 184). Hayek's point is that the historian who views Gresham's Law simply as an empirical proposition "might well be puzzled when he finds that, after good and bad coins had been circulating concurrently for decades without a noticeable deterioration in the average quality, at one point of time the good coins had suddenly begun to grow very scarce" (p. 185). In contrast, the historian who treats Gresham's Law as an instance of compositive social theory, and so is aware of the need to consider the causal mechanism underpinning it, will appreciate the importance of looking for some external cause, such as a deterioration in the balance of payments, that by changing people's actions triggers the mechanism and sets in train the process whereby full-value coins leave circulation: "What theory will tell him is that he must look for some cause which led to a fall of the internal value of both good and bad coins relative to their value in foreign commerce and in industrial uses". Historians who are ignorant of economic theory, however, will lack the encouragement it provides "to look for a cause which either increased the relative supply or decreased the relative demand for coins and their substitutes in internal circulation" and will therefore be at a loss as to how to proceed (p. 185).[70]

"The Dilemma of Specialisation"

Hayek also considers the relationship between economics and other disciplines, including history, in "The Dilemma of Specialisation", an essay prepared for a conference held in 1955 to commemorate the twenty-fifth anniversary of the opening of the Social Science Research Building at the University of Chicago.[71] The background is provided by the fact that Hayek left the London School of Economics in 1950, joining the Committee on Social Thought at the University of Chicago as Professor of Social and Moral Science.[72] The Committee had been established in the 1940s with a view to countering the increasing fragmentation of the social sciences. It was located within the Divi-

---

[70] For more on Hayek's views on the relationship between theory and history, see F. A. Hayek, "The Facts of the Social Sciences" [1943], reprinted as chapter 2 of Hayek, *The Market and Other Orders*, pp. 87–90.

[71] A detailed conference programme, listing all the speakers and commentators, can be found in the appendix to the conference volume, *The State of the Social Sciences*, ed. L. D. White (Chicago: University of Chicago Press, 1956).

[72] The story of Hayek's recruitment to Chicago, and his appointment to the Committee on Social Thought rather than to the Department of Economics, is recounted in D. Mitch, "Morality versus Money: Hayek's Move to the University of Chicago", in *Hayek: A Collaborative Biography, Part IV: England, the Ordinal Revolution and the Road to Serfdom, 1931–50*, ed. R. Leeson (Basingstoke: Palgrave Macmillan, 2015), and on pp. 1727–31 of D. Mitch, "A Year of Transition: Faculty Recruiting at Chicago in 1946", *Journal of Political Economy*, vol. 124, 2016, pp. 1714–34.

sion of Social Sciences, whose creation the conference was intended to mark. The third day of the conference was devoted to "The Role of the Social Scientist", with Hayek's post-dinner lecture being the final one of the entire event. As befitted a member of the Committee, Hayek focused on the implications of the nature of social scientific research for the kind of education graduate students ought to receive, concentrating in particular on the degree of specialisation appropriate for such aspiring scholars.[73]

The 'dilemma' to which Hayek refers is the product of two countervailing imperatives. The first is the need for students to acquire a firm grasp of the criteria by which scholarly work is judged. Such knowledge "can be acquired only through the complete mastery of at least one field . . . which has its own firmly established standards". In the early stages of a postgraduate student's research training, therefore, "a progressive tendency toward specialisation seems to be inevitable" (p. 187). However, a conflicting tendency arises because social scientists are mainly interested in explaining particular events, processes and institutions. Concrete social phenomena are typically multi-faceted, and the product of several causal mechanisms which do not align neatly with one scientific discipline, so that "[t]here is scarcely an individual phenomenon or event in society with which we can deal adequately without knowing a great deal of several disciplines" (p. 189). Hence, in addition to acquiring 'technical' competence in their chosen field, economists should possess some knowledge both of other social sciences and also of history, philosophy and law:

> [I]n the study of society exclusive concentration on a speciality has a peculiarly baneful effect: it . . . may impair our competence in our proper field—or at least for some of the most important tasks we have to perform. The physicist who is only a physicist can still be a first-class physicist and a most valuable member of society. But nobody can be a great economist who is only an economist—and I am even tempted to add that the economist who is only an economist is likely to become a nuisance if not a positive danger. (p. 188)[74]

---

[73] Hayek had already discussed this issue with reference to British undergraduate education, in an address delivered in 1944 to the Students' Union of the LSE. See F. A. Hayek, "On Being an Economist" [1944], published as chapter 2 of Hayek, *The Trend of Economic Thinking*, pp. 41–43. One of the primary reasons why Hayek chose to return to this topic, he stated whilst preparing his Chicago lecture, was "to explain what *I* think the Committee on Social Thought ought to do". See F. A. Hayek to William L. Letwin, October 27, 1955, FAHP 34.1.

[74] Also see Hayek, "On Being an Economist", p. 42, and Hayek, *The Constitution of Liberty*, pp. 49–50. One of the most important examples of the significance of interdisciplinarity concerns the need for economists to possess a knowledge of law if they are to understand the possibility of social order. As Hayek put it in *Law, Legislation and Liberty*, "One of the main themes of this book will be that the rules of just conduct which the lawyer studies serve a kind of order of the character of which the lawyer is largely ignorant; and that this order is studied chiefly by the

It is critical, therefore, that after the initial phase of specialist training has ended, and they have begun work on their doctoral thesis, nascent researchers should also spend considerable time acquiring knowledge of other disciplines. The problem is that the time needed to satisfy both demands far exceeds that available for postgraduate research training. Hayek recommends dealing with the dilemma by establishing an institutional framework that affords individuals the freedom to make their own choices about how to respond: "The main conclusion must thus probably be that there is no single best way and that our main hope is to preserve room for that multiplicity of efforts which true academic freedom makes possible" (p. 199). This is challenging, however, because in most universities academics in one department are often reluctant to countenance their students taking instruction elsewhere. What is needed is a new kind of institution that can offset this parochial outlook and encourage interdisciplinary work by providing "the facilities and the climate for work which is not on well-established lines" (p. 199). This was not merely wishful thinking on Hayek's part. He attempted to establish such a centre, to be called the Institute of Advanced Human Studies, at the University of Vienna in the late 1950s and early 1960s. However, his efforts were unsuccessful.[75]

"Full Employment, Planning and Inflation"

A notable feature of Hayek's 1950 encyclopaedia entry on "Economics" was how little he discussed Keynes's work. He did, however, confront Keynesianism head on in another essay that appeared in the same year, namely "Full Employment, Planning and Inflation". Hayek's topic in that paper, which was published by the Institute of Public Affairs, a liberal Australian think tank, was "the new belief that a higher level of employment can be permanently maintained by monetary pressure than would be possible without it" (p. 200). Defining 'full employment' as "that maximum of employment that can be brought about in the short run by monetary pressure" (p. 201), Hayek argued that pursuit of that goal had necessarily been accompanied both by inflation and by government controls.

Hayek's analysis was informed by his theory of the business cycle, as expounded in *Prices and Production* (1931) and *Monetary Theory and the Trade Cycle* (1933).[76] For Hayek, the cause of the business cycle lay in the malfunctioning of the market for loanable funds. For instance, if the government pursues an

---

economist who in turn is similarly ignorant of the character of the rules of conduct on which the order that he studies rests". See Hayek, *Rules and Order*, pp. 4–5.

[75] See F. A. Hayek, *Hayek on Hayek: An Autobiographical Dialogue*, ed. S. Kresge and L. Wenar (Chicago: University of Chicago Press, 1994), pp. 29, 132.

[76] Now see Hayek, *Business Cycles, Part I*.

expansionary monetary policy, with a view to reducing unemployment, then the market rate of interest will fall below the natural rate, defined as the rate that equalises planned saving and planned investment, leading firms to believe (erroneously) that consumers wish to sacrifice current in favour of future consumption. Firms respond by investing in the capital goods required to satisfy consumers' (supposedly) higher demand for future consumption, as well as hiring the necessary workers, so that resources are bid away from the production of consumption goods. However, consumers have not in fact decided to reduce their current consumption. The resulting excess demand for consumer goods leads to an increase in their price relative to future goods—that is, to an increase in the market rate of interest—which signals to firms that their decision to invest in extra capital goods was mistaken. The new production methods will be seen to be unprofitable and abandoned, leading to an economic crisis as the relevant capital goods, and the workers hired to operate them, become unemployed. Hence Hayek's remark that "during every boom period a greater quantity of factors of production is drawn into the capital goods industries than can be permanently employed there, and that as a result we have normally a greater proportion of our resources specialised in the production of capital goods than corresponds to the share of income which, under full employment, will be saved and be available for investment, seems to [me] the cause of the collapse which has regularly followed a boom" (p. 203).

For Hayek, therefore, the trade cycle is not simply a matter of deficient aggregate demand. Rather, it is the result of a process of intertemporal discoordination that leads to the creation of a capital structure that cannot be sustained by the underlying pattern of demand. Efforts to avoid the ensuing downturn through additional monetary expansion will serve only to prolong and deepen the crisis: "Any attempt to create full employment by drawing labour into occupations where they will remain employed only so long as credit expansion continues creates the dilemma that either credit expansion must be continued indefinitely (which means inflation), or that, when it stops, unemployment will be greater than it would be if the temporary increase in employment had never taken place" (p. 203). Only the passage of time, and the slow process of adapting the capital stock to fit better with consumers' preferences, will cure the malaise.

Hayek also reflects on the difficulties of correcting an erroneously expansionary monetary policy. Especially when it has been pursued for some time, so that the misallocation of resources that must be overcome, and the unemployment that must be endured, are considerable, the reversal of the policy may lead to significant social and political unrest. It might therefore be "an experiment which politically is unbearable" (p. 205). Prefiguring some of the ideas that became central to his work in the 1970s, Hayek contends that the inappropriate use of monetary policy to pursue full employment thus raises "one of the gravest issues of our time: the capacity of democratic institutions to handle the tremendous powers for good and evil which the new instruments of economic policy place in their hands" (p. 208).

"Inflation Resulting from the Downward Inflexibility of Wages"

Hayek returned to some of the same ideas in an essay published eight years later, entitled "Inflation Resulting from the Downward Inflexibility of Wages". The essay appeared in a volume organised by the Committee for Economic Development, an American business-led, non-profit organisation interested in public policy, as part of its effort to stimulate discussion of urgent economic problems. Contributors were asked to "write 2,000 words on the question: 'What is the most important economic problem to be faced by the United States in the next twenty years?'"[77] Hayek chose as his topic the problem of inflation, arguing that inflationary policies had been encouraged by Keynesian economics, in particular by the "decisive assumption on which Keynes' original argument rested and which has since ruled policy . . . [namely] that it is impossible ever to reduce the money wages of a substantial group of workers without causing extensive unemployment" (p. 210). If that is the case, then the restoration of full employment "must be effected by the devious process of reducing the value of money. A society which accepts this is bound for a continuous process of inflation" (p. 210).[78]

Achieving full employment without recourse to the periodic use of inflationary monetary policy will be possible only with "the restoration of a labour market which will produce wages which are compatible with stable money". That in turn requires that "the responsibility for a wage level which is compatible with a high and stable level of employment should again be squarely placed where it belongs: with the trade unions" (p. 213). Monetary policy should be devoted, not to producing whatever level of nominal national income is required to secure full employment, thereby absolving trade unions of responsibility for considering how their wage claims affect employment, but to controlling inflation. Whether this shift in policy would be politically feasible, however, seemed doubtful to Hayek, because it would require a struggle with the unions for which policy-makers were quite unprepared: "The desire to avoid this [struggle] will probably again and again lead politicians to put off the necessity by resorting once more to the temporary way out

---

[77] G. Cowles, "Foreword", in *Problems of United States Economic Development*, ed. by the Committee for Economic Development (New York: Committee for Economic Development, 1958), vol. 1, p. 1.

[78] See Keynes, *The General Theory*, pp. 7–15, 257–71.

which inflation offers as the path of least resistance" (p. 214). Only when the shortcomings of this approach had become so obvious as to produce a change in the climate of opinion in favour of reducing union power would the necessary changes in policy be made.

"Unions, Inflation, and Profits"

Hayek explores similar issues in "Unions, Inflation, and Profits". The essay was based on a guest lecture Hayek delivered in 1958 for a graduate course on labour relations at the University of Virginia. Hayek's main focus was on the demands made by the United Auto Workers (UAW) union in its negotiations with employers in that year's collective bargaining round. There were two main elements to the union's programme. The first saw the union seek a general wage increase, justified in part on the grounds that this would increase mass purchasing power and thereby help extract the American economy in general, and the automobile industry in particular, from the recession in which both were mired at the time.[79] Drawing on theoretical considerations summarised above, Hayek challenged the 'deficient demand' theory of the business cycle that underpinned the union's claims, arguing that wage increases of the kind proposed would not only be inflationary but would also, by deterring private investment, cause higher unemployment (pp. 220–22).

The second demand, to which Hayek devotes most of his attention, applied exclusively to the 'Big Three' car producers, namely Chrysler, Ford and General Motors. It required that one quarter of all pre-tax profits in excess of a 10% return on net capital be given to the union to use as it saw fit. While the UAW viewed this proposal as a logical extension of the profit-sharing plans enjoyed by the executives of the companies in question, Hayek argued that it was fundamentally different, because it did not involve individual union members investing any of their own capital in the firm: "It is not a plan to give the individual worker a determinable share in the ownership of the enterprise and therefore in its profits, but rather a plan to give the union . . . control over, in the first instance, one quarter of the profits in excess of 10 per cent on net capital" (p. 225). Acceptance of the proposal would establish a new and far-reaching general principle, namely "the right of the worker of a firm, *qua* worker, to participate in a share of the profits, irrespective of any contribution he has made to its capital" (p. 228). Once established, there would be nothing

---

[79] By the middle of 1958, some 400,000 out of a total UAW membership of 1,300,000 workers were unemployed. See p. 321 of R. Montgomery, I. Stelzer and R. Roth, "Collective Bargaining over Profit-Sharing: The Automobile Union's Effort to Extend Its Frontier of Control", *The Journal of Business*, vol. 31, 1958, pp. 318–34.

to prevent that principle being invoked time and again to justify the appropriation by workers of an ever-increasing share of those profits, not only in the car industry but elsewhere in the economy. In effect, the principle would establish workers as part-owners of their firms. Hence, the UAW's proposed profit-sharing scheme was "purely socialistic" and, if implemented, "would place us straight on the road to syndicalism" (pp. 228, 230).

It is for this reason that Hayek believed that the UAW's proposals had implications for the character of the entire economic system: "What will be tested when these demands are seriously put forward is the crucial issue of how far the organised groups of industrial workers are to be allowed to use the coercive power they have acquired to force on the rest of this country a change in the basic institutions on which our social and economic system rests" (p. 229). In Hayek's view, it was the task of the economist to bring such long-run consequences, and the issues of principle they raised, to the attention of the general public. The latter had to be persuaded that the long-term benefits of defending private ownership outweighed the short-run costs, reckoned in terms of higher unemployment and lost output, threatened by the prospect of prolonged strike action by the UAW in support of its proposal (pp. 219–20, 229–31).[80]

"The Corporation in a Democratic Society: In Whose Interest Ought It to and Will It Be Run?"

In November 1959, Hayek was invited to participate in a symposium organised to celebrate the 10th anniversary of the Graduate School of Industrial Administration at the Carnegie Institute of Technology. The topic was the probable nature and role of the business corporation twenty-five years hence. Hayek was asked to consider the place of the corporation in democratic society, focusing in particular on the rights and duties that ought to be assigned to corporations and how, to whom, and for what they should be held responsible. Although initially sceptical about participating, on the grounds that he had "never been thinking directly about the problems involved", Hayek shortly after acquiesced, on the condition that he could focus on the specific question, "In whose interest will and ought the corporation be run?"[81] Hayek's thesis was that "if we want effectively to limit the powers of cor-

---

[80] Hayek further discusses the state of public opinion concerning trade unions in *The Constitution of Liberty*, pp. 386–87, 392–93. The UAW's campaign for the Big Three to adopt profit-sharing was unsuccessful. See Montgomery *et al.*, "Collective Bargaining over Profit-Sharing", p. 321.

[81] G. Bach, "An Introductory Note", in *Management and Corporations 1985*, ed. M. Anshen and G. Bach (New York: McGraw-Hill, 1960), pp. 1–2, 9–10, and F. A. Hayek to G. Bach, November 20, 21 and 29, 1959, FAHP 14.10.

porations to where they are beneficial, we shall have to confine them much more than we have yet done to one specific goal, that of the profitable use of the capital entrusted to the management by the stockholders" (p. 232). Failure to focus on profit-maximisation would have damaging and dangerous consequences, both in the short term and over the longer run. The immediate effect would be to afford managers discretion to pursue any goal they regarded as morally or socially good. This would "turn corporations from institutions serving the expressed needs of individual men into institutions determining which ends the efforts of individual men should serve", thereby creating "centres of uncontrollable power never intended by those who provided the capital" (p. 237). In the longer term, however, such power would not go unchallenged. For if it became widely accepted that managers were entitled to use the capital with which they had been entrusted to promote any goal thought to be in the public interest, then it would soon be claimed that their activities ought to be controlled by the representatives of that interest: "The more it comes to be accepted that corporations ought to be directed in the service of specific 'public interests'", Hayek (p. 244) argues, "the more persuasive becomes the contention that, as government is the appointed guardian of the public interest, government should also have power to tell the corporations what they must do". If left unchecked, deviations from profit-maximising behaviour would ultimately lead to increased state control over corporations and the undermining of free enterprise.[82]

Hayek also suggested how these problems might be solved. In his opinion, the divorce between ownership and control that was their root cause was "largely the result of special conditions which the law has created and the law can change", in particular the fact that the individual shareholder "has no legally enforceable claim to his share in the whole profits of the corporation" (pp. 243, 239). Legislation was needed to ensure that corporations "should, to a much greater degree than is the case at present, be governed by regulations which assure that the interest of the stockholder shall be paramount" (p. 239). Hayek offered two examples of the kind of reforms he had in mind. First, he recommended that the law be changed to require that all profits be paid out to shareholders immediately upon the close of the relevant financial period. Shareholders would then decide how much if anything to return to the corporation. "It seems to me that nothing would produce so active an interest of the individual stockholder in the conduct of a corporation, and at the same time give him so much effective power, as to be annually called upon individu-

---

[82] Hayek's argument could hardly have been more different from that advanced by the other presenter in his session, namely lawyer, former senior advisor to U.S. President Franklin D. Roosevelt, and Columbia University Professor Adolph A. Berle. Berle maintained that corporations should temper their pursuit of profit with a concern for a broader range of social responsibilities. See A. Berle, "The Corporation in a Democratic Society", in *Management and Corporations 1985*.

ally to decide what part of his share in the net profits he was willing to reinvest in the corporation", Hayek argued (p. 240). Second, Hayek also suggested that corporations should be prevented from acquiring voting rights in other corporations in which they owned shares. The fact that they could do so created the possibility that by acquiring control of a company which in turn held a controlling interest in another corporation, and so forth across several businesses, a small number of people could exert power over assets whose value far exceeded their own investment. This was "contrary to . . . the conceptions on which the system of private property rests—an artificial separation of ownership and control which may place the individual owner in the position where his capital is used for purposes conflicting with his own" (p. 242). The laws that allowed such a situation to arise "cannot be regarded as satisfactory" and must be changed so as to ensure that, while corporations could still own shares in one another as an investment, they should not bring the right to vote (p. 243).

What we have here are examples of how Hayek thought the law could be improved by legislation. Hayek clearly departs from the doctrine of laissez-faire: he disavows claims that any freely-agreed contract must be accepted (pp. 238–39); and he also distances himself from the view that the laws bequeathed by the past stand in no need of improvement, arguing that "the 'apathy' and lack of influence of the stockholder is largely the result of an institutional set-up which we have wrongly come to regard as the obvious or only possible one" (p. 239). This echoes Hayek's remarks in "'Free' Enterprise and Competitive Order" that liberals should be open to reforming existing institutions so as to make competition work as beneficially as possible. And in arguing that it is only through "bold mental experimentation" (p. 239) about changes in corporate law that profit maximisation can be restored to its rightful place as the over-riding goal of the corporation, Hayek provided a concrete example of the kind of legislation through which he believed government could discharge its positive duty of making the market work more effectively.

"The Non Sequitur *of the 'Dependence Effect'"*

The late 1950s saw the publication of John Kenneth Galbraith's best-selling book *The Affluent Society.*[83] Hailed by its most enthusiastic supporters as a work of political economy whose influence would match that of Keynes's *General*

---

[83] J. K. Galbraith, *The Affluent Society* (London: Hamish Hamilton, 1958). Galbraith had spent the year 1937–38 at Cambridge University, periodically travelling down to London to attend Hayek's seminar at the LSE. See *Interviews with John Kenneth Galbraith*, ed. J. Stanfield and J. Stanfield (Jackson: University Press of Mississippi, 2004), pp. 221–22.

Theory,[84] it is a critique of what Galbraith saw as the excessive material acquisitiveness of post-war capitalism. Its main claim was that, far from being sovereign rulers of the economic realm, modern consumers are vulnerable to manipulation by powerful corporations, which use advertising to cultivate artificial desires that far outstrip people's genuine needs. Galbraith also argued that the belief in the importance of private consumption engendered by corporations had fermented resentment against the taxation needed to provide high-quality public services. The upshot was a privileging of private over public expenditure, leading—in Galbraith's celebrated phrase—to a society characterised by "private opulence and public squalor".[85]

The Affluent Society sold extremely well, reaching the *New York Times* bestseller list in the spring of 1958 and remaining there for the remainder of the year.[86] It also helped to shape political debate. In Great Britain, for example, Galbraith's ideas informed discussions within the Labour Party, whose leaders were seeking ways to justify social democratic policies in the face of rising working-class living standards. One person who was concerned about the growing influence of Galbraith's work was the Secretary of the Mont Pèlerin Society, Albert Hunold, who believed that the Society should counter its influence on public opinion. To that end, Hunold arranged for a panel on *The Affluent Society* to take place on the final day of the Mont Pèlerin Society meeting held at Kassel in 1960.[87] The main speakers were economist George Stigler, author and journalist John Davenport, and Hayek. While it was initially hoped that the panel would spawn a book, it was subsequently decided not to proceed with that project. Hayek's paper was ultimately published in *The Southern Economic Journal* in April 1961.[88]

Hayek focused on what he saw as Galbraith's pivotal argument, namely that in modern societies many wants are not innate but rather arise only through the process by which they are satisfied, a phenomenon Galbraith termed "the

[84] See p. 52 of N. Thompson, "Socialist Political Economy in an Age of Affluence: The Reception of J. K. Galbraith by the British Social-democratic Left in the 1950s and 1960s", *Twentieth Century British History*, vol. 21, 2010, pp. 50–79.

[85] Galbraith, *The Affluent Society*, p. 200.

[86] Thompson, "Socialist Political Economy in an Age of Affluence," pp. 51, 54, and R. Parker, *John Kenneth Galbraith: His Life, His Politics, His Economics* (Toronto: Harper Collins, 2005), p. 292.

[87] See A. Hunold to J. Jewkes, June 9, 1960, box 14, folder 6, Mont Pèlerin Society Records, Hoover Institution Archives.

[88] See "Transcript of Tape Recording", box 16, folder 6, Mont Pèlerin Society Records, and p. 6 of *The Mont Pèlerin Quarterly*, vol. II, no. 3, October 1960, which can be found in box 3, folder 5, of the Mont Pèlerin Society Records. The texts of the talks by Stigler, Davenport, and Hayek were in fact published on pp. 12–26 of *The Mont Pèlerin Quarterly*, vol. III, no. 1/2, April–July 1961, along with a transcript of comments made by members of the audience in Kassel. See box 3, folder 6, of the Mont Pèlerin Society Records.

Dependence Effect".[89] Hayek readily acknowledged that many of our desires are indeed the result of social processes of emulation, imitation and the like, but denied that they must therefore be unimportant. Hayek's critique takes the form of a *reductio* that focuses on goods such as music, painting and literature. It is only because such goods are produced that there is any demand for them. Yet far from being of little worth, they are some of humankind's most valued achievements: "If the fact that people would not feel the need for something if it were not produced did prove that such products are of small value", Hayek (p. 247) wrote, "all those highest products of human endeavour would be of small value". Such a conclusion, that "the whole cultural achievement of man is not important", is "rather absurd" (pp. 246, 247). The fact that one of the goals of public education is to instil in people a taste for the arts only underlined the contradictory nature of Galbraith's position.

Hayek argued that the underlying flaw in Galbraith's argument stemmed from the way he equivocated between arguing that people's wants are influenced by producers and claiming that individual producers can determine people's preferences. Hayek readily conceded that producers can shape people's wants, but claimed that such an admission "would clearly not justify the contention that particular producers can deliberately determine the wants of particular consumers":

> The efforts of all producers will certainly be directed towards that end; but how far any individual producer will succeed will depend not only on what he does but also on what the others do and on a great many other influences operating upon the consumers . . . It is because each individual producer thinks that the consumers can be persuaded to like his products that he endeavours to influence them. But though this effort is part of the influences which shape consumers' tastes, no producer can in any real sense 'determine' them. (pp. 248–49)

For Hayek, therefore, there is sufficient competition to ensure that no one producer can deliberately determine what consumers want, leaving the sovereignty of the consumer largely intact.

"What Is 'Social'? What Does It Mean?"

Hayek's belief that the managers of firms should focus on profit maximisation rather than on 'socially' desirable purposes is an example of a more general

---

[89] Galbraith, *The Affluent Society*, p. 124.

critique of the term 'social' upon which he embarked in the late 1950s.[90] In "What Is 'Social'? What Does It Mean?", which was originally published in German in 1957, Hayek contends that the term 'social' was originally introduced to describe institutions, such as language and the market, that had arisen as the unintended consequences of human action. Over time, however, the word had come to be used to denote many phenomena that had been deliberately designed. The upshot was that "[t]here . . . remains little or nothing in life which is not 'social' in one sense or another, and the word becomes, to all practical intents, meaningless" (p. 257).

Hayek illustrates the pernicious consequences of this development by considering how the term 'social' had gradually come to usurp the place of the word 'moral' in common discourse. According to Hayek, when people speak of someone's 'social conscience', or of their 'social responsibilities'—as distinct from their 'conscience' or 'moral responsibility'—they are claiming that in deciding how to behave people should take into account even very remote consequences of their actions and, in the light of such considerations, choose the action which will best promote the 'social good'. For Hayek, this is quite at odds with traditional rules of morality and justice of the kind that sustain the market order, which refer only to a person's immediate circumstances, of which they can normally be expected to be aware, and require or proscribe certain kinds of action irrespective of their consequences.

The limited epistemic demands made by such long-established rules reflect the way that our reliance on them is an adaptation to the fact that society is too complex for any human mind fully to comprehend it. In making this point, Hayek draws on his account of cultural evolution via group selection, which rose to prominence in his work from 1960 onwards. Hayek's claim is that systems of rules become established through a process of competition between groups of people, where the groups are defined by reference to the rules governing their conduct. Rules that are abstract and general, and which must be followed irrespective of their consequences in any particular case, are well-adapted to the key economic challenge facing complex modern societies, because they afford people the autonomy required to make full use of dispersed knowledge whilst also enabling them to predict one another's actions accurately enough to form mutually compatible plans. Groups adhering to such rules will flourish and grow, while those that do not will lose members and ultimately wither away.[91]

[90] See, for example, Hayek, *The Constitution of Liberty*, pp. 127–28, 145–47. Also see *The Mirage of Social Justice*, pp. 78–80, and *The Fatal Conceit*, pp. 114–17.

[91] See Hayek, *The Constitution of Liberty*, pp. 73–99, 107–32, and F. A. Hayek, "Notes on the Evolution of Systems of Rules of Conduct" [1967], reprinted as chapter 10 of *The Market and Other Orders*. For summaries, see G. Gaus, "Hayek on the Evolution of Society and Mind", in

On this view, evolved social rules are repositories of tacit knowledge, embodying inherited wisdom—accumulated through the countless experiments in living that have taken place down the ages—about how people should behave. They are "genuine social growths" because they are "the results of a process of evolution and selection, the distilled essence of experiences of which we ourselves have no knowledge . . . [and] have acquired general authority because the groups in which they held sway have proved themselves to be more effective than other groups" (pp. 258–59). Those who, labouring under the baleful influence of rationalistic demands for a reasoned justification of all institutions, refuse to obey inherited rules unless the case for doing so has been explicitly made display an unwarranted and hubristic faith in the power of the human mind to master the details of a complex social world. Worse still, by undermining people's willingness to submit to inherited rules, rationalism threatens to destroy the basis for much successful human cooperation, jeopardising the foundations of modern industrial societies.[92]

Hayek argues that the rise of 'social' thinking has undermined two traditional ethical notions in particular, namely 'justice' and 'responsibility' (pp. 259–61). For Hayek, the ambiguity of the word 'social' "robs of its clear meaning every phrase it qualifies and transforms it into a phrase of unlimited elasticity . . . the use of which, as a general rule, serves merely to conceal the lack of real agreement between men regarding a formula upon which, in appearance, they are supposed to be agreed" (p. 253). When used in a phrase like 'social responsibility', the term helps to impose upon people "vague and undefined responsibilities for things that are not clearly apparent" (p. 260). Given that, in Hayek's view, an individual can be held responsible only for the solution of problems that—without too much imaginative effort—she can consider her own, attempts to hold people accountable for outcomes that are so ill-defined and distant from their everyday concerns can only erode people's sense of personal responsibility.[93] Moreover, in an anticipation of arguments that assume greater prominence in his later work, Hayek also notes that the ambiguity of terms such as 'social justice' means that they can easily be turned to suit the purposes of any interest group, rendering them nothing more than "camouflage for aspirations that certainly have nothing to do with the common interest [and] . . . a standing invitation to make further demands or to do good at the expense of others" (pp. 253, 261).

The Cambridge Companion to Hayek, and pp. 1178–86 of P. A. Lewis, "Notions of Order and Process in Hayek: The Significance of Emergence", *Cambridge Journal of Economics*, vol. 39, 2015, pp. 1167–90.

[92] Also see Hayek, "Kinds of Rationalism", p. 50, and F. A. Hayek, "Individualism: True and False" [1946], reprinted as the Prelude to *Studies on the Abuse and Decline of Reason*, pp. 67–69.

[93] Also see Hayek, *The Constitution of Liberty*, pp. 145–47.

"The Moral Element in Free Enterprise"

Hayek elaborates on these issues in "The Moral Element in Free Enterprise". This essay was prepared for presentation at the 66th Annual Congress of American Industry, held in New York in December 1961. The organisers requested that Hayek and three other presenters explore how capitalism might be defended, not simply on the basis of its material benefits, but rather by reference to "the basic concept of human freedom which free enterprise reflects". Almost the entire first day of the Congress was devoted to the four papers, the main interlude being a lunchtime address by President John F. Kennedy.[94]

Drawing on material from *The Constitution of Liberty*, Hayek argued that freedom is essential for the development of morality because it is only when people can choose how to behave that they are able to affirm their commitment to prevailing values and thereby contribute to their continued existence. However, while freedom is necessary for morality, the values which arise need not always be conducive to it: "it is possible", Hayek (p. 264) contends, "in a free society for moral standards to grow up which, if they become general, will destroy freedom and with it the basis of all moral values".[95] Hayek focuses on two moral values, both of which he considered essential for the continued existence of a free society but believed were under threat.

The first is individual responsibility. Contrary to claims that it was legitimate to hold people to account only for actions they had genuinely chosen to undertake, and not for behaviour that was caused by antecedent circumstances, Hayek argues that growing scientific knowledge about how people's actions are shaped by certain kinds of cause supports rather than undermines the case for individual responsibility. Indeed, the whole point of assigning responsibility is to exploit the existence of a reliable causal connection between people's circumstances and their conduct in order to change how they behave, in particular so as "to make it worthwhile for people to act rationally and reasonably and to persuade them that what they would achieve depended chiefly on them" (p. 267).[96] The second moral value considered by Hayek, namely justice, demands "the approval . . . of an arrangement by which material rewards are made to correspond to the value which a person's particular services have to his fellows; not to the esteem in which he is held

---

[94] National Association of Manufacturers, "Introduction", in *The Spiritual and Moral Significance of Free Enterprise*, ed. F. Morley (New York: National Association of Manufacturers, 1962), pp. 3–4.

[95] Also see Hayek, *Rules and Order*, pp. 6–7, and Hayek, *The Political Order of a Free People*, pp. 173–75.

[96] Hayek, *The Constitution of Liberty*, pp. 137–39.

as a whole person for his moral merit" (p. 266). For if society affords individuals the liberty to act as they see fit, in the light of their local knowledge, then because nobody else has that knowledge it will be impossible for others to judge whether someone's success or failure is attributable principally to their own effort and foresight or to luck. In judging a person's actions, therefore, "we must look at results, not intentions or motives, and can allow him to act on his own knowledge only if we also allow him to keep what his fellows are willing to pay him for his services, irrespective of whether we think this reward appropriate to the moral merit he has earned or the esteem in which we hold him as a person" (p. 268).

Remuneration in accordance with the value of an individual's services is often very different from people's views about the moral merits of his or her actions. For if people's wages are to direct their attention to those activities that are most valued by their fellow citizens, then like all prices they must be forward-looking in the sense of indicating what people should do in the future if they are to satisfy others' needs. In a world of unexpected change, therefore, current wages will not necessarily bear any relation to the actions that people have already taken and so cannot serve as a retrospective reward for past conduct:

> Men can be allowed to act on their own knowledge and for their own purposes only if the reward they obtain is dependent in part on circumstances which they can neither control nor foresee . . . In this sense freedom is inseparable from rewards which often have no connection with merit and are therefore felt to be unjust.[97]

This is in Hayek's view the principal source of people's dissatisfaction with the free enterprise system and their demands for distributive justice (p. 268).

The year in which "The Moral Element in Free Enterprise" was published, namely 1962, marks a significant moment in Hayek's career. Not only did he leave Chicago to take up a post at the University of Freiburg, but it was also around this time that he began work on his next major project, an undertaking that would eventually result in *Law, Legislation and Liberty*. In *The Constitution of Liberty*, Hayek had sought to restate the doctrine of classical liberalism, understood as centring on the creation of a protected sphere of individual freedom, defined by rules of just conduct that were enforced by a state whose use of coercion was constitutionally limited by the rule of law. The impetus for his new book came from Hayek's growing realisation that this ideal of liberal constitutionalism was being undermined by intellectual and political

---

[97] Hayek, *The Mirage of Social Justice*, p. 120.

developments that challenged its intellectual foundations and exposed flaws in the institutions in which it had been embodied.[98]

Hayek sought in *Law, Legislation and Liberty* to respond to these challenges, by explaining their intellectual shortcomings and outlining institutional arrangements that would be more effective in preserving individual freedom than those upon which earlier generations of liberals had relied. His response was informed by his view that "the preservation of a society of free men depends on three fundamental insights":

> The first of these is that a self-generating or spontaneous order and an organisation are distinct, and that their distinctiveness is related to the two different kinds of rules or laws which prevail in them. The second is that what today is generally regarded as 'social' or distributive justice has meaning only within the second of these kinds of order, the organisation; but that it is meaningless in, and wholly incompatible with, that spontaneous order which Adam Smith called 'the Great Society', and Sir Karl Popper called 'the Open Society'. The third is that the predominant model of liberal democratic institutions, in which the same representative body lays down the rules of just conduct and directs government, necessarily leads to a gradual transformation of the spontaneous order of a free society into a totalitarian system conducted in the service of some coalition of organised interests.[99]

A first draft of the book was almost entirely completed by the end of 1969, but a period of ill-health from 1969 until 1973 meant that Hayek only finished the work in 1979.[100] During the years when he was writing the book, Hayek incorporated discussions of many of its key themes in various essays, several of which are reproduced below.

"The Principles of a Liberal Social Order"

Hayek set out some of the central issues in a paper presented at a regional meeting of the Mont Pèlerin Society held in Tokyo in September 1966. The essay was entitled "The Principles of a Liberal Social Order" and has been described, not without reason, as "the best short exposition of liberalism by Hayek".[101]

Hayek begins by comparing spontaneous orders, which arise when people

---

[98] Hayek, *Rules and Order*, p. 2.
[99] Hayek, *Rules and Order*, p. 2.
[100] Hayek, *The Political Order of a Free People*, p. xi, and Hayek, *Hayek on Hayek*, pp. 130–32.
[101] Cockett, *Thinking the Unthinkable*, p. 355 n. 5.

interact on the basis of abstract rules that afford them the freedom to pursue their own purposes, with 'organisations'. The latter are social arrangements whereby people pursue a single concrete goal or purpose under the deliberate direction of some leader or planner. In sharp contrast, spontaneous social orders are *abstract*, being defined simply in terms of the compatibility of the diverse plans chosen by the relevant individuals. This leaves open the concrete content of those plans, meaning that a spontaneous social order "can be used for, and will assist in the pursuit of, a great many different, divergent and even conflicting individual purposes" (p. 276). It is in this abstract order, rather than in the achievement of any concrete goal or the advancement of particular interests, that the notion of the common good consists.

The notion of spontaneous social order is also important because it underwrites the liberal conception of justice. Actions are just if they are in conformity with a system of rules that supports a spontaneous social order (or "order of actions", as Hayek also terms it).[102] This has important implications. First, far from being invented in accordance with the arbitrary will of a legislator, rules of just conduct are 'discovered', most notably when judges—faced with the task of reconciling conflicts between existing legal rules that lead people to form inconsistent plans—identify a new law that resolves the conflict and thereby enables people to devise plans that are mutually compatible. The newly discovered law fills a gap in the existing corpus of rules and is in that sense already implicit in that system.[103] Second, the justice of a rule can be tested by reference to its compatibility with the other rules in the legal system. For if a rule were not so compatible, then plans developed in conformity with it would clash with those satisfying the other rules, disrupting the coordination required for social order. Hence Hayek's remark that rules of just conduct "can be developed by consistently applying to whatever such rules a society has inherited the . . . negative test of universal applicability—a test which, in the last resort, is nothing else than the self-consistency of the actions which these rules allow if applied to the circumstances of the real world" (p. 280). Only abstract rules will pass this Kantian test of 'universalisability',

[102] F. A. Hayek, "The Principles of a Liberal Social Order" [1966], republished as chapter 21 of this volume, p. 282; also see Hayek, "Liberalism", pp. 24–25, 28. For an excellent exposition of Hayek's account of justice, see E. Mack, "Hayek on Justice and the Order of Actions", in *The Cambridge Companion to Hayek*.

[103] Hayek contends moreover that, because they must cover an unknown number of future instances, the rules thus discovered are necessarily abstract and general and so qualify as genuine laws. This marks a significant contrast with laws created through conscious legislation, which need not possess such properties. See F. A. Hayek, "Economic Freedom and Representative Government" [1973], reprinted as chapter 24 below, pp. 335–36. Hayek thus distinguishes between *law*—which consists of universal, non-instrumental rules of just conduct that are typically discovered by judges—and *legislation* (involving deliberate acts of government that often aim at specific outcomes).

because they are the only kind of rule that can govern the relation between any members of the Great Society (at least some of whom will have no concrete purposes in common).[104]

Rules of just conduct—which for Hayek typically take the form of prohibitions, especially against behaviour infringing upon an individual's protected domain of free action—must be sharply distinguished from the commands issued by organisations in pursuit of their specific goals. Especially significant amongst the latter are the organisational rules governing governments' efforts to administer the resources placed at their disposal for the provision of certain goods and services inadequately supplied by the market.[105] Such rules, which have been codified in the form of public law, grant government the power to direct its employees to act in particular ways so as to achieve concrete goals. They are therefore quite different from abstract rules of just conduct (as embodied, for Hayek, in private and criminal law). The problem, however, was that—for reasons discussed below—the constitutional arrangements prevailing in Western democracies had made it all too easy for the notion of 'law' as abstract rules equally applicable to all to become confused with the idea—deriving from the realm of public administration—of 'law' as any organisational rule or even command legitimately issued by a legislative body. This mistaken extension of the meaning of the term 'law' to encompass administrative rules stipulating the pursuit of concrete purposes led to a situation where the "conception of the rule of law . . . no longer provides any protection of individual freedom". Indeed, the "progressive displacement of the rules of conduct of private and criminal law by a conception derived from public law" is in Hayek's opinion "the process by which existing liberal societies are progressively transformed into totalitarian societies" (p. 283).

"The Constitution of a Liberal State"

Hayek further discusses this problem in an essay published the following year, namely "The Constitution of a Liberal State", where he explains why one of the devices that liberals had hoped would protect individual freedom, namely the separation of powers, had failed to do so. Hayek summarises his critique at the outset, writing that if it is to constitute an effective safeguard the separation of powers "presupposes a conception of law which defines what is a law

---

[104] The tensions arising from Hayek's attempt to articulate a philosophy of liberalism that combines a Kantian emphasis on the rational justification of the liberal conception of justice with a Humean emphasis on evolutionary processes are explored in C. Kukathas, *Hayek and Modern Liberalism* (Oxford: Clarendon Press, 1990).

[105] Hayek, "Liberalism", pp. 32–33, and Hayek, *The Political Order of a Free People*, pp. 41–64.

by intrinsic criteria and independent from the source from which it springs". In actual fact, however, "we have come to call 'law' not a particular kind of norm or command but almost anything resolved by the agency we call legislature: the current interpretation of the separation of powers rests thus on circular reasoning and makes it a wholly empty concept: only the legislature is to pass laws and it is to possess no other powers, but whatever it resolves is law" (pp. 292–93).

Hayek's explanation of this baleful state of affairs begins with the claim that because for much of history laws were discovered by judges rather than created by legislators, the representative bodies known as 'legislatures' were in fact primarily occupied with matters of government (that is, with administering the resources used for the provision of public goods). However, when the rise of democracy led to demands for the power of formulating rules of just conduct to be placed in the hands of representative assemblies, it was natural that those existing bodies should be used for that purpose. Thus the separation of powers was never in fact achieved, because from the outset of modern constitutional government the powers to make laws and to direct government were vested in the same body. Worse still, given that the assemblies in question were accustomed to devising organisational rules intended to bring about concrete goals, it was all too easy for them to conceptualise their legislative role as involving the enactment of such rules as well as universal rules of just conduct. The upshot was that the term 'law' came to mean any rule of organisation or even any command approved by the constitutionally appointed legislature. This conception of the rule of law, which requires only that laws be issued by the relevant assembly, no longer provides any protection of individual freedom. "In consequence", Hayek (p. 296) concludes, "the ultimate power of government was in no democratic country of modern times ever under the law, because it was always in the hands of a body free to make whatever law it wanted for the particular tasks it desired to undertake".[106]

This problem was exacerbated by two erroneous developments in philosophy. One was the rise of legal positivism, which holds that all law is the product of deliberate legislation and that the expressed will of a legislator is the only criterion of justice. Hence there can be no law standing apart from and constraining the sovereign legislator. Hayek argues that this view can be seen to be mistaken once it is recognised that there exists a body of laws which are the product, not of legislation, but rather of a persistent search for impersonal justice on the part of jurists. Once the role of that system of rules of just conduct in facilitating a spontaneous social order is acknowledged, it

---

[106] Hayek, *Rules and Order*, 89–91, 124–44, and Hayek, *The Political Order of a Free People*, 1–40, 98–107.

becomes clear that the creation of new laws is constrained by the need for them to complement the other rules in the system so to promote the order of actions.[107] The shift away from liberal constitutionalism was further encouraged by "the substitution by Rousseau of popular *will* for general *opinion* and the consequent conception of popular sovereignty, meaning in practice that whatever the majority decided on particular matters was to be binding law for all" (p. 293). Rousseau's work licensed the view that there should be no restrictions on what democratically-elected legislators could call 'law', in which case they would enjoy the authority to coerce individuals into obeying specific commands designed to produce particular outcomes willed by the majority. Hayek rejects this view, arguing that there exists a source of authority that can—and should—limit the power of even the highest legislature, namely public opinion (understood as widely-held beliefs that certain kinds of action are right or wrong, irrespective of their foreseeable consequences in specific situations). Its antonym, in Hayek's lexicon, is the notion of 'will', defined as the desire to produce particular concrete results. For Hayek, the authority of even the highest representative assembly is limited by people's opinion about what kinds of laws are acceptable; if public opinion approves only of general rules of just conduct, then the legislature will be limited to enacting such rules. Hence Hayek's emphasis, expressed in several of the works discussed above, on the importance for the revival of liberalism of shaping public opinion.[108]

"The Confusion of Language in Political Thought"

The notions of 'will' and 'opinion' are one of several pairs of concepts Hayek discusses in "The Confusion of Language in Political Thought". Hayek's goal in that essay, which was published in 1968, was to overcome what he saw as various widespread misunderstandings about the institutions that had made possible the prosperity enjoyed by the inhabitants of modern industrial economies. For Hayek, those institutions were in large part the outcome of an evolutionary process in which they prevailed over alternative arrangements because they were better adapted to the problem of harnessing dispersed knowledge. However, that insight continued to be obscured by the rationalist proclivity for

---

[107] Hayek, *The Mirage of Social Justice*, pp. 44–56, and Hayek, "Liberalism", pp. 28–29.

[108] Opinion in Hayek's sense rests on, or is embodied in, a set of universal rules specifying what kinds of conduct are permissible. As the product of an evolutionary process, the rules are often only tacitly known until they are made explicit by judges seeking to settle disputes arising from people's differing views about what they imply in certain situations. Hayek refers to people's tacit understanding of such rules as their "sense of justice". See F. A. Hayek, "The Confusion of Language in Political Thought" [1968], reprinted as chapter 23 below, p. 311.

interpreting them as the products of deliberate design.[109] This misconception derives from the way that "our thinking is governed by language which reflects an earlier mode of thought" and, in particular, from the use of "words which imply anthropomorphic or personalised explanations of social institutions" (p. 301). His aim is to introduce new terms which "should help us to avoid the prevailing confusion" by making it easier to express and do justice to the spontaneous nature of many of the most important features of society (p. 302).[110]

For example, concerned that the anthropomorphic connotations of the term 'order' would encourage people to conceptualise outcomes produced through spontaneous processes as the result of deliberate organisation—the conscious creations of an actor who brings order to the world—Hayek recommends using the word 'cosmos' to denote features of society that are the product of human action but not of human design. Organisations that are explicitly designed to promote a particular end are to be referred to using the term 'taxis'. Hayek also argues that considerable confusion has been caused by the use of the term 'economy' to designate the spontaneous order produced by the market as well as situations where resources are allocated according to a plan designed to serve a unitary hierarchy of ends (as in organisations such as the household, firm and government). This has encouraged the view that the market order should be made to behave like an economy proper, in particular by being forced to conform to certain ideals of distributive justice. Hayek argues such problems can be avoided by using the term 'catallaxy' to denote the spontaneous market order, with the word 'economy' being reserved for those orders in which the allocation of resources is deliberately arranged.

Hayek likens the catallaxy or market order to a game in which the results for each player depend partly upon his or her skills and the effort (s)he exerts, and partly on chance. Both are rule-governed forms of endeavour, and the rewards earned by individuals in the market, like the outcome of a game, are shaped by circumstances beyond their control (in particular, the dispersed knowledge and specific aims which guide the actions of other individuals). This has important implications for policy, because it suggests that while a reliance on spontaneous forces greatly increases the number of people whose activities can be integrated into a coherent market order, it also necessarily reduces the extent to which anyone can control the details of the outcomes produced.[111] The reason is that the framework of universal rules of just con-

---

[109] See F. A. Hayek, "The Results of Human Action but Not of Human Design" [1967], and F. A. Hayek, "The Errors of Constructivism" [1970], reprinted as chapters 11 and 14 respectively of Hayek, *The Market and Other Orders*.

[110] Also see Hayek, *Rules and Order*, pp. 26–29 and Hayek, *The Fatal Conceit*, pp. 106–19.

[111] See F. A. Hayek, "The Pretence of Knowledge" [1975], reprinted as chapter 16 of Hayek, *The Market and Other Orders*, pp. 365–66, 368–72, and F. A. Hayek, "The Atavism of Social Justice" [1978], reprinted as chapter 27 of this volume, pp. 404–7.

duct, over which policy-makers can exert a measure of control, determines only the general character of the market order. The specific outcomes enjoyed by particular individuals or groups depend upon numerous circumstances which nobody can foresee or determine and which will therefore be left "to 'accident'" (p. 321). "In consequence", Hayek (p. 305) concludes, "the concrete content of such an order will always be unpredictable . . . [and w]e must renounce the power of shaping its particular manifestations according to our desires". Hence, for Hayek, freedom is inseparable from rewards that often have no connection with merit and are often perceived to be unjust.[112]

"Economic Freedom and Representative Government"

Hayek returned to many of the same themes in his Wincott Memorial Lecture of 1973, entitled "Economic Freedom and Representative Government". His thesis was that the political institutions then prevailing in the Western world "necessarily . . . produce a progressive expansion of governmental control of economic life even if the majority of the people wish to preserve a market economy" (p. 330). What Hayek adds to his earlier accounts is a discussion of the political process through which the unlimited power afforded legislatures by the particular form of democratic organisation adopted in modern Western societies comes to be exploited. Where majority power is unlimited by effective constitutional constraints, "a political party hoping to achieve and maintain power will have little choice but to use its powers to buy the support of particular groups":

> They will do so not because the majority is interventionist, but because the ruling party would not retain a majority if it did not buy the support of particular groups by the promise of special benefits. (p. 330)

In this way, the prevalent form of democratic politics gives rise to an expansion of state control over economic affairs even if most people remain in favour of a market system.

Given that the underlying cause of the problem lay in the way that the same representative assembly was responsible both for enacting rules of just conduct and also for directing government, Hayek's solution involved institutional reform.[113] This would centre on the creation of "two distinct represen-

---

[112] Also see Hayek, "Liberalism", pp. 26, 29–30, and Hayek, *The Mirage of Social Justice*, pp. 115–20.

[113] Hayek's proposal was born out of the conviction that the problems of interest group activity, greater government intervention and diminished liberty faced by Western democracies in the 1970s were creating "an impasse from which political leaders will offer to extricate us by desper-

tative assemblies with different tasks, one a true legislative body and the other concerned with government proper" (p. 337). The governmental assembly would closely resemble existing parliaments in its duties, in the method by which its members were elected, and in how it represented the concrete will and particular interests of citizens in securing specific concrete outcomes. It would determine the organisation of government and the use made of the means placed at its disposal for the provision of public services; but its power to coerce citizens would be limited to making them obey laws of just conduct which, having been laid down by a second democratic chamber, it could not itself alter to suit particular purposes.[114]

The determination of the rules of just conduct would be the exclusive preserve of the legislative chamber, to which activity it would be constitutionally restricted. Lacking the authority to issue particular commands, the members of this second assembly would be unable to enact laws that privileged particular groups. To make them representative of public opinion, they would be selected by age group; once in their lives, at the age of forty-five, every citizen would vote for a candidate from his or her own generation. Furthermore, in order to ensure that the legislature's decisions were not shaped by the will of specific groups concerned to promote particular concrete outcomes, Hayek sought to ensure that its members would be immune from the pressure of organised interests: they would enjoy a relatively long term of office (fifteen years); be ineligible for, and so unconcerned about, re-election; and be guaranteed a livelihood after the end of their term of office (freeing them from influences arising from worries about their future). The upshot would be the creation of "a legislature which was not subservient to government and did not produce whatever laws government wanted for the achievement of its momentary purposes, but rather which with the law laid down the permanent limits to the coercive powers of government" (p. 339). In this way, a real separation of powers between two representative bodies would be secured, whereby law-making in the true sense of laying down rules of just conduct and the conduct of government proper would both be carried out democratically, but by two independent agencies. By preventing the legislature from authorising coercion simply to secure benefits for particular groups, such a regime would bring about what Hayek refers to elsewhere as the "dethronement of politics", thereby making it possible to achieve true government

---

ate means". Against that background, Hayek's goal was "to provide a sort of intellectual stand-by equipment for the time, which may not be far away, when the breakdown of the existing institutions becomes unmistakable and when I hope it may show a way out. It should enable us to preserve what is truly valuable in democracy and at the same time free us of its objectionable features". See Hayek, *The Political Order of a Free People*, p. xiii.

[114] Perhaps the earliest presentation of this solution can be found in F. A. Hayek, "New Nations and the Problem of Power", *The Listener*, vol. 64, no. 1650, 1960, pp. 819–21.

under the law and halting the tendency towards greater intervention encouraged by existing political arrangements.[115]

Hayek's model constitution is significant because of what it suggests about the development of his ideas. From the mid-1960s onwards Hayek began to shift away from the position—which characterised his work up to and including *The Constitution of Liberty*—that there is a role for the state in planning the framework of rules within which economic activity occurs towards the common law view that an appropriate legal framework is the product of a spontaneous, evolutionary process.[116] However, while Hayek came to regard judge-made law as more conducive to the preservation of individual liberty than laws created through legislation, he did not entirely abandon the view that legislation might be required to improve the legal framework, either to speed up the adaptation of the law to entirely new circumstances or "to extricate it from the dead ends into which the gradual evolution may lead it, or to deal with altogether new problems."[117] But what Hayek tried to do, through his proposal for constitutional reform, was to recommend changes in the institutional framework that would confine such legislation to the production of universal rules of just conduct. Notwithstanding his increasing emphasis on the importance of evolutionary processes, therefore, even in his later writings Hayek continued to rely significantly on the conscious design of an appropriate institutional and legal framework for a liberal society.[118]

While Hayek might appear to be contradicting himself, by arguing against

---

[115] Hayek, *The Political Order of a Free People*, p. 149. For a helpful attempt to place Hayek's advocacy of his 'model constitution' within the context of the liberal political theory of the 1960s, as well as an insightful critique, see J.-W. Müller, "What, If Anything, Is Wrong with Hayek's Model Constitution?", in *Law, Liberty and State: Oakeshott, Hayek and Schmitt on the Rule of Law*, ed. D. Dyzenhaus and T. Poole (Cambridge: Cambridge University Press, 2015). Also see pp. 45–46 of S. Brittan, "Hayek, the New Right, & the Crisis of Social Democracy", *Encounter*, vol. 54, 1980, pp. 30–46.

[116] This change in Hayek's views arguably reflects the influence of Italian philosopher and lawyer Bruno Leoni (1913–67), who in *Freedom and the Law* (Princeton, NJ: D. Van Nostrand Company, 1961) suggested that the preservation of liberty was better served by a common law system than through law-making via legislation. See J. Shearmur, *Hayek and After: Hayekian Liberalism as a Research Programme* (London and New York: Routledge, 1996), pp. 88–89. Hayek's recollections of Leoni the man, and his assessment of Leoni's scholarly work, can be found on pp. 253–58 of F. A. Hayek, "Bruno Leoni (1913–1967) and Leonard Read (1898–1983)", published as chapter 14 of *The Fortunes of Liberalism*.

[117] Hayek, *Rules and Order*, p. 100; also see pp. 45–46, 88–89, as well as Hayek, "The Principles of a Liberal Social Order", p. 282, and Hayek, "Liberalism", p. 25. It is for this reason that Hayek wrote of Leoni that "although his argument is an effective antidote to the prevailing orthodoxy which believes that only legislation can or ought to alter the law, it has not convinced me that we can dispense with legislation even in the field of private law". See *Rules and Order*, p. 168 n. 35.

[118] Hayek describes himself as addressing "this problem of constitutional design" on p. 4 of *Rules and Order*.

constructivist rationalist attempts to plan the allocation of resources whilst simultaneously contending that the government can design parts of the institutional framework within which spontaneous orders arise, the tension is less acute than it seems.[119] The reason lies in Hayek's work on the economy as a complex system. This sees him develop a set of epistemological concepts—such as the notions of pattern prediction and explanation of the principle—that enable him to argue that people can learn enough about spontaneous orders to be able to understand the principles governing their operation and to identify the conditions under which they promote the common good, whilst also claiming that it is impossible to predict and plan the details of the outcomes produced:

> [S]ometimes, though we may not be able to bring about the particular results we would like, knowledge of the principle of the thing will enable us to make circumstances more favourable to the kind of events we desire . . . An explanation of the principle will thus often enable us to create such favourable circumstances even if it does not allow us to control the outcome. Such activities in which we are guided by a knowledge merely of the principle of the thing should perhaps better be described as the term *cultivation* than by the familiar term 'control.'[120]

Hayek thus counsels against the *abuse* of reason—as manifested in attempts to refashion the institutions of society wholesale—but not against its use *per se*, in particular to inform the design of an over-arching constitutional framework that would make it possible to harness the forces of spontaneous order for the common good. In arguing for his model constitution, Hayek is of course not suggesting a complete redesign of all the operational rules governing society but rather seeking to identify an over-arching set of constitutional and collective choice rules within which the forces of spontaneous order can work to best effect. "Government is of necessity the product of intellectual design", Hayek states, but "[i]f we can give it a shape in which it provides a beneficial framework for the free growth of society, without giving to any one power to control this growth in the particular, we may well hope to see the growth of civilization continue".[121]

---

[119] For an interesting discussion of this issue, see J. Buchanan, "Cultural Evolution and Institutional Reform" [1986], in *Federalism, Liberty, and the Law*, vol. 18 of *The Collected Works of James M. Buchanan* (Indianapolis: Liberty Fund, 2001).

[120] F. A. Hayek, "Degrees of Explanation" [1955], reprinted as chapter 6 of Hayek, *The Market and Other Orders*, p. 210. Also see Hayek, *The Road to Serfdom*, p. 71; Hayek, "Kinds of Rationalism", pp. 50–51; and Hayek, "The Pretence of Knowledge", pp. 371–72.

[121] Hayek, *The Political Order of a Free People*, p. 152. For more recent efforts in this vein, see E. Ostrom, *Governing the Commons: The Evolution of Institutions for Collective Action* (Cambridge: Cam-

"The Campaign against Keynesian Inflation"

Another reform of society's over-arching institutional framework intended to facilitate better use of the forces of spontaneous order is to be found in Hayek's proposal for the denationalisation of money. While Hayek had largely ceased work on monetary economics after the early 1940s, his interest was rekindled by the rising unemployment and accelerating inflation of the early 1970s. His thoughts appeared in a series of newspaper articles and lectures written from 1974 onwards. Four such pieces, originally penned in 1974 and 1975 and first brought together as a chapter of Hayek's *New Studies in Philosophy, Politics, Economics and the History of Ideas*, are reproduced below.[122]

In the earliest of the articles, Hayek draws on his theory of the business cycle to argue that stagflation was the result of an inflationary monetary policy that led to "a misdirection of labour and other resources into employments in which they can be maintained only so long as inflation exceeds expectations" (p. 344). Elaborating on an issue mentioned in "Full Employment, Planning and Inflation", Hayek emphasises the difficulties of conducting an appropriate monetary policy under a democratic political regime. What he had come to believe was that the root cause of inflationary crises was an institutional framework that exposed democratic governments to political pressure to expand the money supply in order to bolster politicians' immediate electoral prospects, either by engineering a boom in the run-up to elections or as a way of raising through inflationary finance the means to confer benefits upon powerful interest groups: "The pressure for more and cheaper money is an ever-present political force which monetary authorities have never been able to resist", Hayek argued, "unless they were in a position credibly to point to an absolute obstacle which made it impossible for them to meet such demands" (p. 372).

For Hayek, therefore, the challenge of ensuring an appropriate monetary policy centres not on the need to solve technical problems in economic analysis but on identifying the right institutional framework to govern policy:

---

bridge University Press, 1990), from pp. 50–52 of which the distinction between operational, collective choice and constitutional rules is taken; D. Colander and R. Kupers, *Complexity and the Art of Public Policy: Solving Society's Problems from the Bottom Up* (Princeton: Princeton University Press, 2014), pp. 19–63; and G. Gaus, "Hayekian 'Classical' Liberalism", in *The Routledge Handbook of Libertarianism*, ed. J. Brennan, B. van der Vossen, and D. Schmidtz (New York: Routledge, 2017).

[122] F. A. Hayek, "The Campaign against Keynesian Inflation" [1978], published as chapter 13 of Hayek, *New Studies*. As Hayek notes at the outset of that essay, much of his 1974 Nobel memorial prize lecture on "The Pretence of Knowledge" was also devoted to the problem of inflation, albeit emphasising the methodological shortcomings of the macroeconomic theories that had informed the conduct of policy since World War Two.

[W]e ought as economists to think much more about the political signifi-cance of institutions which place a restraint on monetary policy and can shelter governments against political pressure, than about the ideal correct-ness of the policy which might be conducted. Central banks and ministers of finance will never be able to implement what the economist would regard as the wise policy. They will always have to act under political pressure, and all we can hope to do is to protect them against this political pressure as well as possible. (p. 364)

On this view, the key to avoiding inflation is to establish an institutional frame-work that will "protect money from politics" (p. 373). What was needed in particular was the removal of the government's exclu-sive right to issue money and to compel people to use it.[123] If the government allows the use within its national boundaries of other countries' currencies, and does not impose any restrictions on the rate at which its currency can be exchanged, then people will be free to choose the currency in which they make contracts and carry out transactions. They will use a particular currency only if they are confident that it will retain its value, and the prospect of los-ing customers will provide the relevant authorities with a powerful incentive to control its supply and preserve its purchasing power:

There could be no more effective check against the abuse of money by the government than if people were free to refuse any money they distrusted and to prefer money in which they had confidence . . . Make it merely legal and people will be very quick indeed to refuse to use the national currency once it depreciates noticeably, and they will make their dealings in a currency they trust. (pp. 374–75)

In this way, competition between the issuers of currencies would give the authorities an incentive to pursue a responsible monetary policy. In particular, it would "deprive government of the power to counteract excessive wage increases, and the unemployment they would cause, by depreciating their currency" and also "prevent employers from conceding such wages in the

---

[123] A fuller account of Hayek's proposal was published by the Institute of Economic Affairs in 1976 as *Denationalisation of Money* (London: Institute of Economic Affairs, 1976), with a second edition appearing in 1978. Now see Hayek, "The Denationalization of Money: An Analysis of the Theory and Practice of Concurrent Currencies" [1978], reprinted as chapter 4 of Hayek, *Good Money, Part II: The Standard*, ed. S. Kresge, vol. 6 (1999) of *The Collected Works of F. A. Hayek*. Hayek's support in these works for the use of spontaneous market forces to supply a satisfactory medium of exchange marks a departure from his earlier skepticism about that possibility. See Hayek, *The Constitution of Liberty*, pp. 451–54. For more on this, see L. White, "Why Didn't Hayek Favour Laissez Faire in Banking?", *History of Political Economy*, vol. 31, 1999, pp. 753–69.

expectation that the national monetary authority would bail them out if they promised more than they could pay" (pp. 375–76). This would in turn place the responsibility for a wage level consistent with full employment where Hayek had long argued it belonged, namely with the trade unions.[124]

"The New Confusion about 'Planning'"

In June 1975, Hayek received a letter from Milton W. Hudson, a Vice President of the Morgan Guaranty Trust Company and editor of *The Morgan Guaranty Survey*, a monthly publication devoted to economic and financial matters. Hudson wrote of the concern he and his colleagues felt about increasing support in the United States for indicative planning. He invited Hayek to contribute an article on that topic, arguing that Hayek could make an important contribution to the debate that was then developing. By September 1975, having examined some of the proposals advanced by the advocates of planning, Hayek had begun work on his essay.[125]

The revival of interest in planning, enthusiasm for which had declined due to the rise of Keynesianism after the Second World War, had been stimulated by the apparent inability of conventional Keynesian policies to deal with stagflation after the 1973 oil price shock.[126] One prominent proposal, upon which Hayek focused, began with the formation on October 14, 1974, of the 'Initiative Committee for National Economic Planning'. The Committee was constituted by eleven prominent businessmen, academics and labour leaders, whose goal was that of "promoting the widest possible public discussion on the need for economic and social planning in the United States, and the drafting of legislation to put such planning into effect".[127] The Committee was co-chaired by the 1973 Nobel Laureate in Economics, Wassily Leontief, and the President of the UAW, Leonard Woodcock. Arguing that "[n]o reliable mechanism in the modern economy relates needs to available manpower, plant, and materials", its members urged that "provision be made for planning at the highest level of the United States government". The broad

---

[124] Also see F. A. Hayek, "Inflation Resulting from the Downward Inflexibility of Wages" [1958], reprinted as chapter 15 of this volume, p. 213.

[125] Milton W. Hudson to F. A. Hayek, June 12, 1975, and F. A. Hayek to Milton W. Hudson, September 12 and September 14, 1975, FAHP 38.46.

[126] C. Goodwin, "Changing Ideas of Planning in the United States", in *National Economic Planning: Six Papers Presented at a Conference in Washington D.C.* (Washington, DC: Chamber of Commerce of the United States, 1976), pp. 20–26.

[127] The quotations are taken from pp. 51–52 of The Initiative Committee for National Economic Planning, "For a National Economic Planning System", *Challenge*, vol. 18, March–April 1975, pp. 51–53.

aim was to establish a form of 'indicative planning' whereby the authorities would signal to employers the quantities of various different kinds of goods that the economy would need to produce in, say, five years' time if various democratically-agreed objectives were to be achieved. The targets, along with the use of a set of policies ranging from "tax incentives and disincentives" to "selective credit controls, guidance of basic capital flows . . . and mandatory resource allocation" would, it was hoped, "induce" firms to act appropriately.

The Committee's proposals were heavily influenced by input-output analysis, an approach developed by Leontief that explored the interdependencies between the various parts of the economy by modelling how each sector's outputs are used not only for final consumption but also as inputs for other sectors.[128] If this model of the structural relationships between different sectors were operationalised using statistical data, then it could be used by the planners to "provide a continuous stream of detailed information about how various sectors of the economy mesh—and are expected to mesh in the future—enabling individual firms, as well as federal, state, and local governments, to make enlightened and coherent decisions about production and consumption".[129] Once a number of detailed possible future growth paths had been identified, the ultimate decision about which one to pursue could be made through a political process.

Hayek's commentary was entitled "The New Confusion about 'Planning'" and published in January 1976. He portrayed Leontief as the chief architect of the proposals, and it is upon Leontief's views that his argument focuses (p. 384). Hayek first examined Leontief's claim that the increasingly complex web of interdependencies in the economy implied a need for greater government intervention to provide actors with the information required to coordinate their plans. Hayek argued to the contrary that "we have been able to achieve a reasonably high degree of order in our economic lives despite modern complexities . . . *only* because our affairs have been guided, not by central direction, but by the operations of the market and competition in securing the mutual adjustment of separate efforts" (p. 389).[130] Furthermore, while input-output analysis shows how the products made by various industries were used by other sectors in the past, such historical data "tell us nothing at all about

[128] W. Leontief, *The Structure of American Economy 1919–1929: An Empirical Application of Equilibrium Analysis* (Cambridge, MA: Harvard University Press, 1941), and W. Leontief, *Input-Output Economics* (New York: Oxford University Press, 1966).

[129] The Initiative Committee for National Economic Planning, "For a National Economic Planning System", p. 53. Also see W. Leontief, "For a National Economic Planning Board", *New York Times*, March 14, 1974, p. 37, and W. Leontief, "Interview: What an Economic Planning Board Should Do," *Challenge*, vol. 17, July–August 1974, pp. 35–40.

[130] For more on Hayek's account of the relationship between the complexity of an economy and the need to rely on spontaneous market forces, see *Rules and Order*, pp. 13–15 and 29–51.

whether that specific combination of inputs or any other combination would be economical under changed conditions" (p. 395). Consequently, there is "no possibility for determining from statistics of the past how much of different materials will be wanted in the future", in which case it is "difficult to see what possible purpose would be served if it were announced beforehand what quantities of the different main classes of goods ought to be produced during a certain period of the future" (pp. 396–97). The information about the scarcity of resources required to make economically efficient resource allocation decisions can be derived only from current market prices. Absent the competitive market process, there were no grounds for believing that planners would be able to acquire the information—about the future needs of consumers, and the consequent requirements for raw materials and equipment—needed to indicate to firms the quantities of the different goods they should produce (pp. 392–95).

"The Atavism of Social Justice"

In October 1974 Hayek was awarded, jointly with Swedish economist Gunnar Myrdal, the Bank of Sweden Nobel Memorial Prize in Economics. The attendant publicity led to an expansion of Hayek's travel schedule as, for the second time in his career, he became a public intellectual, invited to give numerous lectures and interviews around the world. One series of lectures took place in Australia, which Hayek visited between October 3 and November 6, 1976. The moving force behind Hayek's visit was Australian economist and lawyer Roger Randerson, who had known Hayek since he had been a member of the London Economic Club under Hayek's presidency in the late 1930s.[131] During his trip, Hayek kept over sixty appointments, delivering lectures and seminars, appearing in an hour-long nationally-televised discussion programme, and meeting the Australian Prime Minister. Three of his public lectures were subsequently published, namely "The Atavism of Social Justice", "Whither Democracy?" and "Socialism and Science".

Hayek's topic in his first lecture was the notion of social or distributive justice, which he argued was "nothing more than an empty formula, conventionally used to assert that a particular claim is justified without giving any reason" (p. 401). The concept of justice is inapplicable to the results of a market

---

[131] See R. Randerson to F. A. Hayek, September 10, 1963, FAHP 45.5, and R. Randerson, "Hayek – Scholar, Teacher, Liberal" [1979], published as pp. 47–52 of F. A. Hayek, *Social Justice, Socialism & Democracy: 3 Australian Lectures by F. A. Hayek*, CIS Occasional Papers 2 (Turramura: The Centre for Independent Studies, 1979), p. 47. A detailed account of Hayek's visit to Australia is provided by R. Randerson, "Australian 1976 Lecture Tour" [1979], published as pp. 57–61 of the same volume.

economy, Hayek argued, because those outcomes are the unintended consequences of human action and "there can be no distributive justice where no
one distributes" (p. 402). Hence, the results of the market "could neither be
called just nor unjust" (p. 402). To think otherwise is to lapse into unjustified anthropomorphism of the kind Hayek condemned in "The Confusion of
Language in Political Thought".[132]

For Hayek, people's continued belief in 'social justice' reflects deeply
ingrained instincts inherited from earlier forms of society. Prior to the emergence of the Great Society, people had lived in small bands of hunter-
gatherers, organisations in which their actions and the distribution of goods
came under the direction of a leader whose goal was the preservation of the
group in question. This began to change, however, when a few individuals
chose to depart from the norms of their group and trade with outsiders for
profit. Over time, a process of selection led to the gradual displacement of
groups characterised by organisational rules directed towards specific ends by
groups following purpose-independent rules of conduct, ultimately giving rise
to the Great Society.[133]

However, man's ingrained morality has not developed at the same pace
as his methods of social organisation; it is "still governed by the instincts
appropriate to the success of the small hunting band", in particular by feelings of personal loyalty and obligation that enjoin people to meet the visible
needs of the small number of others with whom they are directly acquainted
(p. 405). Those instincts are 'atavistic' in the sense that they are based on
primordial emotions quite at odds with the impersonal morality appropriate
for modern societies, the maintenance of which requires people to do two
things: observe abstract rules of just conduct that are applied equally to close
acquaintances and strangers alike, independently of our views about their

---

[132] For a longer critique, see Hayek, *The Mirage of Social Justice*, pp. 62–102. The merits of
Hayek's argument are discussed in R. Plant, "Hayek on Social Justice: A Critique", in *Hayek,
Coordination and Evolution: His Legacy in Philosophy, Politics, Economics and the History of Ideas*, ed.
J. Birner and R. van Zijp (London and New York: Routledge, 1994), and S. Lukes, "Social Jus-
tice: The Hayekian Challenge", *Critical Review*, vol. 11, 1997, pp. 65–80. The extent to which
Hayek's criticisms of social justice are consistent with his oft-repeated view, expressed for ex-
ample on p. 408 of "The Atavism of Social Justice", that liberals can acknowledge a role for government in providing a minimum income for everyone outside of the market is considered on
pp. 595–600 of A. Tebble, "Hayek and Social Justice: A Critique", *Critical Review of International
Social and Political Philosophy*, vol. 12, 2009, pp. 581–604.

[133] Hayek explores the ideas summarised here at greater length in *The Mirage of Social Justice*,
pp. 133–52, and in *The Political Order of a Free People*, pp. 153–68. For evaluations of Hayek's analysis in the light of more recent developments in evolutionary theory, see F. Faria, "Is Market Liberalism Adaptive? Rethinking F. A. Hayek on Moral Evolution", *Journal of Bioeconomics*, vol. 19,
2017, pp. 307–26, and N. Beck, *Hayek and the Evolution of Capitalism* (Chicago and London: University of Chicago Press, 2018).

particular merits and needs; and pursue financial gain by responding to price signals which lead us unintentionally to serve the needs of many unknown people without having to know anything specific about them. Hence Hayek's remark that "we have all inherited from an earlier different type of society, . . . some now deeply ingrained instincts which are inapplicable to our present civilisation" (pp. 402–3).

In order to form the Great Society, therefore, people had to suppress their innate instincts by following learned rules that facilitated peaceful cooperation between a multitude of diverse individuals.[134] But those instincts were only restrained, not eliminated, and so could be revived. And it is to the moral instincts of the small group that advocates of social justice appeal when they claim that justice is principally a matter of distribution and that organised power should be used to allocate to each person what (s)he deserves. To the extent that their efforts are successful, so that universal rules of just conduct are replaced by rules of organisation that see the authorities treat people differently in order to realise a particular distributive goal, then people are deprived of the freedom required to make good use of their local knowledge, undermining the foundations of the market order: "The trouble is that the aggregate product which [advocates of 'social justice'] think is available for distribution exists only *because* returns for the different efforts are held out by the market with little regard to deserts or needs, and are needed to attract the owners of particular information, material means and personal skills to the points where at each moment they can make the greatest contribution . . . We should not have as much to share if *that* income of an individual were not treated as *just*, the prospects of which induced him to make the largest contribution to the pool" (pp. 408–9).[135]

For Hayek, the demand for social justice more often than not involves

---

[134] Such small-group obligations cannot be universalized and therefore fail to qualify as rules of just conduct. See Hayek, "The Principles of a Liberal Social Order", p. 281, and Hayek, *The Mirage of Social Justice*, pp. 137, 191 n. 10. This aspect of Hayek's thought, according to which liberal societies develop through the gradual extension of rights of membership to outsiders, so that people's interactions centre less on connections binding them into small solidaristic units and more on impersonal connections requiring little sense of shared commitment, also underpins his long-standing unease about nationalism. See C. Kukathas, "Hayek and the State", in Dyzenhaus and Poole, *Law, Liberty and State*.

[135] The revival of such instincts is also encouraged by the fact that many people in modern industrial societies are employed in large, bureaucratic organisations and so have little direct experience of how markets work. As a result, they are prone to support policies that reward people according to the perceived merits of their actions, rather than their results, and are less likely to understand and support policies and parties conducive to the preservation of the market order. See Hayek, *The Constitution of Liberty*, pp. 184–90, and Hayek, *The Mirage of Social Justice*, pp. 134–35.

people trying to protect themselves against declines in their absolute and rela-tive incomes.[136] But in his view such claims are in fact deeply unjust. Those seeking to defend their current position were able to achieve it only because they, and others, submitted in the past to the same kind of market forces that are now tending to diminish their rewards. They can defend their current position only by denying others the same chance of advancement from which they benefitted earlier. Their efforts to maintain their relative position can-not be just, therefore, because they do not satisfy the Kantian standard of being consistent with a rule that could be applied equally to everyone. Rightly understood, justice demands that those who have in the past benefitted from the market process accept the outcomes it produces in the future even when they are less favourable.[137]

The arguments summarized above suggest that Hayek developed a dis-tinctive style of political philosophy, eschewing the traditional approach of first formulating moral standards which are then used to evaluate social sys-tems and to guide their reform in favour of appraising institutional arrange-ments by reference to their epistemic properties (in particular, their capacity to generate and utilise the knowledge required to sustain an extended social order).[138] More specifically, Hayek's approach is social-theoretic in the sense that it centres on an attempt to understand how the character of modern industrial society—in particular, the nature of the economic processes by which it is sustained—limits the kinds of normative ideal that can be realised therein. Hayek's criticisms of the notion of social justice, for example, can be understood—as noted above—as resting on the argument that because efforts to realise particular distributions of material welfare require different people to be treated differently, they involve the replacement of some of the universal rules of just conduct that make modern commercial society possible by rules of organisation designed to ensure that people are rewarded according to the perceived merits of their actions. But in Hayek's view, as we have seen, the substitution of one kind of rule for another undermines the basis of the mar-ket order and the wealth it generates, because the new combination of rules does not form a system that generates the overall order of actions. As Hayek put it in *Law, Legislation and Liberty*, "One of our chief contentions will be that, though spontaneous order and organisation will always coexist, it is still not possible to mix these two principles of order in any manner we like . . . [W]e

---

[136] F. A. Hayek, "Competition as a Discovery Procedure" [1968], reprinted as chapter 12 of *The Market and Other Orders*, p. 311, and Hayek, "The Principles of a Liberal Social Order", p. 286.
[137] Hayek, *The Mirage of Social Justice*, p. 128.
[138] For details of the interpretation summarized here, see Gray, *Hayek on Liberty*, pp. ix–x, 41; Kukathas, *Hayek and Modern Liberalism*, pp. 2–13; J. Shearmur, "Hayek's Politics", in *The Cambridge Companion to Hayek*, pp. 152–54; and Gaus, "Hayekian 'Classical' Liberalism".

are not fully free to pick and choose whatever combination of features we wish our society to possess, or to fit them together into a viable whole, that is . . . we cannot build a desirable social order like a mosaic by selecting whatever particular parts we like best".[139] The advocates of social justice are thus confronted with an unenviable choice between two desirable but mutually incompatible goals, in this case between advancing their normative ideals and sustaining the material prosperity made possible by the extended order of the Great Society.

"Whither Democracy?"

"Whither Democracy?" sees Hayek discuss the nature of, and prospects for, democratic politics. The "true and original meaning" of the term 'democracy' is that it is a method of decision-making which "enables any majority to rid itself of a government it does not like" (p. 413). Understood thus, democracy "is of inestimable value" (p. 413). However, its value is purely instrumental: it is the only peaceful, and therefore the best, way of removing undesirable rules; but it has no intrinsic worth.[140] Hayek also contends that since the widespread adoption of democracy the term's meaning has changed in ways that "have so alarmed even just and reasonable people that a serious reaction against democracy, as such, is a real danger" (p. 413). In particular, 'democracy' is now understood to require not only that ultimate decision-making power should lie in the hands of the majority of the people or their representatives, but also that their power should be unconstrained.

It is against this notion of "unlimited democracy", rather than against 'democracy' as such, that Hayek argues (p. 414). For Hayek, liberalism requires that all power, including majority power, be limited. It is therefore incompatible with unlimited democracy. A legislature with unlimited sovereign power will inevitably use it to confer special benefits on particular groups, because "a majority can be formed only by buying the support of numerous special interests, through granting them such benefits at the expense of a minority" (p. 417). This will erode the rule of law, as politicians use coercive state power to discriminate in favour of some groups in order to retain support. The consequence will be an unacceptable reduction of individual liberty, as the universal rules of just conduct upon which freedom depends are eroded.[141]

---

[139] Hayek, *Rules and Order*, pp. 48, 59.

[140] Hayek, *The Road to Serfdom*, p. 110 and Hayek, *The Constitution of Liberty*, p. 170.

[141] Hayek argues elsewhere that just as the consistent application of liberal principles leads to democracy, because equality before the law spawns the demand that all people should have an equal share in making the law, so the abandonment of liberal principles to which unlimited

Underpinning Hayek's argument is his conviction that democracy and liberalism are distinct doctrines: liberalism is concerned with limiting the coercive powers of government; democracy pertains to the question of who directs government. While Hayek esteems democracy, he ultimately views it as the lesser value:

> Although there is good reason for preferring limited democratic government to a non-democratic one, I must confess to preferring non-democratic government under the law to unlimited (and therefore essentially lawless) democratic government. Government under the law seems to me to be the higher value, which it was once hoped that democratic watch-dogs would preserve. (p. 415)[142]

Of course, one of Hayek's main goals was to bring about the reform of democratic institutions before the pathologies of the current arrangements became so serious that people demanded a return to authoritarianism: "It is important to remember that, if the peculiar institutions of the unlimited democracy we have today should ultimately prove a failure, this need not mean that democracy itself was a mistake, but only that we tried it in the wrong way" (p. 414). Indeed, this was the rationale for Hayek's model constitution, which was intended to show that the problems of contemporary democracies were an artefact of the particular institutional forms through which democratic politics were being conducted rather than an inevitable feature of democracy *per se*, and so could be avoided through a judicious process of institutional reform.[143]

---

democracy leads will ultimately imperil democracy itself. See Hayek, *The Constitution of Liberty*, pp. 182–83, and Hayek, *The Political Order of a Free People*, pp. 137–39.

[142] Hayek at times suggested that there might be circumstances where a temporary dictatorship would be necessary in order to bring about a liberal society. If societal breakdown had led to a situation where there were no recognised social rules stipulating acceptable behaviour, for example, then the use of dictatorial power to impose such rules, including ones that limited the regime's own powers, might be the only hope for restoring a liberal regime. See A. Farrant and E. McPhail, "Can a Dictator Turn a Constitution into a Can-opener? F. A. Hayek and the Alchemy of Transitional Dictatorship in Chile", *Review of Political Economy*, vol. 26, 2014, pp. 331–48, and B. Caldwell and L. Montes, "Friedrich Hayek and His Visits to Chile", *Review of Austrian Economics*, vol. 28, 2015, pp. 261–309.

[143] Hayek was trying "to construct an intellectual emergency equipment which will be available when we have no choice but to replace the tottering structure by some better edifice rather than resort in despair to some sort of dictatorial regime". Hayek, *The Political Order of a Free People*, p. 152. Hayek was far from alone in painting a gloomy portrait of the prospects for democracy in the mid-1970s. For similar views, see S. Brittan, "The Economic Contradictions of Democracy", *British Journal of Political Science*, vol. 5, 1975, pp. 129–59; M. Crozier, S. Huntington and J. Watanuki, *The Crisis of Democracy: Report on the Governability of Democracies to the Trilateral Commission* (New York: New York University Press, 1975); and A. King, "Overload: Problems of Governing in the 1970s", *Political Studies*, vol. 23, 1975, pp. 284–96.

"Socialism and Science"

Hayek's concern in "Socialism and Science" was to examine "the peculiar manner in which most socialists attempt to shield their doctrines against scientific criticism, by claiming that differences from opponents are of a nature which precludes scientific refutation" (p. 427). He maintained that proponents of socialism often dismissed criticism by arguing that it reflected differences in value judgements, something which—they contended—rendered it inadmissible to scientific debate. Hayek countered that his "differences with socialist fellow-economists . . . turn inevitably, not on differences of value, but on differences as to the effects particular measures will have" (p. 427). Even if one accepted for the sake of argument the ethical positions adopted by the socialists, it could be shown that their methods were in fact quite unsuitable for promoting those values.

For instance, the Austrian argument against central planning takes the form of an immanent critique whereby it is shown that the socialists' chosen method—the abolition of private property—will make it impossible for them to achieve their own goals. In claiming that socialism was 'impossible', Hayek states, "Mises obviously meant that the proposed methods of socialism could not achieve what they were supposed to do! We can, of course, try any course of action, but what is questioned is whether any such course of action will produce the effects claimed to follow from it. This undoubtedly *is* a scientific question" (p. 428). This claim reflects the account of the economist's role set out in Hayek's inaugural lecture, where he argued that in criticising policy proposals economists "accepted the ethical postulates on which such proposals were based and tried to demonstrate that these were not conducive to the desired end and that, very often, policies of a radically different nature would bring about the desired result".[144]

Hayek's critique was, he maintained, scientific in the sense of being "based, not on different values or on prejudice, but on unrefuted logical argument" (p. 439). However, his claims continued to be disputed on scientific grounds. Indeed, by the 1970s a consensus had developed in the academic literature that the Austrian critique of socialism had been refuted. A key contribution to that viewpoint was made in the late 1930s by Polish émigré economist Oskar Lange, who argued that it was possible to find a rational way to allocate

---

[144] Hayek, "The Trend of Economic Thinking", p. 20. Also see F. A. Hayek, "Socialist Calculation: The Competitive 'Solution'" [1940], reprinted as chapter 3 of Hayek, *Socialism and War*, p. 130. For a useful analysis of Hayek's emphasis on the importance of immanent critique, which relates it both to his account of the mind as a rule-governed system of classification and also to his analysis of the evolution of the common law, see Gray, *Hayek on Liberty*, pp. 21–26, 42–43.

resources under socialism.[145] The method in question, *market socialism*, would permit free markets in labour and consumer goods; but there would be public ownership of the material means of production, and so no market—and, therefore, no market prices—for capital goods. Lange argued that prices are simply the numerical 'terms on which alternatives are offered' and can therefore be formed in a variety of ways, not all of which involve rivalrous market competition. One alternative would involve a trial-and-error process whereby the planners would announce 'accounting prices' specifying the terms on which capital goods were to be offered to the managers of socialist firms, who would then decide what to do by applying operational rules derived from the characterisation of an efficient allocation of resources provided by marginalist economics (such as producing the level of output at which the marginal cost of production equalled the price paid by consumers). The planners would increase or decrease 'prices' depending on whether the managers' decisions resulted in excess demand or supply. Lange believed that it was possible in this way for the planners to identify equilibrium prices, thereby overcoming Mises's objections to the possibility of socialism.

Hayek first responded to Lange in 1940, advancing what is arguably his most fundamental criticism of market socialism by disputing that socialist plant managers will know such things as the minimum cost of producing all the various possible levels of output. Lange's reliance on equilibrium analysis meant that he was using an approach that focused on situations in which such data had *already* been discovered, thereby assuming away the challenge of generating that knowledge.[146] However, because many economists viewed the calculation debate through an equilibrium-oriented conceptual lens, they were unable fully to appreciate the merits of this argument, which was based on a vision of the market as a dynamic process of rivalrous competition. The upshot was that, by the 1970s and early 1980s, the consensus in the literature on comparative economic systems was that Lange had provided a convincing response to the Austrian critique.[147]

---

[145] O. Lange, "On the Economic Theory of Socialism", *Review of Economic Studies*, vol. 4, no. 1, 1936, pp. 53–71, and vol. 4, no. 2, 1937, pp. 123–42. The publication of Lange's article initiated the second round of the so-called socialist calculation debate, the first round having begun with the publication in 1920 of Mises's article on the impossibility of rational economic calculation under socialism. A fuller account can be found in D. Lavoie, *Rivalry and Central Planning: The Socialist Calculation Debate Reconsidered* (Cambridge: Cambridge University Press, 1985).

[146] As Hayek wrote of Lange's approach, "it is difficult to suppress the suspicion that this particular proposal has been born out of an excessive preoccupation with problems of the pure theory of stationary equilibrium". See Hayek, "Socialist Calculation: The Competitive 'Solution'", p. 123.

[147] See D. Lavoie, "A Critique of the Standard Account of the Socialist Calculation Debate", *Journal of Libertarian Studies*, vol. 5, 1981, pp. 41–87, and Lavoie, *Rivalry and Central Planning*, pp. 1–27.

"Two Pages of Fiction"

Hayek was aware of this, lamenting the "somewhat shameful state of what has become an established part of economic science, the subject of 'economic systems'" (p. 456). Frustrated by what he described as the "endless repetition" (p. 444) of the claim that Lange had successfully refuted the case against planning, Hayek returned to his argument in a paper published in 1982 by the Institute of Economic Affairs. In correspondence with Arthur Seldon, the Editorial Director of the Institute, Hayek stated that his motivation for writing the paper lay in his having been "[g]oaded by the revival of the old nonsense of 'socialist calculation'" and that he was "particularly indignant about the steadily repeated silly talk of Lange having refuted Mises."[148]

Hayek argues that the process through which accounting prices are determined in Lange's model is wholly inadequate to the task of generating the knowledge required to ensure that resources flow to their most-valued uses. For Hayek, that knowledge simply will not exist—it "would *not* be available to anyone in a socialist economy where prices are not provided by the market" (p. 448)—without rivalrous competition in the market for capital goods. What informs entrepreneurs' actions in the market is knowledge of the impact of relatively small variations in factor combinations and output around those at which production has typically taken place in the past:

> [T]he relevant production functions which guide the competitive market are, of course . . . very *specific* relations showing how, in a particular plant under the specific local conditions, changes in the combinations of the particular goods and services employed will affect the size of the output. The individual entrepreneur will not possess or require knowledge of general production functions, but he will currently learn from experience how at any given time variations in the qualities or the relative quantities of the different factors of production he uses will affect his output. (pp. 448–49)

[148] See F. A. Hayek to A. Seldon, December 11, 1981, and February 16, 1982, FAHP 27.6. Hayek was no doubt also motivated by the revival of proposals for planning in the USA in the mid-1970s and by development of a literature on 'resource allocation processes' that seemed to support planning (and to which he refers on p. 455 of his essay). The seeds of the idea for the paper may have been sown by Arthur Seldon, who in a letter to Hayek in 1975 wrote: "Since there have been writings by Lange and other[s] after the War, I wonder whether you had anywhere written a more up-to-date version of 'The State of the Debate' to deal with some of the later arguments . . . The argument on the use of markets under socialism is evidently very much alive". See A. Seldon to F. A. Hayek, February 12, 1975, FAHP 27.6. Also see A. Seldon, "Before and After *The Road to Serfdom*", in *Hayek's 'Serfdom' Revisited* (London: Institute of Economic Affairs, 1984), pp. xxv–xxviii.

And the experience from which entrepreneurs learn is—and only can be—that provided by their participation in the competitive market process. Entrepreneurs gradually broaden their knowledge of production possibilities and costs only because the pressure of competition—the imperative to undercut rivals, or to respond to competitors' efforts to undercut them—encourages them to experiment with new production plans and input combinations. This process of exploration is inextricably bound up with market competition, because producers learn whether those new methods really facilitate lower costs only by implementing their plans and seeing whether they yield profits or losses. This learning process is completely obscured by Lange's assumption that knowledge of the complete range of production techniques and costs is 'given', a claim Hayek describes as an "impermissible falsification" (p. 447). As Hayek states in his 1940 commentary, the problem with market socialism is that "one of the most important forces which in a truly competitive economy brings about the reduction of costs to the minimum discoverable will be absent, namely price competition":

> In the discussion of this sort of problem . . . the question is frequently treated as if the cost curves were objectively given facts. What is forgotten here is that the method which under given conditions is the cheapest is a thing which has to be discovered, and to be discovered anew sometimes almost from day to day, by the entrepreneur . . . The force which in a competitive society brings about the reduction of price to the lowest cost at which the quantity saleable at that cost can be produced is the opportunity for anybody who knows a cheaper method to come in at his own risk and to attract customers by underbidding the other producers. But if prices are fixed by authority this method is excluded.[149]

There is, therefore, a categorical difference between the 'terms of exchange' announced by central planners and the money prices generated through a competitive market process. Only genuine market prices, produced through rivalrous competition in the market for capital goods, and the calculations of profit and loss they facilitate, can provide entrepreneurs with the feedback necessary for them to learn what actually constitutes a cost-minimising method of production.[150]

---

[149] Hayek, "Socialist Calculation: The Competitive 'Solution'", p. 130. Also see F. A. Hayek, "The Meaning of Competition" [1948], reprinted as chapter 4 of *The Market and Other Orders*, p. 108, and Hayek, "Competition as a Discovery Procedure", pp. 306–7.

[150] Notwithstanding Hayek's effort in writing "Two Pages of Fiction", it was arguably only after the publication in the 1980s of revisionist histories of the calculation debate that the merits of the Austrian argument came to be more widely appreciated. These new accounts emphasised

"Letters to The Times, *1931–1981"*

While Hayek had written letters to the editors of national newspapers throughout his career, his correspondence increased significantly after he received the Nobel Prize. He wrote especially often to *The Times* and, by the early 1980s, was in discussion with Arthur Seldon about the publication of a selection of his letters by the Institute of Economic Affairs. However, the proposal did not come to fruition.[151]

Hayek wrote about a wide assortment of issues. Many were often highly controversial, including the rights of minority groups, immigration policy, the relationship between democracy and freedom, the conduct of monetary policy, and the need to curb the power of the trade unions (whose privileges he believed violated the rule of law and whose conduct he saw as encouraging inflation).[152] The prominence of the last three topics is unsurprising, given the context in which Hayek was writing. Policy-makers in Britain were struggling to deal with stagflation, and the shortcomings of standard Keynesian responses afforded an opportunity for alternative approaches—most notably, those falling under the broad heading of 'monetarism'—to gain influence. The efforts of the Conservative government led by Edward Heath to control inflation through incomes policies led in early 1974 to a miners' strike and a three-day working week in British industry.[153] When Heath sought to assert his authority by calling a general election that focused largely on the issue 'Who governs Britain, the government or the miners?', he lost. Heath's

---

that the strengths of Mises and Hayek's position could be fully understood only if their arguments were interpreted from a vantage point that did justice to their vision of the market as a dynamic process. See K. Vaughn, "Economic Calculation under Socialism: The Austrian Contribution", *Economic Inquiry*, vol. 18, 1980, pp. 535–54, and Lavoie, *Rivalry and Central Planning*.

[151] See F. A. Hayek to A. Seldon, June 19, 1981, and A. Seldon to F. A. Hayek, April 13, 1983, FAHP 63.4 and 27.6.

[152] Some of Hayek's remarks make for distinctly uncomfortable reading, in particular his claim that he had "not been able to find a single person even in much maligned Chile who did not agree that personal freedom was much greater under Pinochet than it had been under Allende". See F. A. Hayek, "Freedom of Choice", *The Times*, August 3, 1978, reprinted in chapter 31 below, at p. 497. Hayek had in fact been warned about the human rights abuses taking place in Chile under Pinochet. See R. Raico to F. A. Hayek, June 13, 1977, FAHP 14.20. For additional details, see Farrant and McPhail, "Can a Dictator Turn a Constitution into a Can-opener?", pp. 345–46.

[153] Heath's was only one of several incomes policies—some statutory, some voluntary—to which British governments resorted in their efforts to control inflation in the 1960s and 1970s. Such policies were, of course, anathema to Hayek, who argued that by impeding the adjustment of the relative prices of different kinds of labour they undermined the effective working of the market mechanism. See Hayek, *The Political Order of a Free People*, p. 13, and F. A. Hayek, *1980s Unemployment and the Unions: The Distortion of Relative Prices by Monopoly in the Labour Market*, 2nd edn. (London: Institute of Economic Affairs, 1984), p. 22.

defeat, and the role played in the demise of the ensuing Labour government by a wave of unofficial industrial action during the 'Winter of Discontent' in 1978–79, incited a vigorous debate over whether the unions had become too powerful, to which Hayek of course contributed (as he also did to discussions about the need to use monetary policy to control inflation rather than promote full employment). What we can see here is Hayek seeking, consistent with the approach he adopted in his inaugural lecture almost half a century earlier, to shift public opinion in favour of his preferred policies, especially in this case towards policies designed to curb union power. As he stated in one newspaper article in the late 1970s, "All that I can say with conviction is that so long as general opinion makes it politically impossible to deprive the trade unions of their coercive powers, an economic recovery of Great Britain is also impossible".[154] The swing in public opinion that carried the Conservative Party led by Margaret Thatcher to victory in the 1979 general election provided the basis for a series of legal reforms, introduced gradually over the 1980s, that were designed to reduce union power along the lines—if not at the pace—advocated by Hayek.

The breadth of issues addressed by Hayek in his correspondence is in keeping with the wide range of topics covered by the essays gathered together in this volume of *The Collected Works*. Both include writings on fundamental issues in the methodology of the social sciences and political philosophy, as well as pieces in which those abstract principles are applied to concrete questions of economic and social policy. They leave a picture of Hayek as a thinker who whilst often preoccupied with matters of high theory was also keen to engage in public discussion about how the ideas to which he was committed could be deployed to inform and improve policy. This combination of topics and levels of analysis makes for a fascinating volume that should be of interest to a broad array of readers.

---

[154] F. A. Hayek, "The Powerful Reasons for Curbing Union Powers," *The Times*, October 10, 1978, reprinted in chapter 31 below, at p. 502. Also see Hayek, *1980s Unemployment and the Unions*, pp. 57–58.

ESSAYS ON LIBERALISM
AND THE ECONOMY

ONE

LIBERALISM[1]

Introduction

1. The different concepts of liberalism

The term is now used with a variety of meanings which have little in common beyond describing an openness to new ideas, including some which are directly opposed to those which were originally designated by it during the nineteenth and the earlier parts of the twentieth centuries. What will alone be considered here is that broad stream of political ideals which during that period under the name of liberalism operated as one of the most influential intellectual forces guiding developments in western and central Europe. This movement derives, however, from two distinct sources, and the two traditions to which they gave rise, though generally mixed to various degrees, coexisted only in an uneasy partnership and must be clearly distinguished if the development of the liberal movement is to be understood.

The one tradition, much older than the name 'liberalism', traces back to classical antiquity and took its modern form during the late seventeenth and the eighteenth centuries as the political doctrines of the English Whigs. It provided the model of political institutions which most of the European nineteenth-century liberalism followed. It was the individual liberty which a 'government under the law' had secured to the citizens of Great Britain which inspired the movement for liberty in the countries of the Continent in which absolutism had destroyed most of the medieval liberties which had been largely preserved in Britain. These institutions were, however, interpreted on the Continent in the light of a philosophical tradition very different from the evolutionary conceptions predominant in Britain, namely of a rationalist or constructivistic view which demanded a deliberate reconstruction of

[1] Written in 1973 for the Italian *Enciclopedia del Novecento* where the article will appear in an Italian translation at about the same time as this book. [Published in F. A. Hayek, *New Studies in Philosophy, Politics, Economics and the History of Ideas* (London and Henley: Routledge and Kegan Paul, 1978), pp. 119–51, and also as "Liberalismo", in *Enciclopedia del Novecento*, vol. 3. (Rome: Istituto dell'Enciclopedia Italiana, 1978), pp. 982–93.—Ed.]

the whole of society in accordance with principles of reason. This approach derived from the new rationalist philosophy developed above all by René Descartes (but also by Thomas Hobbes in Britain) and gained its greatest influence in the eighteenth century through the philosophers of the French Enlightenment. Voltaire and J.-J. Rousseau were the two most influential figures of the intellectual movement that culminated in the French Revolution and from which the Continental or constructivistic type of liberalism derives. The core of this movement, unlike the British tradition, was not so much a definite political doctrine as a general mental attitude, a demand for an emancipation from all prejudice and all beliefs which could not be rationally justified, and for an escape from the authority of 'priests and kings'.[2] Its best expression is

[2] [This distinction between the British or evolutionary, and the Continental or rationalist, traditions of social and political thought is a recurrent theme in Hayek's work. It first appears in the distinction Hayek draws between true and false individualism in his 1945 Finlay lecture, "Individualism: True and False" [1946], reprinted as the Prelude to *Studies on the Abuse and Decline of Reason: Text and Documents*, ed. Bruce Caldwell, vol. 13 (2010) of *The Collected Works of F. A. Hayek* (Chicago: University of Chicago Press; London: Routledge). Central to true individualism is the claim that many of the institutions upon which human civilisation rests, and which facilitate peaceful social cooperation and growing prosperity, have developed and operate spontaneously—that is, in the absence of a designing and directing mind—via a process of evolutionary selection. This tradition is exemplified for Hayek by the work of thinkers such as English philosopher John Locke (1632–1704), Dutch physician Bernard Mandeville (1670–1733), the philosopher David Hume (1711–76), Welsh rector and pamphleteer Josiah Tucker (1712–1799), the moral philosopher and historian Adam Ferguson (1723–1816), the Irish statesman and conservative political philosopher Edmund Burke (1729–97), the political economist Adam Smith (1723–90), and the founder of the Austrian school of economics Carl Menger (1840–1921). Later representatives of true individualism are said to include French diplomat, historian and political scientist Alexis de Tocqueville (1805–59) and English historian and Member of Parliament Lord Acton (1834–1902). Hayek's views on Mandeville, Hume and Smith are expressed in the essays entitled "Dr. Bernard Mandeville (1670–1733)" [1966], "The Legal and Political Philosophy of David Hume (1711–1776)" [1963], and "Adam Smith (1723–1790): His Message in Today's Language" [1976], which are reprinted as chapters 6, 7 and 8 of F. A. Hayek, *The Trend of Economic Thinking: Essays on Political Economists and Economic History*, ed. W. W. Bartley III and S. Kresge, vol. 3 (1991) of *The Collected Works of F. A. Hayek*. Hayek discusses Menger in "Carl Menger (1840–1921)" [1934], reprinted as chapter 2 of F. A. Hayek, *The Fortunes of Liberalism: Essays on Austrian Economics and the Ideal of Freedom*, ed. Peter G. Klein, vol. 4 (1992) of *The Collected Works of F. A. Hayek*.

Hayek defines false individualism as the idea that all useful institutions are and should be the deliberate creation of conscious reason. He contends that, while the roots of this 'false' variety of individualism are ultimately to be found in Greek philosophy, its modern influence begins in the sixteenth and seventeenth centuries with the works of English philosopher, and sometime Lord Chancellor of England, Francis Bacon (1561–1626), English philosopher and social contract theorist Thomas Hobbes (1588–1679), and in particular French philosopher René Descartes (1596–1650). Hayek traces the influence of false individualism from Descartes down through Hobbes, via the works of the French writer Voltaire (1694–1778) and French philosopher and political theorist Jean-Jacques Rousseau (1712–78), the physiocrats, the English jurist John Austin (1790–1859), via Hegel and Marx, and ultimately to the market socialists and

probably B. de Spinoza's statement that "he is a free man who lives according to the dictates of reason alone".[3]

These two strands of thought which provided the chief ingredients of what in the nineteenth century came to be called liberalism were on a few essential postulates, such as freedom of thought, of speech, and of the press, in sufficient agreement to create a common opposition to conservative and authoritarian views and therefore to appear as part of a common movement. Most of liberalism's adherents would also profess a belief in individual freedom of action and in some sort of equality of all men, but closer examination shows that this agreement was in part only verbal since the key terms 'freedom' and 'equality' were used with somewhat different meanings. While to the older British tradition the freedom of the individual in the sense of a protection by law against all arbitrary coercion was the chief value, in the Continental tradition the demand for the self-determination of each group concerning its form of government occupied the highest place. This led to an early association and almost identification of the Continental movement with the movement for democracy, which is concerned with a different problem from that which was the chief concern of the liberal tradition of the British type.

During the period of their formation these ideas, which in the nineteenth century came to be known as liberalism, were not yet described by that name. The adjective 'liberal' gradually assumed its political connotation during the later part of the eighteenth century when it was used in such occasional phrases as when Adam Smith wrote of "the liberal plan of equality, liberty and justice".[4] As the name of a political movement liberalism appears, how-

---

Fabian reformers of the twentieth century. The distinction between true and false individualism is recast in Hayek's later writings, as the contrast between the evolutionary and 'constructivist rationalist' modes of thought. See, for instance, the essays entitled "Kinds of Rationalism" [1965], "The Results of Human Action but Not of Human Design" [1967], and "The Errors of Constructivism" [1970], which are reprinted as the Prologue, chapter 11 and chapter 14 respectively, of F. A. Hayek, *The Market and Other Orders*, ed. Bruce Caldwell, vol. 15 (2014) of *The Collected Works of F. A. Hayek*. A full statement can be found in F. A. Hayek, *Rules and Order*, vol. 1 (1973) of *Law, Legislation and Liberty* (Chicago: University of Chicago Press; London: Routledge, 1973–1979), pp. 8–34. Hayek's tendency to divide past thinkers into two categories has not met with universal acclaim. See B. Caldwell, "Introduction", in Hayek, *Studies on the Abuse and Decline of Reason*, p. 40 n. 115.—Ed.]

[3] [Dutch philosopher Benedict de Spinoza (1632–1677) was one of the most important advocates of seventeenth-century rationalism. He took Euclidean geometry as the model for how pure reason enables us to gain access to the truth about the world. The words quoted by Hayek are taken from Spinoza's *Ethics and "De Intellectus Emendatione"*, trans. A. Boyle, ed. E. Rhys, Everyman's Library (London: J. M. Dent, 1910), part IV, proposition 67, p. 187. The full quotation is: "A free man, that is, one who lives according to the dictate of reason alone, is not led by the fear of death . . . but directly desires what is good".—Ed.]

[4] [Adam Smith, *An Enquiry into the Nature and Causes of the Wealth of Nations*, ed. W. B. Todd, vol. 2 of *The Glasgow Edition of the Works and Correspondence of Adam Smith* (Oxford: Oxford University

ever, only at the beginning of the next century, first when in 1812 it was used by the Spanish party of Liberales, and a little later when it was adopted as a party name in France. In Britain it came to be so used only after the Whigs and the Radicals joined in a single party which from the early 1840s came to be known as the Liberal Party. Since the Radicals were inspired largely by what we have described as the Continental tradition, even the English Liberal Party at the time of its greatest influence was based on a fusion of the two traditions mentioned.[5]

In view of these facts it would be misleading to claim the term 'liberal' exclusively for either of the two distinct traditions. They have occasionally been referred to as the 'English', 'classical' or 'evolutionary', and as the 'Continental' or 'constructivistic' types respectively. In the following historical survey both types will be considered, but as only the first has developed a definite political doctrine, the later systematic exposition will have to concentrate on it.

It should be mentioned here that the USA never developed a liberal movement comparable to that which affected most of Europe during the nineteenth century, competing in Europe with the younger movements of nationalism and socialism and reaching the height of its influence in the 1870s and thereafter slowly declining but still determining the climate of public life until 1914. The reason for the absence of a similar movement in the USA is mainly that the chief aspirations of European liberalism were largely embodied in the institutions of the United States since their foundation, and partly that the development of political parties there was unfavourable to the growth of parties based on ideologies. Indeed, what in Europe is or used to be called 'liberal' is

---

Press, 1976; reprinted, Indianapolis, IN: Liberty Fund, 1981), book IV, chapter 9, paragraph 3. The full quote, in which Smith refers to one of Louis XIV's ministers who had embraced mercantilism, is as follows: "The industry and commerce of a great country he endeavoured to regulate upon the same model as the departments of a publick office; and instead of allowing every man to pursue his own interest his own way, upon the liberal plan of equality, liberty and justice, he bestowed upon certain branches of industry extraordinary privileges, while he laid others under as extraordinary restraints".—Ed.]

[5] [The Liberales were members of the Spanish Cortes or parliament which in Cádiz in 1812 established Spain's first constitution. The latter embodied key liberal principles, such as universal male suffrage, freedom of the press, limitations on the power of the monarch to engage in arbitrary acts, and individual property rights. The 'Philosophical Radicals' were a group of early nineteenth-century thinkers who were inspired by the utilitarian political philosophy of English philosopher and jurist Jeremy Bentham (1748–1832) and philosopher James Mill (1773–1836). Their ranks included jurist John Austin, the historian George Grote (1794–1871), and the philosopher and political economist John Stuart Mill (1806–73). Hayek argued that the Radicals were influenced by the French as much as by the British tradition of liberal thought and that their writings, along with the merger of the Whigs and the Radicals to form the Liberal Party, helped to ensure that the two traditions became confused, thereby facilitating the spread of socialist ideas in the second half of the nineteenth century. See Hayek, *Rules and Order*, vol. 1 (1973) of *Law, Legislation and Liberty*, p. 129, and F. A. Hayek, *The Constitution of Liberty*, ed. Ronald Hamowy, vol. 17 (2011) of *The Collected Works of F. A. Hayek*, pp. 109, 259–60.—Ed.]

in the USA today with some justification called 'conservative'; while in recent times the term 'liberal' has been used there to describe what in Europe would be called socialism. But of Europe it is equally true that none of the political parties which use the designation 'liberal' now adhere to the liberal principles of the nineteenth century.

HISTORICAL

2. The classical and medieval roots

The basic principles from which the Old Whigs fashioned their evolutionary liberalism have a long pre-history. The eighteenth-century thinkers who formulated them were indeed greatly assisted by ideas drawn from classical antiquity and by certain medieval traditions which in England had not been extinguished by absolutism.

The first people who had clearly formulated the ideal of individual liberty were the ancient Greeks and particularly the Athenians during the classical period of the fifth and fourth centuries BC. The denial by some nineteenth-century writers that the ancient Greeks knew individual liberty in the modern sense is clearly disproved by such episodes as when the Athenian general at the moment of supreme danger during the Sicilian expedition reminded the soldiers that they were fighting for a country which left them "unfettered discretion to live as they pleased".[6] Their conception of freedom was of freedom under the law, or of a state of affairs in which, as the popular phrase ran, law was king. It found expression, during the early classical periods, in the ideal of *isonomia* or equality before the law which, without using the old name, is still clearly described by Aristotle.[7] This law included a protection of the private

---

[6] [The writers whom Hayek accuses of misrepresenting the views of the ancient Greeks are Franco-Swiss novelist and political author Benjamin Constant (1767–1830), in his essay, "De la liberté des anciens comparée à celle des modernes" [1819], reprinted in *Cours de politique constitutionnelle; ou collection des ouvrages publiés sur le gouvernement représentatif* (Paris: Guillaumin, 1861), vol. 2, pp. 539–60, and the French historian Numa Denis Fustel de Coulanges (1830–89) in *La cité antique* (Paris: Durand, 1864). See Hayek, *The Constitution of Liberty*, p. 238 n. 11. The source of the passage quoted by Hayek is Thucydides, *The History of the Peloponnesian War*, trans. Richard Crawley (London: Longmans, Green, and Co., 1874), book VII, chapter 23, paragraph 69, p. 528. The general is Nicias, and the precise quotation, which was slightly shortened by Hayek, states that he "reminded them of their country, the freest of the free, and of the unfettered discretion left to all to live as they pleased".—Ed.]

[7] [For example, Aristotle writes in his *Politics* that "it is preferable for the law to rule than any one of the citizens" and condemns those governments in which "the multitude is sovereign and not the law". See Aristotle, *Politics*, trans. H. Rackham (Cambridge, MA: Harvard University Press, 1932), book 3, chapter 11, sec. 3, p. 265, and book 4, chapter 4, sec. 3–4, p. 303. He adds in the *Rhetoric*, "First of all, therefore, it is proper that laws, properly enacted, should themselves define the issue of all cases as far as possible, and leave as little as possible to the discretion of the

domain of the citizen against the state which went so far that even under the 'Thirty Tyrants' an Athenian citizen was wholly safe if he stayed at home. Of Crete it is even reported (by Ephorus, quoted by Strabo) that, because liberty was regarded as the state's highest good, the constitution secured "property specifically to those who acquire it, whereas in a condition of slavery everything belongs to the rulers and not to the ruled".[8] In Athens the powers of the popular assembly of changing the law were strictly limited, though we find already the first instances of such an assembly refusing to be restrained by established law from arbitrary action. These liberal ideals were further developed, particularly by the Stoic philosophers who extended them beyond the limits of the city state by their conception of a law of nature which limited the powers of all government, and of the equality of all men before that law.

These Greek ideals of liberty were transmitted to the moderns chiefly through the writings of Roman authors. By far the most important of them, and probably the single figure who more than any other inspired the revival of those ideas at the beginning of the modern era, was Marcus Tullius Cicero. But at least the historian Titus Livius and the emperor Marcus Aurelius must be included among the sources on which the sixteenth- and seventeenth-century thinkers chiefly drew at the beginning of the modern development of liberalism.[9] Rome, in addition, gave at least to the European continent a highly

---

judges . . . But what is most important of all is that the judgement of the legislator does not apply to a particular case, but is universal and applies to the future, whereas the member of the public assembly and the dicast have to decide present and definite issues, and in their case love, hate or personal interest is often involved, so that they are no longer capable of discerning the truth adequately". See Aristotle, *Art of Rhetoric*, trans. John Henry Freese (Cambridge, MA: Harvard University Press, 1926), book 1, chapter 1, pp. 5, 7. Hayek discusses the classical roots of the notion of individual liberty in more detail in *The Constitution of Liberty*, pp. 237–46.—Ed.]

[8] [The Greek geographer and historian Strabo (c. 64 BC–c. 21 BC) wrote of the Cretans in his *Geography*. The precise quote is as follows: "As for their constitution, which is described by Ephorus, it might suffice to tell in a cursory way its most important provisions. The lawgiver, he says, seems to take it for granted that liberty is a state's greatest good, for this alone makes property belong specifically to those who have acquired it, whereas in a condition of slavery everything belongs to the rulers and not to the ruled". See Strabo, *The Geography of Strabo*, ed. H. L. Jones (London: William Heinemann, 1928), vol. 5, p. 145.—Ed.]

[9] [According to Hayek, the Roman statesman, lawyer, scholar, and writer Marcus Tullius Cicero (106 BC–43 BC) provided many of the most effective accounts of various aspects of the notion of freedom under the law, perhaps most notably: the idea that the actions of legislators ought to be governed by general rules; the belief that law and liberty are inseparable, with people obeying the law in order to be free; and the claim that judges discover rather than create the law. On Hayek's account, it was through the works of the Roman historian Titus Livius (59/64 BC–17 AD) that the distinction between government by laws and government by men became known in seventeenth-century England, while it was Livy's translator who introduced the notion of 'isonomia' to England in the late sixteenth century. See Hayek, *The Constitution of Liberty*, pp. 244–45. The Roman Emperor and Stoic philosopher Marcus Aurelius (121 AD–180 AD) praised "the idea of a polity in which there is the same law for all, a polity administered

individualist private law, centring on a very strict conception of private property, a law, moreover, with which, until the codification under Justinian, legislation had very little interfered and which was in consequence regarded more as a restriction on, rather than as an exercise of, the powers of government. The early moderns could draw also on a tradition of liberty under the law which had been preserved through the Middle Ages and was extinguished on the Continent only at the beginning of the modern era by the rise of absolute monarchy. As a modern historian (R. W. Southern) describes it,

> The hatred of that which was governed, not by rule, but by will, went very deep in the Middle Ages, and at no time was this hatred so powerful and practical a force as in the latter half of our period . . . Law was not the enemy of freedom; on the contrary, the outline of liberty was traced by the bewildering variety of law which was slowly evolved during our period . . . High and low alike sought liberty by insisting on enlarging the number of rules under which they lived.[10]

This conception received a strong support from the belief in a law which existed apart from and above government, a conception which on the Continent was conceived as a law of nature but in England existed as the Common Law which was not the product of a legislator but had emerged from a persistent search for impersonal justice. The formal elaboration of these ideas was on the Continent carried on chiefly by the Schoolmen after it had received its first great systematisation, on foundations deriving from Aristotle, at the hands of Thomas Aquinas; by the end of the sixteenth century it had been developed by some of the Spanish Jesuit philosophers into a system of essentially liberal policy, especially in the economic field, where they anticipated much that was revived only by the Scottish philosophers of the eighteenth century.[11]

---

with regard to equal rights and equal freedom of speech, and the idea of a kingly government which respects most of all the freedom of the governed". See Marcus Aurelius Antoninus, *The Thoughts of Marcus Aurelius Antoninus*, trans. G. Long (New York: Scott-Thaw, 1903), p. 6.—Ed.]

[10] [R. W. Southern, *The Making of the Middle Ages* (London: Hutchinson's University Library, 1953), pp. 107–8.—Ed.]

[11] [The Spanish Jesuits of the School of Salamanca, such as Luis de Molina (1535–1600) and Johannes de Lugo (1583–1660), used the term 'naturalis' to denote phenomena that, although social in the sense of depending for their existence on human action, had not been deliberately designed. Thus, they anticipated some of the ideas about spontaneously grown social orders more fully set out by Scottish Enlightenment thinkers such as Ferguson, Hume, and Smith. See in particular Molina's *De iustitia et iure* (Cologne, 1596–1600), in particular tome II, disputatio 347, no. 3, where Molina describes the just price as the competitive market price. Hayek discusses their work in more detail on p. 295 of his essay "The Results of Human Action but Not of Human Design", in *Rules and Order*, p. 21, and in F. A. Hayek, *The Mirage of Social Justice*, vol. 2 (1976) of *Law, Legislation and Liberty*, pp. 178–79 n. 15.—Ed.]

Mention should finally also be made of some of the early developments in the city states of the Italian Renaissance, especially Florence, and in Holland, on which the English development in the seventeenth and eighteenth centuries could largely draw.[12]

3. The English Whig tradition

It was in the course of the debates during the English Civil War and the Commonwealth period that the ideas of the rule or supremacy of law became finally articulated which after the 'Glorious Revolution' of 1688 became the leading principles of the Whig Party that it brought to power. The classical formulations were supplied by John Locke's *Second Treatise on Civil Government* (1689) which, however, in some respects provides a still more rationalist interpretation of institutions than came to be characteristic of eighteenth-century British thinkers. (A fuller account would also have to consider the writings of Algernon Sidney and Gilbert Burnet as early expositors of the Whig doctrine.) It was also during this period that that close association of the British liberal movement and the predominantly non-conformist and Calvinist commercial and industrial classes arose which remained characteristic of British liberalism until recent times. Whether this merely meant that the same classes which developed a spirit of commercial enterprise were also more receptive to Calvinist Protestantism, or whether these religious views led more directly to liberal principles of politics, is a much discussed issue which cannot be further considered here. But the fact that the struggle between initially very intolerant religious sects produced in the end principles of tolerance, and that the British liberal movement remained closely connected with Calvinist Protestantism, is beyond doubt.[13]

---

[12] [For more on these developments, see Hayek, *The Constitution of Liberty*, pp. 232 n. 1 and 430.—Ed.]

[13] [English philosopher John Locke (1632–1704) was the author of *Two Treatises of Government* (London: Awnsham Churchill, 1690), where he developed his accounts of the creation of political society, and of the nature and limits of legitimate government, in terms of a hypothetical social contract between people in a state of nature. For Locke, legitimate governments are those that are established with the consent of the people and which act under the rule of law (that is, under laws that are general, certain, and applied by an independent judiciary). By establishing a sphere in which people can act free from the arbitrary will of others, such laws create, rather than restrain, freedom. Algernon Sidney (1622–83) was an English Whig politician and republican political thinker. He was the author of *Discourses concerning Government* (1698), in which he argued against supporters of an absolute monarchy that people enjoy liberty if they are free from the arbitrary will of another and that laws should be general and certain. Gilbert Burnet (1643–1715) was a Scottish theologian, historian and clergyman who became Bishop of Salisbury. He was the biographer of Sir Matthew Hale and, in his *Enquiry into the Measures of Submission to a Supreme Authority* (1688), argued in favour of the separation of powers and contended that the aim of the law was to preserve, not restrict, liberty. See Hayek, *The Constitution of Liberty*, pp. 251–53.—Ed.]

In the course of the eighteenth century the Whig doctrine of government limited by general rules of law and of severe restrictions on the powers of the executive became characteristic British doctrine. It was made known to the world at large chiefly through Montesquieu's *Esprit des lois* (1748) and the writings of other French authors, notably Voltaire.[14] In Britain the intellectual foundations were further developed chiefly by the Scottish moral philosophers, above all David Hume and Adam Smith, as well as by some of their English contemporaries and immediate successors. Hume not only laid in his philosophical work the foundation of the liberal theory of law, but in his *History of England* (1754–62) also provided an interpretation of English history as the gradual emergence of the Rule of Law which made the conception known far beyond the limits of Britain. Adam Smith's decisive contribution was the account of a self-generating order which formed itself spontaneously if the individuals were restrained by appropriate rules of law. His *Inquiry into the Nature and Causes of the Wealth of Nations* marks perhaps more than any other single work the beginning of the development of modern liberalism. It made people understand that those restrictions on the powers of government which had originated from sheer distrust of all arbitrary power had become the chief cause of Britain's economic prosperity.

The beginnings of a liberal movement in Britain were soon interrupted, however, by a reaction against the French Revolution and a distrust of its admirers in England, who endeavoured to import to England the ideas of Continental or constructivist liberalism. The end of this early English development of liberalism is marked by the work of Edmund Burke who, after his brilliant restatement of the Whig doctrine in defence of the American colonists, violently turned against the ideas of the French Revolution.[15]

It was only after the end of the Napoleonic wars that the development based on the doctrine of the Old Whigs and of Adam Smith was resumed. The further intellectual development was guided largely by a group of disciples of the Scottish moral philosophers who gathered round the *Edinburgh Review*, mostly

[14] [Charles-Louis de Secondat, Baron de la Brède et de Montesquieu (1689–1755), was a French social and political theorist who, in his *De l'esprit des lois* (1748), argued that in the state that most effectively promotes liberty, there must be a separation of powers between the executive, the legislature, and the judiciary. Montesquieu regarded England as the exemplar of such a state. See Montesquieu, *The Spirit of Laws*, trans. Thomas Nugent (London: G. Bell and Sons, 1914). French philosopher and writer François-Marie Arouet (1694–1778), better known as Voltaire, argued against tyranny, cruelty and religious intolerance, and extolled the virtues of the liberalism sustained by English institutions.—Ed.]

[15] [Hayek is alluding to Burke's two parliamentary speeches, "On American Taxation" (1774) and "On Moving His Resolutions for Conciliation with the Colonies" (1775), to his "Letter to the Sheriffs of Bristol, on the Affairs of America" (1777), and to his *Reflections on the Revolution in France* (London: J. Dodsley, 1790). In the latter, Burke argued that liberty would be impossible in France after the Revolution of 1789 because without an aristocratic body there was no barrier against absolutism.—Ed.]

economists in the tradition of Adam Smith; the pure Whig doctrine was once more restated in a form which widely affected Continental thinking by the historian T. B. Macaulay who for the nineteenth century did what Hume in his historical work had done for the eighteenth.[16] Already, however, this development was paralleled by the rapid growth of a radical movement of which the Benthamite 'Philosophical Radicals' became the leaders and which traced back more to the Continental than to the British tradition. It was ultimately from the fusion of these traditions that in the 1830s the political party arose which from about 1842 came to be known as the Liberal Party, and for the rest of the century remained the most important representative of the liberal movement in Europe.

Long before that, however, another decisive contribution had come from America. The explicit formulation by the former British colonists, in a written constitution, of what they understood to be the essentials of the British tradition of liberty, intended to limit the powers of government, and especially the statement of the fundamental liberties in a Bill of Rights, provided a model of political institutions which profoundly affected the development of liberalism in Europe. Though the United States, just because their people felt that they had already embodied the safeguards of liberty in their political institutions, never developed a distinct liberal movement, for the Europeans they became the dreamland of liberty and the example which inspired political aspirations as much as English institutions had done during the eighteenth century.

4. The development of Continental liberalism

The radical ideas of the philosophers of the French Enlightenment, mainly in the form in which they had been applied to political problems by Turgot, Condorcet and the Abbé Sieyès, largely dominated progressive opinion in France and the adjoining countries of the Continent during the Revolu-

---

[16] [The *Edinburgh Review* was a Scottish magazine that was published from 1802 to 1929 and promoted Whig ideas. The economists to whom Hayek refers were John Ramsay McCulloch (1789–1864), a Scottish applied economist, editor, and follower of David Ricardo, and Nassau Senior (1790–1864), an English lawyer, classical economist, and the first Drummond Professor of Political Economy at Oxford University. Thomas Babington Macaulay (1800–1859), Baron Macaulay of Rothley, was an English Whig politician, essayist, poet, and historian. He is best known for his *History of England from the Accession of James II*, 5 vols. (London: Longman, Brown, Green & Longmans, 1849–61), in which he celebrated what he saw as the triumph of the liberal ideal of constitutionally protected personal liberty after the Glorious Revolution of 1688. Accordingly, Macaulay is regarded as one of the founders of the 'Whig interpretation of history'. Hayek elaborates on Macaulay's contribution to the essentially liberal atmosphere of nineteenth-century British politics in his essay "History and Politics" [1954], reprinted as chapter 4 of Hayek, *The Trend of Economic Thinking*, pp. 57–58, and in Hayek, *The Constitution of Liberty*, p. 259.—Ed.]

tionary and Napoleonic periods; but of a definite liberal movement one can speak only after the Restoration.[17] In France it reached its height during the July Monarchy (1830–48), but after that period remained confined to a small élite. It was made up of several different strands of thought. An important attempt to systematise and adapt to Continental conditions what he regarded as the British tradition was made by Benjamin Constant, and was developed further during the 1830s and 1840s by a group known as the 'doctrinaires' under the leadership of F. P. G. Guizot. Their programme, known as 'guarantism', was essentially a doctrine of constitutional limitations of government. For this constitutional doctrine which made up the most important part of the Continental liberal movement of the first half of the nineteenth century, the constitution of 1831 of the newly created Belgian state served as an important model. To this tradition, largely deriving from Britain, also belonged the perhaps most important French liberal thinker, Alexis de Tocqueville.[18]

[17] [Anne Robert Jacques Turgot (1727–81) was a French economist and administrator who, whilst acting as comptroller-general of finance under Louis XVI from 1774 to 1776, made an unsuccessful effort to reduce barriers to trade amongst the French provinces and to abolish the privileges of corporations. French Enlightenment philosopher, mathematician, *encyclopédiste*, and reformer Marie-Jean-Antoine-Nicolas de Caritat, Marquis de Condorcet (1743–94), was an advocate in 1789 of the need for a declaration of rights and later an opponent of utilitarian arguments for transgressing the rights of minorities in the interests of majorities. Condorcet argued in his later work that the history of mankind was one of steady improvement and progress towards a state of ultimate perfection. Hayek regarded the works of Turgot and Condorcet as precursors to—but not thoroughgoing examples of—the positivism, scientism, and rationalism of Saint-Simon and Comte. See Hayek, *Studies on the Abuse and Decline of Reason*, pp. 171–75. Emmanuel-Joseph Sieyès (1748–1836) was a Roman Catholic clergyman and constitutional theorist whose writings on sovereignty, and accounts of various kinds of rights, were influential in guiding the National Assembly in the early stages of the French Revolution.—Ed.]

[18] [In "De la liberté des anciens comparée à celle des modernes", Benjamin Constant drew a distinction between the ancient idea of liberty as the right to participate in collective decision-making and the modern notion of a sphere of personal liberty, guaranteed by the rule of law, within which people are able to act free from arbitrary interference by state or society. On this view, individual liberty and popular democracy are only contingently, not necessarily, related. In his *Principes de politique* (Paris: A. Eymery, 1815), Constant advocated constitutional constraints on all forms of sovereignty, whether popular or divine, and held up England as a model constitutional monarchy. Constant's ideas shaped the thinking of the 'Doctrinaires', a group of French liberal thinkers led by the historian and politician François-Pierre-Guillaume Guizot (1787–1874). The Doctrinaires advocated a system of constitutional checks designed to protect the rights of the individual against encroachment by the state or other social groups ('guarantism'). Guizot extolled the virtues of the English electoral and parliamentary system in his *Histoire des origines du gouvernement représentatif en Europe* (Paris: Didier, 1851) and regarded the changes to the French constitution introduced during the July Monarchy as the French equivalent of England's Glorious Revolution. In *Democracy in America*, trans. H. Reeve, 4 vols. (London: Saunders and Otley, 1835 and 1840) and *The Old Regime and the Revolution*, trans. J. Bonner (New York: Harper & Brothers, 1856), French historian, politician, and political scientist Alexis Charles Henri Clérel de Tocqueville (1805–59) analysed the nature and consequences of the spread of democracy in

The feature, however, which greatly distinguished the type of liberalism predominant on the Continent from the British one was from the beginning what is best described as its free-thinking aspect, which expressed itself in a strong anti-clerical, anti-religious and generally anti-traditionalist attitude. Not only in France, but also in the other Roman Catholic parts of Europe, the continuous conflict with the church of Rome became indeed so characteristic of liberalism that to many people it appeared as its primary characteristic, particularly after, in the second half of the century, the church took up the struggle against 'modernism' and therefore against most demands for liberal reform.

During the first half of the century, up to the revolutions of 1848, the liberal movement in France, as well as in most of the rest of western and central Europe, had also been much more closely allied with the democratic movement than was the case with British liberalism. It was indeed largely displaced by it and by the new socialist movement during the second half of the century. Except for a short period around the middle of the century, when the movement for free trade rallied the liberal groups, liberalism did not again play an important role in the political development of France, nor after 1848 did French thinkers make any important contributions to its doctrine.

A somewhat more important role was played by the liberal movement in Germany, and a more distinct development did take place during the first three quarters of the nineteenth century. Though greatly influenced by the ideas derived from Britain and France, these were transformed by ideas of the three greatest and earliest of the German liberals, the philosopher Immanuel Kant, the scholar and statesman Wilhelm von Humboldt, and the poet Friedrich Schiller. Kant had provided a theory on lines similar to those of David Hume, centred on the concepts of law as the protection of individual freedom and of the Rule of Law (or the *Rechtsstaat*, as it came to be known in Germany); Humboldt had in an early work on *The Sphere and Duties of Government* (1792) developed the picture of a state wholly confined to the maintenance of law and order—a book of which only a small part was published at the

---

the late eighteenth and early nineteenth century. Tocqueville was especially anxious about the potential for democracy to unleash a new kind of despotism, namely the tyranny of the majority. The threat to individual liberty posed by mass democracy was exacerbated, in Tocqueville's eyes, by the increased administrative capacity of the central state, which enhanced the scope for the majority to impose its views on minorities. Accordingly, Tocqueville argued in favour of constitutional bulwarks against the abuse of majority power, including a federal system of government and judicial review of bureaucratic decisions, contrasting the preservation of judicial review and local independence in England with the increasing centralisation of the French state. For more on these issues, see G. de Ruggiero, *The History of European Liberalism*, trans. R. G. Collingwood (London: Oxford University Press, 1927), pp. 159–210, and J. Jennings, *Revolution and the Republic: A History of Political Thought in France since the Eighteenth Century* (Oxford: Oxford University Press, 2011), pp. 147–96, 276–82.—Ed.]

time, but which, when it was finally published (and translated into English) in 1854, exercised wide influence not only in Germany but also on such diverse thinkers as J. S. Mill in England and E. Laboulaye in France. The poet Schiller, finally, probably did more than any other single person to make the whole educated public in Germany familiar with the ideal of personal liberty.[19]

There was an early beginning towards a liberal policy in Prussia during the reforms of Freiherr vom Stein, but it was followed by another period of reaction after the end of the Napoleonic wars. Only in the 1830s did a general liberal movement begin to develop, which from the beginning, however, as was also true in Italy, was closely associated with a nationalist movement aiming at the unification of the country. In general, German liberalism was mainly a constitutionalist movement which in north Germany was somewhat more guided by the British example, while in the south the French model was more influential. This found expression chiefly in a different attitude towards the problem of limiting the discretionary powers of government which in the north produced a fairly strict conception of the Rule of Law (or the *Rechtsstaat*), while in the south it was guided more by the French interpretation of the Separation of Powers that stressed the independence of the administration from the ordinary courts. In the south, however, and especially in Baden and Württemberg, there developed a more active group of liberal

---

[19] [German philosopher Immanuel Kant (1724–1804) argued that people are free if they are able to act autonomously, independent of the will of others. A just society, for Kant, is one in which each individual's freedom is compatible with the freedom of others, so that all people are treated as ends in themselves and never as means to others' ends. On Kant's account, the possibility of freedom and justice requires that people's actions be governed by abstract, universally binding laws. See Immanuel Kant, *Practical Philosophy*, ed. and trans. Mary Gregor (Cambridge: Cambridge University Press, 1996). Wilhelm von Humboldt (1767–1835) was a German philosopher, philologist, diplomat and educational reformer. In *The Sphere and Duties of Government* (1792), also known as *The Limits of State Action*, trans. Joseph Coulthard (London: John Chapman, 1854), Humboldt argued that untrammelled freedom of action and association is critical for human development and that the scope of legitimate state action is therefore confined solely to the enforcement of the laws necessary to defend individual liberty. Johann Christoph Friedrich von Schiller (1759–1805) was one of Germany's foremost poets and dramatists, many of whose works explored issues pertaining to individual freedom. For Schiller, freedom and morality are intimately related, for it is only when people are physically and spiritually free that they can become fully moral. It is interesting to note in this regard that, in an unpublished interview with W. W. Bartley III, labelled "Summer 1984, at St. Blasian", Hayek remarked that "I was reading Schiller, and Goethe's friends and circle at a very early age. I got my liberalism from the great German poets". See Caldwell, "Introduction", in Hayek, *Studies on the Abuse and Decline of Reason*, p. 2. Also see Hayek, *The Constitution of Liberty*, p. 142 n. 10. Édouard de Laboulaye (1811–83) was a liberal French historian, jurist, and abolitionist who edited the writings of Benjamin Constant and sought to distil the lessons of the American Constitution for the government of France. An advocate of liberal democracy, underpinned by constitutional checks against the power of the majority, he is perhaps most commonly remembered for proposing the creation of the Statue of Liberty.—Ed.]

theorists around the *Staatslexicon* of C. von Rotteck and C. T. Welcker, which in the period before the revolution of 1848 became the main centre of German liberal thought. The failure of that revolution brought another short period of reaction, but in the 1860s and early 1870s it seemed for a time as if Germany, too, were rapidly moving towards a liberal order. It was during this period that the constitutional and legal reforms intended definitely to establish the *Rechtsstaat* were brought to completion. The middle of the 1870s must probably be regarded as the time when the liberal movement in Europe had gained its greatest influence and its easternmost expansion. With the German return to protection in 1878, and the new social policies initiated by Bismarck at about the same time, the reversal of the movement began. The liberal party which had flourished for little more than a dozen years rapidly declined.[20]

Both in Germany and in Italy the decline of the liberal movement set in when it lost its association with the movement for national unification, and the achieved unity directed attention to the strengthening of the new states, and when, moreover, the beginnings of a labour movement deprived liberalism of the position of the 'advanced' party which until then the politically active part of the working class had supported.

5. Classical British liberalism

Throughout the greater part of the nineteenth century the European country which seemed nearest to a realisation of the liberal principles was Great Britain. There most of them appeared to be accepted not only by a powerful Liberal Party but by the majority of the population, and even the Conservatives often became the instrument of the achievement of liberal reforms. The great events after which Britain could appear to the rest of Europe as the representative model of a liberal order were the Catholic emancipation of 1829, the Reform Act of 1832, and the repeal of the corn laws by the Conservative, Sir

---

[20] [Heinrich Friedrich Karl Reichsfreiherr vom und zum Stein (1757–1831) was a Prussian statesman whose views were shaped by his understanding of the history and institutions of England and who initiated a series of liberal reforms, including the abolition of serfdom, that laid the ground for the *Rechtsstaat* and for the unification of Germany. See Ruggiero, *The History of European Liberalism*, pp. 215–17, and Hayek, *The Constitution of Liberty*, p. 299 n. 26. Carl von Rotteck (1775–1840) and Karl Theodor Welcker (1790–1869) were constitutional lawyers and politicians who became leaders of the liberal movement in the states of southern Germany in the nineteenth century. Their *Staats-Lexikon oder Enzyklopaedie der Staatswissenschaften*, ed. Karl von Rotteck and Karl T. Welcker, 12 vols. (Altona: Hammerich, 1834–43) was a political encyclopedia in which was elaborated, amongst other things, the ideal of the *Rechtsstaat* (that is, the idea that the administrative apparatus of the state should be placed under the rule of law so as to curb the arbitrary exercise of power by the then-expanding central bureaucracy). See F. A. Hayek, "The Political Ideal of the Rule of Law" [1955], reprinted as chapter 5 of Hayek, *The Market and Other Orders*, p. 151.—Ed.]

Robert Peel, in 1846. Since by then the chief demands of liberalism concerning internal policy were satisfied, agitation concentrated on the establishment of free trade. The movement initiated by the Merchants' Petition of 1820, and carried on from 1836 to 1846 by the Anti-Corn-Law League, was developed particularly by a group of radicals who, under the leadership of Richard Cobden and John Bright, took a somewhat more extreme *laissez faire* position than would have been required by the liberal principles of Adam Smith and the classical economists following him. Their predominant free trade position was combined with a strong anti-imperialist, anti-interventionist and anti-militarist attitude and an aversion to all expansion of governmental powers; the increase of public expenditure was regarded by them as mainly due to undesirable interventions in overseas affairs. Their opposition was directed chiefly against the expansion of the powers of central government, and most improvements were expected from autonomous efforts either of local government or of voluntary organisations. 'Peace, Retrenchment and Reform' became the liberal watchword of this period, with 'reform' referring more to the abolition of old abuses and privileges than the extension of democracy, with which the movement became more closely associated only at the time of the Second Reform Act of 1867. The movement had reached its climax with the Cobden Treaty with France of 1860, a commercial treaty which led to the establishment of free trade in Britain and a widespread expectation that free trade would soon universally prevail.[21] At that time there emerged also in Britain, as the leading figure of the liberal movement, W. E. Gladstone who, first as Chancellor of the Exchequer and then as liberal Prime Minister, came to be widely regarded as the living embodiment of liberal principles, especially, after Palmerston's death in 1865, with regard to foreign policy, with John Bright as his chief associate. With him also the old association of British liberalism with strong moral and religious views revived.[22]

---

[21] [English manufacturer and politician Richard Cobden (1804–65) and English politician John Bright (1811–89) were the leaders of the Anti-Corn Law League and persistent advocates of free trade in nineteenth-century England. After their efforts led to the repeal of the Corn Laws in 1846, Cobden and Bright became the leaders of the Manchester School of economic thought, which advocated a laissez-faire approach to economic policy and exerted a significant influence over the Liberal Party in the mid-nineteenth century. Sir Robert Peel (1788–1850) was Prime Minister of Great Britain (1834–35, 1841–46) and founder of the modern Conservative Party.—Ed.]

[22] [English statesman William Ewart Gladstone (1809–98) became leader of the Liberal Party in 1867 and was an advocate of the classical liberal *desiderata* of free trade, low taxation, and balanced budgets. He served as Prime Minister on four occasions between 1868 and 1894 and, along with his Tory counterpart Benjamin Disraeli, dominated British politics in the Victorian era. Henry John Temple, 3rd Viscount Palmerston (1784–1865), was an English Whig-Liberal statesman. His long career, which included service as Foreign Secretary and Prime Minister, made him a symbol of British nationalism.—Ed.]

In the intellectual sphere during the second half of the nineteenth century the basic principles of liberalism were intensively discussed. In the philosopher Herbert Spencer an extreme advocacy of an individualist minimum state, similar to the position of W. von Humboldt, found an effective expounder.[23] But John Stuart Mill, in his celebrated book *On Liberty* (1859), directed his criticism chiefly against the tyranny of opinion rather than the actions of government, and by his advocacy of distributive justice and a general sympathetic attitude towards socialist aspirations in some of his other works, prepared the gradual transition of a large part of the liberal intellectuals to a moderate socialism. This tendency was noticeably strengthened by the influence of the philosopher T. H. Green who stressed the positive functions of the state against the predominantly negative conception of liberty of the older liberals.[24]

[23] [English sociologist and philosopher Herbert Spencer (1820–1903) rivaled Darwin in importance as a proponent of evolutionary thinking during the Victorian era. The originator of the phrase 'survival of the fittest', Spencer developed a theory of 'social Darwinism' that posited the progressive improvement of mankind via social evolution. Spencer was an individualist who warned against the protean nature of coercive power and in whose version of liberalism the legitimate role of the state was confined to the provision of national defence, the maintenance of law and order, and the enforcement of contracts.—Ed.]

[24] [John Stuart Mill (1806–73) was an English philosopher, political economist, social reformer, and author whose works included *A System of Logic: Ratiocinative and Inductive* (London: John W. Parker, 1843), *Principles of Political Economy: With some of their Applications to Social Philosophy*, 2 vols. (London: J. W. Parker, 1848), and *Utilitarianism* (first published in *Fraser's Magazine*, 1861), as well as *On Liberty* (London: J. W. Parker, 1859). While *On Liberty* saw Mill defend the freedom of the individual against social and political control, Hayek argued nonetheless that in his later writings Mill shifted away from a classical liberal position and displayed greater sympathy towards the aims of socialism, thereby helping to pave the way for the acceptance of socialist ideas amongst the British intelligentsia in the late nineteenth and early twentieth centuries. Hayek attributed the change in Mill's views to the influence both of the French tradition of liberalism, most notably Comte and Saint-Simon, and also of Harriet Taylor, who was a close friend of Mill's from 1830 and who became his wife in 1851. See Hayek, *Studies on the Abuse and Decline of Reason*, pp. 56–57, 71, 238–39. Hayek edited a volume of correspondence between Mill and Taylor, entitled *John Stuart Mill and Harriet Taylor: Their Correspondence and Subsequent Marriage* (Chicago: University of Chicago Press, 1951), now republished—with an amended subtitle, *Their Friendship and Subsequent Marriage*—as part of a Collected Works volume that also contains additional material in which Hayek discusses Taylor's influence on Mill. See F. A. Hayek, *Hayek on Mill: The Mill-Taylor Friendship and Related Writings*, ed. Sandra J. Peart, vol. 16 (2015) of *The Collected Works of F. A. Hayek*. For more on Hayek's ambivalent views about Mill, see B. Caldwell, "Hayek on Mill", *History of Political Economy*, vol. 40, 2008, pp. 689–704.

Thomas Hill Green (1836–82) was an idealist philosopher who argued against the classical liberal idea of freedom as a mere absence of restriction in favour of a notion of freedom as the power or capacity to carry out some worthwhile course of action. For Green, the state had a duty actively to create the conditions in which the exercise of such positive freedom was possible. See his "Lecture on 'Liberal Legislation and Freedom of Contract'", in *Works of Thomas Hill Green*, ed. R. L. Nettleship (London: Longmans, Green & Co., 1888), vol. 3. Green's views

But though the last quarter of the nineteenth century saw already much internal criticism of liberal doctrines within the liberal camp and though the Liberal Party was beginning to lose support to the new labour movement, the predominance of liberal ideas in Great Britain lasted well into the twentieth century and succeeded in defeating a revival of protectionist demands, though the Liberal Party could not avoid a progressive infiltration by interventionist and imperialist elements. Perhaps the government of H. Campbell-Bannerman (1905–8) should be regarded as the last liberal government of the old type, while under his successor, H. H. Asquith, new experiments in social policy were undertaken which were only doubtfully compatible with the older liberal principles. But on the whole it can be said that the liberal era of British policy lasted until the outbreak of the First World War, and that the dominating influence of liberal ideas in Britain was terminated only by the effects of this war.[25]

6. The decline of liberalism

Though some of the elder European statesmen and other leaders in practical affairs after the First World War were still guided by an essentially liberal outlook, and attempts were made at first to restore the political and economic institutions of the pre-war period, several factors brought it about that the influence of liberalism steadily declined until the Second World War. The most important was that socialism, particularly in the opinion of a large part of the intellectuals, had replaced liberalism as the progressive movement. Political discussion was thus carried on mainly between socialists and conservatives, both supporting increasing activities of the state, though with different aims. The economic difficulties, unemployment and unstable currencies,

---

were influential on the thinking of 'new' liberals such as English sociologist and journalist L. T. Hobhouse (1864–1929), whose *Liberalism* (London: Williams and Norgate, 1911) is an attempt to synthesise the ideas of Green and John Stuart Mill in support of extensive government intervention designed to bolster people's positive freedom. Elsewhere, Hayek describes Hobhouse's ideas as an example of constructive rationalism. See Hayek, *Studies on the Abuse and Decline of Reason*, pp. 150–51.—Ed.]

[25] [Scottish politician Sir Henry Campbell-Bannerman (1836–1908) was a Gladstonian liberal, a staunch individualist, and an opponent both of *dirigisme* and of imperialism. He led the Liberal Party in the House of Commons between 1899 and 1908 and was Prime Minister of Great Britain from 1905 to 1908. Henry Herbert Asquith, 1st Earl of Oxford and Asquith (1852–1928), was a Liberal politician and Prime Minister of Great Britain from 1908 to 1916, whose views were shaped by the idealist philosophy of T. H. Green. Asquith's time as Prime Minister saw the implementation of policies, such as the introduction of old-age pensions and unemployment and health insurance, that laid the foundations for the modern welfare state and signalled a shift in the outlook of the Liberal Party away from classical, Gladstonian liberalism towards a more collectivist approach known as 'new' liberalism.—Ed.]

seemed to demand much more economic control by government and led to a revival of protectionism and other nationalistic policies. A rapid growth of the bureaucratic apparatus of government and the acquisition of far-reaching discretionary powers by it was the consequence. These tendencies, already strong during the first post-war decade, became even more marked during the Great Depression following the U.S. crash of 1929. The final abandonment of the gold standard and the return to protection by Great Britain in 1931 seemed to mark the definite end of a free world economy. The rise of dictatorial or totalitarian régimes in large parts of Europe not only extinguished the weak liberal groups which had remained in the countries immediately affected, but the threat of war which it produced led even in Western Europe to an increasing government dominance over economic affairs and a tendency towards national self-sufficiency.

After the end of the Second World War there occurred once more a temporary revival of liberal ideas, due partly to a new awareness of the oppressive character of all kinds of totalitarian régimes, and partly to the recognition that the obstacles to international trade which had grown up during the inter-war period had been largely responsible for the economic depression. The representative achievement was the General Agreement on Tariffs and Trade (GATT) of 1948, but the attempts to create a larger economic unit such as the Common Market and EFTA also ostensibly aimed in the same direction.[26] Yet the most remarkable event which seemed to promise a return to liberal economic principles was the extraordinary economic recovery of the defeated Germany which, on the initiative of Ludwig Erhard, had explicitly committed herself to what was called a 'social market economy', and as a result soon outstripped the victorious nations in prosperity. These events ushered in an unprecedented period of great prosperity which for a time made it seem probable that an essentially liberal economic régime might again durably establish itself in western and central Europe.[27] In the intellectual sphere, too, the period brought renewed efforts to restate and improve the principles of liberal politics. But the endeavours to prolong the prosper-

[26] [The European Free Trade Association (EFTA) is an intergovernmental organisation, founded in 1960, with the goal of promoting free trade and economic integration.—Ed.]

[27] [German statesman Ludwig Erhard (1897–1977) served as economics minister under Chancellor Konrad Adenauer from 1949 to 1963, during which period he was the principal architect of West Germany's postwar economic recovery. A staunch believer in economic liberalism, and member of the Mont Pèlerin Society from 1950, he also served as Chancellor of West Germany (1963–1966). Elsewhere, Hayek writes of Erhard that "I have known many economists with much greater theoretical sophistication and insight, but I have never met another person with as sound an instinct for the right thing to do as Ludwig Erhard". See p. 193 of F. A. Hayek, "The Rediscovery of Freedom: Personal Recollections" [1983], published as the prologue to part II of Hayek, *The Fortunes of Liberalism*.—Ed.]

ity and to secure full employment by means of the expansion of money and credit, in the end created a world-wide inflationary development to which employment so adjusted itself that inflation could not be discontinued without producing extensive unemployment. Yet a functioning market economy cannot be maintained under accelerating inflation, if for no other reason than because governments will soon feel constrained to combat the effects of inflation by the control of prices and wages. Inflation has always and everywhere led to a directed economy, and it is only too likely that the commitment to an inflationary policy will mean the destruction of the market economy and the transition to a centrally directed totalitarian economic and political system.

At present the defenders of the classical liberal position have again shrunk to very small numbers, chiefly economists. And the name 'liberal' is coming to be used, even in Europe, as has for some time been true of the USA, as a name for essentially socialist aspirations, because, in the words of J. A. Schumpeter, "as a supreme, if unintended, compliment, the enemies of the system of private enterprise have thought it wise to appropriate its label".[28]

SYSTEMATIC

7. The liberal conception of freedom

Since only the 'British' or evolutionary type of liberalism has developed a definite political programme, an attempt at a systematic exposition of the principles of liberalism will have to concentrate on it, and the views of the 'Continental' or constructivistic type will be mentioned only occasionally by way of contrast. This fact also demands the rejection of another distinction frequently drawn on the Continent, but inapplicable to the British type, that between political and economic liberalism (elaborated especially by the Italian philosopher, Benedetto Croce, as the distinction between *liberalismo* and *liberismo*). For the British tradition the two are inseparable because the basic principle of the limitation of the coercive powers of government to the enforcement of general rules of just conduct deprives government of the power of directing or controlling the economic activities of the individuals, while the conferment of such powers gives government essentially arbitrary and discretionary power which cannot but restrict even the freedom in the choice of individual aims which all liberals want to secure. Freedom under the law implies eco-

---

[28] [Joseph Alois Schumpeter (1883–1950) was an economist and sociologist best known for his theories of capitalist development and business cycles. The quotation in the text is taken from J. A. Schumpeter, *History of Economic Analysis* (London: Allen and Unwin, 1954), p. 394.—Ed.]

nomic freedom, while economic control, as the control of the means for all purposes, makes a restriction of all freedom possible.[29]

It is in this connection that the apparent agreement of the different kinds of liberalism on the demand for freedom of the individual, and the respect for the individual personality which this implies, conceals an important difference. During the heyday of liberalism this concept of freedom had a fairly definite meaning: it meant primarily that the free person was not subject to arbitrary coercion. But for man living in society protection against such coercion required a restraint on all men, depriving them of the possibility of coercing others. Freedom for all could be achieved only if, in the celebrated formula of Immanuel Kant, the freedom of each did not extend further than was compatible with an equal freedom for all others. The liberal conception of freedom was therefore necessarily one of freedom under a law which limited the freedom of each so as to secure the same freedom for all. It meant not what was sometimes described as the 'natural freedom' of an isolated individual, but the freedom possible in society and restricted by such rules as were necessary to protect the freedom of others. Liberalism in this respect is to be sharply distinguished from anarchism. It recognises that if all are to be as free as possible, coercion cannot be entirely eliminated, but only reduced to that minimum which is necessary to prevent individuals or groups from arbitrarily coercing others. It was a freedom within a domain circumscribed by known rules which made it possible for the individual to avoid being coerced so long as he kept within these limits.

This freedom could also be assured only to those capable of obeying the rules intended to secure it. Only the adult and sane, presumed to be fully responsible for their actions, were regarded as fully entitled to that freedom, while various degrees of tutelage were regarded as appropriate in the case of children and persons not in full possession of their mental faculties. And by infringement of the rules intended to secure the same liberty for all, a person might as penalty forfeit that exemption from coercion which those who obeyed them enjoyed.

This freedom thus conferred on all judged responsible for their actions also held them responsible for their own fate: while the protection of the law was to assist all in the pursuit of their aims, government was not supposed to guarantee to the individuals particular results of their efforts. To enable the indi-

---

[29] [Idealist philosopher, historian, and politician Benedetto Croce (1866–1952) is often, though not entirely uncontroversially, described as a prominent Italian liberal. Accounts of his distinction between *liberalismo* and *liberismo* can be found in B. Croce and L. Einaudi, *Liberismo e Liberalismo*, ed. P. Solari (Milan and Naples: Riccardo Ricciardi Editore, 1957). For Hayek's views on the relation between economic and political freedom, see F. A. Hayek, *The Road to Serfdom: Text and Documents*, ed. B. Caldwell, vol. 2 (2007) of *The Collected Works of F. A. Hayek*, pp. 124–33.—Ed.]

vidual to use his knowledge and abilities in the pursuit of his self-chosen aims was regarded both as the greatest benefit government could secure to all, as well as the best way of inducing these individuals to make the greatest contribution to the welfare of others. To bring forth the best efforts for which an individual was enabled by his particular circumstances and capabilities, of which no authority could know, was thought to be the chief advantage which the freedom of each would confer on all others.

The liberal conception of freedom has often been described as a merely negative conception, and rightly so. Like peace and justice, it refers to the absence of an evil, to a condition opening opportunities but not assuring particular benefits; though it was expected to enhance the probability that the means needed for the purposes pursued by the different individuals would be available. The liberal demand for freedom is thus a demand for the removal of all man-made obstacles to individual efforts, not a claim that the community or the state should supply particular goods. It does not preclude such collective action where it seems necessary, or at least a more effective way for securing certain services, but regards this as a matter of expediency and as such limited by the basic principle of equal freedom under the law. The decline of liberal doctrine, beginning in the 1870s, is closely connected with a re-interpretation of freedom as the command over, and usually the provision by the state of, the means of achieving a great variety of particular ends.

8. The liberal conception of law

The meaning of the liberal conception of liberty under the law, or of absence of arbitrary coercion, turns on the sense which in this context is given to 'law' and 'arbitrary'. It is partly due to differences in the uses of these expressions that within the liberal tradition there exists a conflict between those for whom, as for John Locke, freedom could exist only under the law ("for who could be free, when every other man's humour might domineer over him?") while to many of the Continental liberals and to Jeremy Bentham, as the latter expressed it, "every law is an evil, for every law is an infraction of liberty."[30]

It is of course true that law can be used to destroy liberty. But not every product of legislation is a law in the sense in which John Locke or David Hume or Adam Smith or Immanuel Kant or the later English Whigs regarded law as a safeguard of freedom. What they had in mind when they spoke of law as the indispensable safeguard of freedom were only those rules of just conduct which constitute the private and criminal law, but not every command issued by the legislative authority. To qualify as law, in the sense in which it was used

[30] [Locke, *Two Treatises*, bk. 2, chap. 6, sec. 57. J. Bentham, *Theory of Legislation*, 5th edn. (London: Trübner, 1887), p. 48.—Ed.]

in the British liberal tradition to describe the conditions of freedom, the rules enforced by government had to possess certain attributes which a law like the English Common Law of necessity possessed, but which the products of legislation need not possess: they must be general rules of individual conduct, applicable to all alike in an unknown number of future instances, defining the protected domain of the individuals, and therefore essentially of the nature of prohibitions rather than of specific commands. They are therefore also inseparable from the institution of several property. It was within the limits determined by these rules of just conduct that the individual was supposed to be free to use his own knowledge and skills in the pursuit of his own purposes in any manner which seemed appropriate to him.

The coercive powers of government were thus supposed to be limited to the enforcement of those rules of just conduct. This, except to an extreme wing of the liberal tradition, did not preclude that government should render also other services to the citizens.[31] It meant only that, whatever other services government might be called upon to provide, it could for such purposes use only the resources placed at its disposal, but could not coerce the private citizen; or, in other words, the person and the property of the citizen could not be used by government as a means for the achievement of its particular purposes. In this sense an act of the duly authorised legislature might be as arbitrary as an act of an autocrat, indeed any command or prohibition directed to particular persons or groups, and not following from a rule of universal applicability, would be regarded as arbitrary. What thus makes *an act of coercion* arbitrary, in the sense in which the term is used in the old liberal tradition, is that it serves a particular end of government, is determined by a specific act of will and not by a universal rule needed for the maintenance of that self-generating overall order of actions, which is served by all the other enforced rules of just conduct.

9. Law and the spontaneous order of actions

The importance which liberal theory attached to the rules of just conduct is based on the insight that they are an essential condition for the maintenance of a self-generating or spontaneous order of the actions of the different indi-

---

[31] [The version of this sentence found on p. 135 of *New Studies in Philosophy, Politics, Economics and the History of Ideas* ended as follows: "did not preclude that government should not render also other services to the citizens." The final 'not' in that sentence has been removed from the main text of the essay printed in the current volume, because its presence is inconsistent with the point Hayek was trying to make, namely that for most liberals—including, of course, Hayek himself—a commitment to the rule of law did not preclude government provision of some public services. See, for example, F. A. Hayek, *The Political Order of a Free People*, vol. 3 (1979) of *Law, Legislation and Liberty*, pp. 41–42.—Ed.]

viduals and groups, each of which pursues his own ends on the basis of his own knowledge. At least the great founders of liberal theory in the eighteenth century, David Hume and Adam Smith, did not assume a natural harmony of interests, but rather contended that the divergent interests of the different individuals could be reconciled by the observance of appropriate rules of conduct; or, as their contemporary, Josiah Tucker, expressed it, that "the universal mover in human nature, self-love, may receive such a direction . . . as to promote the public interest by those efforts it shall make towards pursuing its own".[32] Those eighteenth-century writers were indeed as much philosophers of law as students of the economic order, and their conception of law and their theory of the market mechanism are closely connected. They understood that only the recognition of certain principles of law, chiefly the institution of several property and the enforcement of contracts, would secure such a mutual adjustment of the plans of action of the separate individuals that all might have a good chance of carrying out the plans of action which they had formed. It was, as later economic theory brought out more clearly, this mutual adjustment of individual plans which enabled people to serve each other while using their different knowledge and skills in the service of their own ends.[33]

The function of the rules of conduct was thus not to organise the individual efforts for particular agreed purposes, but to secure an overall order of actions within which each should be able to benefit as much as possible from the efforts of others in the pursuit of his own ends. The rules conducive to the formation of such a spontaneous order were regarded as the product of long experimentation in the past. And though they were regarded as capable of improvement, it was thought that such improvement must proceed slowly and step by step as new experience showed it to be desirable.

The great advantage of such a self-generating order was thought to be, not only that it left the individuals free to pursue their own purposes, whether these were egotistic or altruistic. It was also that it made possible the utilisation of the widely dispersed knowledge of particular circumstances of time and place which exists only as the knowledge of those different individuals, and could in no possible way be possessed by some single directing authority. It is this utilisation of more knowledge of particular facts than would be possible under any system of central direction of economic activity, that brings

---

[32] [Josiah Tucker, *The Elements of Commerce and Theory of Taxes* (1755), reprinted in *Josiah Tucker: A Selection from His Economic and Political Writings*, ed. Robert L. Schuyler (New York: Columbia University Press, 1931), p. 92.—Ed.]

[33] [Hayek is alluding here to his own account of the generation of the market order. See F. A. Hayek, "The Use of Knowledge in Society" [1945], reprinted as chapter 3 of Hayek, *The Market and Other Orders*; Hayek, *The Constitution of Liberty*, pp. 215–31; and F. A. Hayek, *The Mirage of Social Justice*, vol. 2 (1976) of *Law, Legislation and Liberty*, pp. 107–32.—Ed.]

about as large an aggregate product of society as can be brought about by any known means.

But while leaving the formation of such an order to the spontaneous forces of the market, operating under the restraint of appropriate rules of law, secures a more comprehensive order and a more complete adaptation to the particular circumstances, it also means that the particular contents of this order will not be subject to deliberate control but are left largely to accident. The framework of rules of law, and all the various special institutions which serve the formation of the market order, can determine only its general or abstract character, but not its specific effects on particular individuals or groups. Though its justification consists in it increasing the chances of all, and in making the position of each in a large measure dependent on his own efforts, it still leaves the outcome for each individual and group dependent also on unforeseen circumstances which neither they nor anybody else can control. Since Adam Smith the process by which the shares of the individuals are determined in a market economy has therefore often been likened to a game in which the results for each depend partly on his skill and effort and partly on chance. The individuals have reason to agree to play this game because it makes the pool from which the individual shares are drawn larger than it can be made by any other method. But at the same time it makes the share of each individual subject to all kinds of accidents and certainly does not secure that it always corresponds to the subjective merits or to the esteem by others of the individual efforts.[34]

Before considering further the problems of the liberal conception of justice which this raises, it is necessary to consider certain constitutional principles in which the liberal conception of law came to be embodied.

10. Natural rights, the separation of powers, and sovereignty

The basic liberal principle of limiting coercion to the enforcement of general rules of just conduct has rarely been stated in this explicit form, but has usually found expression in two conceptions characteristic of liberal constitutionalism, that of indefeasible or natural rights of the individual (also described as fundamental rights or rights of man) and that of the separation of powers. As the French Declaration of the Rights of Man and of the Citizen of 1789, at the same time the most concise and the most influential statement of liberal principles, expressed it: "Any society in which rights are not securely guaranteed, and the separation of powers is not determined, has no constitution."

The idea of specially guaranteeing certain fundamental rights, such as "liberty, property, security and resistance to oppression", and, more specifically,

---

[34] [For more on this, see Hayek, *The Mirage of Social Justice*, pp. 115–20.—Ed.]

such freedoms as those of opinion, of speech, of assembly, of the press, which make their appearance first in the course of the American revolution, is, however, only an application of the general liberal principle to certain rights which were thought to be particularly important and, being confined to enumerated rights, does not go as far as the general principle. That they are merely particular applications of the general principle appears from the fact that none of these basic rights is treated as an absolute right, but that they all extend only so far as they are not limited by general laws. Yet, since according to the most general liberal principle *all* coercive action of government is to be limited to the enforcement of such general rules, all the basic rights listed in any of the catalogues or bills of protected rights, and many others never embodied in such documents, would be secured by a single clause stating that general principle. As is true of economic freedom, all the other freedoms would be secured if the activities of the individuals could not be limited by specific prohibitions (or the requirement of specific permissions) but only by general rules equally applicable to all.

The principle of the separation of powers in its original sense also is an application of the same general principle, but only in so far as in the distinction between the three powers of legislation, jurisdiction and administration the term 'law' is understood, as it undoubtedly was by the early propounders of the principle, in the narrow sense of general rules of just conduct. So long as the legislature could pass only laws in this narrow sense, the courts could only order (and the executive only apply) coercion in order to secure obedience to such general rules. This, however, would be true only in so far as the power of the legislature was confined to laying down such laws in the strict sense (as in the opinion of John Locke it ought to be), but not if the legislature could give to the executive any orders it thought fit, and if any action of the executive authorised in this manner was regarded as legitimate. Where the representative assembly, called the legislature, has become, as it has in all modern states, the supreme governmental authority which directs the action of the executive on particular matters, and the separation of powers merely means that the executive must not do anything not so authorised, this does not secure that the liberty of the individual is restricted only by laws in the strict sense in which liberal theory used the term.

The limitation of the powers of the legislature that was implicit in the original conception of the separation of powers also implies a rejection of the idea of *any* unlimited or sovereign power, or at least of any authority of organised power to do what it likes. The refusal to recognise such a sovereign power, very clear in John Locke and again and again recurring in later liberal doctrine, is one of the chief points where it clashes with the now predominant conceptions of legal positivism. It denies the logical necessity of the derivation of all legitimate power from a single sovereign source, or any organised 'will', on the ground that such a limitation of all organised power may be brought about by a general state of opinion which refuses allegiance to any power (or organised will) which takes action of a *kind* which this general opinion does not authorise. It believes that even a force such as general opinion, though not capable of formulating specific acts of will, may yet limit the legitimate power of all organs of government to actions possessing certain general attributes.

11. Liberalism and justice

Closely connected with the liberal conception of law is the liberal conception of justice. It is different from that now widely held in two important respects: it is founded on a belief in the possibility of discovering objective rules of just conduct independent of particular interests; and it concerns itself only with the justice of human conduct, or the rules governing it, and not with the particular results of such conduct on the position of the different individuals or groups. Especially in contrast to socialism it may be said that liberalism is concerned with commutative justice and not with what is called distributive or now more frequently 'social' justice.

The belief in the existence of rules of just conduct which can be discovered but not arbitrarily created rests on the fact that the great majority of such rules will at all times be unquestioningly accepted, and that any doubt about the justice of a particular rule must be resolved within the context of this body of generally accepted rules, in such a manner that the rule to be accepted will be compatible with the rest: that is, it must serve the formation of the same kind of abstract order of actions which all the other rules of just conduct serve, and must not conflict with the requirements of any one of these rules. The test of the justice of any particular rule is thus whether its universal application is possible because it proves to be consistent with all the other accepted rules.

It is often alleged that this belief of liberalism in a justice independent of particular interests depends on a conception of a law of nature that has been conclusively rejected by modern thought. Yet it can be represented as dependent on a belief in a law of nature only in a very special sense of this term, a sense in which it is by no means true that it has been effectively refuted by legal positivism. It is undeniable that the attacks of legal positivism have done much to discredit this essential part of the traditional liberal creed. Liberal theory is indeed in conflict with legal positivism with regard to the latter's assertion that all law is or must be the product of the (essentially arbitrary) will of a legislator. Yet once the general principle of a self-maintaining order based on several property and the rules of contract is accepted, there will, within the system of generally accepted rules, be required particular answers to specific questions—made necessary by the rationale of the whole system—and the appropriate answers to such questions will have to be discovered rather than arbitrarily invented.[35] It is from this fact that the legitimate conception springs that particular rules rather than others will be required by 'the nature of the case'.

The ideal of distributive justice has frequently attracted liberal thinkers, and has become probably one of the main factors which led so many of them from liberalism to socialism. The reason why it must be rejected by consistent liberals is the double one that there exist no recognised or discoverable general principles of distributive justice, and that, even if such principles could be agreed upon, they could not be put into effect in a society whose productivity rests on the individuals being free to use their own knowledge and abilities for their own purposes. The assurance of particular benefits to particular people as rewards corresponding to their merits or needs, however assessed, requires a kind of order of society altogether different from that spontaneous order which will form itself if individuals are restrained only by general rules of just conduct. It requires an order of the kind (best described as an organisation) in which the individuals are made to serve a common unitary hierarchy of ends, and required to do what is needed in the light of an authoritative plan of action. While a spontaneous order in this sense does not serve any single order of needs, but merely provides the best opportunities for the pursuit of a great variety of individual needs, an organisation presupposes that all its members serve the same system of ends. And the kind of comprehensive single organisation of the whole of society, which would be necessary in order to secure that each gets what some authority thinks he deserves, must produce a society in which each must also do what the same authority prescribes.

12. Liberalism and equality

Liberalism merely demands that so far as the state determines the conditions under which the individuals act it must do so according to the same formal rules for all. It is opposed to all legal privilege, to any conferment by government of specific advantages on some which it does not offer to all. But since, without the power of specific coercion, government can control only a small part of the conditions which determine the prospects of the different individuals, and these individuals are necessarily very different, both in their individual abilities and knowledge as well as in the particular (physical and social) environment in which they find themselves, equal treatment under the same general laws must result in very different positions of the different persons;

---

[35] [Hayek is using the term 'system' in the sense set out in his essay "Notes on the Evolution of Systems of Rules of Conduct" [1967], reprinted as chapter 10 of Hayek, *The Market and Other Orders*.—Ed.]

while in order to make the position or the opportunities of the different persons equal, it would be necessary that government treat them differently. Liberalism, in other words, merely demands that the procedure, or the rules of the game, by which the relative positions of the different individuals are determined, be just (or at least not unjust), but not that the particular results of this process for the different individuals be just; because these results, in a society of free men, will always depend also on the actions of the individuals themselves and on numerous other circumstances which nobody can in their entirety determine or foresee.

In the heyday of classical liberalism, this demand was commonly expressed by the requirement that all careers should be open to talents, or more vaguely and inexactly as 'equality of opportunity'. But this meant in effect only that those obstacles to the rise to higher positions should be removed which were the effect of legal discriminations between persons. It did not mean that thereby the chances of the different individuals could be made the same. Not only their different individual capacities, but above all the inevitable differences of their individual environments, and in particular the family in which they grew up, would still make their prospects very different. For this reason the idea that has proved so attractive to most liberals, that only an order in which the initial chances of all individuals are the same at the start, can be regarded as just, is incapable of realisation in a free society; it would require a deliberate manipulation of the environment in which all the different individuals worked which would be wholly irreconcilable with the ideal of a freedom in which the individuals can use their own knowledge and skill to shape this environment.

But though there are strict limits to the degree of material equality which can be achieved by liberal methods, the struggle for formal equality, i.e. against all discrimination based on social origin, nationality, race, creed, sex, etc., remained one of the strongest characteristics of the liberal tradition. Though it did not believe that it was possible to avoid great differences in material positions, it hoped to remove their sting by a progressive increase of vertical mobility. The chief instrument by which this was to be secured was the provision (where necessary out of public funds) of a universal system of education which would at least place all the young at the foot of the ladder on which they would then be able to rise in accordance with their abilities. It was thus by the provision of certain services to those not yet able to provide for themselves that many liberals endeavoured at least to reduce the social barriers which tied individuals to the class into which they were born.

More doubtfully compatible with the liberal conception of equality is another measure which also gained wide support in liberal circles, namely the use of progressive taxation as a means to effect a redistribution of income in favour of the poorer classes. Since no criterion can be found by which such progression can be made to correspond to a rule which may be said to be the same for all, or which would limit the degree of extra burden on the more wealthy, it would seem that a *generally* progressive taxation is in conflict with the principle of equality before the law and it was in general so regarded by liberals in the nineteenth century.

13. Liberalism and democracy

By the insistence on a law which is the same for all, and the consequent opposition to all legal privilege, liberalism came to be closely associated with the movement for democracy. In the struggle for constitutional government in the nineteenth century, the liberal and the democratic movements indeed were often indistinguishable. Yet in the course of time the consequence of the fact that the two doctrines were in the last resort concerned with different issues became more and more apparent. Liberalism is concerned with the functions of government and particularly with the limitation of all its powers. Democracy is concerned with the question of who is to direct government. Liberalism requires that all power, and therefore also that of the majority, be limited. Democracy came to regard current majority opinion as the only criterion of the legitimacy of the powers of government. The difference between the two principles stands out most clearly if we consider their opposites: with democracy it is authoritarian government; with liberalism it is totalitarianism. Neither of the two systems necessarily excludes the opposite of the other: a democracy may well wield totalitarian powers, and it is at least conceivable that an authoritarian government might act on liberal principles.

Liberalism is thus incompatible with unlimited democracy, just as it is incompatible with all other forms of unlimited government. It presupposes the limitation of the powers even of the representatives of the majority by requiring a commitment to principles either explicitly laid down in a constitution or accepted by general opinion so as to effectively confine legislation.

Thus, though the consistent application of liberal principles leads to democracy, democracy will preserve liberalism only if, and so long as, the majority refrains from using its powers to confer on its supporters special advantages which cannot be similarly offered to all citizens. This might be achieved in a representative assembly whose powers were confined to passing laws in the sense of general rules of just conduct, on which agreement among a majority is likely to exist. But it is most unlikely in an assembly which habitually directs the specific measures of government. In such a representative assembly, which combines true legislative with governmental powers, and which is therefore in the exercise of the latter not limited by rules that it cannot alter, the majority is not likely to be based on true agreement on principles, but will probably consist of coalitions of various organised interests which will mutually concede to each other special advantages. Where, as is almost inevitable in a representative body with unlimited powers, decisions are arrived at by a bartering of special benefits to the different groups, and where the formation of a majority capable of governing depends on such bartering, it is indeed almost inconceivable that these powers will be used only in the true general interests.

But while for these reasons it seems almost certain that unlimited democracy will abandon liberal principles in favour of discriminatory measures benefiting the various groups supporting the majority, it is also doubtful whether in the long run democracy can preserve itself if it abandons liberal principles. If government assumes tasks which are too extensive and complex to be effectively guided by majority decisions, it seems inevitable that effective powers will devolve to a bureaucratic apparatus increasingly independent of democratic control. It is therefore not unlikely that the abandonment of liberalism by democracy will in the long run also lead to the disappearance of democracy. There can, in particular, be little doubt that the kind of directed economy towards which democracy seems to be tending requires for its effective conduct a government with authoritarian powers.[36]

14. The service functions of government

The strict limitation of governmental powers to the enforcement of general rules of just conduct required by liberal principles refers only to the coercive powers of government. Government may render in addition, by the use of the means placed at its disposal, many services which involve no coercion except for the raising of the means by taxation; and apart perhaps from some extreme wings of the liberal movement, the desirability of government undertaking such tasks has never been denied. They were, however, in the nineteenth century still of minor and mainly traditional importance and little discussed by liberal theory which merely stressed that such services had better be left in the hands of local rather than central government. The guiding consideration was a fear that central government would become too powerful, and a hope that competition between the different local authorities would effectively control and direct the development of these services on desirable lines.

The general growth of wealth and the new aspirations whose satisfaction were made possible by it have since led to an enormous growth of those service activities, and have made necessary a much more clear-cut attitude towards them than classical liberalism ever took. There can be no doubt that there are many such services, known to the economists as 'public goods', which are highly desirable but cannot be provided by the market mechanism,

---

[36] [For more on Hayek's views on democracy, see Hayek, *The Constitution of Liberty*, pp. 166–83, and Hayek, *The Political Order of a Free People*, pp. 1–40, 98–104.—Ed.]

because if they are provided they will benefit everybody and cannot be confined to those who are willing to pay for them. From the elementary tasks of the protection against crime or the prevention of the spreading of contagious diseases and other health services, to the great variety of problems which the large urban agglomerations raise most acutely, the required services can only be provided if the means to defray their costs are raised by taxation. This means that, if these services are to be provided at all, at least their finance, if not necessarily also their operation must be placed in the hands of agencies which have the power of taxation. This need not mean that government is given the exclusive right to render these services, and the liberal will wish that the possibility be left open that when ways of providing such services by private enterprise are discovered, this can be done. He will also retain the traditional preference that those services should so far as possible be provided by local rather than central authorities and be paid for by local taxation, since in this manner at least some connection between those who benefit and those who pay for a particular service will be preserved. But beyond this liberalism has developed scarcely any definite principles to guide policy in this wide field of ever increasing importance.

The failure to apply the general principles of liberalism to the new problems showed itself in the course of the development of the modern Welfare State. Though it should have been possible to achieve many of its aims within a liberal framework, this would have required a slow experimental process; yet the desire to achieve them by the most immediately effective path led everywhere to the abandonment of liberal principles. While it should have been possible, in particular, to provide most of the services of social insurance by the development of an institution for true competitive insurance, and while even a minimum income assured to all might have been created within a liberal framework, the decision to make the whole field of social insurance a government monopoly, and to turn the whole apparatus erected for that purpose into a great machinery for the redistribution of incomes, led to a progressive growth of the government controlled sector of the economy and to a steady dwindling of the part of the economy in which liberal principles still prevail.

15. Positive tasks of liberal legislation

Traditional liberal doctrine, however, not only failed to cope adequately with new problems, but also never developed a sufficiently clear programme for the development of a legal framework designed to preserve an effective market order. If the free enterprise system is to work beneficially, it is not sufficient that the laws satisfy the negative criteria sketched earlier. It is also necessary that their positive content be such as to make the market mechanism operate satisfactorily. This requires in particular rules which favour the preservation of competition and restrain, so far as possible, the development of monopolistic positions. These problems were somewhat neglected by nineteenth-century liberal doctrine and were examined systematically only more recently by some of the 'neo-liberal' groups.[37]

It is probable, however, that in the field of enterprise monopoly would never have become a serious problem if government had not assisted its development by tariffs, certain features of the law of corporations and of the law of industrial patents. It is an open question whether, beyond giving the legal framework such a character that it will favour competition, specific measures to combat monopoly are necessary or desirable. If they are, the ancient common law prohibition of conspiracies in restraint of trade might have provided a foundation for such a development which, however, remained long unused. Only comparatively lately, beginning with the Sherman Act of 1890 in the USA, and in Europe mostly only after the Second World War, were attempts made at a deliberate anti-trust and anti-cartel legislation which, because of the discretionary powers which they usually conferred on administrative agencies, were not wholly reconcilable with classical liberal ideals.

The field, however, in which the failure to apply liberal principles led to developments which increasingly impeded the functioning of the market order, is that of the monopoly of organised labour or of the trade unions.

---

[37] [Hayek alludes here to the work of the ordo-liberal or Freiburg School, a group of liberal thinkers established in Germany in the 1930s by economist Walter Eucken (1891–1950) and jurists Hans Großmann-Doerth (1894–1944) and Franz Böhm (1895–1977). The members of the Freiburg School were united by a concern with the constitutional foundations of a free economy and society, arguing that a satisfactory understanding of the working of market economies required an analysis of the system of rules structuring economic activity, informed both by the discipline of law and also by economics. Their work helped to shape the policies used to reconstruct the German economy after World War Two. The Freiburg School is sometimes described as 'neo-liberal' because, in contrast to advocates of a more thoroughgoing commitment to laissez-faire, such as Austrian economist Ludwig von Mises (1881–1973), the ordo-liberals maintained that the development of a legal framework conducive to economic order would not occur spontaneously but rather required state intervention designed to promote competition and to prohibit activities facilitating the growth of monopoly power (an approach to policy known as *Ordnungspolitik*). Hence Hayek's remark that the work of the ordo-liberals constituted "shall we say, a restrained liberalism". See Hayek, "The Rediscovery of Freedom", p. 190. For more on all this, see H. M. Oliver, Jr., "German Neoliberalism", *Quarterly Journal of Economics*, vol. 74, 1960, pp. 117–49, and V. Vanberg, "Markets and Regulation: On the Contrast between Free-Market Liberalism and Constitutional Liberalism", *Constitutional Political Economy*, vol. 10, 1999, pp. 219–43. For Hayek's views on Eucken and Böhm, see his inaugural address as Professor of Political Economy at Freiburg, "The Economy, Science and Politics" [1963], reprinted as chapter 7 of *The Market and Other Orders*, pp. 213–15, 225–26, and "The Rediscovery of Freedom", pp. 189–90. Also see F. A. Hayek, "The Transmission of the Ideals of Economic Freedom" [1951], reprinted as chapter 2 of this volume, pp. 51–53, and F. A. Hayek, "What Is 'Social'? What Does It Mean?" [1967], reprinted as chapter 19 of this volume, pp. 252 n. 2, 254 n. 3.—Ed.]

Classical liberalism had supported the demands of the workers for 'freedom of association', and perhaps for this reason later failed effectively to oppose the development of labour unions into institutions privileged by law to use coercion in a manner not permitted to anybody else. It is this position of the labour unions which has made the market mechanism for the determination of wages largely inoperative, and it is more than doubtful whether a market economy can be preserved if the competitive determination of prices is not also applied to wages. The question whether the market order will continue to exist or whether it will be replaced by a centrally planned economic system may well depend on whether it will prove possible in some manner to restore a competitive labour market.

The effects of these developments show themselves already in the manner in which they have influenced government action in the second main field in which it is generally believed that a functioning market order requires positive government action: the provision of a stable monetary system. While classical liberalism assumed that the gold standard provided an automatic mechanism for the regulation of the supply of money and credit which would be adequate to secure a functioning market order, the historical developments have in fact produced a credit structure which has become to a high degree dependent on the deliberate regulation by a central authority. This control, which for some time had been placed in the hands of independent central banks, has in recent times been in effect transferred to governments, largely because budgetary policy has been made one of the chief instruments of monetary control. Governments have thus become responsible for determining one of the essential conditions on which the working of the market mechanism depends.

In this position governments in all Western countries have been forced, in order to secure adequate employment at the wages driven up by trade union action, to pursue an inflationary policy which makes monetary demand rise faster than the supply of goods. They have been driven by this into an accelerating inflation which in turn they feel bound to counteract by direct controls of prices that threaten to make the market mechanism increasingly inoperative. This seems now to become the way in which, as already indicated in the historical section, the market order which is the foundation of a liberal system will be progressively destroyed.

16. Intellectual and material freedom

The political doctrines of liberalism on which this exposition has concentrated will appear to many who regard themselves as liberals as not the whole or even the most important part of their creed. As has already been indicated, the term 'liberal' has often, and particularly in recent times, been used in a sense in which it describes primarily a general attitude of mind rather than specific views about the proper functions of government. It is therefore appropriate in conclusion to return to the relation between those more general foundations of all liberal thought and the legal and economic doctrines in order to show that the latter are the necessary result of the consistent application of the ideas which led to the demand for intellectual freedom on which all the different strands of liberalism agree.

The central belief from which all liberal postulates may be said to spring is that more successful solutions of the problems of society are to be expected if we do not rely on the application of anyone's given knowledge, but encourage the interpersonal process of the exchange of opinion from which better knowledge can be expected to emerge. It is the discussion and mutual criticism of men's different opinions derived from different experiences which was assumed to facilitate the discovery of truth, or at least the best approximation to truth which could be achieved. Freedom for individual opinion was demanded precisely because every individual was regarded as fallible, and the discovery of the best knowledge was expected only from that continuous testing of all beliefs which free discussion secured. Or, to put this differently, it was not so much from the power of individual reason (which the genuine liberals distrusted), as from the results of the interpersonal process of discussion and criticism, that a progressive advance towards the truth was expected. Even the growth of individual reason and knowledge is regarded as possible only in so far as the individual is part of this process,

That the advance of knowledge, or progress, which intellectual freedom secured, and the consequent increased power of men to achieve their aims, was eminently desirable, was one of the unquestioned presuppositions of the liberal creed. It is sometimes alleged, not quite justly, that its stress was entirely on material progress. Though it is true that it expected the solution of most problems from the advance of scientific and technological knowledge, it combined with this a somewhat uncritical, though probably empirically justified, belief that freedom would also bring progress in the moral sphere; it seems at least true that during periods of advancing civilisation moral views often came to be more widely accepted which in earlier periods had been only imperfectly or partially recognised. (It is perhaps more doubtful whether the rapid intellectual advance that freedom produced also led to a growth of aesthetic susceptibilities; but liberal doctrine never claimed any influence in this respect.)

All the arguments in support of intellectual freedom also apply, however, to the case for the freedom of doing things, or freedom of action. The varied experiences which lead to the differences of opinion from which intellectual growth originates are in turn the result of the different actions taken by different people in different circumstances. As in the intellectual so in the material sphere, competition is the most effective discovery procedure which will lead to the finding of better ways for the pursuit of human aims. Only when a great many different ways of doing things can be tried will there exist such a variety of individual experience, knowledge and skills, that a continuous selection of the most successful will lead to steady improvement. As action is the main source of the individual knowledge on which the social process of the advance of knowledge is based, the case for the freedom of action is as strong as the case for freedom of opinion. And in a modern society based on the division of labour and the market, most of the new forms of action arise in the economic field.

There is, however, yet another reason why freedom of action, especially in the economic field that is so often represented as being of minor importance, is in fact as important as the freedom of the mind. If it is the mind which chooses the ends of human action, their realisation depends on the availability of the required means, and any economic control which gives power over the means also gives power over the ends. There can be no freedom of the press if the instruments of printing are under the control of government, no freedom of assembly if the needed rooms are so controlled, no freedom of movement if the means of transport are a government monopoly, etc. This is the reason why governmental direction of all economic activity, often undertaken in the vain hope of providing more ample means for all purposes, has invariably brought severe restrictions of the ends which the individuals can pursue. It is probably the most significant lesson of the political developments of the twentieth century that control of the material part of life has given government, in what we have learnt to call totalitarian systems, far-reaching powers over the intellectual life. It is the multiplicity of different and independent agencies prepared to supply the means which enables us to choose the ends which we will pursue.

BIBLIOGRAPHY

The best accounts of the liberal movement will be found in some of the histories of the major European countries during the nineteenth century, such as É. Halévy, *Histoire du peuple anglais au XIXe siècle,* 6 vols, Paris, 1912–32, trans. as *History of the English People,* London, 1926, etc.; and F. Schnabel, *Deutsche Geschichte im neunzehnten Jahrhundert,* vol. II, Freiburg, 1933. The fullest survey of the development of the ideals of liberalism is G. de Ruggiero, *Storia del liberalismo europeo,* Bari, 1925, trans. by R. G. Collingwood as *The History of European Liberalism,* Oxford, 1927, which contains an extensive bibliography to which reference must be made for all the works of an earlier date, including the classical works of the founders of modern liberalism. The following list gives in chronological order the more important works of later date dealing with the history of liberal ideas and movements and the present state of liberal doctrine.[38]

Martin, B. Kingsley, 1926, *French Liberal Thought in the Eighteenth Century*, London; new ed. 1954.
Mises, L. von, 1927, *Liberalismus*, Jena.
Croce, B., 1931, *Etica e Politica*, Bari.
Laski, H., 1931, *The Rise of European Liberalism*, London.
Pohlenz, M., 1935, *Die griechische Freiheit*, Heidelberg; trans. as *The Idea of Freedom in Greek Life and Thought*, Dordrecht, 1963.
Lippmann, W., 1937, *An Inquiry into the Principles of the Good Society*, Boston and London.
Sabine, G. H., 1937, *A History of Political Theory*, New York.
McIlwain, C. H., 1939, *Constitutionalism and the Changing World*, New York.
Hallowell, J. H., 1943, *The Decline of Liberalism as an Ideology*, Berkeley, Calif.
Slesser, H., 1943, *A History of the Liberal Party*, London.
Röepke, W., 1944, *Civitas Humana*, Zürich.
Diez del Corral, L., 1945, *El Liberalismo doctrinario*, Madrid.
Popper, K. R., 1945, *The Open Society and Its Enemies*, London.
Rüstow, A., 1945, *Das Versagen des Wirtschaftsliberalismus als religionssoziologisches Problem*, Zürich.
Federici, F., 1946, *Der deutsche Liberalismus*, Zürich.
Watkins, F., 1948, *The Political Tradition of the West*, Cambridge, Mass.
Wormuth, F. D., 1949, *The Origins of Modern Constitutionalism*, New York.
Polanyi, M., 1951, *The Logic of Liberty*, London.
Eucken, W., 1952, *Grundsätze der Wirtschaftspolitik*, Tübingen.
Robbins, L. C., 1952, *The Theory of Economic Policy in English Classical Political Economy*, London.
Talmon, J. L., 1952, *The Origins of Totalitarian Democracy*, London.
Cranston, M., 1953, *Freedom*, London.
Lübtow, U. von, 1953, *Blüte und Verfall der römischen Freiheit*, Berlin.
Neill, T. P., 1953, *Rise and Decline of Liberalism*, Milwaukee, Wis.
Thomas, R. H., 1953, *Liberalism, Nationalism and the German Intellectuals*, Chester Springs, Pa.
Mayer-Maly, T., 1954, "Rechtsgeschichte der Freiheitsidee in Antike und Mittelalter", *Österreichische Zeitschrift für öffentliches Recht*, N.F.VI.
Hartz, L., 1955, *The Liberal Tradition in America*, New York.

[38] [The works recommended by Hayek are as follows: É. Halévy, *Histoire du peuple anglais au XIXᵉ siècle*, 6 vols. (Paris: Hachette, 1912–32); É. Halévy, *A History of the English People in the Nineteenth Century*, trans. E. Watkin, 6 vols. (London: Ernest Benn, 1929–52); F. Schnabel, *Deutsche Geschichte im neunzehnten Jahrhundert*, vol. 2 (Freiburg im Breslau: Herder & Co., 1933); G. de Ruggiero, *Storia del liberalismo Europeo* (Bari: Giuseppe Laterza & Figli, 1925), and Ruggiero, *The History of European Liberalism.*—Ed.]

Bullock, A., and Shock, M., 1956, *The Liberal Tradition from Fox to Keynes*, London.

Wirszubski, C., 1956, *Libertas as a Political Ideal at Rome*, Cambridge.

Feuer, L. S., 1958, *Spinoza and the Rise of Liberalism*, Boston.

Grifò, G., 1958, "Su alcuni aspetti della libertà in Roma", *Archivio Giuridico 'Filippo Serafini'*, 6 serie XXIII.

Grampp, W. D., 1960, *The Manchester School of Economics*, Stanford, Calif.

Hayek, F. A., 1960, *The Constitution of Liberty*, London and Chicago.

Friedman, M., 1962, *Capitalism and Freedom*, Chicago.

Macpherson, C. B., 1962, *The Political Theory of Possessive Individualism: Hobbes to Locke*, Oxford.

Girvetz, H. K., 1963, *The Evolution of Liberalism*, New York.

Schapiro, J. S., 1963, *Condorcet and the Rise of Liberalism*, New York.

Wheeler, 1963, *The Rise and Fall of Liberal Democracy*, Santa Barbara, Calif.

Grampp, W. D., 1965, *Economic Liberalism*, New York.

Böhm, F., 1966, "Privatrechtsgesellschaft und Marktwirtschaft", in *Ordo*, XVII.

Lucas, J. R., 1966, *Principles of Politics*, Oxford.

Vincent, John, 1966, *The Formation of the Liberal Party 1857–1868*, London.

Selinger, M., 1968, *The Liberal Politics of John Locke*, London.

Cumming, R. D., 1971, *Human Nature and History, a Study of the Development of Liberal Thought*, Chicago.

Douglas, R., 1971, *The History of the Liberal Party 1890–1970*, London.

Hamer, D. A., 1972, *Liberal Politics in the Age of Gladstone and Rosebery*, Oxford.[39]

[39] [The complete reference list, arranged in alphabetical order by author and with errors in Hayek's list corrected, is as follows:

Böhm, F., "Privatrechtsgesellschaft und Marktwirtschaft", *Ordo*, vol. 17, 1966, pp. 75–151.

Bullock, A., and M. Shock, eds., *The Liberal Tradition: From Fox to Keynes* (London: Adam & Charles Black, 1956).

Cranston, M., *Freedom: A New Analysis* (London: Longmans, Green and Co., 1953).

Crifò, G., "Su alcuni aspetti della libertà in Roma", *Archivio Giuridico 'Filippo Serafini'*, Série 6, vol. 23, 1958, pp. 3–72.

Croce, B., *Etica e Politica* (Bari: Laterza, 1931).

Cumming, R. D., *Human Nature and History: A Study of the Development of Liberal Political Thought*, 2. vols. (Chicago and London: University of Chicago Press, 1969).

Díez del Corral, L., *El Liberalismo doctrinario* (Madrid: Instituto de Estudios Políticos, 1945).

Douglas, R., *The History of the Liberal Party, 1895–1970* (London: Sidgwick & Jackson, 1971).

Eucken, W., *Grundsätze der Wirtschaftspolitik* (Tübingen: J. C. B. Mohr [Paul Siebeck], 1952).

Federici, F., *Der deutsche Liberalismus: Die Entwicklung einer politischen Idee von Immanuel Kant bis Thomas Mann* (Zürich: Artemiss-Verlag, 1946).

Feuer, L., *Spinoza and the Rise of Liberalism* (Boston: Beacon Press, 1958).

Friedman, M., *Capitalism and Freedom* (Chicago: University of Chicago Press, 1962).

Girvetz, H., *The Evolution of Liberalism* (New York: Collier Books, 1963).

Grampp, W., *Economic Liberalism*, 2 vols. (New York: Random House, 1965).

Grampp, W., *The Manchester School of Economics* (Stanford, CA: Stanford University Press, 1960).

Hallowell, J. H., *The Decline of Liberalism as an Ideology: With Particular Reference to German Politico-Legal Thought* (Berkeley and Los Angeles: University of California Press, 1943).

Hamer, D. A., *Liberal Politics in the Age of Gladstone and Rosebery* (Oxford: Clarendon Press, 1972).

Hartz, L., *The Liberal Tradition in America* (New York: Harcourt, Brace & World, 1955).

Hayek, F. A., *The Constitution of Liberty*, ed. Ronald Hamowy, vol. 17 of *The Collected Works of F. A. Hayek* (Chicago: University of Chicago Press, 2011).

Laski, H., *The Rise of European Liberalism: An Essay in Interpretation* (London: George Allen & Unwin, 1936).

Lippmann, W., *An Inquiry into the Principles of the Good Society* (London: George Allen & Unwin, 1937).

Lübtow, U. von, *Blüte und Verfall der römischen Freiheit: Betrachtungen zur Kultur- und Verfassungsgeschichte des Abendlandes* (Berlin: Blaschker, 1953).

Lucas, J. R., *The Principles of Politics* (Oxford: Clarendon Press, 1966).

Macpherson, C. B., *The Political Theory of Possessive Individualism: Hobbes to Locke* (Oxford: Clarendon Press, 1962).

Martin, K., *French Liberal Thought in the Eighteenth Century: A Study of Political Ideas from Bayle to Condorcet*, 1st edn. (London: Ernest Benn, 1929), 2nd edn. (London: Turnstile Press, 1954).

Mayer-Maly, T., "Zur Rechtsgeschichte der Freiheitsidee in Antike und Mittelalter", *Österreichische Zeitschrift für öffentliches Recht*, vol. 6, 1953–55, pp. 399–428.

McIlwain, C. H., 1939, *Constitutionalism and the Changing World: Collected Papers* (Cambridge: Cambridge University Press, 1939).

Mises, L. von, *Liberalismus* (Jena: Gustav Fischer, 1927).

Neill, T. P., *The Rise and Decline of Liberalism* (Milwaukee: Bruce, 1953).

Pohlenz, M., *Freedom in Greek Life and Thought: The History of an Ideal*, trans. C. Lofmark (Dordrecht: Reidel, 1966).

Pohlenz, M., *Griechische Freiheit: Wesen und Werden eines Lebensideals* (Heidelberg: Quelle & Mayer, 1955).

Polanyi, M., *The Logic of Liberty: Reflections and Rejoinders* (London: Routledge and Kegan Paul, 1951).

Popper, K. R., *The Open Society and Its Enemies*, 2 vols. (London: G. Routledge & Sons, 1945).

Robbins, L., *The Theory of Economic Policy in English Classical Political Economy* (London: Macmillan & Co., 1952).

Röepke, W., *Civitas Humana: Grundfragen der Gesellschafts- und Wirtschaftsreform* (Erlenbach-Zürich: Rentsch, 1944).

Rüstow, A., *Das Versagen des Wirtschaftsliberalismus als religionsgeschichtliches Problem* (Zürich: Europa-Verlag, 1945).

Sabine, G. H., *A History of Political Theory* (New York: Henry Holt and Co., 1937).

Schapiro, J. S., *Condorcet and the Rise of Liberalism* (New York: Octagon Books, 1963).

Seliger, M., *The Liberal Politics of John Locke* (London: George Allen & Unwin, 1968).

Slesser, H., *A History of the Liberal Party* (London: Hutchinson, 1944).

Talmon, J., *The Origins of Totalitarian Democracy* (London: Secker & Warburg, 1952).

Thomas, R. H., *Liberalism, Nationalism and the German Intellectuals (1822–1847)* (Cambridge: W. Heffer & Sons, 1951).

Vincent, J., *The Formation of the Liberal Party, 1857–1868* (London: Constable, 1966).

Watkins, F., *The Political Tradition of the West: A Study in the Development of Modern Liberalism* (Cambridge, MA: Harvard University Press, 1948).

Wheeler, J. *The Rise and Fall of Liberal Democracy* (University of California, Santa Barbara: Center for the Study of Democratic Institutions Occasional Paper, 1966).

Wirszubski, Ch., *Libertas as a Political Idea at Rome during the Late Republic and Early Principate* (Cambridge: Cambridge University Press, 1950).

Wormuth, F., *The Origins of Modern Constitutionalism* (New York: Harper & Brothers, 1949).—Ed.]

THE TRANSMISSION OF THE IDEALS
OF ECONOMIC FREEDOM[1]

At the end of the First World War the spiritual tradition of liberalism was all but dead. True, it was still uppermost in the thoughts of many a leading figure of public and business life, many of whom belonged to a generation which took liberal thought for granted. Their public pronouncements sometimes led the general public to believe that a return to a liberal economy was the ultimate goal desired by the majority of leading men. But the intellectual forces

---

[1] First published in German as a tribute to L. v. Mises on his seventieth birthday, which it was known he did not wish to see formally noticed, in the *Schweizer Monatshefte*, Vol. 31, No. 6, 1951, and later in an English translation in *The Owl*, London, 1951. I should not have wished to reprint this somewhat hastily written occasional piece, if with all its imperfections and errors of translation it had not already been used as a historical source, so that it seems desirable to make a corrected version available.

[The complete reference to the original German version of the essay is F. A. Hayek, "Die Überlieferung der Ideale der Wirtschaftsfreiheit", *Schweizer Monatshefte*, vol. 31, 1951, pp. 333–38. The English translation to which Hayek refers is F. A. Hayek, "The Ideals of Economic Freedom: A Liberal Inheritance", *The Owl*, 1951, pp. 7–12. The essay was subsequently reprinted, under the slightly different title of "The Transmission of the Ideals of Economic Freedom", as chapter 13 of F. A. Hayek, *Studies in Philosophy, Politics and Economics* (London: Routledge & Kegan Paul, 1967). The latter title has been retained here. A very similar essay appeared as F. A. Hayek, "A Rebirth of Liberalism", *The Freeman*, vol. 2, July 1952, pp. 729–31.

Austrian economist Ludwig von Mises (1881–1973) taught at the University of Vienna, before moving in 1934 to the Graduate Institute of International Studies at the University of Geneva. He emigrated to the United States in 1940, where he assumed a position at the Graduate School of Business at New York University. Mises was a staunch advocate of classical liberalism who developed a monetary theory of the business cycle and argued that rational economic calculation would be impossible under socialism. See L. von Mises, *Theorie des Geldes und der Umlaufsmittel* (Munich and Leipzig: Duncker & Humblot, 1912), translated by H. Batson as *The Theory of Money and Credit* (London: Jonathan Cape, 1934), and L. von Mises, *Die Gemeinwirtschaft: Untersuchungen über den Sozialismus* (Jena: Gustav Fischer, 1922), 2nd edn. trans. J. Kahane as *Socialism: An Economic and Sociological Analysis* (London: Jonathan Cape, 1936). Mises was also Hayek's mentor in economics, Hayek having worked under his direction in the Austrian government shortly after World War I and also attended his private seminar in the 1920s and early 1930s. For more on Hayek's views about Mises, see F. A. Hayek, "Ludwig von Mises (1881–1973)", published as chapter 4 of F. A. Hayek, *The Fortunes of Liberalism: Essays on Austrian Economics and the Ideal of Freedom*, ed. Peter G. Klein, vol. 4 (1992) of *The Collected Works of F. A. Hayek* (Chicago: University of Chicago Press; London: Routledge).—Ed.]

then at work had begun to point in quite a different direction. Anyone familiar, thirty years ago, with the thought of the coming generation and especially with the views propounded to the students in their universities, could foresee developments very different from those still hoped for by some of the public figures and the press of the time. There was no longer, at that time, a living world of liberal thought which could have fired the imagination of the young.[2]

Nonetheless, the main body of liberal thought has been safeguarded through that eclipse in the intellectual history of liberalism which lasted throughout the fifteen or twenty years following the First World War; indeed, during that very period the foundations were laid for a new development. This was due, almost exclusively, to the activities of a handful of men about whom I wish to say something here. No doubt, they were not the only ones striving to uphold the liberal tradition. But it seems to me that these men, each working alone and independently of the others, were the only ones who succeeded, by their teaching, in creating the new traditions which more recently have again united in one common stream. The circumstances surrounding the lives of the past generation make it hardly surprising that it should have taken so long for the like-minded efforts of an Englishman, an Austrian and an American to be recognised as such and to be built into the common foundation for the following generation's work. But the new liberal school which does now exist and about which there will be more to say, consciously builds upon the work of these men.

The oldest, and perhaps the least known outside his own country, was the Englishman, Edwin Cannan, who died nearly twenty years ago. The part he played is little known beyond a rather narrow circle. The reason for this may be that his main interests really lay elsewhere and that he dealt with questions of economic policy only in occasional writings; or it may be, perhaps, that he was more interested in practical details than in the basic philosophical questions. Many of his economic essays which he published in two volumes, *The Economic Outlook* (1912) and *An Economist's Protest* (1927), deserve, even now, renewed and wider attention, and translation into other languages. Their simplicity, clarity and sound common sense make them models for the treatment of economic problems, and even some that were written before 1914 are still astonishingly topical. Cannan's greatest merit, however, was the training, over many years, of a group of pupils at the London School of Economics: it was they who later formed what probably became the most important centre of the new liberalism—though, it is true, at a time when such a development had

---

[2] [Hayek offers more detailed recollections of this period in F. A. Hayek, "The Economics of the 1920s as Seen from Vienna" [1963], and on pp. 185–88 of F. A. Hayek, "The Rediscovery of Freedom: Personal Recollections" [1983], published as the Prologues to parts I and II respectively of Hayek, *The Fortunes of Liberalism.*—Ed.]

already been got under way by the work of the Austrian economist of whom we shall presently speak.[3] But first let us say a little more about Cannan's pupils. The oldest is the well-known financial expert, Sir Theodore Gregory.[4] For many years, when holding a chair at the London School of Economics, he too wielded great influence on academic youth; but he gave up teaching a good many years ago. It was Lionel Robbins, who now has held Cannan's chair for twenty-two years, who became the real nucleus of a group of younger economists all very nearly the same age, which emerged at the London School of Economics during the 'thirties. Owing to a rare combination of literary talent and a gift for organising his material, his writings have found a very wide circulation.[5] Robbins' colleague, Sir Arnold Plant, has been teach-

[3] [Edwin Cannan (1861–1935) was a British economist and historian of economic thought. He joined the staff of the London School of Economics (LSE) when the latter opened in 1895 and was Professor of Political Economy from 1907 until 1926. In the two books to which Hayek refers, namely E. Cannan, *The Economic Outlook* (London: T. Fisher Unwin, 1912), and E. Cannan, *An Economist's Protest* (London: P. S. King, 1927), Cannan used economic analysis to address contemporary problems. He is perhaps now best known for his work in the history of economic thought, in particular, his critical edition of Adam Smith's *Wealth of Nations*. See A. Smith, *An Inquiry into the Nature and Causes of the Wealth of Nations*, edited, with an Introduction, Notes, Marginal Summary, and an Enlarged Index, by Edwin Cannan (London: Methuen, 1904). Hayek discusses Cannan and his work in more detail on pp. 51–54 of F. A. Hayek, "The Economics of the 1930s as Seen from London" [1963], published as chapter 1 of F. A. Hayek, *Contra Keynes and Cambridge: Essays, Correspondence*, ed. B. Caldwell, vol. 9 (1995) of *The Collected Works of F. A. Hayek*, and in his obituary of Cannan, namely F. A. Hayek, "Edwin Cannan" [1935], reprinted as the "Addendum" to the aforementioned chapter.—Ed.]

[4] [Sir Theodore Gregory (1890–1970) was a liberal British economist who taught at the LSE between 1913 and 1937, serving as Cassel Professor of Banking and Currency from 1927 until 1937.—Ed.]

[5] [Lionel Robbins (1898–1984), later Lord Robbins of Clare Market, graduated from the LSE with a degree in economics in 1923. In 1929, after periods as Assistant Lecturer and Lecturer at the LSE (1925–27), and as a Fellow of New College, Oxford (1927–29), Robbins returned to the LSE as Professor of Economics and Head of Department. In the latter role, he was instrumental in Hayek's recruitment to the LSE in 1932 as Tooke Professor of Economic Science and Statistics. Robbins's reminiscences of Cannan's teaching can be found in L. Robbins, "A Student's Recollections of Edwin Cannan", *Economic Journal*, vol. 45, 1935, pp. 393–98.

The younger economists to whom Hayek refers included Sir John Hicks (1904–89), R. G. D. Allen (1906–83), Abba P. Lerner (1903–82), and Nicholas Kaldor (1908–86). Hicks was a Lecturer at the London School of Economics (1926–35), later becoming Drummond Professor of Political Economy at Oxford University (1952–65). He made several seminal contributions to economic theory in the 1930s. In a 1934 paper co-authored with his LSE colleague R. G. D. Allen (1906–83), he showed that the notion of the 'marginal rate of substitution' could be used, along with indifference curve analysis, to reformulate the theory of demand without assuming that utility was measurable. See J. R. Hicks and R. G. D. Allen, "A Reconsideration of the Theory of Value", *Economica*, n.s., vol. 1, 1934, pp. 52–76 and 196–219. In 1937, in an effort to clarify and formalise the arguments developed by Keynes in *The General Theory*, Hicks developed the IS-LM approach to the analysis of the determinants of the level of national income, which became one of the most widely used macroeconomic models of the post–World War

ing at the School nearly as long. He, even more than Cannan himself, is wont to hide away his most important contributions in little-known publications, and all his friends have long been looking forward eagerly to a book about the foundations and significance of private property. If he ever publishes it,

---

Two era. See J. Hicks, "Mr. Keynes and the 'Classics'; A Suggested Interpretation", *Econometrica*, vol. 5, 1937, pp. 147–59. Finally, in his 1939 book *Value and Capital: An Inquiry into Some Fundamental Principles of Economic Theory* (Oxford: Clarendon Press, 1939), Hicks not only offered an English-language treatment of general equilibrium theory but also developed an original analysis of the stability and dynamics of the general equilibrium system. In 1972 Hicks was awarded the Nobel Prize in Economics for his contributions to general equilibrium theory and welfare economics.

Born in what is now Romania but raised in Britain, Abba P. Lerner (1903–82) enrolled in the LSE as an evening student in order to understand why, during the Great Depression, the printing shop he had run went out of business. He was an assistant lecturer at the LSE between 1935 and 1937, before moving to the United States, where he worked in various universities. Amongst many important pieces of work, Lerner provided the first clear demonstration of why the equality of price and marginal cost is a condition for the efficient allocation of resources, and of the idea that monopoly is a matter of degree whose magnitude is indicated by the excess of price over marginal cost. See A. P. Lerner, "The Concept of Monopoly and the Measurement of Monopoly Power", *Review of Economic Studies*, vol. 1, 1934, pp. 157–75. The 'marginal conditions' for efficiency, such as price equals marginal cost, that Lerner explored in his work on welfare economics provided the basis for the rules that he, and Polish economist Oskar Lange (1904–65), wished to impose on managers as part of their blueprint for a market socialist society, in which the efficiency of a competitive market process would be reconciled with the redistributive goals of socialism. In this way, ironically, the Paretian approach that Robbins, Hayek, and others at the LSE had been instrumental in introducing into British economics in the 1930s provided a significant foundation for the market socialism they so vigorously opposed. See A. P. Lerner, *The Economics of Control: Principles of Welfare Economics* (New York: Macmillan, 1944). For more on Hayek's views on market socialism, see F. A. Hayek, "Two Pages of Fiction" [1982], reprinted as chapter 30 of this volume, and the references contained therein.

Hungarian-born British economist Nicholas Kaldor, later Baron Kaldor of Newnham, graduated from the LSE in economics in 1930. In 1932 he joined the staff of the School as an Assistant Lecturer. In 1949 he joined Cambridge University, becoming Professor of Economics in 1966, where he remained until his retirement in 1975. During the 1930s, Kaldor wrote important articles on several areas of mainstream neoclassical economic theory, including the theory of the firm, capital theory, the analysis of the stability of market equilibria, and, perhaps most notably, welfare economics, where—along with Hicks—he developed the so-called Kaldor-Hicks compensation criterion for judging the merits of government policies. See N. Kaldor, "Welfare Propositions of Economics and Interpersonal Comparisons of Utility", *Economic Journal*, vol. 49, 1939, pp. 549–52. Whilst initially a follower of Hayek, Kaldor was an early convert to Keynesian economics following the publication of *The General Theory* in 1936 and, from the 1950s in particular, became one of the main architects of the so-called Post-Keynesian school of economics, whose members sought to extend Keynesian modes of thinking to questions of growth and distribution in capitalist economies. See, for instance, N. Kaldor, "Alternative Theories of Distribution", *Review of Economic Studies*, vol. 23, 1955–56, pp. 83–100.

For more detailed accounts of LSE economics in the 1930s, see Hayek, "The Economics of the 1930s as seen from London"; and R. Coase, "Economics at the LSE in the 1930s: A Personal View" [1982], reprinted as chapter 15 of R. Coase, *Essays on Economics and Economists* (Chicago: University of Chicago Press, 1994).—Ed.]

it should become one of the most important contributions to the theory of modern liberalism.[6] We cannot list here all Cannan's pupils who have contributed to the discussion of our problems; just to give an impression of the scope of his influence, let us add the names of F. C. Benham, W. H. Hutt and F. W. Paish—even though the latter was not Cannan's student, he belongs to the same circle.[7]

It could be said with some justification that Cannan really prepared the ground, in England, for the reception of the ideas of a much younger Austrian who has been working since the early 'twenties on the reconstruction of a solid edifice of liberal thought in a more determined, systematic and successful way than anyone else. This is Ludwig von Mises who worked first in

[6] [British economist Sir Arnold Plant (1898–1978) graduated from the LSE with degrees in Commerce (1922) and in Economics (1923). His own commonsense but robust approach to economic analysis and policy reflected the influence of his teacher, Edwin Cannan. In 1930, Plant became Professor of Commerce, a post he retained until his retirement in 1965. Plant published relatively little during his long career, and a combination of ill-health and the burden imposed by administrative duties at the LSE and work on government committees meant that the book on private property to which Hayek refers was never published. For a collection of his essays, see A. Plant, *Selected Economic Essays and Addresses* (London: Routledge and Kegan Paul, 1974).—Ed.]

[7] [After studying as an undergraduate and PhD student at the LSE, English economist Frederic Benham (1900–1962) taught at the University of Sydney before returning to the LSE first as a Lecturer and then as Professor of Commerce. He is best known for his textbook, *Economics: A General Textbook for Students* (London: Sir Isaac Pitman & Sons, 1938). In discussing how he first came to view the economic problem facing society as that of using data that were dispersed throughout the economy, and so not 'given' to anyone in their entirety, Hayek later commented, "My whole thinking on this started with my old friend Freddy Benham joking about economists speaking about given data just to reassure themselves that what was given was really given. That led me, in part, to ask to whom were the data really given. To us it was of course to nobody". See F. A. Hayek, *Hayek on Hayek: An Autobiographical Dialogue*, ed. S. Kresge and L. Wenar (Chicago: University of Chicago Press, 1994), p. 147, and F. A. Hayek, "Economics and Knowledge" [1937], reprinted as chapter 1 of F. A. Hayek, *The Market and Other Orders*, ed. Bruce Caldwell, vol. 15 (2014) of *The Collected Works of F. A. Hayek*.

F. W. Paish (1898–1988) taught at the LSE from 1931 until 1965, becoming Professor of Economics in 1949. His research focused on business finance and his publications included *The Postwar Financial Problem and Other Essays* (London: Macmillan, 1950) and *Business Finance* (London: Sir Isaac Pitman & Sons, 1953).

English classical liberal economist William H. Hutt (1899–1988) graduated from the LSE in 1924. After working for classical liberal author and publisher Sir Ernest Benn (1875–1954) for four years, Hutt joined the Department of Commerce at the University of Cape Town, which at the time was headed by Arnold Plant, where he taught from 1928 until 1965. Hutt opposed both trade union power and Keynesian economic policy, and was an early critic of apartheid. See W. Hutt, *The Economics of the Colour Bar: A Study of the Economic Origins and Consequences of Racial Segregation in South Africa* (London: Andre Deutsch, 1964), along with the references found in n. 15 on p. 87 of F. A. Hayek, "Closing Speech to the 1984 Mont Pèlerin Society Meeting" [1984], published as chapter 5 of this volume.—Ed.]

Vienna, then in Geneva, and who is still very actively at work now in New York. Even before the First World War Mises had become known for his work on monetary theory. Immediately after the war, his prophetic book, *Nation, Staat und Wirtschaft* (1919) initiated a development which had reached its first peak as early as 1922 in *Die Gemeinwirtschaft*,[8] a comprehensive critique of socialism—and at that time, that meant a critique of all the ideologies of any serious consequence in the literature of economic policy.

There is no space here to give the long list of important writings which intervened between this and Mises's second main work which appeared in 1941 in Geneva. This was written in German and was originally called *Nationalökonomie*; its revised American edition, *Human Action*, has achieved almost unique success for a theoretical treatise of such size. Mises's work as a whole covers far more than economics in the narrower sense. His penetrating studies of the philosophical foundations of the social sciences and his remarkable historical knowledge place his work much closer to that of the great eighteenth-century moral philosophers than to the writings of contemporary economists.[9] Mises was strongly attacked from the very beginning because of his relentlessly uncompromising attitude; he made enemies and, above all, did not find academic recognition until late. Yet his work has wielded an influence which is the more lasting and the more extensive for all its slow beginnings. Even some of Mises's own pupils were often inclined to consider as 'exaggerated' that unfaltering tenacity with which he pursued his reasoning to its utmost conclusions; but the apparent pessimism which he habitually displayed in his judgment of the consequences of the economic policies of his time has proved right over and over again, and eventually an ever-widening circle came to appreciate the fundamental importance of his writings which ran counter to the main stream of contemporary thought in nearly every respect. Even when still in Vienna, Mises did not lack close disciples most of whom are now in the United States, like Mises himself; they include Gottfried Haberler (Harvard University), Fritz Machlup (John Hopkins University), and the pres-

---

[8] Translated into English by Jacques Kahane, under the title *Socialism*, London, Jonathan Cape, 1936. [See Mises, *Socialism*. Hayek also refers to L. von Mises, *Nation, Staat und Wirtschaft: Beiträge zur Politik und Geschichte der Zeit* (Vienna and Leipzig: Manzsche Verlags, 1919), translated into English by Yeland B. Yeager as L. von Mises, *Nation, State and Economy: Contributions to the Politics and History of Our Time* (New York: New York University Press, 1983).—Ed.]

[9] [Hayek refers to L. von Mises, *Nationalökonomie: Theories des Handelns und Wirtschaftens* (Geneva: Editions Union, 1940) and L. von Mises, *Human Action: A Treatise on Economics* (New Haven: Yale University Press, 1949). He also alludes to books such as L. von Mises, *Epistemological Problems of Economics* [1933], trans. G. Reisman (Princeton, NJ: D. Van Nostrand, 1960), and L. von Mises, *Theory and History: An Interpretation of Social and Economic Evolution* (New Haven: Yale University Press, 1957). Hayek's reviews of *Nationalökonomie*, and of *Epistemological Problems of Economics*, can be found in Hayek, "Ludwig von Mises (1881–1973)", pp. 147–52.—Ed.]

ent writer.[10] But Mises's influence now reaches beyond the personal sphere to a far greater extent than does that of the two other main personalities with whom we are here concerned. He alone of them has given us a comprehensive treatment ranging over the whole economic and social field. We may or may not agree with him on details, but there is hardly an important question in these fields about which his readers would fail to find real instruction and stimulation.

Mises's influence became important not only for the London group, but equally so for the third, the Chicago, group. This group owes its origins to Professor Frank H. Knight of the University of Chicago, who is Mises's junior by a few years. Like Mises, Knight owes his original reputation to a theoretical monograph; notwithstanding an early lack of recognition, the latter's *Risk, Uncertainty and Profit* (1921) eventually became, and for many years continued to be, one of the most influential textbooks on economic theory, although it had not originally been designed as such. Knight has since written a great deal on questions of economic policy and social philosophy—mostly in articles the majority of which have since been republished in book form. The best-known, and perhaps also the most characteristic, volume is *The Ethics of Competition and Other Essays* (1935).[11] Knight's personal influence, through his teach-

[10] [Gottfried Haberler (1900–1995) studied economics at the University of Vienna in the 1920s, teaching there from 1928 until 1936. He then moved to the United States where he became a Professor at Harvard University (1936–71). Haberler transformed the analysis of international trade by introducing the idea of the production possibility frontier and reformulating the Ricardian account of comparative advantage in terms of the Austrian notion of opportunity cost. He also made significant contributions to business cycle theory, including developing the idea of the 'real-balance effect'. See G. Haberler, *The Theory of International Trade with Its Applications to Commercial Policy*, trans. A. Stonier and F. Benham (London: William Hodge & Co., 1936), and G. Haberler, *Prosperity and Depression: A Theoretical Analysis of Cyclical Movements*, 3rd ed. (Geneva: League of Nations, 1941), respectively.

Fritz Machlup (1902–83) also studied at the University of Vienna in the 1920s, where like Haberler he was taught by Mises, before leaving Germany for the United States on a Rockefeller Fellowship in 1933. He became a Professor at the University of Buffalo (1935–47), at Johns Hopkins University (1947–60), and then at Princeton University (1960–71). After his retirement from Princeton he continued to teach at New York University until his death in 1983. The many topics on which he wrote included industrial organisation, with particular emphasis on the knowledge economy, and the international monetary system. See, for example, F. Machlup, *The Production and Distribution of Knowledge in the United States* (Princeton: Princeton University Press, 1962), and F. Machlup, *International Payments, Debts, and Gold* (New York: Scribner's, 1964). A classical liberal, Machlup was one of the founding members of the Mont Pèlerin Society.—Ed.]

[11] [Frank Knight (1885–1972) was Professor of Economics at the University of Chicago (1928–52) and a dominant figure in the 'old', pre-World War Two Chicago School of Economics. In *Risk, Uncertainty and Profit* (Boston: Houghton-Mifflin, 1921), Knight defined the notion of perfect competition, distinguished the notion of calculable risk from incalculable uncertainty, and argued that profit was the reward entrepreneurs earned for being willing to bear uncer-

ing, exceeds even the influence of his writings. It is hardly an exaggeration to state that nearly all the younger American economists who really understand and advocate a competitive economic system have at one time been Knight's students. From the point of view which interests us here the most important was Henry C. Simons, whose untimely and early death we mourn. In the 'thirties his pamphlet, *A Positive Program for Laissez Faire*, offered a new and common basis for the aspirations of America's young liberals. Hopes for a systematic and comprehensive work from Simons were disappointed; instead, he left a collection of essays which appeared in 1948 under the title *Economic Policy for a Free Society*. This book became very influential owing to its wealth of ideas and to the courage with which Simons discussed such delicate problems as trade unionism.[12] Today, the nucleus of a group of like-minded economists—

---

tainty. Knight's book was widely used by undergraduates reading economics at the LSE in the 1930s, being recommended as a key text by Lionel Robbins for his course on 'General Principles of Economic Analysis'. See Coase, "Economics at the LSE in the 1930s", pp. 212–13. Knight's broader social philosophy was primarily concerned with ascertaining how, by means of a consensus achieved through rational discussion, a liberal society could be created in which the preservation of individual freedom was combined with a satisfactory economic performance. See F. H. Knight, *The Ethics of Competition and Other Essays* (London: Allen & Unwin, 1935), and F. H. Knight, *Freedom and Reform: Essays in Economics and Social Philosophy* (New York: Harper and Brothers, 1947).—Ed.]

[12] [American economist Henry Calvert Simons (1899–1946) taught economics at the University of Iowa from 1922 until 1927, after which he followed his mentor Frank Knight to the University of Chicago, where he was a Professor of Economics first of all (from 1928) in the Department of Economics and subsequently (from 1939) in the Law School. The essay entitled "A Positive Program for Laissez Faire", which Simons published in 1934, was a defence of liberalism against its intellectual opponents, set against the background of economic crisis and a rising tide of collectivism and totalitarianism. Its central claim, indicated by the presence of the word 'positive' in the title, was that if liberalism were to be revived, it had to be viewed not simply as a 'negative' doctrine that aims only to reduce the role of the state in economic life but also as assigning government a 'positive' role in establishing the conditions in which markets could work well. This would involve the state establishing a legal framework that would ensure the "[e]limination of private monopoly in all its forms", whether corporate or union, thereby "maintaining effectively competitive conditions" in both product and labour markets; creating "more definite and adequate 'rules of the game' with respect to money", in order to reduce the scale of the business cycle; and implementing a system of progressive taxation, so as to reduce the concentrations of economic power created by inequalities in the distribution of income and wealth. See H. Simons, "A Positive Program for Laissez Faire: Some Proposals for a Liberal Economic Policy", Public Policy Pamphlet No. 15, ed. H. D. Gideonse (Chicago: University of Chicago Press, 1934). The essay was reprinted as chapter 2 of H. Simons, *Economic Policy for a Free Society* (Chicago: University of Chicago Press, 1948), a posthumously published collection of essays, curated by his friend Aaron Director, in which Simons elaborated on and developed the views summarised above. The words quoted are taken from p. 57 of that book. For more on Hayek's views about Simons, see F. A. Hayek, "'Free' Enterprise and Competitive Order" [1948], reprinted as chapter 6 of this volume, p. 99 n. 11.—Ed.]

no longer confined to Chicago—is formed by Simons' closest friend, Aaron Director, and two of the best-known younger American theoreticians, George Stigler and Milton Friedman. Director has edited Simons' papers and carried on his work.[13]

[13] [Aaron Director (1901–2004) was a PhD student at the University of Chicago and also visited the LSE in 1937, meeting Hayek. He was instrumental in persuading the University of Chicago Press to publish the American edition of Hayek's *Road to Serfdom*. See B. Caldwell, "Introduction", in F. A. Hayek, *The Road to Serfdom: Text and Documents*, ed. B. Caldwell, vol. 2 (2007) of *The Collected Works of F. A. Hayek*, p. 16. In his review of Hayek's book, Director argued, along the same lines as Simons, that the liberal tradition "is not a negative one" and that in a liberal society government "must do many things", including improving "the rules of the game to increase the effectiveness of competition". See A. Director, "The Road to Serfdom. By Friedrich A. Hayek", *American Economic Review*, 35, 1945, pp. 173–75, at p. 174. In 1946 Director joined the faculty of the Law School at the University of Chicago, where he pioneered the application of economic principles to legal reasoning, thereby helping to found the law and economics movement. His appointment to Chicago came about as the result of Hayek and Simons' efforts to establish in the Law School a project, entitled the 'Free Market Study' and financed by the Volker Fund, to examine the legal and institutional foundations for a genuinely competitive market system. See R. Van Horn and P. Mirowski, "The Rise of the Chicago School of Economics and the Birth of Neoliberalism", published as chapter 4 of *The Road from Mont Pèlerin: The Making of the Neoliberal Thought Collective*, ed. P. Mirowski and D. Plehwe (Cambridge: Harvard University Press, 2009), and B. Caldwell, "The Chicago School, Hayek, and Neoliberalism", published as chapter 11 of *Building Chicago Economics: New Perspectives on the History of America's Most Powerful Economics Program*, ed. R. Van Horn, P. Mirowski, and T. Stapleford (Cambridge: Cambridge University Press, 2011).

Nobel Prize-winning economist Milton Friedman (1912–2006) was Hayek's colleague at the University of Chicago from 1950, when Hayek joined the Committee on Social Thought, to 1962, when Hayek left Chicago for Freiburg University. He was the author, amongst many other works, of *Essays in Positive Economics* (Chicago: University of Chicago Press, 1953) and *Capitalism and Freedom* (Chicago: University of Chicago Press, 1962). In an article published in the same year as Hayek's essay, Friedman argued along very similar lines to Simons that there was a need for a "new faith . . . sometimes called neo-liberalism" that would "accept the nineteenth century liberal emphasis on the fundamental importance of the individual, but . . . would substitute for the nineteenth century goal of laissez-faire . . . [that] of providing a framework within which free competition could flourish and the price system operate effectively". See M. Friedman, "Neoliberalism and Its Prospects", *Farmand*, February 17, 1951, pp. 89–93. For an account of Friedman's influence on the development of liberal thought after World War Two, see A. Burgin, *The Great Persuasion: Reinventing Free Markets since the Depression* (Cambridge, MA: Harvard University Press, 2012), pp. 152–213.

American economist George Stigler (1911–91) received his PhD from the University of Chicago in 1938, where he came under the influence not only of Frank Knight and Henry Simons but also of his fellow student Milton Friedman. Stigler subsequently taught at Columbia University (1947–58) and at the University of Chicago (1958–91). Following Simons, Stigler was initially in favour of government intervention to encourage competition. However, from the 1950s onwards Stigler became increasingly sceptical of the merits of state action as a means of curbing monopoly power, arguing that more often than not regulatory agencies were 'captured' by producer interests and used by firms to impose regulations that reduced competition. See, for example, G. Stigler, "The Theory of Economic Regulation", *Bell Journal of Economics and Manage-*

Alas, good manners make it impossible to claim a great nation's head of State for any particular economic school;[14] I should, otherwise, name a fourth scientist whose influence in his own country is of comparable consequence. Instead, I shall complete the picture by turning at once to the last group which interests us here.[15] It is a German group, and differs from the others in that

---

ment Science, vol. 2, 1971, pp. 3–21. In 1982, Stigler was awarded the Nobel Prize in Economics for his work on industrial organisation, the economics of information, and the causes and effects of government regulation.—Ed.]

[14] The reference is, of course, to the late Luigi Einaudi, at the time when this article appeared President of the Italian Republic. [Liberal Italian economist and statesman Luigi Einaudi (1874–1961) was President of the Italian Republic from 1948 until 1955. Collections of his essays include L. Einaudi, *Selected Economic Essays*, ed. L. Einaudi, R. Faucci, and R. Marchionatti (Basingstoke: Palgrave Macmillan, 2006), and L. Einaudi, *Selected Political Essays*, ed. D. da Empoli, C. Malandrino, and V. Zanone (Basingstoke: Palgrave Macmillan, 2014).—Ed.]

[15] In the original version of this sketch I unpardonably omitted to mention a promising beginning of this liberal renaissance which, though cut short by the outbreak of war in 1939, provided many of the personal contacts which after the war were to form the basis of a renewed effort on an international scale. In 1937 Walter Lippmann had delighted and encouraged all liberals by the publication of his brilliant restatement of the fundamental ideals of classic liberalism in his book, *The Good Society*. Recognising the importance of this work as a possible rallying point of dispersed efforts, Professor Louis Rougier of the University of Paris then called a symposium at which at the end of August 1938 about twenty-five students of public affairs from several European countries and the United States met at Paris to discuss the principles stated by Lippmann. They included Louis Baudin, Walter Lippmann, Ludwig von Mises, Michael Polanyi, Lionel Robbins, Wilhelm Röpke, Alexander Rüstow, Marcel van Zeeland and the present author. The meeting approved the proposal for the creation of a Centre International des Etudes pour la Rénovation du Libéralisme—but when its report appeared in print (*Colloque Walter Lippmann*, Paris, 1939), only a few weeks were left before the outbreak of the Second World War and the consequent suspension of all efforts of this kind. [American journalist, author and social commentator Walter Lippmann (1889–1974) was the author of *An Inquiry into the Principles of the Good Society* (Boston: Little, Brown and Co., 1937), in which he sought to restate the principles of liberal thought in a way that would establish its superiority over both collectivism and nineteenth-century laissez-faire. In 1938, French philosopher Louis Rougier (1889–1982), the editor of a series of liberal works in which the French translation of *The Good Society* appeared, organised a colloquium at which Lippmann's arguments were discussed. The twenty-six attendees included classical liberal French economist Louis Baudin (1887–1964), who taught in the law school at the University of Dijon and at the Ecole des Hautes Etudes Commerciales de Paris; Hungarian-British chemist and philosopher Michael Polanyi (1891–1976); German sociologist and economist Alexander Rüstow (1885–1963); German economist Wilhelm Röpke (1899–1966); and Marcel van Zeeland (1898–1972), a Belgian national who worked for the Bank for International Settlements from its foundation in 1930 until 1962, serving as Head of the Banking Department from 1947 until 1962. The proceedings were published as *Compte-rendu des séances du Colloque Walter Lippmann* (Paris: Librairie de Médicis, 1939). For an English translation, see J. Reinhoudt and S. Audier, *The Walter Lippmann Colloquium: The Birth of Neo-Liberalism* (Basingstoke: Palgrave Macmillan, 2018), which also contains a complete list of attendees. Hayek is mistaken in listing Lionel Robbins amongst those who participated in the colloquium; Robbins did not in fact attend. See S. Howson, *Lionel Robbins* (Cambridge: Cambridge University Press, 2011), p. 321. For more on the Colloque Lippmann, see Hayek, "Closing Speech to the 1984 Mont Pèlerin Society Meeting", pp. 82–83.—Ed.]

its origin cannot be traced back directly to any great figure of the preceding generation. It came into being through the association of a number of younger men whose common interest in a liberal economic system brought them together during the years preceding Hitler's seizure of power. There can be no doubt that this group too received decisive stimulus from Mises's writings.[16] This group had not yet made its mark in economic literature by 1933, and at that time some of its members had to leave Germany. There remained, however, one of the group's oldest members, Walter Eucken, who was then as yet relatively little known. Today we realise that his sudden death a little over a year ago robbed the liberal revival of one of its really great men. He had matured slowly, had long refrained from publication and had mainly devoted himself to teaching and to practical problems. It was not until after Germany's collapse that it became apparent how fruitful and beneficial his quiet activities had been during the National Socialist period; for only then was the circle of his friends and students in Germany revealed as the most important bulwark of rational economic thinking. That was also the time when Eucken's first major work began to spread its influence and when he undertook the exposition of his whole economic thought in several other works.[17] The future will show how much of this remains to be recovered from the papers he left at

---

[16] [Hayek refers here to the ordo-liberal or Freiburg School, a group of liberal thinkers who came together in Germany in the early 1930s and whose most significant members included economist Walter Eucken (1891–1950), jurists Hans Großmann-Doerth (1894–1944) and Franz Böhm (1895–1977), as well as Alexander Rüstow and Wilhelm Röpke. The hallmark of ordo-liberalism was its focus on the constitutional foundations of a free society; its advocates argued that liberal philosophy should be grounded in an analysis, informed by the disciplines of law and economics, of the system of rules governing economic activity. While the ordo-liberals' views about the impossibility of central planning and the causes of the business cycle were influenced by Mises's work, they departed from his unwavering commitment to laissez-faire by arguing that the state should prohibit voluntarily agreed contracts that would inhibit competition and thereby promote monopoly power. Indeed, at the Colloque Lippmann Rüstow coined the term 'neo-liberalism' precisely in order to differentiate the version of liberalism to which he and his fellow ordo-liberals subscribed from the 'classical liberalism' of von Mises. Hayek discusses the contributions made by the ordo-liberals to the revival of liberal thinking in Germany in "The Rediscovery of Freedom" and in his own inaugural address as Professor of Political Economy at Freiburg, namely F. A. Hayek, "The Economy, Science and Politics" [1963], reprinted as chapter 7 of *The Market and Other Orders*, pp. 214–15.—Ed.]

[17] [Hayek refers to W. Eucken, *Die Grundlagen der Nationalökonomie* (Jena: Verlag von Gustav Fischer, 1940). An English edition was published in 1950, as W. Eucken, *The Foundations of Economics*, trans. T. Hutchison (London: William Hodge & Co., 1950). Elsewhere, Hayek writes that it was this book that made him "realise for the first time what a towering figure Eucken was and to how great an extent Eucken and his circle embodied the great German liberal tradition, which had unfortunately become defunct". See Hayek, "The Rediscovery of Freedom", p. 189. For a useful summary of Eucken's work, see H. Grossekettler, "On Designing an Economic Order. The Contributions of the Freiburg School", in *Perspectives on the History of Economic Thought*, ed. D. Walker (Aldershot: Edward Elgar, 1989).—Ed.]

his death. The annual *Ordo* which he founded continues to be the most important publication of the entire movement.[18]

The second leading figure of this German group, Wilhelm Röpke, had been in close contact with Eucken from the beginning. By 1933, Röpke had made such a mark in public life that his stay in Hitler's Germany immediately became impossible. He went to Istanbul first, and has now been in Switzerland for many years. He is the most active and the most prolific writer of the whole group and has become known to a wide public.[19]

If the existence of a neo-liberal movement is known far beyond the narrow circles of experts, the credit belongs mainly to Röpke, at least so far as the German-speaking public is concerned.

It has been said above that all these groups which came into being in the course of the last quarter of a century did not really get to know each other until after the Second World War. We then witnessed a lively exchange of ideas. Today, it has almost become a matter of history to speak of separate national groups. For that very reason, this is perhaps the right moment to give a brief outline of this development. Gone is the day when the few remaining liberals each went his own way in solitude and derision; gone the day when they found no response among the young. On the contrary, they bear a heavy responsibility now, because the new generation demands to be told of liberalism's answers to the great problems of our time. An integrated structure of liberal thought is required and its application to the problems of different countries needs to be worked out. This will only be possible by a meeting of minds within a large group. There remain serious difficulties, in many coun-

---

[18] [Eucken's *Grundsätze der Wirtschaftspolitik* (Tübingen: J. C. B. Mohr, 1952) was published after his untimely death in 1950. The journal *Ordo: Jahrbuch für die Ordnung von Wirtschaft und Gesellschaft* was established by Eucken and Franz Böhm in 1948. Hayek was a member of its editorial board from its foundation until 1991.—Ed.]

[19] [Röpke taught in the 1920s at the universities of Jena and Graz, before becoming Professor of Economics at the University of Marburg in 1929. He left Germany in 1933, shortly after Hitler's appointment as Chancellor, and went to the University of Istanbul and then in 1937 to the Graduate Institute of International Studies in Geneva, where he remained until his death in 1966. He published four books in the 1940s, including *The Social Crisis of Our Time* [1942], trans. A. Jacobsohn and P. Jacobsohn (Chicago: University of Chicago Press, 1950), *The Moral Foundations of Civil Society* [1944], trans. C. S. Fox (London: William Hodge and Co., 1948), and *International Order and Economic Integration* [1945], trans. G. Trinks, J. Taylor and C. Kaufer (Dordrecht-Holland: Reidel, 1959). For a helpful overview of Röpke's work, along with that of his fellow exile Rüstow—who also left Germany for Istanbul in 1933, remaining there until 1949—see D. Johnson, "Exiles and Half-Exiles: Wilhelm Röpke, Alexander Rüstow and Walter Eucken", in *German Neo-Liberals and the Social Market Economy*, ed. A. Peacock and H. Willgerodt (London: Macmillan, 1989). Röpke also played a significant part in making available the funds for the first meeting of the Mont Pèlerin Society, as Hayek acknowledges in his "Closing Speech to the 1984 Mont Pèlerin Society Meeting". For more on Hayek's views concerning Röpke, see Hayek, "The Rediscovery of Freedom", pp. 195–97.—Ed.]

tries, with regard to the dissemination of the available literature, and the lack of translations of some of the most important works still stands in the way of a more rapid propagation of these ideas. But there is, today, personal contact between most of their supporters. Twice already Switzerland has been host to the informal, yet cohesive group which met there for the common study of its problems and whose name derives from a Swiss place-name. Another meeting took place in Holland in 1950, and a fourth conference in France in 1951.[20]

The period which we have discussed in this paper can, then, be regarded as closed. Thirty years ago liberalism may still have had some influence among public men, but it had well-nigh disappeared as a spiritual movement. Today its practical influence may be scant, but its problems have once more become a living body of thought. We may feel justified in looking forward with renewed faith to the future of liberalism.

---

[20] [The group to which Hayek refers is, of course, the Mont Pèlerin Society, whose first four meetings were held in Mont Pèlerin, Switzerland (1947); Seelisberg, Switzerland (1949); Bloemendaal, Holland (1950); and Beauvallon, France (1951). See R. M. Hartwell, *A History of the Mont Pelerin Society* (Indianapolis: Liberty Fund, 1995), pp. 81–94. For more on the rationale for the Society, see pp. 207–15 of F. A. Hayek, "Historians and the Future of Europe" [1944], and F. A. Hayek, "Opening Address to a Conference at Mont Pèlerin" [1947], reprinted as chapters 8 and 12 respectively of Hayek, *The Fortunes of Liberalism*, as well as F. A. Hayek, "The Prospects of Freedom" [1946], published as chapter 3 of this collection. Hayek discusses aspects of the work involved in establishing the Society in his "Closing Speech to the 1984 Mont Pèlerin Society Meeting", and the references contained therein. For longer accounts, see Hartwell, *A History of the Mont Pelerin Society*, pp. 3–51, and Burgin, *The Great Persuasion*, pp. 55–122.—Ed.]

THREE

THE PROSPECTS OF FREEDOM[1]

The future student of the history of our time will be puzzled, I believe, by a curious contradiction which pervades the thinking of our generation. On the one hand man prides himself to have become master of his destiny as never before; on the other hand there is an underlying but growing current of fatalism: more and more people feel that we are ineluctably moving towards a kind of social order which nobody wants and which we have yet no power to avert. It seems that with the passage of time the fatalism is slowly gaining ground over the unbounded optimism of not long ago, and it is frequently the same people who quickly change from a violent partisanship of the one to the other point of view—even if they do not, as many Marxists do, hold both views at the same time. Yet, contradictory as these views are, they may still be connected in the sense that the growing fatalism is justified by the kind of action to which we are being led by an exaggerated belief in the power we have over our fate. In other instances it may well be a desire to disclaim responsibility, the search for an alibi, which makes so many, who yesterday urged us on the path on which we are travelling, argue today that we had anyhow no choice in the matter.

Few people will now deny that there are serious dangers on the path on which we are moving, that if we are not careful we may find ourselves saddled with an omnipotent state whose machinery so thoroughly controls the people and their opinions that even the retention of the forms of democracy would not alter its totalitarian character. But there is, of course, nothing inevitable about this development. If it comes, it will be the product of our own doing, the result of our present ambitions and beliefs, and although we are never

[1] [This essay, which was originally delivered as a lecture at Stanford University in 1946, has not previously been published. The version used here can be found in the Hayek Collection, box 61, folder 9, Hoover Institution Archives. An earlier version, which contains just a handful of minor stylistic differences from the one used here, is located in box 107, folder 7, of the Hayek Collection. Hayek wrote the words "Prospects of Freedom" as his diary entry for Tuesday, July 2, 1946, suggesting that was the day the lecture was given. See the Hayek Collection, box 122, folder 4.—Ed.]

fully aware where the many divergent endeavours of any moment will lead us, so long as we are willing to learn and to revise our own ideas, there is no need for us to be driven into a social order we all fear. But if we are at least to be as much masters of our own fate as we can reasonably hope to be, the first condition is that we recognise the enormous power our ideas and our beliefs have on our future, and devote the energy and vigour to the examining and sifting of the ideas which govern our generation which this task deserves in view of its importance.[2]

If it is often doubted that human ideas and beliefs are the main mover of history, the main reason is probably that we all find it is difficult to imagine that our beliefs might be different from what they in fact are. This is probably most true of those beliefs which are most powerful, the most abstract and general ideas which form the presuppositions of all our thinking and pervade all our thought. The conception of inevitable historical trends, of great laws of history which we must obey whether we like it or not, to which I have already referred, is a good illustration of the kind of such preconceptions which determine present-day thought.

I do not propose to undertake here any detailed discussion of the great subject of the power of human ideas. Let me instead quote the words of a great man whom we have recently lost and who, although I do not find myself often agreeing with him, seems to me in this instance to have expressed a profoundly important truth. "The ideas of economists and political philosophers", wrote the late Lord Keynes, "both when they are right and when they are wrong, are more powerful than is commonly understood. Indeed, the world is ruled by little else. Practical men, who believe themselves to be quite exempt from any intellectual influences, are usually the slaves of some defunct economist. Madmen in authority, who hear voices in the air, are distilling their frenzy from some academic scribbler of a few years back. I am sure the power of vested interests is vastly exaggerated compared with the gradual encroachment of ideas. Not, indeed, immediately, but after a certain interval; for in the field of economic and political philosophy there are not many who are influenced by new ideas after they are twenty-five or thirty years of age, so that the ideas which civil servants and politicians and even agitators apply are not

---

[2] [Hayek's claim that "the enormous power our ideas and our beliefs have on our future" implies that there is "nothing inevitable" about government intervention in the economy leading to totalitarianism casts doubt on claims that he believed in the so-called 'inevitability thesis' or 'slippery slope' argument (according to which a society whose government engages in even a small amount of economic planning is doomed to become a totalitarian state). For more on this, see F. A. Hayek, *The Road to Serfdom: Text and Documents*, ed. B. Caldwell, vol. 2 (2007) of *The Collected Works of F. A. Hayek* (Chicago: University of Chicago Press; London: Routledge), in particular pp. 91–170, and F. A. Hayek, "Socialism and Science" [1976], reprinted as chapter 29 of this volume, p. 432 n. 11, and the works referred to there.—Ed.]

likely to be the newest. But, soon or late, it is ideas and not vested interests, which are dangerous for good and evil".[3]

If any man of our generation could speak with authority on this subject, it certainly was Lord Keynes, of whom it might almost be said, as it was said of Adam Smith, that "he has persuaded his own generation and will govern the next". Whether this will be as much to the benefit of mankind as it was in the case of Adam Smith is of course another question.[4]

I have quoted Lord Keynes at length because in that passage he has expressed better than I could another point which is of importance for what I am going to say: the length of the interval between the time when ideas are given currency and the time when they govern action. It is usually a generation, or even more, and that is one reason why on the one hand our present thinking seems so powerless to influence events, and why on the other so much well meant effort at political education and propaganda is misspent, because it is almost invariably aimed at a short run effect. The one important and outstandingly successful exception to this rule is the socialist propaganda of the last hundred years: the socialists have never hesitated to work in this respect for the far distant future, and the extent to which they have succeeded in permeating all our thinking is not least due to their courage to be 'utopian'. It is time that those who cannot share their beliefs learnt in this respect a little from them and became a little more concerned, not with the immediate effect, but with the long period result of their teaching.[5]

What we who still regard personal liberty as the greatest good must learn again is that a stationary creed is a dying creed, that when the intellectual struggle to develop our ideas stops we have lost the battle. It is under this aspect that to the student of the intellectual movements of our time the prospects of freedom seem almost desperate. It cannot be denied that for at least

[3] [Hayek quotes, with a few very minor alterations and omissions, words written by British economist John Maynard Keynes (1883–1946), Baron Keynes of Tilton, on pp. 383–84 of his *magnum opus*, *The General Theory of Employment, Interest and Money* [1936], reprinted as vol. 7 (1973) of *The Collected Writings of John Maynard Keynes* (London: Macmillan for the Royal Economic Society). Hayek's views on Keynesian economics, and on Keynes the man, are set out in more detail in F. A. Hayek, *Contra Keynes and Cambridge: Essays, Correspondence*, ed. B. Caldwell, vol. 9 (1995) of *The Collected Works of F. A. Hayek.*—Ed.]

[4] [Hayek misquotes slightly the phrase used to describe Scottish political economist Adam Smith (1723–90) by one of Smith's former pupils, Scottish politician and property developer Sir William Pulteney (1729–1805). Smith's biographer John Rae (1845–1915) records that, in a speech Pulteney gave in 1797, he quoted an unknown source as saying that Smith "would persuade the present generation and govern the next". See J. Rae, *Life of Adam Smith* (London: Macmillan and Co., 1895), p. 103.—Ed.]

[5] [For more on Hayek's views on these issues, see F. A. Hayek, "The Webbs and Their Work" [1948], reprinted as chapter 4 of this volume, and F. A. Hayek, "The Intellectuals and Socialism" [1949], reprinted as chapter 11 of *Socialism and War: Essays, Documents, Reviews*, ed. B. Caldwell, vol. 10 (1997) of *The Collected Works of F. A. Hayek.*—Ed.]

a generation most of the active and productive thinkers have been moving away from the philosophy of freedom, that almost every so-called progress in social thinking involved some proposal for a restriction on individual freedom to some social good. And though many of you may feel that in these fortunate United States you are still so remote from the horrors of totalitarian government which I have painted elsewhere as not to need to worry, and though in so far as the factual developments are concerned this may be true, I do not feel the same assurance when I study the trend of thought in this country.[6] When I read the more academic discussions about the desirable future order of society, when I talk to young students at the great seats of learning, I find a state of opinion which is alarmingly similar to what I knew on the European Continent twenty-five years ago and in England ten or fifteen years ago. If the state of opinion in these circles is as much an indication of future developments as it has proved elsewhere, the risk that America may go the same road is not negligible.

I have often been told, after I had published a book on the consequences of central economic planning, written mainly with English conditions in mind, that no serious person in this country was advocating the sort of planned economy against which I argued. I wondered whether I could really be so much mistaken in my impression of the American scene and I have since made a little study of the discussion which has taken place here. I am afraid the result is far from re-assuring. I have time here only for one illustration of the kind of thing that was advocated not long ago by men who soon reached responsible position. It comes from a paper of a man who soon after, I understand, became one of the first economic advisers of the New Deal. In this address Mr. Rexford Guy Tugwell unhesitatingly admitted that the planning which he wanted amounted practically to "the abolition of 'business'".[7]

---

[6] [Hayek refers here, and also at the start of the next paragraph, to Hayek, *The Road to Serfdom.*—Ed.]

[7] [American economist Rexford Tugwell (1891–1979) was educated at the University of Pennsylvania, where he fell under the influence of the old institutionalist school of economics, and subsequently taught at Columbia University (1920–36). He was, along with fellow Columbia academics Adolph A. Berle, Jr. (1895–1971) and Raymond Moley (1886–1975), a member of the so-called 'Brain Trust' who advised Franklin D. Roosevelt during his first campaign for the Presidency of the United States (1932). Tugwell subsequently served in the Roosevelt Administration as Under Secretary of Agriculture—he had written extensively on agricultural policy—and head of the Resettlement Administration, and helped to draft the legislation that in 1933 created the National Recovery Administration, the goal of which was to promote cooperation between businesses and thereby help the U.S. economy to recover from the Great Depression. He resigned from government in 1936, subsequently becoming Chairman of the New York City Planning Commission (1938–41), Governor of Puerto Rico (1941–46), and Professor of Political Science at the University of Chicago (1946–57), where he founded and directed the University's Institute for Planning (1946–52). For more on Tugwell, including interesting analyses of his views on planning, see D. Winch, *Economics and Policy: A Historical Study* (London: Hod-

He even warned his hearers that this was "not an overstatement for the sake of emphasis; it is literally meant. The essence of business is its free venture for profits in an unregulated economy. Planning implies guidance of capital uses; this would limit entrance into or expansion of operations. Planning also implies adjustment of production to consumption" etc. etc. Elsewhere in the paper we are informed that "planning for production means planning for consumption too", that we shall have to give up any distinction between private and public or quasi-public employment, that Mr. Tugwell looks forward to a state of affairs in which "industry is government and government is industry" and that "the future is becoming visible in Russia". These few passages from that one document will, perhaps, be sufficient to show what American 'planners' have in store for you. Unfortunately these public announcements of the intentions of the American would-be-dictators seem to be taken as little seriously as other programmes of would-be-dictators have been taken in the past.

This is not to say that I do not recognise the existence of a feeling of apprehension in many quarters. In recent years the awareness that America is by no means immune against the dangers to which other countries have succumbed seems to have become fairly widespread, and there is even plenty of readiness to assist the spreading of 'sound' ideas. But the essential thing seems to me still entirely lacking, perhaps because it is not quite appreciated how ideas grow and gain influence and how far the new philosophy of government has already penetrated everyday thinking. There is little vigorous effort to meet these ideas in their own spiritual sphere, little deliberate effort to develop in opposition to them a true philosophy of freedom, and to make it once again a living and developing philosophy which will enlist the sympathy and support of the young and enthusiastic. Yet there is much hard thinking to be done if we are not soon to be swamped by the trend toward an omnipotent and omnipresent government.

The main reason why we are all drifting and likely to arrive at a social order which almost everybody fears is that we have no coherent social philosophy at all, that we have become afraid of general principles and have committed ourselves to a policy of experimentation without any serious effort to think out beforehand where it will lead us. But in a complex social structure like ours almost any policy which never hesitates to invoke coercion by the government when a particular desirable end is to be achieved is bound to lead us into a system where the government controls everything. If we do not think out beforehand the consequences of what we are doing, we find at every stage our hands

---

der and Stoughton, 1969), pp. 227–32, and M. Namorato, *Rexford G. Tugwell: A Biography* (New York: Praeger, 1988). Hayek quotes from p. 76 of R. Tugwell, "The Principle of Planning and the Institution of Laissez Faire", *American Economic Review, Papers and Proceedings*, vol. 22, 1932, pp. 75–92. The quotations that follow in the remainder of this paragraph are taken from pp. 89, 83, 86 n. 20, and 92 of Tugwell's paper.—Ed.]

forced and our freedom of action limited by the machinery with which we have already encumbered ourselves. What we get in the end is still the product of our wishes, but usually very different from the state of affairs we wanted to achieve.

The worst offenders in this respect are indeed our so-called 'planners'. While in a free system there is some justification if we concern ourselves only with our immediate ends and leave the rest to the impersonal machinery of the market, the planners are the last people entitled to do so. They of all people have no right to rely on any spontaneous forces coming to their aid if they have not provided for everything in their plans. The least thing we must demand from them is that they really think their own plans out beforehand and show us in detail how their planned society would work. Yet they not only persistently refuse to do so—they even bitterly resent it if somebody else tries to do it for them.

The modern proposals for central economic planning raise again great issues, above all that of the relation between power and freedom, on which little thinking has been done during the past two or three generations, because during that period it seemed as if individual liberty were securely established for all time.[8] There is no justification, however, for the confidence that we cannot lose again what we have once gained. There are many achievements of the liberal period which we take so much for granted that we no longer are aware on what they depend, and which we may easily lose if we do not relearn the lessons which those who gained us these liberties understood. We may be able to fight a defensive battle for a time and slow down the process of encroachment on liberty, but we shall not prevent the gradual advance of totalitarian control if we do not succeed in defeating the philosophy which produces it.

This, however, is an intellectual task which we have hardly yet begun, and of the magnitude of which few people have a conception. It is not merely a task of elaborating and popularising an alternative political programme. I have deliberately spoken of a philosophy, or a view of life, because it is not merely our opinions on particular issues, but the whole moral and intellectual climate which at the moment works for ever increased coercion by the state. The current interpretations of recent history as much as the very language in which we now discuss public affairs are so much permeated with the conception that nothing can be satisfactory unless it is 'consciously controlled' by some super-mind, that even if we today defeated all the schemes for government control of economic life existing or proposed, we would tomorrow be faced by another crop, not less dangerous or harmful.

[8] [For more on such plans, and Hayek's response to them, see the essays collected in Hayek, *Socialism and War*.—Ed.]

The first and most urgent task will no doubt have to be largely critical. There is so much sloppy thinking, so much concealed inconsistency in the prevailing convictions, that a somewhat negative approach may be very wholesome. I thoroughly agree in this respect with Wilfred Trotter, the great psychiatrist, who in one of his last essays argued that "at no time, in the history of the intellect, has the sanitary work of destructive criticism been more needful than it is today".[9]

But criticism is not enough. It will not be successful unless we persist in the slower and more arduous task of providing a real alternative to the current beliefs. This is not a task which any single man or small group of men can perform. It is a task, I am convinced, which needs the widest collaboration of all qualified to contribute and anxious to preserve free institutions. Nor is it a task which can ever be left to the economists, or political philosophers, or any group of specialists. What we need is collaboration of all students of human affairs.

I want in particular to stress one point which I know will not be too welcome and which I yet feel is so important that I must dwell upon it, even at the risk of alienating some who may have sympathised with my argument up to this point. The effort I am speaking of must not be confined on national lines, but must be an international effort, in which Americans, and Englishmen, have almost as much to learn as to give. The reason for this is that it is not those who still enjoy full liberty who best understand its value and the conditions for its preservation. If it is true that the same forces are at work here which have destroyed freedom elsewhere, it means that others have learnt in the hard school some lessons which we have not yet comprehended, but from which we must profit if we are to avoid a similar fate. I am, of course, not speaking of the great mass of people, who everywhere are under the sway of the current ideas. But I know that there are, spread all over the world, a number of important and active thinkers, working on similar lines, who as a result

---

[9] [Wilfred Trotter (1872–1939) was a British surgeon and social psychologist best known for his work on the regeneration of sensory nerves in the skin and, in his work on social psychology, for popularising the phrase 'herd instinct'. The words quoted by Hayek are taken from the following passage: "The common tendency to regard destructive criticism as always easy and generally reprehensible is one that I do not share; indeed, I doubt if it could be acquiesced in by any sensible person making a frank survey of the intellectual world of today. We cannot but be struck by the remarkable prevalence of systems of doctrine, by their loudness, their confusion, and their deleterious effect on conduct. In all these systems the most indulgent examination will find little evidence of really enterprising thought, but it will find a great deal of reconditioned lumber, at its best of a low order of reality and now used to justify the lazier, the uglier, and the baser inclinations of the human spirit. At no time in the history of the intellect has the sanitary work of destructive criticism been more needful". See pp. 181–82 of W. Trotter, "Has the Intellect a Function?" [1939], reprinted in W. Trotter, *The Collected Papers of Wilfred Trotter F.R.S.* (London: Oxford University Press, 1941), pp. 165–86.—Ed.]

of the experiences they have gone through, have become wiser and sadder men and who have much to teach us which we can ill afford to disregard.

I am profoundly convinced that if this effort is to be successful, it must be based on much closer international intellectual collaboration than we have at present. There is a tendency in this country to treat the danger as one to what you call the 'American Way of Life' and to meet it in a kind of isolationist and nationalist spirit, to write off the rest of the world as hopeless and to concentrate on preserving Western Civilisation in the United States. This attitude alarms me, not only because of the pessimistic view of Europe which it implies. I believe it would be fatal even for the United States if it prevailed. Just as the ideas which threaten Western Civilisation both in Europe and in America originated to a large extent in Europe, thus an effective counter-offensive will have to extend over the whole area of Western Civilisation. And what is more, though the movement towards the totalitarian state has gone much further in most European countries than it has yet done here, I believe there are in Europe also much more definite signs of an intellectual reaction against this trend to be noticed. There is there already the beginning of a new movement, which stretches from what one might call certain liberal socialist groups at the one extreme to certain liberal catholic groups on the other, composed of men who have learnt once more that personal liberty is the highest political good, more important than security and the other secondary goods on which they had been concentrating. I don't think America can afford not to take part, to profit from and to assist in these endeavours.

The most decisive reason, however, why it seems that such an effort must draw on all who have contributions to make, is that the persons who have learnt to think really independently on these topics are very few, in America no less than elsewhere. This is not a surprising fact. All movements in the fields of ideas have begun with a handful of men. We are no worse off than at other times. What is unique is that the circumstances of the time have brought it about that the people who are working for our goal are in one way or other prevented from being effective, that there is a quite appalling waste of effort in this widespread endeavour to revive the basic tenets of true liberalism.

Yet while in any country the number of men who wrestle with the problems which we must solve is inevitably small, I don't believe there is any absolute lack of men who have contributions to make. I would not presume to speak here as I do if I had not certain knowledge that there are, in almost all countries I know of, including some of those who recently were our enemies, isolated men and women who feel as acutely as anyone the danger to freedom and the need for a thorough re-examination of our social philosophy.[10]

---

[10] [For details of the individuals in question, see F. A. Hayek, "The Transmission of the Ideals of Economic Freedom" [1951], reprinted as chapter 2 of this volume.—Ed.]

Many of them have made important contributions to our common problem. But unlike the advocates of regimentation all those men who want above all to preserve individual liberty and who are working, often on exceedingly similar lines, to develop a truly liberal philosophy for our time, are working in almost complete isolation, without contact among themselves, or opportunity to learn from each other. This may be in fact the result of the individualistic temperament of the lovers of freedom. But I believe there is more in it than that. While socialists and planners never hesitate to unite for the interchange of ideas on the basis of a definite set of values, and to try jointly to study the technical problems which the achievement of their plans raise, the liberal in the old sense has always been over-anxious to keep his intellectual work 'pure', free from 'politics' of any sort, and most of all free from anything which might expose him to the suspicion that he was serving interests which are powerful in the existing order. Thus the problems which arise only after we have agreed on what general sort of social order we want, and the means of achieving such an order are scarcely ever studied systematically. All the 'blue-prints' of a future order of society from which the popularisers, including, I am afraid, not only the press and the radio but also the school and the church largely derive their inspiration, come from the joint efforts of the advocates of a planned society. There are no similar concerted efforts, there are not even the facilities for any such collaboration among the liberals.

This is serious enough in the countries where the scholar still possesses the means and independence to seek out his fellow workers in the same cause. But it is fatal in the impoverished and regimented countries of the European Continent where the individual scholar unless he happens to hold the views approved by his government or one of the big parties, is usually unable to visit foreign counties, to obtain foreign publications, and often even to communicate with his fellow students elsewhere. Even in the English-speaking world the usual channels of communication have been disrupted by the war. It was in a spirit of an international community of scholarship and thought that the in the widest sense liberal, or humanistic atmosphere of the last centuries has been created. It is only if, at least in the world of the mind, we can re-create an open world that we may hope to re-create such a liberal world.

To me it seems therefore one of the most urgent tasks, if we are to preserve a free civilisation, to see that the many efforts in this direction are not wasted, that opportunities for contact and collaboration are created for all those who are striving in the common task of elaborating a workable philosophy for a free society. The organisation which seems to be needed is something half-way between a scholarly association and a political society.[11] It would differ from a

---

[11] [Hayek discusses the need for such an organisation in other papers written in the mid-to-late 1940s. See F. A. Hayek, "Historians and the Future of Europe" [1944], pp. 207–15; F. A.

purely scientific group in that its members would be held together by a basic agreement on the aims for which they are seeking the means. And it would differ from any political organisation in that it would not be concerned with short run policies, or even with the peculiar problems of particular countries, but with the general principles of a liberal order. And it would have a double task: it would not only have to study and discuss the many questions of what would be the best framework in which a free system would work efficiently and beneficially; it would also have to interpret and apply these general principles by the discussion of recent history and contemporary events.[12]

Political philosophy cannot be taught and hardly be discussed in the abstract. We all have acquired most of our political ideals and our standards of public morality from the way in which history has been taught and current events have been interpreted to us. You all know how much political influence e.g. certain new interpretations of the motives and aims of the makers of the American constitution have had in recent years.[13] However much we wish

---

Hayek, "A Plan for the Future of Germany" [1945], pp. 231–33; and in particular F. A. Hayek, "Opening Address to a Conference at Mont Pèlerin" [1947], reprinted as chapters 8, 11 and 12 respectively of F. A. Hayek, *The Fortunes of Liberalism: Essays on Austrian Economics and the Ideal of Freedom*, ed. Peter G. Klein, vol. 4 (1992) of *The Collected Works of F. A. Hayek.*—Ed.]

[12] [For examples of Hayek's own efforts at these tasks, see F. A. Hayek, "'Free' Enterprise and Competitive Order" [1948] and "The Economic Conditions of Inter-state Federalism" [1939], reprinted as chapters 6 and 7 respectively of the present volume.—Ed.]

[13] [Hayek alludes here to the works of the so-called 'progressive' historians of the U.S. Constitution, according to whom the authors of the Constitution were motivated primarily by economic considerations and a desire to preserve the financial position of their class rather than by their disinterested commitment to certain constitutional ideals. A key work in this tradition was American historian Charles Beard's (1874–1948) *An Economic Interpretation of the Constitution of the United States* (New York: Macmillan, 1913), where it is argued that, far from being the product of high-minded patriotism, the Constitution was an instrument designed to serve the financial interests of the Founding Fathers. Later contributions included J. Miller, *Sam Adams, Pioneer in Propaganda* (Stanford: Stanford University Press, 1936), and P. Davidson, *Propaganda and the American Revolution, 1763–1783* (Chapel Hill: University of North Carolina Press, 1941). The progressive analysis was at odds with the emphasis on the importance of constitutional ideas found in the work of older historians such as Charles McIlwain, *The American Revolution: A Constitutional Interpretation* (New York: Macmillan, 1923), according to whom the American revolution occurred because of a clash over the interpretation of the English constitution. McIlwain's writings were frequently cited by Hayek in his account of the American Constitution, as found in F. A. Hayek, *The Constitution of Liberty*, ed. Ronald Hamowy, vol. 17 (2011) of *The Collected Works of F. A. Hayek*, pp. 261–86.

Disputes over the motives of the Founding Fathers were especially prominent in the mid-to-late 1930s, when President Franklin D. Roosevelt sought to make greater use of government intervention in order to deal with the hardship caused by the Great Depression. Conservative jurists claimed that the measures proposed by Roosevelt were unconstitutional, arguing that they were at odds with the Founding Fathers' goal of preventing the creative extension of government power. In stark contrast, Roosevelt and his supporters portrayed the Founding Fathers as exponents of the creative use of government power to solve national problems. One of the

historical scholarship to be non-partisan, historical exposition for the general reader always will, and in a sense must, judge events on certain standards. If this task of teaching political philosophy through history is not undertaken by scholars, it will be done by others and perhaps in a less desirable form. I know that I am touching here on a delicate point. But I am convinced that the historical narrative from which we derive most of our political ideals and standards cannot be ethically neutral. Perhaps I can best get you to consent to my main thesis if for a moment you direct your attention to a slightly different but kindred task which has been much discussed quite recently, although by now it seems again to have been forgotten: Nobody who knows anything about German history can doubt that the teaching of history in that country had much to do with the growth of the ideas which finally culminated in National Socialism, and that the re-education of the Germans will largely have to aim at making them see their own history in a different light. Now this is not a task which can be achieved by a history which is severely scientific in the sense that it never dares to call black black and white white.[14] The historian must have the courage for instance, to say that Hitler was a bad man, or else all the time he spends in 'explaining' him will only serve to the glorification of his misdeeds. Whether he likes it or not, the historian is in fact the main teacher of political ideals and there can be no question that he as much as the economist or political philosopher, of whom I have so far mainly spoken, bears to a large extent the responsibility for what the generation of tomorrow will think. It is of course not a question of distorting history to make it suit a particular political philosophy. But both *what* the general reader knows of history and *how* he *judges* the action of the main figures of history, is largely the product of the approach, I should like to call it the moral approach, of the teachers of history to their subject. I don't think we have reason to be particularly gratified by what in this respect the modern teaching of history has achieved.

---

goals of Beard's followers was to undermine the reverence in which the Founding Fathers were held, the better to overcome claims that increased government intervention violated their 'original intent'. Matters reached a head in 1937 when, frustrated by the way in which the Supreme Court had struck down several pieces of legislation as unconstitutional, the President attempted to reorganise its personnel in order to ease the approval of his preferred policies. His efforts were defeated in the Senate. See R. Bernstein, *The Founding Fathers Reconsidered* (Oxford: Oxford University Press, 2009), pp. 131–32, 161–63. On the implications of all this for the rule of law, see Hayek, *The Constitution of Liberty*, pp. 283–86, 360–62.

Hayek explores similar issues, concerning how political opinion is shaped by the work of historians, in "Historians and the Future of Europe", "A Plan for the Future of Germany", and in F. A. Hayek, "History and Politics" [1954], reprinted as chapter 4 of F. A. Hayek, *The Trend of Economic Thinking: Essays on Political Economists and Economic History*, ed. W. W. Bartley III and S. Kresge, vol. 3 (1991) of *The Collected Works of F. A. Hayek.*—Ed.]

[14] [Also see Hayek, "Historians and the Future of Europe", pp. 207–8, 211–12.—Ed.]

There is so much danger that I may be misunderstood in what I have just said that I should like to give an illustration of what I mean when I speak of the historian as the great teacher of political and moral standards. I want to do so the more as that illustration comes from that great historian to whom I shall presently have to appeal in another connection, Lord Acton, and because it adds something to the little I have been able to say in order to explain what I mean by a fundamentally liberal attitude.[15] The passage deals with the thesis that historical figures must be judged

> unlike other men, with a favourable assumption that they did no wrong. If there is any presumption, it is the other way, against the holder of power, increasing as the power increases. Historic responsibility has to make up for the want of legal responsibility. Power tends to corrupt and absolute power tends to corrupt absolutely. Great men are almost always bad men, even when they exercise influence and not authority, still more when you super-add the tendency or the certainty of corruption by authority. There is no worse heresy than that the office sanctions the holder of it. That is the point at which the negation of Catholicism and the negation of Liberalism meet and keep high festival.[16]

[15] [John Emerich Edward Dalberg-Acton, First Baron Acton (1834–1902), was a classical liberal historian and moralist whose central theme was the 'history of liberty'. Acton was one of the principal exponents of the so-called 'Whig interpretation of history', which portrays past events as constituting an inevitable progression towards greater personal liberty and the expansion of parliamentary authority over the crown, as manifest in the liberal democracy and constitutional monarchy of nineteenth-century England. For more on Hayek's views on Acton, see Hayek, "Historians and the Future of Europe" [1944]; F. A. Hayek, "The Actonian Revival: On Lord Acton (1834–1902)" [1953], reprinted as chapter 9 of Hayek, *The Fortunes of Liberalism*; and F. A. Hayek, "The Principles of a Liberal Social Order" [1966], reprinted as chapter 21 of this volume, p. 272, n. 2.—Ed.]

[16] [The passage to which Hayek refers is found in correspondence between Lord Acton and historian and Anglican bishop Mandell Creighton (1843–1901), who was at the time Dixie Professor of Ecclesiastical History at Cambridge University and editor of the *English Historical Review*. Acton's words, which were only imperfectly reproduced by Hayek, were as follows: "I cannot accept your canon that we are to judge Pope and King unlike other men, with a favourable presumption that they did no wrong. If there is any presumption it is the other way, against the holders of power, increasing as the power increases. Historic responsibility has to make up for the want of legal responsibility. Power tends to corrupt and absolute power corrupts absolutely. Great men are almost always bad men, even when they exercise influence and not authority, still more when you superadd the tendency or the certainty of corruption by authority. There is no worse heresy than that the office sanctifies the holder of it. That is the point at which the negation of Catholicism and the negation of Liberalism meet and keep high festival, and the end learns to justify the means." See J. Dalberg-Acton, "Appendix—Letter to Bishop Creighton" [1887], in J. Dalberg-Acton, *Historical Essays & Studies*, ed. J. Figgis and R. Laurence (London: Macmillan and Co., 1907), p. 504.—Ed.]

This digression about the tasks of the historian in our field was meant merely as an illustration of how other students of society than those I had so far mainly considered have no less to contribute to the common task. I might instead have chosen the lawyer or any field of the humanities for my illustration. But I must go on to sketch the kind of collaboration which I imagine these scholars could undertake in the service of the preservation of human liberty. I like to think of the organisation I have suggested as a kind of International Academy of Political Philosophy, using the term Academy in its original sense of a closed society, whose members would be bound together by common convictions and try both to develop this common philosophy and to spread its understanding.

This is, of course, very far from being an original idea. I know that the need for some such organisation is felt by many, and that it has been discussed in various circles. The great obstacle to its realisation—apart from the question of the funds which such an organisation would need for its work—is the difficulty of giving expression to the basic ideas which would unite such a group, without tying it down beforehand to a ready-made programme. It must of course not be a propaganda organisation but a group of students anxious to learn and to teach. It is a great tradition which we want to continue by this means, not a fixed programme which we want to put over.

I very much doubt whether it would be either wise or practicable to define the aims of such a society in a kind of manifesto drawn up for the purpose. It would either have to be couched in such general terms as to be pretty meaningless, or we should have to accomplish one of our main tasks before we have even begun. After all much thinking has been done on these problems in the past and we cannot hope at once to improve upon the expressions of the great liberal tradition developed by the masters.

But where can we find a statement of those true liberal principles which once seemed destined to conquer the world but during the past two generations have steadily lost their influence? I have long searched for such a statement and I confess I have found this search surprisingly difficult. There is, of course, John Stuart Mill's noble book *On Liberty*, but there are many reasons which make me hesitate to suggest Mill as the symbol for a new liberal movement. Not only did he vacillate a great deal between liberalism and socialism and in the end arrived at a highly unsatisfactory and unstable compromise. What is more serious from our point of view is that he, and his whole group of 19th century liberals or radicals, generally took an intolerant and hostile attitude towards religion which is largely responsible for driving many true friends of liberty from the liberal camp. He also seems to me much too tender towards the incipient nationalist tendencies of the 19th century. If I had time I think I could show how this is largely due to the fact that his inspiration was derived much more from the French and German sources than from that liberal tradition of the English speaking peoples which I have mainly been considering.[17]

Perhaps it would not be inaccurate to describe this tradition of liberty among the English speaking people as the Whig tradition, if we use that term in the sense in which Lord Acton discusses the development of Whig doctrine in the American speeches of Chatham and Camden, in Burke's speeches from 1778 to 1783 and in the *Wealth of Nations*, and shows how the national boundaries were gradually overcome and principles became sacred, irrespective of interest. It was from this point of view that he could say that "the charter of Rhode Island is worth more than the British Constitution, and Whig statesmen toast General Washington, rejoice that America has resisted, and insist on acknowledgement of independence". It is the doctrine which found one of its finest expressions in the *Federalist* papers and became as much the basis of American political ideas as through Burke it became the foundation of English Whiggism and later Liberalism.[18]

[17] [While acknowledging that English philosopher, political economist, and social reformer John Stuart Mill (1806–73) defended individual freedom in *On Liberty* (London: J. W. Parker, 1859), Hayek argued nevertheless that Mill sometimes deviated from classical liberalism. Hayek attributed the variation in Mill's views to the influence both of Continental liberalism, most notably the work of Comte and Saint-Simon, and also of Harriet Taylor, who became Mill's wife in 1851. See F. A. Hayek, *Studies on the Abuse and Decline of Reason: Text and Documents*, ed. Bruce Caldwell, vol. 13 (2010) of *The Collected Works of F. A. Hayek*, pp. 56–57, 71, 238–39, and F. A. Hayek, *Hayek on Mill: The Mill-Taylor Friendship and Related Writings*, ed. Sandra J. Peart, vol. 16 (2015) of *The Collected Works of F. A. Hayek*. In his *Considerations on Representative Government* (London: Parker, Son, and Bourn, 1861), pp. 291–92, Mill expressed nationalist sentiments by writing that "it is in general a necessary condition of free institutions, that the boundaries of governments should coincide in the main with those of nationalities". The 'Philosophical Radicals' were a group of early nineteenth-century thinkers who were inspired by the utilitarian political philosophy of English philosopher and jurist Jeremy Bentham (1748–1832) and philosopher James Mill (1773–1836). Hayek's opinion of Mill is discussed in more detail in B. Caldwell, "Hayek on Mill", *History of Political Economy*, vol. 40, 2008, pp. 689–704.—Ed.]

[18] [Having declared that "The final purpose of the Whigs was not distinct from that of their fathers in the Long Parliament. They desired security against injustice and oppression", Acton then laments the slow development of general Whig principles between the late seventeenth and late eighteenth centuries, arguing that the Whigs "were a little disappointing, a little too fond of the half-way house" and that they "became associated with great interests in English society, with trade, and banking, and the city, with elements that were progressive, but exclusive, and devoted to private, not to national ends. So far as they went, they were in the right, ethically as well as politically. But they proceeded slowly beyond the bare need of the moment . . . General principles were so little apparent in the system that excellent writers suppose that the Whigs were essentially English . . . unfit for exportation over the world. They took long to outgrow the narrow limits of the society in which they arose". Acton goes on to write in the passage to which Hayek refers that, "A hundred years passed before Whiggism assumed the universal and scientific character. In the American speeches of Chatham and Camden, in Burke's

But the problems of these writers are not yet the problems of today; while they created much of the traditions and institutions, they did not yet know

---

writings from 1778 to 1783, in the *Wealth of Nations*, and the tracts of Sir William Jones, there is an immense development. The national bounds are overcome. The principles are sacred, irrespective of interests. The charter of Rhode Island is worth more than the British Constitution, and Whig statesmen toast General Washington, rejoice that America has resisted, and insist on the acknowledgment of independence. The progress is entirely consistent; and Burke's address to the colonists is the logical outcome of the principles of liberty and the notion of a higher law above municipal codes and constitutions, with which Whiggism began". See J. Dalberg-Acton, "The Rise of the Whigs", published as chapter 12 of *Lectures on Modern History*, ed. J. Figgis and R. Laurence (London: Macmillan and Co., 1912), pp. 216–18.

William Pitt (1708–78), first Earl of Chatham, also known as Pitt the Elder, was a British politician who in 1766 opposed the British government policy of taxing its North American colonies, as introduced by the 1765 Stamp Act, arguing that the House of Commons did not represent the colonists and so had no right to impose taxes upon them. Charles Pratt (1714–94), first Earl Camden, was an English lawyer and politician who had a long-standing interest in the role of the constitution as a safeguard of individual liberty. Like Chatham, Camden argued in 1766 that Parliament's right to tax colonies was founded on consent, and therefore depended on representation, while in 1775 he opposed policies designed to coerce the American colonies by crippling their economy. Sir William Jones (1746–94) was an Anglo-Welsh orientalist and jurist who, in his *Speech on the Reformation of Parliament* [1782], reprinted as pp. 501–15 of *The Works of Sir William Jones*, ed. Lord Teignmouth, vol. 8 (Cambridge: Cambridge University Press, 2013), expressed both suspicion of untrammelled aristocratic power and also confidence in market exchange. Elsewhere, Hayek describes Jones as "a lawyer by training and a prominent Whig by persuasion" and claims that he was the first scholar to see clearly that linguistic structures develop spontaneously, through a process of adaptive evolution whereby different languages arise from a common origin. See Hayek, *The Constitution of Liberty*, p. 116 n. 26. Anglo-Irish statesman and conservative political philosopher Edmund Burke (1729–97) attempted to demonstrate the folly of efforts to tax the American colonists without their consent in two parliamentary speeches, namely "On American Taxation" (1774) and "On Moving Resolutions for Conciliation with the Colonies" (1775). See E. Burke, *Burke: Select Works*, vol. 1. *Thoughts on the Present Discontents. The Two Speeches on America*, ed. E. Payne (Oxford: Clarendon Press, 1878). In the late 1770s and early 1780s, Burke sought to eliminate restraints imposed on Irish trade and to secure relief for Roman Catholics by rescinding parts of a penal code that excluded them from political participation and public office. He also drafted the East India Bill of 1783, in which he argued that India should be governed, not—as it had been—by the East India Company, but rather by the same institutions and standards of justice as England. Hayek also refers to Adam Smith's *An Enquiry into the Nature and Causes of the Wealth of Nations*, ed. W. B. Todd, vol. 2 of *The Glasgow Edition of the Works and Correspondence of Adam Smith* (Oxford: Oxford University Press, 1976; reprinted, Indianapolis, IN: Liberty Fund, 1981).

Hayek discusses the Whig tradition to which Acton refers in more detail in *The Constitution of Liberty*, pp. 530–32, where he also approvingly quotes Acton's description of "a higher law above municipal codes and constitutions" as "the supreme achievement of Englishmen, and their bequest to the nations". See Dalberg-Acton, *Lectures on Modern History*, p. 218. For more on Hayek's views on Burke, whom he regarded as an "Old Whig", see F. A. Hayek, "Individualism: True and False" [1946], reprinted as the Prelude to Hayek, *Studies on the Abuse and Decline of Reason*, and Hayek, *The Constitution of Liberty*, pp. 523, 529.—Ed.]

the particular dangers to which they would be exposed or which they would themselves produce. Can we find no later development of their doctrines in a form which is more directly relevant to the problems of today?

My search for a satisfactory statement of the basic liberal philosophy led me in the end to two great historians who seem to me to have achieved the most complete synthesis of the basic principles of a free society and in particular to have developed the Burkean philosophy to the highest point it has yet reached. It was in the fragments of Lord Acton's inachieved great history of freedom and in de Tocqueville's study of American Democracy where I found the ripest fruits of the age-long speculation on that problem of the reconciliation of liberty and government which is again troubling us today. I wish there were still time to give you a fuller account of the system of liberal philosophy which could be constructed from the works of these two writers. But within the remaining minutes I must content myself with selecting a few illustrations, largely because of their immediate relevance to the problems of today, and because they show the amazing foresight of these men which still makes them the best guides to our tasks.

What could be more penetrating than the following discussion by Lord Acton of what today we call totalitarianism?

> Whenever a single definite object is made the supreme end of the State, be it the advantage of a class, the safety or the power of the country, the greatest happiness of the greatest number, or the support of any speculative idea, the State becomes for the time inevitably absolute. Liberty alone demands for its realisation the limitation of the public authority, for liberty is the only object which benefits all alike, and provokes no sincere opposition.[19]

Or his comment on democracy, that

> The true democratic principle, that none shall have power over the people, is taken to mean that none shall be able to restrain or to elude its power. The true democratic principle, that the people shall not be made to do what it does not like, is taken to mean that it shall never be required to tolerate what it does not like. The true democratic principle, that every man's free will shall be as unfettered as possible, is taken to mean that the free will of the collective people shall be fettered in nothing.[20]

[19] [J. Dalberg-Acton, "Nationality" [1862], reprinted as chapter 9 of J. Dalberg-Acton, *The History of Freedom and Other Essays*, ed. J. Figgis and R. Laurence (London: Macmillan and Co., 1909), p. 288.—Ed.]

[20] [J. Dalberg-Acton, "Sir Erskine May's Democracy in Europe" [1878], reprinted as chapter 3 of Dalberg-Acton, *The History of Freedom*, pp. 93–94.—Ed.]

Or take de Tocqueville nearly a hundred years ago commenting on the relationship between democracy and socialism:

> Democracy extends the sphere of individual freedom, socialism restricts it. Democracy attaches all possible value to each man; socialism makes each man a mere agent, a mere number. Democracy and socialism have nothing in common but one word: equality. But notice the difference: while democracy seeks equality in liberty, socialism seeks equality in restraint and servitude.[21]

Or his description of how

> Our contemporaries are constantly excited by two conflicting passions; they want to be led and they wish to remain free: as they cannot destroy either the one or the other of these contrary propensities, they continue to satisfy them both at once. They combine the principle of centralisation and that of popular sovereignty; this gives them a respite; they console themselves for being in tutelage by the reflection that they have chosen their own guardian. Every man allows himself to be put in leading strings, because he sees that it is not a person or a class of persons, but the people at large who hold the end of his chain.[22]

[21] [French historian, politician, and political scientist Alexis Charles Henri Clérel de Tocqueville (1805–59) analysed the nature and consequences of the spread of democracy in the late eighteenth and early nineteenth century, and was particularly concerned about the potential for democracy to unleash a new type of despotism in the form of the tyranny of the majority. The passage quoted by Hayek is taken from A. de Tocqueville, "Discours prononcé à l'Assemblée constituante dans la discussion du projet de constitution (12 Septembre 1848) sur la question du droit au travail", in *Études Économiques, Politiques et Littéraires par Alexis de Tocqueville, Oeuvres complètes d'Alexis de Tocqueville*, vol. 9 (Paris: Michel Lévy Frères, 1866), p. 546. The original passage reads, "La démocratie étend la sphère de l'indépendance individuelle, le socialisme la resserre. La démocratie donne toute sa valeur possible à chaque homme, le socialisme fait de chaque homme un agent, un instrument, un chiffre. La démocratie et le socialisme ne se tiennent que par un mot, l'égalité; mais remarquez la différence: la démocratie veut l'égalité dans la liberté, et le socialisme veut l'égalité dans la gêne et dans la servitude".—Ed.]

[22] [Hayek quotes, with some transcription errors and omissions, from volume 2 of Tocqueville's *Democracy in America*. The actual passage is as follows: "Our contemporaries are constantly excited by two conflicting passions; they want to be led, and they wish to remain free: as they cannot destroy either one or the other of these contrary propensities, they strive to satisfy them both at once. They devise a sole, tutelary, and all-powerful form of government, but elected by the people. They combine the principle of centralisation and that of popular sovereignty; this gives them a respite; they console themselves for being in tutelage by the reflection that they have chosen their own guardians. Every man allows himself to be put in leading-strings, because he sees that it is not a person or a class of persons, but the people at large that holds the end of his chain." A. de Tocqueville, *Democracy in America* [1840], trans. H. Reeve, 2 vols. (London: Longmans, Green, and Co., 1889), vol. 2, pp. 291–92.—Ed.]

Or, finally, take Lord Acton's warning against

> the dogma, that absolute power may, by the hypothesis of a popular origin, be as legitimate as constitutional freedom.[23]

Need I add the amazingly prophetic words, concluding de Tocqueville's *Democracy in America*, in which, comparing Russia and America, he wrote in 1840:

> The Anglo-American relies on personal interest to accomplish his ends, and gives free scope to the unguided exertion and common sense of the citizen; the Russian centres all the authority of society in a single arm: the principal instrument of the former is freedom; of the latter servitude. Their starting point is different, and their courses are not the same; yet each of them seems to be marked out by the will of heaven to sway the destinies of half the globe.[24]

I should have to go on quoting much longer to prove my point that these men were much more aware of the problems we face today than even we are, and that they provide a basic philosophy which might well form the foundation from which our further work can start. I will only add that both men were not only great liberals in the true sense of the word but also profoundly religious. What I have said already must suffice to explain why in my mind I call that international academy of political philosophy of which I dream the Acton-de Tocqueville Society.

But perhaps it has been unwise of me to go so far in discussing a particular proposal and to talk about the organisation of the effort. There are undoubtedly many ways in which my purpose could be accomplished. What I really wanted to stress, and what I think cannot be emphasised too much, is that if we are not to go on moving with bound hands into a new kind of serfdom, if not the fatalists but those who hope to create a better future are to be right, an intense intellectual effort is needed. We must kindle an interest in—and an understanding of—the great principles of social organisation and of the conditions of individual liberty as we have not known it in our life-time. If we are to succeed we must raise and train an army of fighters for freedom, men and women who are prepared to work hard at the hardest of all tasks, the task of re-examining our own prejudices and beliefs, who will insist throughout on the rule of principles in public affairs instead of the rule of expediency,

---

[23] [Dalberg-Acton, "Sir Erskine May's Democracy in Europe", p. 78.—Ed.]

[24] [Hayek quotes, with very minor alterations, from Tocqueville, *Democracy in America*, vol. 1, p. 445.—Ed.]

and who will unhesitatingly oppose any proposals, however popular, which infringe these great principles.

If we do not flinch at this task, if we do not throw up our hands in the face of overwhelming public opinion but work to shape and guide that opinion, our cause is by no means hopeless. But it is late in the day and we have not too much time to spare. I am convinced it is not yet *too* late and that if we really go to work we may still hope to build up or preserve, not an ideal society, but at least a society, in which the essential values are preserved and the door to future advance is not closed.

FOUR

THE WEBBS AND THEIR WORK[1]

It would be difficult to overstate the importance of *Our Partnership* for the understanding of British history in the twentieth century. Beyond this, the story of the Webbs provides a unique lesson of what unselfish and single-minded devotion and the methodical hard work of two people can achieve. The strongest impression left by this second part of Beatrice Webb's memoirs is that she and her husband owed the extent of their influence largely to the fact that they cared only for the success of the ideas in which they believed, without any regard to who got the credit for them, that they were willing to operate through any medium, person or party which allowed itself to be used, and above all, that they fully understood, and knew how to make use of, the decisive position which the intellectuals occupy in shaping public opinion.[2]

[1] A review of *Our Partnership*, by Beatrice Webb. Edited by Barbara Drake and Margaret I. Cole. London: Longmans, Green and Co., 1948; published in *Economica*, August 1948. [This review was first published as F. A. Hayek, "*Our Partnership*. By Beatrice Webb. Edited by Barbara Drake and Margaret I. Cole. London: Longmans, Green, and Co. 1948. xiv + 544 pp. 25s. *Der Sozialismus der Fabier*. By Edgar Reichel. Heidelberg. Verlag Lambert Schneider. 1947. 247 pp.", *Economica*, vol. 15, 1948, pp. 227–30. ©1948 by the London School of Economics and Political Science. Reprinted by permission of John Wiley and Sons. It was subsequently republished, but with the final paragraph of the original *Economica* article omitted, under the title, "The Webbs and their Work", as part of the appendix to F. A. Hayek, *Studies in Philosophy, Politics and Economics* (London: Routledge & Kegan Paul, 1967), pp. 341–44. It is the latter version which is reprinted here.—Ed.]

[2] [English social reformers Beatrice (1858–1943) and Sidney (1859–1947) Webb helped to found both the Fabian Society (in 1884) and the London School of Economics (in 1895). The Fabian Society was established with a view to bringing about a socialist society through gradual political and economic reform, rather than through the revolutionary change traditionally emphasised by Marxists. According to the Fabians, the best way of advancing socialist goals was to educate the masses about the benefits of a socialist society through a variety of means, including meetings, lectures, and discussion groups; the publication of books and pamphlets; and the conduct of academic research into economic and social problems. The Fabians believed that, once the public had been enlightened in this way, their proposed reforms would easily win favour at the ballot box. Hayek's review of the Webbs' book on the Soviet Union, namely S. Webb and B. Webb, *Soviet Communism: A New Civilisation?* (London: Longmans, Green, and Co., 1935), in which they praised what—erroneously, in Hayek's view—they saw as the successful scientific

They had "little faith in the 'average sensual man'" (p. 120). They set out not "to organise the unthinking persons into Socialist societies" but "to make the thinking persons socialistic" (p. 132). "The rank and file of Socialists— especially English Socialists" seemed to them "unusually silly folk" (p. 134). They knew that if they succeeded in "converting the country to the *philosophy* of our scheme . . . the application will follow (whatever persons are in power)" (p. 443). It was because they were known to "have ideas to give away" (p. 402) and because they were always ready to provide articles and memoranda to be used in somebody else's name, that their "behind the scenes intellectual leadership" (p. 116) was so effective.[3] There can indeed be few important organs of the period, from the *Church Times* and the *Christian World* to the *Daily Mail,* which did not, at one time or another, carry unsigned articles by the Webbs (pp. 70, 257), written, if expediency demanded it, in "our best style of modest moderation" (p. 455), and some papers like the *Manchester Guardian* and the *Echo* they came to regard as "practically our organs" (p. 145). They kept the London School of Economics "honestly non-partisan in its theories" (p. 230), and valued its continued prosperity "so long as it remains unbiassed and open to collectivist tendencies" (p. 463), not in spite but because of the fact that they saw in it the centre "from which our views will radiate through personal intercourse" (p. 94). It was part of a scheme which made them "feel assured that with the School as a teaching body, the Fabian Society as a propagandist organisation, the L.C.C. Progressives as an object lesson in electoral success, our books as the only [*sic*] elaborate original work in economic fact and theory, no young man or woman who is anxious to study or to work in public affairs can fail to come under our influence" (p. 145).[4] Towards the end of the period covered by the volume Mrs. Webb was indeed justified in look-

---

planning of the Russian economy, can be found in the appendix to F. A. Hayek, *Socialism and War: Essays, Documents, Reviews*, ed. B. Caldwell, vol. 10 (1997) of *The Collected Works of F. A. Hayek* (Chicago: University of Chicago Press; London: Routledge), pp. 239–42. Hayek explores how the views of intellectuals shape public opinion in F. A. Hayek, "The Intellectuals and Socialism" [1949], reprinted as chapter 11 of *Socialism and War.*—Ed.]

[3] [Hayek has afforded himself a little license in rendering the first of the quotations in this sentence. Referring in 1908 to the "scramble for new constructive ideas" between Conservative, Liberal and Labour Party politicians, Beatrice Webb actually wrote that, "We happen just now to have a good many to give away, hence the eagerness for our company". See Webb, *Our Partnership*, p. 402.—Ed.]

[4] [The insertion in square brackets is Hayek's. The London County Council (L.C.C.) was the main municipal authority for the county of London between 1889 and 1965, and the first ever directly elected local government body for London. The Progressive Party was formed in 1888 by Liberals, trade unionists, Fabians, and socialists to contest local government elections in London. It fought the first L.C.C. elections in 1889 and won six consecutive victories, numbering Sidney Webb as one of its councillors, before losing control of the Council in 1907 to the Municipal Reform Party (an organisation allied to the Conservative Party).—Ed.]

ing forward with confidence to the day when "Hosts of able young men, well trained in Fabian economics and administrative lore, will be crowding into the political arena" (p. 469).

"Behind the scenes" was also the keynote of their direct influence on current politics during the period covered by the volume. (It deals with the years 1892–1911, but the last chapter on "The Plunge into Propaganda, 1909–1911" is really concerned with what is the beginning of the next phase of their life.) Past masters in the art of wire-pulling, of "manipulating", and "—to speak plainly—of intrigue" (p. 259), they knew how to get the most out of the personal contacts for which their social standing provided the opportunity.[5] It is a curious irony that the circumstances which gave the two people the power to contribute so much towards the destruction of the capitalist civilisation which they hated could exist only within that civilisation, and that in the type of society for which they hoped no private persons could wield a similar influence towards its change. It was the "incomparable luxury of freedom from all care for ourselves" (p. 245), provided by an independent income of £1,000 a year, which not only enabled them to devote themselves wholly to the chosen task, but also to employ all the arts of hospitality and to use all the opportunities of social intercourse with the great in the service of their ideals. Even today it is already difficult to appreciate the opportunities which such an income afforded forty or fifty years ago. In the famous ten-roomed house at 41 Grosvenor Road, which they occupied for forty years and ran with two maids, they were for years able to have twelve persons for dinner most weeks (p. 304, cf. p. 339) and to give from time to time receptions for sixty to eighty people. When a person they wanted to use proved recalcitrant he would be asked to dine with a "carefully selected party" (p. 334). "A brilliant little luncheon, typical of the 'Webb' set", might consist of "Dr. Nansen (now Norwegian Minister), Gerald and Lady Betty Balfour, the Bernard Shaws, Bertrand Russells, Masterman and Lady Desborough, typical in its mixture of opinions, classes, interests" (p. 375).[6] Yet to Mrs. Webb this income seemed "not

---

[5] [The phrase "behind the scenes" is used several times by Beatrice Webb to describe the way in which she and her husband influenced elite opinion and policy. See Webb, *Our Partnership*, pp. 6, 7, 17, 116. She describes them as engaging in "wire-pulling" on pp. 58, 182–83 and 213 of that volume. References to them "manipulating" politicians, policy-makers, and trades unionists can be found on pp. 7 and 270 of the book. These aspects of the Webbs' behaviour were described by English Liberal newspaper editor and journalist Alfred George Gardiner (1865–1946), who was famous for his pen portraits of notable figures: "Mr. and Mrs. Webb are always 'managing' you. They sit behind the scenes, touching buttons, pulling wires, making the figures on the stage dance to their rhythms. To their modest table come the great and the powerful to learn their lessons, and to be coached up in their facts". See A. G. Gardiner, *Pillars of Society* (New York: Dodd, Mead & Co., 1914), pp. 205–6.—Ed.]

[6] [Fridtjof Nansen (1861–1930) was a Norwegian zoologist, oceanographer, explorer, and statesman. He served as Norway's Ambassador to Great Britain from 1906 to 1908 and won

much more than a livelihood and working expenses" (p. 339) and only occasionally, as when she smiles at staying "in the cottage of the millionaire,[7] whilst we were composing this great collectivist document" (the Minority Report of the Poor Law) (p. 412), or when, before their world tour in 1898, she is "revelling in buying silks and satins, gloves, underclothing, furs and everything that a sober-minded woman of forty can want to inspire Americans and colonials with a true respect for the refinements of collectivism" (p. 146), some sense of the incongruity of this shows itself.

One may doubt whether any of their contemporaries fully realised the extent of their influence in a world where, as Mrs. Webb noted in her diary, "Every politician one meets wants to be coached—it is really quite comic—it seems to be quite irrelevant whether they are Conservatives, Liberals or Labour Party men" (p. 402). What Mrs. Webb calls with some satisfaction "Perhaps the cleverest caricature—about 1900— . . . a picture of Balfour and Asquith bobbing up and down at the end of wires handled by the 'wily Fabian'" (p. 7) at the time probably seemed an exaggeration; it hardly does so to the reader of *Our Partnership*.[8]

The book is, perhaps inevitably, least informative on what was certainly Mrs. Webb's main occupation during the period covered—their research. We

---

the Nobel Peace Prize in 1922 for his humanitarian work in facilitating the exchange of prisoners after World War One and for directing relief efforts to alleviate the suffering caused by the Russian famine of 1921–22. Gerald Balfour (1853–1945) was a British politician and psychical researcher. His wife, Elizabeth Balfour (1867–1942), Countess of Balfour, was a society hostess and biographer. Playwright and polemicist George Bernard Shaw (1856–1950) was awarded the Nobel Prize for Literature in 1925. He was an early member of the Fabian Society, to which he introduced Sidney Webb, and editor of the landmark volume *Fabian Essays in Socialism* (London: Fabian Society, 1889), in which Fabians such as Shaw and the Webbs set out their views in a systematic fashion. Bertrand Russell (1872–1970) was a British analytical philosopher, writer, journalist, and social reformer. Charles Masterman (1873–1927) was an author, Christian socialist, and New Liberal politician who was instrumental in the framing and passage through Parliament of the 1911 National Insurance Act, which introduced Britain's first-ever system of compulsory insurance against unemployment. Ethel Grenfell (1867–1952), Lady Desborough, was a notable society hostess and a leading member of a group of politically minded intellectuals known as the 'Souls', one of whose leading lights was Tory philosopher, politician, and Prime Minister (1902–5) Arthur James Balfour (1848–1930).—Ed.]

[7] [The "millionaire" was German-born mining magnate, art collector, and philanthropist Sir Julius Charles Wernher (1850–1912).—Ed.]

[8] [Herbert Henry Asquith, 1st Earl of Oxford and Asquith (1852–1928), was a Liberal politician and Prime Minister from 1908 to 1916. The governments led by Asquith implemented a number of reforms, including the introduction of old-age pensions and of unemployment and health insurance, that are commonly regarded as laying the foundations for the modern welfare state. The reforms in question were widely taken, not least by Hayek, as indicating a shift in the outlook of the Liberal Party away from classical, Gladstonian liberalism towards a more collectivist approach referred to as the 'new' liberalism. See F. A. Hayek, "Liberalism" [1978], reprinted as chapter 1 of this volume, p. 19.—Ed.]

do not learn much about their conception of "the scientific method pure and undefiled" (p. 209)[9] which they feel they are practically the first to apply to "the establishment of a science of society" (p. 170), or about the nature of "the sound science of social organisation" at which they aimed.[10] But one need perhaps not be surprised that they felt in retrospect that "every discovery in sociology . . . has strengthened our faith" (p. 16). Certainly, when Mrs. Webb is appointed a member of the Poor Law Commission,[11] strategy and research become curiously intermingled: "Fortunately, we have already discovered our principles of 1907, and we have already devised our scheme for reform. What we are now manufacturing is the heavy artillery of fact that is to drive both principles and scheme home" (p. 399). On one occasion Mrs. Webb confesses to "more or less engineering the evidence in my direction" (p. 370) and on another of practising "tacit deception" on her colleagues on the Commission by carefully selecting those parts of a correspondence which she thought suitable for them to see, "without, be it added, in any way giving the Commission to understand that I had sent them the whole or the part" (p. 393).[12] When after that one finds Mrs. Webb complaining about the

[9] [Webb actually refers to "the scientific method, full and undefiled". See *Our Partnership*, p. 209.—Ed.]

[10] [The phrase "a sound science of social organisation" appears on p. 168 of *Our Partnership*.—Ed.]

[11] [The Royal Commission on the Poor Laws and Relief of Distress was a body established in 1905 by the Conservative government led by Prime Minister Arthur Balfour in order to investigate the possible reform of the Poor Law system, which had governed how relief from poverty and hardship was provided in Britain since 1834. The Commission included Poor Law guardians, members of the Charity Organisation Society, representatives of local government boards and trades unions, and social scientists, as well as Beatrice Webb. The Commission sat for four years, after which its members produced two conflicting reports. The authors of the *Majority Report*, principally Helen Bosanquet (1860–1925), a social theorist, writer on social work, and wife of idealist philosopher and social reformer Bernard Bosanquet (1848–1923), and Scottish economist William Smart (1853–1915), argued that the existing system of poor laws ought to be retained and defended the continued role of organised private charitable activities in the provision of welfare. The *Minority Report*, which was drafted by Beatrice and Sidney Webb, and signed by three Commissioners in addition to Beatrice, contended that the existing system of poor laws should be reformed, with provision being universal rather than selective and funded out of general taxation rather than on a contributory (insurance) basis. While neither report led immediately to legislation, the *Minority Report* is commonly regarded as one of the key influences on the subsequent emergence of the welfare state in Britain.—Ed.]

[12] [The 'confession' to which Hayek refers concerns Beatrice Webb's efforts to collect her own evidence about the provision of medical services and, in particular, her response to the efforts of her fellow-Commissioner Helen Bosanquet to gain access to that evidence in order to discredit Webb's views. The phrase "tacit deception" is in fact used by Webb to describe, not her own behaviour, as Hayek suggests, but rather that of Bosanquet, as Webb's description of what happened after she received Bosanquet's request makes clear: "That evening I looked through the correspondence [about the provision of medical services], took away all the letters that were at all compromising to the authors . . . and bundled the letters and reports off to the Commis-

"packed Commission" (p. 381) one cannot but sympathise a little with the "rude ejaculations" of one of her colleagues whom she heard saying "what cheek" while she questioned a witness (p. 377).[13]

Even with this intimate record of the singularly happy partnership before us, "The Other One" remains a curiously impersonal and shadowy figure whose only distinct trait seems perfect mental efficiency and balance.[14] Sidney Webb has often been described as the prototype of the Commissar, and the description in the diary as a man who "has no kind of qualms", who is "*self-less*" and "has a robust conscience", confirms this just a little.[15] But it is the picture of a very urbane kind of Commissar which emerges and certainly not of a fanatic. One does not feel so certain on the last point about Mrs. Webb herself. She describes herself as "conservative by temperament, and [in her youth] anti-democratic through social environment" (p. 361).[16] 'Authoritarian' would probably have been a better term. With her the belief in the "wholesale and compulsory management" by the expert (p. 120), in the "'higher freedom' of corporate life" (p. 222) is a passion, and the dislike of all views, but particularly Gladstonian Liberalism, which "think in individuals", is a real hatred.[17] It is only expediency which prevents her from attacking "individualism, or, as we prefer to call it, anarchy, in its stronghold of the home and the family" (p. 84), and her craving for a "Church . . . a commu-

---

sion. To be frank, I had qualms of conscience in making any kind of selection of those I did and did not send. But it was clear that Mrs. Bosanquet was not playing the fair game. She did not want to see my correspondence in order to 'inform her own mind'—which was the only legitimate ground for the request; she wanted, as has been proved since, to incriminate me by documents which I supplied of my own free will to the Commission. So I swallowed the tacit deception and sent exactly what I thought fit—without, be it added, in any way giving the Commission to understand that I had sent them the whole or the part. I had, however, left quite enough adverse letters in the bundle to encourage Mrs. Bosanquet in her plan". See *Our Partnership*, pp. 392–93.—Ed.]

[13] [The colleague in question was Sir Charles Stewart Loch (1849–1923). Loch was the longtime secretary of the Charity Organisation Society (1875–1914), an organisation which had been established in 1869 to discourage 'indiscriminate' alms-giving. Accordingly, it pioneered a 'casework' approach that sought to target philanthropic efforts to relieve hardship through the detailed investigation of individual family circumstances, with a view to restricting charity to those with the character to respond favourably to assistance.—Ed.]

[14] [See *Our Partnership*, p. 8, for one example of Beatrice Webb's frequent use of this phrase to describe her husband. For additional details about Hayek's opinion of Sidney Webb, see F. A. Hayek, "The Economics of the 1930s as Seen from London" [1963], published as chapter 1 of F. A. Hayek, *Contra Keynes and Cambridge: Essays, Correspondence*, ed. B. Caldwell, vol. 9 (1995) of *The Collected Works of F. A. Hayek*, pp. 51–52.—Ed.]

[15] [All three phrases can be found on p. 424 of *Our Partnership*.—Ed.]

[16] [The words within the square brackets were added by Hayek.—Ed.]

[17] [Webb's actual words, which have been slightly modified by Hayek, are as follows: "Now the trouble with Gladstonian Liberalism is that, by instinct, by tradition, and by the positive precepts of its past exponents, it 'thinks in individuals'". See *Our Partnership*, p. 222.—Ed.]

nion of those who hold the faith" (p. 366–7), the desire for "constructing a party with a religion and an applied science" (p. 471), fit as well into this fundamentally totalitarian attitude as her personal ascetism which makes her see sins in "all my little self-indulgences—the cup of tea or occasional coffee after a meal" (*ibid.*).[18]

---

[18] [The final paragraph of the version of this article that was published in *Economica* was as follows: "This selection of a few points from a fascinating volume will give an idea of the variety of interest and information it contains. But it is itself merely a selection from the voluminous diaries which Beatrice Webb kept over a period of over seventy years and it is strongly to be hoped that before long these diaries will be published in full. Only then will it be possible to write an adequate history of the small group of people whose ideas have changed Great Britain in the past forty years and rule it at present. Since no even approximately adequate survey of this movement is available in English we must be grateful for the German sketch listed second at the head of this review. Although it is little more than a careful compilation of the more readily available material, prepared as a doctorial dissertation at the University of Zürich but published in Germany, it is useful as a brief survey and helpful by its biographical notes." See n. 1 above for details of the "German sketch" to which Hayek refers.—Ed.]

CLOSING SPEECH TO THE 1984 MONT PÈLERIN SOCIETY MEETING[1]

My Lords, Ladies and Gentlemen.

On the last day of February, it was exactly forty years ago, that in a lecture to the Political Society of King's College, Cambridge, I developed the idea that if, after the war, international contacts were not to be confined to etatists of various sorts, and there should still be private communication between independent thinkers, we ought to consider preparing a society, which I proposed to call the Acton-Tocqueville Society, after two of the great liberal thinkers of the last century.[2] And of course, a few weeks before, I had published in

---

[1] [The following text was delivered by Hayek on March 3, 1984, as the closing remarks of the regional meeting of the Mont Pèlerin Society, held in Paris from February 29 until March 3 of that year. The original version of the text, which can be found in the Hayek Collection, box 110, folder 38, Hoover Institution Archives, contains Hayek's handwritten amendments, which have been incorporated into the text used here. While the lecture has not previously been published in English, a French translation did appear in *Le Figaro* magazine, Saturday, March 10, 1984.—Ed.]

[2] [See F. A. Hayek, "Historians and the Future of Europe" [1944], reprinted as chapter 8 of F. A. Hayek, *The Fortunes of Liberalism: Essays on Austrian Economics and the Ideal of Freedom*, ed. Peter G. Klein, vol. 4 (1992) of *The Collected Works of F. A. Hayek* (Chicago: University of Chicago Press; London: Routledge). Hayek discussed the need for such a society in several other papers written in the mid-1940s, including F. A. Hayek, "A Plan for the Future of Germany" [1945], and F. A. Hayek, "Opening Address to a Conference at Mont Pèlerin" [1947], now published as chapters 11 and 12 of *The Fortunes of Liberalism*, and also in F. A. Hayek, "The Prospects of Freedom" [1946], published as chapter 3 of the current volume.

In all of the aforementioned essays, Hayek suggests that the organisation he was seeking to establish should be called the 'Acton-Tocqueville Society'. John Emerich Edward Dalberg-Acton, First Baron Acton (1834–1902), was a classical liberal historian and moralist, Liberal MP, and leader of the liberal Roman Catholics in England. For additional details concerning Hayek's views on Acton, see Hayek, "The Prospects of Freedom", p. 66 n. 15 and F. A. Hayek, "The Principles of a Liberal Social Order" [1966], reprinted as chapter 21 of this volume, p. 272 n. 2, and the references contained therein. Hayek also refers to French historian, politician and political scientist Alexis Charles Henri Clérel de Tocqueville (1805–59), who analysed the nature and consequences of the spread of democracy in the late eighteenth and early nineteenth centuries, with particular reference to the potential for democracy to unleash a new kind of despotism (namely, the so-called 'tyranny of the majority'). See Hayek, "The Prospects of Freedom",

England a book called *The Road to Serfdom*, which later in that year appeared in the U.S.[3] And only a few weeks after that speech at King's College, a certain gentleman named George Orwell published a review of *The Road to Serfdom*. I won't claim too much. I know, now, that he was already looking for a publisher for his first famous book, but anyhow I think he has contributed much more than *The Road to Serfdom* has in its original form to cause the reaction to totalitarianism of which the history of this Society is of course a very important element.[4] It was a year later, largely as a result of the publication of the American edition, and even more so, of the publication of excerpts of the American edition in *The Reader's Digest*, that I began my extensive travels, first in the U.S. and then elsewhere, lecturing on the topic of *The Road to Serfdom*.[5]

I had then the curious experience, as I moved from place to place, first in the States, then on the European Continent, that in almost each city I went, there was a single person that came up to me afterwards and said, "You know, I agree completely with you, but I am the only person I know who thinks like this, and it's such a pleasure at last to meet a person who holds to that traditional liberal conception."

I think it was a result of that experience that I came to the conclusion that it was essential to bring these people together. I had a very important foundation for such an effort because, shortly before the war, the late Professor Louis Rougier had, in the summer of 1938, organized in Paris a meeting on the

---

p. 71 n. 21, and F. A. Hayek, "Liberalism" [1978], reprinted as chapter 1 of this volume, p. 13 n. 18. Hayek's preferred name for the proposed organisation did not, however, win the favour of those who attended the meeting, held April 1–10, 1947, at the Hotel du Parc on Mont Pèlerin sur Vevey in Switzerland, at which it was established. Instead, after some debate, the suggestion advanced by the German-born, Stanford-based agricultural economist Karl Brandt (1899–1975) that the organisation should be called 'The Mont Pèlerin Society' was accepted. For more on this, see R. M. Hartwell, *A History of the Mont Pelerin Society* (Indianapolis: Liberty Fund, 1995), pp. 42–44.—Ed.]

[3] [Now see F. A. Hayek, *The Road to Serfdom: Text and Documents*, ed. B. Caldwell, vol. 2 (2007) of *The Collected Works of F. A. Hayek*. The story of Hayek's search for an American publisher for his book, and also of how in April 1945 *The Reader's Digest* published and distributed over one million copies of a condensed version, is told by B. Caldwell, 'Introduction', in Hayek, *The Road to Serfdom*, pp. 15–23.—Ed.]

[4] [George Orwell, the pseudonym of Eric Arthur Blair (1903–50), was an English novelist, essayist, and critic whose most famous critiques of collectivism and totalitarianism are *Animal Farm: A Fairy Story* (London: Secker and Warburg, 1945)—to which Hayek refers—and *Nineteen Eighty-Four: A Novel* (London: Secker and Warburg, 1949). For Orwell's review of *The Road to Serfdom*, see "Review: *The Road to Serfdom* by F. A. Hayek, and *The Mirror of the Past*, by Konni Zilliacus" [1944], reprinted in *The Collected Essays, Journalism, and Letters of George Orwell*, ed. S. Orwell and I. Angus (New York: Harcourt, Brace and World, 1968), vol. 3, pp. 117–19.—Ed.]

[5] [The original text of Hayek's speech contained the words "led to" rather than "I began". The latter phrase has been inserted by the editor of this volume in order to render the sentence grammatically correct. The addition is consistent with the version of Hayek's speech that appeared in *Le Figaro*.—Ed.]

occasion of the publication of Walter Lippmann's book on *The Good Society*, the results of which were published in a volume: *Le Colloque Walter Lippmann*. I had made the acquaintance then of a number of the leading thinkers in this field, and the late Professor Rougier had started organising something which might have become the MPS if war had not interfered.[6] After this experience, as perhaps a too typical liberal, I went on saying how nice it would be if we could organise such a society, until I found a curious situation in Switzerland which suddenly produced the means for a first meeting, and I may perhaps tell the story which is in a way tragicomic. This concerns the two men who helped me most in the first dozen years of the Mont Pèlerin Society.

In travelling through Zürich, in my then usual communication between

[6] [Louis Rougier (1889–1982) was a French liberal philosopher and the author of, amongst many other books, *Les mystiques économiques: comment l'on passe des démocraties libérales aux États totalitaires* (Paris: Librairie de Médicis, 1938). In that book, Rougier lamented what he saw as the descent of political debate into a choice between fascism and communism, both of which he believed excluded the beneficial features of a liberal system. He also argued that the market order emerged only against the background of a legal system that, far from being the spontaneous result of 'natural' forces, was created at least in part by the state. Rougier's efforts to elaborate a new form of liberalism that would avoid the extremes of nineteenth-century, Manchester School liberalism, whilst also providing a sturdy bulwark against collectivism, saw him organise in August 1938 a colloquium on American journalist, author and social commentator Walter Lippmann's (1889–1974) recently published book, *An Inquiry into the Principles of the Good Society* (Boston: Little, Brown and Co., 1937). Like Rougier, Lippmann sought to navigate a path between laissez-faire capitalism and socialist planning so as to arrive at a renewed form of liberalism. The colloquium came to be known as the Colloque Walter Lippmann and is widely held to mark the birth of the intellectual and political movement now known as 'neo-liberalism'. In addition to Rougier, Lippmann, and Hayek, the 26 attendees included French sociologist, historian and political commentator Raymond Aron (1905–83); Austrian economist Ludwig von Mises (1881–1973); Hungarian-British chemist and philosopher Michael Polanyi (1891–1976); German economist Wilhelm Röpke (1899–1966); French economist and civil servant Jacques Rueff (1896–1978); Austrian sociologist and philosopher Alfred Schütz (1899–1959); and German sociologist and economist Alexander Rüstow (1885–1963). The proceedings were published as *Compte-rendu des séances du Colloque Walter Lippmann* (Paris: Librairie de Médicis, 1939). For an English translation, and a complete list of participants, see J. Reinhoudt and S. Audier, *The Walter Lippmann Colloquium: The Birth of Neo-Liberalism* (Basingstoke: Palgrave Macmillan, 2018).

Rougier subsequently founded the Centre International d'Études pour la Rénovation du Libéralisme, with a view of continuing the work begun at the colloquium. However, the advent of the Second World War led to the suspension of work on the project. After the war had ended, Röpke attempted to establish a journal that would promote liberal ideas. His efforts received financial support from a group of industrialists led by Swiss businessman Albert Hunold (1899–1981) (who was Secretary of the Mont Pèlerin Society from 1948 to 1960). However, as Hayek recounts below, Röpke and Hunold disagreed over who would exercise control over the journal, causing the project to falter. The money raised by Hunold therefore became available to support the first Mont Pèlerin conference, along with funding obtained from the Volker Foundation. For additional details about the story summarised here, see Hartwell, *A History of the Mont Pelerin Society*, pp. 17–33, and A. Burgin, *The Great Persuasion: Reinventing Free Markets since the Depression* (Cambridge, MA: Harvard University Press, 2012), pp. 55–86, 97–102.—Ed.]

London and Vienna, I encountered a certain gentleman named Albert Hunold to whom, as to many people, I said, "How nice it would be if I could only raise the money to organise such a meeting!" Upon which Dr. Hunold told me, "You know, I have got the money. I have raised it for a similar purpose. I have raised the money in order to enable Professor Röpke to edit a liberal journal. But we have since found we do not sufficiently agree about how to do it. If you can persuade Prof. Röpke to permit me to hand over that money, which was intended for his journal, for the new society, we can hold a meeting". My first task was thus to reconcile Mr. Hunold and Prof. Röpke to raise the funds for that meeting which Dr. Hunold organised on the Mont Pèlerin. Quite extraordinary when I think *The Road to Serfdom* first appeared in the beginning of 1944, my journey in America was in 1945, and we already met on Easter 1947.[7]

I then had a list of 70 people whom I thought would be appropriate members of such a society. I sent invitations to all of them, all approved but only half that number, or more exactly thirty-six, were able to attend and assembled on Mont Pèlerin. We had a long meeting there, leading up to the formal foundation of the Society. The personnel of this first group, the thirty-six who met, were partly the people who had assembled six years before at the Colloque Walter Lippmann. Ultimately the other thirty-five or thirty-four whom I had invited, joined the Society that was created at that moment. I am very sad that of these thirty-six people, a few have left the Society and only ten actual members have survived. And of these ten members I am afraid I am the only one who attends this meeting today.[8]

[7] [For other brief accounts of these events, see Hayek, "Opening Address to a Conference at Mont Pèlerin", pp. 240, 248; F. A. Hayek, "The Rediscovery of Freedom: Personal Recollections" [1983], published as the Prologue to part II of Hayek, *The Fortunes of Liberalism*, p. 191, and F. A. Hayek, *Hayek on Hayek: An Autobiographical Dialogue*, ed. S. Kresge and L. Wenar (Chicago: University of Chicago Press, 1994), p. 133.—Ed.]

[8] [Hayek's account of some of the events discussed in this paragraph is not entirely accurate. The official history of the Mont Pèlerin Society lists 38 attendees at the 1947 meeting, aside from Hayek himself. See Hartwell, *A History of the Mont Pèlerin Society*, pp. 45–46. These included German economist Walter Eucken (1891–1950), American economist Frank Knight (1885–1972), philosopher Karl Popper (1902–94), three future Nobel Laureates in Economics, namely Maurice Allais (1911–2010), Milton Friedman (1912–2006), and George Stigler (1911–91), and British economist Lionel Robbins (1898–1984) (who wrote the Statement of Aims for the Society). Four of the participants, namely Hayek, Mises, Polanyi and Röpke, had also attended the Colloque Lippmann, an event which of course occurred nine years before the meeting at Mont Pèlerin (not six, as Hayek states). The names of 26 people whom Hayek invited to the 1947 meeting, who were unable to attend, but who subsequently joined the Society, can be found on p. 241 of Hayek, "Opening Address to a Conference at Mont Pèlerin". A list of the sixty-four founder members of the Mont Pèlerin Society, which includes the names of Walter Lippmann and Alexander Rüstow, can be found on p. 51 of the Hartwell volume. Hayek's sadness about those members who had left the Society may be a reference to the resignations in 1961–62 of

The Society has, on the whole, done a very good job, when I think of the role which it has played in the undeniable revival of liberalism, but I think nothing is more representative of this event, that now we have a meeting in Paris held by a group of young men.[9] In 1945 all the liberals I could find were old men although at that time by old men I meant usually men older than myself, but now forty years later we can count on a group representing reviving liberalism, in—if I may say so—the intellectual centre of the world where my hope had been least. I have gradually come to recognise that the great obstacle to the preservation of the liberal tradition is a philosophical conviction which overestimates the powers of human reason: Cartesian philosophy which had been largely dominating French political thought, disposed French thinkers to an extent much more than elsewhere to think that our reason is powerful enough to reorganise society and make its structure and efforts more satisfactory than they have been.[10]

I have long doubted that the possibility of turning the efforts which we started in 1947 into an international movement was really a thing to be expected. You will now understand why I say "even in France". But a group of 'nouveaux economistes' of a younger generation have now taken over the message and developed it.[11] I have now become convinced that the task I

Hunold, Röpke, Brandt and Rüstow, amongst others, after a prolonged controversy beginning in the late 1950s over Hunold's role in the running of the Society. Hayek very briefly refers to the problem on p. 133 of *Hayek on Hayek*. For more detailed accounts of the so-called 'Hunold affair', see Hartwell, *A History of the Mont Pelerin Society*, pp. 100–38, and Burgin, *The Great Persuasion*, pp. 124–25, 129–37.—Ed.]

[9] [The Steering Committee of the 1984 regional meeting of the Mont Pèlerin Society was chaired by French industrialist Fred Aftalion (1922–), with the other members of the Committee including Chiaki Nishiyama (1924–2017), a Japanese economist and former doctoral student of Hayek at the University of Chicago, French businessman and at the time executive director of the Institut Economique de Paris Guy Plunier (1930–), and French economist Pascal Salin (1939–). See "1984 Regional Meeting – Paris (Papers Read)", box 78, Mont Pèlerin Society Records, Hoover Institution Archives.—Ed.]

[10] [Hayek discusses the role of Cartesian philosophy in encouraging French and other Continental writers, such as philosopher and political theorist Jean-Jacques Rousseau (1712–78), philosopher and sociologist Auguste Comte (1798–1857), and social reformer Claude Henri de Rouvroy, Comte de Saint-Simon (1760–1825), to think that all institutions and values can and should be consciously planned in F. A. Hayek, *Studies on the Abuse and Decline of Reason: Text and Documents*, ed. Bruce Caldwell, vol. 13 (2010) of *The Collected Works of F. A. Hayek*.—Ed.]

[11] [The group of younger French economists to which Hayek refers, known as the 'Nouveaux Economistes', was founded in 1977 and sought to popularise the ideas of the Austrian, Chicago and Virginia schools in France. Its members included Jacques Garello (1934–), Florin Aftalion (1937–), Pascal Salin, and Henri Lepage (1941–). Members of the group established the Institut Economique de Paris, which they intended to be a think-tank analogous to the London-based Institute of Economic Affairs, and also invited Hayek to speak at the 1984 regional meeting at which his "Closing Speech" was delivered. See H. Lepage to F. A. Hayek, April 14, 1982, and P. Salin to F. A. Hayek, May 13, 1982, and July 26, 1983, Hayek Papers, box 33, folder 9, and

had started so long ago, for which I had received support from a few men in France who were older than myself, where I for a long time had little hope of finding younger people, [is] influential enough to attract public attention, and [to justify organising] a meeting.[12] I don't want to be unjust to a French contribution in the history of the Mont Pèlerin Society. We had at a very early stage a particularly memorable meeting at Beauvallon on the Riviera and in 1976 also in Paris. The first one was I think the first biggish meeting, to me particularly memorable because it was the only occasion on which the President gave a formal presidential address, and I chose to explain the topic, which I think has become rather significant in the history of the Society, which I called my presidential address, the only one I gave in the twelve years I was a president of the Society, "Why I am not a Conservative".[13] I

box 47, folder 31, respectively. For more on the Nouveaux Economistes, see F. Denord, "French Neoliberalism and Its Divisions: From the Colloque Lippmann to the Fifth Republic", in *The Road from Mont Pèlerin: The Making of the Neoliberal Thought Collective*, ed. P. Mirowski and D. Plehwe (Cambridge, MA: Harvard University Press, 2009), p. 62, and S. Audier, "The French Reception of American Neoliberalism in the Late 1970s", in *In Search of the Liberal Moment: Democracy, Anti-totalitarianism, and Intellectual Politics in France since 1950*, ed. S. Sawyer and I. Stewart (Basingstoke: Palgrave Macmillan, 2016).—Ed.]

[12] [In the text of this speech found in the Hayek Papers, the final two clauses of this sentence read, "were influential enough to attract public attention, and to be able to hold a meeting". Since this does not make sense, given the earlier part of the sentence, the words in square brackets have been inserted by the editor of this volume. They are in keeping with the transcript of Hayek's speech published in *Le Figaro*.

The identity of the "few men in France who were older than myself" from whom Hayek received support is unclear. While Hayek might be referring to Jacques Rueff or French monetary economist Charles Rist (1874–1955), perhaps the most plausible candidate is Louis Rougier, on whose work in organising the Colloque Lippmann Hayek built. As Hayek acknowledged elsewhere, Rougier "did much to start the movement for the revival of the basic principles of a free society", in particular because "it was around the group Professor Rougier had brought together that a larger international association of friends of personal liberty [i.e., the Mont Pèlerin Society] was formed". See F. A. Hayek, "Introduction", in L. Rougier, *The Genius of the West* (Los Angeles: Nash Publishing, 1971), p. xvi. Rougier himself did not, however, participate in the early meetings of the Mont Pèlerin Society, having been barred from membership until 1956 because of his wartime association with the Vichy regime in France. See Burgin, *The Great Persuasion*, p. 77.—Ed.]

[13] [Hayek refers to F. A. Hayek, "Why I Am Not a Conservative" [1960], published as the Postscript to F. A. Hayek, *The Constitution of Liberty*, ed. Ronald Hamowy, vol. 17 (2011) of *The Collected Works of F. A. Hayek*. Hayek's account is not, however, completely accurate. A publication did emerge after the Society's 1951 meeting at Beauvallon, but it was a volume, edited by Hayek, containing papers that had been presented at that meeting on the topic of the treatment of capitalism by historians. See *Capitalism and the Historians*, edited and with an introduction by F. A. Hayek (London: Routledge and Kegan Paul, 1954). Hayek gave his paper on 'Why I Am Not a Conservative' at the Society's tenth anniversary meeting, held in September 1957 in St. Moritz, Switzerland. See Hartwell, *A History of the Mont Pelerin Society*, pp. 93–94, 96.—Ed.]

think in a sense this characterises the intellectual development of the MPS. I stress intellectual development, because from the beginning, the MPS was largely concerned with a basic philosophy, and aimed from the beginning not at directly convincing the masses, but those makers of opinion who gradually and in time affect political developments. The MPS has never taken positions on political matters. It hasn't even mainly concerned itself with problems of current policy, but its concern has been largely and predominantly to revive and to adapt to our present day thinking the problems of the basic philosophy of a free society. I think most of us have been aware of this, and most of us have been concerning ourselves chiefly with that basic philosophy.[14]

This is very relevant if I now turn to what must be my main question: how far has the position changed in those forty years? How far has the movement which we tried to initiate been successful? In all these years I have constantly fluctuated between being encouraged by particular steps and being disillusioned and depressed about what governments still actually are doing. I have now arrived at a formula which I want to give you, which I believe provides an answer. I have to admit that the effects on practical politics have been very small. But the effects on the movement of ideas have been absolutely fundamental. There *is* a great change in the attitude of the active younger generation. I used to say, more than 50 years ago, that the only people who still believe in classical liberalism were old men, and in the middle generation there were a handful: Mises and Rueff belonged to the older generation really, for example, and of my contemporaries there were just perhaps Röpke, and Bill Hutt, who is here, and two or three others.[15]

There was a complete lack of liberals among younger people. Liberalism in the classical sense was regarded as something antiquated and no longer up to date. Now this has completely changed, and I am prepared to claim that although they have not yet had much influence on the practice of policy, I

---

[14] [Hayek argued in a number of essays written at around the time of the foundation of the Mont Pèlerin Society that the revival of classical liberal thought would best be furthered by a thorough re-examination of the philosophical foundations, or general principles, of a free society rather than through direct appeals to the general public or the development of concrete policies. See for example Hayek, "The Prospects of Freedom", and F. A. Hayek, "The Intellectuals and Socialism" [1949], reprinted as chapter 11 of *Socialism and War: Essays, Documents, Reviews*, ed. B. Caldwell, vol. 10 (1997) of *The Collected Works of F. A. Hayek.*—Ed.]

[15] [After studying economics under Edwin Cannan at the London School of Economics, William H. Hutt (1899–1988) taught at the University of Cape Town. He was a forceful critic both of the abuse of trade union power and also of Keynesian economics. See, for example, W. H. Hutt, *The Theory of Collective Bargaining: A History, Analysis and Criticism of the Principal Theories Which Have Sought to Explain the Effects of Trade Unions and Employers' Associations upon the Distribution of the Product of Industry* (London: P. S. King & Sons, 1930), and W. H. Hutt, *The Theory of Idle Resources: A Study in Definition* (London: Jonathan Cape, 1939).—Ed.]

think we have contributed at least a great deal to a change of opinion, particularly a change of opinion among the young.[16] Something which 20 years ago would have been unacceptable among the young proves to me these ideas have been influential. When I'm now being asked—and I repeat a formula which many of you will have heard, and which I used many times before—whether I am optimistic about the future, my regular answer is, "If the politicians do not destroy the world in the next fifteen years, there is very good hope indeed". Because there is a new generation coming up, which has rediscovered, not only the material advantages of freedom, but the moral justification of a philosophy of freedom, and I think we can really be quite pleased how things are moving.

There is a new tradition, which teaches one thing, which I think I ought to say in conclusion of what I have just said: "Our task must be not directly to participate in the current practice of politics". When I say "*our*" I mean as a Society. Of course each of us has a duty as a citizen of his particular country to take part in political programmes. But this Society ought to concern itself with a much more important task: with the task of changing opinion. And changing opinion is fundamental, because I think we ought to admit and ought to realise that the class of society which is responsible for things having gone wrong for the past hundred years, was not the Proletariat. It was the Intellectuals. It's the intellectuals who have really created socialism, who have spread socialism, out of the best intentions, because of a factual mistake, out of what in a book on which I am working, I call a fatal conceit, the idea that human reason is strong enough to reorganise society deliberately in the service of known, foreseen ends and purposes.[17] Now this turns out to be an intellectual deception. More and more of the young people see that what is intellectually so fascinating, so attractive, what drove so many, I have to admit, of the best and most intelligent of the young people into the left camp, for the whole period from the middle of the 19th to the middle of the 20th century, has turned out to be factually wrong. We are gradually discovering, and that I regard as my chief task at the present, and should also be our chief task,

---

[16] [For more on the nature and significance of 'opinion', as Hayek understood it, see F. A. Hayek, "The Constitution of a Liberal State" [1967], and F. A. Hayek, "The Confusion of Language in Political Thought" [1968], reprinted as chapters 22 and 23 respectively of the current volume.—Ed.]

[17] [Elsewhere, Hayek defines an 'intellectual' in terms of his or her role as an "intermediary in the spreading of ideas". See Hayek, "The Intellectuals and Socialism", p. 222. In that essay, Hayek sets out in some detail his account of how intellectuals shape public opinion in favour of socialism. His reflections on one particular pair of intellectuals, namely the English social reformers Beatrice (1858–1943) and Sidney (1859–1947) Webb, can be found in F. A. Hayek, "The Webbs and Their Work" [1948], reprinted as chapter 4 of this volume.

Hayek also refers to F. A. Hayek, *The Fatal Conceit: The Errors of Socialism*, ed. W. W. Bartley III, vol. 1 (1988) of *The Collected Works of F. A. Hayek*.—Ed.]

that it is not merely the endowment with intelligence which has enabled us to build up the extensive order of mankind which now can maintain 200 times as many people than existed 5000 years ago on this world, but there is a *second* endowment, equally important, an inheritance which is *not* the product of our reason: a moral inheritance, which is an explanation of the dominance of the western world, a moral inheritance which consists essentially in the belief in property, honesty and the family, all things which we could not and have never been able adequately to justify intellectually. We have to recognise that we owe our civilisation to beliefs which I sometimes have offended some people by calling 'superstitions' and which I now prefer to call 'symbolic truths', truths very different from the truths of reason, which are the result of a process of selection, which made those practical rules of conduct, which enabled societies to grow and to expand and become dominant.[18] We must return to a world in which not only reason, but reason and morals, as equal partners, must govern our lives, where the truth of morals is simply *one* moral tradition, that of the Christian west, which has created morals in modern civilisation.

Thank you.

---

[18] [The process of selection to which Hayek refers, and which is central to his account of cultural evolution as occurring via group selection, is discussed in more detail in Hayek, *The Constitution of Liberty*, pp. 73–99, 107–32; in F. A. Hayek, "Notes on the Evolution of Systems of Rules of Conduct" [1967], reprinted as chapter 10 of F. A. Hayek, *The Market and Other Orders*, ed. Bruce Caldwell, vol. 15 (2014) of *The Collected Works of F. A. Hayek*; and in F. A. Hayek, *The Political Order of a Free People*, vol. 3 (1979) of *Law, Legislation and Liberty* (Chicago: University of Chicago Press; London: Routledge, 1973–79), pp. 155–63. Hayek elaborates on the notion of 'symbolic truths' on pp. 135–40 of *The Fatal Conceit*.—Ed.]

SIX

'FREE' ENTERPRISE AND COMPETITIVE ORDER[1]

I

If during the next few years, that is, during the period with which practical politicians are alone concerned, a continued movement toward more government control in the greater part of the world is almost certain, this is due, more than to anything else, to the lack of a real programme, or perhaps I had better say, a consistent philosophy of the groups which wish to oppose it.[2] The position is even worse than mere lack of programme would imply; the fact is that almost everywhere the groups which pretend to oppose socialism at the same time support policies which, if the principles on which they are based were generalised, would no less lead to socialism than the avowedly socialist policies. There is some justification at least in the taunt that many of the pretending defenders of 'free enterprise' are in fact defenders of privileges and advocates of government activity in their favour rather than opponents of all privilege. In principle the industrial protectionism and government-supported cartels and the agricultural policies of the conservative groups are not different from the proposals for a more far-reaching direction of economic life sponsored by the socialists. It is an illusion when the more conservative interventionists believe that they will be able to confine these government controls to the particular kinds of which they approve. In a democratic society, at any rate, once the principle is admitted that the government undertakes

---

[1] The substance of a paper which served to open a discussion on the subject indicated by its title held at a conference at Mont-Pèlerin, Switzerland, in April, 1947. [The paper was first published as chapter 6 of F. A. Hayek, *Individualism and Economic Order* (Chicago: University of Chicago Press, 1948).—Ed.]

[2] [The version of this sentence found on p. 107 of *Individualism and Economic Order* ended as follows: "to a consistent philosophy of the groups which wish to oppose it." The initial "to" in that clause has been removed from the text of the essay printed here, because its presence would obscure the point Hayek was trying to make, namely that the movement towards greater government control over economic life was facilitated by the fact that its opponents lacked a consistent philosophy. This change to the text is also consistent with the copy of Hayek's paper contained in the Mont Pèlerin Society Records, Hoover Institution Archives, box 140, folder 6, in which the "to" in question does not appear.—Ed.]

responsibility for the status and position of particular groups, it is inevitable that this control will be extended to satisfy the aspirations and prejudices of the great masses.[3] There is no hope of a return to a freer system until the leaders of the movement against state control are prepared first to impose upon themselves that discipline of a competitive market which they ask the masses to accept. The hopelessness of the prospect for the near future indeed is due mainly to the fact that no organised political group anywhere is in favor of a truly free system.

It is more than likely that from their point of view the practical politicians are right and that in the existing state of public opinion nothing else would be practicable. But what to the politicians are fixed limits of practicability imposed by public opinion must not be similar limits to us. Public opinion on these matters is the work of men like ourselves, the economists and political philosophers of the past few generations, who have created the political climate in which the politicians of our time must move. I do not find myself often agreeing with the late Lord Keynes, but he has never said a truer thing than when he wrote, on a subject on which his own experience has singularly qualified him to speak, that "the ideas of economists and political philosophers, both when they are right and when they are wrong, are more powerful than is commonly understood. Indeed the world is ruled by little else [. . .] Madmen in authority, who hear voices in the air, are distilling their frenzy from some academic scribbler of a few years back. I am sure that the power of vested interests is vastly exaggerated compared with the gradual encroachment of ideas. Not, indeed, immediately, but after a certain interval; for in the field of economic and political philosophy there are not many who are influenced by new theories after they are twenty-five or thirty years of age, so that the ideas which civil servants and politicians and even agitators apply [. . .] are not likely to be the newest. But, soon or late, it is ideas, not vested interests, which are dangerous for good or evil."[4]

It is from this long-run point of view that we must look at our task. It is the beliefs which must spread, if a free society is to be preserved, or restored, not what is practicable at the moment, which must be our concern. But, while we

---

[3] [The argument underpinning this claim is set out in F. A. Hayek, *The Road to Serfdom: Text and Documents*, ed. B. Caldwell, vol. 2 (2007) of *The Collected Works of F. A. Hayek* (Chicago: University of Chicago Press; London: Routledge), pp. 134–46.—Ed.]

[4] J. M. Keynes, *The General Theory of Employment, Interest, and Money* (London, 1936), pp. 383–84. [Hayek quotes the words of British economist John Maynard Keynes (1883–1946), Baron Keynes of Tilton. The passage in question is from J. M. Keynes, *The General Theory of Employment, Interest and Money* [1936], reprinted as vol. 7 (1973) of *The Collected Writings of John Maynard Keynes* (London: Macmillan for the Royal Economic Society), pp. 383–84. For more on Hayek's views on Keynes's economics, and also on Keynes the man, see F. A. Hayek, *Contra Keynes and Cambridge: Essays, Correspondence*, ed. B. Caldwell, vol. 9 (1995) of *The Collected Works of F. A. Hayek*.—Ed.]

must emancipate ourselves from that servitude to current prejudices in which the politician is held, we must take a sane view of what persuasion and instruction are likely to achieve. While we may hope that, as regards the means to be employed and the methods to be adopted, the public may in some measure be accessible to reasonable argument, we must probably assume that many of its basic values, its ethical standards, are at least fixed for a much longer time and to some extent entirely beyond the scope of reasoning. To some extent it may be our task even here to show that the aims which our generation has set itself are incompatible or conflicting and that the pursuit of some of them will endanger even greater values. But we shall probably also find that in some respects during the last hundred years certain moral aims have firmly established themselves for the satisfaction of which in a free society suitable techniques can be found. Even if we should not altogether share the new importance attached to some of these newer values, we shall do well to assume that they will determine action for a long time to come and carefully to consider how far a place can be found for them in a free society. It is, of course, mainly the demands for greater security and greater equality I have here in mind. In both respects I believe very careful distinctions will have to be drawn between the sense in which 'security' and 'equality' can and cannot be provided in a free society.

Yet in another sense I think that we shall have to pay deliberate attention to the moral temper of contemporary man if we are to succeed in canalising his energies from the harmful policies to which they are now devoted to a new effort on behalf of individual freedom. Unless we can set a definite task to the reformatory zeal of men, unless we can point out reforms which can be fought for by unselfish men, within a programme for freedom, their moral fervour is certain to be used against freedom. It was probably the most fatal tactical mistake of many nineteenth-century liberals to have given the impression that the abandonment of all harmful or unnecessary state activity was the consummation of all political wisdom and that the question of *how* the state ought to use those powers which nobody denied to it offered no serious and important problems on which reasonable people could differ.

This is, of course, not true of all nineteenth-century liberals. About a hundred years ago John Stuart Mill, then still a true liberal, stated one of our present main problems in unmistakable terms. "The principle of private property has never yet had a fair trial in any country", he wrote in the first edition of his *Political Economy*. "The laws of property have never yet conformed to the principles on which the justification of private property rests. They have made property of things which never ought to be property, and absolute property where only a qualified property ought to exist . . . if the tendency of legislation had been to favour the diffusion, instead of the concentration of wealth, to encourage the subdivision of the large masses, instead of striving to keep them together; the principle of individual property would have been found to have no real connection with the physical and social evils which have made so many minds turn eagerly to any prospect of relief, however desperate".[5] But little was in fact done to make the rules of property conform better to its rationale, and Mill himself, like so many others, soon turned his attention to schemes involving its restriction or abolition rather than its more effective use.

While it would be an exaggeration, it would not be altogether untrue to say that the interpretation of the fundamental principle of liberalism as absence of state activity rather than as a policy which deliberately adopts competition, the market, and prices as its ordering principle and uses the legal framework enforced by the state in order to make competition as effective and beneficial as possible—and to supplement it where, and only where, it cannot be made effective—is as much responsible for the decline of competition as the active support which governments have given directly and indirectly to the growth of monopoly. It is the first general thesis which we shall have to consider that competition can be made more effective and more beneficent by certain activities of government than it would be without them. With regard to some of these activities this has never been denied, although people speak sometimes as if they had forgotten about them. That a functioning market presupposes not only prevention of violence and fraud but the protection of certain rights, such as property, and the enforcement of contracts, is always taken for granted. Where the traditional discussion becomes so unsatisfactory is where it is suggested that, with the recognition of the principles of private property and freedom of contract, which indeed every liberal must recognise, all the issues were settled, as if the law of property and contract were given once and for all in its final and most appropriate form, i.e., in the form which will make the market economy work at its best. It is only after we have agreed on these principles that the real problems begin.

It is this fact which I have wished to emphasise when I called the subject of

---

[5] *Principles of Political Economy* (1st ed.), Book II, chap. 1, §5 (Vol. I, p. 253). [Hayek quotes from English philosopher, political economist, and social reformer John Stuart Mill's *Principles of Political Economy*, 1st ed. (London: J. W. Parker, 1848), vol. 1, book II, chap. 1, section 5, p. 253. As implied by Hayek's remark that Mill was "still a true liberal" at the time he wrote the first edition of the *Principles*, Hayek believed that Mill's views shifted over time, away from the liberalism of his early years towards a more socialist outlook. See F. A. Hayek, *Studies on the Abuse and Decline of Reason: Text and Documents*, ed. Bruce Caldwell, vol. 13 (2010) of *The Collected Works of F. A. Hayek*, pp. 56–57, 71, 238–39, and F. A. Hayek, *The Constitution of Liberty*, ed. Ronald Hamowy, vol. 17 (2011) of *The Collected Works of F. A. Hayek*, pp. 82, 121–22. Hayek's views on Mill are analysed in detail by B. Caldwell, "Hayek on Mill", *History of Political Economy*, vol. 40, 2008, pp. 689–704, and by S. Peart, "Editor's Introduction", in F. A. Hayek, *Hayek on Mill: The Mill-Taylor Friendship and Related Writings*, ed. Sandra J. Peart, vol. 16 (2015) of *The Collected Works of F. A. Hayek.*—Ed.]

this discussion "'Free' Enterprise and Competitive Order". The two names do not necessarily designate the same system, and it is the system described by the second which we want. Perhaps I should at once add that what I mean by 'competitive order' is almost the opposite of what is often called 'ordered competition'. The purpose of a competitive order is to make competition work; that of so-called 'ordered competition', almost always to restrict the effectiveness of competition. Thus understood, this description of our subject at once distinguishes our approach as much from that of the conservative planners as from that of the socialists.

In this introductory survey I must confine myself to enumerating the main problems we shall have to discuss and must leave any detailed examination to later speakers. Perhaps I should begin by emphasising more than I have yet done that, while our main concern must be to make the market work wherever it can work, we must, of course, not forget that there are in a modern community a considerable number of services which are needed, such as sanitary and health measures, and which could not possibly be provided by the market for the obvious reason that no price can be charged to the beneficiaries or, rather, that it is not possible to confine the benefits to those who are willing or able to pay for them. There are some obvious instances of the kind, like the one I have mentioned, but on closer examination we shall find that in some measure this kind of case shades somewhat gradually into those in which the whole of the services rendered can be sold to whoever wants to buy them. At some stage or other we shall certainly have to consider which services of this kind we must always expect the governments to provide *outside the market* and how far the fact that they must do so will also affect the conditions on which the market economy proceeds.

II

There are two other sets of problems which concern preconditions of a competitive order rather than what one might call market policy proper and which I must mention. The first is the question of the kind of monetary and financial policy required to secure adequate economic stability. We are probably all in agreement that any mitigation of cyclical unemployment depends at least in part on monetary policy. When we turn to these problems, one of our main concerns will have to be how far it is possible to make monetary management once more automatic or at least predictable because bound by fixed rule. The second major problem on which we shall have to assume some definite answer without going into detail at this stage is that in modern society we must take it for granted that some sort of provision will be made for the unemployed and the unemployable poor. All that we can usefully consider in this connection is not whether such provision is desirable or not but merely in what form it will least interfere with the functioning of the market.[6]

I have mentioned these points mainly in order more sharply to delimit my main subject. Before I proceed to the bare enumeration with which I must content myself, I will add only that it seems to me highly desirable that liberals shall strongly disagree on these topics, the more the better. What is needed more than anything else is that these questions of a policy for a competitive order should once again become live issues which are being discussed publicly; and we shall have made an important contribution if we succeed in directing interest to them.[7]

III

If I am not mistaken, the main headings under which the measures required to ensure an effective competitive order ought to be considered are the law of property and contract, of corporations and associations, including, in particular, trade-unions, the problems of how to deal with those monopolies or quasi-monopolistic positions which would remain in an otherwise sensibly drawn-up framework, the problems of taxation, and the problems of international trade, particularly, in our time, of the relations between free and planned economies.

As far as the great field of the law of property and contract is concerned, we must, as I have already emphasised, above all beware of the error that the formulas 'private property' and 'freedom of contract' solve our problems. They are not adequate answers because their meaning is ambiguous. Our problems begin when we ask what ought to be the contents of property

[6] [For more on Hayek's views on these two issues, see Hayek, *The Constitution of Liberty*, pp. 451–65 and 405–29 respectively.—Ed.]

[7] [Hayek's wish for greater disagreement between liberals on topics such as the role of the state in sustaining a competitive order was fulfilled. Perhaps most significantly, at the second meeting of the Mont Pèlerin Society, held in Switzerland in 1949, there was a significant clash of opinion between two economists, German ordo-liberal Walter Eucken (1891–1950) and Austrian classical liberal Ludwig von Mises (1881–1973). Whereas Eucken argued that the maintenance of a legal framework conducive to the emergence of economic order required state intervention to promote competition, for example by prohibiting contracts conducive to restraint of trade, Mises argued that freedom of contract was sacrosanct and that no state intervention was justified. For more on these issues, see V. Vanberg, *The Constitution of Markets: Essays in Political Economy* (London: Routledge, 2001), pp. 17–18, and S. Kolev, "Ordoliberalism and the Austrian School", in *The Oxford Handbook of Austrian Economics*, ed. P. Boettke and C. Coyne (Oxford: Oxford University Press, 2015), p. 435. Also see F. A. Hayek, "What Is 'Social'? What Does It Mean?" [1967], reprinted as chapter 19 of the current volume, pp. 252 n. 2 and 254 n. 3, and F. A. Hayek, "Liberalism" [1978], reprinted as chapter 1 of this volume, p. 34 n. 37.—Ed.]

rights, what contracts should be enforceable, and how contracts should be interpreted or, rather, what standard forms of contract should be read into the informal agreements of everyday transactions.

Where the law of property is concerned, it is not difficult to see that the simple rules which are adequate to ordinary mobile 'things' or 'chattel' are not suitable for indefinite extension. We need only turn to the problems which arise in connection with land, particularly with regard to urban land in modern large towns, in order to realise that a conception of property which is based on the assumption that the use of a particular item of property affects only the interests of its owner breaks down. There can be no doubt that a good many, at least, of the problems with which the modern town planner is concerned are genuine problems with which governments or local authorities are bound to concern themselves. Unless we can provide some guidance in fields like this about what are legitimate or necessary government activities and what are its limits, we must not complain if our views are not taken seriously when we oppose other kinds of less justified 'planning.'[8]

The problem of the prevention of monopoly and the preservation of competition is raised much more acutely in certain other fields to which the concept of property has been extended only in recent times. I am thinking here of the extension of the concept of property to such rights and privileges as patents for inventions, copyright, trade-marks, and the like. It seems to me beyond doubt that in these fields a slavish application of the concept of property as it has been developed for material things has done a great deal to foster the growth of monopoly and that here drastic reforms may be required if competition is to be made to work. In the field of industrial patents in particular we shall have seriously to examine whether the award of a monopoly privilege is really the most appropriate and effective form of reward for the kind of risk-bearing which investment in scientific research involves.

Patents, in particular, are specially interesting from our point of view because they provide so clear an illustration of how it is necessary in all such instances not to apply a ready-made formula but to go back to the rationale of the market system and to decide for each class what the precise rights are to be which the government ought to protect. This is a task at least as much

---

[8] [Hayek argues elsewhere that the key criterion for deciding whether or not a policy is legitimate in principle is provided by its consistency, or lack thereof, with the notion of the 'rule of law' (that is, on whether or not it involves the state exercising its coercive powers only to enforce general, purpose-independent rules laid down before the activities they are intended to regulate). See F. A. Hayek, "The Meaning of Government Interference" [1950], published as chapter 8 of this volume, and Hayek, *The Constitution of Liberty*, pp. 329–41. Hayek's attempt to apply this criterion to the case of town planning policy can be found in F. A. Hayek, "The Economics of Development Charges" [1949], reprinted as chapter 9 of this volume, and on pp. 466–81 of *The Constitution of Liberty*.—Ed.]

for economists as for lawyers. Perhaps it is not a waste of your time if I illustrate what I have in mind by quoting a rather well-known decision in which an American judge argued that "as to the suggestion that competitors were excluded from the use of the patent we answer that such exclusion may be said to have been the very essence of the right conferred by the patent" and adds "as it is the privilege of any owner of property to use it or not to use it without any question of motive".[9] It is this last statement which seems to me to be significant for the way in which a mechanical extension of the property concept by lawyers has done so much to create undesirable and harmful privilege.

IV

Another field in which a mechanical extension of the simplified conception of private property has produced undesirable results is in the field of trade-marks and proprietary names. I myself have no doubt that legislation has important tasks to perform in this field and that securing adequate and truthful information concerning the origin of any product is one, but only one, aspect of this. But the exclusive stress on the description of the producer and the neglect of similar provisions concerning the character and quality of the commodity has to some extent helped to create monopolistic conditions because trade-marks have come to be used as a description of the kind of commodity, which then of course only the owner of the trade-mark could produce ('Kodak', 'Coca-Cola'). This difficulty might be solved, for example, if the use of trade-marks were protected only in connection with descriptive names which would be free for all to use.

The situation is rather similar in the field of contract. We cannot regard 'freedom of contract' as a real answer to our problems if we know that not all contracts ought to be made enforceable and in fact are bound to argue that contracts 'in restraint of trade' ought not to be enforced. Once we extend the power to make contracts from natural persons to corporations and the like,

---

[9] *Continental Bag Co.* v. *Eastern Bag Co.,* 210 U.S. 405 (1909). [This case came before the U.S. Supreme Court in 1908 (not, as Hayek states, 1909). The case arose when the Eastern Paper Bag Company sought to prevent one of its competitors, the Continental Paper Bag Company, from using the design for a 'self-opening' paper bag patented by Eastern. Continental argued in its defence that Eastern was not actually using the patented technology but was instead simply using the patent to suppress competition. The Supreme Court rejected Continental's argument, maintaining that patent-holders enjoy an unlimited right *not* to use the technology in question and that patents entitle their holders to prevent others from using a design irrespective of the patent-holder's motivation for doing so. The words quoted with very minor modifications by Hayek come from the Supreme Court's ruling on the case. See *Continental Paper Bag Co.* v. *Eastern Paper Bag Co.,* 210 U.S. 405 (1908).—Ed.]

it no longer can be the contract but it must be the law which decides who is liable and how the property is to be determined and safeguarded which limits the liability of the corporation.

'Freedom of contract' is in fact no solution because in a complex society like ours no contract can explicitly provide against all contingencies and because jurisdiction and legislation evolve standard types of contracts for many purposes which not only tend to become exclusively practicable and intelligible but which determine the interpretation of, and are used to fill the lacunae in, all contracts which can actually be made. A legal system which leaves the kind of contractual obligations on which the order of society rests entirely to the ever new decision of the contracting parties has never existed and probably cannot exist. Here, as much as in the realm of property, the precise content of the permanent legal framework, the rules of civil law, are of the greatest importance for the way in which a competitive market will operate. The extent to which the development of civil law, as much where it is judge-made law as where it is amended by legislation, can determine the developments away from or toward a competitive system, and how much this change in civil law is determined by the dominant ideas of what would be a desirable social order is well illustrated by the development, during the last fifty years, of legislation and jurisdiction on cartels, monopoly, and the restraint of trade generally. It seems to me that no doubt is possible that this development, even where it fully maintained the principle of 'freedom of contract', and partly because it did so, has greatly contributed to the decline of competition. But little intellectual effort has been directed to the question in what way this legal framework should be modified to make competition more effective.

The main field in which these problems arise and the one from which I can best illustrate my point is, of course, the law of corporations and particularly that concerning limited liability. I do not think that there can be much doubt that the particular form legislation has taken in this field has greatly assisted the growth of monopoly or that it was only because of special legislation conferring special rights—not so much to the corporations themselves as to those dealing with corporations—that size of enterprise has become an advantage beyond the point where it is justified by technological facts. It seems to me that, in general, the freedom of the individual by no means need be extended to give all these freedoms to organised groups of individuals, and even that it may on occasion be the duty of government to protect the individual against organised groups. It appears to me also as if historically in the field of the law of corporations we had a situation rather analogous to that in the field of the law of property to which I have already referred. As in the law of property the rules developed for ordinary mobile property were extended uncritically and without appropriate modifications to all sorts of new rights; thus the recognition of corporations as fictitious or legal persons has had the effect that all the rights of a natural person were automatically extended to corporations. There may be valid arguments for so designing corporation law as to impede the indefinite growth of individual corporations; and the ways in which this could be done without setting up any rigid limits or giving the government undesirable powers of direct interference is one of the more interesting problems which we might discuss.

V

I have so far deliberately spoken only of what is required to make competition effective on the side of employers, not because I regard this as of such exclusive importance, but because I am convinced that there is politically no chance to do anything about the other side of the problem—the labour side—until the employers have themselves shown their belief in competition and demonstrated that they are willing to put their own house in order. But we must not delude ourselves that in many ways the most crucial, the most difficult, and the most delicate part of our task consists in formulating an appropriate programme of labour or trade-union policy. In no other respect, I believe, was the development of liberal opinion more inconsistent or more unfortunate or is there more uncertainty and vagueness even among the true liberals of today. Historically liberalism, first, far too long maintained an unjustified opposition against trade-unions as such, only to collapse completely at the beginning of this century and to grant to trade-unions in many respects exemption from the ordinary law and even, to all intents and purposes, to legalise violence, coercion, and intimidation.[10] That, if there is to be any hope of a return to a free economy, the question of how the powers of trade-unions can be appropriately delimited in law as well as in fact is one of the most important of all the questions to which we must give our attention. I have many times already in the course of this outline felt tempted to refer you to the writings of the late Henry Simons, but I want now especially to draw your attention to his "Reflections on Syndicalism", which states this problem with rare courage and lucidity.[11]

[10] [In the United Kingdom, for example, the 1906 Trade Disputes Act provided trade unions with immunity from liability for damages arising from strike action. On this and other examples, see Hayek, *The Constitution of Liberty*, pp. 385–86. Hayek's views on unions are set out in detail on pp. 384–404 of that book.—Ed.]

[11] Henry C. Simons, "Some Reflections on Syndicalism", *Journal of Political Economy*, LII (March, 1944), pp. 1–25; reprinted in his *Economic Policy for a Free Society* (Chicago: University of Chicago Press, 1948), pp. 121–59. [Henry Calvert Simons (1899–1946) was an American economist who spent most of his career at the University of Chicago. In the essay cited by Hayek, Simons contends that the "essence" of liberalism "is a distrust of all concentrations of

CHAPTER SIX

The problem has recently, of course, become even bigger by the assumption on the part of most governments of the responsibility for what is called 'full employment' and by all its implications, and I do not see how we can, when we reach these problems, any longer separate them from the more general problems of monetary policy which I have suggested we should, as far as possible, keep separate. The same is true of the next set of major problems, which I can now only briefly mention—those of international trade, tariffs and foreign exchange control, etc. While on all these our long-run point of view ought not to be in doubt, they do, of course, raise real problems for the immediate future, which, however, we had probably better leave on one side as belonging to the questions of immediate policy rather than long-run principles. The same, I am afraid, we should probably not be entitled to do with regard to that other problem I have already mentioned—the problem of the relation between free and planned economies.

VI

If I am to confine myself to the enunciation of the main problems, I must now hurry to a conclusion and just touch on one more major field—that of taxation. It is, of course, by itself very large. I want to pick out only two aspects of it. The one is the effect of progressive income taxation at the rate which has now been reached and used for extreme egalitarian ends. The two consequences of this which seem to me the most serious are, on the one hand, that it makes for social immobility by making it practically impossible for the successful man to rise by accumulating a fortune and that, on the other, it has come near eliminating that most important element in any free society—the man of independent means, a figure whose essential role in maintaining

power": "The government must not tolerate erection of great private corporate empires or cartel organisations which suppress competition and rival in power great governmental units themselves . . . [M]ost important for the future, it must guard its powers against great trade-unions, both as pressure groups in government and as monopolists outside". See pp. 3–4 of H. Simons, "Some Reflections on Syndicalism", *Journal of Political Economy*, vol. 52, 1944, pp. 1–25. This requires government to provide and enforce a framework of rules that will limit both kinds of concentrations of power, thereby promoting 'effective' competition, and also restrict the scope for discretionary monetary policy, thereby making monetary conditions more predictable for economic actors. Elsewhere, Hayek describes *Economic Policy for a Free Society* as "one of the most important contributions made in recent times to our problem and as just the kind of work which is required to get discussion started on the fundamental issues. Even those who violently disagree with some of its suggestions should welcome it as a contribution which clearly and courageously raises the central problems of our time". See F. A. Hayek, "The Intellectuals and Socialism" [1949], reprinted as chapter 11 of F. A. Hayek, *Socialism and War: Essays, Documents, Reviews*, ed. B. Caldwell, vol. 10 (1997) of *The Collected Works of F. A. Hayek*, p. 234 n. 6.—Ed.]

100

a free opinion and generally the atmosphere of independence from government control we only begin to realise as he is disappearing from the stage.[12] Similar comments apply to modern inheritance taxation and particularly to estate duties as they exist in Great Britain. But, in mentioning this, I ought at once to add that inheritance taxes could, of course, be made an instrument toward greater social mobility and greater dispersion of property and, consequently, may have to be regarded as important tools of a truly liberal policy which ought not to stand condemned by the abuse which has been made of it.

There are many other important problems which I have not even mentioned. But I hope that what I have said will be sufficient to indicate the field which I had in mind when I suggested our present topic for discussion. It is too wide a field to treat the whole of it adequately even if we had much more time at our disposal. But, as I have said before, I hope that these discussions will be only a beginning and that it does not matter a great deal exactly where we start.

[12] [Hayek discusses the importance, and the demise, of the man of independent means at greater length in *The Constitution of Liberty*, pp. 184–96.—Ed.]

SEVEN

THE ECONOMIC CONDITIONS OF INTER-STATE FEDERALISM[1]

I

It is rightly regarded as one of the great advantages of interstate federation that it would do away with the impediments as to the movement of men, goods, and capital between the states and that it would render possible the creation of common rules of law, a uniform monetary system, and common control of communications. The material benefits that would spring from the creation of so large an economic area can hardly be overestimated, and it appears to be taken for granted that economic union and political union would be combined as a matter of course. But, since it will have to be argued here that the establishment of economic union will set very definite limitations to the realisation of widely cherished ambitions, we must begin by showing why the abolition of economic barriers between the members of the federation is not only a welcome concomitant but also an indispensable condition for the achievement of the main purpose of federation.

Unquestionably, the main purpose of interstate federation is to secure peace: to prevent war between the parts of the federation by eliminating causes of friction between them and by providing effective machinery for the settlement of any disputes which may arise between them and to prevent war between the federation and any independent states by making the former so strong as to eliminate any danger of attack from without. If this aim could be achieved by mere political union not extended to the economic sphere, many would probably be content to halt at the creation of a common government for the purpose of defence and the conduct of a common foreign policy,

---

[1] Reprinted from the *New Commonwealth Quarterly*, V, No. 2 (September, 1939), 131–49. [The essay was first published as F. A. von Hayek, "Economic Conditions of Inter-State Federalism", *New Commonwealth Quarterly*, vol. 5, 1939, pp. 131–49. © Commonwealth Education Trust. It was reprinted under the slightly different title "The Economic Conditions of Inter-state Federalism", and with the sub-section headings used in the 1939 version removed, as chapter 12 of F. A. Hayek, *Individualism and Economic Order* (Chicago: University of Chicago Press, 1948). The latter version of the paper is used here.—Ed.]

when a more far-reaching unification might impede the achievement of other ideals.

There are, however, very good reasons why all plans for interstate federation include economic union and even regard it as one of its main objectives and why there is no historical example of countries successfully combining in a common foreign policy and common defence without a common economic regime.[2] Although there are instances of countries concluding customs unions without providing machinery for a common foreign policy and common defence, the decision of several countries to rely upon a common foreign policy and a common defence force, as was the case with the parts of the dual monarchy of Austria-Hungary, has inevitably been combined with a common administration of matters of tariffs, money, and finance.

The relations of the Union with the outside world provide some important reasons for this, since a common representation in foreign countries and a common foreign policy is hardly conceivable without a common fiscal and monetary policy. If international treaties are to be concluded only by the Union, it follows that the Union must have sole power over all foreign relations, including the control of exports and imports, etc. If the Union government is to be responsible for the maintenance of peace, the Union and not its parts must be responsible for all decisions which will harm or benefit other countries.

No less important are the requirements of a common policy for defence. Not only would any interstate barriers to commerce prevent the best utilisation of the available resources and weaken the strength of the Union but the regional interests created by any sort of regional protectionism would inevitably raise obstacles to an effective defence policy. It would be difficult enough to subordinate sectional to Union interests; but should the component states remain separate communities of interest, whose inhabitants gain and suffer together because they are segregated from the rest of the Union by various kinds of barriers, it would be impossible to conduct a defence policy without being hampered at every stage by considerations of local interests. This, however, is only a facet of the wider problem which we must next consider.

The most compelling reasons for extending the union to the economic sphere are provided by the necessity to preserve the internal coherence of the Union. The existence of any measure of economic seclusion or isolation on the part of an individual state produces a solidarity of interests among all its inhabitants and conflicts between their interests and those of the inhabitants of other states which—although we have become so accustomed to such con-

---

[2] To what extent the British Commonwealth of Nations since the Statutes of Westminster constitutes an exception to this statement remains yet to be seen.

flicts as to take them for granted—is by no means a natural or inevitable thing. There is no valid reason why any change which affects a particular industry in a certain territory should impinge more heavily upon all or most of the inhabitants of that territory than upon people elsewhere. This would hold good equally for the territories which now constitute sovereign states and for any other arbitrarily delimited region, if it were not for custom barriers, separate monetary organisations, and all the other impediments to the free movement of men and goods. It is only because of these barriers that the incidence of the various benefits and damages affecting in the first instance a particular group of people will be mainly confined to the inhabitants of a given state and extend to almost all the people living within its frontiers. Such economic frontiers create communities of interest on a regional basis and of a most intimate character: they bring it about that all conflicts of interests tend to become conflicts between the same groups of people, instead of conflicts between groups of constantly varying composition, and that there will in consequence be perpetual conflicts between the inhabitants of a state as such instead of between the various individuals finding themselves arrayed, sometimes with one group of people against another, and at other times on another issue with the second group against the first. We need not stress here the extreme but nevertheless important case that national restriction will lead to considerable changes in the standard of life of the population of one integral state compared with that of another.[3] The mere fact that everybody will find again and again that their interests are closely bound up with those of one constant group of people and antagonistic to that of another group is bound to set up severe frictions between the groups as such. That there will always be communities of interest which will be similarly affected by a particular event or a particular measure is unavoidable. But it is clearly in the interest of unity of the larger whole that these groupings should not be permanent and, more particularly, that the various communities of interest should overlap territorially and never become lastingly identified with the inhabitants of a particular region.

We shall later examine how in existing federal states, even though the states are denied the grosser instruments of protectionism such as tariffs and independent currencies, the more concealed forms of protectionism tend to cause

[3] It is only because, in consequence of these conditions, the standard of life of all the people in a country will tend to move in the same direction that concepts such as the standard of living or the price level of a country cease to be mere statistical abstractions and become very concrete realities. [The word 'compared' has been used in the sentence to which this footnote is appended, in preference both to the phrase "in proportion to" used on p. 134 of the version of this essay published in *New Commonwealth Quarterly* and also to the word 'composed' found on p. 258 of the version published in *Individualism and Economic Order*, on the grounds that it more accurately captures the meaning intended by Hayek.—Ed.]

increasing friction, cumulative retaliation, and even the use of force between the individual states. And it is not difficult to imagine what forms this would take if the individual states were free to use the whole armoury of protectionism. It seems fairly certain that political union between erstwhile sovereign states would not last long unless accompanied by economic union.

II

The absence of tariff walls and the free movements of men and capital between the states of the federation has certain important consequences which are frequently overlooked. They limit to a great extent the scope of the economic policy of the individual states. If goods, men, and money can move freely over the interstate frontiers, it becomes clearly impossible to affect the prices of the different products through action by the individual state. The Union becomes one single market, and prices in its different parts will differ only by the costs of transport. Any change in any part of the Union in the conditions of production of any commodity which can be transported to other parts will affect prices everywhere. Similarly, any change in the opportunities for investment, or the remuneration of labour in any part of the Union, will, more or less promptly, affect the supply and the price of capital and labour in all other parts of the Union.

Now nearly all contemporary economic policy intended to assist particular industries tries to do so by influencing prices. Whether this is done by marketing boards or restriction schemes, by compulsory 'reorganisation' or the destruction of excess capacity of particular industries, the aim is always to limit supply and thus to raise prices. All this will clearly become impossible for the individual states within the Union. The whole armoury of marketing boards and other forms of monopolistic organisations of individual industries will cease to be at the disposal of state governments. If they still want to assist particular groups of producers, they will have to do so by direct subsidies from funds raised by ordinary taxation. But the methods by which, for example, in England, the producers of sugar and milk, bacon and potatoes, cotton yarn, coal, and iron have all been protected in recent years against 'ruinous competition', from within and without, will not be available.

It will also be clear that the states within the Union will not be able to pursue an independent monetary policy. With a common monetary unit, the latitude given to the national central banks will be restricted at least as much as it was under a rigid gold standard—and possibly rather more since, even under the traditional gold standard, the fluctuations in exchanges between countries were greater than those between different parts of a single state, or than would be desirable to allow within the Union.[4] Indeed, it appears doubtful whether, in a Union with a universal monetary system, independent national central banks would continue to exist; they would probably have to be organised into a sort of Federal Reserve System. But, in any case, a national monetary policy which was predominantly guided by the economic and financial conditions of the individual state would inevitably lead to the disruption of the universal monetary system. Clearly, therefore, all monetary policy would have to be a federal and not a state matter.

But even with respect to less thoroughgoing interference with economic life than the regulation of money and prices entails, the possibilities open to the individual states would be severely limited. While the states could, of course, exercise control of the qualities of goods and the methods of production employed, it must not be overlooked that, provided the state could not exclude commodities produced in other parts of the Union, any burden placed on a particular industry by state legislation would put it at a serious disadvantage as opposed to similar industries in other parts of the Union. As has been shown by experience in existing federations, even such legislation as the restriction of child labour or of working hours becomes difficult to carry out for the individual state.

Also, in the purely financial sphere, the methods of raising revenue would be somewhat restricted for the individual states. Not only would the greater mobility between the states make it necessary to avoid all sorts of taxation which would drive capital or labour elsewhere, but there would also be considerable difficulties with many kinds of indirect taxation. In particular if, as would undoubtedly be desirable, the waste of frontier controls between the states were to be avoided, it would prove difficult to tax any commodities which could easily be imported. This would preclude not only such forms of state taxation as, for instance, a tobacco monopoly but probably many excise taxes.

It is not intended here to deal more fully with these limitations which federation would impose upon the economic policy of the individual states. The general effect in this direction has probably been sufficiently illustrated by what has already been said. It is in fact likely that, in order to prevent evasions of the fundamental provisions securing free movement of men, goods, and capital, the restrictions it would be desirable for the constitution of the

[4] On the questions arising in this connection compare the author's *Monetary Nationalism and International Stability* (London, 1937). [Hayek refers to F. A. Hayek, *Monetary Nationalism and International Stability*, Publication No. 18, The Graduate Institute of International Studies, Geneva (Geneva, London, and New York: Longmans, Green, 1937). The five lectures on international monetary issues which compose that work were republished as chapter 1 of F. A. Hayek, *Good Money, Part II: The Standard*, ed. S. Kresge, vol. 6 (1999) of *The Collected Works of F. A. Hayek* (Chicago: University of Chicago Press; London: Routledge).—Ed.]

federation to impose on the freedom of the individual states would have to be even greater than we have hitherto assumed and that their power of independent action would have to be limited still further. We shall have to revert later to this point.

Here it need only be added that these limitations will apply not only to state economic policy but also to economic policy conducted by trade and professional organisations extending over the territory of the state. Once frontiers cease to be closed and free movement is secured, all these national organisations, whether trade-unions, cartels, or professional associations, will lose their monopolistic position and thus, *qua* national organisations, their power to control the supply of their services or products.

III

The reader who has followed the argument so far will probably conclude that if, in a federation, the economic powers of the individual states will be thus limited, the federal government will have to take over the functions which the states can no longer perform and will have to do all the planning and regulating which the states cannot do. But, at this point, new difficulties present themselves. It will be advisable in this short survey to discuss these problems chiefly in connection with the best established form of government intervention in economic life, that is, tariffs. In the main, our remarks on tariffs pertain equally to other forms of restrictive or protective measures. A few references to particular kinds of government regulation will be added later.

In the first instance, protection for the whole of a particular industry within the Union may be of little use to those who now profit from protection, because the producers against whose competition they will desire protection will then be within the Union. The English wheat farmer will have little profit from a tariff which includes him and the Canadian and perhaps also the Argentinean wheat producer in the same free-trade area. The British motor-car manufacturer will have little advantage from a tariff wall which encloses at the same time the American producers. This point need hardly be laboured any further.

But even where, outside the federation, there should be important producers against whose competition a particular industry as a whole wants to be protected, there will arise special difficulties which are not present, to the same extent, within a national tariff system.

It should, perhaps, be pointed out, first, that, in order that a particular industry should benefit from a tariff, it is necessary that the tariff on its products should be higher than the tariffs on the commodities which the producers in that industry consume. A flat tariff at a uniform rate on all imports merely benefits all industries competing with imports at the expense of all others; but the incidence of these benefits is entirely indiscriminate, and they are not likely to assist where help is intended. Although such a tariff would tend to decrease the material wealth of everybody in the Union, it would probably be used to strengthen the political coherence between the members of the federation. There appear, therefore, to be no particular difficulties connected with it.

Difficulties arise only when a tariff is used to assist a particular industry to grow more rapidly than it would do without it or to protect it against adverse influence which would make it decline. In these cases, in order to subsidise one particular group of people, a sacrifice is inevitably imposed on all the other producers and consumers.

In the national state current ideologies make it comparatively easy to persuade the rest of the community that it is in their interest to protect 'their' iron industry or 'their' wheat production or whatever it be. An element of national pride in 'their' industry and considerations of national strength in case of war generally induce people to consent to the sacrifice. The decisive consideration is that their sacrifice benefits compatriots whose position is familiar to them. Will the same motives operate in favour of other members of the Union? Is it likely that the French peasant will be willing to pay more for his fertilizer to help the British chemical industry? Will the Swedish workman be ready to pay more for his oranges to assist the Californian grower? Or the clerk in the city of London be ready to pay more for his shoes or his bicycle to help American or Belgian workmen? Or the South African miner prepared to pay more for his sardines to help the Norwegian fishermen?

It seems clear that, in a federation, the problem of agreeing on a common tariff will raise problems different in kind from those that arise in a national state. It would lack the support of the strong nationalist ideologies, the sympathies with the neighbour; and even the argument of defence would lose much of its power of conviction if the Union were really strong enough to have little to fear. It is difficult to visualise how, in a federation, agreement could be reached on the use of tariffs for the protection of particular industries. The same applies to all other forms of protection. Provided that there is great diversity of conditions among the various countries, as will inevitably be the case in a federation, the obsolescent or declining industry clamouring for assistance will almost invariably encounter, in the same field and within the federation, progressive industries which demand freedom of development. It will be much harder to retard progress in one part of the federation in order to maintain standards of life in another part than to do the same thing in a national state.

But even where it is not simply a question of 'regulating' (i.e., curbing) the progress of one group in order to protect another group from competition, the diversity of conditions and the different stages of economic development reached by the various parts of the federation will raise serious obstacles to federal legislation. Many forms of state interference, welcome in one stage of economic progress, are regarded in another as a great impediment. Even such legislation as the limitation of working hours or compulsory unemployment insurance, or the protection of amenities, will be viewed in a different light in poor and in rich regions and may in the former actually harm and rouse violent opposition from the kind of people who in the richer regions demand it and profit from it. Such legislation will, on the whole, have to be confined to the extent to which it can be applied locally without at the same time imposing any restrictions on mobility, such as a law of settlements.

These problems are, of course, not unfamiliar in national states as we know them. But they are made less difficult by the comparative homogeneity, the common convictions and ideals, and the whole common tradition of the people of a national state. In fact, the existing sovereign national states are mostly of such dimensions and composition as to render possible agreement on an amount of state interference which they would not suffer if they were either much smaller or much larger. In the former instance (and what matters is not merely size in terms of numbers of inhabitants or area but size relative to the existing groups, which are at the same time more or less homogeneous and comparatively self-supporting), the attempts to make the national state self-supporting would be out of the question. If counties, or even smaller districts, were the sovereign units, there would be comparatively few industries in every such unit which would be protected. All the regions which did not possess, and could not create, a particular industry would constitute free markets for the produce of that industry. If, on the other hand, the sovereign units were much larger than they are today, it would be much more difficult to place a burden on the inhabitants of one region in order to assist the inhabitants of a very distant region who might differ from the former not only in language but also in almost every other respect.

Planning, or central direction of economic activity, presupposes the existence of common ideals and common values; and the degree to which planning can be carried is limited to the extent to which agreement on such a common scale of values can be obtained or enforced.[5] It is clear that such

---

[5] Cf. on this and the following the present author's *Freedom and the Economic System* ("Public Policy Pamphlets," No. 29 [Chicago, 1939]), and, more recently, *The Road to Serfdom* (Chicago: University of Chicago Press, 1944). [Hayek refers to F. A. Hayek, "Freedom and the Economic System", Public Policy Pamphlet No. 29, published in a series edited by H. D. Gideonse (Chicago: University of Chicago Press, 1939). It was later republished as chapter 9 of F. A. Hayek, *Socialism and War: Essays, Documents, Reviews*, ed. B. Caldwell, vol. 10 (1997) of *The Collected Works of F. A. Hayek*. This essay, which has its origins in a magazine article with the same title published under Hayek's name in 1938, subsequently formed the basis for Hayek's book *The Road to Serfdom*

agreement will be limited in inverse proportion to the homogeneity and the similarity in outlook and tradition possessed by the inhabitants of an area. Although, in the national state, the submission to the will of a majority will be facilitated by the myth of nationality, it must be clear that people will be reluctant to submit to any interference in their daily affairs when the majority which directs the government is composed of people of different nationalities and different traditions. It is, after all, only common sense that the central government in a federation composed of many different people will have to be restricted in scope if it is to avoid meeting an increasing resistance on the part of the various groups which it includes. But what could interfere more thoroughly with the intimate life of the people than the central direction of economic life, with its inevitable discrimination between groups? There seems to be little possible doubt that the scope for the regulation of economic life will be much narrower for the central government of a federation than for national states. And since, as we have seen, the power of the states which comprise the federation will be yet more limited, much of the interference with economic life to which we have become accustomed will be altogether impracticable under a federal organisation.

The point can be best illustrated if we consider for a moment the problems raised by the most developed form of planning, socialism. Let us first take the question of whether a socialist state, for example, the U.S.S.R., could enter a federation with the Atlantic democratic states. The answer is decisively in the negative—not because the other states would be unwilling to admit Russia but because the U.S.S.R. could never submit to the conditions which federation would impose and permit the free movement of goods, men, and money across her frontiers while, at the same time, retaining her socialist economy.

If, on the other hand, we consider the possibility of a socialist regime for the federation as a whole, including Russia, the impracticability of such a scheme is at once obvious. With the differences in the standard of life, in tradition and education, which would exist in such a federation, it would certainly be impossible to get a democratic solution of the central problems which socialist planning would raise. But even if we consider a federation composed merely of the present democratic states, such as that proposed by Clarence Streit, the difficulties of introducing a common socialist regime would scarcely be smaller.[6]

(Chicago: University of Chicago Press, 1944), now republished as F. A. Hayek, *The Road to Serfdom: Text and Documents*, ed. B. Caldwell, vol. 2 (2007) of *The Collected Works of F. A. Hayek*. See in particular pp. 38, 53 of the latter volume. The relationship between these works is discussed in B. Caldwell, "Introduction", in Hayek, *Socialism and War*, pp. 37–43, and in B. Caldwell, "Introduction", in Hayek, *The Road to Serfdom*, pp. 6–7.—Ed.]

[6] [Clarence Streit (1896–1986) was an American journalist whose experience covering the rise of totalitarian regimes in Europe and the collapse of the League of Nations in the 1930s led him to advocate the creation of a union of democratic countries, modeled on American feder-

That Englishmen or Frenchmen should entrust the safeguarding of their lives, liberty, and property—in short, the functions of the liberal state—to a suprastate organisation is conceivable. But that they should be willing to give the government of a federation the power to regulate their economic life, to decide what they should produce and consume, seems neither probable nor desirable. Yet, at the same time, in a federation these powers could not be left to the national states; therefore, federation would appear to mean that neither government could have powers for socialist planning of economic life.

IV

The conclusion that, in a federation, certain economic powers, which are now generally wielded by the national states, could be exercised neither by the federation nor by the individual states, implies that there would have to be less government all round if federation is to be practicable. Certain forms of economic policy will have to be conducted by the federation or by nobody at all. Whether the federation will exercise these powers will depend on the possibility of reaching true agreement, not only on *whether* these powers are to be used, but on *how* they are to be used. The main point is that, in many cases in which it will prove impossible to reach such agreement, we shall have to resign ourselves rather to have no legislation in a particular field than the state legislation which would break up the economic unity of the federation. Indeed, this readiness to have no legislation at all on some subjects rather than state legislation will be the acid test of whether we are intellectually mature for the achievement of suprastate organisation.

This is a point on which, in existing federations, difficulties have constantly arisen and on which, it must be admitted, the 'progressive' movements have generally sided with the powers of darkness. In the United States, in particular, there has been a strong tendency on the part of all progressives to favour state legislation in all cases where union legislation could not be achieved, irrespective of whether such state legislation was compatible with the preservation of the economic unity of the union. In consequence, in the United States and similarly in Switzerland, the separate economic policies of the individual states have already gone far in the direction of bringing about a gradual disintegration of the common economic area.[7]

---

alism. See C. Streit, *Union Now: A Proposal for a Federal Union of the Democracies of the North Atlantic* (New York: Harper & Brothers, 1939). Hayek also discusses the possibility of federation in *Socialism and War*, pp. 162–64.—Ed.]

[7] For the United States cf. R. L. Buell, *Death by Tariff: Protectionism in State and Federal Legislation* ("Public Policy Pamphlets," No. 27 [Chicago, 1939]), and F. E. Melder, *Barriers to Inter-state Commerce in the United States* (Orono, Me., 1937). [See R. L. Buell, *Death by Tariff: Protectionism in State*

The experience in these federations makes it appear that, to prevent such trends, it is scarcely sufficient to prohibit tariffs and similar obvious impediments to interstate commerce. Evasion of such rules by an individual state which has embarked upon a course of national planning by means of administrative regulations has proved so easy that all the effects of protection can be achieved by means of such provisions as sanitary regulations, requirements of inspection, and the charging of fees for these and other administrative controls. In view of the inventiveness shown by state legislators in this respect, it seems clear that no specific prohibitions in the constitution of the federation would suffice to prevent such developments; the federal government would probably have to be given general restraining powers to this end. This means that the federation will have to possess the negative power of preventing individual states from interfering with economic activity in certain ways, although it may not have the positive power of acting in their stead. In the United States the various clauses of the Constitution safeguarding property and freedom of contract, and particularly the 'due process' clauses of the Fifth and Fourteenth amendments, have, to some extent, fulfilled this function and contributed probably more than is generally realised to prevent an even more rapid disintegration into many separate economic areas; but they have in consequence been the object of persistent attack on the part of all those who demand more rapid extension of state control of economic life.[8]

There will, of course, always be certain kinds of government activity which will be done most efficiently for areas corresponding to the present national states and which, at the same time, can be exercised nationally without endangering the economic unity of the federation. But, on the whole, it is likely that in a federation the weakening of the economic powers of the individual states would and should gradually be carried much further than will at first be evident. Not only will their powers be decreased by the functions taken over by the federation, and by those which cannot be exercised by either federation or states but must be left free from legislative control, but there will probably also be a great deal of devolution of powers from the states to smaller units. There are many activities which are today entrusted to the sovereign states merely in order to strengthen the states as such, but which could really be carried out much more efficiently locally, or, at any rate, by smaller units. In a federation all the arguments for centralisation which are based on the desire to make the

---

and *Federal Legislation*, Public Policy Pamphlet No. 27 (Chicago: University of Chicago Press, 1939), and F. E. Melder, *State and Local Barriers to Interstate Commerce in the United States: A Study in Economic Sectionalism* (Orono: University of Maine, 1937).—Ed.]

[8] [The Fifth and Fourteenth Amendments to the U.S. Constitution require that no citizen should be "deprived of life, liberty or property without due process of law", the latter including the right to appear before a grand jury, the prohibition of double jeopardy, and protection against self-incrimination.—Ed.]

sovereign national states as such as strong as possible disappear—in fact, the converse seems to apply. Not only could most of the desirable forms of planning be conducted by comparatively small territorial units, but the competition between them, together with the impossibility of erecting barriers, would at the same time form a salutary check on their activities and, while leaving the door open for desirable experimentation, would keep it roughly within the appropriate limits.

It should, perhaps, be emphasised that all this does not imply that there will not be ample scope for economic policy in a federation and that there is no need for extreme laissez faire in economic matters. It means only that planning in a federation cannot assume the forms which today are preeminently known under this term; that there must be no substitution of day-to-day interference and regulation for the impersonal forces of the market; and, in particular, that there must be no trace of that "national development by controlled monopolies" to which, as has recently been pointed out in an influential weekly journal, "British leaders are growing accustomed".[9] In a federation economic policy will have to take the form of providing a rational permanent framework within which individual initiative will have the largest possible scope and will be made to work as beneficently as possible; and it will have to supplement the working of the competitive mechanism where, in the nature of the case, certain services cannot be brought forth and be regulated by the price system. But it will, at least in so far as the policy of the federation as such is concerned, essentially have to be a long-term policy, in which the fact that "in the long run we are all dead" is a decided advantage; and it must not be used, as is often the case today, as a pretext for acting on the principle *après nous le déluge*; for the long-term character of the decisions to be taken makes it practically impossible to foresee the incidence of their effects upon individuals and groups and thus prevents the issue from being decided by a struggle between the most powerful 'interests'.[10]

It does not come within the scope of a short article to consider in any detail the positive tasks of the liberal economic policy which a federation would

[9] *Spectator,* March 3, 1939. [The words quoted by Hayek are taken from an unsigned leading article entitled "The Government as a Business Partner", *The Spectator,* no. 5775 (March 3, 1939), p. 337.—Ed.]

[10] [Hayek quotes the words of British economist John Maynard Keynes, Baron Keynes of Tilton (1883–1946). In the course of a discussion of what the quantity theory of money suggests will be the impact on the economy of a change in the quantity of cash circulating within it, Keynes wrote as follows: "[T]his *long run* is a misleading guide to current affairs. *In the long run* we are all dead. Economists set themselves too easy, too useless a task if in tempestuous seasons they can only tell us that when the storm is long past the ocean is flat again". See J. M. Keynes, *A Tract on Monetary Reform* (London: Macmillan and Co., 1923), p. 80. Hayek's opinion of Keynes and his economics can be explored at length by consulting F. A. Hayek, *Contra Keynes and Cambridge: Essays, Correspondence,* ed. B. Caldwell, vol. 9 (1995) of *The Collected Works of F. A. Hayek.*—Ed.]

have to pursue. Nor is it even possible to give here further consideration to such important problems as those of monetary or colonial policy which will, of course, continue to exist in a federation. On the last point it may, however, be added that the question which probably would be raised first, i.e., whether colonies ought to be administered by the states or by the federation, would be of comparatively minor importance. With a real open-door policy for all members of the federation, the economic advantages derived from the possession of colonies, whether the colonies were administered federally or nationally, would be approximately the same to all the members of the federation. But, in general, it would undoubtedly be preferable that their administration should be a federal and not a state matter.

V

Since it has been argued so far that an essentially liberal economic regime is a necessary condition for the success of any interstate federation, it may be added, in conclusion, that the converse is no less true: the abrogation of national sovereignties and the creation of an effective international order of law is a necessary complement and the logical consummation of the liberal programme. In a recent discussion of international liberalism, it has been rightly contended that it was one of the main deficiencies of nineteenth-century liberalism that its advocates did not sufficiently realise that the achievement of the recognised harmony of interests between the inhabitants of the different states was only possible within the framework of international security.[11] The conclusions which Professor Robbins drew from his considerations of these problems and which are summed up in the statement that "there must be neither alliance nor complete unification; neither *Staatenbund* nor *Einheitsstaat* but *Bundesstaat*",[12] are essentially the same as those which have recently been elaborated by Clarence Streit in greater detail in their political aspects.

[11] L. C. Robbins, *Economic Planning and International Order* (1937), p. 240. [Lionel Robbins (1898–1984), Lord Robbins of Clare Market, was Professor of Economics at the London School of Economics and Political Science from 1929 to 1961 and for many years one of Hayek's closest friends and colleagues. On pp. 240–45 of his *Economic Planning and International Order* (London: Macmillan and Co., 1937), Robbins advocated a federation of nation states, arguing that the maintenance of international security required the creation of an international authority to which nation states would surrender the right to wage war. Robbins describes the resulting arrangement as a federation.—Ed.]

[12] *Ibid.*, p. 245. [Hayek misquotes slightly, omitting without acknowledgement two words from the sentence actually penned by Robbins: "There must be neither alliance nor complete unification, but Federation; neither *Staatenbund*, nor *Einheitsstaat*, but *Bundesstaat*." See Robbins, *Economic Planning and International Order*, p. 245.—Ed.]

That nineteenth-century liberalism did not succeed more fully is due largely to its failure to develop in this direction; and the cause is mainly that, because of historical accidents, it successively joined forces first with nationalism and later with socialism, both forces being equally incompatible with its main principle.[13] That liberalism became first allied with nationalism was due to the historical coincidence that, during the nineteenth century, it was nationalism which in Ireland, Greece, Belgium, and Poland and later in Italy and Austro-Hungary fought against the same sort of oppression which liberalism opposed. It later became allied with socialism because agreement as to some of the ultimate ends for a time obscured the utter incompatibility of the methods by which the two movements tried to reach their goal. But now when nationalism and socialism have combined—not only in name—into a powerful organisation which threatens the liberal democracies, and when, even within these democracies, the socialists are becoming steadily more nationalist and the nationalists steadily more socialist, is it too much to hope for a rebirth of real liberalism, true to its ideal of freedom and internationalism and returned from its temporary aberrations into the nationalist and the socialist camps?[14] The idea of interstate federation as the consistent development of the liberal point of view should be able to provide a new *point d'appui* for all those liberals who have despaired of and deserted their creed during the periods of wandering.

[13] This trend can be well observed in John Stuart Mill. His gradual movement toward socialism is, of course, well known, but he also accepted more of the nationalist doctrines than is compatible with his wholly liberal programme. In *Considerations on Representative Government* (p. 298) he states: "it is in general a necessary condition of free institutions, that the boundaries of governments should coincide in the main with those of nationalities". Against this view, Lord Acton argued that "[t]he combination of different nations in one State is as necessary a condition of civilised life as the combination of men in society" and that "[t]his diversity in the same State is a firm barrier against the intrusion of the government beyond the political sphere which is common to all into the social department which escapes legislation and is ruled by spontaneous laws" (*History of Freedom and Other Essays* [1909], p. 290). [The words of philosopher, political economist, and social reformer John Stuart Mill (1806–73) appear on pp. 291–92 of his *Considerations on Representative Government* (London: Parker, Son, and Bourn, 1861). For more on what Hayek saw as Mill's gradual shift towards socialism, see F. A. Hayek, "Liberalism" [1978], reprinted as chapter 1 of this volume, p. 18 n. 24. John Emerich Edward Dalberg-Acton (1834–1902) was a classical liberal historian and moralist, the key theme of whose work was the 'history of liberty'. Hayek quotes from J. Dalberg-Acton, *The History of Freedom and Other Essays*, ed. J. Figgis and R. Laurence (London: Macmillan and Co., 1909), p. 290. In earlier versions of this essay, Hayek misquoted Acton by writing 'intention' rather than 'intrusion', an error corrected here. Hayek discusses Acton in more detail in F. A. Hayek, "Historians and the Future of Europe" [1944] and in "The Actonian Revival: On Lord Acton (1834–1902)" [1953], reprinted as chapters 8 and 9 respectively of F. A. Hayek, *The Fortunes of Liberalism: Essays on Austrian Economics and the Ideal of Freedom,* ed. Peter G. Klein, vol. 4 (1992) of *The Collected Works of F. A. Hayek.*—Ed.]

[14] [Hayek's reflections on National Socialism, to which he alludes here, can be found in *The Road to Serfdom*, pp. 60–63, 144–46, and 181–92.—Ed.]

This liberalism of which we speak is, of course, not a party matter; it is a view which, before World War I, provided a common ground for nearly all the citizens of the Western democracies and which is the basis of democratic government. If one party has perhaps preserved slightly more of this liberal spirit than the others, they have nevertheless all strayed from the fold, some in one direction and some in another. But the realisation of the ideal of an international democratic order demands a resuscitation of the ideal in its true form. Government by agreement is only possible provided that we do not require the government to act in fields other than those in which we can obtain true agreement. If, in the international sphere, democratic government should only prove to be possible if the tasks of the international government are limited to an essentially liberal programme, it would no more than confirm the experience in the national sphere, in which it is daily becoming more obvious that democracy will work only if we do not overload it and if the majorities do not abuse their power of interfering with individual freedom. Yet, if the price we have to pay for an international democratic government is the restriction of the power and scope of government, it is surely not too high a price, and all those who genuinely believe in democracy ought to be prepared to pay it. The democratic principle of "counting heads in order to save breaking them" is, after all, the only method of peaceful change yet invented which has been tried and has not been found wanting.[15] Whatever one may think about the desirability of other aims of government, surely the prevention of war or civil strife ought to take precedence, and, if achievement lies only in limiting government to this and a few other main purposes, these other ideals will have to give place.[16]

[15] [Hayek refers here to the words of English lawyer, journalist, and political philosopher James Fitzjames Stephen (1829–94), who in the course of a critique of the work of John Stuart Mill wrote as follows: "Parliamentary government is simply a mild and disguised form of compulsion. We agree to try strength by counting heads instead of breaking heads, but the principle is exactly the same. It is not the wisest side which wins, but the one which for the time being shows its superior strength (of which no doubt wisdom is one element) by enlisting the largest amount of active sympathy in its support. The minority gives way not because it is convinced that it is wrong, but because it is convinced that it is a minority". See J. Stephen, *Liberty, Equality, Fraternity*, 2nd edn. (London: H. Elder and Co., 1874), p. 31.—Ed.]

[16] [In a later work, Hayek summarises his position as follows: "What we need and can hope to achieve is . . . an international political authority which, without power to direct the different people what they must do, must be able to restrain them from action which will damage others. The powers which must devolve on an international authority are . . . that minimum of powers without which it is impossible to preserve peaceful relationships, i.e., essentially the powers of the ultra-liberal 'laissez-faire' state. And, even more than in the national sphere, it is essential that these powers of the international authority should be strictly circumscribed by the Rule of Law . . . [T]he principle of federation is the only form of association of different peoples which will create an international order without putting an undue strain on their legitimate desire for independence." See Hayek, *The Road to Serfdom*, pp. 231–32.—Ed.]

I make no apology for pointing out obstacles in the way of a goal in whose value I profoundly believe. I am convinced that these difficulties are genuine and that, if we do not admit them from the beginning, they may at a later date form the rock on which all the hopes for international organisation may founder. The sooner we recognise these difficulties, the sooner we can hope to overcome them. If, as it appears to me, ideals shared by many can be realised only by means which few at present favour, neither academic impartiality nor considerations of expediency should prevent one from saying what one recognises to be the right means for the given end—even if these means should happen to be those favoured by a political party.

EIGHT

THE MEANING OF GOVERNMENT INTERFERENCE[1]

The case for a free economy would be so much more effective if it were generally stated in less question-begging terms. In the way in which it is usually stated it is only too easy to distort it into a caricature and expose it to ridicule. Especially the time-honoured phrase about 'non-interference' of government with business can only too easily be misrepresented as a demand for complete inaction of government in economic matters. The advocates of a free economy of course have never meant this in a literal sense. They all count, and must count, on the government enforcing some laws. Although it is really ridiculous that it should be necessary to state this again and again, the opponent of government 'interference' is not an anarchist. The question is not really whether government should ever concern itself with economic matters at all, but what kind of government action is legitimate, what should be its range and how it should be limited.

The instinctive aversion which every believer in a free economy feels about admitting this, is only too understandable. It seems as if, once one abandons the opposition against all government interference, one has let in the thin end of the wedge and there is no way of stopping its spread. But such an indiscriminate opposition to all government action, or even the appearance of such a rigid attitude, can only weaken the case for a free economy. It makes it seem as if in fact those who advocate a free economy are merely opposing those acts of government which are harmful to them personally but approving of those which benefit them. This, of course, is not the case. But in such a position it is essential that a clear principle be stated by which we can distinguish between the objectionable kind of government 'interference' and the kind of government action which, though it may be wise or unwise, harmful or beneficial, is not subject to that objection in principle which applies to all interference in this specific sense.

---

[1] [This essay, which dates from 1950, is hitherto unpublished. The version used here can be found in the Hayek Collection, box 107, folder 13, Hoover Institution Archives. Hayek explores similar themes in another unpublished, and also undated, essay, namely "Planning and Competitive Order", which can be found in the Hayek Collection, box 104, folder 1.—Ed.]

Is there such a principle which would enable us to distinguish between government measures which are *a limine* objectionable and others which will have to be examined for their individual merits; between a type of government action which can be ruled out in all circumstances and another type which may be foolish or wise in the particular instance but which is not subject to the same objection of principle which applies to 'government interference' proper?

I believe there is one very important distinction of the kind, a very old distinction, but one which urgently needs to be revived and to be made again the fundamental touchstone by which we judge the justice or injustice of all laws. This is the old principle of *equality before the law*.[2]

It is closely connected with another distinction which used to be sacred to the tradition of Western Liberalism but which tends to be forgotten: the distinction between government by law and government by men. I believe that if we once again succeeded to limit the activities of government to what can be decided by fixed rules announced in advance, we would eliminate a great deal of those activities which the believer in a free economy thinks objectionable. We would still be far from positively defining the kind of action which was desirable. But we should have erected one important safeguard against that piecemeal encroachment which seems almost inevitable if the opposition against all government action is abandoned and no other principle put in its place.

It is significant that during the last fifty or sixty years this 'merely formal' equality before the law has been the subject of constant attack from all people who regarded themselves as 'progressives'. I believe it was Anatole France who invented the cliché about "the law which, with majestic impartiality, prohibits rich and poor alike to sleep under haystacks or on park benches".[3] The constant ridicule which has since been poured on this fundamental and indispensable maxim of a free society has done much to undermine belief in the possibility of any impartial law. Yet there can be little doubt that it is precisely this majestic impartiality of the law which applies the same principles irrespective of the different circumstances of different people which constitutes the only barrier against arbitrariness of government action.

---

[2] [Hayek discussed the notion of 'equality before the law' at greater length in a set of lectures delivered in Cairo on behalf of the National Bank of Egypt in 1955. See F. A. Hayek, "The Political Ideal of the Rule of Law" [1955], reprinted as chapter 5 of F. A. Hayek, *The Market and Other Orders*, ed. B. Caldwell, vol. 15 (2014) of *The Collected Works of F. A. Hayek* (Chicago: University of Chicago Press; London: Routledge).—Ed.]

[3] [Anatole France, pseudonym for Jacques Anatole Thibault (1844–1924), was a French man of letters. The passage on which Hayek draws can be found on p. 118 of France's *Le Lys Rouge* (Paris: Calmann-Lévy, 1894), where France refers to "la majestueuse égalité des lois, qui interdit au riche comme au pauvre de coucher sous les ponts, de mendier dans les rues et de voler du pain." A more faithful rendition than that provided by Hayek is: "The majestic equality of the law that forbids the rich as well as the poor to sleep under bridges, to beg in the streets and to steal bread".—Ed.]

It also deserves emphasis that exception from equality before the law is the only true meaning of privilege. So long as government action is guided and restricted by abstract rules which apply equally to all people, it would be nonsense to speak of privilege. But if with regard to one person government acts on principles which it is not willing to apply to others, even if it does so to protect weakness or to compensate for misfortune, this is undoubtedly the granting of privilege. The only meaning we can attach to privilege is exception from a general rule in view of personal circumstances.

Similarly, the only meaning of arbitrariness is action which is not in conformity with a general rule which applies equally to all. Whether any action is arbitrary or not can be decided only if there exists a recognised rule which should guide such action. Wherever any authority is given discretion, its action within the limits of this discretion is necessarily arbitrary, and in particular can never be controlled by any judicial revision. A court, by applying a rule may decide whether an authority has acted within the limits of its discretion or not. But if the decision has been within the limits fixed by the law, an administrative decision cannot be impugned, however arbitrary in the true sense it may be.

How far would a strict application of the principle of equality before the law prevent an excessive growth of governmental powers? How many of those acts which are loosely described as 'government interference' would become impossible if the principle were fully adhered to? I believe so large a part that I should like to propose that we should regard the infringement of equality before the law as the best *definition* of 'government interference'.[4] Whether productive government actions which can be carried out by laying down a general rule applying to all people and all times are desirable or not seems to me a matter of expediency. But that government measures which involve discrimination between different people, the application of different rules to different people, are objectionable at all times and should be ruled out altogether, appears to me a matter of general principle. It is a principle which if adopted, would admittedly often preclude government action the immediate effect of which might only be beneficial. But this will often be true of prohibiting lying or even of murder. Unless we are willing to restrict the powers of government even in respects where it might be used for good purposes, we shall not succeed in preventing an indefinite growth of governmental powers. To allow everything which seems expedient for the achievement of a desirable end is to dispense with all moral principles. The submis-

---

[4] [Hayek continued to hold similar views later in his career. See, for example, Hayek, "The Political Ideal of the Rule of Law," p. 178, and F. A. Hayek, *The Mirage of Social Justice*, vol. 2 (1976) of *Law, Legislation and Liberty* (Chicago: University of Chicago Press; London: Routledge, 1973–1979), pp. 128–29.—Ed.]

sion to rules which must be observed irrespective of whether in the particular instance their infringement is harmful or not, is the main condition for the possibility of order in a free society. And to these rules the state should be no less subject than the individual.

It is fairly obvious that most of the controls of economic life which are nowadays employed in the service of government 'planning' could not be enforced if the powers of government were restricted to carrying out fixed general rules. Where the aim of government policy is that other things should be produced than those which would be produced in a free economy, or that the things produced should go to people other than those who would buy them on a free market, it is evidently necessary that the government should discriminate between different people: it will have to allow some people to do things which others are prevented from doing, or compel some people to do things which others need not do. Such discrimination can evidently not be laid down in the form of the general rules which are alone justly called laws. They must take the form of specific orders, which usually will have to be made in the light of the particular circumstances of the moment and for that reason must be left to the executive authorities. These agencies must be given power to do what at a given moment is necessary to achieve a given result, but what specific action in the given circumstances will be most appropriate to achieve that result must be left to their decision.

It is a familiar fact, confirmed everywhere the growth of government control of economic life has proceeded very far, that the discretionary powers of the executive authorities are constantly extended. At first the legislature usually tries to keep these powers within limits by laying down general principles by which their exercise is to be guided. But these limits become constantly wider and wider. In a recent British instance, the Town and Country Planning Act of 1947, Parliament has gone so far as even to provide that the 'general principles' be fixed by ministerial order on which one of the most far reaching tools of control, the so called 'development charges', be levied.[5]

All this is not an accident. If the government by its actions wants to achieve specific results, it must direct particular people to do what it wants done. Direct control however means discrimination. If the government is not allowed to discriminate, it cannot exercise direct controls. It can at most create conditions which will make it attractive to some people by their own choice to do what the government wants done. I do not want to say that these indirect controls are desirable. In most instances quite the contrary. But they are less pernicious than the direct controls. And they interfere of necessity less with the planning of private business. This is so because their effectiveness depends

---

[5] [Hayek examines this case in more detail in F. A. Hayek, "The Economics of Development Charges" [1949], reprinted as chapter 9 of this volume.—Ed.]

on private business being able to adjust itself to the altered conditions created by the government. With direct controls the decision is taken entirely out of the hands of business. With indirect controls the government merely changes the conditions of the choice to be made by business, but still leaves the choice to business management.

Let us briefly survey the kind of government controls which would be precluded if the powers of government were limited to enforcing general rules applying equally to all people. All forms of licenses, permits, allocations, and price fixing would become impossible since all these methods imply that the government has to decide who is to get what. They *ipso facto* involve discrimination. Most forms of quota or subsidies would become equally difficult; it is true, they would not become impossible. It would still be possible, by proclaiming a general rule, to fix a global quota, say of the amount of a commodity to be produced or imported, and then to sell these quotas by auction to the highest bidder. Or to offer the same kind of subsidy to anybody who is willing to produce a certain commodity. As I said before, I believe that these things are almost always undesirable. But they not only give the government less power than the direct controls. They also 'interfere', in a very real sense, less with the private planning of business activities. And what is even more important, they differ only in degree from some other kind of action, such as taxation, which any government must take. I can therefore see no *general* principle on which they can be objected to *in toto*. In so far as they are concerned, every particular measure must be examined on its merit. I shall later try to show that there is still a strong presumption against most actions of this kind undertaken in the service of economic planning. But they cannot, as far as I can see, be objected to simply on the ground that they are government 'interference', that they are of a general type which is in all circumstances undesirable. And it is highly important not to employ this argument where it cannot be defended. Nothing destroys the force of an argument more surely as when it is often used in cases where it is not effective. I think direct controls of the kind I have mentioned, controls which necessarily involve discrimination between persons, should be ruled out of court once and for all. At least in a peace time economy, and perhaps apart from temporary local crises due to natural catastrophes, nothing should be regarded as justifying them.

To enforce rigidly the principle of equality before the law would thus eliminate a large group of government activities as absolutely inadmissible in normal times.[6] Much would be gained if it were generally realised that it is not all

---

[6] [An earlier Hayekian exploration of these ideas can be found in *The Road to Serfdom: Text and Documents*, ed. B. Caldwell, vol. 2 (2007) of *The Collected Works of F. A. Hayek*, pp. 112–23. A later, more extensive discussion can be found in F. A. Hayek, *The Constitution of Liberty*, ed. R. Hamowy, vol, 17 (2011) of *The Collected Works of F. A. Hayek*, pp. 329–41, 367–516.—Ed.]

a matter of degree but that there is such a class of government actions which are just incompatible with a free society. But we must also face the fact that there is another region where we have no such absolute criteria and where the decision about what is admissible and what is not must be in some measure a matter of degree. What can we say about them?

I believe that in practice adherence to the same, or at least to a very similar principle will also provide the solution in most cases. It is true that indirect controls, aiming at influencing the direction of economic activity, can be exercised by the application of general rules. Tariffs and taxes, global quotas sold by auction, and many kinds of subsidies, could be provided for by law in a way that these rules might formally seem to apply equally to all people. But in fact they would of course do so only if they were laid down in advance for long periods and not continuously adjusted to the circumstances of time and the needs of particular people. But legislation, fortunately, is a cumbersome process. At least a great many of the influences which theoretically could be exercised by indirect controls could become effective only if it were possible to alter the terms of these controls at short intervals. A tariff or a tax or a subsidy which could be changed monthly would in fact be almost as powerful a means of control as direct controls. It would be this if alterations could be determined by an administrative authority with discretionary powers. It can be much less so if its alteration depends on legislative action. The main safeguard here, too, is therefore, to prevent delegation of power by the legislature. Legislatures might still erect a great many obstacles to the growth of human productivity. But the wisdom of our governors would have much less chance to thwart the wishes of the consumer and to prevent industry from taking that direction which his wishes indicate.

If beyond this it were possible to persuade legislatures that the norms they are laying down should be intended not only for the day but for long periods, that the criterion for them to apply, when deciding whether a bill ought to go on the statute book, was whether in the light of our present knowledge it ought to be accepted as a permanent rule, we should probably have achieved as much as one could ever hope to achieve in this world. But this is probably already too much to hope for. We ought to be well content if we could succeed in erecting that wall against the further encroachment of overall control by the government which agreed opposition against the kind of interference here defined would represent. It would at least prevent us from sliding by imperceptible steps into a condition which nobody wants but which so many well intentioned people daily help to create.

NINE

THE ECONOMICS OF
DEVELOPMENT CHARGES[1]

I

Few measures of similar importance, at the time they were passed, have probably received so little attention from some of those most affected by them, as was true of the Town and Country Planning Act, 1947.[2] Even now, some nine months after the Act has come into force, few people are aware of its full significance for the economic future of this country. Yet it may well prove to have a decisive and perhaps fatal effect on that increase of industrial efficiency on which our future must depend.

The public can hardly be blamed, however, for not at once appreciating the wider bearing of that measure. One may even doubt whether its drafters and supporters quite understood its implications. The Act applies to a wide field a special theory which has been developed within a narrow circle of town planners with a limited object in view; but the general significance of that theory has never been systematically examined.

This doctrine was first expounded in several reports and documents which

[1] From *The Financial Times*, April 26, 27, 28, 1949. [The first three sections of this chapter correspond to three articles written by Hayek and published in *The Financial Times* on April 26–28, 1949: "A Levy on Increasing Efficiency I. The Economics of Development Charges", *The Financial Times*, April 26, 1949, p. 4; "A Levy on Increasing Efficiency II. Detrimental Effects of Development Charges", *The Financial Times*, April 27, 1949, p. 4; and "A Levy on Increasing Efficiency III. Too Little Evidence of Planning", *The Financial Times*, April 28, 1949, p. 4. The three articles were republished, along with an appendix consisting of a review of C. Haar, *Land Planning Law in a Free Society: A Study of the British Town and Country Planning Act* (Cambridge, MA: Harvard University Press, 1951), as chapter 25 of F. A. Hayek, *Studies in Philosophy, Politics and Economics* (London: Routledge & Kegan Paul, 1967), under the title "The Economics of Development Charges". Hayek returned to some of the issues discussed here in F. A. Hayek, *The Constitution of Liberty*, ed. Ronald Hamowy, vol. 17 (2011) of *The Collected Works of F. A. Hayek* (Chicago: University of Chicago Press; London: Routledge), pp. 466–81.—Ed.]

[2] [*The Town and Country Planning Act, 1947* (10 & 11 Geo. 6. CH. 51) was an Act of Parliament in the United Kingdom. It came into effect on July 1, 1948, and provided the framework within which postwar town and country planning took place. It established in particular that ownership alone was insufficient to confer the right to develop land; planning permission was also required for land development.—Ed.]

were published during the war and which, in consequence, did not receive careful critical examination. The Act itself and its implementation not only went even beyond what was contemplated in those earlier documents; it was also couched in a language so obscure and at the same time so vague that it was scarcely possible to know what some of its most crucial provisions would mean before it was seen how they were administered.

Since on some of the most crucial issues the decisions have not been written into the Act but have been left to the discretion of various government departments, it is only as their policy becomes known that we can form a clearer idea of the probable effects.

On the issue to be considered here, the "development charges", the operation and the interpretation of the Act has been entrusted to the Central Land Board.[3] This Board has recently explained its intentions in a set of *Practice Notes*[4] which is in more than one respect a remarkable document deserving close study.

There will be opportunity later to comment on the curious light it throws on the political and administrative problems raised by this sort of planning. But the indications it gives of how the Board proposes to assess the development charges raise purely economic problems which require careful examination.

As the document puts it, the Central Land Board has been given "a monopoly in development rights" in land. 'Development' means now for this purpose not only the turning of hitherto 'undeveloped' agricultural land to industrial or commercial uses; it includes 'redevelopment', that is all material changes in the use of any already developed land, except when the change takes place within certain narrowly defined classes.[5]

---

[3] [Under the heading "Part VII. Development Charges", paragraph 1 of Section 69 of the Act states the following: "Subject to the provisions of this Act, there shall be paid to the Central Land Board in respect of the carrying out of any operations to which this Part of the Act applies, and in respect of any use of land to which this Part of the Act applies, a development charge of such an amount (if any) as the Board may determine, and accordingly no such operations shall be carried out, and no such use shall be instituted or continued, except with the consent in writing of the Central Land Board, until the amount of the charge (if any) to be paid in respect of those operations or that use has been determined by the Board in accordance with the provisions of this Part of the Act, and the Board have certified that the amount so determined has been paid or secured to their satisfaction in accordance with those provisions". See *Town and Country Planning Act, 1947*, pp. 81–82.—Ed.]

[4] Central Land Board, *Practice Notes (First Series). Being Notes on the Development Charges under the Town and Country Planning Act, 1947*. London: H.M. Stationery Office, 1949. [See Central Land Board, *Practice Notes (First Series). Being Notes on Development Charges under the Town and Country Planning Act, 1947* (London: His Majesty's Stationery Office, 1949).—Ed.]

[5] [The phrase quoted by Hayek can be found on p. 11 of the *Practice Notes*. The authors of the *Notes* set out their understanding of 'development', and explain the relationship between de-

All such changes of use require a previous 'planning permission'. Most of them are also subject to a development charge which must be paid before the change can be made. The principle on which these charges are determined will therefore decide what kind of change will still be practicable.

If anybody should still think that these development charges are intended merely to confiscate some special gain due to the beneficial effect of public policy, of a genuine 'betterment' in the old sense of the term, he will soon be undeceived. The development charge has become something altogether different.

It is intended to absorb any increase in value of a particular piece of land due to the permission to change its use. It constitutes in effect a confiscation of the whole advantage derived from any industrial development for which land hitherto used for a different purpose has to be used.

The development charge is in each instance to be equal to "the difference between the existing use value and the value for the permitted development"; or, in the new terminology introduced, between the "Refusal Value" and the "Consent Value" of the piece of land. Until the planning permission is granted, the land is presumed to derive its value exclusively from the existing use.[6]

So far as the owner is concerned this will indeed be true, whatever its potentialities from a social point of view, since all the potentialities for some different and more valuable use have been expropriated and vested in the Central Land Board.

We are not concerned here with the owner's distant prospect in a share of the £300 million set aside for compensation. That he may hope some day to get a sum of uncertain magnitude does not alter the effect of the price which he will have to pay now for the acquisition or re-acquisition of any development right.

The earlier documents in which this scheme was first outlined had proposed development charges amounting to a certain proportion, something like 75 or 80 per cent, of the increase in value. The Act itself left this point characteristically undecided. But the policy announced by the Minister of Town and Country Planning is to fix the charges at 100 per cent of the increase in value.[7]

---

velopment charges and 'planning permission' to which Hayek refers in the next paragraph, on pp. 1–5 of that document.—Ed.]

[6] [The quotation comes from p. 2 of the *Practice Notes*. The notions of 'refusal value' and 'consent value' are briefly defined on p. ii and discussed in detail on pp. 11–19 of the same document.—Ed.]

[7] [As stated on p. 11 of the *Practice Notes*, "[F]or the normal case, the development charge shall be equal to the additional value of the land due to the planning permission for a particular development".—Ed.]

This means that anyone contemplating a change in the layout of an industrial plant involving a material change in the use of land, before he is allowed to undertake it, will have to hand over the full capitalised value of the expected advantage.

There are, it is true, certain exceptions to this rule. Where the change is confined to an alternation of the use of already existing buildings within certain narrowly defined classes, no charge will arise.[8] But where it involves a change in the use of land between any such categories as office buildings, 'light' industrial buildings, 'general' industrial buildings, or any one of five classes of 'special' industrial buildings, the full charge is due. The exceptions somewhat limit the incidence of the charge. But they do not alter the principle or the general effects of its application.

This principle amounts to nothing less than that the whole of any advantage derived from the reorganisation of a manufacturing process which involves a material change in the use of land shall be absorbed by the development charge. What is taken away is thus not merely the special advantage which a particular piece of land may offer compared with others, because of its situation or special qualities.

Since any land, except that already devoted to a certain kind of use, will be available for this use only after the payment of a development charge, the 'advantage' for which the price has to be paid will be the possibility of introducing a new process anywhere.

Since the permission will be granted only with respect to a particular piece of land, that possibility becomes artificially attached to that piece of land and the value of the possibility to introduce the new process becomes similarly tied to the value of that piece of land.

The significance of the new monopoly element thus introduced will be seen more clearly if we consider for a moment how the price of land in a similar situation was determined in the past. Take the problems raised by the expansion of an industrial undertaking surrounded by agricultural land. If the land on all sides was of the same agricultural quality, was owned by different people, and offered the same opportunities to the plant, the pieces needed could have been bought for a price representing its agricultural use value.

This would in most instances have correctly represented the social cost of the change: the loss of the agricultural value would have been the loss to society which would have to be more than offset by the gain from its industrial use if the change was to be beneficial.

Only if some of the land surrounding the plant offered to the undertaking greater advantages than the rest would the owner of that piece of land have been able to hold out for a correspondingly higher price. The undertaking

---

[8] [The exceptions are outlined on pp. 3, 5–10 of the *Practice Notes.*—Ed.]

might have had to pay extra, over and above what it would have had to pay for any other land, for any special advantage the particular site offered to it. But this payment would have had to be made for a differential advantage of that piece of land—not for the possibility of expanding at all, but for being able to expand in a particular direction.

Contrast this with the situation where all the land surrounding the plant belonged to one owner; it would then have been the possibility of expanding at all, not merely the possibility of expanding on a particular piece of land, which would depend on the landowner's willingness to sell. He would be in a position to extort a price equal to nearly the whole gain from the expansion. Any piece of land he was prepared to sell would for the undertaking possess the full value of the gain to be expected from expanding on the existing site.

The monopoly of the Land Board will be even more complete than that of such a single owner of all the land surrounding an existing plant. The Board will also control the only two alternatives to expanding on adjoining land: development within the given area—for example, by building higher—or moving the whole plant elsewhere.

All opportunities for expansion will depend on its permission and since only land with a planning permission can be used for the expansion, the 'Consent Value' of any such land will include the whole value of the gain to be expected from the expansion.

It is true that in its *Practice Notes* the Board disclaims the intention of exacting monopoly values. But since at the same time it states that it means to take into account the special value of land to an only possible purchaser, that assurance evidently cannot be taken literally. It is indeed difficult to see how under its instructions the Board can do anything but charge monopoly values. Since what it confers are essentially monopoly values, its consent also has a monopoly value.[9]

The Board has in effect been given "a monopoly in development rights" not only *in land*, but, in so far as any development requires some land and since the Board controls all land, it has a monopoly of all industrial development of the kind.

II

Land is a factor which is indispensable in all industrial activity and all change in industrial activity therefore involves a change in the use of land. To make

[9] [The word 'consent', which appeared in Hayek's original newspaper article, has been preferred here to the term 'concept' erroneously used on p. 325 of the version of this essay published in *Studies*. Hayek refers in this paragraph to p. 11 of the *Practice Notes*, which states that, "The Board have a monopoly in development rights and could then exact monopoly values" but "do not propose to value" on that basis.—Ed.]

some such changes dependent upon permission and on the payment of a price is to make industrial adjustment to that extent dependent on a permission and the payment of a price. And to fix this price with regard to the advantage depending on the permission amounts in effect to a confiscation of the gain from such industrial change. This is a principle introduced by the Town and Country Planning Act.

The term 'gain', however, in this connection, is rather misleading; it suggests less serious effects of the development charges than they are likely to have. They will not only eliminate a main incentive to socially desirable changes. They will impose an artificial cost on such change to which no genuine social costs correspond. The changes in question may be necessary merely to preserve the usefulness of the land or to maintain the solvency of an enterprise.

It may merely be a question of avoiding loss. Yet where the avoidance of the loss depends on a change made in the use of land, the permission to make it will be worth the whole loss which is thereby avoided, and the development charge will have to be fixed accordingly. Even where the gain expected from the change is a net gain, its value will have to be laid out beforehand and a new risk will be created which the investor will have to incur without any compensating prospect of gain.

Land used for industrial purposes will over long periods retain its value only in so far as its use is adjusted to changing conditions. The value of a particular piece of land for a given purpose constantly changes, and if it were permanently tied to a particular purpose its value would be certain sooner or later to fall. Such losses are usually avoided by switching the land to a different use when its former use becomes less valuable.

Under the new arrangements such a loss must be wholly borne by the owner of the land, since he no longer owns the right to change the use but will have to purchase his right at a price corresponding to the amount he recovers by the change. The land may in the new use be worth less than it has been before the opportunity for its former use disappeared.

Nevertheless, once the value in its former use has fallen, the opportunity of recovering part of the losses by changing the use belongs to the State. In the example given in the *Practice Notes*, "The slum cottage is to have only its existing use value as a cottage until planning permission is given for redevelopment. Then on payment of the development charge, representing the extra value due to that permission, the value jumps at one bound to that for the new permitted use".[10]

In other words, the owner will first have to suffer the loss of obsolescence imposed on him by the prohibition of the change in the use (or because the versatility of his asset has been artificially restricted by law); and he is then deprived of any gain which he might make when the change is permitted.

[10] [*Practice Notes*, p. 2.—Ed.]

One wonders indeed whether the inventors of the whole scheme have ever reflected on what it will mean if the development charge makes a change unprofitable, or whether it has ever occurred to them that it will frequently do so.

It should be obvious both that *any* development charge may prevent some desirable change, and that, whenever it has that effect, it will prevent a more productive use of the available resources.

The only exception to this would be where the development charge happened to be equal in value to some indirect damage done by the development to other property, a damage which otherwise would not have been taken into account in calculating the net benefit to be expected. But there is no intention and no practical possibility of relating the development charges to such detrimental effects of the change. We can therefore neglect the possibility of a purely accidental coincidence.

Let us consider a particular case. Suppose an undertaking owns some workers' houses close to its manufacturing plant. If the houses had not already been there, it might long have been advantageous to use the site for some process ancillary to manufacture. But as the houses already exist, the value of their services has to be set against the advantage of having that process on the particular spot.

But sooner or later, as the value of the houses declines, the point will come when that advantage is greater than the value of the services which the houses will give. They will be demolished and the site turned to manufacture precisely when this brings some net saving in the combined costs of producing both the housing services and the industrial product.

This saving of costs may be small, and it will certainly stand in no relation to the difference in value between other similar land in the neighbourhood used for housing and for manufacture respectively. Yet it is on the cumulative effect of many small savings in costs such as this that improvements in industrial efficiency depend.

If in a case like this a development charge is levied, the effect can be only that the change is delayed and perhaps altogether prevented. In future, it will be necessary that the saving in costs should exceed the value of the existing use value, according to established valuation practices, by as much as land available for manufacturing purposes exceeds in value land used for dwelling houses.

The same applies to all similar changes designed to bring about a saving in costs. Such changes will be either prevented or at least the incentive to make them greatly reduced.

This would be bad enough if the gain were only confiscated after it has in fact materialised. Carried out consistently, it would deprive the owners of all interest in cost-saving changes of the kind. We should have to rely on their public spirit for their constantly striving to keep costs as low as possible.

The fact that the development charge has to be paid before the change is made and irrespective of whether the expected benefit actually matures makes the effect, however, even worse. It creates a new private risk which the individual developer has to bear, but to which no social risk corresponds.

The developer must be willing to stake an amount equal to the hoped-for gain, certain that he will lose if his hopes are not fulfilled, but without any prospect of advantage if his expectations prove correct. A grosser form of penalising risk can hardly be imagined. Wherever there is uncertainty about the outcome it will become much safer to stay put than to sink capital in buying a permission which may prove of little value.

What the whole scheme amounts to is that a penalty is placed upon industrial change. Every adjustment to changed conditions which involves a 'material' change in the use of land is made the occasion for a levy which in effect expropriates the gain that might be expected. The more rapidly and the more often an undertaking tries to meet changes in conditions, the more often part of its capital will be confiscated.

Wherever the gain it can expect from a change is smaller than the Central Land Board thinks it ought to be, the change will be altogether impossible. And only when a firm can persuade the Board that the gain from the change will be smaller than it in fact expects it to be, will there be any pecuniary advantage in undertaking it.

Let it once more be stressed that in all this 'gain' does not necessarily mean an absolute gain. What is confiscated is the gain relative to the position if the change were prohibited. The change may aim merely at a lowering of costs in line with what foreign competitors are doing. Or it may be necessary because a change in demand requires an alteration of the product.

It does not matter. So long as a material change in the use of land is necessary the benefit from the change is taken away. Can there be much doubt that if this principle is carried out as now announced, it cannot but prove to be one of the most serious blows administered to the prospects of increasing the efficiency of British industry?

III

It has been suggested in the first part of this article that the authors of the Town and Country Planning Act did not know what they were planning. After examining the practical significance of the development charges as now interpreted, one must almost hope that this was so.

It is becoming only too clear that the whole scheme has not been adequately thought out beforehand, and that we have been committed to an experiment, of the outcome of which nobody has formed a clear conception. It appears that the unprecedented blanket powers which the Act conferred on the Minister of Town and Country Planning and the Central Land Board were the result of a lack of any clear idea of how these powers were to be used.

The advocates of central planning always assure us that democratic legislation is an adequate safeguard against controls becoming arbitrary. What are we, then, to think of an Act which explicitly leaves undetermined the *general principles* on which the authorities are to use one of the most powerful tools of economic control ever put into their hands?

Yet this is exactly what the Town and Country Planning Act (Sub-section 3 of Section 70) did when it provided that "regulations made under this Act with the consent of the Treasury may prescribe general principles to be followed by the Central Land Board in determining . . . whether any and if so what development charge is to be paid".[11]

It was under this provision that it was left to the Minister of Town and Country Planning unexpectedly to issue a Regulation according to which the development charges were normally "not to be less" than the whole additional value of the land accruing from the planning permission for a particular development.[12]

The general principle stated in that Regulation, however, still provides no more than the most general framework within which the Board must formulate its own policies.

The position in which the Central Land Board has thereby been placed is well illustrated by the Preface which its chairman has contributed to the *Practice Notes* in which it has summed up the principles it proposes to follow. These notes, he explains, "are meant to describe the principles and working rules in accordance with which any applicant can confidently assume his case will be dealt". This sounds reassuring until one reads on and finds that the sentence continues: "unless either he shows good cause for different treatment, or the Board inform him that for special reasons the normal rules do not apply".[13]

What confidence can there be in any rules if no principles are stated on which it will be decided that the general rules do not apply in a particular case? The Board even explicitly refuses to be tied by a fixed rule: "a general working rule must always be variable if it does not fit a particular case".

The Board also refuses to be bound by precedent and announces that "we have no doubt that from time to time we shall vary our policy" and that such future variations "can only operate for new cases and cannot reopen old".

Why this continued vagueness if there is a clear aim? Can it be that the absurdity of the general principle is already half recognised and that it is

---

[11] [The *Town and Country Planning Act*, p. 84.—Ed.]

[12] [See *Town and Country Planning (Development Charge) Regulations* (S.I. 1189, 1948).—Ed.]

[13] [The words quoted by Hayek in this and the following two paragraphs are taken from the *Practice Notes*, pp. ii–iii.—Ed.]

intended to mitigate the bad effects by concessions in the negotiations with individual applicants? Certain statements made in Parliament and some passages in the Preface to the *Practice Notes* suggest that this may be the intention.[14]

Is a more dangerous procedure imaginable than first to burden the authorities with the duty of imposing enormous charges on a principle which it is known cannot be consistently applied, and then to leave it to their discretion to modify their claims when it appears that the effects are all too harmful?

The Preface to the *Practice Notes* almost seems to invite precisely this sort of bargaining and to suggest that the Board will always be willing to listen to special considerations if they are pressed hard enough.

The fact is that the task of administering the development charges not only 'fairly' but in such a manner that they do not impede desirable industrial development is an impossible one. In determining the development charge the Board is, in fact, deciding whether a particular development ought to take place or not. It could do so intelligently only if it were in a position to plan the whole industrial development of the country.

In order that it should be in a position to judge the effects of its decisions on industrial efficiency, it would have to have at its disposal, and have to be able to judge, all the data which the individual developer takes into account.

Indeed, if the development charges are to be anything but a harmful obstacle to development, they would have to be used according to a detailed overall plan, which lays down in what form and in which direction each industry, and each plant in each industry, ought to be developed.

This, however, is of course neither the intention nor a practical possibility.[15] Instead, the Land Board is charged with determining one of the essential conditions on which the decision of the private developer must depend, without any possibility (other than the owner's statement) of judging how its action will affect that decision, or what that decision ought to be in the national interest.

Neither the Land Board nor the developer will be able to base his decisions on the objective merits of the situation. Whether the development will take place is made dependent on an artificially created conflict of interests to which no economic facts correspond and which must be detrimental to a wise solution of the genuine economic problems involved.

There exists indeed no *rationale* for the development charges as now conceived. Far from introducing a rational element into the decisions about the use of land, it introduces a completely meaningless factor and falsifies the

---

[14] [See the long passage from p. iii of the *Practice Notes* quoted by Hayek in the main text on p. 142 below.—Ed.]

[15] [Hayek argues that widespread industrial planning is impossible in F. A. Hayek, *Socialism and War: Essays, Documents, Reviews*, ed. B. Caldwell, vol. 10 (1997) of *The Collected Works of F. A. Hayek*, pp. 53–147.—Ed.]

data on which the developer will have to base his decisions. The costs he will have to take into account will correspond less to the true social costs than ever before.

His opportunity to plan wisely and the likelihood of his serving the best social interest will be greatly decreased. And his energies will have to be bent, not so much to discovering the real facts of the situation, as to finding arguments which will appear plausible to those who have to fix the terms on which he will be allowed to go ahead with his plans.

The direction of industrial progress will more than ever become dependent on the powers of persuasion, the accidents of contacts, and the vicissitudes of official procedure where the most careful calculation ought to decide. The most efficient and conscientious civil service cannot prevent this where no clear direction can be laid down for its actions.

Nobody has yet suggested what these directions ought to be if the development charges are to be beneficial to the increase of industrial efficiency. The only rule which would have that effect would be that there should be no development charges.[16]

APPENDIX

A Review of Charles M. Haar, *Land Planning Law in a Free Society: A Study of the British Town and Country Planning Act.*[17] Cambridge, Mass., Harvard University Press, 1951.

[16] [A note at the end of the third *Financial Times* article penned by Hayek directed readers to a short editorial comment, which reads as follows: "When the Town and Country Planning Act was passed, it was insufficiently understood, either by its proposers or by the country as a whole. The powers which the Act placed in the hands of the Ministry and of the Central Land Board over the development of industry, go far beyond those which Parliament appeared to appreciate at the time. It is clear from the series of articles by Professor Hayek, concluded today, that the Board, when determining the development charge on land, is, in fact, deciding whether a particular industrial expansion should take place or not. It was never intended that the Act should give the Board such power and control. There is only one way in which the Act can fulfil its proper purpose—namely, by the repeal of the development charge. That charge is a hindrance to development on every front. It must go." See Editorial Comment, "Town & Country Planning", *The Financial Times*, April 28, 1949, p. 4.—Ed.]

[17] Reprinted from the *University of Chicago Law Review*, XIX/3, Spring 1952. [The full reference is F. A. Hayek and A. Dunham, "Land Planning Law in a Free Society: A Study of the British Town and Country Planning Act. By Charles M. Haar. Cambridge: Harvard University Press, 1951. Pp. xiii, 213. $4.00," *University of Chicago Law Review*, vol. 19, 1952, pp. 620–31. Hayek's review of Haar's book comprises Part "I" of the publication (pp. 620–26) and is reprinted here with permission from the *University of Chicago Law Review* and the University of Chicago Law School. Part "II" (pp. 626–31) was written by Allison Dunham (1914–92), Arnold I. Shure Professor of Urban Law at the University of Chicago (1951–83) and Director of the Univer-

One of the inevitable effects of the progressive extension of government control over economic life is that economic problems are increasingly disposed of by lawyers, technologists and experts in 'administration'. It might be expected that this would lead to an increased understanding of economics in these professions. This expectation has generally been frustrated—it almost seems as if those who ardently believe that they can solve economic problems by central planning in most instances do so precisely because they are unaware of what the economic problems are.

There is no better illustration of this than town planning—a subject which, it must be admitted, has been sadly neglected by economists. And there could be hardly a more telling demonstration of the complete lack of comprehension of the economic problems which the use of land raises for society than the present careful and painstaking study of the new British Town and Country Planning Act of 1947 by an American student of Public Administration.[18] While the book presents a sympathetic interpretation of that experiment, in the sense that Mr. Haar fully shares the outlook which inspires it, it is as devoid of any appreciation of the wider economic issues involved as were the group of architects and administrators who, in the peculiar circumstances of Britain between 1940 and 1947, were almost exclusively responsible for this piece of legislation. The book does not even take notice of the few critical analyses of the Act which appeared when the British economists were at last released from the more important preoccupation of winning the war. In particular the author ignores the masterly analysis of the problem by Sir Arnold Plant[19] and the severe criticism which the measure has received from groups

---

sity's Center for Urban Studies (1971–77). The early parts of Dunham's review see him consider the relevance of Haar's account of the British Town and Country Planning Act for an American audience (pp. 626–29). However, Dunham then goes on to challenge the soundness of some of Hayek's own claims about the impact of the Act, arguing for example that "Mr. Hayek's assertion, in his review of the book and in other writings, that under a 'free market' system all advantage of a change in use of a piece of land goes to the developer of the new use and that under the British Planning Act all such advantage will go to the government is unsound in both aspects" and that "Mr. Hayek's sweeping generalizations demonstrate that . . . economists . . . need a little more understanding of the operation of legal and economic institutions". See Hayek and Dunning, pp. 629–30, in particular p. 629.—Ed.]

[18] [Charles M Haar (1920–2012) was a Professor of Law at Harvard Law School and an advocate of robust government regulation of urban development.—Ed.]

[19] A. Plant, 'Land Planning and the Economic Functions of Ownership', *Journal Chartered Auctioneers and Estate Agents Inst.*, Vol. XXX (1949). [British economist Professor Sir Arnold Plant (1898–1978) was Professor of Commerce at the London School of Economics (1930–65). The full reference to his essay is Sir A. Plant, "Land Planning and the Economic Functions of Ownership", *The Journal of the Chartered Auctioneers' and Estate Agents' Institute*, vol. 29, 1949, pp. 284–305. For more on Plant, see F. A. Hayek, "The Transmission of the Ideals of Economic Freedom" [1951], reprinted as chapter 2 of the current volume, p. 46, n. 6.—Ed.]

which one might expect to be sympathetic towards it, such as the followers of Henry George.[20]

After reading the book one feels some doubt whether the author, any more than the legislators or the British public at large, is fully aware of how completely the Act has changed the whole character of the British economic system. While entirely suspending the operation of the price mechanism with regard to land (outside agricultural uses) it has put nothing in its place except arbitrary decision without even a general principle to guide it. What the Act has decreed is nothing less than that all advantage which a private owner could derive from any change in the use made of a piece of land (if it was to be devoted to other than agricultural purposes) shall in future be confiscated by the government, and that, therefore, if the principles of the Act can be consistently applied, no private person or corporation will have any incentive to improve economic efficiency, where this involves a change in the use of land.

To anyone familiar with the history of the Act and the effects which it is producing, the most curious aspect of the present book is that it attempts to emphasise throughout the democratic character of the measure and its compatibility with free institutions, while on the basis of the facts provided by the book itself both are at best pious hopes of highly questionable value. If the author is unaware of the threat to freedom involved, this is probably because he seems equally oblivious to the fact that consistent application of the principles of the Act in the long run implies central direction of all economic

---

[20] Cf. especially their journal, *Land and Liberty*, London, 1948 and 1949. [American economist and social reformer Henry George (1839–97) is best remembered for his advocacy of the 'single tax' on land. For George, the state should raise all of its revenue via a tax levied on the unimproved value of land (that is, on the value of land exclusive of any efforts to augment its value by increasing its fertility, constructing buildings on it, etc.). George argued that because the supply of such land is fixed, taxes on it will not distort people's behaviour and therefore constitute the most efficient way for the government to raise revenue. Moreover, the elimination of all other taxes—on earned income—would increase efficiency, enrich workers, and lead to a more equitable distribution of income. See H. George, *Progress and Poverty: An Inquiry into the Cause of Industrial Depressions and of Increase of Want with Increase of Wealth—The Remedy* (New York: Sterling Publishing Company, 1879). George's ideas influenced both the progressive movement in the United States and the Fabian socialists in Great Britain. The journal *Land and Liberty* was established by George's followers in 1894 in order to promote his principles. The volumes for 1948 and 1949 contain several articles criticising the 1947 Act, of which the following are merely examples: A. Madsen, "Town Planning—Fulfilment or Frustration?", *Land and Liberty*, vols. 646–47, March & April 1948, pp. 122–24; E. Johnson, "The Disastrous Town Planning Act", *Land and Liberty*, vol. 656, January 1949, p. 6; and A. Madsen, "Wreck of the Planning Act", *Land and Liberty*, vols. 657–58, February & March 1949, pp. 17–18. Copies of the first and third articles can be found in the Hayek Collection, box 113, folder 2, Hoover Institution Archives, suggesting that it is to them that Hayek was referring.—Ed.]

activity. Characterisation of the measure as particularly democratic squares ill with the admitted facts that when it was discussed in Parliament almost nobody understood the practically unlimited discretionary powers it conferred on administrative agencies. "[T]he Opposition often felt in the position of Joseph who was asked not only to interpret a dream, but to say what the dream was" (p. 177).[21] Furthermore, after the Act had placed in the power of a minister unlimited discretion to lay down even the 'general principle' on which its most important provision was to be administered, the minister in fact issued regulations which "represent a complete change of mind since the time of the debates on the Act" (p. 111). We shall later have to consider the issue in question. From a lawyer one might also have expected a little more concern about the fact, mentioned like many of the less appealing features of the legislation in the small print of the notes, that "Throughout, the Act seeks to avoid any recourse to the courts" (p. 188).

The discussion of the economically most important provisions of the Act is compressed almost entirely into a few pages of Mr. Haar's book (pp. 98–117), and in a brief review we must concentrate on these. As is made abundantly clear throughout the exposition, the basic motive behind all legislation of this kind is "the ever-present fear of need to pay compensation which constitutes an ever-present threat to bold planning" (p. 101; cf. pp. 157 and 167). In other words, it is the desire of the town planners to be relieved of the necessity of counting the cost of their activities, and it is freely admitted that many of the things which they regard as desirable would prove impossible if the whole costs, as they are measured in a market economy, had to be paid. The central aim is therefore to enable the planning authorities to acquire control over land below the price it would fetch on a free market. The argument used to justify this aim betrays a complete failure to understand the significance of these costs. We shall not stop to examine at length the arguments used in the present book to show why these costs can in fact not be paid.

The significance of the market value of land as an indicator of the social costs of its use for particular purposes is a more fundamental issue. In town planning literature generally, as in the present book, this question is generally represented as a purely fiscal problem: how these costs are to be met. It is regarded as solved if the burden can be placed on a particular group by a partial expropriation of the landowners. But this is not at all the main social problem involved. The crux of the matter lies in making sure that generally, and in every particular instance, the advantages derived from planning exceed the losses of the developments which the planning restrictions prevent. Pay-

---

[21] [This quotation, and all otherwise unattributed references in this and the next three paragraphs, are from Haar, *Land Planning Law in a Free Society*.—Ed.]

ing the owner less than the full value of the land uses which are taken from him does not reduce the costs for society one whit. It merely makes it possible to disregard them and go ahead with planning schemes regardless of whether they repay their total costs. Unless it can be shown that the market prices of land reflect more than the value of the alternative services to the consumers which the land would render if allowed to be put to its more profitable use, the direction of the land to other purposes can be justified only if it can be demonstrated that it will make a contribution to public welfare which is greater than the value lost. This is what the planners can so rarely demonstrate. But, like most planners, the town planners, while pretending to take a more comprehensive view, are usually interested only in a limited range of values and wish to escape the trammels of considerations which they neither understand nor care for, and which probably no central plan could adequately take into account. As the present book characteristically puts it, their hope is that in the future the "decision on the proper use of a piece of land will not be distorted by either the excessive cost of high development value or of the need of avoiding the payment of compensation, but will be taken strictly on planning merits" (p. 102).

The only serious attempt to justify this approach was made by one of the British commissions of inquiry which preceded the 1947 legislation, the 'Uthwatt Report' on Compensation and Betterment of 1942.[22] This report developed a curious theory of 'floating' and 'shifting' values which, though I doubt whether it is taken seriously by a single reputable economist, appears to have made a considerable impression on town planners and administrators. It is based on the assumption that the total value of all the land in a country is a fixed magnitude, independent of the uses to which the individual pieces of land are put, and that, in consequence, the control of the use of land has only "the effect of shifting land values: in other words, it increases the value of some land and decreases the value of other land, but it does not destroy land values" (p. 99, quoted from the Uthwatt Report). Now this is not merely, as Mr. Haar suggests, a theory which "may be open to question on the ground of lack of empiric proof" (*ibid.*). It is sheer nonsense, which empirically could

---

[22] [The Expert Committee on Compensation and Betterment, chaired by Augustus Uthwatt (1879–1949), a British judge and Law Lord, was charged in 1941 with the task of analysing issues associated, first of all, with the need to pay compensation to landowners for the loss of development value due to the state acquiring land or imposing restrictions on its use, and second, with the principle that people whose property has increased in value due to the carrying out of public works should help to pay for the latter (an occurrence known as 'betterment'). The Committee's final report, which was published in 1942, is commonly referred to as the "Uthwatt Report". See Ministry of Works and Planning, *Expert Committee on Compensation and Betterment: Final Report*, Cmd. 6386 (London: His Majesty's Stationary Office, 1942).—Ed.]

neither be proved nor disproved. There is no useful meaning of the term 'value' of which it could possibly be true. The situation is not much better with regard to the theory of 'floating value': the assertion that as a rule the expectation of impending development will affect the value of more land than will in fact be developed and increase it by more than the value of the actual developments. Yet even though it may occasionally be true that the market value of land on the margin of a town may be based on expectations which cannot all be valid, this surely is a difficulty which could be met by appropriate principles of valuation and which does not justify complete disregard of market values.

All this does not mean that we want to belittle the difficulty caused by the fact that while the cost of planning through reducing the value of some land is not too difficult to recognise and the bearers of the loss are certain to claim compensation, the 'betterment', i.e., the increases in the value of land due to the same planning measures, is much more difficult to ascertain. Nor can there be much question that, so far as specific betterments of this kind are ascertainable, it is desirable that the beneficiaries should be made to contribute to the cost of planning in proportion. There is much to be said for taxing away increments of land value which are demonstrably due to public activity. Indeed, of all kinds of socialism, the nationalisation of land would have most to recommend it if it were practicable to distinguish the value of the Ricardian "indestructible and permanent powers of the soil", to which alone the argument applies, from that value which the efforts of the owner have contributed.[23] The difficulties here are essentially of a practical nature: the impossibility of distinguishing between these two parts of the value of a piece of land, and the problem of so adjusting rent contracts as to give the user of the land the appropriate inducements for investment. However, though 'only' practical, these difficulties have nevertheless proved insuperable.

In effect, this was recognised by the Uthwatt Report which, by a "bold departure from precedent"[24] on which the authors specially prided themselves, started a new development which in the end perverted that reasonable but impracticable idea of the taxation of betterment values into its opposite: instead of using the taxation of land values as a means of forcing the owners to put their land to the best use, the Town and Country Planning Act of 1947, under the name of the Development Charge, in effect imposed a penalty, on anyone putting land to better use, amounting to the whole gain to be

[23] [Hayek quotes from p. 53 of English economist David Ricardo's book *On the Principles of Political Economy, and Taxation*, 3rd edn. (London: John Murray, 1821), where Ricardo defines rent as "that portion of the produce of the earth, which is paid to the landlord for the use of the original and indestructible powers of the soil".—Ed.]

[24] [See *Expert Committee on Compensation and Betterment*, p. 112.—Ed.]

derived from it. This transformation of the initial idea began with the Uthwatt Committee's decision "to cut the Gordian knot by taking for the community some fixed proportion of the whole of any increase in site values without any attempt at precise analysis of the causes to which it may be due" (p. 98, quoted from the Uthwatt Report).[25] The further steps leading from this to the 1947 Act were that this principle, which the Uthwatt Report intended to apply only to as yet undeveloped land, was extended to include all redevelopment of land already used for non-agricultural purposes; that, instead of making the value at a fixed date the basis for determining the increment, the value of any piece of land in the particular use to which it was devoted at any given time became the measure of the 'gain' due to a change in that use—apparently even if the 'existing use value' had fallen to zero; and finally that, after the measure had been passed by Parliament in the general belief that some 75 or 80 per cent of the difference between the value in the old use and the value in the new use would be taxed away, the minister empowered to fix the percentage decided that it should be 100 per cent. The result is that, as the law now stands, the Central Land Board, entrusted with levying the development charges, is instructed to make it a condition for permitting any development on land that the whole gain derived from it be handed over to the government. It would not seem unfair to sum up this curious evolution by saying that, since what might have made sense theoretically proved practically impossible, and since we must have planning whatever the costs ("even only fairly good planning is to be preferred over the past chaos"—p. 169),[26] even the most nonsensical principle, if it is only administratively feasible, must be adopted.

It will now be clear that what the British government has undertaken is no less than to remove the incentive from practically any change in industrial and commercial activity which involves any substantial change in the use of land (the exceptions are so insignificant that we can disregard them for the present purpose). This is a task which cannot rationally be consummated unless the government takes responsibility for practically all investment decisions. If it were to be consistently carried out, land planning would in the end mean central direction of all commercial and industrial activity. No private person or corporation would have any interest in putting a piece of land to better use or in starting anything new on British soil, because the gain, which can only be obtained by using some British land for new purposes, would have to go to the government. Even worse is the fact that since the prospective value of the development must be paid for in cash before the development can be started, the risk of any uncertain venture will be greatly increased. Sir Arnold Plant,

[25] [Haar, *Land Planning Law in a Free Society*, p. 98.—Ed.]
[26] [Haar, *Land Planning Law in a Free Society*, p. 169.—Ed.]

in the address already mentioned, put it mildly when he concluded that the
Act, in its present form,

> threatens to ossify our industrial and commercial structure at the very points
> at which flexibility and speed of redeployment are the indispensable require-
> ments of successful enterprise in a competitive system.

The illustrations which Sir Arnold offers demonstrate, perhaps better than
general discussion, just what the Act means in practice:

> Thus the ground floor of a commercial building cannot be changed over
> from use as an office to use as a shop, a retail shop cannot undertake new
> wholesale business, a wholesale warehouse cannot be used for light industry,
> or *vice versa* [i.e. without previous planning permission and payment of de-
> velopment charges]. You will be pleased to know, if you have not yet caught
> up with Statutory Instrument No. 195 of 9th February, 1949, that although a
> shop cannot begin to serve its customers with a meal cooked on the premises,
> a restaurant may now be turned into a shop. The managements of our great
> department stores may not yet all be aware that if they increase the propor-
> tion of their floor space devoted to the restaurant by more than 10 per cent,
> without first securing the permission of the local planning authority and
> paying any development charge demanded by the Central Land Board, they
> are apparently breaking the law.[27]

Any number of similar illustrations could be given from the actual decisions of the Central Land Board. It is one of the most serious defects of Mr.
Haar's book that it gives scarcely any idea of what the application of the new
law means in concrete terms. The fact is that it would no longer be worth
while to make any changes in the use of land if the law were followed literally and the development charges so fixed as to absorb the whole advantage
of the change. But it is scarcely more reassuring for the prospects of preserving a free society that in fact all future 'developments' will depend on the Central Land Board authoritatively so fixing the development charges in each particular instance that those developments it wishes to proceed will still remain
profitable while all others become impossible. We cannot attempt to demonstrate here in detail that the two magnitudes whose difference is to determine the development charge, the 'refusal value' (i.e., the value of a piece of
land for which permission for *any* development is refused) and the 'consent
value' (the value of this land after permission for a particular development has

---

[27] [Both quotations are taken from Plant, "Land Planning and the Economic Functions of
Ownership", p. 298. The insertion in square brackets in the second quotation is Hayek's.—Ed.]

been granted), are not objective magnitudes, ascertainable, as the legislator believed, by "normal processes of valuation".[28] As there can be no longer a market for development values there will also exist no basis for their valuation.[29] The fixing of the development charges of necessity becomes an arbitrary affair, exempt from any objective test, and is bound to degenerate into a process of bargaining. The American observer will have no difficulty in seeing where this is likely to lead when he reads the following remarkable paragraph from the preface to the pamphlet called *Practice Notes*, in which the chairman of the Central Land Board announced the 'principles' which the Board proposed to follow in fixing development charges:

> The State now owns the value of all development rights in land. We are the managing agents and have to collect the additional value given to a piece of land by the permission given to develop it for a particular purpose. My colleagues and I are very conscious of the responsibilities of this new task. A study of these Notes will show that 'value' has many meanings and that to adopt one common meaning for all cases must produce absurd results in some. We have been given the discretion to decide which is the fairest to adopt in each case, and have stated some of our present views in these Notes. Each case, however, must depend on its own facts and a general working rule must always be variable if it does not fit a particular case. We have given instructions to our staff and to our advisers to suggest the fairest value possible for the case in question and to consider with care the views of any developer who takes an opposite view. We promise to try to give our own decisions with these points always in mind.[30]

[28] [The phrase "normal processes of valuation" is used here instead of the words "normal processes of evaluation" found on p. 337 of *Studies*, because it is used in Hayek's original review and also because it appears in the *Practice Notes*, p. 17, and on p. 111 of Haar's book, where it is attributed to paragraph 2 of the *Town and Country Planning (Development Charge) Regulations.*—Ed.]

[29] [Hayek draws here on the argument developed by Austrian economist Ludwig von Mises (1881–1973) concerning the impossibility of rational economic calculation in a socialist economy. Mises argued that if the means of production were commonly rather than privately owned, as would be the case under socialism, then there would be no market for capital goods. Consequently, there would be no competitive market process through which the prices of those goods could be established. And without monetary prices to inform them of the relative scarcity of resources, and (therefore) of the opportunity costs of different business projects, people would be unable to evaluate which of the many technically feasible projects constituted the most cost-effective means of satisfying people's desires. Under socialism, therefore, there would be no basis for the rational appraisal of alternative business ventures. See L. von Mises, "Economic Calculation in the Socialist Commonwealth" [1920], in *Collectivist Economic Planning*, ed. F. A. Hayek (London: Routledge and Kegan Paul, 1935). Hayek argues analogously that the absence of a market for development opportunities would leave people bereft of any basis for evaluating the merits of different development projects.—Ed.]

[30] *I Series, Central Land Board, Practice Notes* (1949) at III. [See the *Practice Notes*, p. iii.—Ed.]

Could the invitation to bargaining be stated in much plainer terms?

There is indeed much that must be explained both to the British and to the American public about this "daring experiment in social control of the environment" (p. 1) into which the British people appear to have stumbled even more unknowingly than into any of the undesigned institutions which grew up as the result of free development. If Mr. Haar's prediction be true, "that the fifties in the United States will be marked by a struggle over land planning in much the same fashion as public housing was the issue in the forties", certainly the British experiment should be carefully studied in this country. Mr. Haar has faithfully presented the legislative foundations. Perhaps, as the book appears to be based on a single visit to Britain in 1949, when the Act had only just come into force, we should not expect more than a descriptive account of its provisions and antecedents. We ought to be grateful to Mr. Haar for offering, in readable form, the essence of the "massive document of 10 Parts, 120 long and involved sections, subdivided into 405 subsections . . . [which] runs to no less than 206 pages in the King's Printer's copy" and which still left "many of the more important provisions . . . for Regulations, Directions, and Orders to be issued by the Minister of Town and Country Planning" which, even at the time of the writing of the book, had become more voluminous and complex than the Act itself (p. 8).[31] Yet, convenient as it is to have available an intelligible account of the British arrangements, the concern with the administrative details tends to obscure rather than point up the wider significance of the measure. Where a definite goal is set the technique of achieving it is a matter of legitimate interest. But where, as appears to be true in the present case, administrative expediency and the narrow considerations of a group of specialists have been allowed to decide one of the most general issues of economic policy, exclusive concern with machinery has little value except as a warning. Few readers will derive from the present book the main lesson the British experience has to teach: the acute danger that a small group of technical specialists may, in suitable circumstances, succeed in leading a democracy into legislation which few of those affected by it would have approved if they had understood what it meant.

---

[31] [The three quotations in this paragraph come from Haar, *Land Planning Law in a Free Society*, pp. 1, 10 and 8 respectively. The insertion in square brackets is Hayek's.—Ed.]

TEN

EFFECTS OF RENT CONTROL[1]

Ladies and Gentlemen,

Thanks to the thorough preparation for today's topic in the Association's publications and to Mr. Zimmermann's overview of all the related problems that you have just heard, I can address myself without further preliminaries to the narrower subject of my report: the consequences of rent control, or, more accurately, the consequences of interventions of all kinds in the matter of rents.[2] I have been asked by our board to devote my report to the theoretical aspects of this issue. There are two reasons, I believe, why they have a considerable bearing on the practical problems with which we are more directly concerned. The first is that the problem of tenant protection tends to be viewed exclusively in terms of its direct effects on renters and landlords, while the more pervasive effects of rent control and its sometimes profound impact on the global economy are often neglected or trivialised. And the second is that—to the extent that these pervasive effects are considered at all—inaccurate and even erroneous views that have gained public acceptance sometimes turn up even in scientific discussions and are in urgent need of reexamination. Since I am lucky enough to have no quarrel at all with

[1] [This essay is based on a lecture given to the German Economic Association in Königsberg in September 1930. It was first published as F. A. Hayek, "Wirkungen der Mietzinsbeschränkungen", in *Verhandlungen des Vereins für Sozialpolitik in Königsberg 1930: Grundlagen und Grenzen der Sozialpolitik. Deutsche Agrarnot. Städtische Wohn- und Siedelwirtschaft*, ed. F. Boese (Munich and Leipzig: Duncker & Humblot), *Schriften des Vereins für Sozialpolitik*, vol. 182, 1931, pp. 253–70. It was subsequently republished as chapter 14 of F. A. Hayek, *Wirtschaft, Wissenschaft und Politik: Aufsätze zur Wirtschaftspolitik*, ed. V. Vanberg (Tübingen: Mohr Siebeck, 2001). A rough translation was published as F. A. Hayek, "The Repercussions of Rent Restrictions", in F. A. Hayek, M. Friedman and G. Stigler, B. de Jouvenal, F. Paish, and S. Rydenfelt, *Verdict on Rent Control: Essays on the Economic Consequences of Political Action to Restrict Rents in Five Countries* (London: Institute of Economic Affairs, 1972). The version presented here was translated by Dr. Grete Heinz in 1995.—Ed.]

[2] [Waldemar Zimmermann (1876–1963) was Professor of Economics at the University of Hamburg. Hayek refers to W. Zimmermann, "Die Grenzen der Wohnungszwangswirtschaft", in *Verhandlungen des Vereins für Sozialpolitik in Königsberg 1930*, pp. 229–53.—Ed.]

the introductory remarks, I can deal more extensively with those matters that Mr. Zimmermann could treat only summarily in his talk.

I will therefore try to summarise in order the most important consequences of legally established rent control or of rents depressed below the market level through public construction projects. I will concentrate primarily on how these interventions influence the global supply of rental space as well as its composition, how they affect the apportioning of this supply among those looking for housing, and what is their impact on income distribution and production conditions in general, notably the supply of capital and the wage level. In keeping with the topic chosen for today, I will deal exclusively with tenant protection for private dwellings and will not concern myself with the closely related and highly important problem of the impact of tenant protection on business rentals, which I have on a previous occasion discussed in conjunction with this topic.[3]

Let me make one more preliminary remark. Should you find my presentation of the consequences of rent control to be somewhat overemphatic in certain respects, you must bear in mind that my views are strongly coloured, perforce, by conditions in Vienna. You undoubtedly realise that these differ from conditions in Germany. Suffice it to say that it will take another two years before average rents in Vienna attain their tentative maximum level, which will be 30% of the prewar level, and that at present there exists no right to reclaim one's apartment or select its tenant, in short, that managerial rights are in fact non-existent. I believe, however, that the relevance of my theoretical considerations to conditions in Germany is not in the least diminished by my personal experience. What is true for the situation in Vienna, where things stand out more clearly, must be just as true in principle for places where rent control is less stringent. My conclusions could just as well be deduced theoretically, and in reality the Viennese case merely serves as a particularly apt illustration. The Viennese case is in fact not extreme in every respect: the decline in the Viennese population diminishes the severity of certain consequences that would otherwise have been very harsh.

To come to the theoretical problems as such. Obvious as this point may seem, the problem that we face here is of a different nature than the problem of price control for other kinds of goods. I am referring to the fact that wartime controls on housing have not as yet been lifted, in contrast to all

---

[3] F. A. Hayek, "Das Mieterschutzproblem. Nationalökonomische Betrachtungen" (*Bibliothek für Volkswirtschaft und Politik*, No. 2) Vienna 1929. To a large extent the paper which follows is based on the earlier, more detailed study. [F. A. Hayek, *Das Mieterschutzproblem, Nationalökonomische Betrachtungen* (Vienna: Steyrermühl-Verlag, 1929) (*Bibliothek für Volkswirtschaft und Politik*, no. 2, 1929). The German version of this pamphlet was reprinted as chapter 13 of Hayek, *Wirtschaft, Wissenschaft und Politik.*—Ed.]

other types of control, not because housing needs are perhaps more press-ing than nutritional needs, nor because they are intrinsically more difficult or more expensive to fill. The only reason that apartments have been singled out, in contrast to almost all other consumption goods, is the fact that they are durable goods that can continue to remain in use for decades once they have been constructed and for this reason are more amenable to coercive measures than potatoes or lard. This peculiarity of dwellings obscures the most unpleas-ant consequence of any kind of price fixing, namely its effect on supply. This effect on apartments has not as yet been widely felt or generally noticed. But if we wish to evaluate the significance of tenant protection not only as a short-lived emergency measure but as a permanent state of affairs, we cannot en-visage it—as we might do if it were of limited duration—as a mere question of distributing and possibly supplementing available housing units. Instead, we must settle the basic question as to how the entire demand for housing at reduced rents can be satisfied.

In resolving this question, people, in my opinion, do not sufficiently rec-ognise how much the demand for housing increases in response to any given reduction in rent below the free-market level. This is not merely a matter of an elastic housing demand, one that increases disproportionately when rents are lowered for any reason whatever, even lowered building costs. A hous-ing shortage develops from any limitation on rents and is reflected in the dif-ficulty of finding a new apartment. This situation converts possession of an apartment into an economic asset and reinforces the tenant's urge to hold on to his apartment, even assuming that he might be willing to give it up at the reduced price, were he assured of finding a new apartment when the need arose. Almost all the collaborators in the introductory studies took due note of this phenomenon, but even so it is startling to read Wolff's findings. In quantifying the number of "continued occupancies of dwellings that pre-viously would have been vacated", he determined that it constituted almost a third of the new demand for apartments (about 80,000 to 85,000 out of 265,000). Yet elsewhere in this same study, Wolff complains that construction activity fell short of this annual demand by about one-quarter, namely 75,000 apartments.[4]

Under these circumstances, even in the absence of an increase in popula-tion, a huge unfilled housing need, which could be met only by public con-struction projects, was bound to materialise. Wherever a very large dispar-ity between legally set rents and free-market rents continues to exist, there is

---

[4] Cf. *Schriften* 177, I, pp. 91, 94, 156. [Hellmuth Wolff (1876–1961) was a German stat-istician. Hayek refers the reader to pp. 91, 94 and 156 of H. Wolff, "Wohnungsbedarf und Wohnungsangebot", in *Beiträge zur städtischen Wohn- und Siedelwirtschaft*, ed. W. Zimmermann (Munich and Leipzig: Duncker & Humblot), *Schriften des Vereins für Sozialpolitik*, vol. 177 (I), 1930, pp. 87–158.—Ed.]

almost certainly no prospect that the demand associated with reduced rents can ever be met. Although population has diminished by about one-seventh and apartments have probably increased by one-tenth—there are no reliable statistics on this score—there can be no question in this instance of a decline in the housing shortage. But even in Germany the housing shortage is primarily attributable to the increase in demand resulting from reduced rents, and in this light today's housing shortage is a consequence of tenant protection, as is clearly demonstrated by the fact that in almost all German cities housing density has declined, compared to prewar years—a fact also corroborated by Wolff.[5] I will later have more to say about how these calculations of average housing density should be interpreted in view of today's conditions.

This additional demand, which can be filled only by public building activity, is exacerbated not only by potential population growth, but also—and here we come at last to the problems created by permanently maintained housing control—demand created by the deterioration of existing dwelling units. When housing control served as an emergency measure, one could envisage construction activity as supplementing the stock of buildings previously erected by private means. In the long run, however, the entire housing stock will have to be supplied from public funds, if the increased housing demand generated by the global reduction in rents is to be met by public construction activity. We must stress that as long as rents remain below the market level, public construction cannot confine itself to providing for the supposed extra housing demand; in the end, public funds will have to assume responsibility for the entire demand. As the literature on the subject demonstrates, this point is by no means self-evident.

Aside from the fact that this outcome would pose nearly insurmountable financial problems, no representative body would wish to assume responsibility for the provision of all categories of apartments for which there might be demand. Of necessity, public construction activity will tend to be limited to certain more modest types of apartments, to which tenant protection would then logically have to be restricted. Limiting tenant protection to certain categories of apartments raises further difficulties, however, which, in my opinion, are very often overlooked. If public building activity and provision of apartments at below-cost rents are consistently confined, as it would have to be, to the most modest categories of dwellings, all of which would be dependent on public funds, the quality of these apartments must be such that they are suitable only for those population groups for whom society wishes to provide, and not wealthier segments of the population. For this reason it is illusory to expect that with funds available for public housing construction one can all at once eliminate the dearth of housing for the poorest part of the population

---

[5] Ibid., pp. 129–30. [Wolff, "Wohnungsbedarf und Wohnungsangebot", pp. 129–30.—Ed.]

and build apartments that are far above the housing standards of the bulk of the population. Better quality apartments may possibly be built from public funds, where available, as model buildings, but any attempt to reduce rents in this category below the level required to pay interest and amortization of the capital required for construction is bound to fail, as long as public funds are not adequate in the long run for meeting the entire demand for apartments in this category. It should be kept in mind, furthermore, that even when public construction activity is confined to the housing needs of the poorest segment of the population which it alone can fully meet, there is no way to avoid a significant and undesirable side effect. A rather substantial discrepancy is bound to arise between the rents of the best apartments erected with public funds and the slightly superior apartments constructed with private funds, with the result that a large number of people who, if rents were evenly graduated, might still have been willing to pay for a slightly higher-quality apartment, will be tempted by the relatively larger savings to settle for a poorer-quality apartment.

My speaking time is too short to examine in detail the impact of rent control on the volume and composition of the global housing supply. I will therefore limit myself to the composition of the existing supply. Most experts simply label the utilisation of living space under tenant protection as 'calcification' for which they give brief illustrations. I think that the phenomena subsumed under this phrase deserve closer attention, since almost all the 'more pervasive consequences' of tenant protection can be attributed thereto. All the other consequences are predicated on from the fact that, as is now the case, rent control applies to apartments of all quality levels and that therefore, as previously mentioned, the apartment shortage created by rent control continues to manifest itself. Under these conditions, whoever has an apartment with reduced rent remains subject to the conditions that prevailed before tenant protection was enacted. It is obvious that this historically determined distribution of rental space corresponds less and less to changing needs the longer tenant protection remains in effect, and labour mobility in particular suffers from this situation. Before examining these consequences more closely, however, I would first like to examine the limits to this 'calcification' and how it can be shattered. One of the ways to circumvent calcification is the subletting of a protected tenant's living space to a subtenant, another is the 'sale of apartments'—legally, if possible or de facto if not—that is, the transfer of the protected apartment in exchange for a relinquishing fee, a term that could be extended to cover most cases of exchanges between two apartments of unequal quality. However, for reasons mentioned above, not all renters who would have been content with smaller apartments in the absence of rent control are necessarily willing to sublet their apartments or enter into an exchange. Consequently persons whose only option for satisfying their housing needs is to become subtenants or to buy or trade apartments have a much smaller housing supply at their disposal than if they were freely competing for their share in a free housing market. The relationship between supply and demand is necessarily less favorable for the renter in these segmented markets than in markets where prices are freely established. The steadily increasing segment of the population that does not dispose of any protected apartment and is not eligible for public housing is worse off than it would be without tenant protection. In practical terms this means that a large part of the younger generation has to pay tribute to the older generation, which still disposes of apartments dating from the prewar period, and this tribute exceeds the rent which it would pay to the landlord without tenant protection.

These expedients are certainly of little avail in reestablishing mobility. The large majority of the population is severely tied down to whatever living space it has happened to obtain and is in no position to adapt this space in terms of size, location, and quality to its changing needs. Consequently there are such great variations in the number of persons per apartment that the customary statistical information about average housing density has practically lost its significance. This fact explains, on the other hand, why there is a greater housing shortage than there would be in a free housing market, even with the same housing density, that is, for a given housing supply.

Aside from the poor utilisation of available space for the satisfaction of different needs, reduced mobility of labour in terms of its deployment and replacement has had more severe consequences than has generally been realised. Geographic shifts in industrial labour demand have required very extensive labour movements, which have been hampered in the last decade by tenant protection, and this at a time when very substantial industrial shifts occurred. With unrestricted wage formation, this immobility would have interfered with equalisation of the wage level in different localities and would have caused a larger differential between local wages. Under current conditions of wage setting by collective bargaining, which prevents such large differences in most cases, there are two other consequences. To the extent that the new workplace can be reached from the old apartment by daily or weekly commuting, these alternatives replace moving to a new apartment, but the result is by no means equally advantageous. For a worker who is unable to move, there results a higher expenditure in time and money for these trips and a consequent reduction in his salary, an indirect manifestation of the inequality in wages. From a systemic economic point of view these and many other additional expenditures caused by the inability to move away from the old apartment represent pure wastefulness. Kautsky[6] points out that the doubling

---

[6] *Schriften* 177, III, pp. 70–71. [Benedikt Kautsky (1894–1960) was a German-born, Austrian economist and the son of Marxist theorist and politician Karl Kautsky (1854–1938). Hayek

of street car traffic in Vienna between 1913 and 1928 despite a simultaneous decline in the population was induced primarily by this restricted mobility, and Vas[7] estimates—with some exaggeration—that these coercive measures have extorted (from the Vienna population) added transportation expenses of 63 million Schillings per year, equivalent to two-thirds of the annual budget for municipal housing construction.

However, insofar as commuting instead of moving to a new apartment is not an option, then under today's conditions the result is unemployment. If I am not mistaken, Schumpeter once emphasised in the "Deutsche Volkswirt" that lack of labour mobility is a very significant source of unemployment.[8] I believe that this consequence is of the greatest importance. Let me report just one example that came to my attention just a few days ago. A manufacturer who is a friend of mine has a factory about five hours from Vienna and an office in Vienna itself. He asked for an electrician for the factory at the employment agency. About twenty men, some of them electricians who had been out of work for long periods, applied for the job, but they all turned it down with the comment that they would have to give up their protected apartments in Vienna in exchange for unprotected apartments at the factory. The factory owner has not been able to fill the position within the past several weeks despite intensive recruiting. Every manufacturer outside the large industrial localities in Austria can tell a similar tale.

I would almost say that matters become even worse when the policy of making housing cheaper is successful in actually making such lower-cost apartments available to persons moving to big cities. It should not be forgotten that migrations occur not only among the urban population that lives in rental dwellings. Thus every time urban apartments become cheaper, the attraction toward the city, the flight from the country, is reinforced. I would imagine that nobody would favour, for economic or social reasons, the artificial promotion of huge urban centers, yet that is precisely what occurs when the brake on this movement created by high rents is circumvented by these measures. Such migrations generally take place in periods of economic upswing,

---

refers to pp. 70–71 of B. Kautsky, "Die wirtschlaftlichen und sozialen Folgen des Wohnungsrechtes in Österreich", in *Beiträge zur städtischen Wohn- und Siedelwirtschaft*, ed. J. Bunzel (Munich and Leipzig: Duncker & Humblot), *Schriften des Vereins für Sozialpolitik*, vol. 177 (III), 1930, pp. 59–88.—Ed.]

[7] Ph. Vas, *Die Wiener Wohnungszwangswirtschaft von 1917–1927*, Jena 1928, p. 35. [See P. Vas, *Die Wiener Wohnungszwangswirtschaft von 1917–1927* (Jena: Fischer, 1928), p. 35.—Ed.]

[8] [Joseph Schumpeter (1883–1950) was an Austrian economist and sociologist who in the late 1920s contributed several articles to *Der Deutsche Volkswirt*, an economics and business weekly founded in 1926 by economist and journalist Gustav Stolper (1888–1947). The article to which Hayek refers is J. Schumpeter, "Die Arbeitslosigkeit", *Der Deutsche Volkswirt*, I.1 (March, 1927), pp. 729–32.—Ed.]

and when lowered rents foster urban migration, unemployment is likely to be exacerbated in the downswing that will inevitably ensue. Thus even sharply increased rents in boom times have something in their favor.

One final point to mention in passing. It is at the very least highly questionable whether persons with small means should be encouraged to bear children at the expense of the better-off and whether the urban population should be subsidised by the rural population, all of which undoubtedly results when measures are taken to prevent apartment size from being a function of income and when the urban growth is supported by federal funds.

I will later revert to a final point, which is very closely tied to the uneconomical distribution of the available living space, namely the inability to assess accurately the real demand for new buildings in terms of location and quality.

Our previous remarks have already clarified, implicitly, many of the consequences of rent control for the distribution of income, but I want to expound more fully one point on which erroneous views, I believe, are particularly widespread, namely, the issue of the effects of rent control on the wage level. This is certainly a very difficult issue, if the various indirect effects are kept in mind, but nevertheless the widespread opinion, which strangely enough, even Pribram espouses unquestioningly and without further justification in the volume under preparation,[9] namely that tenant protection has helped to keep wages low, is completely unfounded. I am referring here to the relative wage level compared to all other prices, not to the specific increase in purchasing power for individual workers in terms of living space. It is not surprising that the layman interprets the demand for higher wages in response to higher rents as implying that higher rents necessarily imply higher wages. Economists who espouse this reasoning, however, seem to be completely oblivious to their specialised knowledge. Pribram for instance exemplifies this erroneous view by writing in the above-mentioned publication that "to the extent that wages were determined (!) *on the basis of* (!) rents legally set by tenant protection regulations rather than the free-market rents, the prices of all products in which labour costs are a factor were kept lower" etc. The remarks we have quoted in this passage make it quite obvious that Pribram is not interested in analysing how wages are determined—presumably a pointless exercise—and only has

---

[9] *Schriften* 177 I, especially pp. 172–73. (The emphasis is mine.) [Economist and historian of economic thought Karl Pribram (1877–1973) taught economics at the University of Vienna, worked as head of the statistical office at the International Labour Office and at the time of writing the article mentioned here was Professor of Economics at the University of Frankfurt am Main. The quotation later in this paragraph comes from p. 173 of K. Pribram, "Die volkswirtschaftlichen Probleme der deutschen Wohnungswirtschaft", in *Beiträge zur städtischen Wohn- und Siedelwirtschaft*, ed. W. Zimmermann (Munich and Leipzig: Duncker & Humblot), *Schriften des Vereins für Sozialpolitik*, vol. 177 (I), 1930, pp. 159–272.—Ed.]

in mind the determination of something like a fair wage. His line of reasoning, which also underlies the widespread argument that tenant protection fosters production and exports, can be explained no other way.

For my part, I am absolutely certain that a cost theory of wages, which Pribram may have had somewhere at the back of his mind, is totally beside the point in connection with a relatively short-run phenomenon of this kind. With the labour market as it now exists and collective bargaining decisive for wage determination, we must start out from the assumption that at a given wage level only a certain number of workers can be employed. The magnitude of the wage increases that labour unions can win hinges on the strength of worker solidarity or on whether the level of unemployment support is high enough to prevent workers from underbidding the higher wages when they lose their jobs as a result of these wage increases. It goes without saying that industry could not employ more workers at a given wage level just because rents are higher. On the other hand, there is no reason to assume that a uniform increase in rents commensurate with increases in all the other prices would significantly modify the position of the labour unions. However, the assured possession of an apartment at a reduced rent is certainly equivalent to a very substantial increase in unemployment support for unemployed workers. The existence of tenant protection therefore mitigates the pressure of the unemployed on the labour market to the same extent as an increase in unemployment support. For this reason it is more plausible that on the supply side tenant protection exerts an upward rather than a downward pressure on wages, assuming that rent increases are of the same order of magnitude as increases in all other prices. Sudden increases in rents, perhaps in the wake of a sudden repeal of tenant protection, could well produce such drastic changes in workers' outlook that labour unions might demand higher wages at the risk of increasing unemployment, something that would previously have been unacceptable. But this is quite a different matter from insisting, as has been done repeatedly, that tenant protection inherently contributes to maintaining lower production costs.

It seems to me, in any case, that the direct impact of rent control on the wage level by its bearing on labour supply, irrespective of its direction, has been vastly overestimated. In my opinion certain indirect effects which influence the capacity of industry to pay high wages play a much greater role by affecting the demand side of the equation. I need hardly emphasise that any downward pressure tenant protection may have exerted on the wage level from this angle is an altogether different story from its much heralded contribution to keeping wages down. The effects to which I refer—and these are in every way deleterious effects—relate to the supply of capital. These effects are reinforced by the combined impact of all the other wastefulness to which I have already alluded and to which I will still refer, notably the uneconomic utilisation of available productive resources entailed by tenant protection. All of these must by the very nature of things, have an adverse effect on the demand price for human resources.

The current housing policy has had a two-fold effect on the supply of capital. One is that it has shrunk the supply of capital that would have been available, had nothing interfered with the amortization of existing housing property and that can now no longer be reserved from property income. This fact is very important for industry because under present conditions a large part of these amortization reserves would not have been plowed back into housing construction but would have been invested in the rest of the economy at least during a transition period. The second and even more important factor in shrinking the supply of capital for the economy has been the enormous amount of capital absorbed by public building activity and thus invested in a way that did not contribute as much to the productivity of human labour as would have happened without the housing policy adopted.

How much capital has been absorbed by the construction of public housing—without its having even come close to eliminating the existing housing shortage—is most clearly indicated by the fact that 700 million Schillings were invested by the city of Vienna since the war in the construction of apartment buildings, while the global amount of share capital of all Austrian companies registered at the Vienna stock exchange comes to no more than 961 million Schillings, based on the calculated average for 1929 as estimated by the Austrian Institute for Business Cycle Research. This amount has since then dropped by about 25% and now probably barely exceeds 700 million Schillings.

There can be no question that spending an amount exceeding the value of the entire productive capital of Austrian industry—if we include all the expenditures by the Bund and by the other Bundeslaender as well as the whole administrative costs of the current housing policy—must have had a substantial impact. Even if we assume that only a part of this amount would have been converted into industrial capital, had taxes not had to be raised for the purpose of public housing, it is unquestionable that the final impact on the productivity of human labour and hence on the wage level was quite significant.

One's position on a question that can be addressed here only briefly does play a critical role in evaluating these expenditures of capital and even the housing policy as a whole. Anyone who holds the view that the economic difficulties of the postwar years and particularly the high rate of unemployment can be dealt with successfully by reinforcing consumption, anyone who believes that there is no shortage of durable productive resources but that inadequate consumer income stands in the way of fully utilising available productive capital and that therefore any kind of public works can be expected to have an invigorating effect on the economy, any such person will view more favorably than I am inclined to do the expenditure of capital in the construction of housing and the built-in tendency of the entire current housing policy to reinforce consumption at the expense of capital formation. As I have already mentioned, I unfortunately do not have the time here to refute these widely held and most pernicious fallacies in economic theory, whose main source is the United States. All I can do here is to point out that differences in interpretation on this score cannot be divorced from positions taken on problems that lie far beyond the narrower scope of my talk.

Leaving aside the consequences of withdrawing capital from the rest of the economy, the question must be addressed whether the amounts of capital devoted to housing construction contribute at least as effectively to the satisfaction of housing needs under rental restrictions as the same amounts spent under freely determined rents. I must come back here to the question raised earlier and at the same time focus on one of the most serious problems of the prevailing housing policy. What was stated earlier about the wasteful distribution of preexisting living space applies with equal force to construction activity deprived of the guidance of freely determined prices. The fact that there are no rental restrictions on new buildings is of no consequence here. What is decisive in reality is that the needs of persons who, today, happen not to have any apartment and for whom new buildings are primarily intended, are not identical with the needs that would arise if there were a sensible distribution of available living space at this point. On economic grounds, it would generally make most sense that those who presently lack apartments would take over existing apartments and that at the same time apartments in really short supply of quite a different sort or in quite a different location would be built instead. But today we have no idea for what size and what quality apartments there exists a real need. Construction therefore does not complement existing housing in an organic fashion. It is as though existing apartments were under no circumstance suitable for the persons in need of housing and, conversely, the housing needs of persons in a protected apartment were unchangeable for an indefinite future. Just because, for example, a certain number of young couples happen to be looking for an apartment in a certain locality or city district, construction now occurs there, though far more people already live in that locality than want to do so and the needed apartments would become vacant if mobility were unrestricted. Or else apartments are being constructed that are primarily intended for families with children, because no suitable apartments are available for them, although far more older couples live in such apartments and no longer need them.

The enormous wastefulness represented by such unplanned building activity makes it highly questionable whether one should defer the repeal of rent control until supply and demand have equalised in the housing market, as

Kruschwitz[10] believes, or that, indeed, such a state of affairs can ever materialise under these conditions. Even before the war and thus quite independently of a controlled economy, Adolf Weber recognised "the basic cause of housing problems . . . to be the distorted relationship between the highly volatile economic relations of modern times and the rigidity of the housing market".[11] Can we really hope to eliminate housing shortages today while we continue to deprive ourselves even of the opportunity to adapt new construction to changing needs?

I hope to have accomplished herewith the actual objective of my report, which was to give a systematic review of the consequences of rent control within the short time allotted for my talk. If the enumeration of these consequences as revealed by a theoretical investigation is identical with a listing of the sins of tenant protection, this should not, in my opinion, be blamed on the fact that a theoretical treatment of the problem and a liberal approach to the subject are bound to give identical results—a view held by the gentleman who invited me to give this lecture in the name of the board members. I do not see how anyone examining the problem from a theoretical standpoint could arrive at different results, irrespective of his economic policy views. The reason that a theoretical analysis reveals only negative consequences is that everyone clearly understands the immediate favorable effects for the sake of which tenant protection was introduced in the first place, while the unintended consequences of any intervention of this sort can be clarified only with the help of theory. That these unintended consequences are all unfavorable is hardly surprising after all. Everyone is free to opt for tenant protection after weighing these unfavorable effects against its favorable aspects. Pointing out the unfavorable effects does not necessarily imply a definite stand against tenant protection. Only if one knows the consequences can one decide for or against it.

As to my conclusions about future policy from the findings that I have presented here, that is a different matter. On this score I must state, first of all, that after weighing all the pros and cons, I am convinced that without an early restoration of a free housing market there is no way out of our current difficulties. But even given this final objective, what can a fuller grasp of the current situation teach us in dealing with the transition period? The conviction that the restoration of a free housing market is inherently desirable does not

---

[10] *Schriften* 177 I, p. 48. [See H. Kruschwitz, "Deutsche Wohnungswirtschaft und Wohnungspolitik seit 1913", in *Beiträge zur städtischen Wohn- und Siedelwirtschaft*, ed. W. Zimmermann (Munich and Leipzig: Duncker & Humblot), *Schriften des Vereins für Sozialpolitik*, vol. 177 (I), 1930, pp. 1–48.—Ed.]

[11] Adolf Weber, *Die Wohnungsproduktion*, Gr. d. S, p. 354 (Tübingen 1914). [Adolf Weber (1876–1963) was a German economist. The complete reference of the work cited by Hayek is A. Weber, "Die Wohnungsproduktion," *Grundriss der Sozialökonomik*, VI. *Abteilung. Industrie, Bergwesen, Bauwesen.* (Tübingen: J. C. B. Mohr (Paul Siebeck), 1914), p. 354.—Ed.]

by any means suggest that the immediate repeal of tenant protection is the most appropriate way to reach this goal. As we have seen, tenant protection does not just mean that renters pay a lower rent than would otherwise be the case. One important side effect is the fact that the distribution of available living space today is quite different from what it would have been under free-market conditions, so that freeing the housing market would result not only in a greater burden on the tenant but would also lead to a change in the distribution of living space. A sudden repeal of tenant protection would then trigger such extensive changes as to trigger a total disorganisation of the market and would threaten all the concomitant dangers implied thereby. It would suddenly become apparent that a vast disproportion exists between the composition of demand on the one hand and of supply on the other. Certain kinds of apartments and dwellings in certain localities would increase in price quite disproportionately to their cost. The situation would undoubtedly be especially difficult in the case of small apartments, since demand for smaller units on the part of those forced by rent increases to vacate their current larger apartments would greatly exceed the demand for the vacated and probably relatively cheap larger apartments. At first there would also be no yardstick for appropriate rent levels and attempts would certainly be made to raise rents excessively, a maneuver that might well be successful during the initial chaotic period.

The stepwise raising of rents, which is the most widely used procedure, would not in my opinion do much to alleviate these problems. Under this procedure, at the time the critical point—the attainment of free market prices, the convergence of supply and demand and hence full mobility—would be reached, no correction in the current distribution of dwellings would as yet have taken place to ease the transition. An expedient, in my opinion, would be to allow as large as possible a free market to coexist with the controlled apartments, in other words, to expand gradually as far as possible the existing free market (that is, apartments not covered by tenant protection on the one hand, sublet apartments or apartments offered for sale on the other). The basis for this approach already exists today, since a growing part of the population no longer enjoys the advantages of tenant protection. What is essential is to avoid the establishment of new tenant entitlements and the related misdirection of newly arising demand and at the same time to channel as many existing apartments as possible into this free market without creating a new demand by the eviction of old tenants. I hope that this brief outline conveys the underlying idea well enough that I need only sketch out in key words, mainly for the sake of illustration, what measures in this direction seem most promising.

The first would certainly be to convert tenant protection from something tied to a given living space to a personal right of the tenant, that is, a right tied to him personally and to those truly dependent on him, thereby terminating the heritability and transferability of protected apartments. Tenant protection should be eliminated, furthermore, for apartments that are very large in absolute terms and large in terms of the size of the main tenant's family. It should be eliminated, finally, for sublet apartments and parts of apartments to the extent that the home owner himself sets aside this part of the dwelling as an independent rental unit. The partitioning of large existing apartments should be especially encouraged, although the opportunity to rent under free-market conditions the separated-off unit of an apartment previously under tenant protection would by itself be a strong incentive. To enhance the supply even further, an acceptable form of pressure would be to apply a rental tax or similar fee for vacant apartments as well, according to their estimated value. In addition, since the whole new procedure would benefit landlords, the unfavorable market situation of tenants during this transitional period might be mitigated by forcing landlords to give considerable advance notice before terminating tenants' leases, while tenants for their part would be entitled to give short notice before terminating the lease.

It is particularly important that the rents emerging in these partial markets serve as the sole guideposts for subsequent building activity. Under these circumstances public funds will probably be required to foster building activity, so as to prevent rents in certain localities and for certain categories of dwellings from exceeding the level that they would gradually reach for privately constructed dwellings. In any case, these resources should be applied only where there is at least a prospect of relative profitability, and it should be required that in all publicly supported construction projects rents be set at whatever level could eventually be maintained after the elimination of tenant protection.

And to the extent that public funds continue to be applied in housing construction for the sake of rent reduction, these resources should be reserved for the construction of very modest small apartments, in line with the arguments presented earlier.

(loud applause)

ELEVEN

ECONOMICS[1]

Economics, as a theoretical discipline, aims at explaining those uniformities in the economic activities of society which are not the result of deliberate design but the produce of the interplay of the separate decisions of individuals and groups. As a name for this theoretical science 'economics' has since about 1880 gradually replaced the older term 'political economy', and it is often also used in a wider sense which includes the allied descriptive and 'applied' studies which serve more directly the needs of current policy and for which the older name was perhaps more appropriate.

Development of Economics

Some of the central problems of economic theory have been discussed ever since classical antiquity, and a good deal of technical knowledge on particular economic phenomena has been gradually accumulated since. Moral and political philosophers on the one hand and business men and administrators on the other contributed to this in their different ways. On the origin of value the views expressed by some of the Greek philosophers remained long the standard views, while in the field of money interesting contributions were made by some mediaeval and early modern writers, particularly in Italy.[2]

---

[1] [F. A. Hayek, "Economics", *Chambers's Encyclopaedia*, volume IV (London: George Newnes, 1950), pp. 771–75.—Ed.]

[2] [Prominent amongst the anticipations of economic thought to which Hayek alludes are the views of Aristotle (384–322 BC) on household management, for which art he reserved the term 'economy', trade, and justice. In book I of the *Politics*, Aristotle distinguishes between the natural or proper art of acquisition, whereby people trade with one another in order to obtain the goods they need to live a good life, and trading for the purpose of making money or profit, which he condemns as improper and unnatural (reserving particular scorn for the lending of money at interest). Book V of the *Nicomachean Ethics* sees Aristotle consider the principles of justice, including those pertaining to the exchange and distribution of goods (reciprocal or commutative justice). The influence of Aristotle's ideas—perhaps most notably, his distinction between the use value and the exchange value of a good, his notion of a 'just price' as involving the equivalence of the values given and received in exchange, and his condemnation of trading for profit in general and usury in particular—can be seen in the writings of mediaeval thinkers such

Early Economic Theorists

The theoretical questions raised by the problems of economic policy however began to attract serious attention only in the 17th century when the passing of the feudal system and the rise of the centralised national states made the financial and economic strength of the states a matter of great importance. It was in the course of the discussions of this period, concerned with the effects of foreign trade, the stimulation of manufacturing industry and particularly with money, that the rudiments of the science were developed. Yet, although the 'mercantilists', as the writers of this period are called, were concerned with a common set of problems, they can hardly be regarded as a definite school with a common doctrine.[3]

---

as Saint Thomas Aquinas (1225–74). In his *Summa Theologiae* [1265–73], Aquinas argued that there was something base about commerce, excoriated usury, and set great store by the notion of a 'just price'. Hayek's views on Aristotle, whom he criticises for ignoring the possibility of spontaneously-grown orders and for failing to discern how the pursuit of personal gain makes possible the extended pattern of market trade upon which Athenian society depended, can be found in F. A. Hayek, *The Fatal Conceit: The Errors of Socialism*, ed. W. W. Bartley III, vol. 1 (1988) of *The Collected Works of F. A. Hayek* (Chicago: University of Chicago Press; London: Routledge), pp. 45–48.

The most notable writer on money from the medieval and early modern era was French Roman Catholic Bishop and Scholastic philosopher, mathematician, and economist Nicole Oresme (c. 1320–82). Oresme translated Aristotle's *Ethics* and *Politics* from Latin into French and wrote on theology and mathematics, as well as on economics. In his *De origine, natura, jure et mutationibus monetarum* [c. 1360], Oresme developed an Aristotelian perspective on the nature and origins of money, setting out a version of what later became known as 'Gresham's law'— the idea that bad money drives out good—and condemning the destructive effects on a nation's economy of the debasement of its currency. See N. Oresme, *The De Moneta of Nicholas Oresme and English Mint Documents*, trans. C. Johnson (London: Thomas Nelson and Sons, 1956), part I. French lawyer and political philosopher Jean Bodin (1530–96) is widely credited with introducing into legal and political thought the theory of state sovereignty, and treated the right of coinage as one of the most important parts of sovereignty. See J. Bodin, *Les six livres de la République* (1576), trans. R. Knolles as *The Six Bookes of a Commonweale* (London: Impensis G. Bishop, 1606). He also, in his *Response to the Paradoxes of Malestroit* [1568/1578], trans. H. Tudor and R. W. Dyson (Bristol: Thoemmes, 1997), offered one of the earliest formulations of the quantity theory of money. According to Hayek, Bodin, "understood more about money than most of his contemporaries". See F. A. Hayek, "The Denationalization of Money" [1978], reprinted as chapter 4 of F. A. Hayek, *Good Money, Part II: The Standard*, ed. S. Kresge, vol. 6 (1999) of *The Collected Works of F. A. Hayek*, p. 137. Early modern Italian writers on money included: banker Gasparo Scaruffi (1519–84), whose monograph *L'Alitinonfo: per fare ragione e concordanza d'oro e d'argento* (Reggio: Hercoliano Bartoli, 1582) explored the functions of money and contained a proposal for a universal currency referenced by Hayek in "The Denationalization of Money", p. 151 n. 40; and Florentine merchant, translator of Tacitus, and economist Bernardo Davanzati (1529–1606), who in *Lezione delle monete* [1588], trans. J. Toland as *A Discourse upon Coins* (London: A. and J. Churchill, 1696), treated money as a social convention and set out a version of the quantity theory.—Ed.]

[3] ['Mercantilism' was a broad set of ideas and policies, common from the sixteenth to the eighteenth century, that centred on the use of government intervention in the economy in order to promote the power of the domestic state at the expense of rival foreign powers. Mercantil-

We can scarcely speak of systematic attempts to join the various bits of knowledge into a coherent discipline before the 18th century. The end of the 17th century, however, saw some vigorous attempts to collect empirical information on the part of Sir William Petty and some of his fellow 'political arithmeticians', while at the same time moral philosophers like John Locke, and the European theorists of the 'law of nature' devoted increasing parts of their more comprehensive systems to the discussion of economic topics.[4]

The first of the 18th-century authors who successfully singled out the greater part of what today is the field of economics was Richard Cantillon (c. 1680–1734), a banker of Irish origin who lived in Paris and London and whose *Essai sur la nature du commerce en général* (originally written in English) appeared only in 1755 in a French translation.[5] While on special points impor-

---

ist policies included efforts to develop domestic industry, to generate a surplus of exports over imports, and to accumulate stocks of precious metals. Prominent seventeenth-century mercantilists included English businessman and writer Thomas Mun (1571–1641) and Italian economist Antonio Serra (dates unknown), who both contributed significantly to the economic analysis of the balance of trade, and Jean-Baptiste Colbert (1619–83), controller of finance under Louis XIV, who sought to increase French power through policies designed to increase France's share of international trade. The term 'mercantilism' was popularised by the Scottish political economist Adam Smith (1723–90) as a label for such policies, of which he was highly critical. See A. Smith, *An Inquiry into the Nature and Causes of the Wealth of Nations*, ed. W. B. Todd, vol. 2 of *The Glasgow Edition of the Works and Correspondence of Adam Smith* (Oxford: Oxford University Press, 1976; reprinted, Indianapolis, IN: Liberty Fund, 1981), book IV.—Ed.]

[4] [English doctor, administrator and political economist Sir William Petty (1623–87) is best known as the founder of 'political arithmetic', defined as the production and statistical analysis of quantitative data concerning population and wealth for the purpose of state governance. See W. Petty, *Political Arithmetick* (London: For Robert Clavel, and Hen. Mortlock, 1690). Other pioneers in this emerging field included English statistician and demographer John Graunt (1620–74), who estimated the population of London; English herald and political economist Gregory King (1648–1712), who improved upon the estimates of population and wealth provided by Graunt and Petty; and English government official and political economist Charles Davenant (1656–1714), who examined questions of taxation.

English philosopher John Locke (1632–1704) wrote on various issues in monetary economics in his *Some Considerations of the Consequences of the Lowering of Interest, and Raising the Value of Money* [1691], and in *Further Considerations Concerning Raising the Value of Money* [1695], both reprinted in J. Locke, *Several Papers Relating to Money, Interest and Trade, &c* (London: Printed for A. and J. Churchill and others, 1696) and in *The Works of John Locke, in Nine Volumes*, 12th edn., vol. 4 (London: C. and J. Rivington, 1824). Hayek's views on Locke's economics are discussed in more detail in F. A. Hayek, "The Dilemma of Specialisation" [1956], reprinted as chapter 13 of the current volume, p. 197 n. 12.

Prominent seventeenth-century natural law theorists who dealt with economic subjects include Dutch statesman and jurist Hugo Grotius (1583–1645) and German jurist and historian Samuel Pufendorf (1632–94), both of whom wrote on value and just price. See H. Grotius, *The Rights of War and Peace* [1625], trans. A. C. Campbell (London and New York: M. Walter Dunne, 1901), book II, chapter 12, and S. Pufendorf, *The Law of Nature and Nations* [1672], trans. B. Kennet (Oxford: A. and J. Churchill and others, 1703), book V, chapters 1–8.—Ed.]

[5] [Irish economist and banker Richard Cantillon (c. 1680–1734) spent most of his life in France. His *Essai*, first written around 1730–34 but published only posthumously, provides a sys-

tant contributions were made by many of the other brilliant writers on economics, in which the middle of the century is particularly rich and of whom David Hume, Ferdinando Galiani and A. R. J. Turgot are the outstanding figures, the only other comprehensive system which was achieved before Adam Smith is that of the French 'physiocrats' or *économistes*. This group, under the leadership of François Quesnay (1694–1774) attracted for a time great attention and, although on some of the central theoretical questions distinctly inferior to its immediate predecessors and contemporaries, made a real and influential contribution by its attempt to picture the process of the circulation of wealth as a whole.[6]

---

tematic treatment of many subjects in economics, including the nature and sources of wealth, the theory of value, the analysis of population, entrepreneurship, the determination of prices, wages, and interest, monetary theory, foreign trade and currency, and banking and credit. See R. Cantillon, *Essai sur la nature du commerce en général* [1755], edited with an English translation and other material by H. Higgs (London: Macmillan for the Royal Economic Society, 1931). The book had some influence in its day, being cited by Adam Smith in *The Wealth of Nations*, but it became famous only after it was rediscovered in the late nineteenth century by William Stanley Jevons. See W. S. Jevons, "Richard Cantillon and the Nationality of Political Economy" [1881], reprinted in Cantillon, *Essai*, pp. 333–60. Elsewhere, Hayek describes the *Essai* as "the first great theoretical work of our science [of economics]". See F. A. Hayek, "The Economy, Science and Politics" [1963], reprinted as chapter 7 of Hayek, *The Market and Other Orders*, ed. Bruce Caldwell, vol. 15 (2014) of *The Collected Works of F. A. Hayek*, p. 221. Hayek discusses Cantillon at length in F. A. Hayek, "Richard Cantillon (c. 1680–1734)" [1931], reprinted as chapter 13 of F. A. Hayek, *The Trend of Economic Thinking: Essays on Political Economists and Economic History*, ed. W.W. Bartley III and S. Kresge, vol. 3 (1991) of *The Collected Works of F. A. Hayek.*—Ed.]

[6] [Scottish philosopher David Hume's (1711–76) writings on money and international trade can be found in part II of D. Hume, *Essays: Moral, Political, and Literary* [1777], ed. E. F. Miller (Indianapolis, IN: Liberty Fund, 1987).

Italian civil servant and economist Ferdinando Galiani (1728–87) developed a subjective theory of value based on the notions of utility and scarcity, thereby foreshadowing some of the key ideas of modern value theory as it developed after the marginal revolution of the 1870s. See F. Galiani, *Della moneta* (Naples: G. Raimondi, 1750), now available as *On Money*, trans. P. Toscano (Ann Arbor: University Microfilms International, 1977). For Hayek, this made Galiani "the greatest of the early anticipators of modern theory". See F. A. Hayek, "The Austrian School of Economics" [1968], reprinted as chapter 1 of F. A. Hayek, *The Fortunes of Liberalism: Essays on Austrian Economics and the Ideal of Freedom*, ed. Peter G. Klein, vol. 4 (1992) of *The Collected Works of F. A. Hayek*, p. 43.

French administrator and economist Anne Robert Jacques Turgot (1727–81) was comptroller-general of finance under Louis XVI from 1774 to 1776. His most famous work is his *Réflexions sur la formation et la distribution des richesses*, which is perhaps most notable for Turgot's analysis of the nature of wealth and of the relations between capital accumulation, savings and the rate of interest. See A. Turgot, "Reflections on the Formation and Distribution of Wealth" [1766], reprinted as chapter 5 of *The Economics of A. R. J. Turgot*, edited and translated with an introduction by P. D. Groenewegen (The Hague: Martinus Nijhoff, 1977). In the unfinished "Value and Money" [1769], reprinted as chapter 9 of the same volume, Turgot analysed the value of a good, along subjectivist lines, as depending on its fitness to serve the purposes for which it was intended and the difficulty of obtaining it.

In his *Tableau Économique* [1758], French lawyer and physician François Quesney (1694–1774)

The temporary success of this sect was soon eclipsed however by the immediate and lasting success of Adam Smith's *Inquiry into the Nature and Causes of the Wealth of Nations*, published in 1776.[7] The great importance of this work is due less to any contributions to the details of theoretical analysis, which are comparatively few, than to the broad sweep of its treatment, its historical and philosophical perspective and its literary excellence. Indebted mainly to the rich school of Scottish moral philosophers of which it is itself the crowning achievement, the work effectively summed up the state of knowledge of the time, and by the views it adopted or discarded determined what was to be the basis for the development of economics for at least a hundred years. It created for the first time a widespread understanding of the forces through which the market process directed the distribution of resources between the different industries, and of the manner in which competition produced a kind of order based on specialisation and the division of labour. The predominantly practical aim brought it about that Smith's theoretical argument was closely connected with his strong advocacy of freedom of trade and his severe criticism of most restrictions of competition, whether by government regulations or by combinations of producers. But while Smith was a convinced believer in free trade, he not only regarded as chimerical any hope of establishing free trade but also qualified his argument for *laissez-faire* by several important exceptions.[8]

---

compared the flow of wealth through a nation to the circulation of blood within the human body. See *Quesnay's Tableau Economique* [1759], 3rd edn., ed. M. Kucznyski and R. Meek (London: Macmillan for the Royal Economic Society, 1972). The physiocrats argued that land is the source of all wealth and that government should not interfere with the operation of natural economic laws, and constituted the first systematic school of political economy. Their ranks also included French political economist Victor Riquetti (1715–89), Marquis de Mirabeau, whose interesting use of Cantillon's *Essai* is discussed at length in Hayek's aforementioned essay on Cantillon, pp. 249–51, 273–78.—Ed.]

[7] [See Smith, *An Inquiry into the Nature and Causes of the Wealth of Nations.*—Ed.]

[8] [The Scottish moral philosophers to whom Hayek refers included lawyer and philosopher Henry Home, Lord Kames (1696–1782), philosopher and historian David Hume, and philosopher and historian Adam Ferguson (1723–1816). The common thread running through their work, and that of Smith, is the idea that many social institutions have not been consciously designed but rather have arisen spontaneously. They are, in the words of Adam Ferguson, "the result of human action, but not the execution of any human design". See A. Ferguson, *An Essay on the History of Civil Society* (Edinburgh: Printed for A. Millar and T. Caddel, London, and A. Kincaid and J. Bell, Edinburgh, 1767), p. 187. In that book, Ferguson portrays the development of private property and government as being the result of an evolutionary process rather than of deliberate design. Likewise, in book III of his *Treatise of Human Nature*, "Of Morals", Hume explores how general rules of justice arise as the unintended consequence of individual action. See D. Hume, *A Treatise of Human Nature: Being an Attempt to Introduce the Experimental Method of Reasoning into Moral Subjects* [1739–40], ed. L. A. Selby-Bigge (Oxford: Clarendon Press, 1896). Similarly, Lord Kames explains the emergence of a formal system of government, and of property in land, as the unplanned outcome of a four-stage process of social evolution. See his *Essays on the Principles of Morality and Natural Religion*, 2nd edn. (London: Printed for C. Hitch & L. Hawes,

The success of the *Wealth of Nations* gave Smith's teaching lasting influence, even on those theoretical questions where his analysis was less satisfactory than that of some of his predecessors and contemporaries. This proved to be particularly significant with respect to the theory of value, where Smith had half-heartedly adopted a theory which explained the value of commodities in terms of the quantity of labour employed in their production. It was due to him that the labour theory of value secured a firm position in English political economy and became an essential part of its so-called 'classical school', while in Europe the utility approach, initiated by F. Galiani and developed by Smith's contemporary É. B. de Condillac, retained its influence and finally produced developments which superseded the central doctrines of the 'classical' school.[9]

'Classical' School

This school took definite shape in the efforts to master the new problems raised by the progress of the industrial revolution and by the grave economic disturbances caused by the Napoleonic wars. During the forty years following the appearance of the *Wealth of Nations* substantial advances were made in the study of particular problems, especially in the field of monetary theory. Some of the essential foundations of the new school were provided by T. R. Malthus's *Essay on the Principle of Population* (1798), the development of Jeremy Bentham's utilitarian philosophy, and J. B. Say's elegant systematisation of the body of economic knowledge in his *Traité d'économie politique* (1803). But the decisive event which led to the formation of a definite school was the publication of David Ricardo's *Principles of Political Economy and Taxation* in 1817. He and his mentor James Mill, to whose tuition it was largely due that the successful stockbroker and financial expert developed into one of the most powerful abstract thinkers economics has known, must be regarded as the founders of modern economic theory. It was Ricardo's misfortune however that he built his rigorously deductive system on the inadequate foundations provided by Adam Smith's theory of value. His theories consequently suffered from seri-

---

R. & J. Dodsley, J. Rivington & J. Fletcher, and J. Richardson, 1758). For Hayek's views on the broader evolutionary tradition of thought of which these Scottish Enlightenment thinkers form a part, see for example F. A. Hayek, "Individualism: True and False" [1946], reprinted as the Prelude to *Studies on the Abuse and Decline of Reason: Text and Documents*, ed. Bruce Caldwell, vol. 13 (2010) of *The Collected Works of F. A. Hayek*, and F. A. Hayek, "The Results of Human Action but Not of Human Design" [1967], reprinted as chapter 11 of *The Market and Other Orders.*—Ed.]

[9] [French philosopher, psychologist, logician, and economist Étienne Bonnot de Condillac, Abbé de Mureau (1714–80), developed a subjective theory of value, according to which the exchange value of a good depends upon the utility it yields, in his *Le commerce et le gouvernement, considérés relativement l'un à l'autre* (Amsterdam: Jombert and Cellot, 1776).—Ed.]

ous defects of which, towards the end of his life, Ricardo became more clearly aware than most of his pupils. Even so his method of reasoning and the problems which he selected, particularly the central position which he gave the theory of value and of the distribution of incomes, have remained characteristic of most economic theory until recent times. Although the details of his theory never commanded general assent his views remained on the whole dominant during that particularly fertile twenty-five years of discussion which followed his death. This 'classical' tradition finally received a new lease of life when John Stuart Mill incorporated its main ideas into his *Principles of Political Economy* (1848) in which the bare bones of economic theory were expounded against the background of a comprehensive social philosophy. It remained the most influential book on the subject for the second half of the 19th century.[10]

[10] [Thomas Robert Malthus (1766–1834) was an English clergyman, economist and demographer best known for his theory that population growth will tend to outrun the supply of food, so that the betterment of mankind is impossible without limits on reproduction. See T. Malthus, *An Essay on the Principle of Population As It Affects the Future Improvement of Society, with Remarks on the Speculations of Mr. Godwin, M. Condorcet, and Other Writers* (London: Printed for J. Johnson, 1798). In contrast to Malthus's 'under-consumptionist' thesis that downturns in the trade cycle are caused by excessive savings, French economist Jean-Baptiste Say (1767–1832) denied that there could be a shortage of demand in general, a counter-argument commonly known as 'Say's law'. Although Say was the best-known interpreter of Adam Smith's views in both Europe and the United States, he departed from Smith's cost-of-production theory of value, adopting instead a subjectivist approach according to which the value of a good derives from the utility it affords its user. See J.-B. Say, *Traité d'économie politique* [1803], 3rd edn., 2 vols. (Paris: Deterville, 1817).

English philosopher, jurist, and reformer Jeremy Bentham (1748–1832) set out his utilitarian philosophy in *An Introduction to the Principles of Morals and Legislation* (London: Printed for T. Payne and Son, 1789). Bentham was a 'philosophical radical' who, like both James and John Stuart Mill, used utilitarianism as a basis for criticising and reforming social institutions. Bentham's most famous work in economics is his *Defence of Usury* (London: Payne and Foss, 1787), where he takes Adam Smith to task for his reluctance to countenance free trade in the lending of money at interest. Bentham's economic writings are collected in W. Stark, ed., *Jeremy Bentham's Economic Writings*, 3 vols. (London: George Allen and Unwin, 1952–54).

David Ricardo (1772–1823) was an English stockbroker and economist who, in his *On the Principles of Political Economy and Taxation* (London: John Murray, 1817), analysed the laws governing the distribution of national income between rent, wages and profits (that is, between landlords, workers, and the owners of capital). James Mill (1773–1836) was a Scottish philosopher, historian and economist, and mentor to Ricardo. Mill's *Elements of Political Economy* (London: Printed for Baldwin, Cradock, and Joy, 1821) expounded Ricardo's ideas and summarised the philosophical radicals' views on economics. English philosopher and political economist John Stuart Mill's (1806–73) *Principles of Political Economy* expounded a modified version of Ricardian economics and became the leading introductory text in English until it was superseded by Alfred Marshall's *Principles of Economics*, vol. 1 (London: Macmillan and Co., 1890). See J. S. Mill, *Principles of Political Economy with some of their applications to Social Philosophy* [1848], vols. 2 (1965) and 3 (1965) of the *Collected Works of John Stuart Mill*, ed. J. M. Robson (Toronto: Toronto University Press; reprinted, Indianapolis: Liberty Fund, 2006). According to Hayek, in his later writings Mill shifted away from classical liberalism towards socialism, thereby helping to pave the way for the acceptance of socialist ideas amongst the British intelligentsia in the late nineteenth and

'Marginal' Revolution

Less influential and somewhat outside the orthodox classical tradition was a group of economists at Oxford and Dublin, of whom N. W. Senior (*An Outline of the Science of Political Economy*, 1836) was the best known figure and who on the central subject of value approached much closer both to modern theory and to European thought of the time.[11] Outside England the utility approach had always retained a stronger hold and in the beginning of the 1870s Carl Menger in Austria and Léon Walras in Switzerland began to expound, almost simultaneously with W. S. Jevons in England, the new 'marginal utility' theory of value which was finally to displace the 'classical' labour theory of value, which has survived almost exclusively among some disciples of Karl Marx and in the form which the latter had given it. The achievement

---

early twentieth century. See Hayek, *Studies on the Abuse and Decline of Reason*, pp. 56–57, 71, 238–39. For a more detailed analysis of Hayek's opinions about Mill, see B. Caldwell, "Hayek on Mill", *History of Political Economy*, vol. 40, 2008, pp. 689–704.—Ed.]

[11] [Nassau Senior (1790–1864) was an English lawyer, classical economist, and the first incumbent of the Drummond Chair of Political Economy at Oxford University (1825–30, 1847–52), whose ideas helped to prepare the way for the marginalist revolution. In particular, Senior is often credited with introducing both the idea that profit is the reward enjoyed by capitalists for their decision to abstain from consuming their wealth, and also the notion of diminishing marginal utility, thereby anticipating—albeit without fully working out the implications of—concepts that later were central to the marginalist theory of value. See N. Senior, *An Outline of the Science of Political Economy* (London: W. Clowes and Sons, 1836). Aside from Senior, the "group of economists at Oxford and Dublin" included Anglican clergyman and social reformer Richard Whately (1787–1863) and English political economist William Forster Lloyd (1794–1852). Whately was a close friend of Senior, having taught him at Oxford, and succeeded him as Drummond Professor (1829–31). Whately favoured a subjectivist over a labour theory of value, arguing that, "It is not that pearls fetch a high price *because* men have dived for them; but on the contrary, men dive for them because they fetch a high price". He was also the first person to use the term 'catallactics' to describe the science that studies market exchanges. See R. Whately, *Introductory Lectures on Political Economy*, 2nd edn. (London: B. Fellowes, 1832), pp. 253, 6. Whately became Anglican Archbishop of Dublin in 1831 and, one year later, established a Chair in Political Economy at Trinity College, Dublin. Its first incumbent was Irish judge and economist Mountifort Longfield (1802–84), who criticised the labour theory of value and offered in its place a supply-and-demand analysis of market price underpinned by something very close to the theory of marginal utility. See M. Longfield, *Lectures on Political Economy: Delivered in Trinity and Michaelmas Terms, 1833* (Dublin: Richard Milliken & Son, 1834). William Forster Lloyd was Drummond Professor of Political Economy at Oxford from 1832 to 1837, during which time he delivered a series of lectures in which he distinguished marginal from total utility and argued that the exchange value of a good depends upon its marginal utility. See W. Lloyd, *Lectures on Population, Value, Poor-Laws and Rent* (London: Roake and Varty, 1837). For more on Hayek's views on those scholars, such as Galiani, Condillac, Lloyd, and Longfield, who anticipated some of the ideas systematised in the marginal revolution, see Hayek, "The Austrian School of Economics", pp. 43–45, and F. A. Hayek, "Carl Menger (1840–1921)" [1934], reprinted as chapter 2 of *The Fortunes of Liberalism*, pp. 64, 97–98.—Ed.]

of Jevons, Menger and Walras is commonly referred to as the 'marginal' revolution because they at last solved the apparent conflict between value and utility by recognising that it was the specific utility depending on the last available or 'marginal' unit of the commodity, and not the generic utility of a given kind of commodity, which determined its value.[12] Its wider significance however consists in the fact that it opened the way for a consistently 'subjectivist' restatement of the whole of economic theory. This development was at first carried on mainly by a group of Austrians, particularly Menger's pupils E. von Böhm-Bawerk and F. von Wieser,[13] while in England Alfred Marshall (*Prin-*

[12] [Hayek refers to the independent, and almost simultaneous, discovery of the principle of marginal utility by William Stanley Jevons and by Carl Menger, in 1871, and by Léon Walras, in 1874. French economist Léon Walras's (1834–1910) *Eléments d'économie politique pure; ou, théorie de la richesse sociale* (Lausanne: L. Corbaz, 1874) was a foundational text in general equilibrium theory and established him as one of the co-founders of the marginalist revolution. English economist and philosopher of science William Stanley Jevons (1835–82) gave his account of the principle of marginal utility in *The Theory of Political Economy* (London and New York: Macmillan and Co., 1871). Carl Menger (1840–1921), the founder of the Austrian school of economics, set out his subjectivist approach to the theory of value in his *Grundsätze der Volkswirtschaftslehre* (Vienna: W. Braumüller, 1871), translated by J. Dingwall and B. Hoselitz as *Principles of Economics* (Glencoe, IL: Free Press, 1950). In his second book, *Untersuchungen über die Methode der Sozialwissenschaften und der politischen Oekonomie insbesondere* (Leipzig: Dunker & Humblot, 1883), translated by F. Nock as *Investigations into the Method of the Social Sciences with Special Reference to Economics* (New York: New York University Press, 1985), Menger strove to demonstrate the indispensable role of theory in the social sciences by showing how social institutions that promote the common welfare, such as money, the market, and the law, can be explained as the unintended outcome of individual actions directed at quite different goals. Publication of this book initiated the so-called *Methodenstreit*, or battle of methods, between Menger and the representatives of the German Historical School. Hayek discusses Menger and his work in more detail in Hayek, "Carl Menger (1840–1921)". The work of Walras, Jevons, and Menger marks a major shift in the methodology of economics. However, while all three thinkers argued that the exchange value or price of a good was determined by its marginal utility, there remain important differences between them. Menger in particular placed more emphasis on the causal processes through which prices are changed, and the uncertainty faced by economic actors in the course of that process of disequilibrium adjustment, than did the more equilibrium-oriented Walras and Jevons. See W. Jaffé, "Menger, Jevons and Walras De-Homogenized", *Economic Inquiry*, vol. 14, 1976, pp. 511–24.—Ed.]

[13] [Friedrich von Wieser (1851–1926) and Eugen von Böhm-Bawerk (1851–1914) were the two most prominent members of the generation of Austrian economists that followed Carl Menger. After Menger's retirement in 1903, Wieser assumed his chair at the University of Vienna, where he subsequently taught Hayek. Wieser's most important theoretical contribution was his subjectivist interpretation of cost as foregone utility (or 'opportunity cost', as the concept later came to be known). See F. Wieser, *Über den Ursprung und die Hauptgesetze des wirtschaftlichen Werthes* (Vienna: A. Hölder, 1884), in which he also coined the term 'marginal utility' (*Grenznutzen*). His *Theorie der gesellschaftlichen Wirtschaft* (Tübingen: J. C. B. Mohr, 1914), translated by A. F. Hinrichs as *Social Economics* (London: Allen and Unwin, 1927), was the first systematic treatise on economics produced by the Austrian school. A longer account of Hayek's views on Wieser can be found in F. A. Hayek, "Friedrich von Wieser (1851–1926)" [1926], now published as chapter 3 of Hayek, *The Fortunes of Liberalism*, while Hayek's account of "The Austrian School of Eco-

ciples of Economics, 1890) combined a somewhat more conservative attitude on the problem of value with important contributions of his own, based in part on the work of certain earlier European thinkers such as the Frenchman A. A. Cournot (the founder of the mathematical theory of monopoly price) and the German J. H. von Thünen. Marshall's *Principles* (succeeding J. S. Mill's) remained for almost another half-century the most influential single exposition of economic theory and provided many of the theoretical tools which are still in current use.[14]

---

nomics", of whose second generation Wieser and Böhm-Bawerk were the most prominent members, is reprinted as chapter 1 of the same volume. Böhm-Bawerk was Austrian finance minister on three occasions and a Professor at the University of Vienna. He is best known for his theory of capital, central to which is the idea that time is a factor of production so that production processes that are longer or more 'roundabout' are more productive than shorter or less roundabout ones. See E. Böhm-Bawerk, *Kapital und Kapitalzins* [1884–1921], 3 vols., 4th edn. (Jena: Gustav Fischer, 1921), translated by G. D. Huncke and H. Sennholz as *Capital and Interest*, 3 vols. (South Holland, IL: Libertarian Press, 1959). Discussions of the influence of Böhm-Bawerk's ideas on Hayek's capital theory and business cycle theory are provided by L. White, "Editor's Introduction", in F. A. Hayek, *The Pure Theory of Capital*, ed. L. White, vol. 12 (2007) of *The Collected Works of F. A. Hayek*, pp. xxi–xxviii, and by H. Klausinger, "Introduction", in F. A. Hayek, *Business Cycles, Part I*, ed. H. Klausinger, vol. 7 (2012) of *The Collected Works of F. A. Hayek*, pp. 25–27.—Ed.]

[14] [Antoine-Augustin Cournot (1801–77) was a university administrator and, briefly, Professor of Analysis and Mechanics at the University of Lyon. He was one of the first economists to deploy mathematics to analyse economic problems, using it to establish the equilibrium conditions for industries under monopoly, duopoly, and perfect competition. Cournot was also the first economist to use a diagram to illustrate how the interplay of supply and demand determines price in a competitive market. His *Recherches sur les principes mathématiques de la théorie des richesses* (Paris: L. Hachette, 1838), translated by N. Bacon as *Researches into the Mathematical Principles of the Theory of Wealth* (New York: Macmillan, 1927), is commonly regarded as the first great work of mathematical economics. German landowner Johann Heinrich von Thünen (1783–1850) was, like Cournot, a pioneer in the use of mathematical methods for the study of economic issues. He is best known for his analysis of the location of economic activity and for developing a marginal productivity theory of distribution. See J. von Thünen, *Der isolierte Staat in Beziehung auf Landwirtschaft und Nationalökonomie* [1826–63], 3 vols. (Jena: G. Fischer, 1910), translated by C. Wartenberg and edited by P. Hall as *Von Thünen's Isolated State: An English Edition of Der Isolierte Staat* (Oxford: Pergamon Press, 1966).

Alfred Marshall (1842–1924), Professor of Political Economy at Cambridge University from 1884 until 1908, was the dominant figure in British economics between J. S. Mill and John Maynard Keynes. He devised many of the concepts that have become standard in modern economics, including the notions of elasticity and consumer surplus, and the distinction between short-run and long-run time periods. The origin of Marshall's *Principles of Economics* lay in an effort to translate the ideas of Ricardo and Mill into mathematics, and he was less overtly critical of the theory of value espoused by the classical economists than were the founders of the marginal revolution. He was for that reason described as a 'neo-classical' economist. Nonetheless, drawing on Cournot and von Thünen, Marshall in the *Principles* linked the derivation of the demand curve to the notion of marginal utility, before setting out a theoretical framework that incorporated both demand and supply as determinants of the market price of a good. For more on this,

Twentieth-Century Developments[15]

In the period between the two world wars this traditional body of knowledge was gradually developed by the introduction of various improvements which derived either from the earlier Austrians through P. H. Wicksteed, K. Wicksell, F. H. Knight and L. von Mises,[16] or from Léon Walras and the later

---

see G. F. Shove, "The Place of Marshall's *Principles* in the Development of Economic Theory", *Economic Journal*, vol. 52, 1942, pp. 294–329.—Ed.]

[15] [Hayek considers the developments in economics that took place in the interwar years at greater length in F. A. Hayek, "The Economics of the 1930s as Seen from London" [1963], published as chapter 1 of F. A. Hayek, *Contra Keynes and Cambridge: Essays, Correspondence*, ed. B. Caldwell, vol. 9 (1995) of *The Collected Works of F. A. Hayek*. Also see Hayek, "The Austrian School of Economics", pp. 53–56. —Ed.]

[16] [Philip Wicksteed (1844–1927) was an English Unitarian minister and exponent of marginalist economics who, in his *Essay on the Co-ordination of the Laws of Distribution* (London: Macmillan & Co., 1894), developed a marginal productivity theory of distribution according to which different types of input are paid according to the value of the extra amount each of them adds to total output. His book *The Common Sense of Political Economy* is notable for articulating a consistently subjectivist theory of choice. See P. Wicksteed, *The Common Sense of Political Economy* [1910], 2nd. edn., vol. 1, ed. L. Robbins (London: Routledge and Kegan Paul, 1933). For more on Wicksteed, see F. A. Hayek, "Two Pages of Fiction" [1982], reprinted as chapter 30 of the current volume, p. 445, n. 3.

Swedish economist Knut Wicksell (1851–1926) was one of the major architects of early twentieth-century work on capital, money and business cycles. In his first book, *Über Wert, Kapital und Rente* (Jena: Gustav Fischer, 1893), Wicksell sought to integrate Walras's general equilibrium theory with Böhm-Bawerk's analysis of capital in order to develop a marginal productivity theory of distribution. See K. Wicksell, *Value, Capital and Rent*, trans. S. Frowein (London: Allen and Unwin, 1954). Wicksell subsequently used this general equilibrium model of a capital-using economy in order to argue that the trade cycle is the result of differences between the natural rate of interest—that is, the rate that equates savings and investment—and actual or market rate of interest. See K. Wicksell, *Geldzins und Güterpreise: Eine Studie über die den Tauschwert des Geldes bestimmenden Ursachen* (Jena: Fischer, 1898), translated by R. F. Kahn as *Interest and Prices: A Study of the Causes Regulating the Value of Money* (London: Macmillan, 1936). Both John Maynard Keynes, in *A Treatise on Money* (1930), and Hayek, in *Monetary Theory and the Trade Cycle* [1933] and *Prices and Production* [1935], used Wicksell's distinction between the natural and market rates of interest as the basis for their models of the business cycle. See J. M. Keynes, *A Treatise on Money* [1930], reprinted as vols. 5–6 (1971) of *The Collected Writings of John Maynard Keynes* (London: Macmillan for the Royal Economic Society), and Hayek, *Business Cycles, Part I*. For more on the ensuing debate between the two, in which Hayek argued that Keynes's analysis was flawed because he had failed to integrate Wicksell's capital theory into his account of the working of the economy, see Hayek, *Contra Keynes and Cambridge*.

American economist Frank Knight (1885–1972) was a Professor of Economics at the University of Chicago (1928–52) and a dominant figure in the 'old', pre–World War Two Chicago School of Economics. In *Risk, Uncertainty and Profit* (Boston: Houghton-Mifflin, 1921), Knight articulated and defended the concept of perfect competition, differentiated the notion of risk from that of uncertainty, on the grounds that the former can be measured and expressed in terms of probabilities whereas the latter cannot, and conceptualised the role of the entrepreneur as the person who bears uncertainty in the economic process in return for the prospect of

mathematical economists, particularly V. Pareto, F. Y. Edgeworth and Irving Fisher.[17] Perhaps the most far-reaching single step of this development was

profit. Knight criticised Austrian capital theory, as presented in Hayek's *Prices and Production*, in F. H. Knight, "Capital, Time, and the Interest Rate," *Economica*, n.s., vol. 1, 1934, pp. 257–86. Hayek's response, along with Knight's rejoinder and a further article by Hayek, are reprinted as chapters 6–8 of F. A. Hayek, *Capital and Interest*, ed. L. White, vol. 11 (2015) of *The Collected Works of F. A. Hayek*. For an overview of the debate, see A. Cohen, "The Hayek/Knight Capital Controversy: The Irrelevance of Roundaboutness, or Purging Processes in Time?" *History of Political Economy*, vol. 35, 2003, pp. 469–90.

In his *Theorie des Geldes und der Umlaufsmittel* (Munich and Leipzig: Duncker & Humblot, 1912), translated by H. Batson as *The Theory of Money and Credit* (London: Jonathan Cape, 1934), Austrian economist Ludwig von Mises (1881–1973) set out a monetary theory of the business cycle based on Wicksell's capital theory. Mises later argued that rational economic calculation is impossible under socialism, thereby setting in train the so-called 'socialist calculation debate'. See L. von Mises, *Die Gemeinwirtschaft: Untersuchungen über den Sozialismus* (Jena: Gustav Fischer, 1922), 2nd edn. translated by J. Kahane as *Socialism: An Economic and Sociological Analysis* (London: Jonathan Cape, 1936). Also see F. A. Hayek, "The New Confusion about 'Planning'" [1976], reprinted as chapter 26 of the present volume and Hayek, "Two Pages of Fiction" and the notes and references contained therein.—Ed.]

[17] [Irish economist and statistician Francis Ysidro Edgeworth (1845–1926) was Drummond Professor of Political Economy at Oxford University from 1891 to 1922, editor of the *Economic Journal* from 1890 to 1911, and co-editor, with John Maynard Keynes, from 1919 until his death. Edgeworth pioneered the use of mathematical and statistical analysis in economics, and is best known for inventing several concepts—such as indifference curves, contract curves, and the Edgeworth box—that have subsequently become part of the standard theoretical machinery of economics. See F. Edgeworth, *Mathematical Psychics: An Essay on the Application of Mathematics to the Moral Sciences* (London: Kegan Paul, 1881). Now also see *F. Y. Edgeworth's 'Mathematical Psychics' and Further Papers on Political Economy*, ed. P. Newman (Oxford: Oxford University Press for the Royal Economic Society, 2003).

American economist Irving Fisher (1867–1947), Professor of Political Economy at Yale University (1898–1935) and the first president of the Econometric Society, is best known for his work on capital theory and monetary theory, where his contributions included the distinction between real and nominal interest rates; an analysis of the real rate of interest as the outcome of the interplay between people's 'time preference' for current over future consumption and the extra income that could be generated by postponing consumption in order to invest resources in some productive asset (the 'marginal productivity of capital'); and the use of the so-called 'equation of exchange' (MV = PT) as a framework for analysing the purchasing power of money. See I. Fisher, *Appreciation and Interest* (New York: Macmillan Co., 1896); I. Fisher, *The Purchasing Power of Money* (New York: Macmillan Co., 1911); and I. Fisher, *The Theory of Interest* (New York: Macmillan Co., 1930). Earlier in his career, Fisher's doctoral dissertation at Yale, subsequently published as *Mathematical Investigations in the Theory of Value and Prices* (New Haven: Yale University Press, 1925), offered a rigorous mathematical treatment of the marginal utility theory of value, couched in term of indifference curves, that stripped the notion of utility of any hedonistic, psychological content.

Italian economist and sociologist Vilfredo Pareto (1848–1923) succeeded Walras as professor of Political Economy at the University of Lausanne in 1893. Building on the work of Edgeworth and, in particular, of Walras, Pareto used the notion of an 'indifference curve' to illustrate how an individual's preferences over various combinations of goods can be represented without making reference to the psychologistic notion of 'utility' and also laid the foundations of modern

that the concept of utility as an absolute magnitude has been almost entirely eliminated and a consistently relative conception of utility (as manifested in the acts of choice or preference) taken its place. This has been fully achieved in recent restatements of the central core of economic theory, such as J. R. Hicks's *Value and Capital* (1939), which incorporate elements from all the various sources. At about the same time the development of a theory of 'imperfect' and 'monopolistic' competition by Joan Robinson and E. H. Chamberlin in 1933 somewhat extended the scope of this kind of theory.[18]

In spite of these changes in some of its central doctrines the predominant interest of economic theory in the factors determining value and price, the allocation of resources and the distribution of income, and connected with this its concentration on a hypothetical state of equilibrium, had remained its characteristic features from the time of Ricardo through the first third of the 20th century. Throughout this period the theory of money had a somewhat separate existence with an extensive literature of its own; there had also been many attempts to create side by side with equilibrium analysis a general theory

welfare economics by outlining what has subsequently become known as the concept of 'Pareto efficiency'. See V. Pareto, *Manuel d'économie politique* (Paris: V. Giard and E. Brière, 1909), translated by A. Schwier as *Manual of Political Economy* (New York: Augustus M. Kelley, 1971).—Ed.]

[18] [Sir John Hicks (1904–89) was a Lecturer at the London School of Economics (1926–35) and later Drummond Professor of Political Economy at Oxford University (1952–65). Along with British economist R. G. D. Allen (1906–83), Hicks built on the earlier work of Fisher and Edgeworth in order to show, using the concept of the 'marginal rate of substitution', how indifference curve analysis could be used to reformulate the theory of demand without reference to the notion of cardinal utility. See J. R. Hicks and R. G. D. Allen, "A Reconsideration of the Theory of Value", *Economica*, n.s., vol. 1, 1934, pp. 52–76 and 196–219. In *Value and Capital*, 1st ed. (Oxford: Clarendon Press, 1939), Hicks not only offered an English-language treatment of general equilibrium theory but also developed an original analysis of the stability and dynamics of the general equilibrium system. Hicks is also famous for having developed, in "Mr. Keynes and the 'Classics'", *Econometrica*, vol. 5, 1937, pp. 147–59, the IS-LM model of the relationship between savings, investment, income, and the rate of interest, which he used to formalise the arguments advanced by Keynes in *The General Theory*. In 1972, Hicks was awarded the Nobel Prize, jointly with American economist Kenneth Arrow, for his pioneering work on general equilibrium theory and welfare economics. Hayek later expressed the esteem in which he held *Value and Capital* in more fulsome terms, describing it as "absolutely first-class work" and concluding, "I think it's the final formulation of the theory of value". See F. A. Hayek, *Hayek on Hayek: An Autobiographical Dialogue*, ed. S. Kresge and L. Wenar (Chicago: University of Chicago Press, 1994), p. 87.

In two books, both of which were published in 1933, Edward H. Chamberlin (1899–1967), Professor of Economics at Harvard University (1937–67), and Joan Robinson (1903–83), Professor of Economics at Cambridge University (1965–79), analysed the behaviour of firms that produced differentiated products and so enjoyed a measure of market power, thereby developing the theory of imperfect or monopolistic competition. See E. Chamberlin, *The Theory of Monopolistic Competition* (Cambridge, MA: Harvard University Press, 1933), and J. Robinson, *The Economics of Imperfect Competition* (London: Macmillan, 1933).—Ed.]

of economic 'dynamics'. Somewhat more successful than these latter attempts were the more specialised efforts to understand the causes of the recurrent periods of industrial depressions and unemployment. But only the impact of the great depression which followed the crisis of 1929 led to a radical shift of emphasis. Increasingly the factors determining the total volume of production and employment, rather than those determining the distribution of resources between industries and the distribution of the social product between the factors, began to occupy the attention of the economists. The decision point in this development was the publication in 1936 of Lord Keynes's *General Theory of Employment, Interest, and Money,* of which it can almost be said, as it was said of the *Wealth of Nations,* that through it its author has persuaded his own generation and will govern the next (see EMPLOYMENT, THEORY OF).[19] It remains yet to be seen whether this will abound as much to the benefit of the world as it did in the case of Adam Smith. While undoubtedly what has come to be known as 'orthodox' economics sometimes led to unrealistic conclusions by arguing as if the available resources were normally fully occupied, and as if in consequence the production of one thing could be increased only at the expense of the production of another, the new orthodoxy tends to go to the opposite extreme and to argue as if the scarcity of resources were no longer the basic factor which governs all economic activity.

Character and Method of Economic Theory

As economics is the most highly developed among the theoretical social sciences a few words may be said here about the points on which all these disciplines differ from the more familiar natural sciences. If the layman tends to be sceptical about the possibility of any theoretical generalisations about social phenomena, while those trained in the sciences often do not regard subjects like economics as sciences at all, these doubts have their common ground in the fact that in some respects the problems of the social sciences differ fundamentally from those of the natural sciences. It is not for want of trying but because the nature of their subject-matter has forced it upon them that econo-

---

[19] [Hayek refers to the *magnum opus* of British economist John Maynard Keynes (1883–1946), Baron Keynes of Tilton, namely *The General Theory of Employment, Interest, and Money* [1936], reprinted as vol. 7 (1973) of *The Collected Writings of John Maynard Keynes.* For more on Hayek's opinions about Keynes's economics, and also for his views on Keynes himself, see Hayek, *Contra Keynes and Cambridge.* Hayek also refers the reader to the entry on "Employment, Theory of", in *Chambers's Encyclopaedia,* vol. V, pp. 171–75. The entry was written by British economist Thomas Wilson (1916–2001), Adam Smith Chair of Political Economy at Glasgow University (1958–85).—Ed.]

mists have developed methods of theoretical analysis which differ markedly from those of the natural sciences.[20]

A common misunderstanding, which has to be cleared out of the way first and for which the language often employed by economists is partly responsible, is that economics attempts to 'explain' human behaviour. There is ground for doubt whether we shall ever be able fully to explain why individuals act as they do; and in so far as we can arrive at valid generalisations about the causes of human action, this is a task for psychology and not for economics. The specific problem of economics and of all social theory is not why people act as they do, but what are the unintended consequences of their actions when they live in societies in which the individuals and groups act according to their own individual decisions and plans.[21] They deal, in the phrase of an 18th-century writer (Adam Ferguson), with phenomena which are "the result of human action but not of human design".[22] If there is often reluctance to admit that this is the characteristic problem of all social theory, this is still a consequence of the fact that in the hands of some of the earlier writers this approach had become too closely connected with their admiration for the beneficial character of the order which thus spontaneously establishes itself. The character of the problem is however the same if we ask why such and such action regularly produces unemployment or leads to the waste of resources, although in neither case was this result intended by those whose actions brought it about. Both the extent to which the separate actions of different people produce an order or desirable pattern, and the extent to which they fail to do so, raise problems to which social theory has to supply an answer. Questions of a similar nature are raised by the growth of language or of any other social formation or institution. In all questions of this sort the answer involves not only the knowledge of a unique historical process but also the understanding of a

[20] [Hayek expresses here the belief, which was central to his thinking in the 1940s, that there is sharp distinction between the methods appropriate for the study of the social and natural worlds. See F. A. Hayek, "The Facts of the Social Sciences" [1943], reprinted as chapter 2 of Hayek, *The Market and Other Orders*, and Hayek, *Studies on the Abuse and Decline of Reason*, pp. 75–166. However, from the early 1950s onwards, Hayek ceased to draw a sharp dividing line between the natural and social sciences, preferring instead to categorise disciplines by reference to whether their subject-matter is simple or complex (a criterion that cuts across the distinction between the natural and social worlds). See F. A. Hayek, "Degrees of Explanation" [1955] and F. A. Hayek, "The Theory of Complex Phenomena" [1964], reprinted as chapters 6 and 9 of *The Market and Other Orders*. For more on this shift in Hayek's thinking, see B. Caldwell, "Introduction", in Hayek, *The Market and Other Orders*, pp. 14–16, 23–24.]

[21] [Hayek refers here to what elsewhere he describes as the compositive method. This involves the social scientist showing how the subjective beliefs held by individual people lead them to act in ways that give rise, unintentionally, to the structures that help to make up the social world. See Hayek, *Studies on the Abuse and Decline of Reason*, pp. 91–107.—Ed.]

[22] [On Adam Ferguson, see n. 8 above.—Ed.]

kind of mechanism which may operate in a similar manner at different times, in other words a theoretical scheme of explanation.[23]

Problems Involved

The specific set of problems which is singled out for treatment by economics as a distinct discipline arises from the circumstance that in most of their activities men are constrained to choose between the various ends they would wish to achieve, because the available means which can be used for a variety of these ends are limited in quantity and insufficient to satisfy all requirements. Economics has for this reason been defined as "the science which studies human behaviour as a relationship between ends and scarce means which have alternative uses" (L. Robbins).[24]

While this definition correctly describes the nature of the human activities from which the problems of economic theory arise, it says hardly enough about its task. Problems which allow an answer in terms of cause and effect and which therefore give rise to a science properly speaking, only arise when this kind of activity takes place in a group in which each person's decisions have to be adjusted to, and modified as a result of, the actions of other people. So far as individual action is concerned economics strictly speaking can do no more than provide a convenient apparatus for describing the different attitudes of individual men in their economically relevant aspects. This involves

[23] [Hayek elaborates on how explanations in social science involve the use of theoretical models to develop simplified representations of the causal mechanisms underlying the formation of spontaneously emerging social phenomena in various papers. Some, such as "The Facts of the Social Sciences" [1943], predate the essay under consideration here. Others postdate it, and see Hayek place increasing emphasis on the importance of evolutionary models. See, for example, Hayek, "Degrees of Explanation", Hayek, "The Results of Human Action but Not of Human Design", and F. A. Hayek, "Notes on the Evolution of Systems of Rules of Conduct" [1967], reprinted as chapter 10 of *The Market and Other Orders*. In the latter essay, Hayek describes the explanation of spontaneous orders as an example of, "Conjectural history . . . the reconstruction of a hypothetical kind of process which may never have been observed but which, if it had taken place, would have produced phenomena of the kind we observe" (p. 287). For more on Hayek's views on the relationship between theory and history, see Hayek, "The Facts of the Social Sciences", pp. 87–90, and F. A. Hayek, "The Uses of 'Gresham's Law' as an Illustration of 'Historical Theory'" [1962], reprinted as chapter 12 of this volume.—Ed.]

[24] [Lionel Robbins (1898–1984), later Lord Robbins of Clare Market, was Professor of Economics at the London School of Economics and Political Science and for many years one of Hayek's closest friends and colleagues. The phrase quoted by Hayek comes from L. Robbins, *An Essay on the Nature and Significance of Economic Science*, 2nd edn. (London: Macmillan, 1935), p. 16. Later in his career, Hayek came to believe that Robbins' definition of economics was misleading when used to describe the economy as a whole, because the ends served by the market order or catallaxy are not given in their totality to anyone. See F. A. Hayek, "The Confusion of Language in Political Thought" [1968], reprinted as chapter 23 of the current volume, p. 319 n. 28.—Ed.]

a classification of the objects of economic activity which must differ in two respects from the manner in which they would be considered as physical objects. Since we are interested in understanding human action, it will not be the properties which the things possess in some objective sense, but the views which the acting people hold about these things, which must form our starting-point; and, secondly, we shall never be concerned in this type of analysis with the properties of individual objects in isolation, but with their significance in particular situations. The first of these peculiarities is common to all social sciences, since in dealing with intelligible action we must necessarily regard the objects of such action from the point of view of the persons whose actions we are trying to understand.[25] The second is the distinguishing characteristic of the problems of economics. The considerations which are significant in this connexion are whether a good or service is regarded as useful for many different purposes or for only a few, whether it can be easily replaced by other goods or not, whether in view of the whole situation more or less important needs depend on the availability of the whole quantity of it, etc. It depends on whether the various goods and services are similar to each other or different from each other in these formal regards, and not on their specific physical properties, whether they give rise to the same or different economic problems.

The technique which has been developed for describing the context of human action in a manner which brings out the interrelation of the parts of a single plan of action is sometimes described as the theory of economic planning. Since it does not assert anything about facts, however, but, like logic or mathematics, is simply a technique for working out the implications of given assumptions, it would perhaps be better to describe it as the 'economic calculus'.[26] It contains, as a method of describing the ways in which goods and ser-

[25] [Hayek justifies this 'subjectivist' approach to social sciences at greater length in "The Facts of the Social Sciences" and in *Studies on the Abuse and Decline of Reason*, pp. 88–98, arguing in the latter that "it is probably no exaggeration to say that every important advance in economic theory during the last hundred years was a further step in the consistent application of subjectivism" (p. 94).—Ed.]

[26] [In his 1937 paper "Economics and Knowledge", Hayek distinguishes between two kinds of economic analysis. The first, which he refers to as the "Pure Logic of Choice", involves the economist assuming that people know both their own preferences and also the constraints they face, in which case it is possible simply to deduce what actions they will take. Accordingly, the pure logic of choice consists of a "series of propositions which are necessarily true because they are merely transformations from the assumptions from which we start". The second approach, by contrast, introduces "the empirical element in economic theory" and involves "the investigation of causal processes", concerning in particular how people acquire the knowledge required to act in the way postulated by the economic calculus. See F. A. Hayek, "Economics and Knowledge" [1937], reprinted as chapter 1 of Hayek, *The Market and Other Orders*, pp. 57–59. It is the first of these two approaches that Hayek describes elsewhere as the "economic calculus". See F. A. Hayek, "The Use of Knowledge in Society" [1945], reprinted as chapter 3 of *The Mar-*

vices may differ in their usefulness and the decisions about their use which follow from given views about the relative importance of different needs, most of the theory of utility and (subjective) value and of the theory of production. The strictly formal apparatus which it supplies can be used to describe the economically relevant aspects of any kind of action and involves no specific assumptions about motivations, such as, for example, 'rational' behaviour or the existence of an 'economic man'.

While this economic calculus must take up a considerable space in any systematic exposition of economic theory, it is still merely a preliminary to its main task. If, indeed, all activity in an economic system were directed by a single plan, the contribution the economist could make towards its understanding would here be at an end. He could strictly speaking not explain anything, except perhaps in so far as the planner actually availed himself of this technique. He could merely provide a concise form for stating the problems which the planner would have to solve and a technique by which he might try to solve them.

Equilibrium Analysis

The main purpose for which the economic calculus has been evolved is to provide a starting-point for the analysis of a complex economic system in which the separate plans of individuals and groups must be adjusted to one another if their aims are to be achieved. From the elements supplied by the economic calculus mental models can be constructed which will show how attempts to carry out these separate plans will interact, and which will enable us to determine the conditions which must be satisfied if all the individuals are to be able to carry out their plans. If these conditions are satisfied the economic system is said to be in a 'state of equilibrium'. This equilibrium may never be fully achieved in real life. It is nevertheless significant not only because the absence of equilibrium will mean that some or all members of the community will be unable to carry out their plans and will therefore have to change them, but also because experience shows that in the absence of too violent change in the external data the spontaneous forces of the market do bring about a fairly close approach to the equilibrium position. Even if it cannot be shown that there will normally exist a 'tendency' towards equilibrium in the sense that, if enough time were allowed without unforeseen changes, the hypothetical state of equilibrium would be fully achieved, there is empirical justification for

ket and Other Orders, pp. 93, 99, and F. A. Hayek, "A New Look at Economic Theory" [1961], reprinted as Appendix A of The Market and Other Orders, pp. 382–85, 387–401. For a discussion, see B. Caldwell, "F. A. Hayek and the Economic Calculus", History of Political Economy, vol. 48, 2016, pp. 151–80.—Ed.]

speaking of such a tendency in the sense that prices and quantities are at any given moment more likely to be at a figure near the equilibrium point than at figures more remote from it.[27]

The main questions which equilibrium analysis of a market economy endeavours to answer may be grouped under five headings: (1) why are the different resources allocated in the given proportions between the different uses? (2) what determines the different shares of different individuals in the aggregate product of society? (3) what determines the distribution of production over time, or the extent to which current activities are devoted to the needs of different future dates? (4) what determines the choice between the various alternative techniques of producing particular goods and services? And (5) what determines the spatial distribution of the different activities or the location of the different industries? On examination the answers to all these different questions prove to be closely interconnected, indeed to be no more than different aspects of the same problem which in a market economy is solved by the same forces by which the prices of the different commodities and services are determined.

The impersonal forces, which this type of analysis aims to make intelligible, show themselves most clearly, because the influence which can be exerted by the decision of any single person is reduced to a minimum, in a free system in which numerous comparatively small units compete with each other. This kind of theory has therefore been developed in the first instance and most completely for a system which is fully competitive, i.e. for a system in which to the individual the prices established in the market are given facts to which he

---

[27] [Hayek's own path-breaking account of the state of general economic equilibrium, understood as a situation that is orderly in the sense that people's plans are mutually compatible, can be found in his 1937 essay "Economics and Knowledge". Hayek made significant headway in explaining the causal processes through which plan coordination is brought about in his 1945 article on "The Use of Knowledge in Society", where he explained how (changes in) market prices inform people about (variations in) the scarcity of different goods, thereby helping them to adjust their plans to one another in such a way that they can still all be brought to a successful conclusion. However, Hayek arguably completed his account of the generation of social order in decentralised market economies only in his later writings, ostensibly on political philosophy and the law, where he argued that the dissemination of knowledge required for plan coordination is also facilitated by systems of formal legal rules and informal norms that enable people to form reasonably accurate expectations of each other's future conduct and thereby to devise plans that have a reasonable chance of coming to fruition. See, for example, F. A. Hayek, *The Mirage of Social Justice*, vol. 2 (1976) of *Law, Legislation and Liberty* (Chicago: University of Chicago Press; London: Routledge, 1973–1979), pp. 107–32. For more on this, see K. Vaughn, "Hayek's Implicit Economics: Rules and the Problem of Order", *Review of Austrian Economics*, vol. 11, 1999, pp. 129–44, and P. Lewis, "Hayek: From Economics as Equilibrium Analysis to Economics as Social Theory", in the *Elgar Companion to Hayekian Economics*, ed. R. Garrison and N. Barry (Cheltenham: Edward Elgar, 2014).—Ed.]

has to adjust himself, and in which therefore the whole or nearly the whole of all economic activity is guided by competitive markets.

Limitations of Analysis

Modern economic theory fully recognises however that this 'perfect' market is no more than an ideal type or an extreme limiting case, and that any existing economic system always is (and in some measure must be) something intermediate between a purely competitive system and a system in which prices and quantities are fixed by deliberate human decision.[28] There are two reasons for this: one is that regulation or outright direction of economic activity by the state may displace the forces of the market to a greater or smaller degree; the other that in a particular market one or a few of the parties may have monopolistic or near-monopolistic positions and may be able to exercise deliberate control over quantities and prices. As each of these two forces may be present in different degrees in different parts of the economic system, and the two combined in a great variety of ways, so as to leave only a restricted field to the spontaneous social forces, which also must operate within a framework determined by the former, there is an almost infinite variety of possible forms of economic organisation. Economic theory tries to meet this difficulty by elaborating certain standard models; but the variety of possible combinations of elements is so great that the application of the tools, which theory provides, to particular situations must be left largely to the students of particular historical conditions.

Another limitation of equilibrium analysis in its traditional form is due to the fact that by its assumption it is forced to a large extent to abstract from the existence of money and to proceed in what is called 'real' terms. It is at least doubtful whether with the hypothetical assumptions on which traditional equilibrium analysis is based, particularly with the assumption of complete certainty about the future, there could be a place for money, while on the other hand it is scarcely conceivable that without money even an approach to market equilibrium could be achieved.

Widening of Scope

It is one of the achievements of the theoretical work done between the two world wars that this difficulty has been largely overcome and that the theory

---

[28] [Hayek provides an extended critique of the notion of 'perfect competition' in F. A. Hayek, "The Meaning of Competition" [1948], reprinted as chapter 4 of *The Market and Other Orders*.—Ed.]

of money has been more fully integrated with the general body of theory. This was made possible in the first instance by a more adequate analysis of the factors determining the demand for holding money which assimilated it into the established scheme for analysing the demand for commodities.[29] The widening of the scope of economic theory which this made possible led however to more far-reaching changes in the whole theoretical approach. The most important of these are that the concept of equilibrium has come to be explicitly used merely as a step towards an analysis of the process in time, represented as a sequence of successive periods in each of which the 'data' can be accounted for as the result of the process which took place during the preceding period;[30] and that, for a time at any rate, a new emphasis on demand for commodities in general and on the size and changes of the total stream of money income has led to the substitution of social or aggregate magnitudes for the description of individual behaviour which used to form the starting-point of theoretical analysis. This new type of analysis, sometimes described as 'macro-dynamics' as distinguished from the 'micro-statics' of the traditional type of theory, appears to some economists to offer new opportunities for empirical research on the lines of the natural sciences, for investigations based on quantitative measurement which are thus at last to make their long-hoped-for contribution to economic theory. Whether new theoretical results can be expected from this approach depends mainly on the much-disputed question whether the so-called statistical 'constants' which may be determined for a particular moment can be regarded as true constants and therefore as significant for positions other than those for which they have been ascertained. Although there exists a large and flourishing school of 'econometricians' who under the motto 'science is measurement' devote their energies to this type of investigation, it would still seem as if the important work done

[29] [Hayek alludes to J. Hicks, "A Suggestion for Simplifying the Theory of Money", *Economica*, n.s., vol. 2, 1935, pp. 1–19. In that paper, Hicks sought to integrate monetary and value theory by treating the demand for money as arising from people's decisions about how to allocate their wealth between a variety of assets, and then subjecting those decisions to marginal analysis in order to develop what he refers to as a "marginal utility theory of money" (p. 2). In later correspondence with Hicks, Hayek wrote of the development of the economic analysis of the demand for money that, "The main achievement in the right direction was your 'A Suggestion for Simplifying the Theory of Money'." F. A. Hayek to John Hicks, December 4, 1967, quoted in S. Kresge, "Afterword", in F. A. Hayek, *Good Money, Part I: The New World*, ed. S. Kresge, vol. 5 (1999) of *The Collected Works of F. A. Hayek*, p. 247 n. 5.—Ed.]

[30] [Hayek refers here to the notion of 'temporary equilibrium', developed and used by Sir John Hicks in parts III and IV of *Value and Capital* as a means of combining general equilibrium theory, the theory of capital and interest, and the theory of the trade cycle. For a helpful discussion, which highlights the connections between Hicks's work and Hayek's, see B. Ingrao and G. Israel, *The Invisible Hand: Economic Equilibrium in the History of Science* (Cambridge, MA: MIT Press, 1990), pp. 217–44.—Ed.]

in this field belongs more properly to the next heading rather than that of economic theory.[31]

[31] [Notable contributors to the literature on 'macrodynamics' included the Oxford economist Sir Roy Harrod (1900–78), who developed a Keynesian macroeconomic model of economic growth, couched in terms of the notion of a moving equilibrium growth path for the economy as a whole—the so-called 'warranted growth path'—and American Nobel Laureate Paul Samuelson (1915–2009), developer of the multiplier-accelerator model of the trade cycle. See R. Harrod, "An Essay in Dynamic Theory", *Economic Journal*, vol. 49, 1939, pp. 14–33; R. Harrod, *Towards a Dynamic Economics: Some Recent Developments of Economic Theory and Their Application to Policy* (London: Macmillan, 1948); and P. Samuelson, "Interactions between the Multiplier Analysis and the Principle of Acceleration", *Review of Economics and Statistics*, vol. 21, 1939, pp. 75–8. In the course of working out his ideas, Harrod drew on the 'acceleration principle'—or 'the Relation', as he termed it—according to which the stock of capital goods in the economy is proportional to the level of output, so that increases in output lead to increases in the demand for capital goods and, therefore, to investment. Hayek argued that the operation of the 'acceleration principle' is not uniform over time, with the capital-output ratio varying inversely with final consumer demand. See F. A. Hayek, *Business Cycles, Part II*, ed. H. Klausinger, vol. 8 (2012) of *The Collected Works of F. A. Hayek*, pp. 222–23, and Hayek, *The Pure Theory of Capital*, p. 352, n. 15.

Another prominent early contribution to macrodynamic analysis was the theory of the trade cycle developed by Norwegian economist and econometrician Ragnar Frisch (1895–1973), who constructed a model of how an economy might respond to (or propagate) the external shocks (or impulses) impinging upon it in such a way as to give rise to a cyclical pattern of economic activity akin to that witnessed in the business cycle. See R. Frisch, "Propagation Problems and Impulse Problems in Dynamic Economics", in *Economic Essays in Honour of Gustav Cassel* (London: Allen and Unwin, 1933). Significantly, Frisch's model consisted of a set of simultaneous equations whose parameters could be estimated, prefiguring his later work on national income accounting and large-scale statistical models of the economy. Indeed, Frisch was a pioneer in the application of mathematical models and statistical methods to economic data (for which work he coined the term 'econometrics'). In 1969, Frisch was awarded the first Nobel Memorial Prize in Economic Science, jointly with Dutch economist and econometrician Jan Tinbergen (1903–94), for their efforts in developing and applying dynamic models of economic processes. Tinbergen had developed in the 1930s a theoretically-informed, multi-equation model of the macroeconomy whose parameters he estimated, first for Holland and subsequently for the United States and the United Kingdom. See in particular J. Tinbergen, *Statistical Testing of Business-Cycle Theories*, 2 vols. (Geneva: League of Nations, 1939).

The 'school of econometricians' to which Hayek refers, whose early motto was Lord Kelvin's dictum that 'science is measurement', was the Cowles Commission for Research in Economics. This was a centre for mathematical and statistical research in economics that was established in 1932 and was based at the University of Chicago from 1939 until 1955, and at Yale University thereafter. A notable member of the Commission was one of Frisch's former Research Assistants, Norwegian economist Trygve Haavelmo (1911–99). Haavelmo, who won the 1989 Nobel Prize in Economic Science, argued that in order to be meaningful the statistical methods used to analyse economic data needed to be grounded in models derived from the theory of probability. See T. Haavelmo, "The Statistical Implications of a System of Simultaneous Equations", *Econometrica*, vol. 11, 1943, pp. 1–12, and T. Haavelmo, "The Probability Approach in Econometrics", Supplement to *Econometrica*, vol. 12, 1944, pp. S1–115. The Director of the Cowles Commission from 1943 to 1948, during which time its central focus was on the development of statistical models for the predictive and structural analysis of the economy as a whole, was Russian-American economist Jacob Marschak (1898–1977), who late in 1943 penned one of the

Descriptive and Applied Economics

While in a survey like the present the emphasis must be on the tools of theoretical analysis which are common to all the different branches of economic research, the making of these tools is of course the concern of only a small proportion of the economists, while the majority are concerned with the study of the particular conditions of a given time and place.

Importance of Empirical Research

For this task economists have developed their special techniques (mainly statistical) for ascertaining the facts and diagnosing concrete situations. But while this empirical work is at least as important in economics as it is in the natural sciences, it occupies a somewhat different position. This difference is a consequence of the fact that, contrary to the position in the natural sciences, in the social sciences it is the elements of the complex situations which are familiar to everyday experience and can be made the bases of theoretical constructions, while the complex phenomena cannot be directly perceived but only pieced together by mental reconstruction from their elements. Hence the task of empirical research in the social sciences is not to discover regularities or laws in the behaviour of the complex phenomena, but mainly to ascertain the particular facts for the interpretation of which theory is required. But while this position is widely understood in theory, it is still true that much of the work of the applied economists (as is similarly true of much historical research) is misdirected and its value impaired by the mistaken belief that in order to be 'scientific' it must aim at discovering empirical laws, particularly 'laws of development' of those social 'wholes' which in fact cannot be directly observed but only reconstructed with the help of theory. The character of most of the work of the so-called 'historical school' of economists of the 19th century and much of Marxist economics of the 20th century has suffered from this fallacy.[32]

---

referee reports on the manuscript of Hayek's *Road to Serfdom* for the University of Chicago Press. See F. A. Hayek, *The Road to Serfdom: Text and Documents*, ed. B. Caldwell, vol. 2 (2007) of *The Collected Works of F. A. Hayek*, pp. 251–52.

Hayek expresses scepticism concerning the usefulness of statistics for understanding complex social phenomena, and also about claims that science should concern itself exclusively with measurable factors, in "The Theory of Complex Phenomena", pp. 264–66, and in his Nobel Memorial Lecture on "The Pretence of Knowledge" [1975], reprinted as chapter 16 of *The Market and Other Orders*, especially pp. 363–68.—Ed.]

[32] [Hayek in this paragraph raises issues that he discusses at greater length in his essay on "Scientism and the Study of Society". See Hayek, *Studies in the Abuse and Decline of Reason*, pp. 75–166.—Ed.]

Empirical Studies

Even if these more ambitious goals of empirical research are abandoned there remains almost unlimited scope for empirical studies in the field of what is usually called applied economics. As a continuous effort to observe and interpret an ever-changing world this wide field of investigations does not lend itself to systematic or comprehensive exposition. Every branch of industry and trade, every period, country or section of the population, and every measure of public policy raises problems which require, apart from the tools of economic theory, detailed factual knowledge which can be acquired only through a considerable degree of specialisation.[33] These studies are usually 'applied' not only in the sense that they refer to a particular situation, but also in the sense that they are directed at finding suitable means for achieving some given social objectives. While economics as a theoretical science is necessarily neutral between the ultimate goals of economic policy, there is much that it has to say about the appropriateness of different courses of action once the ends to be achieved are given. And though in many instances it would be merely pedantic to emphasise that any recommendation the economist can make must remain conditional upon the desirability of the ends at which he aims, it is nevertheless important to keep these two questions distinct, particularly as the choice between alternative courses of action will almost always depend not merely on whether a particular result is desirable but also on its relative importance compared with other desirable objectives which may have to be sacrificed if the one in question is to be attained. The answer to this sort of question can never be taken for granted by the economist without incurring considerable risk of mixing up scientific conclusions with his personal preferences. It would, for instance, not be correct to say that economics as a science proves that free trade is desirable, even though most economists were inclined to favour free trade. While their differences from the protectionists may be due to a difference about the effects which free trade would produce, and therefore capable of resolution by scientific argument, they may also be due to differences of opinion about the desirability of these effects. In the latter case the task of the economist ends with setting out what these results are, while the ultimate choice must be left to political decision which will depend on value judgments which cannot be scientifically demonstrated.[34]

For separate articles on different economic theories, see CAPITAL, THEORY OF; DEMAND; DISTRIBUTION, THEORY OF; INTEREST;

---

[33] [Hayek sets out his views on this issue, and also on other aspects of specialisation in the social sciences, in more detail in Hayek, "The Dilemma of Specialisation".—Ed.]

[34] [For more on Hayek's views on the place of value judgments in scientific debate, see F. A. Hayek, "Socialism and Science" [1976], reprinted as chapter 29 of the current volume, pp. 428–29.—Ed.]

INTERNATIONAL TRADE; MONEY; MONOPOLY AND COMPE-
TITION; PRODUCTION, THEORY OF; PROFIT; RENT; VALUE;
WAGES, THEORY OF

For descriptions of systems of economic policy see ECONOMIC SYS-
TEMS. See also lives of KEYNES, J. M., MARSHALL, A., RICARDO,
D., SMITH, A., etc.

In addition to the books already mentioned see F. Benham, *Economics* (4th
ed. 1948) for an elementary statement, and K. E. Boulding, *Economic Analysis*
(1941), G. J. Stigler, *Theory of Price* (1946) and G. N. Halm, *Monetary Theory* (2nd
ed. 1946) for somewhat more advanced expositions of the present state of
economic theory. A discussion of the central theoretical problems on a somewhat more difficult level will be found in J. R. Hicks, *Value and Capital* (2nd ed.
1946). For the method and character of economic theory, see L. C. Robbins,
The Nature and Significance of Economic Science (2nd ed. 1935) and W. Eucken,
Die Grundlagen der Nationalökonomie (4th ed. 1944); for surveys of the history of
economics A. Gray, *The Development of Economic Doctrine* (1931), E. Cannan, *A
Review of Economic Theory* (1929) and C. Gide and C. Rist, *A History of Economic
Doctrines* (1915) for the earlier period, and G. J. Stigler, *Production and Distribution
Theories* (1941) for the last fifty years.[35]

---

[35] [The full references of the books to which Hayek refers are as follows: F. Benham, *Economics: A General Textbook for Students*, 4th edn. (London: Sir Isaac Pitman & Sons, 1948); K. Boulding, *Economic Analysis* (New York: Harper and Brothers, 1941); G. J. Stigler, *Theory of Price* (New
York: Macmillan, 1946); G. N. Halm, *Monetary Theory: A Modern Treatment of the Essentials of Money
and Banking*, 2nd edn. (Philadelphia: Blakiston Company, 1946); J. R. Hicks, *Value and Capital*, 2nd
edn. (Oxford: Clarendon Press, 1946); L. Robbins, *An Essay on the Nature and Significance of Economic
Science*, 2nd edn. (London: Macmillan, 1935); W. Eucken, *Die Grundlagen der Nationalökonomie*, 4th
edn. (Jena: Gustav Fischer, 1944); A. Gray, *The Development of Economic Doctrine: An Introductory Survey* (London: Longmans, Green, and Co., 1931); E. Cannan, *A Review of Economic Theory* (London: P. S. King and Son, 1929); C. Gide and C. Rist, *A History of Economic Doctrines from the Time
of the Physiocrats to the Present Day*, trans. R. Richards (London: George G. Harrap & Co., 1915);
and G. J. Stigler, *Production and Distribution Theories: The Formative Period* (New York: Macmillan
Co., 1941).—Ed.]

TWELVE

THE USES OF 'GRESHAM'S LAW' AS AN ILLUSTRATION OF 'HISTORICAL THEORY'[1]

Mr. A. L. Burns' use of Gresham's Law as an illustration[2] provides a good example for showing how useful it would be for the historian if he examined what Gresham's Law amounts to as a theoretical statement and not merely as an empirical generalisation. The empirical generalisation that 'bad money drives out good' of course goes back to classical antiquity, when it seems to have been so familiar that Aristophanes (*Frogs*, 891–898)[3] could assume that he would be readily understood when he applied the idea to good and bad politicians. It is pure accident that this empirical rule became attached to the name of Gresham.[4] And as a mere empirical rule it is practically valueless. I remember that in the monetary disturbances of the early 1920's, when people began to use dollars and other solid currencies in the place of the rapidly depreciating mark, a Dutch financier (if I remember rightly, Mr. Vissering)

---

[1] Reprinted from *History and Theory*, Vol. II, 1962. [The essay was first published as F. A. Hayek, "The Uses of 'Gresham's Law' as an Illustration in Historical Theory", *History and Theory*, vol. 2, 1962, pp. 101–2. It was reprinted, with the slightly different title of "The Uses of 'Gresham's Law' as an Illustration of 'Historical Theory'", as chapter 24 of F. A. Hayek, *Studies in Philosophy, Politics and Economics* (London: Routledge & Kegan Paul, 1967). The latter title has been retained here.—Ed.]

[2] Arthur Lee Burns, 'International Theory and Historical Explanation', *History and Theory*, I, 1 (1960), 62–6. [The page references given by Hayek refer to Burns' discussion of Gresham's law as an instance of a particular kind of historical explanation of how unintended consequences can arise, rather than to his article as a whole. The full reference is A. L. Burns, "International Theory and Historical Explanation", *History and Theory*, vol. 1, 1960, pp. 55–74.—Ed.]

[3] [See Aristophanes, *The Frogs*, trans. J. H. Frere (London: W. Nicol, 1839), lines 891–98. Hayek quotes the relevant lines in F. A. Hayek, "The Campaign against Keynesian Inflation" [1978], reprinted as chapter 25 of the present volume, p. 375 n. 42.—Ed.]

[4] [Sir Thomas Gresham (c.1518–79) was an English merchant and financier who, in his capacity as financial agent to Queen Elizabeth I, advised her upon her accession to the throne in 1558 to re-coin the currency after it had been debased with inferior metal by her father, Henry VIII. While, as Hayek's reference to Aristophanes shows, the propensity for bad money to drive out good was recognised long before Gresham, the latter's account of it prompted Scottish economist Henry Dunning Macleod (1821–1902) to argue that the tendency should be referred to as 'Gresham's law', which name became widespread thereafter. See H. D. Macleod, *The Elements of Political Economy* (London: Longman, Brown, Green, Longmans, and Roberts, 1858), pp. 475–77.—Ed.]

asserted that Gresham's Law was wrong and that it was in fact the other way round and it was the good money that drove out the bad.[5]

If Gresham's Law is properly stated with the conditions in which it applies, it will appear that as a proposition of compositive social theory it can indeed provide a useful tool of historical explanation.[6] The essential condition is that there must be two kinds of money which are of equivalent value for some purposes and of different value for others. The typical instance about which the empirical generalisation developed is the simultaneous circulation of a particular coin, say a gold ducat, in a new and a worn state. If such a coin is legal tender in a country, the two different forms are of the same value for the discharge of internal debts. But they may not be for foreign payments, and are clearly not of the same value for the industrial use of the gold contained in them. The two kinds of coin may for a long time circulate side by side and be accepted as equivalent not only internally but even externally if there is a net influx of money into the country concerned. But as soon as its balance of payments turns against it, the position will change. The worn coins will now have only the value which they have as currency of the country using them in its regular internal trade. But in international trade the new and full-weight coins may well have a higher value and the same will apply to the internal industrial uses (by goldsmiths) of the gold contained in them. In certain transactions which take coins out of the internal circulation new full-weight coins will therefore be more useful than worn coins, and the former will tend to go out of circulation.

---

[5] [Gerard Vissering (1865–1937) was President of the Bank of the Netherlands from 1912 until 1932 and the younger brother of Willem Vissering, whose work on Chinese currency Hayek references in F. A. Hayek, "The Denationalization of Money: An Analysis of the Theory and Practice of Concurrent Currencies" [1978], reprinted as chapter 4 of F. A. Hayek, *Good Money, Part II: The Standard*, ed. Stephen Kresge, vol. 6 (1999) of *The Collected Works of F. A. Hayek* (Chicago: University of Chicago Press; London: Routledge), pp. 143, 146, 160. It was at Gerard Vissering's instigation that economists from several nations, including John Maynard Keynes, met in Amsterdam in 1919 to discuss how to restore normal economic conditions in Europe in the aftermath of World War One. See R. Skidelsky, *John Maynard Keynes*, vol. I: *Hopes Betrayed 1883–1920* (London: Macmillan, 1983), p. 382.—Ed.]

[6] [The method of compositive social theory involves the social scientist showing how the subjective beliefs held by individual people lead them to act in ways that give rise, often unintentionally, to the structures or wholes that constitute the social world. See F. A. Hayek, *Studies on the Abuse and Decline of Reason: Text and Documents*, ed. Bruce Caldwell, vol. 13 (2010) of *The Collected Works of F. A. Hayek*, pp. 91–107. On this account—as Hayek puts it elsewhere, in an essay referenced by Burns on p. 65 of his article—the task of social theory is "to *constitute* these wholes, to provide schemes of structural relationships which the historian can use when he has to attempt to fit together into a meaningful whole the elements [i.e. the individual beliefs] which he actually finds". See F. A. Hayek, "The Facts of the Social Sciences" [1943], reprinted as chapter 2 of F. A. Hayek, *The Market and Other Orders*, ed. Bruce Caldwell, vol. 15 (2014) of *The Collected Works of F. A. Hayek*, p. 90.—Ed.]

It would not be a very useful approach to the problem to say "that at some reasonably brief interval before the specie disappeared from circulation, it had become public knowledge that it was under-valued by a certain amount in terms of the rest of the currency".[7] No change of this sort need have become newly known. Foreign merchants and goldsmiths may always have been using only new coins. But while as many gold coins (or as much gold to be coined) came into the country as went out, this would not lead to a reduction of the proportion of good coins in circulation. Only when the conditions of a net inflow turned into conditions of a net outflow would a change in the relative composition of the circulation manifest itself.

The historian who knows of Gresham's Law merely as an empirical proposition might well be puzzled when he finds that, after good and bad coins had been circulating concurrently for decades without a noticeable deterioration in the average quality, at one point of time the good coins had suddenly begun to grow very scarce. He would not be able to discover any new information which had become available concerning the 'undervaluation' of one kind of coin. Indeed if he were able to ask those immediately concerned they would tell him that they merely continued to do exactly what they had done before. What theory will tell him is that he must look for some cause which led to a fall of the internal value of both good and bad coins relative to their value in foreign commerce and in industrial uses. He will have to understand that neither wear and tear nor clipping can have caused this relative depreciation. He will have to look for a cause which either increased the relative supply or decreased the relative demand for coins and their substitutes in internal circulation. One need merely read the usual accounts of the events during the 'Kipper and Wipper' period (1621–23) in Germany, or of those preceding the English re-coinage of 1696, in order to see how easy it is to go wrong without some knowledge of monetary theory.[8] Like most of the theory which is

---

[7] Ibid., 65. [See Burns, "International Theory and Historical Explanation", p. 65.—Ed.]

[8] [The Kipper- und Wipperzeit (1619–23) was a monetary crisis that occurred shortly after the outset of the Thirty Years War. Princes in rival German states debased the currency used in everyday transactions, both in an effort to raise funds to pay for the war and also—by exchanging the debased coins for good ones in neighbouring territories—in an attempt to undermine the finances of their enemies. The period took its name, which loosely means 'the time of short measure in weighing', from the actions of the money-changers sent out by the princes, who rigged their scales as they sought to exchange their bad money for the good currency initially possessed by naive peasants, shopkeepers, and craftsmen. Escalating debasement spread from state to state until the coins used in daily transactions became almost worthless. See C. P. Kindleberger and R. Aliber, *Panics, Manias and Crashes: A History of Financial Crashes*, 6th edn. (Basingstoke: Palgrave Macmillan, 2011), pp. 157–58.

The re-coinage of 1696 was a response to the debased state into which much English currency had fallen in the late seventeenth century. Drawing on proposals developed by English philosopher and economist John Locke (1632–1704) in his *Further Considerations Concerning Rais-*

likely to be useful to the historian, it is only very simple and elementary theory which is required; and the usual conception of Gresham's Law is a very good illustration of how theory may and how it will not help the historian.

ing the Value of Money [1695], reprinted in his *Several Papers Relating to Money, Interest and Trade, &c* (London: Printed for A. and J. Churchill and others, 1696), the government withdrew from circulation coins that were counterfeit or had been clipped, issuing in their place new, full-weight coins. However, the implementation of Locke's proposals precipitated a shortage of silver money and an economic crisis. Hayek's account of this episode in monetary history can be found on pp. 127–47 of F. A. Hayek, "Genesis of the Gold Standard in Response to English Coinage Policy in the 17th and 18th Centuries" [1929], published as chapter 9 of F. A. Hayek, *The Trend of Economic Thinking: Essays on Political Economists and Economic History*, ed. W. W. Bartley III and S. Kresge, vol. 3 (1991) of *The Collected Works of F. A. Hayek.*—Ed.]

THIRTEEN

THE DILEMMA OF SPECIALISATION[1]

We have been commemorating the foundation of a research centre within our University, and our thoughts have inevitably often touched upon the problems of the relation between research and education, and of education for research. It may therefore be fitting if this last evening is devoted to a problem in this field which must give concern to many of us. Research, of necessity, requires specialisation, often in a very minute field. It is probably also true that those exacting standards which fruitful scientific work demands can be acquired only through the complete mastery of at least one field, which today means that it must be a narrow field and, also, that it ought to be one which has its own firmly established standards. Thus a progressive tendency toward specialisation seems to be inevitable, bound to continue and to grow, both in research and in university education.

This applies, of course, to all branches of science and is not peculiar to the study of society, which is our particular concern. It is so conspicuous a fact that the sad joke about the scientific specialist who knows more and more about less and less has become about the one thing which everybody believes to know about science. There seem to me to exist, however, in this respect important differences among the various fields, special circumstances which ought to warn us not to accept too readily in the social sciences a tendency which natural scientists can treat as a regrettable necessity to which they may submit with impunity. It may well be that the chemist or physiologist is right

[1] A lecture delivered at the celebration of the twenty-fifth anniversary of the opening of the Social Science Research Building of the University of Chicago and now reprinted from Leonard D. White (ed.): *The State of the Social Sciences* (University of Chicago Press, 1956). [Hayek's lecture was delivered as the centerpiece of the final session of the conference, on November 12, 1955. It was first published as F. A. Hayek, "The Dilemma of Specialisation", in *The State of the Social Sciences*, ed. L. D. White (Chicago: University of Chicago Press, 1956), pp. 462–73. Other speakers, whose essays appear in the same volume, included economists Frank Knight (1885–1972) and George Stigler (1911–91), economist and historian of economic thought Jacob Viner (1892–1970), organisational theorist Herbert Simon (1916–2001), journalist and author Walter Lippmann (1889–1974), and behavioural scientist James Grier Miller (1916–2002). Hayek's essay was reprinted with minor stylistic changes as chapter 8 of F. A. Hayek, *Studies in Philosophy, Politics and Economics* (London: Routledge & Kegan Paul, 1967), the version used here.—Ed.]

when he decides that he will become a better chemist or physiologist if he concentrates on his subject at the expense of his general education. But in the study of society exclusive concentration on a speciality has a peculiarly baneful effect: it will not merely prevent us from being attractive company or good citizens but may impair our competence in our proper field—or at least for some of the most important tasks we have to perform. The physicist who is only a physicist can still be a first-class physicist and a most valuable member of society. But nobody can be a great economist who is only an economist—and I am even tempted to add that the economist who is only an economist is likely to become a nuisance if not a positive danger.

I do not wish to exaggerate a difference which in the last resort, of course, is one of degree; but it still seems to me so great that what in one field is a venal offence is a cardinal sin in the other. What we face is a true dilemma imposed upon us by the nature of our subject or, perhaps I should say, by the different significance we must attach to the concrete and particular as against the general and theoretical. Although the logical relation between theory and its application, of course, is the same in all sciences and although theory is quite as indispensable in our field as anywhere, there is no denying that the interest of the natural scientist is concentrated on the general laws, while our interest in the end is mainly in the particular, individual, and unique event, and that in a sense our theories are more remote from reality—requiring much more additional knowledge before they can be applied to particular instances.

One result of this is that in the natural sciences specialisation is predominantly what might he called systematic specialisation—specialisation in a theoretical discipline—while at least in research in the social sciences topical specialisation is more common. Of course this contrast is again not absolute. The expert in the topography of Mars, in the ecology of Nyasaland, or in the fauna of the Triassic is as much a topical specialist as anyone in the social sciences; yet even there the share of general knowledge which qualifies the specialist is probably much greater in the natural sciences than in the social. The ecologist will need to learn less when he shifts from Nyasaland to Alaska than the archaeologist when he shifts from Crete to Peru. The former is readily done, while the latter requires almost a new training.

A further consequence is that the disparity between the age at which the human mind works at its best and the age at which one can have accumulated the knowledge demanded from the competent specialist becomes greater and greater as we move from the purely theoretical subjects to those in which the concern with the concrete is the main part. Every one of us probably lives for most of his life on the original ideas which he conceived when very young. But while this means for the mathematician or logician that he may do his most brilliant work at eighteen, the historian, to go to the other extreme, may do his best work at eighty.

I trust I shall not be misunderstood as identifying the difference between the natural and the social sciences with that between the theoretical and the historical. This is certainly not my view. I am not defending what I regard as the erroneous view that the study of society is nothing but history, but I merely want to stress that the need for understanding history arises in every application of our knowledge.[2] The degree of abstraction which the theoretical disciplines in our field require makes them at least as theoretical, if not more so, than any in the natural sciences. This, however, is precisely the source of our difficulty. Not only is the individual concrete instance much more important to us than it is in the natural sciences, but the way from the theoretical construction to the explanation of the particular is also much longer.

For almost any application of our knowledge to concrete instances, the knowledge of one discipline, and even of all the scientific knowledge we can bring to bear on the topic, will be only a small part of the foundations of our opinions. Let me speak first of the need of using the results of scientific disciplines other than our own, though this is far from all that is required. That concrete reality is not divisible into distinct objects corresponding to the various scientific disciplines is a commonplace, yet a commonplace which severely limits our competence to pronounce as scientists on any particular event. There is scarcely an individual phenomenon or event in society with which we can deal adequately without knowing a great deal of several disciplines, not to speak of the knowledge of particular facts that will be required. None of us can feel but very humble when he reflects what he really ought to know in order to account for even the simplest social process or to be able to give sensible advice on almost any political issue. We are probably so used to this impossibility of knowing what we ideally ought to know that we are rarely fully aware of the magnitude of our shortcomings. In an ideal world an economist who knows no law, an anthropologist who knows no economics, a psychologist who knows no philosophy, or a historian who does not know almost every subject should be inconceivable; yet the fact is, of course, that the limitations of our capacities make such deficiencies the rule. We can do no better than be guided by the particular topic which we take up for research and gradually acquire whatever special technical equipment is demanded by it. Indeed, most successful research work will require a very particular combination of diverse kinds of knowledge and accomplishments, and it may take half a lifetime before we are better than amateurs in three-quarters of the knowledge demanded by the task we have set ourselves. In this sense, fruitful research undoubtedly demands the most intense specialisation—so intense, indeed,

---

[2] [Hayek discusses the relationship between history and theory in F. A. Hayek, "The Uses of 'Gresham's Law' as an Illustration of 'Historical Theory'" [1962], reprinted as chapter 12 of the current volume.—Ed.]

that those who practise it may soon cease to be of much use in teaching the whole of any one of the conventional subjects. That such specialists are badly needed, that today the advance of knowledge depends largely on them, and that a great university cannot have enough of them is as true in our fields as it is in the natural sciences.

Yet professors, curiously enough, want students, and preferably students all of whose work they direct. Thus the multiplicity of research specialisations tends to produce a proliferation of teaching departments. It is here that the educational aspects of our problem begin. Not every legitimate research speciality is equally suitable as a scientific education. Even if we look at it entirely as education for research, it must be doubtful whether the composite knowledge demanded by a particular empirical object ought to be taught as a whole in those decisive years during which a student must learn what real competence is, during which his standards are set and the conscience of a scholar is formed. It seems to me that at this stage the complete mastery of one clearly circumscribed field, of the whole of a systematically coherent subject, should be acquired. It cannot always be, as I am a little inclined to wish, a theoretical field, because some of the descriptive and historical disciplines have, of course, their own highly developed techniques which it takes years to master. But it ought to be a field that has its own firmly established standards and where it is not true that most workers, except those who have already spent a lifetime in it, are inevitably more or less amateurs in much of the field.

Let me illustrate what I mean from a subject which, for my present purpose, has the advantage of not being represented in this University, so that I shall not offend any susceptibilities. It is ancient economic history, which to me has always seemed not only a particularly fascinating subject but also one of great importance for the understanding of our own civilization. I very much wish it were represented and taught here. But by this I do not mean that there ought to exist a separate department of ancient economic history in which students should from the beginning of their graduate career divide their energies among the variety of disciplines and accomplishments which a competent ancient economic historian must command. I believe, rather, that the men who will do good work in such a field will do much better if, in the first instance, they get a thorough training in the classics, or in ancient history, or in archaeology, or in economics; and, only when they are really competent in that one field and start to work largely on their own, begin to work seriously on the other subjects.

When I stress here the need of intense systematic specialisation during a certain phase of education, I do not, of course, approve of the system of prescribed courses or lectures which leaves the student no time for exploring anything else and which often prevents him from following that intellectual curiosity which ought to gain him more education than anything which is formally offered.[3] If there is anything I somewhat miss in the great American universities, it is that attitude of intellectual adventure among the students, an attitude which leads them, concurrently with their specialised work, to range over wide fields, to sample a great variety of courses, and to make them feel that the university and not their department is their intellectual home. I do not believe that this is so much the fault of the students as of university organisation, which keeps the students largely ignorant of what happens outside their departments in the form of extra fees or rigid departmental schedules, and tends even to put obstacles in the way of their inclinations. It is only by the greatest freedom in this respect that the student will discover his true vocation.

What I do mean is that there must be a period or phase in his education when the chief object is to acquire complete mastery of one well-defined subject and when he will learn to distrust superficial knowledge and facile generalisations. But I am speaking only of one necessary phase in the process of education for research. My chief point is that different things are true of different phases. If it seems to me to be untrue that all the recognised research specialities are equally suitable as a basic training, it seems to be no less untrue that the advanced work usually leading to a Ph.D. thesis must fit into any one of the already established research specialities. What I am arguing is that only certain kinds of specialisations deserve the name of 'disciplines' in the original sense of a discipline of the mind, and even that it is not so important which discipline of this kind a mind has undergone as that it has experienced all the rigour and strictness of such a schooling. I can even see some merit in the belief on which English higher education used to be based that a man who has thoroughly studied either mathematics or the classics can be presumed to be capable of learning on his own almost any other subject. The number of true disciplines which achieve this object may today be much larger; but I do not think that it has become co-extensive with the number of research specialities.

There is another side to this which I can best explain with reference to my own field. I happen to believe that economic theory is one of those true disciplines of the mind, but I regret that most of those whose basic training is in pure economic theory tend to remain specialists in this field. What I have said implies that those of us who teach such subjects ought to do so in the aware-

[3] [Hayek raises in this paragraph and the next issues that he had also discussed some years earlier, in an address given to the Students' Union of the London School of Economics in February 1944. See F. A. Hayek, "On Being an Economist" [1944], first published as chapter 2 of F. A. Hayek, *The Trend of Economic Thinking: Essays on Political Economists and Economic History*, ed. W. W. Bartley III and S. Kresge, vol. 3 (1991) of *The Collected Works of F. A. Hayek* (Chicago: University of Chicago Press; London: Routledge), pp. 41–43. A slightly later discussion is to be found in his inaugural lecture at Freiburg University, delivered in 1962. See F. A. Hayek, "The Economy, Science and Politics" [1963], reprinted as chapter 7 of F. A. Hayek, *The Market and Other Orders*, ed. Bruce Caldwell, vol. 15 (2014) of *The Collected Works of F. A. Hayek*, pp. 228–29.—Ed.]

ness and the hope, and even with the deliberate aim, that those whom we train as specialists ought not to remain specialists in this field but should use their competence for some other, realistic or topical, specialisation. I would be happier to see even the majority of the economic theorists we turn out become economic historians, or specialists in labour economics or agricultural economics—though I must admit to some doubts about the suitability of these topics as a basic training.

Please note that what I have said about such composite subjects is said in no slighting spirit but rather from an appreciation of the very high demands which they put on our mental equipment. It is based on the recognition that for most worthwhile research subjects we ought to be masters of more than one systematic subject, and on the belief that we are more likely to achieve this if we use the short period during which we work under close guidance to become real masters of one. I am also pleading for such a period of intense specialisation only on the assumption that it is preceded by a good general education which, I am afraid, American schools hardly provide and which our College so manfully struggles to supply. But my main emphasis, of course, is on how far we still are, at the end of such an indispensable period of specialisation, from being competent to deal with most of the problems the study of human civilization raises. So far I have spoken only of the limited and modest tasks which most of us can reasonably set ourselves and where still the ideal after which we must strive far exceeds our powers. I have not spoken of the need for synthesis, of efforts to understand our civilization, or any other civilization, as a whole, and still less of the even more ambitious conception of a comparative study of civilizations. I will not comment on such efforts beyond saying that it is fortunate that there do still occasionally arise exceptional men who have the power and the courage to make the human universe their province. You will have the privilege, later this evening, of listening to a great scholar who has probably come nearer than any other living man to achieve the seemingly impossible in this field.[4]

We certainly ought to feel nothing but admiration for the mature scholar who is willing to run the serious risk of disregarding all the boundaries of specialisation in order to venture on tasks for which perhaps no man can claim full competence. While I sympathise with the healthy prejudice which brings it about that the scholar who produces a best seller thereby rather lowers him-

---

[4] This lecture was followed by one by Arnold J. Toynbee. [English historian Arnold Toynbee (1889–1975) advanced a philosophy of history based on an analysis of the cyclical development and decline of civilizations. At the time of the Chicago conference, Toynbee was Director of Studies at the Royal Institute of International Affairs and Research Professor of International History at the London School of Economics. The 'Program' for the conference lists Toynbee as the first of three commentators on Hayek's lecture, the other two being Herrlee G. Creel, Professor of Early Chinese Literature and Institutions, and Gustave E. von Grunebaum, Professor of Arabic, both at the University of Chicago. See *The State of the Social Sciences*, p. 480—Ed.]

self in the estimation of his peers—and sometimes even wish that there were more of it in this country—the suspicion of boundary violations as such must not go so far as to discourage attempts which are beyond the scope of any specialist.[5] I would go even further, although the economist suffers perhaps more from—and tends, therefore, also to be more intolerant of—intrusions into his preserve than other social scientists. It is perhaps not unjust to suggest that in other subjects, too, there is a little too much of a clannish spirit among the representatives of the recognised specialities, which makes them almost resent an attempt at a serious contribution even from a man in a neighbouring field—although the basic kinship of all our disciplines makes it more than likely that ideas conceived in one field may prove fertile in another.[6]

The grand efforts toward a comprehension of civilization as a whole, of which I have just spoken, are specially significant in our context in one respect: they raise particularly clearly one difficulty which to a lesser degree affects all our efforts. I have so far spoken only of the constant need to draw on knowledge belonging to specialisations other than our own. But, though the need to know many disciplines presents a formidable difficulty, it is only part of our problem. Even where we study only some part or aspect of a civilization of which we and our whole way of thinking are a part, this means, of course, that we cannot take for granted much that in the normal course of life we must unquestioningly accept if we are to get our work done, or even if we are to remain sane; it means that we must question systematically all the presuppositions which in acting we accept unreflectingly; it means, in short, that in order to be strictly scientific we ought to see, as it were, from the outside what we can never see as a whole in such a manner; and, in practice, it means that we have constantly to deal with many important questions to which we have no scientific answer, where the knowledge on which we must draw is either the kind of knowledge of men and the world which only rich and varied experience can give, or the accumulated wisdom of the past, the inherited cultural treasures of our civilization, which to us must thus at the same time be tools which we use in orienting ourselves in our world and objects of critical study. This means that in most of our tasks we need not only be competent scientists

---

[5] [Hayek himself had some experience of the "healthy prejudice" in question, having produced his own best-seller in the form of *The Road to Serfdom*. For more on that book's success, see B. Caldwell, "Introduction", in F. A. Hayek, *The Road to Serfdom: Text and Documents*, ed. B. Caldwell, vol. 2 (2007) of *The Collected Works of F. A. Hayek*, pp. 18–23. Hayek alludes to the damage he believed that book did to his professional reputation in F. A. Hayek, *Hayek on Hayek: An Autobiographical Dialogue*, ed. S. Kresge and L. Wenar (Chicago: University of Chicago Press, 1994), pp. 152–53.—Ed.]

[6] [Hayek may well be lamenting here the limited attention paid to his 1952 book on theoretical psychology, *The Sensory Order*. See F. A. Hayek, *The Sensory Order and Other Writings on the Foundations of Theoretical Psychology*, ed. V. Vanberg, vol. 14 (2017) of *The Collected Works of F. A. Hayek*.—Ed.]

and scholars but ought also to be experienced men of the world and, in some measure, philosophers.

Before I develop these points, let me briefly remind you of one respect where with us specialisation goes less far than in the natural sciences: we do not know as sharp a division between the theoretician and the practitioner as there exists between the physicist and the engineer or between the physiologist and the doctor. This is not an accident or merely an earlier stage of development but a necessary consequence of the nature of our subject. It is due to the fact that the task of recognising the presence in the real world of the conditions corresponding to the various assumptions of our theoretical schemes is often more difficult than the theory itself, an art which only those will acquire to whom the theoretical schemes have become second nature. We cannot state simple, almost mechanical criteria by which a certain type of theoretical situation can be identified, but we have to develop something like a sense for the physiognomy of events.[7] We can, therefore, only rarely delegate the application of our knowledge to others, but must be our own practitioners, doctors as well as physiologists.

The factual knowledge, the familiarity with particular circumstances, which we cannot leave to our 'engineers' but must ourselves acquire, is, moreover, only in part of the kind which can be ascertained by established techniques. Although we endeavour to add by systematic effort to the knowledge of the world and of man, this effort can neither displace nor make unnecessary that knowledge of the world which is acquired only by extensive experience and a steepening in the wisdom contained in great literature and in our whole cultural tradition.

I need not say more about the necessity of a knowledge of the world in the usual sense, of the variety of human situations and characters with which we ought to be familiar. But I must say a word about what seems to me the unfortunate effect of the separation of what we now call the social *sciences* from the other human studies. By this I do not mean merely such paradoxical results as that so scientific a discipline as linguistics, from whose method and approach the other social sciences might well profit, should, for purely historical reasons, be counted among the humanities. What I have in mind is mainly a question of the climate in which our work will prosper; the question whether the atmosphere created by the pursuit of the humanities proper, of literature and the arts, is not quite as indispensable to us as the austerity of the scientific one. I am not sure that the results of the ambition to share in the prestige, and the funds, available for scientific research have always been fortunate, and that the separation of the social sciences from the humanities, of which this build-

---

[7] [For related themes, see F. A. Hayek, "Degrees of Explanation" [1955], reprinted as chapter 6 of *The Market and Other Orders*, p. 209, and F. A. Hayek, "Rules, Perception and Intelligibility" [1962], reprinted as chapter 8 of *The Market and Other Orders*, pp. 235–36, 243–45.—Ed.]

ing is a symbol, was altogether a gain. I do not wish to overstress this point, and I will readily admit that, if I were speaking to a European rather than to an American audience, I might well stress the opposite view. But that here the separation of the humanities from what we mean to dignify by the name of social sciences may have gone too far ought not to be forgotten when we are looking back at twenty-five years of existence in a separate home.

We must admit, however, that there is one respect in which our attitude does differ from that of the humanities and in which we may even be disturbing and unwelcome in their circle. It is that our approach to the traditions which they cultivate must in some measure always be a critical and dissecting one; that there is no value which we must not on occasion question and analyse, though we can, of course, never do so for all values at the same time.[8] Since our aim must be to discover what role particular institutions and traditions play in the functioning of society, we must constantly put the dissolving acid of reason to values and customs which not only are dear to others but are also so largely the cement which keeps society together. Especially in the study of that experience of the human race which is not preserved as explicit human knowledge but rather implicit in habits and institutions, in morals and mores—in short, in the study of those adaptations of the human race which act as non-conscious factors, of whose significance we are not normally aware, and which we may never fully understand, we are bound all the time to question fundamentals. This, I need hardly add, is, of course, the opposite to following intellectual fashions. While it must be our privilege to be radical, this ought not to mean 'advanced' in the sense that we claim to know which is the only forward direction.

Such constant practice is a heady wine which, if not paired with modesty, may make us little better than a nuisance. If we are not to become a mainly destructive element, we must also be wise enough to understand that we cannot do without beliefs and institutions whose significance we do not understand and which, therefore, may seem meaningless to us. If life is to proceed, we must, in practice, accept much which we cannot justify, and resign ourselves to the fact that reason cannot always be the ultimate judge in human affairs.[9] This is, though not the only, yet perhaps the main, point where,

---

[8] [On the last point, see F. A. Hayek, *The Constitution of Liberty*, ed. Ronald Hamowy, vol. 17 (2011) of *The Collected Works of F. A. Hayek*, pp. 124–25, and "The Errors of Constructivism" [1970], reprinted as chapter 14 of *The Market and Other Orders*, pp. 353–56.—Ed.]

[9] [Hayek draws here on the insights of what he terms elsewhere the 'British' or 'evolutionary' tradition of social theory, whose principal exponents include Scottish philosopher David Hume (1711–76), moral philosopher and historian Adam Ferguson (1723–1816), Irish statesman and conservative political philosopher Edmund Burke (1729–97), and Scottish political economist Adam Smith (1723–90). The central insight gleaned by these thinkers, Hayek contends, is that order is possible in modern societies only if people's decisions about how to act are guided by inherited rules, values and institutions that, having developed through a process of evolutionary selection and thereby become adapted to the context in which people find them-

whether we want it or not, we must in some measure be philosophers. By philosophy I mean here, in the first instance, not so much those problems which, like those of logic, have themselves already become the subjects of highly specialised and technical disciplines, but rather that remaining body of inchoate knowledge from which the distinct disciplines only gradually detach themselves and which has always been the province of philosophers. But there are also two fully developed branches of philosophy to which we cannot afford to be total strangers. The problems of ethics are constantly with us, and questions of scientific method are bound to be more troublesome for us than in most other fields. What Einstein once said about science, "Without epistemology—insofar as it is thinkable at all—it is primitive and muddled", applies even more to our subjects.[10]

Rather than be slightly ashamed of this connection, I feel we ought to be proud of the intimate relation which for centuries has existed between the

---

selves, embody more wisdom about appropriate behaviour than is accessible to any one individual. However, because the social formations in question are the outcome of human action but not the product of human design, they are only imperfectly understood by those who rely on them. This has rendered them vulnerable to criticism by thinkers in what Hayek terms the 'constructivist' rationalist tradition of thought, an approach whose modern roots Hayek traces back to French philosopher René Descartes (1596–1650) and whose exponents include English philosopher Thomas Hobbes (1588–1679); French sociologist Auguste Comte (1798–1857); utilitarians of various kinds including English philosopher and jurist Jeremy Bentham (1748–1832) and Cambridge philosopher G. E. Moore (1873–1958); legal positivists such as English jurist John Austin (1790–1859) and Austrian jurist and philosopher Hans Kelsen (1881–1973); and logical positivist philosophers such as Rudolph Carnap (1891–1970) and Sir Alfred Ayer (1910–89). What unites these thinkers, Hayek claims, is their belief that only those institutions whose purpose can be explicitly recognised and justified should have a place in a rational social order. Given, however, that people lack the knowledge required to make such rational assessments, this has led to what Hayek described in 1973 as "that destruction of values by scientific error which has increasingly come to seem to me the great tragedy of our time—a tragedy, because the values which scientific error tends to dethrone are the indispensable foundation of all our civilization . . . The tendency of constructivism to represent those values which it cannot explain as determined by arbitrary human decisions, or acts of will, or mere emotions, rather than as the necessary conditions of facts which are taken for granted by its expounders, has done much to shake the foundations of civilization, and of science itself, which also rests on a system of values which cannot be scientifically proved". See F. A. Hayek, *Rules and Order*, vol. 1 (1973) of *Law, Legislation and Liberty* (Chicago: University of Chicago Press; London: Routledge, 1973–1979), pp. 6–7. For more on the evolutionary and constructivist traditions of social and moral thought, see Hayek, *The Constitution of Liberty*, pp. 107–32, Hayek, "The Errors of Constructivism", and Hayek, *Rules and Order*, pp. 8–34.—Ed.]

[10] [See A. Einstein, "Remarks Concerning the Essays Brought Together in This Co-operative Volume", in *Albert Einstein: Philosopher-Scientist*, Library of Living Philosophers, vol. 7, ed. P. A. Schilpp (Evanston, IL: Library of Living Philosophers, 1949), p. 684. Einstein's actual words, which have been slightly modified by Hayek, were as follows: "Science without epistemology is—insofar as it is thinkable at all—primitive and muddled."—Ed.]

social sciences and philosophy.[11] It is certainly no accident that, so far as economics is concerned, in England, the country which has so long been leading in the subject, a list of her great economists, if we leave out only two major figures, might readily be taken for a list of her great philosophers: Locke, Hume, Adam Smith, Bentham, James and John Stuart Mill, Samuel Bailey, W. S. Jevons, Henry Sidgwick, to John Neville and John Maynard Keynes—all occupy equally honoured places in the history of economics as in that of philosophy or of scientific method. I see little reason to doubt that other social sciences would equally profit if they could attract a similar array of philosophic talent.[12]

[11] [Hayek elaborates briefly on the issues discussed in this paragraph in his 1962 inaugural lecture, "The Economy, Science and Politics", pp. 229–30. A more extended treatment can be found in a series of lectures Hayek delivered at the University of Chicago in 1963, under the sponsorship of the Charles R. Walgreen Foundation. The lectures have now been published for the first time as F. A. Hayek, "Economists and Philosophers" [1963], Appendix B of *The Market and Other Orders*, pp. 427–37 in particular.—Ed.]

[12] [English philosopher John Locke (1632–1704) set out his empiricist philosophy in his *Essay Concerning Human Understanding* [1689], reprinted in *The Works of John Locke, in Nine Volumes*, 12th edn., vols. 1 and 2 (London: C. and J. Rivington and others, 1824). Locke wrote on interest rates, and on the relationship between the quantity of money and the general price level in an economy, in *Some Considerations of the Consequences of the Lowering of Interest, and Raising the Value of Money* [1691] and in *Further Considerations Concerning Raising the Value of Money* [1695], both reprinted in his *Several Papers Relating to Money, Interest and Trade, &c* (London: Printed for A. and J. Churchill and others, 1696) and in *The Works of John Locke, in Nine Volumes*, 12th edn., vol. 4. Hayek's assessment of Locke's monetary economics can be found in F. A. Hayek, "Genesis of the Gold Standard in Response to English Coinage Policy in the 17th and 18th Centuries" [1929], now to be found as chapter 9 of Hayek, *The Trend of Economic Thinking*.

David Hume's (1711–76) writings on money and international trade can be found in part II of D. Hume, *Essays: Moral, Political, and Literary* [1777], ed. E. F. Miller (Indianapolis, IN: Liberty Fund, 1987), while his mature philosophical system is set out in D. Hume, *Enquiries Concerning the Human Understanding and Concerning the Principles of Morals* [1777], ed. L. A. Selby-Bigge, 2nd edn. (Oxford: Clarendon Press, 1902). Adam Smith (1723–90) presents his views on scientific method in "The History of Astronomy" [1795], reprinted in A. Smith, *Essays on Philosophical Subjects*, ed. W. P. D. Wightman and J. C. Bryce, vol. 3 (1980) of *The Works and Correspondence of Adam Smith* (Indianapolis, IN: Liberty Fund, 1982), pp. 33–105. Smith's economics is set out in his *An Inquiry into the Nature and Causes of the Wealth of Nations*, ed. W. B. Todd, vol. 2 of *The Glasgow Edition of the Works and Correspondence of Adam Smith* (Oxford: Oxford University Press, 1976; reprinted, Indianapolis, IN: Liberty Fund, 1981).

English philosopher, jurist, and reformer Jeremy Bentham (1748–1832) expounded his utilitarian philosophy in *An Introduction to the Principles of Morals and Legislation* (London: Printed for T. Payne and Son, 1789). His most famous work in economics is his *Defence of Usury* (London: Payne and Foss, 1787), a critique of Adam Smith's reluctance in *The Wealth of Nations* to advocate free trade in the lending of money at interest. A collection of Bentham's economic writings can be found in *Jeremy Bentham's Economic Writings*, ed. W. Stark, 3 vols. (London: George Allen and Unwin, 1952–54). Along with others including James and John Stuart Mill, Bentham was a philosophical radical who employed utilitarianism as a basis for criticising and reforming social institutions.

James Mill (1773–1836) was a Scottish philosopher, historian and economist. A follower of

David Ricardo, Mill in his *Elements of Political Economy* (London: Printed for Baldwin, Cradock, and Joy, 1821) expounded Ricardo's ideas and summarised the philosophical radicals' views on economics. Mill's *Analysis of the Phenomena of the Human Mind*, 2 vols. (London: Baldwin and Cradock, 1829) developed an associationist perspective on psychology and the philosophy of mind. English philosopher and political economist John Stuart Mill (1806–73) examined the principles of the natural and social sciences in his *A System of Logic: Ratiocinative and Inductive* [1843], vols. 7 (1974) and 8 (1974) of the *Collected Works of John Stuart Mill*, ed. J. M. Robson (Toronto University Press; reprinted, Indianapolis: Liberty Fund, 2006). Mill's *Principles of Political Economy with some of their applications to Social Philosophy* [1848], vols. 2 (1965) and 3 (1965) of the *Collected Works of John Stuart Mill*, saw him set out a modified version of Ricardo's approach and became the leading introductory economics text in English until it was superseded by Alfred Marshall's *Principles of Economics*, vol. 1 (London: Macmillan and Co., 1890).

British economist and philosopher Samuel Bailey (1791–1870) wrote on banking and on the theory of value, where he argued contrary to Ricardo that value is a subjective phenomenon, depending not on costs but on the esteem in which an object is held. See S. Bailey, *Money and its Vicissitudes in Value; as they affect National Industry and Pecuniary Contracts; with a Postscript on Joint-Stock Banks* (London: E. Wilson, 1837), and S. Bailey, *A Critical Dissertation on the Nature, Measure, and Causes of Value; Chiefly in Reference to the Writings of Mr. David Ricardo and his Followers* (London: R. Hunter, 1825). Bailey's philosophical works include *A Review of Berkeley's Theory of Vision* (London: James Ridgway, 1842) and *The Theory of Reasoning* (London: Longman, Brown, Green, and Longmans, 1851).

English economist and philosopher of science William Stanley Jevons (1835–82) was the author of *The Theory of Political Economy* (London and New York: Macmillan and Co., 1871), in which he built on Bentham's utilitarianism to argue that value depends entirely upon utility. The book became one of the founding texts of the marginal revolution in economics. Jevons's writings on philosophy and scientific method included *Logic* (London: Macmillan, 1876) and *The Principles of Science: A Treatise on Logic and Scientific Method*, 2nd edn. (London: Macmillan, 1877).

Cambridge philosopher and political economist Henry Sidgwick (1838–1900) wrote on moral philosophy, most notably in his classic *The Methods of Ethics* (London: Macmillan, 1874), and on economics, exploring in *The Principles of Political Economy* (London: Macmillan and Co., 1883) the role of the state in economic life. John Neville Keynes (1852–1949) was a logician, economist, and university administrator. He was the author both of *Studies and Exercises in Formal Logic* (London: Macmillan and Co., 1884), a textbook which became a classic in the field of deductive logic, and also of *The Scope and Method of Political Economy* (London: Macmillan and Co., 1891), in which he integrated inductive and deductive approaches to economics so successfully that he was widely regarded as bringing to a close the famous *Methodenstreit*. The economist John Maynard Keynes (1883–1946) was the author of *A Treatise on Probability* [1921] and of *The General Theory of Employment, Interest and Money* [1936], now reprinted as vol. 8 (1973) and vol. 7 (1973) respectively of *The Collected Writings of John Maynard Keynes* (London: Macmillan for the Royal Economic Society). For more on Hayek's views about Keynes, see F. A. Hayek, *Contra Keynes and Cambridge: Essays, Correspondence*, ed. B. Caldwell, vol. 9 (1995) of *The Collected Works of F. A. Hayek*.

In his inaugural lecture as Professor of Political Economy at the University of Freiburg, Hayek remarked that the "two conspicuous exceptions" to the trend for great British economists also to be great philosophers are David Ricardo (1772–1823) and Alfred Marshall (1842–1924). In that lecture, Hayek also added one more name to the list of distinguished practitioners of economics and philosophy, namely Anglican Bishop George Berkeley (1685–1753), best known for his immaterialist or subjective idealist philosophy, as expressed in *A Treatise Concerning the Principles of Human Knowledge* (Dublin: Aaron Rhames, 1710). Berkeley's principal contribution to economics was a pamphlet entitled *The Querist* (Dublin: Anonymous, 1735–37), in which he condemned

I have said enough, however, to describe our dilemma and must hasten to my conclusion. A true dilemma, of course, has no perfect solution, and my main point has been that we *are* faced by a true dilemma—that our task puts conflicting demands upon us which we cannot all satisfy. The choice imposed upon us by our imperfections remains a choice between evils. The main conclusion must thus probably be that there is no single best way and that our main hope is to preserve room for that multiplicity of efforts which true academic freedom makes possible.

But as a norm for academic education some general principles seem to emerge. We probably all agree that the main need for students who enter upon their graduate careers is a good general education. I have been arguing for the need for a following period of intense specialisation in one of a somewhat limited number of subjects. But this, I feel, ought not regularly to continue to the end of the graduate work—and, if my contention is accepted that not all topical specialisations are equally suitable as basic training, cannot always mean the end. Many students will of course continue to do their specialised research in the field of their basic training. But they should not have to do so or in their majority do so. At least for those who are willing to shoulder the extra burden, there ought to be opportunities to work, wherever possible under the guidance of competent specialists, on any suitable combination of knowledge. There ought to be opportunities for men who want to strike out in their own new field on some new combination of specialism or some other borderline problem. There is clearly an urgent need for a place in the University where the specialisms again meet, which provides the facilities and the climate for work which is not on well-established lines, and where requirements are flexible enough to be adapted to the individual tasks. The whole position in the field which I have been surveying seems to me to call for a sort of College of Advanced Human Studies as a recognised part of the organisation of the social sciences and the humanities, some such institution as our chairman[13] has so devotedly and judiciously striven to provide with his pathbreaking conception of the Committee on Social Thought.

English exploitation of the Irish economy. See Hayek, "The Economy, Science and Politics", p. 229.—Ed.]

[13] Professor John U. Nef. [American economic historian John Ulric Nef (1899–1988) co-founded the University of Chicago's Committee on Social Thought in 1941 and served as its Chairman from 1945 until 1964. Hayek obtained an independently-funded position on the Committee as Professor of Social and Moral Thought when he moved to Chicago in 1950. Nef's role in the recruitment of Hayek to the University of Chicago is discussed in D. Mitch, "A Year of Transition: Faculty Recruiting at Chicago in 1946", *Journal of Political Economy*, vol. 124, 2016, pp. 1714–34, and in D. Mitch, "Morality versus Money: Hayek's Move to the University of Chicago", in *Hayek: A Collaborative Biography, Part IV: England, the Ordinal Revolution and the Road to Serfdom, 1931–50*, ed. R. Leeson (Basingstoke: Palgrave Macmillan, 2015).—Ed.]

FOURTEEN

FULL EMPLOYMENT, PLANNING AND INFLATION[1]

I

In the years that have elapsed since the war, central planning, 'full employment', and inflationary pressure have been the three features which have dominated economic policy in the greater part of the world. Of these only full employment can be regarded as desirable in itself. Central planning, direction, or government controls, however we care to call it, is at best a means which must be judged by the results. Inflation, even 'repressed inflation', is undoubtedly an evil, though some would say a necessary evil if other desirable aims are to be achieved. It is part of the price we pay for having committed ourselves to a policy of full employment and central planning.

The new fact which has brought about this situation is not a greater desire to avoid unemployment than existed before the war. It is the new belief that a higher level of employment can be permanently maintained by monetary pressure than would be possible without it. The pursuit of a policy based on these beliefs has somewhat unexpectedly shown that inflation and government controls are its necessary accompaniments—unexpected not by all, but by probably the majority of those who advocated those policies.

Full employment policies as now understood are thus the dominant factor of which the other characteristic features of contemporary economic policy are mainly the consequence. Before we can further examine the manner in which central planning, full employment, and inflation interact, we must become clear about what precisely the full employment policies as now practised mean.

---

[1] Reprinted from the *Institute of Public Affairs Review*, Melbourne, Vol. IV, 1950. [This essay was first published as F. A. Hayek, "Full Employment, Planning and Inflation", *Institute of Public Affairs Review*, vol. 4, 1950, pp. 174–84. It was subsequently reprinted as chapter 19 of F. A. Hayek, *Studies in Philosophy, Politics and Economics* (London: Routledge & Kegan Paul, 1967). In the version published in 1950, the first sentence began, "In the five years that have elapsed since the war".—Ed.]

II

Full employment has come to mean that maximum of employment that can be brought about in the short run by monetary pressure. This may not be the original meaning of the theoretical concept, but it was inevitable that it should have come to mean this in practice. Once it was admitted that the momentary state of employment should form the main guide to monetary policy, it was inevitable that any degree of unemployment which might be removed by monetary pressure should be regarded as sufficient justification for applying such pressure. That in most situations employment can be temporarily increased by monetary expansion has long been known.[2] If this possibility has not always been used, this was because it was thought that by such measures not only other dangers were created, but that long-term stability of employment itself might be endangered by them. What is new about present beliefs is that it is now widely held that so long as monetary expansion creates additional employment, it is innocuous or at least will cause more benefit than harm.

Yet while in practice full employment policies merely mean that in the short run employment is kept somewhat higher than it would otherwise be, it is at least doubtful whether over longer periods they will not in fact lower the level of employment which can be permanently maintained without progressive monetary expansion. These policies are, however, constantly represented as if the practical problem were not this, but as if the choice were between full employment thus defined and the lasting mass unemployment of the 1930's.

The habit of thinking in terms of an alternative between 'full employment' and a state of affairs in which there are unemployed factors of all kinds available is perhaps the most dangerous legacy which we owe to the great influence of the late Lord Keynes.[3] That so long as a state of *general* unemployment prevails, in the sense that unused resources of *all* kinds exist, monetary expan-

---

[2] [Here, and elsewhere in this essay, Hayek draws on his monetary theory of the business cycle, which is in turn underwritten by his theory of capital. See F. A. Hayek, *Business Cycles, Part I*, ed. H. Klausinger, vol. 7 (2012) of *The Collected Works of F. A. Hayek* (Chicago: University of Chicago Press; London: Routledge), and F. A. Hayek, *The Pure Theory of Capital*, ed. L. White, vol. 12 (2007) of *The Collected Works of F. A. Hayek.*—Ed.]

[3] [Hayek refers to British economist John Maynard Keynes (1883–1946), Baron Keynes of Tilton, and alludes in particular to Keynes's book *The General Theory of Employment, Interest, and Money* [1936], reprinted as vol. 7 (1973) of *The Collected Writings of John Maynard Keynes* (London: Macmillan for the Royal Economic Society). Hayek considers both Keynes's economics, and also Keynes the man, at length in F. A. Hayek, *Contra Keynes and Cambridge: Essays, Correspondence*, ed. B. Caldwell, vol. 9 (1995) of *The Collected Works of F. A. Hayek.*—Ed.]

sion can be only beneficial, few people will deny.[4] But such a state of general unemployment is something rather exceptional, and it is by no means evident that a policy which will be beneficial in such a state will also always and necessarily be so in the kind of intermediate position in which an economic system finds itself most of the time, when significant unemployment is confined to certain industries, occupations or localities.

Of a system in a state of general unemployment it is roughly true that employment will fluctuate in proportion with money income, and that if we succeed in increasing money income we shall also in the same proportion increase employment. But it is just not true that all unemployment is in this manner due to an insufficiency of aggregate demand and can be lastingly cured by increasing demand. The causal connection between income and employment is not a simple one-way connection so that by raising income by a certain ratio we can always raise employment by the same ratio. It is all too naive a way of thinking to believe that, since, if all workmen were employed at current wages, total income would reach such and such a figure, therefore, if we can bring income to that figure, we shall also necessarily have full employment. Where unemployment is not evenly spread, there is no certainty that additional expenditure will go where it will create additional employment. At least the amount of extra expenditure which would have to be incurred before the demand for the kind of services is raised which the unemployed offer may have to be of such a magnitude as to produce major inflationary effects before it substantially increases employment.

If expenditure is distributed between industries and occupations in a proportion different from that in which labour is distributed, a mere increase in expenditure need not increase employment. Unemployment can evidently be the consequence of the fact that the distribution of labour is different from the distribution of demand. In this case the low aggregate money income would have to be considered as a consequence rather than as a cause of unemployment. Even though, during the process of increasing incomes, enough expenditure may 'spill over' into the depressed sectors temporarily there to cure unemployment, as soon as the expansion comes to an end the discrepancy between the distribution of demand *and* the distribution of supply will again show itself. Where the cause of unemployment and of low aggregate incomes is such a discrepancy, only a re-allocation of labour can lastingly solve the problem in a free economy.

---

[4] [The first set of italics found in this sentence were present in Hayek's original 1950 paper, but not in the version reprinted in 1967. The same is also true of the italicised words found both towards the end of this section and also in section VI below.—Ed.]

III

This raises one of the most crucial and most difficult problems in the whole field: is an inappropriate distribution of labour more likely to be corrected under more or less stable or under expanding monetary conditions? This involves in fact two separate problems: the first is whether demand conditions during a process of expansion are such that, if the distribution of labour adjusted itself to the then existing distribution of demand, this would create employment which would continue after expansion has stopped; the second problem is whether the distribution of labour is more likely to adapt itself promptly to any given distribution of demand under stable or under expansionary monetary conditions, or, in other words, whether labour is more mobile under expanding or under stable monetary conditions.

The answer to the first of these questions is fairly clear. During a process of expansion the direction of demand is to some extent necessarily different from what it will be after expansion has stopped. Labour will be attracted to the particular occupations on which the extra expenditure is made in the first instance. So long as expansion lasts, demand there will always run a step ahead of the consequential increases of demand elsewhere. And in so far as this temporary stimulus to demand in particular sectors leads to a movement of labour, it may well become the cause of unemployment as soon as the expansion comes to an end.

Some people may feel doubt about the importance of this phenomenon. To the present writer it seems the main cause of the recurrent waves of unemployment. That during every boom period a greater quantity of factors of production is drawn into the capital goods industries than can be permanently employed there, and that as a result we have normally a greater proportion of our resources specialised in the production of capital goods than corresponds to the share of income which, under full employment, will be saved and be available for investment, seems to him the cause of the collapse which has regularly followed a boom. Any attempt to create full employment by drawing labour into occupations where they will remain employed only so long as credit expansion continues creates the dilemma that either credit expansion must be continued indefinitely (which means inflation), or that, when it stops, unemployment will be greater than it would be if the temporary increase in employment had never taken place.

If the real cause of unemployment is that the distribution of labour does not correspond with the distribution of demand, the only way to create stable conditions of high employment which is not dependent on continued inflation (or physical controls) is to bring about a distribution of labour which matches the manner in which a stable money income will be spent. This depends of course not only on whether during the process of adaptation the distribution of demand is approximately what it will remain, but also on whether conditions in general are conducive to easy and rapid movements of labour.

IV

This leads to the second and more difficult part of our question to which, perhaps, no certain answer can be given, though the probability seems to us to point clearly in one direction. This is the question whether workers will on the whole be more willing to move to new occupations or new localities when general demand is rising, or whether mobility is likely to be greater when total demand is approximately constant. The main difference between the two cases is that in the former the inducement to move will be the attraction of a higher wage elsewhere, while in the second case it will be the inability to earn the accustomed wages or to find any employment in the former occupation which will exercise a push. The former method is, of course, the more pleasant, and it is usually also represented as the more effective. It is this latter belief which I am inclined to question.

That the same wage differentials which in the long run would attract the necessary greater number of new recruits to one industry rather than another will not suffice to tempt workers already established in the latter to move is in itself not surprising. As a rule the movement from job to job involves expenditure and sacrifices which may not be justified by a mere increase in wages. So long as the worker can count on his accustomed money wage in his current job, he will be understandably reluctant to move. Even if, as would be inevitable under an expansionist policy which aimed at bringing about the adjustment entirely by raising some wages without allowing others to fall, the constant money wages meant a lower real wage, the habit of thinking in terms of money wages would deprive such a fall of real wages of most of its effectiveness. It is curious that those disciples of Lord Keynes who in other connections make such constant use of this consideration regularly fail to see its significance in this context.[5]

To aim at securing to men who in the social interest ought to move elsewhere the continued receipt of their former wages can only delay movements

[5] [Hayek refers to the Keynesian view that it would be easier to reduce workers' real wages indirectly, by engineering a rise in the general price level, than by reducing their nominal or money wages directly. Hayek's criticism of this approach can be found in F. A. Hayek, "Unions, Inflation, and Profits" [1959], reprinted as chapter 16 of the present volume, and in F. A. Hayek, *The Constitution of Liberty*, ed. Ronald Hamowy, vol. 17 (2011) of *The Collected Works of F. A. Hayek*, pp. 398–400.—Ed.]

which ultimately must take place. It should also not be forgotten that in order to give all the men formerly employed continued employment in a relatively declining industry, the general level of wages in that industry will have to fall more than would be necessary if some of the workers moved away from it.

What is so difficult here for the layman to understand is that to protect the individual against the loss of his job may not be a way to decrease unemployment but may over longer periods rather decrease the number which can be employed at given wages. If a policy is pursued over a long period which postpones and delays movements, which keeps people in their old jobs who ought to move elsewhere, the result must be that what ought to have been a gradual process of change becomes in the end a problem of the necessity of mass transfers within a short period. Continued monetary pressure which has helped people to earn an unchanged money wage in jobs which they ought to have left will have created accumulated arrears of necessary changes which, as soon as monetary pressure ceases, will have to be made up in a much shorter space of time and then result in a period of acute mass unemployment which might have been avoided.

All this applies not only to those maldistributions of labour which arise in the course of ordinary industrial fluctuations, but even more to the task of large-scale re-allocations of labour such as arise after a great war or as a result of a major change in the channels of international trade. It seems highly doubtful whether the expansionist policies pursued since the war in most countries have helped and not rather hindered that adjustment to radically changed conditions of world trade which has become necessary. Especially in the case of Great Britain the low unemployment figures during recent years may be more a sign of a delay in necessary change than of true economic balance.

The great problem in all those instances is whether such a policy, once it has been pursued for years, can still be reversed without serious political and social disturbances. As a result of these policies, what not very long ago might merely have meant a slightly higher unemployment figure, might now, when the employment of large numbers has become dependent on the continuation of these policies, be indeed an experiment which politically is unbearable.

V

Full employment policies, as at present practised, attempt the quick and easy way of giving men employment where they happen to be, while the real problem is to bring about a distribution of labour which makes continuous high employment without artificial stimulus possible. What this distribution is we can never know beforehand. The only way to find out is to let the unhampered market act under conditions which will bring about a stable equilibrium between demand and supply. But the very full employment policies make it almost inevitable that we must constantly interfere with the free play of the forces of the market and that the prices which rule during such an expansionary policy, and to which supply will adapt itself, will not represent a lasting condition. These difficulties, as we have seen, arise from the fact that unemployment is never evenly spread throughout the economic system, but that, at the time when there may still be substantial unemployment in some sectors, there may exist acute scarcities in others. The purely fiscal and monetary measures on which current full employment policies rely are, however, by themselves indiscriminate in their effects on the different parts of the economic system. The same monetary pressure which in some parts of the system might merely reduce unemployment will in others produce definite inflationary effects. If not checked by other measures, such monetary pressure might well set up an inflationary spiral of prices and wages long before unemployment has disappeared, and—with present nation-wide wage bargaining—the rise of wages may threaten the results of the full employment policy even before it has been achieved.

As is regularly the case in such circumstances, the governments will then find themselves forced to take measures to counteract the effects of their own policy. The effects of the inflation have to be contained or 'repressed' by direct controls of prices and of quantities produced and sold: the rise of prices has to be prevented by imposing maximum prices and the resulting scarcities must be met by a system of rationing, priorities and allocations.

The manner in which inflation leads a government into a system of overall controls and central planning is by now too well known to need elaboration. It is usually a particularly pernicious kind of planning, because not thought out beforehand but applied piecemeal as the unwelcome results of inflation manifest themselves. A government which uses inflation as an instrument of policy but wants it to produce only the desired effects is soon driven to control ever increasing parts of the economy.[6]

---

[6] [The way in which the price controls to which governments sometimes resort as a means of dealing with inflation themselves precipitate further intervention is discussed by Austrian economist Ludwig von Mises (1881–1973) in his *Kritik des Interventionismus: Untersuchungen zur Wirtschaftspolitik und Wirtschaftsideologie der Gegenwart* (Jena: G. Fischer, 1929), translated by H. Sennholz as *A Critique of Interventionism: Inquiries into Present Day Economic Policy and Ideology* (Irvington-on-Hudson: Foundation for Economic Education, 1976), pp. 99–106. Also see L. von Mises, *Interventionism: An Economic Analysis* [1940], ed. B. Bien Greaves (Indianapolis: Liberty Fund, 2011), pp. 24–31, 47–49.—Ed.]

VI

The connection between inflation and controls and central planning is, however, not only a one-way connection. That inflation leads to controls is nowadays widely seen. But that once an economic system has become cluttered up and encumbered with all sorts of controls and restrictions, continued inflationary pressure is required to keep it going is not yet generally understood but no less important. It is indeed a fact of crucial importance for the understanding of the self-perpetuating and self-accentuating character of the modern tendencies in economic policy.

Since the measures intended to counteract inflation are designed to damp the uplift which the inflationary stimulus would cause, it is inevitable that they should also act as a damper to the spontaneous forces of recovery as soon as the inflationary pressure is relaxed. If most of the post-war economies do not show a greater resilience and spontaneous strength, this is largely due to the fact that they are smothered by controls and that, whenever improvement flags, instead of a removal of all those hindrances an even stronger dose of inflation is demanded which sooner or later leads to further controls.

This tendency of the existing controls to produce a further demand for inflationary pressure is especially important in view of the widely held opinion that, if only the inflationary tendencies can be brought under control, the restrictive measures will subsequently prove unnecessary and be readily removed. If the connection between inflation and controls is a mutual one as here suggested, this view would prove to be erroneous, and to act on it would necessarily lead to failure. Unless the controls are removed *at the same time* that expansion is discontinued, the pressure for its resumption will probably be irresistible as soon as the deadening effect of the controls makes itself felt.

An economy paralysed by controls needs the extra stimulus of inflation to keep going at anything near full rate. Where the controls deprive the entrepreneur of all scope for initiative, freedom of choice and the assumption of responsibility, where the government in effect decides what and how much he is to produce, he must at least be assured of a certain sale if it is to be worth his while to carry on. It is because extensive government controls have almost always been accompanied by more or less inflationary conditions that they have not as completely paralysed economic activity as seems inevitable to the outside observer who learns of the maze of permits and licences through which any manufacturer who wants to do anything has to find his way.

To such an observer it seems at first impossible that an entrepreneur so largely deprived of the control of his costs and the nature and the quantity of his products should still be willing to run any risks. The answer is that he is in fact relieved of the main risk by the creation of conditions in which almost anything which can be produced can also be sold. The inefficiency of such a 'planned economy' is concealed by the effects of inflation.

But as soon as inflationary pressure disappears, the whole force of all these impediments to successful production makes itself felt. The very controls which in the first instance were imposed to keep the effects of inflation under control make it thus more difficult to stop inflation. If, while the controls remain, stable monetary conditions were restored, unemployment would at once reappear. The impression would be created that continued expansion is an indispensable condition for maintaining a high level of employment, while in fact what is needed is the removal of the controls which hamper trade, even if as a result some of the hitherto concealed effects of inflation should become apparent.

VII

If these considerations are correct, they cannot but make one feel very pessimistic about the prospects of a reasonable economic policy being adopted in the foreseeable future. In the present state of public opinion they are most unlikely to be listened to. The habit of inflation has often been compared to the addiction to a stimulating drug. But the position of a society which has become addicted to the drug of inflation is even worse than that of an individual in the corresponding case. One has to conceive of a position in which the administration of, say, morphia to sufferers were to be decided under the influence of mass psychology and where every demagogue who knows just a little more about these things than the crowd would be able to offer an effective means of relieving present suffering while the more remote harm his remedy causes is understood only by few.

The rapidity with which the full employment ideology has taken hold of the public imagination, the manner in which in the process a subtle although probably mistaken theoretical reasoning has been turned into a crude dogma, and not least the way in which certain bigots of the new doctrine who ought to know better represent the issue as if it were a choice between long-lasting mass unemployment and the wholesale application of their prescriptions, make one sometimes despair about one of the gravest issues of our time: the capacity of democratic institutions to handle the tremendous powers for good and evil which the new instruments of economic policy place in their hands.

If the outcome of economic policy is not to be altogether different from what has been desired, if we are not to be driven from one expedient to another, economic policy, more even than any other, must be long-range policy, governed less by the pressing needs of the moment than by an understanding of the long-period effects. It was certainly wise that at a time when the scope and objectives of monetary policy were much more limited, its direction was placed in the hands of bodies not directly subject to political control. It is understandable and perhaps inevitable that once the much greater use of these powers is recognised, it should become a major political issue. But it must appear more than doubtful whether in the nature of democratic institutions it is possible that democratic governments will ever learn to exercise that restraint which is the essence of economic wisdom of not using palliatives for present evils which not only create worse problems later but also constantly restrict the freedom of further action.[7]

[7] [For a slightly later account of Hayek's views about the kind of rules that ought to govern the conduct of monetary policy in a democratic society, see *The Constitution of Liberty*, pp. 460–65.—Ed.]

FIFTEEN

INFLATION RESULTING FROM THE DOWNWARD INFLEXIBILITY OF WAGES[1]

Contrary to what is widely believed, the crucial result of the 'Keynesian Revolution' is the general acceptance of a factual assumption and, what is more, of an assumption which becomes true as a result of its being generally accepted. The Keynesian theory, as it has developed during the last twenty years, has become a formal apparatus which may or may not be more convenient to deal with the facts than classical monetary theory; this is not our concern here. The decisive assumption on which Keynes' original argument rested and which has since ruled policy is that it is impossible ever to reduce the money wages of a substantial group of workers without causing extensive unemployment. The conclusion which Lord Keynes drew from this, and which the whole of his theoretical system was intended to justify, was that since money wages can in practice not be lowered, the adjustment necessary, whenever wages have become too high to allow 'full employment', must be effected by the devious process of reducing the value of money. A society which accepts this is bound for a continuous process of inflation.[2]

[1] Reprinted from *Problems of United States Economic Development*, ed. by the Committee for Economic Development, New York, 1958, Vol. 1, pp. 147–52. [The essay was first published as F. A. Hayek, "Inflation Resulting from the Downward Inflexibility of Wages", in *Problems of United States Economic Development*, ed. Committee for Economic Development (New York: Committee for Economic Development, 1958), vol. 1, pp. 147–52. The first volume of that work consisted of 48 papers whose authors had been asked to "write 2,000 words on the question: 'What is the most important economic problem to be faced by the United States in the next twenty years?'" See *Problems of United States Economic Development*, p. 1. In addition to Hayek, contributors included the Harvard economist and public servant John Kenneth Galbraith (1908–2006); Harvard-based economist Gottfried Haberler (1900–1995), who had been a friend of Hayek's since his student days; Nobel Prize-winning economists Milton Friedman (1912–2006), Paul Samuelson (1915–2009), and Jan Tinbergen (1903–94); English economists Roy Harrod (1900–78) and Lionel Robbins (1898–1984); and Hungarian-born British economist Nicholas Kaldor (1908–86). Hayek's essay was subsequently reprinted as chapter 21 of F. A. Hayek, *Studies in Philosophy, Politics and Economics* (London: Routledge & Kegan Paul, 1967).—Ed.]

[2] [For more on this, see F. A. Hayek, "Unions, Inflation, and Profits" [1959], reprinted as chapter 16 of the present volume, especially pp. 216–18, and F. A. Hayek, *The Constitution of Liberty*, ed. Ronald Hamowy, vol. 17 (2011) of *The Collected Works of F. A. Hayek* (Chicago: University of Chicago Press; London: Routledge), pp. 398–400.—Ed.]

This consequence is not at once apparent within the Keynesian system because Keynes and most of his followers are arguing in terms of a general wage level while the chief problem appears only if we think in terms of the relative wages of the different (sectional or regional) groups of workers. Relative wages of the different groups are bound to change substantially in the course of economic development. But if the money wage of no important group is to fall, the adjustment of the relative position must be brought about exclusively by raising all other money wages. The effect must be a continuous rise in the level of money wages greater than the rise of real wages, i.e., inflation. One need only consider the normal year-by-year dispersion of wage changes of the different groups in order to realise how important this factor must be.

The twelve years since the end of the war have in fact in the whole Western world been a period of more or less continuous inflation. It does not matter how far this was entirely the result of deliberate policy or the product of the exigencies of government finance. It certainly has been a very popular policy since it has been accompanied by great prosperity over a period of probably unprecedented length. The great problem is whether by the same means prosperity can be maintained indefinitely—or whether an attempt to do so is not bound sooner or later to produce other results which in the end must become unbearable.

The point which tends to be overlooked in current discussion is that inflation acts as a stimulus to business only in so far as it is unforeseen, or greater than expected. Rising prices by themselves, as has often been seen, are not necessarily a guarantee of prosperity. Prices must turn out to be higher than they were expected to be, in order to produce profits larger than normal. Once a further rise of prices is expected with certainty, competition for the factors of production will drive up costs in anticipation. If prices rise no more than expected there will be no extra profits, and if they rise less, the effect will be the same as if prices fell when they had been expected to be stable.[3]

On the whole the post-war inflation has been unexpected or has lasted longer than expected. But the longer inflation lasts, the more it will be generally expected to continue; and the more people count on a continued rise of prices, the more must prices rise in order to secure adequate profits not only to those who would earn them without inflation but also to those who would not. Inflation greater than expected secures general prosperity only because those who without it would make no profit and be forced to turn to something

---

[3] [Here, and elsewhere in the essay, Hayek draws on ideas explained more fully in his capital-theoretic analysis of the trade cycle. See F. A. Hayek, *Business Cycles, Part I* and *Part II*, ed. H. Klausinger, vols. 7 (2012) and 8 (2012) of *The Collected Works of F. A. Hayek*, and F. A. Hayek, *The Pure Theory of Capital*, ed. L. White, vol. 12 (2007) of *The Collected Works of F. A. Hayek*. For a brief account, published shortly after this essay, see Hayek, *The Constitution of Liberty*, pp. 457–61.—Ed.]

else are enabled to continue with their present activities. A cumulative inflation at a progressive rate will probably secure prosperity for a fairly long time,
but not inflation at a constant rate. We need hardly inquire why inflation at
a progressive rate cannot be continued indefinitely: long before it becomes so
fast as to make any reasonable calculation in the expanding currency impracticable and before it will be spontaneously replaced by some other medium
of exchange, the inconvenience and injustice of the rapidly falling value of
all fixed payments will produce irresistible demands for a halt—irresistible,
at least, when people understand what is happening and realise that a government can always stop inflation. (The hyper-inflations after the First World
War were tolerated only because people were deluded into believing that the
increase of the quantity of money was not a cause but a necessary consequence of the rise of prices.)

We can therefore not expect inflation-born prosperity to last indefinitely.
We are bound to reach a point at which the source of prosperity which inflation now constitutes will no longer be available. Nobody can predict when
this point will be reached, but come it will. Few things should give us greater
concern than the need to secure an arrangement of our productive resources
which we can hope to maintain at a reasonable level of activity and employment when the stimulus of inflation ceases to operate.

Yet the longer we have relied on inflationary expansion to secure prosperity, the more difficult that task will be. We shall be faced not only with an accumulated backlog of delayed adjustments—all those businesses which have
been kept above water only by continued inflation. Inflation also becomes the
active cause of new 'misdirections' of production, i.e., it induces new activities which will continue to be profitable only so long as inflation lasts. Especially when the additional money first becomes available for investment activities, these will be increased to a volume which cannot be maintained once
only current savings are available to feed them.

The conception that we can maintain prosperity by keeping final demand
always increasing a jump ahead of costs must sooner or later prove an illusion, because costs are not an independent magnitude but are in the long
run determined by the expectations of what final demand will be. And to
secure 'full employment' even an excess of 'aggregate demand' over 'aggregate costs' may not lastingly be sufficient, since the volume of employment
depends largely on the magnitude of investment and beyond a certain point
an excessive final demand may act as a deterrent rather than as a stimulus to
investment.

I fear that those who believe that we have solved the problem of permanent full employment are in for a serious disillusionment. This is not to say
that we need have a major depression. A transition to more stable monetary
conditions by gradually slowing down inflation is probably still possible. But it

will hardly be possible without a significant decrease of employment of some duration. The difficulty is that in the present state of opinion any noticeable increase of unemployment will at once be met by renewed inflation. Such attempts to cure unemployment by further doses of inflation will probably be temporarily successful and may even succeed several times if the inflationary pressure is massive enough. But this will merely postpone the problem and in the meantime aggravate the inherent instability of the situation.

In a short paper on the twenty years' outlook there is no space to consider the serious but essentially short-term problem of how to get out of a particular inflationary spell without producing a major depression. The long-term problem is how we are to stop the long-term and periodically accelerated inflationary trend which will again and again raise that problem. The essential point is that it must be once more realised that the employment problem is a wage problem and that the Keynesian device of lowering real wages by reducing the value of money when wages have become too high for full employment will work only so long as the workers let themselves be deceived by it. It was an attempt to get round what is called the 'rigidity' of wages which could work for a time but which in the long run has only made this obstacle to a stable monetary system greater than it had been. What is needed is that the responsibility for a wage level which is compatible with a high and stable level of employment should again be squarely placed where it belongs: with the trade unions. The present division of responsibility where each union is concerned only with obtaining the maximum rate of money wages without regard to the effect on employment, and the monetary authorities are expected to supply whatever increases of money income are required to secure full employment at the resulting wage level, must lead to continuous and progressive inflation. We are discovering that by refusing to face the wage problem and temporarily evading the consequences by monetary deception, we have merely made the whole problem much more difficult. The long-run problem remains the restoration of a labour market which will produce wages which are compatible with stable money. This means that the full and exclusive responsibility of the monetary authorities for inflation must once more be recognised. Though it is true that, so long as it is regarded as their duty to supply enough money to secure full employment at any wage level, they have no choice and their role becomes a purely passive one, it is this very conception which is bound to produce continuous inflation. Stable monetary conditions require that the stream of money expenditure is the fixed datum to which prices and wages have to adapt themselves, and not the other way round.[4]

---

[4] [A longer account of Hayek's views on the appropriate monetary framework, written at around the same time as the current essay, can be found in Hayek, *The Constitution of Liberty*, pp. 451–65.—Ed.]

Such a change of policy as would be required to prevent progressive inflation, and the instability and recurrent crises it is bound to produce, presupposes, however, a change in the still predominant state of opinion. Though a 7 per cent bank rate in the country where they originated and were most consistently practised proclaims loudly the bankruptcy of Keynesian principles, there is yet little sign that they have lost their sway over the generation that grew up in their heyday. But quite apart from this intellectual power that they still exercise, they have contributed so much to strengthen the position of one of the politically most powerful elements in the country, that their abandonment is not likely to come without a severe political struggle. The desire to avoid this will probably again and again lead politicians to put off the necessity by resorting once more to the temporary way out which inflation offers as the path of least resistance. It will probably be only when the dangers of this path have become much more obvious than they are now that the fundamental underlying problem of union power will really be faced.[5]

[5] [For more on Hayek's views on unions, see F. A. Hayek "'Free' Enterprise and Competitive Order" [1948], reprinted as chapter 6 of this book, especially pp. 99–100, and Hayek, *The Constitution of Liberty*, pp. 384–404.—Ed.]

SIXTEEN

UNIONS, INFLATION, AND PROFITS[1]

Tendencies are observable in the field of labour economics which most seriously threaten our future prosperity. The developments which are bringing this about are not of recent date. They extend at least over the last twenty-five years. But for most of that time, and particularly during the long period of great prosperity through which we have recently passed, it may have seemed as if the United States could take in its stride even those new hurdles which only a few alarmists regarded as serious. But there are strong reasons for thinking that things will soon be coming to a head. It may be that already those new demands of labour which I want later to examine in some detail will prove to be the critical point. Or Walter Reuther may decide that this is not a favourable moment for a decisive test of strength and the fatal struggle will be deferred a little further.[2] Whichever it will be, I have little doubt that we shall soon have to face fundamental issues which we have managed to avoid for so long and which have not become easier to solve because the practices and institutions which raise them have been allowed to continue for such a long time.

---

[1] Reprinted from *The Public Stake in Union Power*, edited by Philip D. Bradley, New York, 1959. [The essay was written as a guest lecture for a course on labour relations offered by the Graduate School of Business Administration at the University of Virginia in the spring of 1958. A letter from Hayek to James Buchanan, who was chairman of the Department of Economics at the University of Virginia at the time, indicates that the lecture took place on March 17, 1958. See F. A. Hayek to J. Buchanan, March 8, 1958, Hayek Papers, box 72, folder 43, Hoover Institution Archives. Other guest lecturers included Frank Knight (1885–1972), a prominent figure in the 'old', pre–World War II, Chicago School of Economics; Harvard-based economist Gottfried Haberler (1900–1995), who had been a friend of Hayek's since his days as a university student; and 'new' Chicago School economist and Nobel Laureate in economics Gary Becker (1930–2014). Hayek's essay was first published as chapter 3 of the edited volume based on the lecture series, namely *The Public Stake in Union Power*, ed. P. D. Bradley (Charlottesville: University of Virginia Press, 1959), and is © 1959 by the Rector and Visitors of the University of Virginia and reprinted by permission of the University of Virginia Press. It was subsequently republished as chapter 20 of F. A. Hayek, *Studies in Philosophy, Politics and Economics* (London: Routledge & Kegan Paul, 1967).—Ed.]

[2] [Walter Reuther (1907–70) was President of the United Automobile Workers Union (UAW) from 1946 to 1970.—Ed.]

Before turning to the more specific problems which the new union demands raise, I must explain how I see the more general problem of policy which the powers of modern labour unions create, and describe the character of the particular phase of business fluctuations in which it seems those problems will now have to be decided.

The first of these tasks divides itself into two distinct yet closely connected ones: the character which labour organisations have gradually assumed, and the new powers they have obtained, not as a result of anything *they* can do, but as a result of the new conceptions of the tasks of credit and fiscal policy. With regard to the first, though it contains the crux of the union problem, I can be very brief. The essential facts are here so well known that I need merely mention the chief points. Unions have not achieved their present magnitude and power by merely achieving the right of association. They have become what they are largely in consequence of the grant, by legislation and jurisdiction, of unique privileges which no other associations or individuals enjoy. They are the one institution where government has signally failed in its first task, that of preventing coercion of men by other men—and by coercion I do not mean primarily the coercion of employers but the coercion of workers by their fellow workers. It is only because of the coercive powers unions have been allowed to exercise over those willing to work at terms not approved by the union, that the latter has become able to exercise harmful coercion of the employer. All this has become possible because in the field of labour relations it has come to be accepted belief that the ends justify the means, and that, because of the public approval of the aims of union effort, they ought to be exempted from the ordinary rules of law. The whole modern development of unionism has been made possible mainly by the fact that public policy was guided by the belief that it was in the public interest that labour should be as comprehensively and completely organised as possible, and that in the pursuit of this aim the unions should be as little restricted as possible. This is certainly not in the public interest. But all this has been so admirably treated by Professor Sylvester Petro of New York University in his recent book *The Labor Policy of the Free Society*[3] that I need merely refer to that work.

I must take a little longer in discussing the particular circumstances which have made the power of unions over wages so especially dangerous in the present world. It is often said that successful general union pressure for higher

[3] New York, 1957. [Sylvester Petro (1917–2007) was a libertarian Professor of Law at New York University (1950–72), specialising in labour, anti-trust and contract law, and a member of the Mont Pèlerin Society. Hayek refers to S. Petro, *The Labor Policy of the Free Society* (New York: Ronald Press Company, 1957). Hayek sets out his own views on trade unions at greater length in F. A. Hayek, *The Constitution of Liberty*, ed. Ronald Hamowy, vol. 17 (2011) of *The Collected Works of F. A. Hayek* (Chicago: University of Chicago Press; London: Routledge), pp. 384–404.—Ed.]

wages necessarily produces inflation. This is not correct as a general proposition. It is, however, only too true under the particular conditions under which we now live. Since it has become the generally accepted doctrine that it is the duty of the monetary authorities to provide enough credit to secure full employment, whatever the wage level, and this duty has in fact been imposed upon the monetary authorities by statute, the power of the unions to push up money wages cannot but lead to continuous, progressive inflation. It is the blessing that J. M. Keynes has showered on us which we enjoy in this respect.

We are not concerned here with the niceties of his theory. What we are concerned with is the factual assumption on which his whole argument rests: that it is easier to cheat workers out of a gain in real wages by a reduction in the value of money than to reduce money wages; and his contention that this method ought to be employed every time real wages have become too high to allow of 'full employment'. Where Lord Keynes went wrong was in the naive belief that workers would let themselves be deceived by this for any length of time, and that the lowering of the purchasing power of wages would not at once produce new demands for higher wages—demands which would be even more irresistible when it was recognised that they would not be allowed to have any effect on employment.[4]

What we have achieved is a division of responsibilities under which one group can enforce a wage level without regard to the effects on employment, and another agency is responsible for providing whatever amount of money

---

[4] [Hayek refers to the work of British economist John Maynard Keynes (1883–1946). Keynes advanced two main reasons why it would be easier to reduce workers' real wages through a rise in the general price level—"a reduction in the value of money", as Hayek puts it—than by reducing their nominal or money wages directly. First, Keynes argued that in bargaining over money wages groups of workers are concerned primarily to preserve their position in the wage distribution. In the absence of guarantees that other groups of workers will consent to a simultaneous and equal reduction in their nominal wages, each group's concern to protect its relative wage makes it reluctant to countenance a reduction in its own nominal wage (which, if unmatched by other groups, would lead to a deterioration in its place in the wage distribution). Workers would be more willing to accept reductions in real wages caused by rises in the general price level, Keynes believed, because the all-round character of this method of changing real wages, with all groups being affected simultaneously, would leave relative wages unchanged and so provoke less resistance. Second, Keynes argued that even if reductions in nominal wages were achieved, they might not lead to a reduction in real wages, because an all-round reduction in nominal wages would lead to a corresponding fall in prices, leaving real wages unchanged. Such difficulties would not arise, Keynes believed, if real wages were reduced via a rise in the general price level. See J. M. Keynes, *The General Theory of Employment, Interest and Money* [1936], reprinted as vol. 7 (1973) of *The Collected Writings of John Maynard Keynes* (London: Macmillan for the Royal Economic Society), pp. 7–15, 257–71. For more on Hayek's views on Keynes and his economics, see F. A. Hayek, *Contra Keynes and Cambridge: Essays, Correspondence*, ed. B. Caldwell, vol. 9 (1995) of *The Collected Works of F. A. Hayek.*—Ed.]

is needed to secure full employment at that wage level. So long as this is the accepted principle, it is true that the monetary authorities have no choice but to pursue a policy resulting in continuous inflation, however little they may like it. But the fact that in the existing state of opinion they cannot do anything else does not alter the fact that, as always, it is monetary policy and nothing else which is the cause of inflation.

We have behind us the first long period of such cost-push inflation, as it has come to be called. It has been one of the longest periods of high prosperity on record. But, though the upward trend of wages has not yet stopped, the forces which have been making for prosperity have been flagging for some time. We have probably reached the point when we must reap the inevitable harvest of a period of inflation. Nobody can be certain about this. It may well be that another massive dose of inflation may once more get us rapidly out of the recession. But that, in my opinion, would merely postpone the evil day—and make the ultimate result much worse. Inflation-born prosperity has never been and never will be lasting prosperity. It depends on factors which are nourished, not simply by inflation, but by an increase in the rate of inflation. And though we may have permanent inflation, we clearly cannot for very long have inflation at a progressive rate.

Such inflation-fed prosperity neither comes to an end because final demand becomes insufficient to take the whole product off the market, nor can be perpetuated by simply keeping final demand at a sufficiently high level. The decline always begins, and did begin this time, in the field of investment, and it is only as a consequence of the decline of incomes in the investment goods industries that final demand is later affected. It is true that this secondary shrinkage in final demand may become cumulative and tend to become the controlling factor; it may then turn what would otherwise be merely a period of recession and readjustment into a major depression. There is, therefore, every reason to counteract these tendencies and to prevent them from setting up a deflationary spiral. But this does not mean that by merely maintaining final demand at a sufficiently high level we can secure continued full employment and avoid the readjustment and incidental unemployment made necessary by the transition from inflationary to stable monetary conditions. The reason for this is that investment is not, as is often naively believed, coupled in any simple manner with final demand; a given volume of final demand does not always evoke a proportional, or perhaps even more than proportional, change in investment in the same direction. There are other factors operating within the whole price-cost structure which determine what rate of investment will be evoked by a given level of demand. It is a change in these factors which brings about the primary decline in investment and incomes which then produces a decline of final demand.

I cannot here examine this highly complex and very controversial mechanism in detail.[5] I will confine myself to two considerations which seem to me to prove that the predominant 'lack of buying power' theory of depression is just wrong. One is the empirical fact that not only have declines of investment often started when final demand and prices are rising rapidly, but also that attempts to revive investment by stimulating final demand have almost invariably failed. The great depression of the 'thirties was indeed the first occasion when, under the influence of such 'purchasing power theories', deliberate efforts were made from the very beginning to maintain wages and purchasing power; and we managed to turn it into the longest and most severe depression on record. The second point is that the whole argument on which the purchasing power view rests suffers from an inherent contradiction. It proceeds as if, even under conditions of full or nearly full employment, an increase in the demand for final products would lead to a switching of resources from producing final goods to producing investment goods. Indeed, it suggests that if at any one time the demand for consumers' goods should become very urgent, the immediate effect would be that fewer consumers' goods and more investment goods would be produced. I suppose it means that in the extreme case, because people want more consumers' goods very urgently, no consumers' goods and only investment goods would be produced. Clearly there must be a mechanism which will bring it about that the opposite happens. But unless we understand that mechanism, we cannot be sure that it may not also operate under conditions of less than full employment. We evidently cannot accept the current popular view on these matters, which not only offers no answer to that crucial problem, but which, if consistently pursued, leads into absurdities.

I now come to my main subject. The reason why I have spent so much time in diagnosing the economic situation in which the new demands of labour are presented is partly that they are presented both as non-inflationary and as a safeguard against (or a remedy for) depression, but mainly because in the present situation the greatest pressure will be brought on the employers to avoid a labour dispute, which at this juncture may have very serious consequences.

---

[5] [Hayek refers here and in the previous paragraph to his capital-theoretic analysis of the business cycle, as expounded in F. A. Hayek, *Business Cycles, Part I* and *Part II*, ed. H. Klausinger, vols. 7 (2012) and 8 (2012) of *The Collected Works of F. A. Hayek*. Hayek discusses the possibility of a "secondary shrinkage in final demand", as he puts it here, or "secondary deflation" as he terms it elsewhere, in F. A. Hayek, "The Present State and Immediate Prospects of the Study of Industrial Fluctuations" [1933], reprinted as chapter 4 of *Business Cycles, Part II*, pp. 175–77. For a further discussion, see H. Klausinger, "Introduction", in *Business Cycles, Part II*, pp. 9–13. For a useful comparison of the views Hayek held on these matters in the 1930s and the 1970s, see A. Magliulo, "Hayek and the Great Depression of 1929: Did He Really Change His Mind?", *European Journal of the History of Economic Thought*, vol. 23, 2016, pp. 31–58.—Ed.]

But the decisions which the corporations facing the new demands will have to make are decisions of principle which may have tremendous long-term effects, indeed, may do much to shape the future of our society. They should be made entirely in consideration of their long-run significance and not be affected by the desire to get out of our momentary difficulties. But with the power the unions have acquired, the capacity of the corporations to resist any harmful demands depends on what support they get from public opinion. It is therefore of the greatest importance that we clearly understand what these demands really imply, what their satisfaction and the general acceptance of the principle underlying them would mean for the future character of our economy.

As will be remembered, Mr. Reuther has presented the demands of the United Automobile Workers for 1958 as a "two-package" programme, consisting of a set of "minimum basic demands which will be common for all employers" and of supplementary demands "in addition to the minimum for those corporations or companies in a more favoured economic position"—or, in other words, one set of demands applying to the automobile industry generally, and further demands directed to the Big Three. The first package constitutes in general only 'more of the same as before'—although we have been told that it will be the biggest wage increase demanded in the history of the automobile industry—and I shall consider it only briefly as an illustration of what I have already said about the inflationary character of these demands and especially about their significance in the present phase of business conditions. It is the second package which raises the interesting new problems and, I believe, constitutes a real threat to the future of our economy.[6]

Of the first part of the demands, I want to examine only the claims that wage increases proportional to the increase in average output per head of the employed are non-inflationary, and that "increasing mass purchasing power"[7] through wage increases is an effective means of combating depres-

---

[6] [Hayek does not provide a reference to the document from which the words he attributes to Walter Reuther are taken. Most of them can be found in a letter written by Walter Reuther to local branches of the United Auto Workers Union on January 13, 1958, setting out for approval by delegates attending the union's 1958 special convention the leadership's recommended demands for the 1958 round of bargaining with employers. The letter was reproduced, along with brief responses from the Presidents of General Motors and Chrysler, and the Chairman of Ford, the so-called 'Big Three' car manufacturers, in "Text of Reuther Proposals on Auto Contracts and Companies' Replies", *New York Times*, January 14, 1958, p. 36. The three phrases quoted by Hayek at the start of this paragraph can be found in column 2 of that article. Hayek has modified slightly the wording of the second phrase; the original Reuther letter refers to a "minimum basic economic demand, which will be common for all employers". The phrase 'more of the same as before' does not appear in Reuther's letter; its source remains unknown.—Ed.]

[7] [See "Text of Reuther Proposals", column 2.—Ed.]

sion. They are easy to dispose of. Changes in output per head are, of course, not the same as changes in the productivity of labour. To see this clearly we need merely consider an extreme but by no means impracticable case, such as the replacement of present power stations by highly automatised atomic energy stations. Once one of these modern stations is erected, a handful of men would appear to be the sole producers of a colossal amount of electric energy and their output per head may have increased hundreds of times. But that does not mean that the productivity of labour in that industry has significantly increased in any sense relevant to our problem, or that in that industry the marginal product of a given number of workers has increased at all. The increase in average productivity of labour in the industry is the result of the investment made and in no way reflects the value which a man's work contributes to its product. To raise wages in proportion to the increase in average productivity in that industry would raise them to many times their marginal product in other industries of the economy. Unless we assume that the particular men employed in that industry acquire a vested right in a share of the product of that investment and are entitled to earn much more than exactly similar labour earns elsewhere, it will mean a general rise in money wages far in excess of what can be paid without a general rise in money incomes, that is, without inflation.

This does not mean, of course, that labour may not succeed in pushing up money wages to that level, but it means that this would be highly inflationary and could not mean a significant increase of the real wages for the workers of this kind as a whole. Since the illustration just given throws much light on one of the crucial aspects of the power of modern labour monopoly, I will dwell on it just a little longer. Where very large and very durable investments have once been made, it is today the owner of these investments who is almost completely at the mercy of an effective monopoly of the supply of labour. Once such plants have been created, and so long as they can be kept going without substantial renewal or re-investment, labour is in a position to appropriate almost any share of the returns due to the investment of the capital. The demand for a definite share in the increase in the average productivity of labour due to the investment of capital amounts, in fact, to nothing less than an attempt to expropriate that capital. There is no reason why a really powerful union monopoly should not succeed in this to a large extent so far as investments irrevocably committed to a particular purpose are concerned.

This, however, is only a relatively short-run effect and the advantages that labour as a whole can derive from such policies look very different when we consider what effects such policies must have on the attractiveness of new investment once they come to be anticipated. Personally, I am convinced that this power of union monopolies is, together with contemporary methods of taxation, the chief deterrent to private investment in productive equipment which we have allowed to grow up. We must not be surprised that private investment dries up as soon as uncertainty about the future increases after we have created a situation in which most of the gain of a large, risky and successful investment goes to the unions and the government, while any loss has to be borne by the investor. Man is so made that in times of great prosperity he still tends to forget about these deterrents. But we must not be surprised that as soon as prospects darken a little, these reasonable fears revive in full strength and we face another apparent 'exhaustion of investment opportunities' which is entirely the result of our own follies.

This brings me to the second aspect of the general demands of the UAW: their significance at a time of threatening depression. It is contended that an increase of wages at this juncture will result in an overall increase in purchasing power and thereby reverse the tendency towards a shrinkage of incomes. I do not wish to deny that, at a time when there is danger that we may be entering a deflationary spiral, it is desirable that aggregate spending power should be prevented from falling further. What I question is that raising wages is a sensible or effective method of achieving this. What we need in the first instance is not that some people should earn more, but that more people should earn an income, and particularly that employment should revive in the capital goods industries. There is every likelihood that in the present phase of business an increase of wages will lead immediately to a decrease of employment in the industries concerned—even if it is not achieved through a labour dispute and work stoppage which, at present, would react even more rapidly on employment. And it seems certain to have even more harmful indirect effects on employment in the investment industries. I believe that under conditions of more or less full employment an increase of real wages of the final producers may act as an incentive to investment—crudely speaking because it induces the producer to substitute machinery for labour. But this is certainly *not* true in a situation where a large part of the capacity of the existing equipment is unused. In such a situation, investment does depend solely on how much of the final product can be sold at a profit, and that prospect can only be worsened by raising money costs first.

I must not enlarge any further, however, on the first part of Mr. Reuther's 'packages' since, after all, they do not raise any problems with which we have not been long familiar. Even if some of the considerations I have mentioned cannot be stated often enough, or emphasised strongly enough, there is nothing new in them.

The interesting part of the proposals is the second 'package', the special discriminatory terms for the more successful enterprises in the automobile industry. It is not quite easy to say what their aim is or what Mr. Reuther expects to achieve by them. But it is well worth while to ask what the consequences would be if they were successful.

It will doubtless be remembered that before the UAW put forward this demand they had asked that the Big Three reduce the price of their cars by $100.00 and promised that if this were done, the UAW would take this into account in formulating their new demands.[8] The fact that this suggestion has not been acted upon is now advanced as a justification for the new demands. I do not believe that that demand for price reduction ought to be taken very seriously, and it is probably more correctly seen as a public relations job— intended to prepare public opinion for the demands subsequently to be put forward. The union had, in fact, used exactly the same tactics twelve years earlier.[9] But it will help to understand the present issue if we examine for a moment the significance of that demand.

For the purposes of the argument, let us assume that General Motors and perhaps also the two other big automobile manufacturers could, in fact, profitably sell their cars at the reduced price, and that perhaps over a limited period this would even turn out to their advantage. There seems very little question but that this would rapidly mean the end of the remaining independent producers and leave the Big Three alone in the field. If that is so, the first question on which we must form an opinion is why they do not go ahead and reduce their prices. One obvious answer is, of course, that such action would probably bring them soon into conflict with the anti-trust authorities. We have reached the ridiculous position where an attempt to act competitively will lay a particularly efficient organisation open to the charge of aiming at monopoly. I do not know what advantages Mr. Reuther imagines his workers would reap from this result, if he really wanted it. I merely mention this to point out that it would almost certainly bring about results which are contrary to one of the accepted objects of public policy.

In fact, it seems very doubtful whether the Big Three regard it as really in their interest that the independent producers should be eliminated. If any one of them did think it desirable, he could quickly force the others into a course of action which would have that result. But it seems to me much more likely that a concern like General Motors, which takes such pains to preserve active

---

[8] [The demand was made in letters sent by Walter Reuther to the Presidents of Chrysler, Ford, and General Motors, on January 17, 1957. The letter to the President of the Chrysler Corporation, along with portions of otherwise identical letters to the Presidents of Ford and General Motors, was reproduced in "Reuther's Letters Proposing That Big Three Auto Companies Cut Price on '58 Cars", *New York Times*, August 18, 1957, p. 80.—Ed.]

[9] [See "Reuther's Letters", column 3, where Reuther notes that in 1945–46 the UAW was willing to reduce its demands in order to avoid creating the need for price rises. During that period, Reuther led a 113-day UAW strike against General Motors in an attempt to win a 30 per cent wage increase without an increase in the retail price of cars, his goal being to protect workers' real wages against inflation. Reuther challenged the company to 'open its books' to prove the union's demands impossible. General Motors refused, but ultimately offered an 18.5 per cent wage increase, which the UAW accepted.—Ed.]

competition between its divisions, would for the same reasons regard it in its long-run interest to preserve the independent experimentation of the smaller producers. After all, the men inside the big corporations probably understand better than many outside observers that the exceptional efficiency of a particular organisation is not the necessary result of size, but rather that size is the result of the exceptional efficiency of a particular organisation. They doubtless know also that such exceptional efficiency does not only not follow automatically from size, or from any device or design which can be established once and for all, but only from a constant and ever-renewed effort to do better than can be done by any other known method. I feel very strongly that in this sphere the simplified schemes which the economic theorist legitimately uses as a first approach, which treat costs as a function of size and approach the problem in terms of economics of scale, have become an obstacle to a realistic understanding of the important factors. Many of the individual and unique features of a particular corporation which make for its success are of the same character as the similar features of an individual person; they exist largely as an intangible tradition of an approach to problems, based on a tradition which is handed on but ever changing, and which, though it may secure superiority for long periods, may be challenged at any time by a new and even more effective corporate personality.[10] I must say that if I were responsible for the fate of one of these corporations, I would not only feel that I was acting in the best interest of the corporation if I sacrificed the temporary gain from the control of an even larger share of the market in order to preserve the stimulus which has kept the organisation on tip-toe so long; I should also feel that, in my efforts to prolong this leadership as long as possible, and use for this purpose part of the differential profits which this greater efficiency allowed my corporation to earn, I was acting in the interest of the community at large. An advantage of an individual or a corporation which cannot be duplicated remains an advantage to society even though nobody else has it; it ought to be made full use of, so long as nobody else is prevented from bettering the result by different and even greater advantages. To think of such positions in terms which are appropriate to monopolies based on obstacles to entry into an industry leads to an altogether distorted approach to the problems of policy.

It will be useful to remember this when we now turn to the specific demands of the automobile workers directed only to the three dominant corporations. I am not a little puzzled to understand what Mr. Reuther really expects to

---

[10] [For related points, see F. A. Hayek, "The Present State of the Debate" [1935], p. 95, and F. A. Hayek, "Socialist Calculation: The Competitive 'Solution'" [1940], p. 130, reprinted as chapters 2 and 3 respectively of F. A. Hayek, *Socialism and War: Essays, Documents, Reviews*, ed. B. Caldwell, vol. 10 (1997) of *The Collected Works of F. A. Hayek*.—Ed.]

achieve by them, and from what parts of them he expects to derive any real benefit for the employees, and what part has been put in rather for its optical effect, that is, to gain the support of public opinion. The result of the acceptance of these demands would depend on certain decisions on the part of the management of the corporations, the character of which is by no means obvious. I shall, therefore, have to consider the consequences of these demands being accepted on the basis of alternative assumptions concerning how the corporations respond to the new conditions.

The "supplementary economic demands" directed to the Big Three are that one half of all profits in excess of 10 per cent on what is called "net capital" should be divided equally between employees and the consumers so that one quarter of these "excess profits" during any one year should be given as a rebate to the buyers of cars, while another quarter should be handed over *to the unions* to do with it as they please.[11] It is this last feature which distinguishes the proposal from all other profit-sharing plans and particularly from the profit-sharing plan which was offered by some automobile manufacturers to the workers and was turned down by them.[12] It is not a plan to give the individual worker a determinable share in the ownership of the enterprise and therefore in its profits, but rather a plan to give the union, or the representatives of the workers employed in the corporation at a given time, control over, in the first instance, one quarter of the profits in excess of 10 per cent on net capital.

There are various grounds why the idea seems attractive that the workers in a corporation should be given a favoured opportunity to invest their savings in the corporation, and there are also good reasons why the great hopes which some people have set on such plans have scarcely ever been borne out by the result. Though the worker may find greater satisfaction in working for a corporation where he has a share in the profits, however small, and may take a greater interest in the prosperity of the corporation, it is also natural that, if he has any savings to invest, he will normally prefer not to stake them on the same enterprise on the prosperity of which all the rest of his income depends.

---

[11] [The phrases quoted by Hayek in this paragraph can all be found in a sub-section entitled "Collective Bargaining Program for 1958" of R. Reuther, *Price Policy and Public Responsibility: Administered Prices in the Automobile Industry. Statement Prepared for Presentation by Walter P. Reuther, President, United Automobile, Aircraft and Agricultural Implement Workers of America, to the Subcommittee on Antitrust and Monopoly of the Committee on the Judiciary, United States Senate, Senator Estes Kefauver, Chairman, January 28, 1958* (Detroit: UAW Publications Department, 1958), pp. 23–29.—Ed.]

[12] [As noted in Reuther's 1958 letter to the Big Three, the 1955 negotiations saw both Ford and General Motors offer their employees a stock-participation plan. This was rejected by the workers on the grounds that those with the lowest incomes and greatest family responsibilities would be unable to afford to participate. See "Text of Reuther Proposals", column 3.—Ed.]

It is, however, an entirely different matter if it is demanded that the body of workers employed by a firm at any one time, without having contributed to its capital, be given a share in the profits. The effect will in part depend on how this share is to be distributed among the workers or otherwise used for their benefit. On this the proposal, as published, leaves us largely in the dark. It merely tells us that the workers of any company "would determine democratically how they chose to allocate the money available from their particular companies through this supplementary package",[13] and adds a list of purposes for which they may be used which ends with "any other purposes which they deem advisable".[14] I sometimes wonder whether this is not the most ominous sentence in the whole document, since it leaves open the possibility that the individual worker may get little, if anything, for his free disposal, and that the money will be used mainly for the collective purposes of the union, i.e., further to increase its power.

So far as the effects on the position of the companies affected are concerned, we must distinguish between the short- and the long-run effects. In the relatively short run, the companies would have the choice between absorbing the loss of net profits and continuing essentially the same price policies as before, or at once trying to recoup themselves by an adjustment of prices. The former would mean that they would both be in a stronger position in the labour market compared with their weaker competitors, and would also offer the consumers what amounts to a lower price—though how significant the expectation of an uncertain and at best small rebate at the end of the year would be in affecting the choice of the purchaser seems doubtful. At any rate, so long as they followed this policy, the tendency would necessarily be to strengthen their superiority over the less successful companies and to increase the likelihood of the elimination of the latter. If, on the other hand, the companies concerned decided that they could not afford the reduction of profits but that it was expedient to raise prices sufficiently so as to restore them (so far as practicable), the car buyers would not only have no advantage at all—they would have to pay more than before, because they would have to provide the additional profits which would have to be obtained to satisfy the demands of labour.

In the long run, however, the managements of the corporations would have no such choice. Mr. Reuther is here obscuring the main issue by calling all profits in excess of ten per cent on "net capital" before taxation (i.e.,

---

[13] [See Reuther, *Price Policy and Public Responsibility*, p. 26.—Ed.]

[14] [See "Text of Reuther Proposals", column 3. The list of purposes to which Hayek refers includes "additional wage increases", "added hospital-medical insurance", and "added protection against short work weeks and layoffs".—Ed.]

4.8 per cent after taxation) "excess profits". I will not examine here the diffi-culties which the vague concept of 'net capital' raises in this connection but, for the purposes of the argument, shall assume that it can be given a suffi-ciently definite meaning. Whatever this basis of calculation, it is difficult to see in what sense the profits actually earned by the successful industries can be called 'excessive'. It is true they are high in comparison with those com-panies in the industry that are struggling for survival, but hardly in any other sense. The commonly accepted measures of profitability scarcely suggest that the profits earned by the three companies are more than is necessary in such a highly risky field to make the investment of new capital attractive: at the end of last year the value of the shares of both Ford and Chrysler was below the book value of the assets of these companies, and only the price of General Motors shares exceeded the book value of the assets by more than the average for all the companies included in the Dow-Jones index number of the prices of industrial stocks.[15] But even if it could be seriously maintained that the profits of these companies were in some meaningful sense "excessive",[16] surely this would only constitute a case that, in the general interest, more capital should be invested in the companies concerned, and not a case for making investment in them less profitable. Or, assuming there were any grounds on which it could be contended that the big firms in the automobile industry were making 'monopoly profits', this would seem to me the strongest possible case against giving the workers a vested interest in the preservation of such monopoly profits.[17]

This brings me at last to the general principle involved in those demands,

---

[15] See the Statement by Theodore O. Yntema, Vice-President-Finance, Ford Motor Com-pany, before the Subcommittee on Anti-trust and Monopoly of the Committee on the Judiciary, United States Senate, Washington D.C., February 4–5, 1958. [For a contemporaneous analysis of the likely economic implications of the proposed profit-sharing plan, see R. Montgomery, I. Stelzer and R. Roth, "Collective Bargaining over Profit-Sharing: The Automobile Union's Effort to Extend Its Frontier of Control", *The Journal of Business*, vol. 31, 1958, pp. 318–34.—Ed.]

[16] [The phrase "excessive profits" appears on pp. 23 and 78 of Reuther, *Price Policy and Public Responsibility*.—Ed.]

[17] [The phrase 'monopoly profits' appears neither in the "Text of Reuther Proposals" nor in *Price Policy and Public Responsibility*. However, there are in the latter document several sub-sections lamenting what is seen as the uncompetitive nature of the U.S. car market. It is argued there that "the automobile industry in some way has found exemption from what used to be con-sidered the natural laws of a competitive economic system", the consequence of which has been "to give each producer a measure of individual monopoly". The outcome is a situation in which "the price charged for each product will tend to be the same as would be charged by one single monopolist controlling the entire market". As a result, the Big Three firms enjoy "abnor-mally high" and "exorbitant" profits. See Reuther, *Price Policy and Public Responsibility*, pp. 74–82. Hayek's use of the term 'monopoly profits' appears, therefore, to capture the spirit, if not the precise wording, of Reuther's views on the nature of the U.S. car market.—Ed.]

the question of what would be the significance for the character of our whole economic system if the principle underlying them were applied generally. This is a question which must be examined without any regard to the particular figures mentioned in Mr. Reuther's 'packages'. If it is in any sense right that the employees of a particular firm should get one quarter of the profits in excess of 10 per cent, it would seem equally right that next time they should demand one half, or that they should claim some even larger percentage of all profits. It is, of course, a familiar and an only too often successful practice to establish a new principle by putting forward at first what may quantitatively seem a not very important demand, and only when the principle has been established to push its application further and further. It may be that Mr. Reuther was not very wise in asking in the first instance as much as one quarter of what he calls excess profits. The danger that he would gain his point would probably be much greater if in the first instance he had asked a modest 10 per cent and only after the principle had been established had pushed for a higher participation. Perhaps because he has on the first occasion asked for as much as he did, the public will be more ready to grasp what the establishment of the principle would mean.

The recognition of the right of the worker of a firm, *qua* worker, to participate in a share of the profits, irrespective of any contribution he has made to its capital, establishes him as a part owner of this firm. In this sense the demand is, of course, purely socialistic and, what is more, not based on any socialist theory of the more sophisticated and rational kind, but on the crudest type of socialism, commonly known as syndicalism. It is the form in which socialist demands usually first appear but which, because of their absurd consequences, have been abandoned by all of the theorists of socialism. It is at least possible to put up a rational argument in favour of nationalising all industrial capital (though I believe it can be demonstrated—and is confirmed by all experience—that the consequences of such a policy would be disastrous). But it is not even possible to construct a rational argument in support of the contention that the workers employed at any one time in a firm or industry should collectively own the equipment of that industry. Any attempt to think through the consequences of such an arrangement soon shows that it is utterly incompatible with any rational use of the resources of society, and would soon lead to complete disorganisation of the economic system.[18] The final outcome

---

[18] [Hayek alludes to the critique of collective ownership advanced by Austrian economist Ludwig von Mises (1881–1973). Mises argued that, by eliminating the possibility of a market in which the prices of capital goods could be established, the nationalisation of industrial capital would leave people unable to identify the relative scarcities of the various resources at their disposal and so incapable of acting in a rational way. See L. von Mises, "Economic Calculation in the Socialist Commonwealth" [1920], in *Collectivist Economic Planning*, ed. F. A. Hayek (London:

would, no doubt, merely be that some new closed group of established workers would entrench themselves as the new proprietors and endeavour to get out of the seized property as much for their benefit as they could. The expropriation of one group of capitalists would have been achieved, but only to give some other group an equally exclusive (and probably equally temporary) right to the particular assets.

This is not the proper place to demonstrate the unworkability of a syndicalist system, nor should it be necessary once more to attempt to do so. What needs to be brought out is that the fulfilment of Mr. Reuther's demand would be a step towards syndicalism and that, once the first step was taken, it is difficult to see how further demands in the same direction could be resisted. If the UAW have now the power to appropriate part of the capital of some of the biggest enterprises in the country, there is no reason why the same power should not next time be used to appropriate more and in the end all of it, and why the same should not happen in other industries. Nothing, indeed, brings home more vividly the dangers of the situation we have allowed to grow up over the last twenty-five years than the fact that it is necessary to examine such demands seriously and to explain at length why they must on no account be accepted if we are to preserve the fundamental character of our economy. I hope it is owing to the fact that most people believe that these demands will not be pressed seriously and that, at least this time, they have been put forward as a bargaining manoeuvre, that they have not caused more concern. But I fear that it may be more owing to the fact that the public have not yet realised that much more is at stake than the prosperity of three big corporations. What will be tested when these demands are seriously put forward is the crucial issue of how far the organised groups of industrial workers are to be allowed to use the coercive power they have acquired to force on the rest of this country a change in the basic institutions on which our social and economic system rests. This is no longer a situation where we can afford the detached view which assumes that in a conflict of interests there is always something to be said for both sides and a compromise to be desired. It is a situation in which even the fear of the grave consequences which at this juncture a prolonged labour dispute and perhaps a long stoppage of production might have must not be allowed to influence our position. It is, it seems to me, a moment at which all who desire the preservation of the market system based on free enterprise must unambiguously desire and support an outright rejec-

---

Routledge and Kegan Paul, 1935). Hayek's views on Mises's argument, and on attempts to rebut it, can be found in Hayek, *Socialism and War*, F. A. Hayek, "The New Confusion about 'Planning'" [1976], and F. A. Hayek, "Two Pages of Fiction" [1982], reprinted as chapters 26 and 30 respectively of the current volume.—Ed.]

tion of these demands without flinching at the short-run consequences this may produce.

Many people probably still feel that the great automobile manufacturers are able to take care of themselves and that we need not concern ourselves about their problems. This is scarcely any longer true. The fact is that we have permitted a situation to develop in which the unions have grown so powerful, and at the same time the employers have been deprived of any effective defence, that there must be grave doubt about the outcome if Mr. Reuther, according to his favourite practice, singles out one of the Big Three for attack. We have reached a point when the question of how we can still enable one such corporation effectively to resist demands which, if satisfied, would place us straight on the road to syndicalism must be a major public concern. Mr. Reuther may, indeed, be in a position to bring most severe pressure, not only on that corporation but on the public at large, because it may depend on him whether the present decline is turned into a major depression. It should be clearly recognised that the responsibility is entirely his and that no threat will frighten the public into a compromise which in the long run could be even more fatal. It seems to me that in this situation the economist must not shirk this duty of speaking plainly. This is not a pleasant task for one who as a scientist must aim at being impartial and whose inclination is either not to take sides in a particular dispute of interests or, if he has to, to favour the side on which are the relatively poorer. I have to admit that I have my doubts whether the predominant concern of so many economists with what they regard as justice in the particular case rather than with the consequences of a measure for the structure of society in general has on the whole been beneficial. But I am quite sure that the present issue has nothing at all to do with questions of justice between the particular parties involved but raises a question of principle which should be decided in the light of the consequences which its general adoption would have for our society. If this means that the economist, whose chief duty it is to think through and explain the long-run consequences, has to take what may be the unpopular side, particularly the side which is likely to be unpopular among the general class of intellectuals to which he belongs, I feel it becomes even more his duty to do so unreservedly and unequivocally. Perhaps I may conclude with the words of one of the wisest and most detached of economists, which have been quoted before at the head of a well-known essay called 'Reflections on Syndicalism' and which is now proving to have been dreadfully prophetic. The passage by Alfred Marshall which Henry Simons quoted at the head of that essay runs as follows: "Students of social science must fear popular approval; evil is with them when all men speak well of them. If there is any set of opinions by the advocacy of which a newspaper can increase its sales, the student, who wishes to leave the world in general and his country in particular better than it would be if he had not been born, is bound to dwell on the limitations and defects and errors, if any, in that set of opinions: and never to advocate unconditionally even in an *ad hoc* discussion. It is almost impossible for a student to be a true patriot and to have the reputation of being one in his own time."[19] It is probably equally impossible in our time for a student to be a true friend of labour and to have the reputation of being one.

[19] Henry C. Simons, "Some Reflections on Syndicalism", *Journal of Political Economy*, Vol. LII, No. 1 (March 1944), p. 1. [In the essay to which Hayek refers, American economist Henry Calvert Simons (1899–1946) argues that the hallmark of liberalism is its opposition to concentrations of power and that accordingly one of the principal tasks of government is to establish and enforce a framework of rules designed to prevent corporations and trade unions from accumulating such power. See Henry C. Simons, "Some Reflections on Syndicalism", *Journal of Political Economy*, vol. 52, 1944, pp. 1–25. For more on Hayek's views on Simons, and on syndicalism, see Hayek, "'Free' Enterprise and Competitive Order" [1948], reprinted as chapter 6 of this book, pp. 99–100, especially n. 11.

The quotation from British economist Alfred Marshall (1842–1924), Professor of Political Economy at Cambridge University (1885–1908), found at the head of Simons' essay is in fact a little different from that reported by Hayek, reading as follows: "Students of social science must fear popular approval; evil is with them when all men speak well of them. If there is any set of opinions by the advocacy of which a newspaper can increase its sales, then the student . . . is bound to dwell on the limitations and defects and errors, if any, in that set of opinions; and never to advocate them unconditionally even in an *ad hoc* discussion. It is almost impossible for a student to be a true patriot and to have the reputation of being one at the same time". See Simons, "Some Reflections on Syndicalism", p. 1. Simons in turn took the quote, verbatim, from A. C. Pigou, *Economics in Practice* (London: Macmillan and Co., 1935), pp. 10–11. The longer version of the passage quoted by Hayek can be found on p. 89 of A. C. Pigou, "In Memoriam: Alfred Marshall", in *Memorials of Alfred Marshall*, ed. A. C. Pigou (London: Macmillan and Co., 1925). Hayek explores the dangers run by economists who are too keen to win public approval in an essay entitled "On Being an Economist" [1944], first published as chapter 2 of F. A. Hayek, *The Trend of Economic Thinking: Essays on Political Economists and Economic History*, ed. W. W. Bartley III and S. Kresge, vol. 3 (1991) of *The Collected Works of F. A. Hayek.*—Ed.]

SEVENTEEN

THE CORPORATION IN A
DEMOCRATIC SOCIETY

In Whose Interest Ought It to and Will It Be Run?[1]

I

For the questions on which I intend to concentrate here the 'ought' and the 'will' cannot be separated. Twenty-five years is a period long enough for the outcome of the developments to depend on what we will do to shape it. I believe that we have the power to avert some of the unpleasant prospects which current tendencies seem to create. Whether we will succeed in doing so depends on whether we clearly recognise the problem and take appropriate action. All I can attempt here is to indicate the channels into which we ought to try to steer developments.

My thesis will be that if we want effectively to limit the powers of corporations to where they are beneficial, we shall have to confine them much more than we have yet done to one specific goal, that of the profitable use of the capital entrusted to the management by the stockholders. I shall argue that it is precisely the tendency to allow and even to impel the corporations to use their resources for specific ends other than those of a long-run maximisation of the return on the capital placed under their control that tends to confer upon them undesirable and socially dangerous powers, and that the fashion-

[1] Reprinted from M. Anshen and G. L. Bach (eds.), *Management and Corporations, 1985*. New York (McGraw-Hill Company), 1960. [Hayek's essay was prepared for a symposium held to mark the tenth anniversary of the Graduate School of Industrial Administration at the Carnegie Institute of Technology, and was first published as F. A. Hayek, "The Corporation in a Democratic Society: In Whose Interest Ought It and Will It Be Run?", in *Management and Corporations 1985*, ed. M. Anshen and G. Bach (New York: McGraw-Hill, 1960), pp. 99–117. Other participants in the symposium included organisational theorist and Nobel Laureate in Economics Herbert Simon (1916–2001), sociologist Robert K. Merton (1910–2003), and American lawyer and sometime political advisor to President Franklin D. Roosevelt, Adolph A. Berle, Jr. (1895–1971). Both Berle and Hayek were commissioned to address the topic of 'The Corporation in a Democratic Society'. Consequently, although rather different in their substantive claims, their papers bore the same title. Hayek's essay was subsequently reprinted, under the slightly different title that stands at the head of this essay, as chapter 22 of F. A. Hayek, *Studies in Philosophy, Politics and Economics* (London: Routledge & Kegan Paul, 1967). This later version, which omits the section headings found in the original essay, is used here.—Ed.]

able doctrine that their policy should be guided by 'social considerations' is likely to produce most undesirable results.

I should like, however, to emphasise at once that when I contend that the only specific purpose which corporations ought to serve is to secure the highest long-term return on their capital, this does not mean that in the pursuit of this end they ought not to be restrained by general legal *and* moral rules. There is an important distinction to be drawn between specific goals and the framework of rules within which the specific aims are to be pursued. In this respect certain generally accepted rules of decency and perhaps even charitableness should probably be regarded as no less binding on corporations than the strict rules of law. But while these rules limit what corporations may do in the pursuit of their concrete aims, this does not mean that they are entitled to use their resources for particular purposes which have nothing to do with their proper aim.

Power, in the objectionable sense of the word, is the capacity to direct the energy and resources of others to the service of values which those others do not share. The corporation that has the sole task of putting assets to the most profitable use has no power to choose between values: it administers resources in the service of the values of others. It is perhaps only natural that management should desire to be able to pursue values which they think are important and that they need little encouragement from public opinion to indulge in these 'idealistic' aims. But it is just in this that the danger rests of their acquiring real and uncontrollable power. Even the largest aggregation of potential power, the largest accumulation of resources under a single control, is comparatively innocuous so long as those who exercise such power are entitled to use it only for one specific purpose and have no right to use it for other aims, however desirable in themselves. I shall maintain, therefore, that the old-fashioned conception which regards management as the trustee of the stockholders and leaves to the individual stockholder the decision whether any of the proceeds of the activities of the corporation are to be used in the service of higher values is the most important safeguard against the acquisition of arbitrary and politically dangerous powers by corporations.

I need hardly stop to point out how much in recent times policy (especially tax policy), public opinion, and the traditions growing inside the corporations, have tended in the opposite direction, and to what extent most of the agitation for reform is actually directed towards making corporations act more deliberately in 'the public interest'. These demands appear to me to be radically mistaken and their satisfaction more likely to aggravate than to reduce the dangers against which they are directed. There can be little doubt, however, that the conception that corporations ought to pursue public as well as private aims has become so widely accepted even by managements that it seems doubtful whether Adam Smith's comment still applies that the affectation to trade for the public good is "not very common among merchants, and very few words need be employed in dissuading them from it".[2]

II

There are four groups on whose behalf it might be claimed that the corporations ought to be run in their interest: management, labour, stockholders, and 'the public' at large. So far as management is concerned we can dismiss it briefly with the observation that, though it is perhaps a danger to be guarded against, nobody would probably seriously contend that it is desirable that corporations should be run primarily in their interest.

The interest of 'labour' demands only a little longer consideration. As soon as it is made clear that it is not a question of the interest of workers in general but of the special interests of the employees of a particular corporation, it is fairly obvious that it would not be in the interest of 'society' or even of labour in general that the corporation should be run mainly for the benefit of any particular closed group of people employed by it. Though it may be in the interest of the corporation to tie its employees as closely to it as possible, the tendencies in this direction give ground for serious concern. It is the increasing dependence on the particular corporation by which a person is employed which gives the corporations increasing power over the employees, a power against which there can be no other safeguard than the facility the individual has of changing his employment.[3]

That corporations tend to develop from an aggregation of material resources directed and operated by a body of men hired for that purpose into what is primarily a group of men held together by common experience and traditions, and even developing something like a distinct personality, is an important and probably inevitable fact. Nor can it be denied that some of the features which make a particular corporation especially efficient do not rest entirely with the management but would be destroyed if its whole operating personnel were at a given moment replaced by new men. The performance and very existence of a corporation is thus often bound up with the preservation of a certain continuity in its personnel, the preservation of at least an inner core of men right down the line who are familiar with its peculiar traditions and concrete tasks. The 'going concern' differs from the material struc-

---

[2] [Adam Smith, *An Enquiry into the Nature and Causes of the Wealth of Nations*, ed. W. B. Todd, vol. 2 of *The Glasgow Edition of the Works and Correspondence of Adam Smith* (Oxford: Oxford University Press, 1976; reprinted, Indianapolis, IN: Liberty Fund, 1981), book IV, chapter 2, paragraph 9.—Ed.].

[3] [For more on this point, see F. A. Hayek, *The Constitution of Liberty*, ed. Ronald Hamowy, vol. 17 (2011) of *The Collected Works of F. A. Hayek* (Chicago: University of Chicago Press; London: Routledge), pp. 184–90.—Ed.]

ture which will still exist after operations have ceased mainly by the mutually adjusted knowledge and habits of those who operate it.

Nevertheless, in a free system (i.e., in a system of free labour) it is necessary in the interest of the efficient use of resources that the corporation be regarded primarily as an aggregate of material assets. It is they and not the men whom the management can at will allocate to different purposes, they which alone are the means which it is the task of corporations to put to the best use, while the individual must in the last resort himself remain free to decide whether the best use of his energies is within the particular corporation or elsewhere.

The fact is that an enterprise cannot be conducted in the interest of some permanent distinct body of workers if it is at the same time to serve the interest of the consumers. The management will take the decisions it ought to take in the interest of society only if its primary concern is the right use of those resources which it entirely controls, on which the risk of their decisions permanently falls, i.e., the equity capital, and if it treats all other resources it buys or hires as items which it must use only so long as it can make better use of them than anybody else. So long as the individual is free to decide whether he wants to serve this or that corporation, the corporation itself must primarily be concerned with the best use of those resources which are permanently associated with it.

The conception that a corporation ought to be run in the interest of the distinct body of people working in it raises all the problems discussed in connection with the syndicalist type of socialism.[4] I have no space here to enter into a full discussion of these and will merely mention that these could be satisfactorily solved only if not merely this body of people became owners of the material resources of the corporation but if they were also able to hire other workers at the going rate of wages. The result would thus in effect be merely a change in the persons owning the enterprise but not an elimination of the class of wage earners. Whether it is really in the interest of the workers that, if they are also to be capitalists, their investment should be in the same concern which gives them employment is at least questionable.

III

There remain then as possible claimants for the position of the dominating interest in whose service the individual corporation ought to be conducted the

---

[4] [Syndicalism is a form of socialism whereby firms are owned and managed by workers. Hayek elaborates on his criticism of syndicalism in F. A. Hayek, "'Free' Enterprise and Competitive Order" [1948], reprinted as chapter 6 of this volume, pp. 99–100, and in F. A. Hayek, "Unions, Inflation, and Profits" [1959], reprinted as chapter 16 of this volume, pp. 228–29.—Ed.]

owners of the equity and the public at large. (I pass over such other possible claimants as the creditors or the local community to whom the arguments discussed in connection with labour apply *a fortiori.*) The traditional reconciliation of those two interests rested on the assumption that the general rules of law can be given such form that an enterprise, by aiming at long-run maximum return, will also serve the public interest best. There are certain familiar difficulties which arise where property rights cannot be readily so delimited that the direct benefits or disadvantages consequent upon the use made of a particular piece of property will fall exclusively on the owner. These special difficulties, which we must try to remedy as far as possible by a gradual improvement of the law, I shall here disregard as not connected with the special problem of corporations.

Apart from these special instances, the general case for free enterprise and the division of labour rests on a recognition of the fact that, so long as each item of resources gets into the control of the enterprise willing to pay the highest price for it, it will, on the whole, also be used where it will make the largest contribution to the aggregate product of society.

This contention is based on the assumption that each firm will in its decisions consider only such results as will affect, directly or indirectly, the value of its assets and that it will not directly concern itself with the question of whether a particular use is 'socially beneficial'. I believe this is both necessary and right under a regime based on the division of labour, and that the aggregation of assets brought together for the specific purpose of putting them to the most productive use is not a proper source for expenditure which is thought to be generally socially desirable. Such expenditure should be defrayed either by the voluntary payment of individuals out of their income or capital or out of funds raised by taxation.

Rather than further argue this case positively I will briefly consider the consequences which would follow if it were to become the accepted view that the managements of corporations are entitled to spend corporation funds on what they regard as socially desirable purposes. The range of such purposes which might come to be regarded as legitimate objects of corporation expenditure is very wide: political, charitable, educational and in fact everything which can be brought under the vague and almost meaningless term 'social'.[5] I propose

---

[5] [Elsewhere, Hayek describes the term 'social' as one of those "weasel word[s]" that can "deprive of content any term to which they are prefixed while seemingly leaving them untouched". Such words are, Hayek contends, "used to draw the teeth from a concept one is obliged to employ, but from which one wishes to eliminate all implications that challenge one's ideology". See F. A. Hayek, *The Fatal Conceit: The Errors of Socialism*, ed. W. W. Bartley III, vol. 1 (1988) of *The Collected Works of F. A. Hayek*, pp. 116–17. For longer expositions of Hayek's critique of the term 'social', see F. A. Hayek, "What Is 'Social'? What Does It Mean?" [1967], reprinted as chapter 19 of the present volume and the references contained in note 2 of that essay. An

to consider this question mainly with reference to the use of corporation funds in the support of higher education and research, since in this instance my personal interest is most likely biased in favour of such practices. All that is to be said in this connection applies equally to all the other fields mentioned.

The popular view of these matters is, of course, connected with the idea that corporations are 'rich' and therefore have special duties. What ought to be stressed here is that in the sense in which an individual may be rich, that is in the sense of having a large disposable income or capital he is free to devote to what seems to him most important, a corporation cannot be rich. In the strict sense the corporation has no more an income of its own than a trustee has in his capacity of trustee. That its management has been entrusted with large resources for a particular purpose does not mean that it is entitled to use it for other purposes. This is, of course, relevant in many other connections than that which concerns me here, especially in connection with taxation.

In fact, the only argument I can discover in favour of allowing corporations to devote their funds to such purposes as higher education and research—not in instances where this is likely to make it a profitable investment for their stockholders, but because this is regarded as a generally desirable purpose—is that in existing circumstances this seems to be the easiest way to raise adequate funds for what many influential people regard as important ends. This, however, seems to me not to be an adequate argument when we consider the consequences that would follow if it were to become generally recognised that managements have such power. If the large aggregations of capital which the corporations represent could, at the discretion of the management, be used for any purpose approved as morally or socially good, if the opinion of the management that a certain end was intellectually or aesthetically, scientifically or artistically desirable, were to justify expenditure by the corporation for such purposes, this would turn corporations from institutions serving the expressed needs of individual men into institutions determining which ends the efforts of individual men should serve. To allow the management to be guided in the use of funds, entrusted to them for the purpose of putting them to the materially most productive use, by what they regard as their social responsibility, would create centres of uncontrollable power never intended by those who provided the capital. It seems to me therefore clearly not desirable that generally higher education or research should be regarded as legitimate purposes of corporation expenditure, because this would not only vest powers over cultural decisions in men selected for capacities in an entirely different field, but

---

important instance of this misuse of language, Hayek argues, is to be found in the term 'social justice', Hayek's critique of which can be found in F. A. Hayek, *The Mirage of Social Justice*, vol. 2 (1976) of *Law, Legislation and Liberty* (Chicago: University of Chicago Press; London: Routledge, 1973–1979), pp. 62–106.—Ed.]

would also establish a principle which, if generally applied, would enormously enhance the actual powers of corporations.

This, at least, would be the immediate effect. Yet not the least serious consequence of such a development would be that such powers would not long be left uncontrolled. So long as the management is supposed to serve the interest of the stockholders, it is reasonable to leave the control of its action to the stockholders. But if the management is supposed to serve wider public interests, it becomes merely a logical consequence of this conception that the appointed representatives of the public interest should control the management. The argument against specific interference of government into the conduct of business corporations rests on the assumption that they are constrained to use the resources under their control for a specific purpose. If this assumption becomes invalid, the argument for exemption from specific direction by the representatives of the public interest also lapses.

IV

If ideally corporations ought to be conducted primarily in the interest of the stockholders, this does not mean that the law as it stands fully achieves this, or even that, if they were left unregulated by law, the market would necessarily produce such developments as to make the interest of the stockholders prevail. The general philosophy of government from which I am approaching these problems makes it probably expedient that, before I proceed to ask what particular legal arrangements would seem desirable, I devote a few paragraphs to the question why there should be a need for any special regulation of corporations and why we should not be content to let the market develop appropriate institutions under the general principle of freedom of contract.

Historically, the need for the deliberate creation of special legal institutions in this field arose, of course, out of the problem of limited liability and the desire to protect the creditors. The creation of a legal person capable of entering contracts, for which only the separate property of the corporation and not all the property of the owners was liable, required special legislative action. In this sense limited liability is a privilege and it is a valid argument to say that it is for the law to decide on which conditions this privilege is to be granted.

I shall also state only briefly what I have argued at length in another connection,[6] that 'freedom of contracts', like most freedoms of this kind, does not mean that any contract must be permitted or be made enforceable, but merely that the permissibility or enforceability of a contract is to be

---

[6] *The Constitution of Liberty*, 1960, pp. 230–1. [See now the *Collected Works* edition of *The Constitution of Liberty*, pp. 339–40.—Ed.]

decided by the general rules of law and that no authority has power to allow or disallow a contract on the basis of the merits of its specific contents. I am not at all sure that in the field of corporations any kind of contract should be generally prohibited or declared generally invalid. But I am firmly convinced that modern use of the corporate form of organisation requires that there should be a standard type of rules applying to all corporations bearing a description reserved to this type so that, for example, any corporation designated by the addition of 'Inc.' to its name should thereby subject itself to a known standard type of rules. I see little reason for making such rules strictly mandatory, or not allowing other types of corporations explicitly described as 'special'. If the public is thus warned that in the particular case the standard rules do not apply, it will probably look very carefully at the provisions of any corporate charter which differs from the standard type.

The problem I want to consider is, thus, whether the rules for the standard type of corporation should, to a much greater degree than is the case at present, be governed by regulations which assure that the interest of the stockholder shall be paramount. I believe this to be the case and wish here to indulge in some bold mental experimentation with regard to the means of giving the stockholders greater powers in this respect. It seems to me that in this field the possibilities of arrangements different from those to which we are accustomed are all too little considered, and that the 'apathy' and lack of influence of the stockholder is largely the result of an institutional set-up which we have wrongly come to regard as the obvious or only possible one. I shall not be surprised if the experts on corporation law should at first regard my suggestions as wildly impracticable and am even prepared to admit that, under the present system of taxation and under current monetary policies, at least the first of the two possibilities I shall consider may do more harm than good. This, however, is no reason for not seriously examining these possibilities, even if it were only in order to free ourselves from the belief that the developments which have taken place were inevitable. It is probable that, on the two chief points I want to consider, the existing arrangements were adopted, not by deliberate choice and in awareness of the consequences, but because the alternatives were never seriously considered.

V

If today the actual influence of the stockholder on the conduct of the corporation is small and often negligible, this is probably due, more than to any other fact, to the circumstance that he has no legally enforceable claim to his share in the whole profits of the corporation. We have come to regard it as natural that a majority decides for all what part of the profits is to be distributed and what part to be reinvested in the corporation, and that on this question the stockholders will normally act on the recommendation of the management. It seems to me that nothing would produce so active an interest of the individual stockholder in the conduct of a corporation, and at the same time give him so much effective power, as to be annually called upon individually to decide what part of his share in the net profits he was willing to reinvest in the corporation.[7] It would still be for the management to say what part of the profits it thought it could profitably use as additional capital and to recommend that additional shares be offered to stockholders who wish to reinvest part or all of their profits in the corporation. But it should normally be for the individual stockholder to decide whether he wants to make use of this opportunity or not.

It is evident that this would be desirable only in conditions of a stable currency where paper profits corresponded to real profits and under a system of taxation different from the present. But disregarding for the moment these obstacles to the present adoption of the principle, it seems to me that this one change would go very far towards making stockholder control of the corporation a reality, and that it would at the same time limit the growth (and probably even the existence) of individual corporations to what is economically desirable. I need not ask here how far the allegations about an excessive expansion of corporations through ploughing back of profits are in fact justified. That with the existing arrangements this is at least a distinct possibility and that the natural bias of the management will tend in this direction can hardly be denied.

It might at first be thought that the striving for the power which an increase of total assets confers on management will also make it aim at maximising

---

[7] Cf. Louis O. Kelso and Mortimer Adler, *The Capitalist Manifesto*, New York (Random House), 1958, p. 210. [Mortimer Adler (1902–2001) was an American philosopher and educator and an advocate of liberal education via the reading of the great books of the Western canon. Louis Kelso (1913–1991) was an American political economist and the inventor and pioneer of employee share ownership plans. In *The Capitalist Manifesto: A Revolutionary Plan for a Capitalistic Distribution of Wealth to Preserve Our Free Society* (New York: Random House, 1958), Kelso and Adler analyse the changing nature of the institution of private property, consider its implications for individual responsibility and political freedom, and make the case for employee share ownership. Hayek alludes to p. 210 of the book, where Kelso and Adler write: "The essence of property in productive wealth is the right to receive its product. Legal recognition of this right would consist in the legal requirement that the entire net income of a mature corporation during or immediately after the close of each financial period be paid out in dividends to its stockholders . . . Failure to apply the laws of private property to the capital owned by stockholders permits corporate managers in effect to hire capital at a price dictated by themselves. The voice of the stockholder is ineffective unless he receives the entire product of his capital and then determines, by his own affirmative action, whether he will return any part of such earnings to the corporation as a further investment of capital. No other conceivable arrangement can force corporate management to justify its performance".—Ed.]

profits. This, however, is true only in a sense of this term different from that in which we have used it and in which it can be maintained that maximising profits is socially desirable. The interest of a management striving for control of more resources will be to maximise aggregate profits of the corporation, not profits per unit of capital invested. It is the latter, however, which should be maximised if the best use of the resources is to be secured.

VI

So far as the individual stockholder is concerned, it is in general to be assumed that his interest is solely to obtain the maximum direct return from his holdings of the shares of a particular corporation, whether this be in the form of dividends or of appreciation, or in the short or in the long run. It is conceivable that even an individual stockholder may use a controlling influence to direct the activities of a corporation so that the gain will accrue mainly, not to that corporation, but to another corporation or firm where his share of the profit thus obtained would be even greater. Though possible, this is not a very likely situation to occur in the case of individual stockholders, not only because it would require very large resources but even more because such a manoeuvre would probably be rather transparent and would be regarded as dishonest.

The situation is different, however, where the shares of one corporation are owned by another corporation, and nobody seriously questions that any control thus exercised by the second corporation over the first can legitimately be employed to increase the profits of the second. In such a situation it is clearly possible, and not unlikely, that the control over the policy of the first corporation will be used to channel the gains from its operations to the second, and that the first would be run, not in the interest of all its stockholders but only in the interest of the controlling majority. When the other stockholders discover this it will be too late for them to apply any remedy. The only possibility they will have is to sell out—which may be just what the corporate stockholder wants.

I must admit that I have never quite understood the *rationale* or justification of allowing corporations to have voting rights in other corporations of which they own shares. So far as I can discover, this was never deliberately decided upon in full awareness of all its applications, but came about simply as a result of the conception that, if legal personality was conferred upon the corporation, it was natural to confer upon it all powers which natural persons possessed. But this seems to me by no means a natural or obvious consequence. On the contrary, it turns the institution of property into something quite different from what it is normally supposed to be. The corporation thereby becomes, instead of an association of partners with a common interest, an association of groups whose interest may be in strong conflict; and the possibility appears that a group which directly owns assets amounting only to a small fraction of those of the corporation, may, through a pyramiding of holdings, acquire control of assets amounting to a multiple of what they own themselves. By owning a controlling interest in a corporation which owns a controlling interest in another corporation and so on, a comparatively small amount owned by a person or group may control a very much bigger aggregation of capital.

There seems to me to exist no reason why a corporation should not be allowed to own stock of another corporation purely as an investment. But it also seems to me that such stock, so long as it is owned by another corporation, should cease to confer a right to vote. Technically this could perhaps be effectively enforced only by permanently setting aside some part of the stock as non-voting shares and permitting only those to be held by other corporations. I am not concerned, here, however, with the practical details. The point I want to bring out is simply that the possibility of the control of one corporation by another opens up the possibility of the complete and perfectly legal control of large resources by persons who own only a small fraction of them, and of the use of such control in the interest of that group only.

The possibility of such an indirect, chainwise ownership of the stock of corporations is probably the second factor which has accentuated the separation of ownership from control and has given management, i.e., a few individuals, powers far exceeding those which their individually owned property could ever confer upon them. This development has nothing to do with the essence of the institution of the corporation as such, or with the reasons for which the privilege of limited liability was conferred upon them. In fact, if anything, it seems to me to be contrary to, rather than a consequence of, the conceptions on which the system of private property rests—an artificial separation of ownership and control which may place the individual owner in the position where his capital is used for purposes conflicting with his own and without his even being able to ascertain who, in fact, possesses the majority of votes. With the grant of voting rights to corporate stockholders the general presumption that the corporation will be run by persons whose interests are the same as those of the individual stockholder is no longer valid.

I will not pursue this possibility further to ask whether these considerations suggest that merely industrial corporations should be deprived of the voting power on the stock of other industrial corporations which they hold, or whether the principle should be extended also to financial corporations. Offhand I can see no reason for allowing such a distinction. Whatever desirable financial activities require that a firm should exercise the voting rights in a corporation could probably be performed without the privilege of limited liability.

Perhaps I should add that it seems to me that in recent years economists have been looking at corporation law (so far as they did so at all!) much too exclusively from the angle of whether it favoured the creation of monopoly positions. No doubt this is one important consideration which we ought to keep in mind. But it is certainly not the only one and perhaps not even the most important. The justification of the corporation is based on the conception that its managers will have to run it in such a manner that the whole of the capital it raises will be used in the most profitable way, and the public at large is certainly under the impression that the law is designed to assure this. So long as the corporations are run by representatives of the majority of the true owners, there is at least a strong probability that this will be the case. But somebody who represents merely the majority of a majority, and whose interests may well be better served if he does not have to share the profit from his control of the corporation with those who have provided the greater part of the capital, may well pursue different aims. A legal situation which makes it theoretically possible that this position may arise in any corporation after the stockholders have committed their capital to it and have no remedy cannot be regarded as satisfactory.

VII

I have considered these two possibilities of changes in corporation law not so much because of their specific merit but as illustrations of the degree to which future developments depend on the legal framework we provide for them. They were meant to show that the complete separation of management from ownership, the lack of real power of the stockholders, and the tendency of corporations to develop into self-willed and possibly irresponsible empires, aggregates of enormous and largely uncontrollable power, is not a fact which we must accept as inevitable, but largely the result of special conditions which the law has created and the law can change. We have it in our power to halt and reverse this process if we want to. Even the two changes in the law I have considered would probably be much more far-reaching in this respect than is at first apparent or could be indicated in a few paragraphs.

Let me repeat, in conclusion, that to me the chief merit of these changes would seem to be that they would tie management much more effectively than is now the case to the single task of employing the capital of their stockholders in the most profitable manner and would deprive them of the power of using it in the service of some 'public interest'. The present tendency not only to allow but to encourage such use of corporate resources appears to me as dangerous in its short-run as in its long-run consequences. The immediate effect is greatly to extend the powers of the management of corporations over cultural, political, and moral issues for which proven ability to use resources efficiently in production does not necessarily confer special competence; and at the same time to substitute a vague and indefinable 'social responsibility' for a specific and controllable task. But while in the short run the effect is to increase an irresponsible power, in the long run the effect is bound to be increased control of corporations by the power of the state. The more it comes to be accepted that corporations ought to be directed in the service of specific 'public interests', the more persuasive becomes the contention that, as government is the appointed guardian of the public interest, government should also have power to tell the corporations what they must do. Their power to do good according to their own judgment is bound to be a merely transitory stage. The price they would soon have to pay for this short-lived freedom will be that they will have to take instructions from the political authority which is supposed to represent the public interest. Unless we believe that the corporations serve the public interest best by devoting their resources to the single aim of securing the largest return in terms of long-run profits, the case for free enterprise breaks down.

I cannot better sum up what I have been trying to say than by quoting a brief statement in which my colleague Professor Milton Friedman expressed the chief contention two years ago: "If anything is certain to destroy our free society, to undermine its very foundations, it would be a wide-spread acceptance by management of social responsibilities in some sense other than to make as much money as possible. This is a fundamentally subversive doctrine."[8]

---

[8] The Social Science Reporter's Eighth Social Science Seminar on "Three Major Factors in Business Management: Leadership, Decision Making, and Social Responsibility", March 19, 1958. Summary by Walter A. Diehm, Graduate School of Business, Stanford University. [Nobel Prize-winning economist Milton Friedman (1912–2006) was Hayek's colleague at the University of Chicago from 1950, when Hayek joined the Committee on Social Thought, to 1962, when Hayek left Chicago for Freiburg University. While it has proven impossible to find the "Summary" referred to by Hayek, a similar passage can be found in Friedman's *Capitalism and Freedom* (Chicago: University of Chicago Press, 1962), p. 133: "Few trends could so thoroughly undermine the very foundations of our free society as the acceptance by corporate officials of a social responsibility other than to make as much money for their stockholders as possible. This is a fundamentally subversive doctrine". For more on Hayek's views on the notion of 'social responsibility', see Hayek, "What Is 'Social'? What does It Mean?".—Ed.]

EIGHTEEN

THE *NON SEQUITUR* OF THE 'DEPENDENCE EFFECT'[1]

For well over a hundred years the critics of the free enterprise system have resorted to the argument that if production were only organised rationally, there would be no economic problem. Rather than face the problem which scarcity creates, socialist reformers have tended to deny that scarcity existed. Ever since the Saint-Simonians their contention has been that the problem of production has been solved and only the problem of distribution remains.[2] However absurd this contention must appear to us with respect to the time when it was first advanced, it still has some persuasive power when repeated with reference to the present.

The latest form of this old contention is expounded in *The Affluent Society* by Professor J. K. Galbraith. He attempts to demonstrate that in our affluent society the important private needs are already satisfied and the urgent need is therefore no longer a further expansion of the output of commodities but an increase of those services which are supplied (and presumably can be supplied only) by government. Though his book has been extensively discussed since its publication in 1958, its central thesis still requires some further examination.[3]

---

[1] Reprinted from *The Southern Economic Journal*, Vol. XXVII, No. 4, April 1961. [The article was first published as F. A. Hayek, "The *Non Sequitur* of the 'Dependence Effect'", *Southern Economic Journal*, vol. 27, 1961, pp. 346–48. It was subsequently reprinted under the same title, with very minor stylistic changes, as chapter 23 of F. A. Hayek, *Studies in Philosophy, Politics and Economics* (London: Routledge & Kegan Paul, 1967). The latter is the version used here.—Ed.]

[2] [The 'Saint-Simonians' were the followers of the French social reformer and founder of French socialism Claude Henri de Rouvroy, Comte de Saint-Simon (1760–1825). They included French philosopher, and founder of sociology and positivism, Auguste Comte (1798–1857), and French social reformers Saint-Amand Bazard (1791–1832) and Barthélemy-Prosper Enfantin (1796–1864). Hayek argued that Saint-Simon's writings contain the origins both of 'scientism'—that is, the slavish, and inappropriate, imitation by those investigating the social world of the methods and language of the natural sciences—and also of modern socialist planning. See F. A. Hayek, *Studies on the Abuse and Decline of Reason: Text and Documents*, ed. Bruce Caldwell, vol. 13 (2010) of *The Collected Works of F. A. Hayek* (Chicago: University of Chicago Press; London: Routledge), pp. 187–255.—Ed.]

[3] [John Kenneth Galbraith (1908–2006) was a Canadian-born, American economist and public servant who taught at Harvard University and was an advisor to President John F. Kennedy. His best known works include *American Capitalism: The Concept of Countervailing Power* (Boston:

I believe the author would agree that his argument turns upon the 'Dependence Effect' explained in Chapter XI of the book. The argument of this chapter starts from the assertion that a great part of the wants which are still unsatisfied in modern society are not wants which would be experienced spontaneously by the individual if left to himself, but are wants which are created by the process by which they are satisfied. It is then represented as self-evident that for this reason such wants cannot be urgent or important. This crucial conclusion appears to be a complete *non sequitur* and it would seem that with it the whole argument of the book collapses.

The first part of the argument is of course perfectly true: we would not desire any of the amenities of civilization—or even of the most primitive culture—if we did not live in a society in which others provide them. The innate wants are probably confined to food, shelter, and sex. All the rest we learn to desire because we see others enjoying various things. To say that a desire is not important because it is not innate is to say that the whole cultural achievement of man is not important.

This cultural origin of practically all the needs of civilized life must of course not be confused with the fact that there are some desires which aim at a satisfaction derived directly not from the use of an object, but only from the status which its consumption is expected to confer. In a passage which Professor Galbraith quotes (p. 118), Lord Keynes seems to treat the latter sort of Veblenesque conspicuous consumption as the only alternative to "those needs which are absolute in the sense that we feel them whatever the situation of our fellow human beings may be".[4] If this phrase is interpreted to exclude all the needs for goods which are felt only because these goods are known to be pro-

---

Houghton Mifflin, 1952), *The Affluent Society* (London: Hamish Hamilton, 1958), and *The New Industrial State* (Boston: Houghton Mifflin, 1967). In *The Affluent Society*, probably his most famous book, Galbraith argued against satisfying all consumer demands, on the grounds that "If the individual's wants are to be urgent they must be original with himself. They cannot be urgent if they must be contrived for him. And above all they must not be contrived by the process of production by which they are satisfied. For this means that the whole case for the urgency of production, based on the urgency of wants, falls to the ground. One cannot defend production as satisfying wants if that production creates the wants." It is "the way wants depend on the process by which they are satisfied" that Galbraith refers to as "the Dependence Effect". See *The Affluent Society*, pp. 119, 124. All the references to Galbraith's work made in the main text of Hayek's essay are to this book.—Ed.]

[4] [Galbraith quotes from the work of British economist John Maynard Keynes (1883–1946), who wrote that the needs of human beings "fall into two classes—those needs which are absolute in the sense that we feel them whatever the situation of our fellow human beings may be, and those which are relative in the sense that we feel them only if their satisfaction lifts us above, makes us feel superior to, our fellows". See J. M. Keynes, "Economic Possibilities for Our Grandchildren" [1930], reprinted in J. M. Keynes, *Essays in Persuasion*, vol. 9 (1972) of *The Collected Writings of John Maynard Keynes* (London: Macmillan for the Royal Economic Society), p. 326.—Ed.]

duced, these two Keynesian classes describe of course only extreme types of wants, but disregard the overwhelming majority of goods on which civilized life rests. Very few needs indeed are "absolute" in the sense that they are independent of social environment or of the example of others and that their satisfaction is an indispensable condition for the preservation of the individual or of the species. Most needs which make us act are needs for things of which only civilization teaches us that they exist at all, and these things are wanted by us because they produce feelings or emotions which we would not know if it were not for our cultural inheritance. Are not in this sense probably all our aesthetic feelings 'acquired tastes'?[5]

How complete a *non sequitur* Professor Galbraith's conclusion represents is seen most clearly if we apply the argument to any product of the arts, be it music, painting, or literature. If the fact that people would not feel the need for something if it were not produced did prove that such products are of small value, all those highest products of human endeavour would be of small value. Professor Galbraith's argument could be easily employed, without any change of the essential terms, to demonstrate the worthlessness of literature or any other form of art. Surely an individual's want for literature is not original with himself in the sense that he would experience it if literature were not produced. Does this then mean that the production of literature cannot be defended as satisfying a want because it is only the production which provokes the demand? In this, as in the case of all cultural needs, it is unquestionably, in Professor Galbraith's words, "the process of satisfying wants that creates the wants". There have never been "independently determined desires for" literature before literature has been produced and books certainly do not serve the "simple modes of enjoyment which require no previous conditioning of the consumer" (p. 217). Clearly my taste for the novels of Jane Austen or Anthony Trollope or C. P. Snow is not "original with myself".[6] But is it not rather absurd to conclude from this that it is less important than, say, the need for education? Public education, indeed, seems to regard it as one of its tasks to instil a taste for literature in the young and even employs producers of literature for that purpose. Is this want-creation by the producer reprehensible? Or does the fact that some of the pupils may possess a taste for poetry only because of the efforts of their teachers prove that since "it does not arise in

[5] [The term 'acquired tastes' is Hayek's, appearing in neither Galbraith's book nor Keynes's essay.—Ed.]

[6] [The first two quotations in this paragraph, which were not referenced by Hayek in his original article, come from pp. 120 and 121 of *The Affluent Society*. The expression "original with myself" was not used by Galbraith and is presumably a modification, made by Hayek to serve his own stylistic purposes, of the phrase "original with himself" that can be found on p. 119 of Galbraith's book.—Ed.]

spontaneous consumer need and the demand would not exist were it not contrived, its utility or urgency, ex contrivance, is zero"?[7]

The appearance that the conclusions follow from the admitted facts is produced by an obscurity of the wording of the argument with respect to which it is difficult to know whether the author is himself the victim of a confusion or whether he skilfully uses ambiguous terms to make his conclusion appear plausible. The obscurity concerns the implied assertion that the wants of the consumers are determined by the producers. Professor Galbraith avoids in this connection any terms as crude and definite as 'determine'. The expressions he employs, such as that wants are "dependent on" or the "fruits of" production, or that "production creates the wants", do, of course, suggest determination but avoid saying so in plain terms.[8] After what has already been said it is of course obvious that the knowledge of what is being produced is one of the many factors on which it depends what people will want. It would scarcely be an exaggeration to say that contemporary man, in all fields where he has not yet formed firm habits, tends to find out what he wants by looking at what his neighbours do and at various displays of goods (physical or in catalogues or advertisements) and then choosing what he likes best.[9]

In this sense the tastes of man, as is also true of his opinions and beliefs and indeed much of his personality, are shaped in great measure by his cultural environment. But though in some contexts it would perhaps be legitimate to express this by a phrase like "production creates the wants", the circumstances mentioned would clearly not justify the contention that particular producers can deliberately determine the wants of particular consumers. The efforts of all producers will certainly be directed towards that end; but how far any individual producer will succeed will depend not only on what he does but also

[7] [Hayek has again modified Galbraith's words, running together parts of separate sentences. Commenting on the way that tastes are formed as society becomes wealthier, Galbraith actually writes: "[O]ur concern for goods . . . does not arise in spontaneous consumer need. Rather, the dependence effect means that it grows out of the process of production itself. If production is to increase, the wants must be effectively contrived. In the absence of the contrivance the increase would not occur. This is not true of all goods, but that it is true of a substantial part is sufficient. It means that since the demand for this part would not exist, were it not contrived, its utility or urgency, ex contrivance, is zero. Clearly the attitudes and values which make production the central achievement of our society have some exceptionally twisted roots". See *The Affluent Society*, p. 125.—Ed.]

[8] [For these expressions, see *The Affluent Society*, pp. 122, 124 and, in the final case, pp. 119 and 120, respectively.—Ed.]

[9] [Hayek explores the kinds of issues raised here, such as the role of advertising and imitation in the formation of consumer tastes, in more detail in F. A. Hayek, "The Meaning of Competition" [1948], reprinted as chapter 4 of F. A. Hayek, *The Market and Other Orders*, ed. Bruce Caldwell, vol. 15 (2014) of *The Collected Works of F. A. Hayek*, pp. 105–08, and in F. A. Hayek, *The Constitution of Liberty*, ed. Ronald Hamowy, vol. 17 (2011) of *The Collected Works of F. A. Hayek*, pp. 96–98.—Ed.]

on what the others do and on a great many other influences operating upon the consumers. The joint but unco-ordinated efforts of the producers merely create one element of the environment by which the wants of the consumers are shaped. It is because each individual producer thinks that the consumers can be persuaded to like his products that he endeavours to influence them. But though this effort is part of the influences which shape consumers' tastes, no producer can in any real sense 'determine' them. This, however, is clearly implied in such statements as that wants are "both passively and deliberately the fruits of the process by which they are satisfied" (p. 124). If the producer could in fact deliberately determine what the consumers will want, Professor Galbraith's conclusions would have some validity. But though this is skilfully suggested, it is nowhere made credible, and could hardly be made credible because it is not true. Though the range of choice open to the consumers is the joint result of, among other things, the efforts of all producers who vie with each other to make their respective products appear more attractive than those of their competitors, every particular consumer still has the choice between all those different offers.

A fuller examination of this process would, of course, have to consider how, after the efforts of some producers have actually swayed some consumers, it becomes the example of the various consumers thus persuaded which will influence the remaining consumers. This can be mentioned here only to emphasise that even if each consumer were exposed to pressure of only one producer, the harmful effects which are apprehended from this would soon be offset by the much more influential example of his fellows. It is of course fashionable to treat this influence of the example of others (or, what comes to the same thing, the learning from the experience made by others) as if it amounted all to an attempt at keeping up with the Joneses and for that reason was to be regarded as detrimental. It seems to me that not only is the importance of this factor usually greatly exaggerated, but also that it is not really relevant to Professor Galbraith's main thesis. But it might be worthwhile briefly to ask what it would really prove if some expenditure were actually determined solely by the desire to keep up with the Joneses. At least in Europe we used to be familiar with a type of person who often denied himself even enough food in order to maintain an appearance of respectability or gentility in dress and style of life. We may regard this as a misguided effort, but surely it would not prove that the income of such persons was larger than they knew how to use wisely. That the appearance of success, or wealth, may to some people seem more important than many other needs, does in no way prove that the needs they sacrifice to the former are unimportant. In the same way, even though people are often persuaded to spend unwisely, this surely is no evidence that they do not still have important unsatisfied needs.

Professor Galbraith's attempt to give an apparent scientific proof of the contention that the need for the production of more commodities has greatly decreased seems to me to have broken down completely. With it goes the claim to have produced a valid argument which justifies the use of coercion to make people employ their income for those purposes of which he approves. It is not to be denied that there is some originality in this latest version of the old socialist argument. For over a hundred years we have been exhorted to embrace socialism because it would give us more goods. Since it has so lamentably failed to achieve this where it has been tried, we are now urged to adopt it because more goods after all are not important. The aim is still progressively to increase the share of the resources whose use is determined by political authority and the coercion of any dissenting minority. It is not surprising, therefore, that Professor Galbraith's thesis has been most enthusiastically received by the intellectuals of the British Labour Party, among whom his influence bids fair to displace that of the late Lord Keynes.[10] It is more curious that in this country it is not recognised as an outright socialist argument and often seems to appeal to people on the opposite end of the political spectrum. But this is probably only another instance of the familiar fact that on these matters the extremes frequently meet.

[10] [Hayek's intuitions about Galbraith's influence appear to have been sound. A survey conducted in 1962 revealed that Galbraith was one of three authors mentioned by at least 40 per cent of Labour Members of Parliament when asked who was a major influence on their thinking. See K. Alexander and A. Hobbs, "What Influences Labour MPs?", *New Society*, December 13, 1962, pp. 11–14. To take a prominent example, in a pamphlet whose title was explicitly drawn from Galbraith's book, Labour politician and diarist Richard Crossman (1906–74) described *The Affluent Society* as "the most iconoclastic study of political economy since Keynes's *General Theory of Employment, Interest and Money*". See R. Crossman, *Labour in the Affluent Society*, Fabian Tract 325 (London: The Fabian Society, 1960), p. 1. In a similar vein, socialist theorist and Labour politician John Strachey (1901–63) wrote of Galbraith's book that "twenty years after its publication, *The Affluent Society* will be exercising an influence comparable, though of a very different kind, to that exercised by *The General Theory* today". See p. 80 of J. Strachey, "Unconventional Wisdom", *Encounter*, vol. 11, October 1958, pp. 73–80. For an interesting analysis of Galbraith's influence on the Labour Party, on which this brief summary draws, see N. Thompson, "Socialist Political Economy in an Age of Affluence: The Reception of J. K. Galbraith by the British Social-democratic Left in the 1950s and 1960s", *Twentieth Century British History*, vol. 21, 2010, pp. 50–79.—Ed.]

NINETEEN

WHAT IS 'SOCIAL'? WHAT DOES IT MEAN?[1]

Except in the fields of philology and logic, there are probably few cases in which one would be justified in devoting a whole article to the meaning of a single word. Sometimes, however, such a little word not only throws light upon the process of the evolution of ideas and the story of human error, but often also exercises an irrational power which becomes apparent only when, by analysis, we lay bare its true meaning. I doubt whether there exists a better example of the little understood influence that may be exercised by a single word than that afforded by the role which for a hundred years the word 'social' has played in the whole sphere of political problems—and is still playing. We are so familiar with it, we accept it so much as a matter of course, that we are hardly conscious of any problem regarding its meaning. We have accepted it for so long as the natural description of good behaviour and sincere thinking, that it seems almost sacrilege even to ask what this word really means which so many men consider as the guiding star of their moral aspirations. Indeed, I rather suspect that the majority of my readers, though they may not be quite sure what 'social' means, nevertheless have little doubt that it does indicate an ideal by which all good men should regulate their conduct, and that they will hope that I shall now tell them exactly what it does mean. Let me say at once that in this respect I shall disappoint them; for the primary conclusion to which a meticulous scrutiny of the word and its meaning has led me is that even so exceptionally potent a word as this can be incredibly empty of meaning and offer us no answer to our question.

---

[1] First published in German in *Masse und Demokratie* (ed. A. Hunold), Zurich, 1957 and then in an unauthorised translation in *Freedom and Serfdom* (ed. A. Hunold), Dordrecht, 1961. The present reprint is a revised version of that translation which in parts gravely misrepresented the meaning of the original. [The version of the essay found here is taken from F. A. Hayek, "What Is 'Social'? What Does It Mean?", published as chapter 17 of F. A. Hayek, *Studies in Philosophy, Politics and Economics* (London: Routledge & Kegan Paul, 1967). The earlier versions to which Hayek refers are F. A. Hayek, "Was ist und was heisst 'sozial'?", in *Masse und Demokratie*, ed. A. Hunold (Erlenbach-Zürich and Stuttgart: Eugen Rentsch, 1957), and F. A. Hayek, "What Is 'Social' – What Does It Mean?", in *Freedom and Serfdom: An Anthology of Western Thought*, ed. A. Hunold (Dordrecht: D. Reidel Publishing Company, 1961).—Ed.]

Generally speaking, I am no friend of the new sport of semantics which derives particular satisfaction from dissecting the meaning of words that are familiar to us all. Equally I have no desire to turn the tables and, for once, to employ against the concepts of the radical reformers the technique which has hitherto been used almost exclusively against the traditional values of the free world. Nevertheless, I see in the ambiguity of the word and the slovenly manner in which it is normally used a very real danger to any clear thinking, to any possibility of reasoned discussion with regard to a great number of our most serious problems. It is, I admit, no pleasant task to have to brush aside the roseate veil in which such a 'good' word has been able to envelop all our discussions on problems of internal policy; but it is a very important task, and one that must be undertaken. The fact that for three or four generations it has been regarded almost as the hall-mark of good men that they make constant use of it, must not be allowed to disguise the other fact that very soon avoidance of its use will inevitably come to be regarded as the hall-mark of clear thinking.

Perhaps it would be as well if, at this juncture, I explained how it came about that, as far as I myself am concerned, a certain *malaise* regarding the use of the word 'social' was transformed into open hostility that caused me to regard it as a real danger. It was the fact that not only did many of my friends in Germany deem it appropriate and desirable to qualify the term 'free market economy' by calling it 'social market economy', but that even the constitution of the Federal German Republic, instead of adhering to the clear and traditional conception of a *Rechtsstaat*, used the new and ambiguous phrase 'a social *Rechtsstaat*'. I doubt very much whether anyone could really explain what the addition of this adjectival frill is supposed to denote. But in any case, it gave me a great deal to think about, and the second of the two instances I have quoted will furnish lawyers in the future with plenty of hard nuts to crack.[2]

---

[2] [The term 'social market economy' (*soziale Marktwirtschaft*) is often used to describe a distinctive form of capitalism, developed in Germany after the Second World War, that sought to combine free-market competition under the rule of law, sustained if necessary by state intervention to curb excessive concentrations of economic power, with the use of social policy to ameliorate problems of poverty and inequality and thereby to ensure the long-term political viability of the market order. Accordingly, the expression *sozialer Rechtsstaat* or 'social rule of law' was employed in 1949 in the constitution of the Federal Republic of Germany. The "friends" to whom Hayek refers, in whose work the notion of the 'social market economy' has its origins, seem likely to have included the following: legal scholar Franz Böhm (1895–1977); economist Walter Eucken (1891–1950); economist Leonhard Miksch (1901–50); economist and politician Alfred Müller-Armack (1901–78), who in 1946 was the first person to use in print the phrase 'social market economy'; economist Wilhelm Röpke (1899–1966); and sociologist and economist Alexander Rüstow (1885–1963), who in 1938 coined the term 'neo-liberalism' to describe the work of this

Be that as it may, the final conclusion emerging from my deliberations has been that the word 'social' has become an adjective which robs of its clear meaning every phrase it qualifies and transforms it into a phrase of unlimited elasticity, the implications of which can always be distorted if they are unacceptable, and the use of which, as a general rule, serves merely to conceal the lack of real agreement between men regarding a formula upon which, in appearance, they are supposed to be agreed. To a large extent it seems to me that it is to the result of this attempt to dress up political slogans in a guise acceptable to all tastes that phrases like 'social market economy' and the like owe their existence. When we all use a word which always confuses and never clarifies the issue, which pretends to give an answer where no answer exists and, even worse, which is so often used as camouflage for aspirations that certainly have nothing to do with the common interest, then the time has obviously come for a radical operation which will free us from the confusing influence of this magical incantation.

Nothing brings more clearly to light the role played in our thinking by our interpretation of the meaning of 'social' than the significant fact that in the course of the last few decades the word has, in all languages known to me, to an ever increasing degree taken the place of the word 'moral' or simply 'good'. An interesting light is thrown on the whole issue if we ask ourselves what, exactly, does it mean when we speak of 'social' feeling or conduct, where our grandparents or great-grandparents would simply have said that a man was a good man or that his conduct was ethical? Once upon a time a man was good if he obeyed the ethical rules, or was a good citizen when he acted faithfully according to the laws of his country. What, then, was implied in this new demand, which the freshly awakened 'social conscience' made of

---

group of ordo-liberal thinkers. There was significant variety in the policies advocated by the members of this group, with Müller-Armack being most committed to intervention designed to increase equality. See N. Goldschmidt and M. Wohlgemuth, "Social Market Economy: Origins, Meanings and Interpretations", *Constitutional Political Economy*, vol. 19, pp. 261–76, especially pp. 269–73. Selections of their writings can be found in *Standard Texts on the Social Market Economy*, ed. H. Wünsche (Stuttgart and New York: Gustav Fischer, 1982), and in *Germany's Social Market Economy: Origins and Evolution*, ed. A. Peacock and H. Willgerodt (London: Macmillan for the Trade Policy Research Centre, 1989). Hayek's reminiscences of many of these figures can be found in F. A. Hayek, "The Rediscovery of Freedom: Personal Recollections" [1983], published as the "Prologue" to part II of F. A. Hayek, *The Fortunes of Liberalism: Essays on Austrian Economics and the Ideal of Freedom*, ed. Peter G. Klein, vol. 4 (1992) of *The Collected Works of F. A. Hayek* (Chicago: University of Chicago Press; London: Routledge). For more on Hayek's views on the term 'social', see F. A. Hayek, *The Constitution of Liberty*, ed. Ronald Hamowy, vol. 17 (2011) of *The Collected Works of F. A. Hayek*, pp. 127–28; F. A. Hayek, *The Mirage of Social Justice*, vol. 2 (1976) of *Law, Legislation and Liberty* (Chicago: University of Chicago Press; London: Routledge, 1973–79), pp. 78–80; and F. A. Hayek, *The Fatal Conceit: The Errors of Socialism*, ed. W. W. Bartley III, vol. 1 (1988) of *The Collected Works of F. A. Hayek*, pp. 114–17.—Ed.]

us and which has led to a distinction being drawn between 'mere' morality and a 'social' sense?

Primarily, it was doubtless a praiseworthy appeal that we should carry our thinking further than we had been in the habit of doing, that in our actions and our attitude we should take into consideration the situation and the problems of *all* the members of our society. In order, however, fully to understand what was meant by this, we must go back to the situation as it was when the 'social question' first became the subject of public discussion.[3] This, in the middle of the last century, was, roughly speaking, a situation in which both political discussion and the taking of political decisions were confined to a small upper class; and there were good grounds for reminding this upper class that they were responsible for the fate of "the most numerous and poorest" sections of the community, who themselves had little or no part in the government of the country. It was at that time—when the civilized world had discovered that there existed an 'underworld', which it felt itself called upon to 'raise', if it were not to be engulfed by it, and before the era of modern democracy and universal suffrage—that 'social' came to assume the meaning of the taking care of those who were incapable of grasping where their own interests lay—a concept which seems somewhat of an anachronism in an age when it is the masses who wield political power.[4]

---

[3] [The term 'the social question' (*die soziale Frage*) refers to the challenge posed by the problems of poverty, inequality, and social unrest that accompanied the rise of modern industrial society in mid-nineteenth-century Germany. One response to the social question was the creation in the 1880s by Prussian Prime Minister Otto von Bismarck (1815–98) of the world's first modern social security system, involving the provision of sickness, accident, and old-age insurance with a view to alleviating the problems just mentioned and thereby improving social cohesion. A reformulated version of 'the social question' arose after World War Two, centring on the question of how to avoid the subservience of the individual to the power of interest groups and the ruling elite. A response can be found in the efforts of the ordo-liberals to establish in Germany after World War Two a social market economy characterised by a strong state that would create and enforce rules that safeguarded individual freedom against the power of interest groups while simultaneously promoting social integration through the use of social policy, thereby securing the future of the market system. See, for example, W. Eucken, "The Social Question" [1948], reprinted in *Standard Texts on the Social Market Economy*, pp. 267–76. For useful overviews, see R. Sally, "Ordoliberalism and the Social Market: Classical Political Economy from Germany", *New Political Economy*, vol. 1, 1996, pp. 233–57, and R. Ptak, "Neoliberalism in Germany: Revisiting the Ordoliberal Foundations of the Social Market Economy", in *The Road from Mont Pèlerin: The Making of the Neoliberal Thought Collective*, ed. P. Mirowski and D. Plehwe (Cambridge: Harvard University Press, 2009).—Ed.]

[4] [The expression "most numerous and poorest" is normally attributed to French social reformer Claude Henri de Rouvroy, Comte de Saint-Simon (1760–1825). See *Oeuvres de Saint-Simon et d'Enfantin*, 2nd edn., vol. 1 (Paris, 1865), pp. vii, 114. The original French reads as follows: "Toutes les institutions sociales doivent avoir pour but l'amélioration du sort moral, intellectuel et physique de la classe la plus nombreuse et la plus pauvre". The phrase also appeared as part of the motto of *L'Organisateur* (Paris, 1829–31), a weekly journal in which the views of

Side by side with this challenge to deal with problems of whose existence many had until then been unaware, there was, however, another, though kindred, school of thought, which drew a distinction between the necessity for 'social' thinking and conduct and the demands of the traditionally accepted ethical standards. The rules of the latter referred to the concrete and recognised situation in which a man found himself, and prescribed the things he should in bounden duty do or refrain from doing, regardless of the consequences. (A man, for example, did not lie or cheat, even though it might be to his or someone else's advantage that he should do so.) But the demand for 'social' thinking contained also the demand that we should consciously take into consideration even the very remote consequences of our actions and should order our conduct accordingly.

In this respect the demand for social conduct differed fundamentally from the traditionally accepted tenets of morality and justice, which, on principle, expect a man to give due consideration only to those consequences of his actions which in normal circumstances would be readily apparent to him; from this it easily followed that a man came to regard it as desirable that he should be instructed as to what he should or could do in any given case by someone endowed with greater knowledge and judgment than himself. This whole conception of social conduct is most closely linked, therefore, with a desire for a comprehensive blueprint of the social scene as a whole and a code of social conduct based upon it in accordance with a uniform and orderly plan. Implicit in this conception is also the desire to see all individual activity directed towards defined 'social' aims and tasks and subordinated to the interests of the 'community'. These tasks and aims may or may not be recognisable to the individual, but they will not, in any case, be achieved if the individual, even though his actions may consistently be governed by the traditional rules of conduct and justice, devotes his activities solely to the promotion of his own aspirations.

As long as forty years ago, the Cologne sociologist, Leopold von Wiese, drew attention to this somewhat peculiar interpretation of the social idea. In an essay published in January 1917[5] he remarked: "Only those who were

---

Saint-Simon's followers were published, appearing immediately below the title of that publication. An English translation is as follows: "All social institutions must aim at the amelioration of the moral, physical and intellectual condition of the most numerous and poorest class". In his account of 'scientism' and the 'abuse of reason', Hayek described Saint-Simon as a "megalomanic visionary". See F. A. Hayek, *Studies on the Abuse and Decline of Reason: Text and Documents*, ed. Bruce Caldwell, vol. 13 (2010) of *The Collected Works of F. A. Hayek*, p. 193. The editor of the current volume was unable to find references for Hayek's use of the terms 'underworld' and 'raise'.—Ed.]

[5] *Der Liberalismus in Vergangenheit und Zukunft*, Berlin, 1917, p. 115. [The complete reference is L. von Wiese, *Der Liberalismus in Vergangenheit und Zukunft* (Berlin: S. Fischer, 1917), p. 115. The original German reads as follows: "Man muss 'das soziale Zeitalter', die letzten Jahrzehnte vor

young men in the 'social age'—the decades immediately before the war—can appreciate how strong was the inclination to regard the social sphere as a substitute for the religious. In those days there existed a dramatic manifestation— the social pastors. Even the philosophers fell under their spell. One particularly loquacious gentleman wrote a voluminous book, entitled *The Social Question in the Light of Philosophy* . . . In the meanwhile, throughout Europe, and particularly in Germany, social work had been crowned with a halo. Rationally assessed, the relative value of all social policies and charitable activities is very considerable; but their limitations must be very clearly recognised. To be 'social' is not the same as being good or 'righteous in the eyes of the Lord'".

That this use of the word 'social' instead of simply saying 'moral' constitutes a complete change, indeed, almost a complete reversal, of its original meaning becomes apparent only when we go back some two hundred years to the era in which the concept of society was first discovered—or at any rate first became the subject of scientific discussion—and ask ourselves what, exactly, it was supposed to denote. It was, of course, introduced to describe that order of human relationships which had developed spontaneously, as distinct from the deliberate organisation of the State. We still use the word in its original sense when we talk about 'social forces' or 'social structures', such as language and customs, or rights that have gradually come to be recognised in contrast to rights that have been deliberately granted; and the object thereof was to show that these things were not the creations of an individual will, but the unforeseen results of the haphazard activities of countless individuals and generations. The truly social in this sense is, of its very nature, anonymous, non-rational and not the result of logical reasoning, but the outcome of a supra-individual process of evolution and selection, to which the individual, admittedly, makes his contribution, but the component parts of which cannot be mastered by any one single intelligence.

---

dem Kriege als junger Mensch erlebt haben, um zu wissen, wie stark die Neigung war, die soziale Sphäre zu einem Ersatze der religiösen zu machen. Es gab in dieser Zeit ein dramatisches Kapitel: die sozialen Pastoren. Auch die Philosophen verfielen dem Banne. Ein besonders redseliger unter ihnen schrieb ein dickes Buch: Die soziale Frage im Lichte der Philosophie . . . Indessen umgab man im modernen Europa, besonders in Deutschland, die 'soziale Arbeit' mit einem Strahlenkranze. Richtig eingeschätzt, wird der relative Wert aller Sozialpolitik und Wohlfahrtspflege gross genug erscheinen; jedoch sollte man seine Grenze klarer erkennen. Sozial zu sein ist nicht dasselbe wie gut oder vor Gott gerecht zu sein." Leopold von Wiese (1876–1969) was a German liberal sociologist and economist who believed that the aim of sociology is the study of the universal forms of social phenomena and who examined the links between various interpretations of 'the social question' and the development of social policy. In addition to recognising Wiese's historical analysis of the use and influence of the term 'social', Hayek also credited him with an early recognition of the fact that competition is a process of discovery. See Hayek, *The Mirage of Social Justice*, p. 180 n. 22; Hayek, *The Fatal Conceit*, p. 114; and F. A. Hayek, *The Political Order of a Free People*, vol. 3 (1979) of *Law, Legislation and Liberty*, pp. 68, 189 n. 2.—Ed.]

It came to be realised that there existed forces working quite independently of the aspirations of mankind, and that the combination of their activities gave birth to structures which furthered the endeavours of the individual, even though they had not been designed for the purpose; and it was this realisation that led to the introduction of the concept of society, as distinct from the deliberately created and directed State.

How quickly the meaning of the word has changed until it has been transformed almost into the very opposite of its original meaning, becomes clear when we consider what it denotes in the very frequently used phrase, 'the social order'. This phrase *can*, of course, be used exclusively in the sense of something created spontaneously *by* society itself. Mostly, however, the word 'social' in this connection denotes nothing more than something or other *connected with* the community, if not, indeed, primarily the only sort of order which so many people are capable of envisaging, namely, a social structure which has been forcibly imposed, as it were, on the community from without. How few there are today who understand Ortega y Gasset's dictum that "order is not a pressure imposed upon society from without, but an equilibrium which is set up from within".[6]

If we are content to designate as social not only those co-ordinating forces which come into being as the result of the independent activities of the individual in the community, but also everything else which has in any way anything to do with the community, then the whole essential difference becomes completely obliterated. There then remains little or nothing in life which is not 'social' in one sense or another, and the word becomes, to all practical intents, meaningless. It is therefore high time that these various meanings were sorted out. Let us for the moment adhere to the meaning 'peculiar to society' or 'arising out of a specifically social process'—the sense in which we use it when speaking of social structures and social forces. This is a sense in which we have urgent need of the word, and the true sense, which I should like to see reserved for it. It is obviously quite different from the sense in which we use it in such phrases as 'social awareness', 'social conscience', 'social responsibility', 'social activities', 'social welfare', 'social policy', 'social legislation' or 'social justice', or from the other sense implicit in the terms 'social insurance', 'social rights' or 'social control'. One of the most astonishing, albeit most familiar, combinations of this kind is 'social democracy'—I should very much like to know what aims of a democracy can be said to be not social, and why! That, however, is by the way.

[6] [José Ortega y Gasset (1883–1955) was a Spanish liberal philosopher, social theorist, essayist, and editor. The quotation is taken from José Ortega y Gasset, *Mirabeau o El político* (1927), in *Obras completas* (Madrid: Revista de Occidente, 1947), vol. 3, p. 603: "Orden no es una presión que desde fuera se ejerce sobre la sociedad, sino un equilibrio que se suscita en su interior".—Ed.]

The really important point is, that all these combinations have but little to do with the specific character of social forces, and that, in particular, the difference between that which has developed spontaneously and that which has been deliberately organised by the State has completely disappeared. In so far as 'social' is not taken to mean merely 'communal', the word, obviously, should mean either 'in the interest of society' or 'in accordance with the will of society', i.e., of the majority, or sometimes perhaps 'an obligation on society' as such, *vis-à-vis* the relatively less fortunate minority. I do not propose here to discuss the question why the rather indefinite word 'society' should be preferred to such precise and concrete terms as 'the people', 'the nation' or 'the citizens of a State', although it is these latter that are meant. The important thing, to me, is that in all these uses the word 'social' *presupposes* the existence of known and common aims behind the activities of a community, *but does not define them*. It is simply assumed that 'society' has certain concrete tasks that are known to all and are acknowledged by all, and that 'society' should direct the endeavours of its individual members to the accomplishment of these tasks. 'Society' thus assumes a dual personality: it is firstly a thinking, collective entity with aspirations of its own that are different from those of the individuals of whom it is composed; and secondly, by identifying it with them, it becomes the personification of the views held on these social aspirations by certain individuals who claim to be endowed with a more profound insight or to possess a stronger sense of moral values. Frequently enough a speaker will claim that his own views and aspirations are 'social', while those of his opponent are brushed aside as 'anti-social'. There is, I think, no need for me further to emphasise that, when 'social' is used in the sense of 'serving the interests of society', it certainly raises a problem, but provides no solution. It concedes precedence to certain values to which society should adhere, but it does not describe them. Were the word strictly used in this sense, there would, I think, be but little objection. In point of fact, however, not only does it compete in many ways with existing ethical values, but it has also undermined their prestige and influence. Indeed, I am coming more and more to the belief that the substitution of this rubber word, 'social', to denote values we have always described as 'moral', may well be one of the main causes of the general degeneration of moral sense in the world.

The first great difference, at which I have already hinted, stems from the fact that the tenets of ethical behaviour consist of abstract, general rules which we are called upon to obey, regardless of what the consequences may be and very often without our even knowing why it is desirable that we should act in one particular way and in no other. These rules have never been invented, and no one, so far, has ever succeeded in producing a rational foundation of the whole of the existing system of ethical behaviour. As I see them, these rules are genuine social growths, the results of a process of evolution and selection, the distilled essence of experiences of which we ourselves have no knowledge. They have acquired general authority because the groups in which they held sway have proved themselves to be more effective than other groups. Their claim to be observed is not based upon the fact that the individual is aware of the consequences of disregarding them, but they exemplify a recognition of the fundamental fact that the majority of these concrete consequences are beyond our ken and that our actions will not lead to constant conflict with our fellow men only when they are guided by rules which pay due regard to the circumstances under which we commit them. But it is against the very nature of *all* these rules of ethical behaviour and justice that this bogus rationalism to which the concept of 'social interest' owes its origin, transgresses. Rationalism refuses to be guided by anything it does not completely understand; it reserves to itself the right to decide what is desirable in each individual case, because it claims to be fully aware of all possible consequences; it refuses to obey any rules, but insists on pursuing definite, concrete aims. But by so doing, it transgresses against every fundamental principle of ethical behaviour, for agreement regarding the importance of any aspiration is only possible if it is reached in unison and in accordance with accepted general rules which themselves are impervious to rationalisation. Thus, by undermining respect for rules and 'plain' ethical behaviour, this demand for 'social behaviour' is destroying the foundations on which it is itself built.

This dependence of the conception of what is 'social' on ethical rules which are not explicitly stated or simply disregarded is shown most clearly by the fact that it leads to an extension of the concept of justice to fields to which it is not applicable.[7] The demand for a just or more equal distribution of the world's goods has today become one of the primary 'social' demands. The application of the concept of justice to distribution requires, however, reward according to merit or desert, and merit cannot be measured by achievement but only by the extent to which known rules of ethics have been observed. Reward according to merit thus presupposes that we know all the circumstances which led to a particular performance. But in a free society we allow the individual to decide himself about his actions because we do not know those very circumstances which determine how meritorious his achievement is. It is therefore necessary in a free society to reward the individuals according to the value of the services actually rendered to their fellows, a value which

---

[7] The extent to which the misuse of the word 'social' has been pushed in this connection seems at last to have provoked protests in other quarters; and it was with great satisfaction that, shortly after delivering this lecture, I read in a book review by Charles Curran in *The Spectator* of July 6, 1956 (p. 8) the sentence: "Social Justice is a semantic fraud from the same stable as People's Democracy". [See p. 8 of C. Curran, "Political Commentary", *The Spectator*, July 6, 1956, pp. 7–8. Curran was reviewing The Socialist Union, *Twentieth Century Socialism: The Economy of Tomorrow* (London: Penguin, 1956).—Ed.]

has often little relation to the subjective merit they have earned in rendering them. The concept of justice has application only in so far as all will be equally rewarded according to the value of the objective results of their efforts and not according to someone's judgment of the merit they have thereby acquired. The demand for the latter, for a reward according to merit, is a demand which cannot be met in a free society, because we cannot know or isolate all the circumstances which determine merit. The attempt at a partial application of the principle of reward according to merit can, however, lead only to general injustice, because it would mean that different people were rewarded according to different principles. Such abuse of the concept of justice must ultimately lead to a destruction of the sense of justice.

In reality, things in this connection are even worse. Since in questions of distribution there exists no yardstick of justice, other and less noble feelings inevitably and unexpectedly insinuate themselves when decisions come to be taken. That the social concept in this context is only too frequently used as a cloak for envy, that a sentiment which John Stuart Mill has rightly described as the most anti-social of all passions,[8] should be able to make its appearance, decked in the beautifying form of an ethical demand, is one of the worst consequences for which we have to thank the unthinking use of the word 'social'.

The third point in which the predominance of the idea of the 'social' has had an anti-ethical effect is the destruction of the feeling of personal responsibility to which it has led. Originally, the appeal to the social sense was expected to lead to a more widely spread acceptance of personal responsibility. But the confusion that arose between the further aims to which the individual man should aspire, between the taking-into-consideration of social repercussions and social—in the sense of collective—behaviour, and between the moral obligations of the individual to the community and his claims upon it, has gradually undermined that sense of personal responsibility which is the foundation of all ethics. To this, all kinds of intellectual movements have made their contributions, into which I cannot go in any detail, but which, like 'social psychology', in most cases sail under the 'social' flag. Indeed, there seems to me to be very little doubt that this whole process which has thoroughly confused the issue as regards personal responsibility, absolving the individual on the one hand of all responsibility as regards his immediate environment and, on the other hand, placing upon him vague and undefined responsibilities for things that are not clearly apparent, has, by and large, led to a marked diminution of man's sense of personal responsibility. Without placing upon the individual any new and clear obligations which he has to fulfil by his own per-

---

[8] John Stuart Mill, *On Liberty*, 1859 (p. 10). [Mill refers to "that most anti-social and odious of all passions, envy" on p. 140 of *On Liberty*, 2nd edn. (London: John Parker and Son, 1859). For more on Hayek's views on envy, see Hayek, *The Constitution of Liberty*, pp. 154–56.—Ed.]

sonal endeavours, it has expunged the boundaries of all responsibility and has become a standing invitation to make further demands or to do good at the expense of others.

Fourthly, with their emphasis on concrete aims and on the claims of expediency, these 'social movements' have hindered more than they have promoted the very essential emergence of genuine principles of political ethics. All ethics and justice are based, surely, on the application of general, abstract principles to concrete cases; and the dictum that the end justifies the means has for a long time been justly regarded as a negation of all that is ethical. It is, however, just this that is, in fact, very often meant by the plea, so frequently heard nowadays, that due consideration must be given to 'the social aspect'. As regards the genuine products of social evolution, such as justice and ethics, it is claimed on behalf of the social will of the moment that it is justified in neglecting those principles in favour of its own immediate aims.

I have, unfortunately, insufficient space to go in any detail into the reasons why the rules of political ethics, like all other rules of ethics, are, of their nature, long-term principles, and for that reason must not be judged on the evidence of their effect upon an individual case. More important from our point of view is the fact that it is only as the result of a long and unfettered process of evolution that these rules are able to come into being and to acquire authority. Only when adherence to a principle comes, as a matter of course, to be regarded as more important than success in any individual case, and only when we acknowledge that the use of compulsion is justifiable solely when it is applied in accordance with general principles, and never when it is used as an expedient in the pursuit of a concrete aim, can we hope that a general principle of political ethics will gradually come to be accepted by all. Any 'social' code of ethics must be based upon rules which are binding on the collective behaviour of society, and to me it seems that we are further from a recognition of this fact today than we were in the past.

For there certainly *was* a time when a conscious sense of what was just and right imposed ethical limits on the use of compulsion by society for its own ends. The ideal of the freedom of the individual was one, and, indeed, the most important, of these ethical rules of political behaviour which, at one time, enjoyed universal recognition. But it is just this ideal that those who march under the 'social' standard have been attacking with ever increasing vehemence. The ideals of freedom and independence, of being answerable to one's own conscience and of respect for the individual, have all gone by the board under the dominant pressure of the conception of the 'social'. But in reality, it is the nurturing of the spontaneous forces of freedom that truly constitutes a service to society—to that which has grown, as distinct from that which has been deliberately created—and to the further strengthening of the creative forces of the social process. What we have experienced under the banner of the social concept has been a metamorphosis from service *to* society to a demand for an absolute control *of* society, from a demand for the subordination of the State to the free forces of society to a demand for the subordination of society to the State. If the human intellect is allowed to impose a preconceived pattern on society, if our powers of reasoning are allowed to lay claim to a monopoly of creative effort (and hence to recognition only of premeditated results), then we must not be surprised if society, as such, ceases to function as a creative force. And in particular we must not be surprised if, from a policy based upon the ideal of material equality, there emerges a mass society, admittedly more thoroughly organised, but devoid of any spontaneous articulation. True service to the social concept is not rendered by the imposition of absolute authority or leadership, nor does it even consist of common endeavour towards a common aim, but rather of the contribution that each and every one of us makes to a process which is greater than any one of us, from which there constantly emerges something new, something unforeseen, and which can flourish only in freedom. In the last resort we find ourselves constrained to repudiate the ideal of the social concept because it has become the ideal of those who, on principle, deny the existence of a true society and whose longing is for the artificially constructed and the rationally controlled. In this context, it seems to me that a great deal of what today professes to be social is, in the deeper and truer sense of the word, thoroughly and completely anti-social.

TWENTY

THE MORAL ELEMENT IN
FREE ENTERPRISE[1]

Economic activity provides the material means for all our ends. At the same time, most of our individual efforts are directed to providing means for the ends of others in order that they, in turn, may provide us with the means for our ends. It is only because we are free in the choice of our means that we are also free in the choice of our ends.

Economic freedom is thus an indispensable condition of all other freedom, and free enterprise both a necessary condition and a consequence of personal freedom. In discussing The Moral Element in Free Enterprise I shall therefore not confine myself to the problems of economic life but consider the general relations between freedom and morals.

By freedom in this connection I mean, in the great Anglo-Saxon tradition, independence of the arbitrary will of another. This is the classical conception of freedom under the law, a state of affairs in which a man may be coerced only where coercion is required by the general rules of law, equally applicable to all, and never by the discretionary decision of administrative authority.[2]

The relationship between this freedom and moral values is mutual and

---

[1] An address to the 66th Congress of American Industry organised by The National Association of Manufacturers, New York, December 6, 1961 and first printed with similar addresses by Felix Morley, Merrell De Graff and John Davenport under the title *The Spiritual and Moral Significance of Free Enterprise*, New York, 1962. [The essay was first published as F. A. Hayek, "The Moral Element in Free Enterprise", in *The Spiritual and Moral Significance of Free Enterprise*, ed. F. Morley (New York: National Association of Manufacturers, 1962), pp. 26–33. It was reprinted, with the same title and with several sets of italics removed, as chapter 16 of F. A. Hayek, *Studies in Philosophy, Politics and Economics* (London: Routledge & Kegan Paul, 1967), the version used here. The other presenters were Herrell DeGraff (1908–86), Professor of Food Economics at Cornell University; journalist John Davenport (1904–87), a founder member of the Mont Pèlerin Society who at the time of the Congress was Assistant Managing Editor of *Fortune* magazine; and author, journalist and founder member of the Mont Pèlerin Society Felix Morley (1894–1982). Morley had been editor of the *Washington Post* from 1933 to 1940, winning a Pulitzer Prize for his editorials, many of which expressed his 'Old Right' criticisms of the New Deal, and was by the early 1960s writing for the *Nation's Business* magazine.—Ed.]

[2] [For a more detailed account of the concepts of 'freedom' and 'coercion', see F. A. Hayek, *The Constitution of Liberty*, ed. Ronald Hamowy, vol. 17 (2011) of *The Collected Works of F. A. Hayek* (Chicago: University of Chicago Press; London: Routledge), pp. 57–72, 199–214.—Ed.]

complex. I shall therefore have to confine myself to bringing out the salient points in something like telegram style.

It is, on the one hand, an old discovery that morals and moral values will grow only in an environment of freedom, and that, in general, moral standards of people and classes are high only where they have long enjoyed freedom—and proportional to the amount of freedom they have possessed. It is also an old insight that a free society will work well only where free action is guided by strong moral beliefs, and, therefore, that we shall enjoy all the benefits of freedom only where freedom is already well established.[3] To this I want to add that freedom, if it is to work well, requires not only strong moral standards but moral standards of a particular kind, and that it is possible in a free society for moral standards to grow up which, if they become general, will destroy freedom and with it the basis of all moral values.

Before I turn to this point which is not generally understood, I must briefly elaborate upon the two old truths which ought to be familiar but which are often forgotten. That freedom is the matrix required for the growth of moral values—indeed not merely one value among many but the source of all values—is almost self-evident. It is only where the individual has choice, and its inherent responsibility, that he has occasion to affirm existing values, to contribute to their further growth, and to earn moral merit. Obedience has moral value only where it is a matter of choice and not of coercion. It is in the order in which we rank our different ends that our moral sense manifests itself; and in applying the general rules of morals to particular situations each individual is constantly called upon to interpret and apply the general principles and in doing so to create particular values.

I have no time here for showing how this has in fact brought it about that free societies not only have generally been law-abiding societies, but also in modern times have been the source of all the great humanitarian movements aiming at active help to the weak, the ill, and the oppressed. Unfree societies,

---

[3] [In "Individualism: True and False" [1946], reprinted as the Prelude to *Studies on the Abuse and Decline of Reason: Text and Documents*, ed. Bruce Caldwell, vol. 13 (2010) of *The Collected Works of F. A. Hayek*, p. 67 n. 31, Hayek cites Irish statesman and political philosopher Edmund Burke (1729–97) as someone who recognised this "old insight". In the passage quoted by Hayek, Burke writes as follows: "Men are qualified for civil liberty, in exact proportion to their disposition to put moral chains upon their own appetites: in proportion as their love to justice is above their rapacity; in proportion as their soundness and sobriety of understanding is above their vanity and presumption; in proportion as they are more disposed to listen to the counsels of the wise and good, in preference to the flattery of knaves". See E. Burke, "A Letter to a Member of the National Assembly" [1791], in E. Burke, *Further Reflections on the Revolution in France*, ed. D. Ritchie (Indianapolis: Liberty Fund, 1992), p. 69. Elsewhere, Hayek also mentions James Madison (1751–1836), one of the Founding Fathers of the American Constitution and the fourth President of the United States, and French historian and political scientist Alexis Charles Henri Clérel de Tocqueville (1805–59), as holding similar views. See Hayek, *The Constitution of Liberty*, p. 123 n. 38.—Ed.]

on the other hand, have as regularly developed a disrespect for the law, a callous attitude to suffering, and even sympathy for the malefactor.

I must turn to the other side of the medal. It should also be obvious that the results of freedom must depend on the values which free individuals pursue. It would be impossible to assert that a free society will always and necessarily develop values of which we would approve, or even, as we shall see, that it will maintain values which are compatible with the preservation of freedom. All that we can say is that the values we hold are the product of freedom, that in particular the Christian values had to assert themselves through men who successfully resisted coercion by government, and that it is to the desire to be able to follow one's own moral convictions that we owe the modern safeguards of individual freedom. Perhaps we can add to this that only societies which hold moral values essentially similar to our own have survived as free societies, while in others freedom has perished.

All this provides strong argument why it is most important that a free society be based on strong moral convictions and why if we want to preserve freedom and morals, we should do all in our power to spread the appropriate moral convictions. But what I am mainly concerned with is the error that men must first be good before they can be granted freedom.

It is true that a free society lacking a moral foundation would be a very unpleasant society in which to live. But it would even so be better than a society which is unfree and immoral; and it at least offers the hope of a gradual emergence of moral convictions which an unfree society prevents. On this point I am afraid I strongly disagree with John Stuart Mill who maintained that until men have attained the capacity of being guided to their own improvement by conviction or persuasion, "there is nothing for them but implicit obedience to an Akbar or a Charlemagne, if they are so fortunate as to find one". Here I believe T. B. Macaulay expressed the much greater wisdom of an older tradition, when he wrote that "Many politicians of our time are in the habit of laying it down as a self-evident proposition, that no people are to be free till they are fit to use their freedom. The maxim is worthy of the fool in the old story, who resolved not to go into the water till he had learnt to swim. If men are to wait for liberty till they become wise and good, they may indeed wait forever".[4]

But I must now turn from what is merely the re-affirmation of old wisdom to more critical issues. I have said that liberty, to work well, requires not

---

[4] [The quotation from English philosopher, political economist, and social reformer John Stuart Mill (1806–73) is taken from J. S. Mill, *On Liberty*, 2nd edn. (London: John Parker and Son, 1859), p. 23. The second passage quoted by Hayek comes from the writings of English politician, essayist, and historian Thomas Babington Macaulay (1800–1859), specifically his essay on "Milton" [1825], reprinted in Thomas Babbington Macaulay, *Critical and Historical Essays, Contributed to the Edinburgh Review*, vol. 1 (London: Longman, Brown, Green, and Longmans, 1848), p. 42. The final sentence of the passage from Macaulay actually reads, "If men are to wait for liberty till they become wise and good in slavery, they may indeed wait forever".—Ed.]

merely the existence of strong moral convictions but also the acceptance of particular moral views. By this I do not mean that within limits utilitarian considerations will contribute to alter moral views on particular issues. Nor do I mean that, as Edwin Cannan expressed it, "of the two principles, Equity and Economy, Equity is ultimately the weaker . . . the judgment of mankind about what is equitable is liable to change, and . . . one of the forces which cause it to change is mankind's discovery from time to time that what was supposed to be quite just and equitable in some particular matter has become, or perhaps always was, uneconomical".[5]

This is also true and important, though it may not be a commendation to all people. I am concerned rather with some more general conceptions which seem to me an essential condition of a free society and without which it cannot survive. The two crucial ones seem to me the belief in individual responsibility and the approval as just of an arrangement by which material rewards are made to correspond to the value which a person's particular services have to his fellows; not to the esteem in which he is held as a whole person for his moral merit.

I must be brief on the first point—which I find very difficult. Modern developments here are part of the story of the destruction of moral value by scientific error which has recently been my chief concern—and what a scholar happens to be working on at the moment tends to appear to him as the most important subject in the world.[6] But I shall try to say what belongs here in a very few words.[7]

[5] [Edwin Cannan (1861–1935) was a British economist and historian of economic thought, and Professor of Political Economy at the London School of Economics from 1907 until 1926. The passage on which Hayek draws comes from E. Cannan, *The History of Local Rates in England*, 2nd edn. (London: P. S. King & Son, 1912), p. 173. For more on Cannan, see F. A. Hayek, "The Transmission of the Ideals of Economic Freedom" [1951], reprinted as chapter 2 of the current volume, p. 44, n. 3.—Ed.]

[6] [The more general "story of the destruction of moral value by scientific error" to which Hayek refers concerns how certain thinkers, termed by Hayek 'Cartesian' or 'constructivist' rationalists, rejected all those moral rules and values that were not consciously justified and adhered to for a known purpose, arguing instead that in the field of morals and values "we should only accept as binding what we could recognise as a rational design for a recognisable purpose". See F. A. Hayek, "The Errors of Constructivism" [1970], reprinted as chapter 14 of F. A. Hayek, *The Market and Other Orders*, ed. Bruce Caldwell, vol. 15 (2014) of *The Collected Works of F. A. Hayek*, p. 340. According to Hayek, such thinkers failed to recognise that complex modern societies are sustainable only because people's actions are guided by various social formations, including moral rules and values, that have developed through a process of evolutionary selection and so embody more knowledge about appropriate kinds of action than any one person can grasp. However, because the rules and values in question are the unintended consequence of human action, rather than the conscious product of human design, they are only imperfectly understood by those who behave in accordance with them. In seeking to exclude such rules and values from any rationally designed social order, Cartesian rationalists threaten to undermine the foundations of modern society. For more details, see F. A. Hayek, "The Dilemma of Specialisation" [1956], reprinted as chapter 13 of this volume, p. 195 n. 9 and the references contained therein, and p. 267 n. 8 below.—Ed.]

[7] [A fuller exposition of Hayek's views on individual responsibility, the subject of his first point, can be found in Hayek, *The Constitution of Liberty*, pp. 133–47.—Ed.]

Free societies have always been societies in which the belief in individual responsibility has been strong. They have allowed individuals to act on their knowledge and beliefs and have treated the results achieved as due to them. The aim was to make it worthwhile for people to act rationally and reasonably and to persuade them that what they would achieve depended chiefly on them. This last belief is undoubtedly not entirely correct, but it certainly had a wonderful effect in developing both initiative and circumspection.

By a curious confusion it has come to be thought that this belief in individual responsibility has been refuted by growing insight into the manner in which events generally, and human actions in particular, are determined by certain classes of causes. It is probably true that we have gained increasing understanding of the kinds of circumstances which affect human action— but no more. We can certainly not say that a particular conscious act of any man is the necessary result of particular circumstances that we can specify— leaving out his peculiar individuality built up by the whole of his history. Of our generic knowledge as to how human action can be influenced we make use in assessing praise and blame—which we do for the purpose of making people behave in a desirable fashion. It is on this limited determinism—as much as our knowledge in fact justifies—that the belief in responsibility is based, while only a belief in some metaphysical self which stands outside the chain of cause and effect could justify the contention that it is useless to hold the individual responsible for his actions.

Yet, crude as is the fallacy underlying the opposite and supposedly scientific view, it has had the most profound effect in destroying the chief device which society has developed to assure decent conduct—the pressure of opinion making people observe the rules of the game. And it has ended in that *Myth of Mental Illness* which a distinguished psychiatrist, Dr. T. S. Szasz, has recently justly castigated in a book so titled.[8] We have probably not yet dis-

---

[8] [Thomas Szasz (1920–2012) was a Hungarian-American psychiatrist and a prominent writer on the moral and scientific foundations of psychiatry. In his most famous work, *The Myth of Mental Illness: Foundations of a Theory of Personal Conduct* (New York: Hoeber-Harper, 1961), Szasz argued that there is no such thing as 'mental illness'. While physical illnesses are the result of a disease, Szasz contended, there is no such underlying cause in the case of mental problems; the term 'mental illness' is merely a metaphor, used to describe behaviour that is deemed offensive or shocking. Szasz's concern was to undermine the use of the notion of mental 'illness' to give false legitimacy to coercive psychiatry (e.g. involuntary incarceration in mental hospitals) and to the so-called 'insanity defence' for crimes (which, he believed, illegitimately absolved the guilty of responsibility for their actions). Szasz viewed people as free agents, fully responsible for their conduct, and denounced any incursions on their liberty in the name of psychiatry. As Hayek elaborates in a later work, he viewed Szasz's work as supporting his own critique of various pseudo-scientific, constructivist rationalist efforts to undermine the culturally inherited moral rules that facilitate orderly human action in advanced economies. See F. A. Hayek, *The Political Order of a Free People*, vol. 3 (1979) of *Law, Legislation and Liberty* (Chicago: University of Chicago Press; London: Routledge, 1973–1979), pp. 173–75. Also see Hayek, "The Errors of Constructivism", pp. 350–51, and n. 6 on p. 266 above.—Ed.]

covered the best way of teaching people to live according to rules which make life in society for them and their fellows not too unpleasant. But in our present state of knowledge I am sure that we shall never build up a successful free society without that pressure of praise and blame which treats the individual as responsible for his conduct and also makes him bear the consequences of even innocent error.

But if it is essential for a free society that the esteem in which a person is held by his fellows depends on how far he lives up to the demand for moral law, it is also essential that material reward should not be determined by the opinion of his fellows of his moral merits but by the value which they attach to the particular services he renders them. This brings me to my second chief point: the conception of social justice which must prevail if a free society is to be preserved. This is the point on which the defenders of a free society and the advocates of a collectivist system are chiefly divided. And on this point, while the advocates of the socialist conception of distributive justice are usually very outspoken, the upholders of freedom are unnecessarily shy about stating bluntly the implications of their ideal.

The simple facts are these: We want the individual to have liberty because only if he can decide what to do can he also use all his unique combination of information, skills and capacities which nobody else can fully appreciate. To enable the individual to fulfil his potential we must also allow him to act on his own estimates of the various chances and probabilities. Since we do not know what he knows, we cannot decide whether his decisions were justified; nor can we know whether his success or failure was due to his efforts and foresight, or to good luck. In other words, we must look at results, not intentions or motives, and can allow him to act on his own knowledge only if we also allow him to keep what his fellows are willing to pay him for his services, irrespective of whether we think this reward appropriate to the moral merit he has earned or the esteem in which we hold him as a person.

Such remuneration, in accordance with the value of a man's services, inevitably is often very different from what we think of his moral merit. This, I believe, is the chief source of the dissatisfaction with a free enterprise system and of the clamour for 'distributive justice'. It is neither honest nor effective to deny that there is such a discrepancy between the moral merit and esteem which a person may earn by his actions and, on the other hand, the value of the services for which we pay him. We place ourselves in an entirely false position if we try to gloss over this fact or to disguise it. Nor have we any need to do so.

It seems to me one of the great merits of a free society that material reward is not dependent on whether the majority of our fellows like or esteem us personally.[9] This means that, so long as we keep within the accepted rules,

[9] [Hayek draws here on arguments developed at greater length in *The Constitution of Liberty*, pp. 148–65.—Ed.]

moral pressure can be brought on us only through the esteem of those whom we ourselves respect and not through the allocation of material reward by a social authority. It is of the essence of a free society that we should be materially rewarded not for doing what others order us to do, but for giving some others what they want. Our conduct ought certainly to be guided by our desire for their esteem. But we are free because the success of our daily efforts does not depend on whether particular people like us, or our principles, or our religion, or our manners, and because we can decide whether the material reward others are prepared to pay for our services makes it worthwhile for us to render them.

We seldom know whether a brilliant idea which a man suddenly conceives, and which may greatly benefit his fellows, is the result of years of effort and preparatory investment, or whether it is a sudden inspiration induced by an accidental combination of knowledge and circumstance. But we do know that, where in a given instance it has been the former, it would not have been worthwhile to take the risk if the discoverer were not allowed to reap the benefit. And since we do not know how to distinguish one case from the other, we must also allow a man to get the gain when his good fortune is a matter of luck.

I do not wish to deny, I rather wish to emphasise, that in our society personal esteem and material success are much too closely bound together. We ought to be much more aware that if we regard a man as entitled to a high material reward that in itself does not necessarily entitle him to high esteem. And, though we are often confused on this point, it does not mean that this confusion is a necessary result of the free enterprise system—or that in general the free enterprise system is more materialistic than other social orders. Indeed, and this brings me to the last point I want to make, it seems to me in many respects considerably less so.

In fact, free enterprise has developed the only kind of society which, while it provides us with ample material means, if that is what we mainly want, still leaves the individual free to choose between material and non-material reward. The confusion of which I have been speaking—between the value which a man's services have to his fellows and the esteem he deserves for his moral merit—may well make a free enterprise society materialistic. But the way to prevent this is certainly not to place the control of all material means under a single direction, to make the distribution of material goods the chief concern of all common effort and thus to get politics and economics inextricably mixed.

It is at least possible for a free enterprise society to be in this respect a pluralistic society which knows no single order of rank but has many different principles on which esteem is based; where worldly success is neither the only evidence nor regarded as certain proof of individual merit. It may well be true that periods of a very rapid increase of wealth in which many enjoy the benefits of wealth for the first time, tend to produce for a time a predominant concern with material improvement. Until the recent European upsurge many members of the more comfortable classes there used to decry as materialistic the economically more active periods to which they owed the material comfort which had made it easy for them to devote themselves to other things.

Periods of great cultural and artistic creativity have generally followed, rather than coincided with, the periods of the most rapid increase in wealth. To my mind this shows not that a free society must be dominated by material concerns, but rather that with freedom it is the moral atmosphere in the widest sense, the values which people hold, that will determine the chief direction of their activities. Individuals as well as communities, when they feel that other things have become more important than material advance, can turn to them. It is certainly not by the endeavour to make material reward correspond to all merit, but only by frankly recognising that there are other and often more important goals than material success, that we can guard ourselves against becoming too materialistic.

Surely it is unjust to blame a system as more materialistic because it leaves it to the individual to decide whether he prefers material gain to other kinds of excellence, instead of having this decided for him. There is indeed little merit in being idealistic if the provision of the material means required for these idealistic aims is left to somebody else. It is only where a person can himself choose to make a material sacrifice for a non-material end that he deserves credit. The desire to be relieved of the choice, and of any need for personal sacrifice, certainly does not seem to me particularly idealistic.

I must say that I find the atmosphere of the advanced Welfare State in every sense more materialistic than that of a free enterprise society.[10] If the latter gives individuals much more scope to serve their fellows by the pursuit of purely materialistic aims, it also gives them the opportunity to pursue any other aim they regard as more important. One must remember, however, that the pure idealism of an aim is questionable whenever the material means necessary for its fulfilment have been created by others.

In conclusion I want for a moment to return to the point from which I started. When we defend the free enterprise system we must always remember that it deals only with means. What we make of our freedom is up to us. We must not confuse efficiency in providing means with the purposes which they serve. A society which has no other standard than efficiency will indeed waste that efficiency. If men are to be free to use their talents to provide us with the means we want, we must remunerate them in accordance with the value these means have to us. Nevertheless, we ought to esteem them only in accordance with the use they make of the means at their disposal.

---

[10] [For more on Hayek's views on the welfare state, see *The Constitution of Liberty*, pp. 373–79.—Ed.]

Let us encourage usefulness to one's fellows by all means, but let us not confuse it with the importance of the ends which men ultimately serve. It is the glory of the free enterprise system that it makes it at least possible that each individual, while serving his fellows, can do so for his own ends. But the system is itself only a means, and its infinite possibilities must be used in the service of ends which exist apart.

TWENTY-ONE

THE PRINCIPLES OF A LIBERAL
SOCIAL ORDER[1]

By 'liberalism' I shall understand here the conception of a desirable political order which in the first instance was developed in England from the time of the Old Whigs in the later part of the seventeenth century to that of Gladstone at the end of the nineteenth. David Hume, Adam Smith, Edmund Burke, T. B. Macaulay and Lord Acton may be regarded as its typical representatives in England. It was this conception of individual liberty under the law which in the first instance inspired the liberal movements on the Continent and which became the basis of the American political tradition. A few of the leading political thinkers in those countries like B. Constant and A. de Tocqueville in France, Immanuel Kant, Friedrich von Schiller and Wilhelm von Humboldt in Germany, and James Madison, John Marshall and Daniel Webster in the United States belong wholly to it.[2]

[1] A paper submitted to the Tokyo Meeting of the Mont Pèlerin Society, September 1966, and published in *Il Politico*, December 1966. [The paper was originally published as F. A. Hayek, "The Principles of a Liberal Social Order", *Il Politico*, vol. 31, 1966, pp. 601–18. It was reprinted with minor stylistic changes as chapter 11 of F. A. Hayek, *Studies in Philosophy, Politics and Economics* (London: Routledge & Kegan Paul, 1967), the version used here. In the versions of the paper published in *Il Politico* and *Studies*, each paragraph of the essay was numbered. Those numbers have been removed from the *Collected Works* edition of the essay.—Ed.]

[2] [John Emerich Edward Dalberg-Acton, First Baron Acton (1834–1902), was a classical liberal historian and moralist, Liberal MP, leader of the liberal Roman Catholics in England, and founder-editor of the *Cambridge Modern History*. The key theme of his work was the 'history of liberty'. While Acton's projected volume of that name remained unfinished, passages from his published essays, book reviews and lectures were frequently quoted by Hayek in support of his views on the importance of private property, on the relationship between liberty and equality, on nationalism, on the merits of federalism, and on the need for constitutional restraints on the power of democratic majorities to impose their will on minorities. See, for instance, F. A. Hayek, "Individualism: True and False" [1946], reprinted as the Prelude to F. A. Hayek, *Studies on the Abuse and Decline of Reason: Text and Documents*, ed. Bruce Caldwell, vol. 13 (2010) of *The Collected Works of F. A. Hayek* (Chicago: University of Chicago Press; London: Routledge), pp. 70–73. Along with Macaulay, Acton is regarded as one of the principal representatives of the so-called 'Whig interpretation of history', according to which the events of the past constitute an inevitable progression towards greater personal liberty and the expansion of parliamentary authority over the crown, culminating in the liberal democracy and constitutional monarchy of nineteenth-century England. For Hayek's views on Acton, see "Historians and the Future of

This liberalism must be clearly distinguished from another, originally Continental European tradition, also called 'liberalism' of which what now claims this name in the United States is a direct descendant. This latter view, though beginning with an attempt to imitate the first tradition, interpreted it in the spirit of a constructivist rationalism prevalent in France and thereby made of it something very different, and in the end, instead of advocating limitations on the powers of government, ended up with the ideal of the unlimited powers of the majority. This is the tradition of Voltaire, Rousseau, Condorcet and the French Revolution which became the ancestor of modern socialism. English utilitarianism has taken over much of this Continental tradition and the late-nineteenth-century British liberal party, resulting from a fusion of the liberal Whigs and the utilitarian Radicals, was also a product of this mixture.

Liberalism and democracy, although compatible, are not the same. The first is concerned with the extent of governmental power, the second with who holds this power. The difference is best seen if we consider their opposites: the opposite of liberalism is totalitarianism, while the opposite of democracy is authoritarianism. In consequence, it is at least possible in principle that a democratic government may be totalitarian and that an authoritarian government may act on liberal principles. The second kind of 'liberalism' mentioned before has in effect become democratism rather than liberalism and, demanding *unlimited* power of the majority, has become essentially anti-liberal.

It should be specially emphasised that the two political philosophies which both describe themselves as 'liberalism' and lead in a few respects to similar

---

Europe" [1944] and "The Actonian Revival: On Lord Acton (1834–1902)" [1953], reprinted as chapters 8 and 9 respectively of F. A. Hayek, *The Fortunes of Liberalism: Essays on Austrian Economics and the Ideal of Freedom*, ed. Peter G. Klein, vol. 4 (1992) of *The Collected Works of F. A. Hayek*.

James Madison (1751–1836) was one of the architects of the U.S. Constitution at the Constitutional Convention of 1787, one of the authors of the *Federalist Papers* (1787–88), the sponsor of the first ten amendments to the Constitution (commonly known as the Bill of Rights), and the fourth President of the United States (1809–17). John Marshall (1755–1835) was the fourth Chief Justice of the United States of America and the main founder of the U.S. system of constitutional law. Under his direction, the Supreme Court established in 1803 its right to exercise judicial review and to invalidate federal laws and acts that were found to be in conflict with the Constitution. Daniel Webster (1782–1852) was an American lawyer, statesman and orator who, in the course of winning several celebrated cases before the Supreme Court, became one of the most influential interpreters of the Constitution. Webster emphasised the importance of constitutional limits to the exercise of temporary majority power. Hayek discusses the contributions made by these three men to efforts in America to limit the power of the government and thereby secure the liberty of the individual against arbitrary coercion in F. A. Hayek, *The Constitution of Liberty*, ed. Ronald Hamowy, vol. 17 (2011) of *The Collected Works of F. A. Hayek*, pp. 261–86.

Brief accounts of the other representatives of the liberal tradition listed by Hayek in this paragraph, and also of the exponents of constructive rationalism mentioned in the following paragraph, can be found in F. A. Hayek, "Liberalism" [1978], reproduced as chapter 1 of the current volume.—Ed.]

conclusions, rest on altogether different philosophical foundations. The first is based on an evolutionary interpretation of all phenomena of culture and mind and on an insight into the limits of the powers of the human reason. The second rests on what I have called 'constructivist' rationalism, a conception which leads to the treatment of all cultural phenomena as the product of deliberate design, and on the belief that it is both possible and desirable to reconstruct all grown institutions in accordance with a preconceived plan. The first kind is consequently reverent of tradition and recognises that all knowledge and all civilisation rest on tradition, while the second type is contemptuous of tradition because it regards an independently existing reason as capable of designing civilisation. (Cf. the statement by Voltaire: "If you want good laws, burn those you have and make new ones".)[3] The first is also an essentially modest creed, relying on abstraction as the only available means to extend the limited powers of reason, while the second refuses to recognise any such limits and believes that reason alone can prove the desirability of particular concrete arrangements.[4]

(It is a result of this difference that the first kind of liberalism is at least not incompatible with religious beliefs and has often been held and even been developed by men holding strong religious beliefs, while the 'Continental' type of liberalism has always been antagonistic to all religion and politically in constant conflict with organised religions.)

The first kind of liberalism, which we shall henceforth alone consider, is itself not the result of a theoretical construction but arose from the desire to extend and generalise the beneficial effects which unexpectedly had followed on the limitations placed on the powers of government out of sheer distrust of the rulers. Only after it was found that the unquestioned greater personal liberty which the Englishman enjoyed in the eighteenth century had produced

---

[3] [Voltaire, *Dictionnaire Philosophique*, s.v. "Lois", reprinted in *Oeuvres complètes de Voltaire*, new edition (Paris: Garnier frères, 1879), vol. 19, p. 614: "Voulez-vous avoir de bonnes lois; brûlez les vôtres, et faites-en de nouvelles".—Ed.]

[4] [For more on the evolutionary and constructivist rationalist traditions, see Hayek, "Liberalism", p. 4 n. 2 and the references contained therein. Hayek elaborates on the contrast between the view that people ought to be guided by rules of action that are abstract in the sense of specifying only the broad type of response they should make to every situation of a particular kind, irrespective of any differences in the details of those situations, and the constructivist rationalist claim that determining the appropriate response to any given set of circumstances requires such details to be taken explicitly into account, in the essays entitled, "Kinds of Rationalism" [1965], pp. 47–51, and "The Errors of Constructivism" [1970], pp. 342–44, reprinted as the Prologue and chapter 14 respectively of F. A. Hayek, *The Market and Other Orders*, ed. Bruce Caldwell, vol. 15 (2014) of *The Collected Works of F. A. Hayek*. The connection between people's reliance on abstract rules and the generation of the spontaneous market order or catallaxy is discussed in detail in Hayek, *The Constitution of Liberty*, pp. 215–31, and in F. A. Hayek, *The Mirage of Social Justice*, vol. 2 (1976) of *Law, Legislation and Liberty* (Chicago: University of Chicago Press; London: Routledge, 1973–79), pp. 107–32.—Ed.]

an unprecedented material prosperity were attempts made to develop a systematic theory of liberalism, attempts which in England never were carried very far while the Continental interpretations largely changed the meaning of the English tradition.

Liberalism thus derives from the discovery of a self-generating or spontaneous order in social affairs (the same discovery which led to the recognition that there existed an object for theoretical social sciences), an order which made it possible to utilise the knowledge and skill of all members of society to a much greater extent than would be possible in any order created by central direction, and the consequent desire to make as full use of these powerful spontaneous ordering forces as possible.

It was thus in their efforts to make explicit the principles of an order already existing but only in an imperfect form that Adam Smith and his followers developed the basic principles of liberalism in order to demonstrate the desirability of their general application. In doing this they were able to presuppose familiarity with the common law conception of justice and with the ideals of the rule of law and of government under the law which were little understood outside the Anglo-Saxon world; with the result that not only were their ideas not fully understood outside the English-speaking countries, but that they ceased to be fully understood even in England when Bentham and his followers replaced the English legal tradition by a constructivist utilitarianism derived more from Continental rationalism than from the evolutionary conception of the English tradition.[5]

The central concept of liberalism is that under the enforcement of universal rules of just conduct, protecting a recognisable private domain of individuals, a spontaneous order of human activities of much greater complexity will form itself than could ever be produced by deliberate arrangement, and that in consequence the coercive activities of government should be limited to the enforcement of such rules, whatever other services government may at the same time render by administering those particular resources which have been placed at its disposal for those purposes.

The distinction between a *spontaneous order* based on abstract rules which leave individuals free to use their own knowledge for their own purposes, and

---

[5] [Prominent amongst the followers of Bentham was the English jurist and legal positivist John Austin (1790–1859) who, like Bentham, argued that every legal rule must have originated in a conscious act of legislation. See J. Austin, *Lectures on Jurisprudence, or The Philosophy of Positive Law*, 4th edn. (London: John Murray, 1873). Hayek argues to the contrary that many laws have grown spontaneously, arising from custom and precedent rather than from explicit legislative acts, so that law precedes and constrains legislation rather than being created according to the unfettered will of some sovereign legislative body. See Hayek, *The Constitution of Liberty*, pp. 110–15, 234–36, 345–55; F. A. Hayek, *Rules and Order*, vol. 1 (1973) of *Law, Legislation and Liberty*, pp. 72–93, 128–29; and Hayek, *The Mirage of Social Justice*, pp. 44–56.—Ed.]

an *organisation* or *arrangement* based on commands, is of central importance for the understanding of the principles of a free society and must in the following paragraphs be explained in some detail, especially as the spontaneous order of a free society will contain many organisations (including the biggest organisation, government), but the two principles of order cannot be mixed in any manner we may wish.

The first peculiarity of a spontaneous order is that by using its ordering forces (the regularity of the conduct of its members) we can achieve an order of a much more complex set of facts than we could ever achieve by deliberate arrangement, but that, while availing ourselves of this possibility of inducing an order of much greater extent than we otherwise could, we at the same time limit our power over the details of that order. We shall say that when using the former principle we shall have power only over the abstract character but not over the concrete detail of that order.[6]

No less important is the fact that, in contrast to an organisation, neither has a spontaneous order a purpose nor need there be agreement on the concrete results it will produce in order to agree on the desirability of such an order, because, being independent of any particular purpose, it can be used for, and will assist in the pursuit of, a great many different, divergent and even conflicting individual purposes. Thus the order of the market, in particular, rests not on common purposes but on reciprocity, that is on the reconciliation of different purposes for the mutual benefit of the participants.

The conception of the common welfare or of the public good of a free society can therefore never be defined as a sum of known particular results to be achieved, but only as an abstract order which as a whole is not oriented on any particular concrete ends but provides merely the best chance for any member selected at random successfully to use his knowledge for his purposes. Adopting a term of Professor Michael Oakeshott (London), we may call such a free society a *nomocratic* (law-governed) as distinguished from an unfree *telocratic* (purpose-governed) social order.[7]

The great importance of the spontaneous order or nomocracy rests on the fact that it extends the possibility of peaceful co-existence of men for their

---

[6] [Hayek treats at length the issue of the relationship between the abstract nature of the rules characteristic of liberal society, and the degree of complexity of the order that can be sustained therein, in Hayek, *Rules and Order*, pp. 29–71. On the significance of this emphasis on abstraction for Hayek's political philosophy, see E. Mack, "Hayek on Justice and the Order of Actions", in *The Cambridge Companion to Hayek*, ed. E. Feser (Cambridge: Cambridge University Press, 2006). For Hayek's account of complexity, see F. A. Hayek, "The Theory of Complex Phenomena" [1964], reprinted as chapter 9 of Hayek, *The Market and Other Orders.*—Ed.]

[7] [M. Oakeshott, *Lectures in the History of Political Thought*, ed. T. Nardin and L. O'Sullivan (Exeter: Imprint Academic, 2006), pp. 469–97. Also see F. A. Hayek. "The Confusion of Language in Political Thought" [1968], reprinted as chapter 23 of the current volume, p. 317 n. 25.—Ed.]

mutual benefit beyond the small group whose members have concrete common purposes, or were subject to a common superior, and that it thus made the appearance of the *Great* or *Open Society* possible.[8] This order which has progressively grown beyond the organisations of the family, the horde, the clan and the tribe, the principalities and even the empire or national state, and has produced at least the beginning of a world society, is based on the adoption— without and often against the desire of political authority—of rules which came to prevail because the groups who observed them were more successful; and it has existed and grown in extent long before men were aware of its existence or understood its operation.[9]

The spontaneous order of the market, based on reciprocity or mutual benefits, is commonly described as an economic order; and in the vulgar sense of the term 'economic' the Great Society is indeed held together entirely by what are commonly called economic forces. But it is exceedingly misleading, and has become one of the chief sources of confusion and misunderstanding, to call this order an economy as we do when we speak of a national, social, or world economy. This is at least one of the chief sources of most socialist endeavour to turn the spontaneous order of the market into a deliberately run organisation serving an agreed system of common ends.

An economy in the strict sense of the word in which we can call a household, a farm, an enterprise or even the financial administration of government an economy, is indeed an organisation or a deliberate arrangement of a given stock of resources in the service of a unitary order of purposes. It rests on a system of coherent decisions in which a single view of the relative importance of the different competing purposes determines the uses to be made of the different resources.

The spontaneous order of the market resulting from the interaction of many such economies is something so fundamentally different from an economy proper that it must be regarded as a great misfortune that it has ever been called by the same name. I have become convinced that this practice so

---

[8] [Hayek used Adam Smith's term 'Great Society' to describe those large modern civilisations characterized by an advanced division of labour and a correspondingly elaborate division of knowledge, in which people's plans are co-ordinated by abstract rules and relative price signals. Hayek treats the phrase 'Open Society', coined by philosopher Sir Karl Popper (1902– 94), as a synonym for Smith's term. See Hayek, *Rules and Order*, pp. 14, 148 n. 11. Also see Adam Smith, *An Enquiry into the Nature and Causes of the Wealth of Nations*, ed. W. B. Todd, vol. 2 of *The Glasgow Edition of the Works and Correspondence of Adam Smith* (Oxford: Oxford University Press, 1976; reprinted, Indianapolis, IN: Liberty Fund, 1981), book II, Introduction, p. 278, and book IV, chapter 2, p. 453, and K. Popper, *The Open Society and Its Enemies*, 2 vols. (London: George Routledge, 1945), vol. 1, pp. 1, 151–55.—Ed.]

[9] [Hayek draws here on his theory of cultural evolution via group selection, additional details about which can be found in his essay "Notes on the Evolution of Systems of Rules of Conduct" [1967], reprinted as chapter 10 of Hayek, *The Market and Other Orders.*—Ed.]

constantly misleads people that it is necessary to invent a new technical term for it. I propose that we call this spontaneous order of the market a *catallaxy* in analogy to the term 'catallactics', which has often been proposed as a substitute for the term 'economics'. (Both 'catallaxy' and 'catallactics' derive from the ancient Greek verb *katallattein* which, significantly, means not only 'to barter' and 'to exchange' but also 'to admit into the community' and 'to turn from enemy into friend'.)[10]

The chief point about the catallaxy is that, as a spontaneous order, its orderliness does *not* rest on its orientation on a single hierarchy of ends, and that, therefore, it will *not* secure that for it as a whole the more important comes before the less important. This is the chief cause of its condemnation by its opponents, and it could be said that most of the socialist demands amount to nothing less than that the catallaxy should be turned into an economy proper (i.e., the purposeless spontaneous order into a purpose-oriented organisation) in order to assure that the more important be never sacrificed to the less important. The defence of the free society must therefore show that it is due to the fact that we do not enforce a unitary scale of concrete ends, nor attempt to secure that some particular view about what is more and what is less important governs the whole of society, that the members of such a free society have as good a chance successfully to use their individual knowledge for the achievement of their individual purposes as they in fact have.

The extension of an order of peace beyond the small purpose-oriented organisation became thus possible by the extension of purpose-independent ('formal') rules of just conduct to the relations with other men who did not pursue the same concrete ends or hold the same values except those abstract rules—rules which did not impose obligations for particular actions (which always presuppose a concrete end) but consisted solely in prohibitions from infringing the protected domain of each which these rules enable us to determine.[11] Liberalism is therefore inseparable from the institution of private property which is the name we usually give to the material part of this protected individual domain.

But if liberalism presupposes the enforcement of rules of just conduct and expects a desirable spontaneous order to form itself only if appropriate rules of just conduct are in fact observed, it also wants to restrict the *coercive* powers

[10] [The term 'catallactics' was first used to denote the science that studies market exchanges by sometime Archbishop of Dublin and Drummond Professor of Political Economy at Oxford University, Richard Whately (1787–1863). See R. Whately, *Introductory Lectures on Political Economy*, 2nd edn. (London: B. Fellowes, 1832), p. 6. The term was also used by Austrian economist Ludwig von Mises (1881–1973). See Ludwig von Mises, *Human Action: A Treatise on Economics*, 3rd revised ed. (New Haven: Yale University Press, 1966), pp. 3, 232–34. Also see Hayek, "The Confusion of Language in Political Thought", p. 320 n. 29.—Ed.]

[11] [For more on the notion of 'formal' rules, see F. A. Hayek, *The Road to Serfdom: Text and Documents*, ed. B. Caldwell, vol. 2 (2007) of *The Collected Works of F. A. Hayek*, pp. 112–23.—Ed.]

of government to the enforcement of such rules of just conduct, including at least one prescribing a positive duty, namely, the rule requiring citizens to contribute according to uniform principles not only to the cost of enforcing those rules but also to the costs of the non-coercive service functions of government which we shall presently consider. Liberalism is therefore the same as the demand for the rule of law in the classical sense of the term according to which the coercive functions of government are strictly limited to the enforcement of uniform rules of law, meaning uniform rules of just conduct towards one's fellows. (The 'rule of law' corresponds here to what in German is called *materieller Rechtsstaat* as distinguished from the mere *formelle Rechtsstaat* which requires only that each act of government is authorised by legislation, whether such a law consists of a general rule of just conduct or not.)

Liberalism recognises that there are certain other services which for various reasons the spontaneous forces of the market may not produce or may not produce adequately, and that for this reason it is desirable to put at the disposal of government a clearly circumscribed body of resources with which it can render such services to the citizens in general. This requires a sharp distinction between the coercive powers of government, in which its actions are strictly limited to the enforcement of rules of just conduct and in the exercise of which all discretion is excluded, and the provision of services by government, for which it can use only the resources put at its disposal for this purpose, has no coercive power or monopoly, but in the use of which resources it enjoys wide discretion.

It is significant that such a conception of a liberal order has arisen only in countries in which, in ancient Greece and Rome no less than in modern Britain, justice was conceived as something to be discovered by the efforts of judges or scholars and not as determined by the arbitrary will of any authority; that it always had difficulty in taking roots in countries in which law was conceived primarily as the product of deliberate legislation, and that it has everywhere declined under the joint influence of legal positivism and of democratic doctrine, both of which know no other criterion of justice than the will of the legislator.

Liberalism has indeed inherited from the theories of the common law and from the older (pre-rationalist) theories of the law of nature, and also presupposes, a conception of justice which allows us to distinguish between such rules of just individual conduct as are implied in the conception of the 'rule of law' and are required for the formation of a spontaneous order on the one hand, and all the particular commands issued by authority for the purpose of organisation on the other. This essential distinction has been made explicit in the legal theories of two of the greatest philosophers of modern times, David Hume and Immanuel Kant, but has not been adequately restated since and is wholly uncongenial to the governing legal theories of our day.

The essential points of this conception of justice are (a) that justice can be meaningfully attributed only to human action and not to any state of affairs as such without reference to the question whether it has been, or could have been, deliberately brought about by somebody; (b) that the rules of justice have essentially the nature of prohibitions, or, in other words, that injustice is really the primary concept and the aim of rules of just conduct is to prevent unjust action; (c) that the injustice to be prevented is the infringement of the protected domain of one's fellow men, a domain which is to be ascertained by means of these rules of justice; and (d) that these rules of just conduct which are in themselves negative can be developed by consistently applying to whatever such rules a society has inherited the equally negative test of universal applicability—a test which, in the last resort, is nothing else than the self-consistency of the actions which these rules allow if applied to the circumstances of the real world. These four crucial points must be developed further in the following paragraphs.[12]

Ad(a): Rules of just conduct can require the individual to take into account in his decisions only such consequences of his actions as he himself can foresee. The concrete results of the catallaxy for particular people are, however, essentially unpredictable; and since they are not the effect of anyone's design or intentions, it is meaningless to describe the manner in which the market distributed the good things of this world among particular people as just or unjust. This, however, is what the so-called 'social' or 'distributive' justice aims at in the name of which the liberal order of law is progressively destroyed. We shall later see that no test or criteria have been found or can be found by which such rules of 'social justice' can be assessed, and that, in consequence, and in contrast to the rules of just conduct, they would have to be determined by the arbitrary will of the holders of power.

Ad(b): No particular human action is fully determined without a concrete purpose it is meant to achieve. Free men who are to be allowed to use their own means and their own knowledge for their own purposes must therefore not be subject to rules which tell them what they must positively do, but only to rules which tell them what they must not do; except for the discharge of obligations an individual has voluntarily incurred, the rules of just conduct thus merely delimit the range of permissible actions but do not determine the particular actions a man must take at a particular moment. (There are certain rare exceptions to this, like actions to save or protect life, prevent catastrophes, and the like, where either rules of justice actually do require, or would at least generally be accepted as just rules if they required, some positive action. It would lead far to discuss here the position of such rules in the system.) The generally negative character of the rules of just conduct, and the corresponding primacy of the injustice which is prohibited, has often been noticed but scarcely ever been thought through to its logical consequences.

---

[12] [For a more detailed treatment, see Hayek, *The Mirage of Social Justice*, pp. 1–44.—Ed.]

Ad(c): The injustice which is prohibited by rules of just conduct is any encroachment on the protected domain of other individuals, and they must therefore enable us to ascertain what is the protected sphere of others. Since the time of John Locke it is customary to describe this protected domain as property (which Locke himself had defined as "the life, liberty, and possessions of a man".)[13] This term suggests, however, a much too narrow and purely material conception of the protected domain which includes not only material goods but also various claims on others and certain expectations. If the concept of property is, however, (with Locke) interpreted in this wide sense, it is true that law, in the sense of rules of justice, and the institution of property are inseparable.

Ad(d): It is impossible to decide about the justice of any one particular rule of just conduct except within the framework of a whole system of such rules, most of which must for this purpose be regarded as unquestioned: values can always be tested only in terms of other values. The test of the justice of a rule is usually (since Kant) described as that of its 'universalisability', i.e., of the possibility of willing that the rules should be applied to all instances that correspond to the conditions stated in it (the 'categorical imperative'). What this amounts to is that in applying it to any concrete circumstances it will not conflict with any other accepted rules. The test is thus in the last resort one of the compatibility or non-contradictoriness of the whole system of rules, not merely in a logical sense but in the sense that the system of actions which the rules permit will not lead to conflict.

It will be noticed that only purpose-independent ('formal') rules pass this test because, as rules which have originally been developed in small, purpose-connected groups ('organisations') are progressively extended to larger and larger groups and finally universalised to apply to the relations between any members of an Open Society who have no concrete purposes in common and merely submit to the same abstract rules, they will in this process have to shed all references to particular purposes.

The growth from the tribal organisation, all of whose members served common purposes, to the spontaneous order of the Open Society in which people are allowed to pursue their own purposes in peace, may thus be said to have commenced when for the first time a savage placed some goods at the boundary of his tribe in the hope that some member of another tribe would find them and leave in turn behind some other goods to secure the repetition of the offer. From the first establishment of such a practice which served reciprocal but not common purposes, a process has been going on for millennia which, by making rules of conduct independent of the particular purposes of

---

[13] [Hayek alludes here to the second volume of *Two Treatises of Government* (London: Awnsham Churchill, 1690), chapter 9, section 123, where Locke refers to people's "lives, liberties and estates, which I call by the general name, property".—Ed.]

those concerned, made it possible to extend these rules to ever wider circles of undetermined persons and eventually might make possible a universal peaceful order of the world.

The character of those universal rules of just individual conduct, which liberalism presupposes and wishes to improve as much as possible, has been obscured by confusion with that other part of law which determines the organisation of government and guides it in the administration of the resources placed at its disposal. It is a characteristic of liberal society that the private individual can be coerced to obey only the rules of private and criminal law; and the progressive permeation of private law by public law in the course of the last eighty or hundred years, which means a progressive replacement of rules of conduct by rules of organisation, is one of the main ways in which the destruction of the liberal order has been effected. A German scholar (Franz Böhm) has for this reason recently described the liberal order very justly as the *Privatrechtsgesellschaft* (private law society).[14]

The difference between the order at which the rules of conduct of private and criminal law aim, and the order at which the rules of organisation of public law aim, comes out most clearly if we consider that rules of conduct will determine an order of action only in combination with the particular knowledge and aims of the acting individuals, while the rules of organisation of public law determine directly such concrete action in the light of particular purposes, or, rather, give some authority power to do so. The confusion between rules of conduct and rules of organisation has been assisted by an erroneous identification of what is often called the 'order of law' with the order of actions, which in a free system is not fully determined by the system of laws but merely presupposes such a system of laws as one of the conditions required for its formation. Not every system of rules of conduct which secures uniformity of action (which is how the 'order of law' is frequently interpreted) will, however, secure an order of action in the sense that the actions permitted by the rules will not conflict.

---

[14] [Franz Böhm (1895–1977) was a German jurist and politician who, along with German economist Walter Eucken (1891–1950) and German jurist Hans Großmann-Doerth (1894–1944), was one of the founders in the 1930s of the liberal Freiburg School of law and economics. In 1948, Böhm and Eucken established as the principal outlet for the work of the Freiburg School the journal *Ordo: Jahrbuch für die Ordnung von Wirtschaft und Gesellschaft*, on whose editorial board Hayek sat from 1948 until 1991 and in which he published several papers. It was in that journal that Böhm published the essay in which he outlined the notion of the 'private law society', namely F. Böhm, "Privatrechtsgesellschaft und Marktwirtschaft", *Ordo*, vol. 17, 1966, pp. 75–151. For an English translation, see F. Böhm, "Rule of Law in a Market Economy", in *Germany's Social Market Economy: Origins and Evolution*, ed. A. Peacock and G. Willgerodt (London: Macmillan, 1989). A useful discussion of the relation between Böhm's and Hayek's ideas about the law can be found on pp. 242–44 of R. Sally, "Ordoliberalism and the Social Market: Classical Political Economy from Germany", *New Political Economy*, vol. 1, 1996, pp. 233–57.—Ed.]

The progressive displacement of the rules of conduct of private and criminal law by a conception derived from public law is the process by which existing liberal societies are progressively transformed into totalitarian societies. This tendency has been most explicitly seen and supported by Adolf Hitler's 'crown jurist' Carl Schmitt who consistently advocated the replacement of the 'normative' thinking of liberal law by a conception of law which regards as its purpose the 'concrete order formation' (*konkretes Ordnungsdenken*).[15]

Historically this development has become possible as a result of the fact that the same representative assemblies have been charged with the two different tasks of laying down rules of individual conduct and laying down rules and giving orders concerning the organisation and conduct of government. The consequence of this has been that the term 'law' itself, which in the older conception of the 'rule of law' had meant only rules of conduct equally applicable to all, came to mean any rule of organisation or even any particular command approved by the constitutionally appointed legislature. Such a conception of the rule of law which merely demands that a command be legitimately issued and not that it be a rule of justice equally applicable to all (what the Germans call the merely *formelle Rechtsstaat*), of course no longer provides any protection of individual freedom.

If it was the nature of the constitutional arrangements prevailing in all Western democracies which made this development possible, the driving force which guided it in the particular direction was the growing recognition that the application of uniform or equal rules to the conduct of individuals who were in fact very different in many respects, inevitably produced very different results for the different individuals; and that in order to bring about by government action a reduction in these unintended but inevitable differences in the material position of different people, it would be necessary to treat them not according to the same but according to different rules. This gave rise to a new and altogether different conception of justice, namely that usually described as 'social' or 'distributive' justice, a conception of justice which did not confine itself to rules of conduct for the individual but aimed at particular results for

---

[15] [Conservative legal, constitutional and political theorist Carl Schmitt (1888–1985) is widely regarded as one of the most important critics of liberalism and parliamentary democracy. A defender of the authoritarian state, Schmitt was a prominent apologist for the Nazi regime in the mid-1930s. In his *Über die drei Arten des rechtswissenschaftlichen Denkens* (Hamburg: Hanseatische Verlagsanstalt, 1934), p. 11 *et seq.*, Schmitt argued that, far from consisting of a set of abstract rules which constrain the actions of the state and make possible the formation of a spontaneous order through the freely-chosen actions of individuals, the law is an instrument of organisation by which individuals are made to serve concrete purposes chosen by others. Now see C. Schmitt, *On the Three Types of Juristic Thought* [1934], trans. J. W. Bendersky (Westport, CT: Praeger Publishers, 2004). For more on Hayek's views on Schmitt, see *Rules and Order*, p. 71. Hayek elaborates on the decline of the rule of law in Germany from the late nineteenth century in *The Constitution of Liberty*, pp. 342–50.—Ed.]

particular people, and which therefore could be achieved only in a purpose-governed organisation but not in a purpose-independent spontaneous order.

The concepts of a 'just price', a 'just remuneration' or a 'just distribution of incomes' are of course very old; it deserves notice, however, that in the course of the efforts of two thousand years in which philosophers have speculated about the meaning of these concepts, not a single rule has been discovered which would allow us to determine what is in this sense just in a market order. Indeed the one group of scholars which have most persistently pursued the question, the Schoolmen of the later Middle Ages and early modern times, were finally driven to define the just price or wage as that price or wage which would form itself on a market in the absence of fraud, violence or privilege—thus referring back to the rules of just conduct and accepting as a just result whatever was brought about by the just conduct of all individuals concerned. This negative conclusion of all the speculations about 'social' or 'distributive' justice was, as we shall see, inevitable, because a just remuneration or distribution has meaning only within an organisation whose members act under command in the service of a common system of ends, but can have no meaning whatever in a catallaxy or spontaneous order which can have no such common system of ends.[16]

A state of affairs as such, as we have seen, cannot be just or unjust as a mere fact. Only in so far as it has been brought about designedly or could be so brought about does it make sense to call just or unjust the actions of those who have created it or permitted it to arise. In the catallaxy, the spontaneous order of the market, nobody can foresee, however, what each participant will get, and the results for particular people are not determined by anyone's intentions; nor is anyone responsible for particular people getting particular things. We might therefore question whether a deliberate choice of the market order as the method for guiding economic activities, with the unpredictable and in a great measure chance incidence of its benefits, is a just decision, but certainly not whether, once we have decided to avail ourselves of the catallaxy for that purpose, the particular results it produces for particular people are just or unjust.

That the concept of justice is nevertheless so commonly and readily applied to the distribution of incomes is entirely the effect of an erroneous anthropomorphic interpretation of society as an organisation rather than as a spontaneous order. The term 'distribution' is in this sense quite as misleading as the term 'economy', since it also suggests that something is the result of deliberate action which in fact is the result of spontaneous ordering forces. Nobody dis-

---

[16] [For more on the Spanish Schoolmen, see Hayek, *The Mirage of Social Justice*, pp. 73–74, and Hayek, "Liberalism", p. 9 n. 11. A lengthier account of Hayek's critique of social justice appears in *The Mirage of Social Justice*, pp. 62–106.—Ed.]

tributes income in a market order (as would have to be done in an organisation) and to speak, with respect to the former, of a just or unjust distribution is therefore simple nonsense. It would be less misleading to speak in this respect of a 'dispersion' rather than a 'distribution' of incomes.

All endeavours to secure a 'just' distribution must thus be directed towards turning the spontaneous order of the market into an organisation or, in other words, into a totalitarian order. It was this striving after a new conception of justice which produced the various steps by which rules of organisation ('public law'), which were designed to make people aim at particular results, came to supersede the purpose-independent rules of just individual conduct, and which thereby gradually destroyed the foundations on which a spontaneous order must rest.[17]

The ideal of using the coercive powers of government to achieve 'positive' (i.e., social or distributive) justice leads, however, not only necessarily to the destruction of individual freedom, which some might not think too high a price, but it also proves on examination a mirage or an illusion which cannot be achieved in any circumstances, because it presupposes an agreement on the relative importance of the different concrete ends which cannot exist in a great society whose members do not know each other or the same particular facts. It is sometimes believed that the fact that most people today desire social justice demonstrates that this ideal has a determinable content. But it is unfortunately only too possible to chase a mirage, and the consequence of this is always that the result of one's striving will be utterly different from what one had intended.

There can be no rules which determine how much everybody 'ought' to have unless we make some unitary conception of relative 'merits' or 'needs' of the different individuals, for which there exists no objective measure, the basis of a central allocation of all goods and services—which would make it necessary that each individual, instead of using *his* knowledge for *his* purposes, were made to fulfil a duty imposed upon him by somebody else, and were remunerated according to how well he has, in the opinion of others, performed this duty. This is the method of remuneration appropriate to a closed organisation, such as an army, but irreconcilable with the forces which maintain a spontaneous order.

It ought to be freely admitted that the market order does not bring about any close correspondence between subjective merit or individual needs and rewards. It operates on the principle of a combined game of skill and chance in which the results for each individual may be as much determined by circumstances wholly beyond his control as by his skill or effort. Each is remu-

---

[17] [Hayek discusses the process whereby public law supersedes private law in more detail in *Rules and Order*, pp. 131–34, 141–44, and in *The Mirage of Social Justice*, pp. 46–47.—Ed.]

nerated according to the value his particular services have to the particular people to whom he renders them, and this value of his services stands in no necessary relation to anything which we could appropriately call his merits and still less to his needs.[18]

It deserves special emphasis that, strictly speaking, it is meaningless to speak of a value 'to society' when what is in question is the value of some services to certain people, services which may be of no interest to anybody else. A violin virtuoso presumably renders services to entirely different people from those whom a football star entertains, and the maker of pipes altogether different people from the maker of perfumes. The whole conception of a 'value to society' is in a free order as illegitimate an anthropomorphic term as its description as 'one economy' in the strict sense, as an entity which 'treats' people justly or unjustly, or 'distributes' among them. The results of the market process for particular individuals are neither the result of anybody's will that they should have so much, nor even foreseeable by those who have decided upon or support the maintenance of this kind of order.

Of all the complaints about the injustice of the results of the market order the one which appears to have had the greatest effect on actual policy, and to have produced a progressive destruction of the equal rules of just conduct and their replacement by a 'social' law aiming at 'social justice', however, was not the extent of the inequality of the rewards, nor their disproportion with recognisable merits, needs, efforts, pains incurred, or whatever else has been chiefly stressed by social philosophers, but the demands for protection against an undeserved descent from an already achieved position. More than by anything else the market order has been distorted by efforts to protect groups from a decline from their former position; and when government interference is demanded in the name of 'social justice' this now means, more often than not, the demand for the protection of the existing relative position of some group. 'Social justice' has thus become little more than a demand for the protection of vested interests and the creation of new privilege, such as when in the name of social justice the farmer is assured 'parity' with the industrial worker.

The important facts to be stressed here are that the positions thus protected were the result of the same sort of forces as those which now reduce the relative position of the same people, that their position for which they now demand protection was no more deserved or earned than the diminished position now in prospect for them, and that their former position could

---

[18] [Hayek elaborates on his view of the market order as a 'game of catallaxy', and draws out in detail its implications for the notion of justice, in *The Mirage of Social Justice*, pp. 71–73, 107–32.—Ed.]

in the changed position be secured to them only by denying to others the same chances of ascent to which they owed their former position. In a market order the fact that a group of persons has achieved a certain relative position cannot give them a claim in justice to maintain it, because this cannot be defended by a rule which could be equally applied to all.

The aim of economic policy of a free society can therefore never be to assure particular results to particular people, and its success cannot be measured by any attempt at adding up the value of such particular results. In this respect the aim of what is called 'welfare economics' is fundamentally mistaken, not only because no meaningful sum can be formed of the satisfactions provided for different people, but because its basic idea of a maximum of need-fulfilment (or a maximum social product) is appropriate only to an economy proper which serves a single hierarchy of ends, but not to the spontaneous order of a catallaxy which has no common concrete ends.

Though it is widely believed that the conception of an optimal economic policy (or any judgment whether one economic policy is better than another) presupposes such a conception of maximising aggregate real social income (which is possible only in value terms and therefore implies an illegitimate comparison of the utility to different persons), this is in fact not so. An optimal policy in a catallaxy may aim, and ought to aim, at increasing the chances of any member of society taken at random of having a high income, or, what amounts to the same thing, the chance that, whatever his share in total income may be, the real equivalent of this share will be as large as we know how to make it.

This condition will be approached as closely as we can manage, irrespective of the dispersion of incomes, if everything which is produced is being produced by persons or organisations who can produce it more cheaply than (or at least as cheaply as) anybody who does not produce it, and is sold at a price lower than that at which it would be possible to offer it for anybody who does not in fact so offer it. (This allows for persons or organisations to whom the costs of producing one commodity or service are lower than they are for those who actually produce it and who still produce something else instead, because their comparative advantage in that other production is still greater; in this case the total costs of their producing the first commodity would have to include the loss of the one which is not produced.)

It will be noticed that this optimum does not presuppose what economic theory calls 'perfect competition' but only that there are no obstacles to the entry into each trade and that the market functions adequately in spreading information about opportunities. It should also be specially observed that this modest and achievable goal has never yet been fully achieved because at all times and everywhere governments have both restricted access to some occupations and tolerated persons and organisations deterring others from entering occupations when this would have been to the advantage of the latter.

This optimum position means that as much will be produced of whatever combination of products and services is in fact produced as can be produced by any method that we know, because we can through such a use of the market mechanism bring more of the dispersed knowledge of the members of society into play than by any other. But it will be achieved only if we leave the share in the total, which each member will get, to be determined by the market mechanism and all its accidents, because it is only through the market determination of incomes that each is led to do what this result requires.

We owe, in other words, our chances that our unpredictable share in the total product of society represents as large an aggregate of goods and services as it does to the fact that thousands of others constantly submit to the adjustments which the market forces on them; and it is consequently also our duty to accept the same kind of changes in our income and position, even if it means a decline in our accustomed position and is due to circumstances we could not have foreseen and for which we are not responsible. The conception that we have 'earned' (in the sense of morally deserved) the income we had when we were more fortunate, and that we are therefore entitled to it so long as we strive as honestly as before and had no warning to turn elsewhere, is wholly mistaken. Everybody, rich or poor, owes his income to the outcome of a mixed game of skill and chance, the aggregate result of which and the shares in which are as high as they are only because we have agreed to play that game. And once we have agreed to play the game and profited from its results, it is a moral obligation on us to abide by the results even if they turn against us.

There can be little doubt that in modern society all but the most unfortunate and those who in a different kind of society might have enjoyed a legal privilege, owe to the adoption of that method an income much larger than they could otherwise enjoy. There is of course no reason why a society which, thanks to the market, is as rich as modern society should not provide *outside the market* a minimum security for all who in the market fall below a certain standard.[19] Our point was merely that considerations of justice provide no justification for 'correcting' the results of the market and that justice, in the sense of treatment under the same rules, requires that each takes what a market provides in which every participant behaves fairly. There is only a justice of individual conduct but not a separate 'social justice'.

We cannot consider here the legitimate tasks of government in the administration of the resources placed at its disposal for the rendering of services

---

[19] [For Hayek's arguments on this point, see Hayek, *The Road to Serfdom*, pp. 147–48, 156, and Hayek, *The Mirage of Social Justice*, p. 87.—Ed.]

to the citizens.[20] With regard to these functions, for the discharge of which the government is given money, we will here only say that in exercising them government should be under the same rules as every private citizen, that it should possess no monopoly for a particular service of the kind, that it should discharge these functions in such a manner as not to disturb the much more comprehensive spontaneously ordered efforts of society, and that the means should be raised according to a rule which applies uniformly to all. (This, in my opinion, precludes an overall progression of the burden of taxation of the individuals, since such a use of taxation for purposes of redistribution could be justified only by such arguments as we have just excluded.) In the remaining paragraphs we shall be concerned only with some of the functions of government for the discharge of which it is given not merely money but power to enforce rules of private conduct.

The only part of these coercive functions of government which we can further consider in this outline are those which are concerned with the preservation of a functioning market order. They concern primarily the conditions which must be provided by law to secure the degree of competition required to steer the market efficiently. We shall briefly consider this question first with regard to enterprise and then with regard to labour.

With regard to enterprise the first point which needs underlining is that it is more important that government refrain from assisting monopolies than that it combat monopoly. If today the market order is confined only to a part of the economic activities of men, this is largely the result of deliberate government restrictions of competition. It is indeed doubtful whether, if government consistently refrained from creating monopolies and from assisting them through protective tariffs and the character of the law of patents for inventions and of the law of corporations, there would remain an element of monopoly significant enough to require special measures. What must be chiefly remembered in this connection is, firstly, that monopolistic positions are always undesirable but often unavoidable for objective reasons which we cannot or do not wish to alter; and, secondly, that all government-supervised monopolies tend to become government-protected monopolies which will persist when their justification has disappeared.

Current conceptions of anti-monopoly policy are largely misguided by the application of certain conceptions developed by the theory of perfect competition which are irrelevant to conditions where the factual presuppositions of the theory of perfect competition are absent. The theory of perfect competition shows that if on a market the number of buyers and sellers is sufficiently large to make it impossible for any one of them deliberately to influ-

---

[20] [See Hayek, *The Constitution of Liberty*, pp. 329–41, 405–29, and F. A. Hayek, *The Political Order of a Free People*, vol. 3 (1979) of *Law, Legislation and Liberty*, pp. 41–64.—Ed.]

ence prices, such quantities will be sold at prices which will equal marginal costs. This does not mean, however, that it is either possible or even necessarily desirable everywhere to bring about a state of affairs where large numbers buy and sell the same uniform commodity. The idea that in situations where we cannot, or do not wish to, bring about such a state, the producers should be held to conduct themselves as if perfect competition existed, or to sell at a price which would rule under perfect competition, is meaningless, because we do not know what would be the particular conduct required, or the price which would be formed, if perfect competition existed.[21]

Where the conditions for perfect competition do not exist, what competition still can and ought to be made to achieve is nevertheless very remarkable and important, namely the conditions described on pages 287–88 above. It was pointed out then that this state will tend to be approached if nobody can be prevented by government or others to enter any trade or occupation he desired.

This condition would, I believe, be approached as closely as it is possible to secure this if, *firstly*, all agreements to restrain trade were without exception (not prohibited, but merely) made void and unenforceable, and, *secondly*, all discriminatory or other aimed actions towards an actual or potential competitor intended to make him observe certain rules of market conduct were to make liable for multiple damages. It seems to me that such a modest aim would produce a much more effective law than actual prohibitions under penalties, because no exceptions need to be made from such a declaration as invalid or unenforceable of all contracts in restraint of trade, while, as experience has shown, the more ambitious attempts are bound to be qualified by so many exceptions as to make them much less effective.

The application of this same principle that all agreements in restraint of trade should be invalid and unenforceable and that every individual should be protected against all attempts to enforce them by violence or aimed discrimination, is even more important with regard to labour. The monopolistic practices which threaten the functioning of the market are today much more serious on the side of labour than on the side of enterprise, and the preservation of the market order will depend, more than on anything else, on whether we succeed in curbing the latter.

The reason for this is that the developments in this field are bound to force government, and are already forcing many governments, into two kinds of measures which are wholly destructive of the market order: attempts authoritatively to determine the appropriate incomes of the various groups (by what

---

[21] [Hayek is relying here, as elsewhere in this essay, on arguments developed at greater length in F. A. Hayek, "The Meaning of Competition" [1948] and in "Competition as a Discovery Procedure" [1968], reprinted as chapters 4 and 12 of *The Market and Other Orders*.—Ed.]

is called an 'incomes policy') and efforts to overcome the wage 'rigidities' by an inflationary monetary policy. But since this evasion of the real issue by only temporarily effective monetary means must have the effect that those 'rigidities' will constantly increase, they are a mere palliative which can only postpone but not solve the central problem.

Monetary and financial policy is outside the scope of this paper. Its problems were mentioned only to point out that its fundamental and in the present situation insoluble dilemmas cannot be solved by any monetary means but only by a restoration of the market as an effective instrument for determining wages.[22]

In conclusion, the basic principles of a liberal society may he summed up by saying that in such a society all coercive functions of government must be guided by the overruling importance of what I like to call THE THREE GREAT NEGATIVES: PEACE, JUSTICE AND LIBERTY. Their achievement requires that in its coercive functions government shall be confined to the enforcement of such prohibitions (stated as abstract rules) as can be equally applied to all, and to exacting under the same uniform rules from all a share of the costs of the other, non-coercive services it may decide to render to the citizens with the material and personal means thereby placed at its disposal.[23]

---

[22] [For more on Hayek's views on these issues, see for example F. A. Hayek, "Full Employment, Planning and Inflation" [1950], and F. A. Hayek, "The Campaign against Keynesian Inflation" [1978], reprinted as chapters 14 and 25 respectively of the present volume.—Ed.]

[23] [In the version of this paper found in the Mont Pèlerin Society Records, the following words appeared after Hayek's signature:

Is this all so very different
From what Lao-Tzu says
In his fifty-seventh poem?:
    "If I keep from meddling with people
        They take care of themselves,
    If I keep from commanding people,
        They behave themselves,
    If I keep from imposing on people,
        They become themselves."

The lines in quotation marks are taken from the *Tao Te Ching* by Chinese philosopher Lao-Tzu. The quotation omits the following phrase, which appears in the original poem: "If I keep from preaching at people, they improve themselves". See *31 Papers Presented at the Special Meeting*, ed. B. Leoni (Turin: Mont Pèlerin Society, 1966), which can be found in box 17, folder 9, of the Mont Pèlerin Society Records, Hoover Institution Archives. The lines quoted above were retained in the version of Hayek's essay that was published in *Il Politico* but were omitted from the reprint that appeared in *Studies in Philosophy, Politics and Economics*.—Ed.]

TWENTY-TWO

THE CONSTITUTION OF A
LIBERAL STATE[1]

The device by which the founders of liberal constitutionalism had hoped to protect individual liberty was the separation of powers.[2] The idea behind this was that coercion should be permissible only for the enforcement of universal rules of individual conduct sanctioned by the legislature. The separation of powers as we know it has failed to achieve this end. To be meaningful this principle presupposes a conception of law which defines what is a law by intrinsic criteria and independent from the source from which it springs; only if by 'law-making' a particular kind of activity is meant do any significant consequences follow from reserving this kind of activity to a particular agency and at the same time confining the powers of this agency to this activity.

In fact we have come to call 'law' not a particular kind of norm or command but almost anything resolved by the agency we call legislature: the current interpretation of the separation of powers rests thus on circular reason-

---

[1] First published in *Il Politico*, Turin, 1967. [The article was first published as F. A. Hayek, "The Constitution of a Liberal State", *Il Politico*, vol. 32, 1967, pp. 455–61. A version containing corrections to typesetting errors, minor stylistic changes, and extra references in footnotes 2 and 6 appeared as chapter 7 of F. A. Hayek, *New Studies in Philosophy, Politics, Economics and the History of Ideas* (London: Routledge & Kegan Paul, 1978). The later version is used here. The paragraph numbers found in earlier versions have been removed from the *Collected Works* edition.—Ed.]

[2] On the general subject of the separation of powers I would like to draw attention to two important recent works: M. J. C. Vile, *Constitutionalism and the Separation of Powers*, Oxford, 1967, and W. B. Gwyn, *The Meaning of the Separation of Powers*, The Hague and New Orleans, 1965. See now also H. Rausch (ed.), *Zur heutigen Problematik der Gewaltentrennung*, Darmstadt, 1969. [The full references are as follows: M. Vile, *Constitutionalism and the Separation of Powers* (Oxford: Clarendon Press, 1967); W. B. Gwyn, *The Meaning of the Separation of Powers: An Analysis of the Doctrine from Its Origin to the Adoption of the United States Constitution* (The Hague: Martinus Nijhoff; New Orleans: Tulane University Press, 1965); and H. Rausch (ed.), *Zur heutigen Problematik der Gewaltentrennung* (Darmstadt: Wissenschaftliche Buchgesellschaft, 1969). Hayek draws on Vile's book in particular for his account of "the process by which the original conception of the nature of democratic constitutions gradually was replaced by that of the unlimited power of the democratically elected assembly". See F. A. Hayek, *The Political Order of a Free People*, vol. 3 (1979) of *Law, Legislation and Liberty* (Chicago: University of Chicago Press; London: Routledge, 1973–79), p. 20.—Ed.]

ing and makes it a wholly empty concept: only the legislature is to pass laws and it is to possess no other powers, but whatever it resolves is law.

This development has resulted from the rise of democratic government interpreted as unlimited government, and from the legal philosophy congenial to it, legal positivism, which attempts to trace all law to the expressed will of a legislator. In the last resort it rests on the misconception that the ultimate 'sovereign' power must be unlimited, because, it is thought, power can be checked only by another power. This would be correct if the substantive content of the actions of a given power were to be limited. But it is not true if the power is to be limited to a *kind* of action recognisable by objective tests.

The basic conception on which the classical distinction between lawmaking and the issue of particular commands rests is that the lawmaker had to prove his belief in the justice of his pronouncements by committing himself to their universal application to an unknown number of future instances and renouncing the power of modifying their application to particular cases. In this sense law was to rest on the *opinion* that certain kinds of actions were right or wrong and *not* on the *will* to bring about particular results. And the authority of the legislator rested on the *opinion* of the people that so long as in this manner he provided evidence of his belief in the justice of his rulings, his considered pronouncements deserved support.[3]

The current misconception of democratic theory derives from the substitution by Rousseau of popular *will* for general *opinion* and the consequent conception of popular sovereignty, meaning in practice that whatever the majority decided on particular matters was to be binding law for all.[4] There is, however, neither need for such an unlimited power, nor can its existence be reconciled with individual freedom. It is true that so far as government is entrusted

---

[3] [Hayek discusses the notions of 'will' and 'opinion' in greater detail in F. A. Hayek, "The Confusion of Language in Political Thought" [1968], reprinted as chapter 23 of the current volume, section 4, and in F. A. Hayek, *The Mirage of Social Justice*, vol. 2 (1976) of *Law, Legislation and Liberty*, pp. 12–14. He deploys those concepts to expose the shortcomings of the notion of popular sovereignty in *The Political Order of a Free People*, pp. 3–5, 33–35, and in F. A. Hayek, *Rules and Order*, vol. 1 (1973) of *Law, Legislation and Liberty*, pp. 91–93.—Ed.]

[4] [Hayek viewed French philosopher and political theorist Jean-Jacques Rousseau (1712–78) as a prominent exponent of 'rationalist constructivism' (that is, the view that all useful human institutions are and should be the deliberate creation of conscious reason). Rousseau's claims, made in his book *The Social Contract* [1762], that there is no law except that willed by living men, and that there is no need for any constraint on the power of democratic majorities, exemplify for Hayek the constructivist rationalist view that society is deliberately made by men for an intended purpose. See J.-J. Rousseau, *The Social Contract and the Discourses*, trans. G. D. H. Cole (London: Everyman's Library, 1973). For more on Hayek's opinion of Rousseau, see F. A. Hayek, *The Constitution of Liberty*, ed. Ronald Hamowy, vol. 17 (2011) of *The Collected Works of F. A. Hayek* (Chicago: University of Chicago Press; London: Routledge), pp. 110–14, 172.—Ed.]

with the administration of the personal and material resources placed at its disposal, its activities cannot be fully determined by general rules of just conduct. But the essence of a free society is that the private individual is not one of the resources which government administers, and that a free person can count on using a known domain of such resources on the basis of his knowledge and for his purposes. Government under the law meant to the theorists of representative government that, in directing the administrative machinery, government could not use it to coerce private persons except to make them observe the universal rules of just conduct.[5]

The rise of the democratic ideal brought it about that it was desired that the representatives of the people should be able to decide not only on the laying down of rules of just conduct but also on the current activities of government in providing services by means of the resources placed at its disposal. This, however, need not have meant that both activities be placed in the hands of the same representative assembly. Democratic legislation and democratic government are probably both desirable, but to place these functions in the hands of the same body destroys the safeguard of individual liberty which the separation of powers meant to provide. Such democratic government necessarily ceases to be government under the law in the sense in which this expression was meant, if the same assembly that directs government can make whatever laws it likes to suit the purposes of government. Legislation thus understood wholly loses that legitimation which the supreme power derives from its commitment to universal rules.

An assembly with unlimited powers is in a position to use that power to favour particular groups or individuals and it is an inevitable consequence that it will come to be constituted of coalitions of particular interests offering particular benefits to their supporters. The whole modern development of the rise of 'para-government', the organised interests pressuring the legislature to intervene in their favour, is a necessary and inevitable result of, and only of, giving the supreme authority unlimited power to coerce particular individuals or groups in the service of particular ends. A legislative assembly confined to the articulation of universally applicable rules of just conduct, whose effects on particular individuals or groups would be unforeseeable, would not be under such pressure (lobbying, etc., is thus the product of government intervention and must assume ever increasing dimensions as the legislature assumes power to intervene on behalf of particular groups).

It would take too much space here to show how this development is connected with the rise of the concept of 'social justice'. I must confine myself

[5] [For an account of the relevant notions of 'freedom' and 'coercion', see Hayek, *The Constitution of Liberty*, pp. 57–72, 199–214.—Ed.]

to refer in this respect to my paper submitted last year to the Tokyo conference of the Mont Pèlerin society and to quote an instructive passage from a
recent work:[6]

> the evolution in modern times of three major procedures of government
> reflected the importance attached to three dominant values in the Western
> World—efficiency, democracy, and justice. Over the past hundred years,
> however, a new value emerged which could not be subordinated to these—
> social justice. It is the concern with social justice which above all else has
> disrupted the earlier triad of government functions and agencies, and has
> added a new dimension to modern government.

Historically, individual liberty has arisen only in countries in which law was
not conceived to be a matter of arbitrary will of anybody but arose from
the efforts of judges or jurisconsults to articulate as general rules the principles which governed the sense of justice. Legislation intended to alter the
general rules of just conduct is a comparatively new phenomenon in history and has justly been described as "among all inventions of man the one
wrought with the gravest consequences, more far-reaching even than that of
fire and gunpowder".[7] Most of what in earlier times was done by deliberate 'legislation' referred in fact to the organisation and conduct of government rather than to the rules of just conduct. Law in the latter sense was long
regarded as unalterably given and requiring only recurrent restoration to its
pristine purity. Even early forms of representative assemblies were created
principally for decisions on matters of government proper, especially taxation,
rather than for the formulation of law in the sense of universal rules of just
conduct.

It was thus natural that when it was demanded that the power of articulating general rules of just conduct be placed in the hands of representative
or democratic assemblies, it was placed in the hands of assemblies already

---

[6] See my *Studies in Philosophy, etc.*, p. 160 and M. J. C. Vile, *loc. cit.*, p. 347. [The passage quoted
by Hayek comes from Vile, *Constitutionalism and the Separation of Powers*, p. 347. The paper that
Hayek presented at the 1966 meeting of the Mont Pèlerin Society, held in Tokyo, was "The
Principles of a Liberal Social Order". The paper was reprinted as chapter 11 of F. A. Hayek,
Studies in Philosophy, Politics and Economics (London: Routledge & Kegan Paul, 1967), and can also
be found as chapter 21 of the current volume. Hayek elaborates at length on his critique of
'social justice' in Hayek, *The Mirage of Social Justice*, pp. 62–106.—Ed.]

[7] B. Rehfeldt, *Die Wurzeln des Rechtes*, Berlin, 1951, p. 68. [The original German sentence
on which Hayek drew reads as follows: "An dieser Vorstellung gemessen ist die Erfindung der
Gesetzgebung vielleicht die folgenschwerste gewesen, die je gemacht worden, folgenschwerer als
die des Feuermachens oder des Schießpulvers". See B. Rehfeldt, *Die Wurzeln des Rechtes* (Berlin:
Duncker and Humblot, 1951), p. 68.—Ed.]

existing for the purpose of directing government. It were only the theorists, especially Locke, Montesquieu and the Fathers of the American Constitution, who allowed themselves to be deceived by the description of these assemblies as 'legislatures' into believing that they were concerned only with what these theorists then understood by law, i.e. the universal rules of just conduct to the enforcement of which they hoped to confine coercion. From the very beginning these 'legislative' assemblies were however primarily occupied with the organisation and conduct of government and they have increasingly become so.[8] A purely 'legislative' assembly in the sense in which the theorists of the separation of powers conceived it has never existed—at least not since the *nomothetai* of ancient Athens who appear to have possessed only the exclusive power of altering the rules of just conduct.[9]

The separation of powers has thus never been achieved because from the beginning of the modern development of constitutional government the power of making law, in the sense presupposed by that conception, and the power of directing government were combined in the same representative assemblies. In consequence, the ultimate power of government was in no democratic country of modern times ever under the law, because it was always in the hands of a body free to make whatever law it wanted for the particular tasks it desired to undertake.

To achieve its aim the separation of powers in a democratic system would require two distinct representative assemblies charged with altogether different tasks and acting independently of each other.[10] This would evidently not be achieved by two assemblies of the same composition and acting in collusion. Since the assembly which was to be truly law-giving (in the sense of the theory of the separation of powers) would have to establish rules limiting the powers of the governmental assembly which would be under the law laid down by the first, the second must not be subservient to the other, as it would be if it were

---

[8] [Hayek discusses at greater length how the assignment to representative bodies concerned primarily with matters of government—that is, with raising and directing resources for specific purposes, connected in particular with providing services for citizens—of the legislative function of establishing rules of just conduct led to the gradual erosion of constitutional restraints on the exercise of sovereign power, thereby undermining the ideal of government under the law, in *Rules and Order*, pp. 89–91, 124–44, and in *The Political Order of a Free People*, pp. 1–40, 98–107. Also see F. A. Hayek, "Whither Democracy?" [1978], reprinted as chapter 28 of the current volume.—Ed.]

[9] [Hayek christens the group of people who set the *nomoi* or rules of just conduct 'nomothetae'. For more on the meaning and history of that term, see Hayek, "The Confusion of Language in Political Thought", p. 324, and Hayek, *The Political Order of a Free People*, pp. 111–17. Hayek discusses the notion of 'nomos' at greater length in *Rules and Order*, pp. 94–123.—Ed.]

[10] [A more detailed description of Hayek's 'model constitution' can be found in Hayek, *The Political Order of a Free People*, pp. 105–27.—Ed.]

composed of the representatives of the same coalitions of interests or parties as the former. In the terms used before, the law-making assembly should be concerned with *opinion* about what is right and *not* with *will* about particular objectives of government.

Existing democratic institutions have been shaped entirely by the needs of democratic government rather than by the needs of discovering the appropriate systems of rules of justice or law as the theory of the separation of powers understood it. For the purposes of democratic government an organised body dedicated to the realisation of a particular system of concrete ends is undoubtedly necessary. Democratic *government* thus requires parties and there is therefore no reason why the governmental assembly should not be organised on party lines—with the executive committee of the majority acting as government, as is the rule in parliamentary systems.

On the other hand, the distrust of 'factions' or organised interests, so characteristic of the older theorists of representative government, is wholly justified so far as law-making, as they understood it, is concerned. Where not a sum of particular concrete interests but the true public interest is concerned, "which is no other than common right and justice, excluding all partiality or privat interest" and which "may be call'd the empire of laws, and not of men" (James Harrington),[11] an assembly is wanted which represents not interests but opinion about what is right. Here we need a 'representative sample' of the people—and if possible men and women particularly respected for their probity and wisdom but not delegates required to look after the particular interest of their constituents.

Though elected by the people as representatives of opinion of what is just, the members of the law-making assembly should thus not be dependent on will and interest and certainly not be bound by party discipline. This can be secured by electing them for long periods after which they would not be re-eligible. To make them nevertheless representative of current opinion I have suggested a system of representation by age groups: each generation electing once in their lives, say in their fortieth year, representatives to serve for 15 years and to be secured thereafter continued occupation as lay judges. The law-making assembly would thus be composed of men and women between their fortieth and fifty-fifth year (and thus of an average age probably considerably lower than in existing assemblies!), elected by their contempo-

---

[11] [James Harrington (1611–77) was an English classical republican political theorist whose major work, *The Commonwealth of Oceana* (London: J. Streater, 1656), set out an ideal constitution designed to undergird the creation of a utopian republic. The words quoted by Hayek are from Harrington's *The Prerogative of Popular Government* [1658], in *The Oceana and Other Works of James Harrington, with an Account of his Life by John Toland* (London: Printed for T. Becket. and T. Cadell, 1771), p. 224.—Ed.]

raries after they had an opportunity to prove themselves in ordinary life and required to leave their business concerns for a honorific position for the rest of their lives. I imagine that such a system of election by the contemporaries, who are always the best judges of a man's ability, as a sort of prize awarded to 'the most successful member of the class', would come nearer producing the ideal of the political theorists, a senate of the wise, than any system yet tried. It would certainly for the first time make possible a real separation of powers, a government under the law and an effective rule of law.

The manner of operation of such a system is best seen if we consider the way in which it would apply to tax legislation. Taxation is a coercive activity and the principles on which each individual would be required to contribute to the common purse, or the manner in which a given amount to be raised would be pro-rated among the different individuals, would have to be determined by a general rule which it would be for the legislative assembly to determine. The annual amount to be spent and therefore to be raised by taxation would be a matter for the governmental assembly to decide. But in doing so it would know that every additional expenditure would have to be borne by themselves and their constituents in a manner they had no power to alter. Every attempt to shift the burden of additional expenditure to other shoulders would be precluded. I can conceive of no more wholesome restraint on politicians than this knowledge that every penny they spent would be pro-rated according to a predetermined universal scale which they could not alter.

Government as a service agency limited to the use of the means it could raise in this manner (or which were permanently placed at its disposal) could still provide whatever collective good the majority was willing to pay for. What it could not do would be to deflect the general stream of goods and services produced by the market for the benefit of particular groups. Apart from contributing his share of the common expenses, determined by a uniform rule, the individual citizen would merely be held to observe those universal rules of just conduct required to delimit everybody's protected domain, but could not be required to do, or be prohibited from doing, particular things or serving particular ends.

If, as some maintain, democracy has now definitely come to mean unlimited power of the majority, we may have to invent a new word to describe a system of government in which, though there would be no power higher than that of the majority, even that power would be limited by the principle that it possessed coercive power only to the extent that it was prepared to commit itself to general rules. I suggest that we call such a system of government a *demarchy*—a system of government in which the *demos* has no brute power (*kratos*) but is confined to ruling (*archein*) by "established standing laws, promulgated and known to the people, and not by extemporary decrees" (John

Locke)—and reminding us of the error we committed by sweeping away all the safeguards by which we had learnt effectively to hedge about constitutional *monarchy* under the illusion that once the will of the people governed there was no longer any need for the majority to prove that it regarded as just what it decided.[12]

---

[12] [Hayek discusses the term 'demarchy' at greater length in *The Political Order of a Free People*, pp. 38–40. The phrase quoted by Hayek is from J. Locke, *Two Treatises of Government*, ed. P. Laslett (Cambridge: Cambridge University Press, 1960), p. 371.—Ed.]

THE CONFUSION OF LANGUAGE
IN POLITICAL THOUGHT[1]

Homo non intelligendo fit omnia.

G. Vico

Introduction

Modern civilisation has given man undreamt of powers largely because, without understanding it, he has developed methods of utilising more knowledge and resources than any one mind is aware of. The fundamental condition from which any intelligent discussion of the order of all social activities should start is the constitutional and irremediable ignorance both of the acting persons and of the scientist studying this order, of the multiplicity of particular, concrete facts which enter this order of human activities because they are known to *some* of its members. As the motto above expresses it, "man has become all he is without understanding what happened".[2] This insight

---

[1] A lecture originally delivered in 1967 in German to the Walter Eucken Institute at Freiburg im Breisgau, and published in 1968 as an Occasional Paper by the Institute of Economic Affairs in London. [See F. A. Hayek, *The Confusion of Language in Political Thought: With Some Suggestions for Remedying It*. Occasional Paper 20 (London: The Institute of Economic Affairs, 1968), reprinted as chapter 6 of F. A. Hayek, *New Studies in Philosophy, Politics, Economics and the History of Ideas* (London and Henley: Routledge & Kegan Paul, 1978).—Ed.]

[2] The passage from Giambattista Vico used as a motto is taken from *Opere*, ed. G. Ferrari, 2nd ed. Milan, 1854, vol. V, p. 183. [Italian historian, rhetorician, and philosopher of cultural history and law Giambattista Vico (1668–1744) was Professor of Rhetoric at the University of Naples and a prominent critic of Cartesian rationalism. Hayek regarded Vico as one of the founders of anti-rationalist social theory. See F. A. Hayek, "Individualism: True and False" [1946], reprinted as the Prelude to F. A. Hayek, *Studies on the Abuse and Decline of Reason: Text and Documents*, ed. Bruce Caldwell, vol. 13 (2010) of *The Collected Works of F. A. Hayek* (Chicago: University of Chicago Press; London: Routledge), p. 55 n. 16. The full reference to the phrase quoted by Hayek is G. Vico, *Opere* [1834], ed. G. Ferrari, 2nd edn. (Milan: Società tipographica de' classici italiani, 1854), vol. 5, p. 183. The phrase is usually translated as "man becomes all things by *not* understanding them." See G. Vico, *The New Science of Giambattista Vico*, trans. T. G. Bergin and M. H. Fisch (Ithaca and London: Cornell University Press, 1968), p. 130. —Ed.]

should not be a cause of shame but a source of pride in having discovered a method that enables us to overcome the limitations of individual knowledge. And it is an incentive deliberately to cultivate institutions which have opened up those possibilities.

The great achievement of the eighteenth-century social philosophers was to replace the naive constructivistic rationalism of earlier periods,[3] which interpreted all institutions as the products of deliberate design for a foreseeable purpose, by a critical and evolutionary rationalism that examined the conditions and limitations of the effective use of conscious reason.

We are still very far, however, from making full use of the possibilities which those insights open to us, largely because our thinking is governed by language which reflects an earlier mode of thought. The important problems are in large measure obscured by the use of words which imply anthropomorphic or personalised explanations of social institutions. These explanations interpret the general rules which guide action directed at particular purposes. In practice such institutions are successful adaptations to the irremediable limitations of our knowledge, adaptations which have prevailed over alternative forms of order because they proved more effective methods for dealing with that incomplete, dispersed knowledge which is man's unalterable lot.

The extent to which serious discussion has been vitiated by the ambiguity of some of the key terms, which for lack of more precise ones we have constantly to use, has been vividly brought home to me in the course of a still incomplete investigation of the relations between law, legislation, and liberty on which I have been engaged for some time.[4] In an endeavour to achieve clarity I have been driven to introduce sharp distinctions for which current usage has no accepted or readily intelligible terms. The purpose of the fol-

---

[3] Cf. my *Studies in Philosophy, Politics and Economics,* London and Chicago, 1967, especially chapters 4, 5 and 6, as well as my lecture "Dr Bernard Mandeville", reprinted as chapter 15 of this book. [Hayek is referring to the following essays: F. A. Hayek, "Notes on the Evolution of Systems of Rules of Conduct" [1967], F. A. Hayek, "Kinds of Rationalism" [1965], and F. A. Hayek, "The Results of Human Action but Not of Human Design" [1967], which were published as chapters 4, 5 and 6 respectively of F. A. Hayek, *Studies in Philosophy, Politics and Economics* (London: Routledge and Kegan Paul, 1967). They have now been reprinted as chapter 10, the Prologue, and chapter 11 respectively of F. A. Hayek, *The Market and Other Orders,* ed. Bruce Caldwell, vol. 15 (2014) of *The Collected Works of F. A. Hayek.* Hayek also refers to F. A. Hayek, "Dr Bernard Mandeville" [1966], reprinted as chapter 15 of *New Studies in Philosophy, Politics, Economics and the History of Ideas,* and subsequently reprinted again under the slightly different title of "Dr. Bernard Mandeville (1670–1733)" as chapter 6 of F. A. Hayek, *The Trend of Economic Thinking: Essays on Political Economists and Economic History,* ed. W. W. Bartley III and S. Kresge, vol. 3 (1991) of *The Collected Works of F. A. Hayek.*—Ed.]

[4] [F. A. Hayek, *Law, Legislation and Liberty,* 3 vols. (Chicago: University of Chicago Press, 1973–79).—Ed.]

lowing sketch is to demonstrate the importance of these distinctions which I found essential and to suggest terms which should help us to avoid the prevailing confusion.

1 Cosmos and Taxis

The achievement of human purposes is possible only because we recognise the world we live in as orderly. This order manifests itself in our ability to learn, from the (spatial or temporal) parts of the world we know, rules which enable us to form expectations about other parts. And we anticipate that these rules stand a good chance of being borne out by events. Without the knowledge of such an order of the world in which we live, purposive action would be impossible.

This applies as much to the social as to the physical environment. But while the order of the physical environment is given to us independently of human will, the order of our social environment is partly, but only partly, the result of human design. The temptation to regard it *all* as the intended product of human action is one of the main sources of error. The insight that *not all order that results from the interplay of human actions is the result of design* is indeed the beginning of social theory. Yet the anthropomorphic connotations of the term 'order' are apt to conceal the fundamental truth that all deliberate efforts to bring about a social order by arrangement or organisation (i.e. by assigning to particular elements specified functions or tasks) take place within a more comprehensive spontaneous order which is not the result of such design.

While we have the terms 'arrangement' or 'organisation' to describe a *made* order, we have no single distinctive word to describe an order which has formed *spontaneously*. The ancient Greeks were more fortunate in this respect. An arrangement produced by man deliberately putting the elements in their place or assigning them distinctive tasks they called *taxis*, while an order which existed or formed itself independent of any human will directed to that end they called *cosmos*. Though they generally confined the latter term to the order of nature, it seems equally appropriate for any spontaneous social order and has often, though never systematically, been used for that purpose.[5]

---

[5] For example, J. A. Schumpeter, *History of Economic Analysis,* New York, 1954, p. 67, where he speaks of A. A. Cournot and H. von Thünen as the first two authors "to visualise the general interdependence of all economic quantities and the necessity of representing this cosmos by a system of equations." [The correct reference is to p. 467 of J. A. Schumpeter, *History of Economic Analysis* (London: Allen and Unwin, 1954). French economist, mathematician and philosopher Antoine-Augustin Cournot (1801–77) is commonly described as the first mathematical economist. His principal work in economics, in which he developed the concept of general economic equilibrium to which Hayek alludes, is *Recherches sur les principes mathématiques de la théorie des richesses*

The advantage of possessing an unambiguous term to distinguish this kind of order from a made order should outweigh the hesitation we may feel about endowing a social order which we often do not like with a name which conveys the sense of admiration and awe with which man regards the *cosmos* of nature.

The same is in some measure true of the term 'order' itself. Though one of the oldest terms of political theory, it has been somewhat out of fashion for some time. But it is an indispensable term which, on the definition we have given it—a condition of affairs in which we can successfully form expectations and hypoteses about the future—refers to objective facts and not to values. Indeed, the first important difference between a spontaneous order or *cosmos* and an organisation (arrangement) or *taxis* is that, not having been deliberately made by men, a *cosmos* has no purpose.[6] This does not mean that its existence may not be exceedingly serviceable in the pursuit of many purposes: the existence of such an order, not only in nature but also in society, is indeed indispensable for the pursuit of any aim. But the order of nature and aspects of the social order not being deliberately created by men, cannot properly be said to have a purpose, though both can be used by men for many different, divergent and even conflicting purposes.

While a *cosmos* or spontaneous order has thus no purpose, every *taxis* (arrangement, organisation) presupposes a particular end, and men forming such an organisation must serve the same purposes. A *cosmos* will result from regularities of the behaviour of the elements which it comprises. It is in this sense endogenous, intrinsic or, as the cyberneticians say, a 'self-regulating' or 'self-organising' system.[7] A *taxis*, on the other hand, is determined by an

---

(Paris: L. Hachette, 1838). Johann Heinrich von Thünen (1783–1850) was a German agriculturalist and agricultural economist best known for his work on the optimal location of economic activity and for developing a marginal productivity theory of distribution. See his *Der isolierte Staat in Beziehung auf Landwirtschaft und Nationalökonomie* [1826–63], 3 vols. (Jena: G. Fischer, 1910), translated by C. Wartenberg and edited by P. Hall as *Von Thünen's Isolated State: An English Edition of Der Isolierte Staat* (Oxford: Pergamon Press, 1966).—Ed.]

[6] The only passage known to me in which the error, usually only implicit, that "order supposes an end" is explicitly stated in these words occurs, significantly, in the writings of Jeremy Bentham, "An essay on political tactics", first published in *Works*, ed. Bowring, vol. II, p. 399. [In the original essay by Bentham, the words "order" and "end" are italicised. The full reference is J. Bentham, "An Essay on Political Tactics" [1843], in J. Bentham, *The Works of Jeremy Bentham, Published under the superintendence of his executor, John Bowring* (Edinburgh: William Tait, 1843), vol. 2, p. 301. Hayek viewed English utilitarian philosopher and jurist Jeremy Bentham (1748–1832) as an exponent of constructivistic rationalism. See, for example, F. A. Hayek, "Liberalism" [1978], reprinted as chapter 1 of this volume, p. 6 n. 5.—Ed.]

[7] The idea of the formation of spontaneous or self-determining orders, like the connected idea of evolution, has been developed by the social sciences before it was adopted by the natural sciences and here developed as cybernetics. This is beginning to be seen by the biologists. For example, G. Hardin, *Nature and Man's Fate* (1959), Mentor edn., New York, 1961, p. 54: "But long

agency which stands outside the order and is in the same sense exogenous or imposed. Such an external factor may induce the formation of a spontaneous order also by imposing upon the elements such regularities in their responses to the facts of their environment that a spontaneous order will form itself. Such an indirect method of securing the formation of an order possesses important advantages over the direct method: it can be applied in circumstances where what is to affect the order is not known as a whole to anyone. Nor is it necessary that the rules of behaviour within the *cosmos* be deliberately created: they, too, *may* emerge as the product of spontaneous growth or of evolution.[8]

It is therefore important to distinguish clearly between the spontaneity of the order and the spontaneous origin of regularities in the behaviour of elements determining it. A spontaneous order may rest in part on regularities which are not spontaneous but imposed. For policy purposes there results thus the alternative whether it is preferable to secure the formation of an order by a strategy of indirect approach, or by directly assigning a place for each element and describing its function in detail.

Where we are concerned solely with the alternative social orders, the first important corollary of this distinction is that in a *cosmos* knowledge of the facts and purposes which will guide individual action will be those of the acting individuals, while in a *taxis* the knowledge and purposes of the organiser will determine the resulting order. The knowledge that can be utilised in such an organisation will therefore always be more limited than in a spontaneous order where all the knowledge possessed by the elements can be taken

---

before [Claude Bernard, Clerk Maxwell, Walter B. Cannon or Norbert Wiener] Adam Smith had just as clearly used the idea [of cybernetics] . . . The 'invisible hand' that regulates prices to a nicety is clearly this idea. In a free market, says Smith in effect, prices are regulated by negative feedback". [Garrett Hardin (1915–2003) was an American ecologist, most famous for his work on the tragedy of the commons. The passage quoted by Hayek can be found in G. Hardin, *Nature and Man's Fate* (New York: A Mentor Book, 1961), pp. 54–55. The insertions in square brackets are Hayek's. On the page cited by Hayek, Hardin refers only to Bernard and Clerk Maxwell; the references to Cannon and Wiener come earlier, on pp. 51–53. Claude Bernard (1813–78) was a French physiologist whose research contributed to the scientific understanding of homeostasis (that is, the way in which the self-regulation of vital processes in the human body enables it to maintain constant internal conditions in the face of a changing external environment). American physiologist Walter Bradford Cannon (1871–1945) built on Bernard's work, developing and popularising the notion of homeostasis in his book *The Wisdom of the Body* (New York: W. W. Norton, 1932). Best known for developing the theory of electromagnetism, the Scottish physicist James Clerk Maxwell (1831–79) also wrote a paper on speed governors that is commonly regarded as the foundation of the discipline of cybernetics. Norbert Wiener (1894–1964) was an American mathematician who, in his book *Cybernetics: Or Control and Communication in the Animal and the Machine* (Cambridge, MA: MIT Press, 1948), established cybernetics as an independent science.—Ed.]

[8] [As argued by Hayek in, for example, his "Notes on the Evolution of Systems of Rules of Conduct".—Ed.]

into account in forming the order without this knowledge first being transmitted to a central organiser. And while the complexity of activities which can be ordered as a *taxis* is necessarily limited to what can be known to the organiser, there is no similar limit in a spontaneous order.

While the deliberate use of spontaneous ordering forces (that is, of the rules of individual conduct which lead to the formation of a spontaneous general order) thus considerably extends the range and complexity of actions which can be integrated into a single order, it also reduces the power anyone can exercise over it without destroying the order. The regularities in the conduct of the elements in a *cosmos* determine merely its most general and abstract features. The detailed characteristics will be determined by the facts and aims which guide the actions of individual elements, though they are confined by the general rules within a certain permissible range. In consequence, the concrete content of such an order will always be unpredictable, though it may be the only method of achieving an order of wide scope. We must renounce the power of shaping its particular manifestations according to our desires. For example, the position which each individual will occupy in such an order will be largely determined by what to us must appear as accident. Though such a *cosmos* will serve all human purposes to some degree, it will not give anyone the power to determine whom it will favour more and whom less.

In an arrangement or *taxis*, on the other hand, the organiser can, within the restricted range achievable by this method, try to make the results conform to his preferences to any degree he likes. A *taxis* is necessarily designed for the achievement of particular ends or of a particular hierarchy of ends; and to the extent that the organiser can master the information about the available means, and effectively control their use, he may be able to make the arrangement correspond to his wishes in considerable detail. Since it will be *his* purposes that will govern the arrangement, he can attach any valuation to each element of the order and place it so as to make its position correspond to what he regards as its merits.

Where it is a question of using limited resources known to the organiser in the service of a unitary hierarchy of ends, an arrangement or organisation (*taxis*) will be the more effective method. But where the task involves using knowledge dispersed among and accessible only to thousands or millions of separate individuals, the use of spontaneous ordering forces (*cosmos*) will be superior. More importantly, people who have few or no ends in common, especially people who do not know one another or one another's circumstances, will be able to form a mutually beneficial and peaceful spontaneous order by submitting to the same abstract rules, but they can form an organisation only by submitting to somebody's concrete will. To form a common *cosmos* they need agree only on abstract rules, while to form an organisation they must either agree or be made to submit to a common hierarchy of ends. Only a *cosmos* can thus constitute an open society, while a political order conceived as an organisation must remain closed or tribal.

2 *Nomos* and *Thesis*

Two distinct kinds of rules or norms correspond respectively to *cosmos* or *taxis* which the elements must obey in order that the corresponding kind of order be formed. Since here, too, modern European languages lack terms which express the required distinction clearly and unambiguously, and since we have come to use the word 'law' or its equivalents ambiguously for both, we shall again propose Greek terms which, at least in the classic usage of Athens in the fourth and fifth centuries BC, conveyed approximately the required distinction.[9]

By *nomos* we shall describe a universal rule of just conduct applying to an unknown number of future instances and equally to all persons in the objective circumstances described by the rule, irrespective of the effects which observance of the rule will produce in a particular situation. Such rules demarcate protected individual domains by enabling each person or organised group to know which means they may employ in the pursuit of their purposes, and thus to prevent conflict between the actions of the different persons. Such rules are generally described as 'abstract' and are independent of individual ends.[10] They lead to the formation of an equally abstract and end-independent spontaneous order or *cosmos*.

---

[9] *Thesis* must not be confused with *thesmos*, a Greek term for 'law' older than *nomos* but, at least in classical times, meaning rather the law laid down by a ruler than the impersonal rules of conduct. *Thesis*, by contrast, means the particular act of setting up an arrangement. It is significant that the ancient Greeks could never make up their minds whether the proper opposite to what was determined by nature (*physei*) was what was determined *nomō* or what was determined *thesei*. On this problem see chapter 6 of the volume of essays and the lecture mentioned in footnote 3 of this chapter. [Hayek refers to "The Results of Human Action but Not of Human Design" and to "Dr. Bernard Mandeville (1670–1733)".—Ed.]

[10] The end-independent character of rules of just conduct has been demonstrated clearly by David Hume and most systematically developed by Immanuel Kant. Cf. D. Hume, "An enquiry concerning the principles of Morals", in *Essays, Moral, Political, and Literary*, ed. T. H. Green and T. H. Grose, London, 1875, vol. II, p. 273: "the benefit, resulting from [the social virtues of justice and fidelity], is not the consequence of every individual single act; but arises from the whole scheme or system, concurred in by the whole, or the greater part of the society. General peace and order are the attendants of justice or a general abstinence from the possessions of others: But a particular regard to the particular right of one individual citizen may frequently, considered in itself, be productive of pernicious consequences. The result of the individual acts is here, in many instances, directly opposite to that of the whole system of actions; and the former may be extremely hurtful, while the latter is, to the highest degree, advantageous." [The square brackets were added by Hayek; the inserted words are from the sentence in Hume's essay imme-

In contrast, we shall use *thesis* to mean any rule which is applicable only to particular people or in the service of the ends of rulers. Though such rules may still be general to various degrees and refer to a multiplicity of particular instances, they will shade imperceptibly from rules in the usual sense to particular commands. They are the necessary instrument of running an organisation or *taxis*.

The reason why an organisation must to some extent rely on rules and not be directed by particular commands only also explains why a spontaneous order can achieve results which organisations cannot. By restricting actions of individuals only by general rules they can use information which the authority does not possess. The agencies to which the head of an organisation delegates functions can adapt to changing circumstances known only to them, and therefore the commands of authority will generally take the form of general instructions rather than of specific orders.

In two important respects, however, the rules governing the members of an organisation will necessarily differ from rules on which a spontaneous order rests: rules for an organisation presuppose the assignment of particular tasks, targets or functions to individual people by commands; and most of the rules of an organisation will apply only to the persons charged with particular responsibilities. The rules of organisation will therefore never be universal in intent or end-independent, but always subsidiary to the commands by which roles are assigned and tasks or aims prescribed. They do not serve the spontaneous formation of an abstract order in which each individual must find his place and is able to build up a protected domain. The purpose and general outline of the organisation or arrangement must be determined by the organiser.

---

diately preceding the one quoted. The reference is D. Hume, "An Enquiry Concerning the Principles of Morals", in *Essays: Moral, Political, and Literary*, ed. T. H. Green and T. H. Grose, 2 vols. (London: Longmans, Green and Co., 1875), vol. 2, p. 273.—Ed.] See also his *Treatise on Human Nature* (same ed.), vol. II, p. 318: "It is evident, that if men were to regulate their conduct by the view of a particular *interest*, they would involve themselves in endless confusion." [The full quote, which Hayek edited somewhat, is as follows: "'tis evident, that if men were to regulate their conduct in this particular [the appointment of magistrates], by the view of a peculiar *interest*, either public or private, they wou'd involve themselves in endless confusion, and wou'd render all government, in a great measure, ineffectual". See D. Hume, *A Treatise on Human Nature*, ed. T. H. Green and T. H. Grose, 2 vols. (London: Longmans, Green and Co., 1878), vol. 2, p. 318.—Ed.] For I. Kant see the excellent exposition in Mary Gregor, *Laws of Freedom,* Oxford, 1963, especially pp. 38–42 and 81. [M. Gregor, *Laws of Freedom: A Study of Kant's Method of Applying the Categorical Imperative in the Metaphysik der Sitten* (Oxford: Basil Blackwell, 1963), pp. 38–42, 81. Elsewhere, Hayek explains that it was through reading Gregor's book that he realised that in his legal philosophy Kant used the categorical imperative as a negative test whereby the justice of a rule can be established by considering its compatibility with all of the other rules in which a set of people believe. See F. A. Hayek, *The Mirage of Social Justice*, vol. 2 (1976) of *Law, Legislation and Liberty*, pp. 166–67 n. 24.—Ed.]

This distinction between the *nomoi* as universal rules of conduct and the *theseis* as rules of organisation corresponds roughly to the familiar distinction between private (including criminal) and public (constitutional and administrative) law. There exists much confusion between these two kinds of rules of law. This confusion is fostered by the terms employed and by the misleading theories of legal positivism (in turn the consequence of the predominant role of public lawyers in the development of jurisprudence). Both represent the public law as in some sense primary and as alone serving the public interest; while private law is regarded, not only as secondary and derived from the former, but also as serving not general but individual interests. The opposite, however, would be nearer the truth. Public law is the law of organisation, of the superstructure of government originally erected only to ensure the enforcement of private law. It has been truly said that public law passes, but private law persists.[11] Whatever the changing structure of government, the basic structure of society resting on the rules of conduct persists. Government therefore owes its authority and has a claim to the allegiance of the citizens only if it maintains the foundations of that spontaneous order on which the working of society's everyday life rests.

The belief in the pre-eminence of public law is a result of the fact that it has indeed been deliberately created for particular purposes by acts of will, while private law is the result of an evolutionary process and has never been invented or designed as a whole by anybody. It was in the sphere of public law where law-making emerged while, for millennia, in the sphere of private law development proceeded through a process of law-finding in which judges and jurists endeavoured to articulate the rules which had already for long periods governed action and the 'sense of justice'.

Even though we must turn to public law to discover which rules of conduct an organisation will in practice enforce, it is not necessarily the public law to which the private law owes its authority. In so far as there is a spontaneously ordered society, public law merely organises the apparatus required for the better functioning of that more comprehensive spontaneous order. It determines a sort of superstructure erected primarily to protect a pre-existing spontaneous order and to enforce the rules on which it rests.

It is instructive to remember that the conception of law in the sense of *nomos* (i.e. of an abstract rule not due to anybody's concrete will, applicable in particular cases irrespective of the consequences, a law which could be 'found' and was not made for particular foreseeable purposes) has existed and been preserved together with the ideal of individual liberty only in countries such as ancient Rome and modern Britain, in which the development of private

---

[11] H. Huber, *Recht, Staat, und Gesellschaft*, Bern, 1954, p. 5: "Staatsrecht vergeht, Privatrecht besteht". [H. Huber, *Recht, Staat, und Gesellschaft* (Bern: Herbert Lang, 1954), p. 5.—Ed.]

law was based on case law and not on statute law, that is, was in the hands of judges or jurists and not of legislators. Both the conception of law as *nomos* and the ideal of individual liberty have rapidly disappeared whenever the law came to be conceived as the instrument of a government's own ends.[12]

What is not generally understood in this connection is that, as a necessary consequence of case law procedure, law based on precedent must consist exclusively of end-independent abstract rules of conduct of universal intent which the judges and jurists attempt to distil from earlier decisions. There is no such built-in limitation to the norms established by a legislator; and he is therefore less likely to submit to such limitations as the chief task which occupies him. For a long time before alterations in the *nomos* were seriously contemplated, legislators were almost exclusively concerned with laying down the rules of organisation which regulate the apparatus of government. The traditional conception of the law as *nomos* underlies ideals like those of the Rule of Law, a Government under the Law, and the Separation of Powers. In consequence, when representative bodies, initially concerned solely with matters of government proper, such as taxation, began to be regarded also as the sources of the *nomos* (the private law, or the universal rules of conduct), this traditional concept was soon replaced by the idea that law was whatever the will of the authorised legislator laid down on particular matters.[13]

Few insights more clearly reveal the governing tendencies of our time than understanding that the progressive permeation and displacement of private by public law is part of the process of transformation of a free, spontaneous order of society into an organisation or *taxis*. This transformation is the result of two factors which have been governing development for more than a century: on the one hand, of the increasing replacement of rules of just individual conduct (guided by 'commutative justice') by conceptions of 'social' or 'distributive' justice, and on the other hand, of the placing of the power of laying down *nomoi* (i.e. rules of just conduct) in the hands of the body charged with the direction of government. It has been largely this fusion of these two essentially different tasks in the same 'legislative' assemblies which has almost wholly destroyed the distinction between law as a universal rule of

---

[12] [Hayek expands on these claims in F. A. Hayek, *Rules and Order*, vol. 1 (1973) of *Law, Legislation and Liberty*, pp. 72–144.—Ed.]

[13] A revealing description of the difference between the law with which the judge is concerned and the law of modern legislation is to be found in an essay by the distinguished American public lawyer P. A. Freund in R. B. Brandt (ed.), *Social Justice*, New York, 1962, p. 94: "The judge addresses himself to standards of consistency, equivalence, predictability, the legislator to fair shares, social utility, and equitable distribution". [Paul A. Freund (1908–92) was an American jurist and professor of constitutional law who for most of his life taught at Harvard Law School. The full reference is: P. A. Freund, "Social Justice and the Law", in *Social Justice*, ed. R. B. Brandt (Englewood Cliffs, NJ: Prentice-Hall, 1962), p. 94.—Ed.]

conduct and law as an instruction to government on what to do in particular instances.

The socialist aim of a just distribution of incomes must lead to such a transformation of the spontaneous order into an organisation; for only in an organisation, directed towards a common hierarchy of ends, and in which the individuals have to perform assigned duties, can the conception of a 'just' reward be given meaning. In a spontaneous order nobody 'allocates', or can even foresee, the results which changes in circumstances will produce for particular individuals or groups, and it can know justice only as rules of just individual conduct but not in results. Such a society certainly presupposes the belief that justice, in the sense of rules of just conduct, is not an empty word—but 'social justice' must remain an empty concept so long as the spontaneous order is not wholly transformed into a totalitarian organisation in which rewards are given by authority for merit earned in performing duties assigned by that authority. 'Social' or 'distributive' justice is the justice of organisation but meaningless in a spontaneous order.[14]

3 A Digression on Articulated and Non-articulated Rules

Though the distinction to be considered next is not quite on the same plane with the others examined here, it will be expedient to insert some remarks on the sense in which we are employing the term 'rule'. As we have used it it covers two distinct meanings, the difference between which is often confused with, or concealed by, the more familiar and closely related distinction between written and unwritten, or between customary and statute, law. The point to be emphasised is that a rule may effectively govern action in the sense that from knowing it we can predict how people will act, without it being known as a verbal formula to the actors. Men may 'know how' to act, and the manner of their action may be correctly described by an articulated rule, without their explicitly 'knowing that' the rule is such and such; that is, they need not be able to state the rule in words in order to be able to conform to it in their actions, or to recognise whether others have or have not done so.[15]

---

[14] [Hayek develops his critique of social justice at greater length in *The Mirage of Social Justice*, pp. 62–106.—Ed.]

[15] [Hayek draws here on the work of Oxford linguistic philosopher Gilbert Ryle (1900–1976), most notably "Knowing How and Knowing That", *Proceedings of the Aristotelian Society*, vol. 46, 1946, pp. 1–16, and *The Concept of Mind* (London: Hutchinson's University Library, 1949), chapter 2. The issues mentioned in this paragraph, and in the remainder of the section, are discussed at greater length in F. A. Hayek, "Rules, Perception and Intelligibility" [1962] and F. A. Hayek, "The Primacy of the Abstract" [1969], reprinted as chapters 8 and 13 respectively of *The Market and Other Orders*, and in Hayek, *Rules and Order*, pp. 72–123.—Ed.]

There can be no doubt that, both in early society and since, many of the rules which manifest themselves in consistent judicial decisions are not known to anyone as verbal formulae, and that even the rules which are known in articulated form will often be merely imperfect efforts to express in words principles which guide action and are expressed in approval or disapproval of the actions of others. What we call the 'sense of justice' is nothing but that capacity to act in accordance with non-articulated rules, and what is described as finding or discovering justice consists in trying to express in words the yet unarticulated rules by which a particular decision is judged.

This capacity to act, and to recognise whether others act, in accordance with non-articulated rules probably always exists before attempts are made to articulate such rules; and most articulated rules are merely more or less successful attempts to put into words what has been acted upon before, and will continue to form the basis for judging the results of the application of the articulated rules.

Of course, once particular articulations of rules of conduct have become accepted, they will be the chief means of transmitting such rules; and the development of articulated and unarticulated rules will constantly interact. Yet it seems probable that no system of articulated rules can exist or be fully understood without a background of unarticulated rules which will be drawn upon when gaps are discovered in the system of articulated rules.

This governing influence of a background of unarticulated rules explains why the application of general rules to particular instances will rarely take the form of a syllogism, since only articulated rules can serve as explicit premises of such a syllogism. Conclusions derived from the articulated rules only will not be tolerated if they conflict with the conclusions to which yet unarticulated rules lead. Equity develops by the side of the already fully articulated rules of strict law through this familiar process.

There is in this respect much less difference between the unwritten or customary law which is handed down in the form of articulated verbal rules and the written law, than there is between articulated and unarticulated rules. Much of the unwritten or customary law may already be articulated in orally transmitted verbal formulae. Yet, even when all law that can be said to be explicitly known has been articulated, this need not mean that the process of articulating the rules that in practice guide decisions has already been completed.

4 Opinion and Will, Values and Ends

We come now to a pair of important distinctions for which the available terms are particularly inadequate and for which even classical Greek does not provide us with readily intelligible expressions. Yet the substitution by Rousseau, Hegel, and their followers down to T. H. Green, of the term 'will' for what older authors had described as 'opinion',[16] and still earlier ones contrasted as *ratio* to *voluntas*, was probably the most fateful terminological innovation in the history of political thinking.

This substitution of the term 'will' for 'opinion' was the product of a constructivistic rationalism[17] which imagined that all laws were invented for a known purpose rather than the articulation or improved formulation of practices that had prevailed because they produced a more viable order than those current in competing groups. The term 'opinion' at the same time became increasingly suspect because it was contrasted with incontrovertible knowledge of cause and effect and a growing tendency to discard all statements incapable of proof. 'Mere opinion' became one of the chief targets of rationalist critique; 'will' seemed to refer to rational purposive action, while 'opinion' came to be regarded as something typically uncertain and incapable of rational discussion.

Yet the order of an open society and all modern civilisation rests largely on opinions which have been effective in producing such an order long before people knew why they held them; and in a great measure it still rests on such beliefs. Even when people began to ask how the rules of conduct which they observed might be improved, the effects which they produced, and in the light of which they might be revised, were only dimly understood. The difficulty lay in the fact that any attempt to assess an action by its foreseeable results in the particular case is the very opposite of the function which opinions about the permissibility or non-permissibility of a kind of action play in the formation of an overall order.

Our insight into these circumstances is much obscured by the rationalistic

---

[16] The term 'opinion' has been most consistently used in this sense by David Hume particularly in *Essays, loc. cit.*, vol. I, p. 125: "It may farther be said, that, though men be much governed by interest; yet even interest itself, and all human affairs, are entirely governed by *opinion*"; and *ibid.*, p. 110: "[A]s FORCE is always on the side of the governed, the governors have nothing to support them but opinion. It is therefore, on opinion only that government is founded; and this maxim extends to the most despotic military governments, as well as to the most free and most popular". [See Hume, *Essays: Moral, Political and Literary*, vol. 1, pp. 125, 110.—Ed.] It seems that this use of the term 'opinion' derives from the great political debates of the seventeenth century; this is at least suggested by the text of a broadside of 1641 with an engraving by Wenceslaus Hollar (reproduced as frontispiece to vol. I of William Haller (ed.), *Tracts on Liberty in the Puritan Revolution 1638–1747*, New York, 1934) which is headed "The world is ruled and governed by opinion". [*Tracts on Liberty in the Puritan Revolution*, ed. W. Haller, 3 vols. (New York: Columbia University Press, 1934).—Ed.]

[17] The Cartesian foundations of Rousseau's thinking in these respects are clearly brought out in Robert Derathé, *Le Rationalisme de J.-J. Rousseau*, Paris, 1948. [R. Derathé, *Le rationalisme de J.-J. Rousseau* (Paris: Presses Universitaires de France, 1948).—Ed.]

prejudice that intelligent behaviour is governed exclusively by a knowledge of the relations between cause and effect, and by the associated belief that 'reason' manifests itself only in deductions derived from such knowledge. The only kind of rational action constructivistic rationalism recognises is action guided by such considerations as 'If I want X then I must do Y'. Human action, however, is in fact as much guided by rules which limit it to permissible kinds of actions—rules which generally preclude certain *kinds* of action irrespective of their foreseeable particular results. Our capacity to act successfully in our natural and social environment rests as much on such knowledge of what *not* to do (usually without awareness of the consequences which would follow if we did it) as on our knowledge of the particular effects of what we do. In fact, our positive knowledge serves us effectively only thanks to rules which confine our actions to the limited range within which we are able to foresee relevant consequences. It prevents us from overstepping these limits. Fear of the unknown, and avoidance of actions with unforeseeable consequences, has as important a function to perform in making our actions 'rational' in the sense of successful as positive knowledge.[18] If the term 'reason' is confined to knowledge of positive facts and excludes knowledge of the 'ought not', a large part of the rules which guide human action so as to enable the individuals or groups to persist in the environment in which they live is excluded from 'reason'. Much of the accumulated experience of the human race would fall outside what is described as 'reason' if this concept is arbitrarily confined to positive knowledge of the rules of cause and effect which govern particular events in our environment.

Before the rationalist revolution of the sixteenth and seventeenth centuries, however, the term 'reason' included and even gave first place to the knowledge of appropriate rules of conduct. When *ratio* was contrasted with *voluntas*, the former referred pre-eminently to opinion about the permissibility or non-permissibility of the kinds of conduct which *voluntas* indicated as the most obvious means of achieving a particular result.[19] What was described as reason was thus not so much knowledge that in particular circumstances particular actions would produce particular results, but a capacity to avoid

[18] The extension of knowledge is largely due to persons who transcended these limits, but of those who did many more probably perished or endangered their fellows than added to the common stock of positive knowledge.

[19] John Locke, *Essays on the Law of Nature* (1676), ed. W. von Leyden, Oxford, 1954, p. 111: "By reason . . . I do not think is meant here that faculty of the understanding which forms trains of thought and deduces proofs, but certain definite principles of action from which spring all virtues and whatever is necessary for the proper moulding of morals . . . reason does not so much establish and pronounce this law of nature as search for it and discover it . . . Neither is reason so much the maker of that law as its interpreter". [J. Locke, *Essays on the Law of Nature* [1676], ed. W. von Leyden (Oxford: Clarendon Press, 1954), p. 111.—Ed.]

actions of a kind whose foreseeable results seemed desirable, but which were likely to lead to the destruction of the order on which the achievements of the human race rested.

We are familiar with the crucial point that the general order of society into which individual actions are integrated results not from the concrete purposes which individuals pursue but from their observing rules which limit the range of their actions. It does not really matter for the formation of this order what are the concrete purposes pursued by the individuals; they may in many instances be wholly absurd, yet so long as the individuals pursue their purposes within the limits of those rules, they may in doing so contribute to the needs of others. It is not the purposive but the rule-governed aspect of individual actions which integrates them into the order on which civilisation rests.[20]

To describe the content of a rule, or of a law defining just conduct, as the expression of a *will*[21] (popular or other) is thus wholly misleading. Legislators approving the text of a statute articulating a rule of conduct, or legal draftsmen deciding the wording of such a bill, will be guided by a will aiming at a particular result; but the particular form of words is not the content of such a law. *Will* always refers to particular actions serving particular ends, and the will ceases when the action is taken and the end (terminus) reached. But nobody can have a *will* in this sense concerning what shall happen in an unknown number of future instances.

Opinions, on the other hand, have no purpose known to those who hold them—indeed, we should rightly suspect an opinion on matters of right and wrong if we found that it was held for a purpose. Most of the beneficial opinions held by individuals are held by them without their having any known reasons for them except that they are the traditions of the society in which they have grown up. *Opinion* about what is right and wrong has therefore nothing to do with *will* in the precise sense in which it is necessary to use the term if confusion is to be avoided. We all know only too well that our will may often

---

[20] The distinction between what we call here the 'purposive' and the 'rule-governed' aspects of action is probably the same as Max Weber's distinction between what he calls *zweckrational* and *wertrational*. If this is so it should, however, be clear that hardly any action could be guided by only either the one or the other kind of consideration, but that considerations of the effectiveness of the means according to the rules of cause and effect will normally be combined with considerations of their appropriateness according to the normative rules about the permissibility of the means. [German sociologist and political economist Max Weber (1864–1920) distinguished between the instrumentally-rational (*zweckrational*) and value-rational (*wertrational*) forms of action in M. Weber, *Economy and Society: An Outline of Interpretive Sociology*, ed. G. Roth and C. Wittich (Berkeley: University of California Press, 1968), vol. 1, pp. 24–26.—Ed.]

[21] This is a confusion against which the ancient Greeks were protected by their language, since the only word they had to express what we describe as willing, *bouleuomai*, clearly referred only to particular concrete actions. (M. Pohlenz, *Der Hellenische Mensch*, Göttingen, 1946, p. 210.) [M. Pohlenz, *Der Hellenische Mensch* (Göttingen: Vandenhoeck und Ruprecht, 1946), p. 210.—Ed.]

be in conflict with what we think is right, and this applies no less to a group of people aiming at a common concrete purpose than to any individual.

While an act of will is always determined by a particular concrete *end* (terminus) and the state of willing ceases when the end is achieved, the manner in which the end is pursued does also depend on *dispositions* which are more or less permanent properties of the acting person.[22] These dispositions are complexes of built-in rules which say either which kinds of actions will lead to a certain kind of result or which are generally to be avoided. This is not the place to enter into a discussion of the highly complex hierarchic structure of those systems of dispositions which govern our thinking and which include dispositions to change dispositions, etc., as well as those which govern all actions of a particular organism and others which are only evoked in particular circumstances.[23]

What is of importance is that among the dispositions which will govern the manner of action of a particular organism there will always be, in addition to dispositions to the kind of actions likely to produce particular results, many negative dispositions which rule out some kinds of action. These inhibitions against types of actions likely to be harmful to the individual or the group are probably among the most important adaptations which all organisms, and especially all individuals living in groups, must possess to make life possible. 'Taboos' are as much a necessary basis of successful existence of a social animal as positive knowledge of what kind of action will produce a given result.

If we are systematically to distinguish the *will* directed to a particular *end* (terminus) and disappearing when that particular end has been reached, from the *opinion* in the sense of a lasting or permanent disposition towards (or against) *kinds* of conduct, it will be expedient to adopt also a distinct name for the generalised aims towards which *opinions* are directed. It is suggested that

[22] Cf chapter 3 of *Studies in Philosophy, Politics and Economics,* London and Chicago, 1967. [Hayek refers to his essay "Rules, Perception and Intelligibility". Also see Hayek, "The Primacy of the Abstract", and F. A. Hayek, "The Sensory Order after 25 Years" [1982], reprinted on pp. 382–89 of F. A. Hayek, *The Sensory Order and Other Writings on the Foundations of Theoretical Psychology,* ed. V. Vanberg, vol. 14 (2017) of *The Collected Works of F. A. Hayek.*—Ed.]

[23] It is the basic mistake of particularistic utilitarianism to assume that rules of just conduct aim at particular concrete ends and must be judged by them. I know of no clearer expression of this fundamental error of constructivist rationalism than the statement by Hastings Rashdall (*The Theory of Good and Evil,* London, 1948, vol. I, p. 184) that "all moral judgements are ultimately judgements as to the value of ends". This is precisely what they are *not.* They do not refer to concrete ends but to kinds of actions or, in other words, they are judgments about means based on a presumed probability that a kind of action will produce undesirable effects, but are applicable in spite of our factual ignorance in most particular instances of whether they will do so or not. [Hastings Rashdall (1858–1924) was an English moral philosopher, theologian, and historian whose 'ideal utilitarianism' drew on the work of Henry Sidgwick and T. H. Green. The words quoted by Hayek can be found on p. 184 of vol. 1 of H. Rashdall, *The Theory of Good and Evil: A Treatise on Moral Philosophy,* 2 vols. (Oxford: Clarendon Press, 1907).—Ed.]

among the available terms the one which corresponds to *opinion* in the same way in which *end* corresponds to *will* is the term *value*.[24] It is of course not used currently only in this narrow sense; and we are all apt to describe the importance of a particular concrete end as its value. Nevertheless, at least in its plural form *values*, the term seems as closely to approach the needed meaning as any other term available.

It is therefore expedient to describe as values what may guide a person's actions throughout most of his life as distinct from the concrete ends which determine his actions at particular moments. Values in this sense, moreover, are largely culturally transmitted and will guide the action even of persons who are not consciously aware of them, while the end which most of the time will be the focus of conscious attention will normally be the result of the particular circumstances in which he finds himself at any moment. In the sense in which the term 'value' is most generally used it certainly does not refer to particular objects, persons, or events, but to attributes which many different objects, persons, or events may possess at different times and different places and which, if we endeavour to describe them, we will usually describe by stating a rule to which these objects, persons or actions conform. The importance of a value is related to the urgency of a need or of a particular end in the same manner in which the universal or abstract is related to the particular or concrete.

It should be noted that these more or less permanent dispositions which we describe as *opinions about values* are something very different from the emotions with which they are sometimes connected. Emotions, like needs, are evoked by and directed towards particular concrete objects and rapidly disappear with their disappearance. They are, unlike opinions and values, *temporary* dispositions which will guide actions with regard to particular things but not a framework which controls all actions. Like a particular end an emotion may overpower the restraints of opinion which refer not to the particular but to the abstract and general features of the situation. In this respect opinion, being abstract, is much more akin to knowledge of cause and effect and therefore deserves to be included with the latter as part of reason.

All moral problems, in the widest sense of the term, arise from a conflict between a knowledge that particular desirable results can be achieved in a given way and the rules which tell us that some *kinds* of actions are to be avoided. It is the extent of our ignorance which makes it necessary that in the use of knowledge we should be limited and should refrain from many

[24] Cf. W. Shakespeare, *Troilus and Cressida*, II, 2, 52:
But value dwells not in particular will;
It holds his estimate and dignity
As well wherein 'tis precious of itself
As in the prizer.

actions whose unpredictable consequences might place us outside the order within which alone the world is tolerably safe for us. It is only thanks to such restraints that our limited knowledge of positive facts serves us as a reliable guide in the sea of ignorance in which we move. The actions of a person who insisted on being guided only by calculable results and refused to respect opinions about what is prudent or permissible would soon prove unsuccessful and in this sense be irrational to the highest degree.

The understanding of this distinction has been badly blurred by the words at our disposal. But it is of fundamental importance because the possibility of the required agreement, and therefore of a peaceful existence of the order of an Open Society, rests on it. Our thinking and our vocabulary are still determined largely by the problems and needs of the small group concerned with specific ends known to all its members. The confusion and harm caused by the application of these conceptions to the problems of the Open Society are immense. They have been preserved particularly through the dominance in moral philosophy of a Platonic tribalism which in modern times has received strong support from the preference of people engaged in empirical research for the problems of the observable and tangible small groups and from their distaste for the intangible, more comprehensive order of the social cosmos—an order which can be only mentally reconstructed but never intuitively perceived or observed as a whole.

The possibility of an Open Society rests on its members possessing common opinions, rules and values, and its existence becomes impossible if we insist that it must possess a common will issuing commands directing its members to particular ends. The larger the groups within which we hope to live in peace, the more the common values which are enforced must be confined to abstract and general rules of conduct. The members of an Open Society have and can have in common only *opinions* on values but *not* a *will* on concrete ends. In consequence the possibility of an order of peace based on agreement, especially in a democracy, rests on coercion being confined to the enforcement of abstract rules of just conduct.

5 Nomocracy and Teleocracy

The first two of the distinctions we have drawn (in sections 1 and 2) have been conveniently combined by Professor Michael Oakeshott into the two concepts of *nomocracy* and *teleocracy*,[25] which need now hardly any further expla-

---

[25] So far as I know these terms have been used by Professor Oakeshott only in his oral teaching but not in any published work. For reasons which will become clear in section 7, I should have preferred to employ the term *nomarchy* rather than *nomocracy*, if the former were not too easily

nation. A *nomocracy* corresponds to our *cosmos* resting entirely on general rules or *nomoi*, while a *teleocracy* corresponds to a *taxis* (arrangement or organisation) directed towards particular ends or *teloi*. For the former the 'public good' or 'general welfare' consists solely in the preservation of that abstract and end-independent order which is secured by obedience to abstract rules of just conduct: that "public interest which is no other than common right and justice excluding all partiality or private interest [which may be] called the empire of laws and not of men".[26] For a teleocracy, on the other hand, the common good consists of the sum of the particular interests, that is, the sum of the concrete foreseeable results affecting particular people or groups. It was this latter conception which seemed more acceptable to the naive constructivistic rationalism whose criterion of rationality is a recognisable concrete order serving known particular purposes. Such a teleocratic order, however, is incompatible with the development of an Open Society comprising numerous people having no known concrete purposes in common; and the attempt to impose it on the grown order or a nomocracy leads back from the Open Society to the Tribal Society of the small group. And since all conceptions of the 'merit' according to which individuals should be 'rewarded' must derive from concrete and particular ends towards which the common efforts of a group are directed, all efforts towards a 'distributive' or 'social' justice must lead to the replacement of the nomocracy by a teleocracy, and thus to a return from the Open to the Tribal Society.[27]

---

confused with 'monarchy'. [Michael Oakeshott (1901–1990) was a conservative political theorist and philosopher who, in lectures on the history of political thought delivered at the London School of Economics in the late 1960s, used the terms 'nomocratic' and 'teleocratic' to describe different kinds of state. See M. Oakeshott, *Lectures in the History of Political Thought*, ed. T. Nardin and L. O'Sullivan (Exeter: Imprint Academic, 2006), pp. 469–97. Oakeshott later recast this distinction as that between civil and enterprise associations. See M. Oakeshott, *On Human Conduct* (Oxford: Clarendon Press, 1975), pp. 108–18.—Ed.]

[26] James Harrington, *The Prerogative of Popular Government* (1658), in *The Oceana and His Other Works*, ed. J. Toland, London, 1771, p. 224. [The addition in square brackets is Hayek's. The full quote is: "That interests also being of one, or more, or of all; those of one man, or of a few men, where laws are made accordingly, being more privat than coms duly up to the law, the nature wherof lys not in partiality but in justice, may be call'd the empire of men, and not of laws: and that of the whole people coming up to the public interest (which is no other than common right and justice, excluding all partiality or privat interest) may be call'd the empire of laws, and not of men". See J. Harrington, "The Prerogative of Popular Government" [1658], in *The Oceana and Other Works of James Harrington, with an Account of his Life by John Toland* (London: T. Becket and T. Cadell, 1771), bk. 1, chap. 2, p. 224. James Harrington (1611–77) was an English classical republican political theorist whose major work, *The Commonwealth of Oceana* (London: J. Streater, 1656), set out an ideal constitution that would facilitate the creation of a utopian republic.—Ed.]

[27] [Hayek draws here, and in the previous section, on the distinction drawn by philosopher Sir Karl Popper (1902–94) between 'closed' or tribal societies, whose inhabitants think of institutions as being determined by magical forces beyond their control, and 'open societies', where

6 *Catallaxy* and Economy

The instance in which the use of the same term for two different kinds of order has caused most confusion, and is still constantly misleading even serious thinkers, is probably that of the use of the word 'economy' for both the deliberate arrangement or organisation of resources in the service of a unitary hierarchy of ends, such as a household, an enterprise, or any other organisation including government, and the structure of many interrelated economies of this kind which we call a social, or national, or world 'economy' and often also simply an 'economy'. The ordered structure which the market produces is, however, not an organisation but a spontaneous order or cosmos, and is for this reason in many respects fundamentally different from that arrangement or organisation originally and properly called an economy.[28]

---

institutions are held to be man-made and therefore subject to critical evaluation, where individuals have significant freedom to decide how to behave, and where people must therefore take personal responsibility for their actions. See K. Popper, *The Open Society and Its Enemies*, vol. I: *The Spell of Plato* (London: George Routledge, 1945), pp. 1, 151–55. Also see F. A. Hayek, *The Political Order of a Free People*, vol. 3 (1979) of *Law, Legislation and Liberty*, pp. 161–68.—Ed.]

[28] I now find somewhat misleading the definition of the science of economics as "the study of the disposal of scarce means towards the realisation of given ends", which has been so effectively expounded by Lord Robbins and which I should long have defended. It seems to me appropriate only to that preliminary part of catallactics which consists in the study of what has sometimes been called 'simple economies' and to which also Aristotle's *Oeconomica* is exclusively devoted: the study of the dispositions of a single household or firm, sometimes described as the economic calculus or the pure logic of choice. (What is now called economics but had better be described as catallactics Aristotle described as *chrematistike* or the science of wealth.) The reason why Robbins' widely accepted definition now seems to me to be misleading is that the ends which a catallaxy serves are not *given* in their totality to anyone, that is, are not known either to any individual participant in the process or to the scientist studying it.

[Lionel Robbins (1898–1984), later Lord Robbins of Clare Market, was Professor of Economics at the London School of Economics and Political Science and for many years one of Hayek's closest friends and colleagues. The phrase to which Hayek refers does not appear in either the first or the second editions of Robbins' most famous work, namely *An Essay on the Nature and Significance of Economic Science*. The phrase "disposal of scarce means" appears once in the first edition of that book, on p. 15, and twice in the second edition, on pp. 16 and 22, but never as part of the sentence quoted by Hayek. The term "given ends" appears on seven occasions in the first edition, and eight in the second, but again never as part of the sentence reported by Hayek. It seems likely that Hayek was thinking of sentences such as that found on p. 23 of the first edition of that book, where Robbins states that economics is "concerned with that aspect of behaviour which arises from the scarcity of means to achieve given ends", and also such as those found on p. 15 of that edition where, having observed that "[s]carcity of means to satisfy given ends is an almost ubiquitous condition of human behaviour", Robbins offers his famous definition of economics: "Here, then, is the unity of subject of Economic Science, the forms assumed by human behaviour in disposing of scarce means . . . Economics is the science which studies human behaviour as a relationship between ends and scarce means which have alternative uses". See L. Robbins, *An Essay on the Nature and Significance of Economic Science*, 1st edn. (Lon-

The belief, largely due to this use of the same term for both, that the market order ought to be made to behave as if it were an economy proper, and that its performance can and ought to be judged by the same criteria, has become the source of so many errors and fallacies that it seems necessary to adopt a new technical term to describe the order of the market which spontaneously forms itself. By analogy with the term *catallactics* which has often been proposed as a replacement for the term 'economics' as the name for the theory of the market order, we could describe that order itself as a *catallaxy*. Both expressions are derived from the Greek verb *katallatein* (or *katallassein*) which significantly means not only 'to exchange' but also 'to receive into the community' and 'to turn from enemy into friend'.[29]

The chief aim of this neologism is to emphasise that a *catallaxy* neither ought nor can be made to serve a particular hierarchy of concrete ends, and that therefore its performance cannot be judged in terms of a sum of particular results. Yet all the aims of socialism, all attempts to enforce 'social' or 'distributive' justice, and the whole of so-called 'welfare economics', are directed towards turning the *cosmos* of the spontaneous order of the market into an arrangement or *taxis*, or the *catallaxy* into an economy proper. Apparently the belief that the *catallaxy* ought to be made to behave as if it were an economy seems so obvious and unquestionable to many economists that they never examine its validity. They treat it as the indisputable presupposition for rational examination of the desirability of any order, an assumption without

---

don: Macmillan, 1932), pp. 23, 15. In arguing that the ends served by a catallaxy are not given to anyone in their entirety, Hayek was drawing on arguments about the importance of dispersed knowledge first aired in F. A. Hayek, "Economics and Knowledge" [1937], reprinted as chapter 1 of *The Market and Other Orders*. A similar critique of Robbins was made by Hayek's fellow Nobel Laureate in economics, James Buchanan (1919–2013). See J. Buchanan, "What Should Economists Do?" [1964], in J. Buchanan, *What Should Economists Do?* (Indianapolis, IN: Liberty Fund, 1979), especially pp. 18–28.

Aristotle distinguished 'household management' (*oikonomia*) from the art of acquisition in general and of money in particular (*chrematistike*) in his *Politics*. See Aristotle, *Politics*, trans. Sir Ernest Barker (Oxford: Oxford University Press, 2009), 1256a1–1258a35. According to Hayek, Aristotle's emphasis on the economics of the household blinded him to the possibility of the spontaneous formation of social order on a larger scale (that is, to the possibility of a catallaxy). See F. A. Hayek, *The Fatal Conceit: The Errors of Socialism*, ed. W. W. Bartley III, vol. 1 (1988) of *The Collected Works of F. A. Hayek*, pp. 45–47.—Ed.]

[29] See H. G. Liddell and R. Scott, *A Greek-English Lexicon,* new ed., Oxford, 1940, s.v. *Katallásso.* [H. G. Liddell and R. Scott, *A Greek-English Lexicon,* 9th edn. (Oxford: Clarendon Press, 1940), p. 899. The entry referenced by Hayek records that the term 'catallaxy' can mean to "exchange, esp. of money", to "exchange one thing for another", and to "change a person from enmity to friendship". There is no reference to 'receive into the community' or to 'admit into the community'. Nor does a search of the online version of the *Lexicon* reveal any such references. Also see F. A. Hayek, "The Principles of a Liberal Social Order" [1966], reprinted as chapter 21 of the current volume, p. 278 n. 10.—Ed.]

which no judgment of the expediency or worth of alternative institutions is possible. The belief that the efficiency of the market order can be judged only in terms of the degree of the achievement of a known hierarchy of particular ends is, however, wholly erroneous. Indeed, since these ends are in their totality not known to anybody, any discussion in such terms is necessarily empty. The discovery procedure which we call competition aims at the closest approach we can achieve by any means known to us to a somewhat more modest aim which is nevertheless highly important: namely a state of affairs in which all that is in fact produced is produced at the lowest possible costs.[30] This means that of that particular combination of commodities and services which will be produced more will be made available than could be done by any other known means; and that in consequence, though the share in that product which the different individuals will get is left to be determined by circumstances nobody can foresee and in this sense to 'accident', each will get for the share he wins in the game (which is partly a game of skill and partly a game of chance) as large a real equivalent as can be secured. We allow the individual share to be determined partly by luck in order to make the total to be shared as large as possible.

The utilisation of the spontaneous ordering forces of the market to achieve this kind of optimum, and leaving the determination of the relative shares of the different individuals to what must appear as accident, are inseparable. Only because the market induces every individual to use his unique knowledge of particular opportunities and possibilities for his purposes can an overall order be achieved that uses in its totality the dispersed knowledge which is not accessible as a whole to anyone. The 'maximisation' of the total product in the above sense, and its distribution by the market, cannot be separated because it is through the determination of the prices of the factors of production that the overall order of the market is brought about. If incomes are not determined by factor pricing within the output, then output cannot be maximised relative to individual preferences.

This does not preclude, of course, that *outside* the market government may use distinct means placed at its disposal for the purpose of assisting people who, for one reason or another, cannot through the market earn a minimum income.[31] A society relying on the market order for the efficient use of its resources is likely fairly soon to reach an overall level of wealth which makes it possible for this minimum to be at an adequate level. But it should not be

[30] [See F. A. Hayek, "Competition as a Discovery Procedure" [1968], reprinted as chapter 12 of *The Market and Other Orders.*—Ed.]

[31] [Also see F. A. Hayek, *The Road to Serfdom: Text and Documents*, ed. B. Caldwell, vol. 2 (2007) of *The Collected Works of F. A. Hayek*, pp. 147–48, 156, and Hayek, *The Political Order of a Free People*, pp. 54–55.—Ed.]

achieved by manipulating the spontaneous order in such a manner as to make the income earned on the market conform to some ideal of 'distributive justice'. Such efforts will reduce the total in which all can share.

7 Demarchy and Democracy

This, unfortunately, does not exhaust the neologisms which seem necessary to escape the confusion which dominates current political thought. Another instance of the prevailing confusion of language is the almost universal use of the term 'democracy' for a special kind of democracy which is by no means a necessary consequence of the basic ideal originally described by that name. Indeed Aristotle questioned whether this form should even be called 'democracy'.[32] The appeal of the original ideal has been transferred to the particular form of democracy which now prevails everywhere, although this is very far from corresponding to what the original conception aimed at.

Initially the term 'democracy' meant no more than that whatever ultimate power there is should be in the hands of the majority of the people or their representatives. *But it said nothing about the extent of that power.* It is often mistakenly suggested that any ultimate power must be unlimited. From the demand that the *opinion* of the majority should prevail it by no means follows that their *will* on particular matters should be unlimited. Indeed the classical theory of the separation of powers presupposes that the 'legislation' which was to be in the hands of a representative assembly should be concerned only with the passing of 'laws' (which were presumed to be distinguishable from particular commands by some intrinsic property), and that particular decisions did not become laws (in the sense of *nomoi*) merely because they emanated from the 'legislature'. Without this distinction the idea that a separation of powers involved the attribution of particular functions to distinct bodies would have been meaningless and indeed circular.[33]

---

[32] Aristotle, *Politics*, Iv IV 4, 1,292a, Loeb, ed. Rackham, Cambridge, Mass., and London, 1950, p. 305: "And it would seem . . . a reasonable criticism to say that such a democracy is not a constitution at all; for where the laws do not govern there is no constitution, as the law ought to govern all things while the magistrates control particulars, and we ought to judge this to be constitutional government; if then democracy really is one of the forms of constitution, it is manifest that an organisation of this kind, in which all things are administered by resolutions of the assembly, is not even a democracy in the proper sense, for it is impossible for a voted resolution to be a universal rule". [The passage quoted can be found on p. 305 of Aristotle, *Politics*, trans. H. Rackham, Loeb Classical Library 264 (Cambridge, MA: Harvard University Press, 1932).—Ed.]

[33] Cf. above what is said under '*Nomos* and *Thesis*' on the difference between private and public law; and on what follows now also the important work by M. J. C. Vile, *Constitutionalism and*

If the legislature only can make new law and can do nothing else but make law, whether a particular resolution of that body is valid law must be determinable by a recognisable property of that resolution. Its source alone does not constitute a sufficient criterion of validity.

There can be no doubt that what the great theorists of representative government and of liberal constitutionalism meant by law when they demanded a separation of powers was what we have called *nomos*. That they spoiled their aim by entrusting to the same representative assemblies also the task of making laws in another sense, namely that of the rules of organisation determining the structure and conduct of government, is another story which we cannot further pursue here. Nor can we further consider the inevitable consequence of an institutional arrangement under which a legislature which is not confined to laying down universal rules of just conduct must be driven by organised interests to use its power of 'legislation' to serve particular private ends.[34] All we are here concerned with is that it is not necessary that the supreme authority possesses this sort of power. To limit power does *not* require that there be another power to limit it. If all power rests on *opinion*, and opinion recognises no other ultimate power than one that proves its belief in the justice of its actions *by committing itself to universal rules* (the application of which to particular cases it cannot control), the supreme power loses its authority as soon as it oversteps these limits.

The supreme power thus need not be an unlimited power—it may be a power which loses the indispensable support of opinion as soon as it pronounces anything which does not possess the substantive character of *nomos* in the sense of a universal rule of just conduct. Just as the Pope in Roman Catholic doctrine is deemed to be infallible only *dum ex cathedra loquitur*, that is, so long as he lays down dogma and not in his decision of particular matters, so a legislature may be supreme only when it exercises the capacity of legislating in the strict sense of stating the valid *nomos*. And it can be so limited because there exist objective tests (however difficult they may be to apply in particular instances) by which independent and impartial courts, not concerned with any particular aims of government, can decide whether what the legislature resolves has the character of a *nomos* or not, and therefore also whether it is binding law. All that is needed is a court of justice which can say whether the acts of the legislature do or do not possess certain formal proper-

---

the *Separation of Powers*, Oxford, 1967. [M. J. C. Vile, *Constitutionalism and the Separation of Powers* (Oxford: Clarendon Press, 1967).—Ed.]

[34] [Hayek explores these issues further in *Rules and Order*, pp. 89–91, 124–44, and in *The Political Order of a Free People*, pp. 1–40, 98–107. Also see F. A. Hayek, "The Constitution of a Liberal State" [1967], and F. A. Hayek, "Economic Freedom and Representative Government" [1973], which are reprinted as chapters 22 and 24 respectively of the present volume.—Ed.]

ties which every valid law must possess. But this court need possess no positive power to issue any commands.

The majority of a representative assembly may thus well be the *supreme* power and yet not possess *unlimited* power. If its power is limited to acting as (to revive another Greek term which appealed both to the seventeenth-century English theorists of democracy and to John Stuart Mill)[35] *nomothetae*, or as the setters of the *nomos*, without power to issue particular commands, no privilege or discrimination in favour of particular groups which it attempted to make law would have the force of law. This sort of power would simply not exist because whoever exercised supreme power would have to prove the legitimacy of its acts by committing himself to universal rules.

If we want democratic determination not only of the coercive rules which bind the private citizen as well as the government, but also of the administration of the government apparatus, we need some representative body to do the latter. But this body need not and should not be the *same* as that which lays down the *nomos*. It should itself be *under* the *nomos* laid down by another representative body, which would determine the limits of the power which this body could not alter. Such a governmental or directive (but in the strict sense *not* legislative) representative body would then indeed be concerned with matters of the *will* of the majority (i.e. with the achievement of particular concrete purposes) for the pursuit of which it would employ governmental powers. It would not be concerned with questions of *opinion* about what was

---

[35] Cf. Philip Hunton, *A Treatise of Monarchie*, London, 1643, p. 5, and John Stuart Mill, *On Liberty and Considerations of Representative Government*, ed. R. B. McCallum, Oxford, 1946, p. 171. [Philip Hunton (c.1602–82) was an English clergyman and political pamphleteer who, in *A Treatise of Monarchie*, advanced a theory according to which sovereign power was held jointly— though not necessarily equally—by the King, the House of Lords, and the House of Commons. Consequently, none of those bodies enjoyed absolute authority. On the page to which Hayek refers, Hunton writes that the "Power of Magistracie" has two degrees, namely the "*Nomotheticall* or *Architechtonicall* and the *Gubernative* or *Executive*". He goes on to state later in the same work that the Nomotheticall power is "the power of making, and authentick expounding Lawes" and is limited by being jointly held ("mixed") by the Monarch, Lords and Commons: "he who knowes how farre this Government is limited, will soon discerne how farre it is mixed, for the Limitation is mostly affected by the mixture". See P. Hunton, *A Treatise on Monarchy* (London: John Bellamy and Ralph Smith, 1643), pp. 5, 46 (also see p. 38).

In the course of a discussion of the shortcomings of Parliament in framing laws, and the consequent need for a Commission of legislation charged with that task, Mill writes: "The necessity of some provision corresponding to this was felt even in the Athenian democracy, where, in the time of its most complete ascendency, the popular Ecclesia could pass Psephisms (mostly decrees on single matters of policy), but laws, so called, could only be made or altered by a different and less numerous body, renewed annually, called the Nomothetae, whose duty it also was to revise the whole of the laws, and keep them consistent with one another". See J. S. Mill, *On Liberty and Considerations on Representative Government*, ed. R. B. McCallum (Oxford: Basil Blackwell, 1946), p. 171.—Ed.]

right and wrong. It would be devoted to the satisfaction of concrete foresee-able needs by the use of separate resources set aside for the purpose.

The fathers of liberal constitutionalism were surely right when they thought that in the supreme assemblies concerned with what they regarded as legis-lation proper, that is, with laying down the *nomos*, those coalitions of organ-ised interests which they called factions and which we call parties should have no place. Parties are indeed concerned with matters of concrete *will*, the sat-isfaction of the particular interest of the people who combine to form them, but legislation proper should express *opinion* and therefore not be placed in the hands of representatives of particular interests but in the hands of a rep-resentative sample of the prevailing opinion, persons who should be secured against all pressure of particular interests.

I have elsewhere suggested[36] a method of electing such a representative body that would make it independent of the organised parties though they would still remain necessary for the effective democratic conduct of gov-ernment proper. It requires the election of members for long periods after which they would not be re-eligible. To make them nevertheless representa-tive of current opinion a representation by age groups might be used: each generation electing once in their lives, say, in their fortieth year, representa-tives to serve for 15 years and thereafter assured of continued occupation as lay judges. The law-making assembly would then be composed of men and women between 40 and 55 (and thus probably of an average age somewhat lower than the existing representative assemblies!), elected by their contem-poraries after they had opportunity to prove themselves in ordinary life, and required on election to abandon their private occupations for an honorific position for the rest of their active life.

Such a system of election by the contemporaries (who usually are the best judges of a person's ability) would come nearer to producing that ideal of the political theorists, a senate of wise and honourable men, than any system yet tried. The restriction of the power of such a body to legislation proper would for the first time make possible that real separation of powers which has never yet existed, and with it a true government under the law and an effective rule of law. The governmental or directive assembly, on the other hand, subject to the law laid down by the former, and concerned with the provision of par-ticular services, might well continue to be elected on established party lines.

Such a basic change in existing constitutional arrangements presupposes

---

[36] Most recently in the two essays reprinted as the next two chapters of this volume. [Hayek refers to "The Constitution of a Liberal State" and "Economic Freedom and Representative Government", which were reprinted as chapters 7 and 8 respectively of *New Studies in Philosophy, Politics, Economics and the History of Ideas* and now appear as chapters 22 and 24 respectively of the current volume. The reference to the second of these essays appeared only in the 1978 reprint of this chapter. Also see Hayek, *The Political Order of a Free People*, pp. 105–27.—Ed.]

that we finally shed the illusion that the safeguards men once painfully devised to prevent abuse of government power are all unnecessary once that power is placed in the hands of the majority of the people. There is no reason whatever to expect that an omnipotent democratic government will always serve the general rather than particular interests. Democratic government free to benefit particular groups is bound to be dominated by coalitions of organised interests, rather than serve the general interest in the classical sense of 'common right and justice, excluding all partial or private interests'.[37]

It is greatly to be regretted that the word democracy should have become indissolubly connected with the conception of the unlimited power of the majority on particular matters.[38] But if this is so we need a new word to denote the ideal which democracy originally expressed, the ideal of a rule of the popular *opinion* on what is just, but not of a popular *will* concerning whatever concrete measures seem desirable to the coalition of organised interests governing at the moment. If democracy and limited government have become irreconcilable conceptions, we must find a new word for what once might have been called limited democracy. We want the *opinion* of the *demos* to be the ultimate authority, but not allow the naked power of the majority, its *kratos*, to do rule-less violence to individuals. The majority should then *rule* (*archein*) by "established *standing laws*, promulgated and known to the people, and not by extemporary decrees".[39] We might perhaps describe such a political order by linking *demos* with *archein* and call *demarchy* such a limited government in which the opinion but not the particular will of the people is the highest authority. The particular scheme considered above was meant to suggest one possible way to secure such a *demarchy*.

If it is insisted upon that democracy must be unlimited government, I do indeed *not* believe in democracy, but I am and shall remain a profoundly convinced demarchist in the sense indicated. If we can by such a change of the name free ourselves from the errors that have unfortunately come to be so closely associated with the conception of democracy, we might thereby suc-

---

[37] [Hayek paraphrases here the words of James Harrington, on which see n. 26 above. Hayek's account of 'the general interest' is set out in more detail in Hayek, *The Mirage of Social Justice*, pp. 1–30.—Ed.]

[38] Cf. R. Wollheim, "A paradox in the theory of democracy", in P. Laslett and W. G. Runciman (eds.), *Philosophy, Politics, and Society*, 2nd series, London, 1962, p. 72: "the modern conception of Democracy is of a form of government in which no restriction is placed upon the governing body". [R. Wollheim, "A Paradox in the Theory of Democracy", in P. Laslett and W. G. Runciman, eds., *Philosophy, Politics and Society*, 2nd series (Oxford: Basil Blackwell, 1962), p. 72.—Ed.]

[39] John Locke, *Second Treatise on Government*, sect. 131, ed. P. Laslett, Cambridge, 1960, p. 371. [Hayek refers to Locke's *Second Treatise*, in which the passage he quotes appears. However, the actual title of Laslett's edition is that of Locke's complete work, namely *Two Treatises of Government*. The correct reference is therefore J. Locke, *Two Treatises of Government*, ed. P. Laslett (Cambridge: Cambridge University Press, 1960), p. 371.—Ed.]

ceed in avoiding the dangers which have plagued democracy from its very beginning and have again and again led to its destruction. It is the problem which arose in the memorable episode of which Xenophon tells us, when the Athenian Assembly wanted to vote the punishment of particular individuals and[40]

> the greater number cried out that it was monstrous if the people were to be prevented from doing whatever they wished . . . Then the Prytanes, stricken with fear, agreed to put the question,—all of them except Socrates, the son of Sophroniscus; and he said that in no case would he act except in accordance with the law.

---

[40] Xenophon, *Hellenica*, I, vii, 15, Loeb ed. by C. L. Brownson, Cambridge, Mass., and London, 1918, p. 73. [Xenophon, *Hellenica, Volume I, Books 1–4*, trans. C. L. Brownson, Loeb Classical Library 88 (Cambridge, MA: Harvard University Press, 1918), p. 73.—Ed.]

ECONOMIC FREEDOM AND REPRESENTATIVE GOVERNMENT[1]

1 The Seeds of Destruction

Thirty years ago I wrote a book[2] which, in a manner which many regarded as unduly alarmist, described the dangers that the then visible collectivist tendencies created for personal freedom. I am glad that these fears so far have not materialised, but I do not think this has proved me wrong. In the first instance I did not, as many misunderstood me, contend that if government interfered at all with economic affairs it was bound to go the whole way to a totalitarian system. I was trying to argue rather what in more homely terms is expressed by saying "if you don't mend your principles you will go to the devil".

In the event developments since the war, in Britain as well as in the rest of the Western world, have gone much less in the direction which the prevalent collectivist doctrines seemed to suggest was likely. Indeed, the first 20 years after the war saw a revival of a free market economy much stronger than even its most enthusiastic supporters could have hoped. Although I like to think that those who worked for this consummation in the intellectual sphere, such as Harold Wincott, to whose memory this lecture is dedicated, have contributed to it, I do not overrate what intellectual debate can achieve.[3] At least

[1] The Fourth Wincott Memorial Lecture, delivered at the Royal Society of Arts in London on 31 October 1973, and published as Occasional Paper 39 by the Institute of Economic Affairs. As in the case of chapter 6, I am much indebted to the Editorial Director of that institute, Mr. Arthur Seldon, for his careful and sympathetic editing of my text. [See F. A. Hayek, *Economic Freedom and Representative Government*, Occasional Paper 39 (London: The Institute of Economic Affairs, 1973), reprinted with some sub-headings removed and minor changes to the text as chapter 8 of F. A. Hayek, *New Studies in Philosophy, Politics, Economics and the History of Ideas* (London and Henley: Routledge & Kegan Paul, 1978). The latter version is used here. Classical liberal economist Arthur Seldon (1916–2005) was Editorial Director of the Institute of Economic Affairs from 1957 until 1988.—Ed.]

[2] *The Road to Serfdom,* London, 1944. [F. A. Hayek, *The Road to Serfdom: Text and Documents*, ed. B. Caldwell, vol. 2 (2007) of *The Collected Works of F. A. Hayek* (Chicago: University of Chicago Press; London: Routledge).—Ed.]

[3] [British economic journalist Harold Wincott (1906–69) edited the *Investors Chronicle*, was a columnist for the *Financial Times,* and was a staunch supporter of the Institute of Economic Affairs in its early years.—Ed.]

as important were probably the experiences of Germany, relying on a market economy, rapidly becoming the strongest economic power of Europe—and to some extent the practical efforts for a removal of the obstacles to international trade, such as GATT and perhaps in some measure the intentions if not the practice of the EEC.

The result was the Great Prosperity of the last 20 to 25 years which, I fear, will in the future appear as an event as unique as the Great Depression of the 1930s now appears to us. To me at least it seems clear that, until six or eight years ago, this prosperity was due entirely to the freeing of the spontaneous forces of the economic system and not, as in the later years, to inflation. Since this is today often forgotten I may perhaps remind you that, in the most remarkable burst of prosperity of this period, that of the German Federal Republic, the average annual rise of prices remained below 2 per cent until 1966.

I believe that even this modest rate of inflation would not have been necessary to secure the prosperity, and indeed that we should all today have better prospects of continuing prosperity if we had been content with what was achieved without inflation and had not attempted to stimulate it further by an expansionist credit policy. Instead such a policy has created a situation in which it is thought necessary to impose controls which will destroy the main foundations of the prosperity, namely the functioning market. Indeed the measures supposedly necessary to combat inflation—as if inflation were something which attacks us and not something which we create—threaten to destroy the free economy in the near future.

We find ourselves in the paradoxical situation that, after a period during which the market economy has been more successful than ever before in rapidly raising living standards in the Western world, the prospects of its continuance even for the next few years must appear slight. I have indeed never felt so pessimistic about the chances of preserving a functioning market economy as I do at this moment—and this means also of the prospects of preserving a free political order. Although the threat to free institutions now comes from a source different from that with which I was concerned 30 years ago, it has become even more acute than it was then.

That a systematically pursued incomes policy means the suspension of the price mechanism and before long the replacement of the market by a centrally directed economy seems to me beyond doubt. I cannot here discuss the ways in which we may still avoid this course, or the chances that we may still do so. Although I regard it as at this time the chief duty of every economist to fight inflation—and to explain why a repressed inflation is even worse than an open inflation—I devote this lecture to another task. As I see it, inflation has merely speeded up the process of the destruction of the market economy which has been going on for other reasons, and brought much nearer the moment when, seeing the economic, political and moral consequences of a centrally directed economy, we shall have to think how we can re-establish a market economy on a firmer and more durable basis.

2 The Danger of Unlimited Government

For some time I have been convinced that it is not only the deliberate attempts of the various kinds of collectivists to replace the market economy by a planned system, nor the consequences of the new monetary policies, which threaten to destroy the market economy: the political institutions prevailing in the Western world necessarily produce a drift in this direction which can be halted or prevented only by changing these institutions. I have belatedly come to agree with Joseph Schumpeter who 30 years ago argued[4] that there was an irreconcilable conflict between democracy and capitalism—except that it is not democracy as such but the particular forms of democratic organisation, now regarded as the only possible forms of democracy, which will produce a progressive expansion of governmental control of economic life even if the majority of the people wish to preserve a market economy.

The reason is that it is now generally taken for granted that in a democracy the powers of the majority must be unlimited, and that a government with unlimited powers will be forced to secure the continued support of a majority, to use its unlimited powers in the service of special interests—such groups as particular trades, the inhabitants of particular regions, etc. We shall see this most clearly if we consider the situation in a community in which the mass of the people are in favour of a market order and against government direction, but, as will normally happen, most of the groups wish an exception to be made in their favour. In such conditions a political party hoping to achieve and maintain power will have little choice but to use its powers to buy the support of particular groups. They will do so not because the majority is interventionist, but because the ruling party would not retain a majority if it did not buy the support of particular groups by the promise of special benefits. This means in practice that even a statesman wholly devoted to the common interest of all the citizens will be under the constant necessity of satisfying special interests, because only thus will he be able to retain the support of a majority which he needs to achieve what is really important to him.

The root of the evil is thus the unlimited power of the legislature in modern democracies, a power which the majority will be constantly forced to use in a manner that most of its members may not desire. What we call the

---

[4] *Capitalism, Socialism and Democracy*, London, 1943 (Unwin University Books, no. 28, 3rd ed., 1950). [J. A. Schumpeter, *Capitalism, Socialism and Democracy* (London: George Allen & Unwin, 3rd edn., 1950).—Ed.]

will of the majority is thus really an artefact of the existing institutions, and particularly of the omnipotence of the sovereign legislature, which by the mechanics of the political process will be driven to do things that most of its members do not really want, simply because there are no formal limits to its powers.

It is widely believed that this omnipotence of the representative legislature is a necessary attribute of democracy because the will of the representative assembly could be limited only by placing another will above it. Legal positivism, the most influential current theory of jurisprudence, particularly represents this sovereignty of the legislature as logically necessary. This, however, was by no means the view of the classical theorists of representative government. John Locke made it very clear that in a free state even the power of the legislative body should be limited in a definite manner, namely to the passing of laws in the specific sense of general rules of just conduct equally applicable to all citizens. That all coercion would be legitimate only if it meant the application of general rules of law in this sense became the basic principle of liberalism. For Locke, and for the later theorists of Whiggism and the separation of powers, it was not so much the source from which the laws originated as their character of general rules of just conduct equally applicable to all which justified their coercive application.[5]

This older liberal conception of the necessary limitation of all power by requiring the legislature to commit itself to general rules has, in the course of the last century, been replaced gradually and almost imperceptibly by the altogether different though not easily distinguished conception that it was the approval of the majority which was the only and sufficient restraint on legislation. And the older conception was not only forgotten but no longer even understood. It was thought that any substantive limitation of the legislative power was unnecessary once this power was placed in the hands of the majority, because approval by it was regarded as an adequate test of justice. In practice this majority opinion usually represents no more than the result of bargaining rather than a genuine agreement on principles. Even the concept of the arbitrariness which democratic government was supposed to prevent changed its content: its opposite was no longer the general rules equally applicable to all but the approval of a command by the majority—as if a majority might not treat a minority arbitrarily.

---

[5] [Hayek alludes to Locke's *Second Treatise of Government* (1689) and to the ideas of such thinkers as David Hume, Montesquieu, and Thomas Babington Macaulay. See, for example, F. A. Hayek, "Liberalism" [1978], reprinted as chapter 1 of the current volume, and F. A. Hayek, *The Constitution of Liberty*, ed. Ronald Hamowy, vol. 17 (2011) of *The Collected Works of F. A. Hayek*, pp. 246–60. Hayek's critique of legal positivism can be found in *The Constitution of Liberty*, pp. 345–55, and in F. A. Hayek, *The Mirage of Social Justice*, vol. 2 (1976) of *Law, Legislation and Liberty* (Chicago: University of Chicago Press; London: Routledge, 1973–79), pp. 44–60.—Ed.]

3 The Fundamental Principle

Today it is rarely understood that the limitation of all coercion to the enforcement of general rules of just conduct was the fundamental principle of classical liberalism, or, I would almost say, its definition of liberty. This is largely a consequence of the fact that the substantive (or 'material') conception of law (as distinguished from a purely formal one) which underlies it, and which alone gives a clear meaning to such ideas as that of the separation of powers, of the rule of law or of a government under the law, had been rarely stated explicitly but merely tacitly presupposed by most of the classical writers. There are few passages in their seventeenth- and eighteenth-century writings in which they explicitly say what they mean by 'law'. Many uses of the term, however, make sense only if it is interpreted to mean exclusively general rules of just conduct and not every expression of the will of the duly authorised representative body.

Though the older conception of law survives in limited connections, it is certainly no longer generally understood, and in consequence has ceased to be an effective limit on legislation. While in the theoretical concept of the separation of powers the legislature derived its authority from the circumstance that it committed itself to general rules and was supposed to impose only general rules, there are now no limits on what a legislature may command and so claim to be 'law'. While its power was thus once supposed not to be limited by a superior will but by a generally recognised principle, there are now no limits whatever. There is therefore also no reason why the coalitions of organised interests on which the governing majorities rest should not discriminate against any widely disliked group. Differences in wealth, education, tradition, religion, language or race may today become the cause of differential treatment on the pretext of a pretended principle of social justice or of public necessity. Once such discrimination is recognised as legitimate, all the safeguards of individual freedom of the liberal tradition are gone. If it is assumed that whatever the majority decides is just, even if what it lays down is not a general rule, but aims at affecting particular people, it would be expecting too much to believe that a sense of justice will restrain the caprice of the majority: in any group it is soon believed that what is desired by the group is just. And since the theoreticians of democracy have for over a hundred years taught the majorities that whatever they desire is just, we must not be surprised if the majorities no longer even ask whether what they decide is just. Legal positivism has powerfully contributed to this development by its contention that law is not dependent on justice but determines what is just.

Unfortunately, we have not only failed to impose upon legislatures the limitations inherent in the necessity of committing themselves to general rules.

We have also charged them with tasks which they can perform only if they are not thus limited but are free to use coercion in the discriminatory manner that is required to assure benefits to particular people or groups. This they are constantly asked to do in the name of what is called social or distributive justice, a conception which has largely taken the place of the justice of individual action. It requires that not the individuals but 'society' be just in determining the share of individuals in the social product; and in order to realise any particular distribution of the social product regarded as just it is necessary that government directs individuals in what they must do.

Indeed, in a market economy in which no single person or group determines who gets what, and the shares of individuals always depend on many circumstances which nobody could have foreseen, the whole conception of social or distributive justice is empty and meaningless; and there will therefore never exist agreement on what is just in this sense. I am not sure that the concept has a definite meaning even in a centrally directed economy, or that in such a system people would ever agree on what distribution is just. I am certain, however, that nothing has done so much to destroy the juridical safeguards of individual freedom as the striving after this mirage of social justice. An adequate treatment of the topic of this lecture would indeed presuppose a careful dissection of this ideal which almost everybody seems to believe to have a definite meaning but which proves more completely devoid of such meaning the more one thinks about it. But the main subject of this lecture is what we have to do, if we ever again get a chance, to stop those tendencies inherent in the existing political systems which drive us towards a totalitarian order.[6]

Before I turn to this main problem, I should correct a widespread misunderstanding. The basic principle of the liberal tradition, that all the coercive action of government must be limited to the enforcement of general rules of just conduct, does not preclude government from rendering many other services for which, except for raising the necessary finance, it need not rely on coercion. It is true that in the nineteenth century a deep and not wholly unjustified distrust of government often made liberals wish to restrain government much more narrowly. But even then, of course, certain collective wants were recognised which only an agency possessing the power of taxation could satisfy. I am the last person to deny that increased wealth and the increased density of population have enlarged the number of collective needs which government can and should satisfy. Such government services are entirely compatible with liberal principles so long as,

---

[6] [Hayek argues at length that the concept of 'justice' is inapplicable to the unintended outcomes produced as the result of impersonal market processes, so that the notion 'social justice' is meaningless, in *The Mirage of Social Justice*, pp. 62–106.—Ed.]

(1) government does not claim a monopoly and new methods of rendering services through the market (for example, in some now covered by social insurance) are not prevented;

(2) the means are raised by taxation on uniform principles and taxation is not used as an instrument for the redistribution of income; and,

(3) the wants satisfied are collective wants of the community as a whole and not merely collective wants of particular groups.

Not every collective want deserves to be satisfied: the desire of the small boot-makers to be protected against the competition of the factories is also a collective need of the bootmakers, but clearly not one which in a liberal economic system could be satisfied.[7]

Nineteenth-century liberalism in general attempted to keep the growth of these service activities of government in check by entrusting them to local rather than central government in the hope that competition between the local authorities would control their extent. I cannot consider here how far this principle had to be abandoned and mention it only as another part of the traditional liberal doctrine whose rationale is no longer understood.

I had to consider these points to make it clear that those checks on government activity with which for the rest of this lecture I shall be exclusively concerned refer only to its powers of coercion but not to the necessary services we today expect government to render to the citizens.

I hope that what I have said so far has made it clear that the task we shall have to perform if we are to re-establish and preserve a free society is in the first instance an intellectual task: it presupposes that we not only recover conceptions which we have largely lost and which must once again become generally understood, but also that we design new institutional safeguards which will prevent a repetition of the process of gradual erosion of the safeguards which the theory of liberal constitutionalism had meant to provide.

4 The Separation of Powers

The device to which the theorists of liberal constitutionalism had looked to guarantee individual liberty and the prevention of all arbitrariness was the separation of powers. If the legislature laid down only general rules equally applicable to all and the executive could use coercion only to enforce obedience to these general rules, personal liberty would indeed be secure. This pre-

---

[7] [Hayek elaborates on these issues in *The Constitution of Liberty*, pp. 329–41, 405–29, and in F. A. Hayek, *The Political Order of a Free People*, vol. 3 (1979) of *Law, Legislation and Liberty*, pp. 41–64.—Ed.]

supposes, however, that the legislature is confined to laying down such general rules. But, instead of confining parliament to making laws in this sense, we have given it unlimited power simply by calling 'law' everything which it proclaims: a legislature is now not a body that makes laws; a law is whatever is resolved by a legislature.

This state of affairs was brought about by the loss of the old meaning of 'law' and by the desire to make government democratic by placing the direction and control of government in the hands of the legislatures, which are in consequence constantly called upon to order all sorts of specific actions—to issue commands which are called laws, although in character they are wholly different from those laws to the production of which the theory of the separation of powers had intended to confine the legislatures.

Although the task of designing and establishing new institutions must appear difficult and almost hopeless, the task of reviving and making once more generally understood a lost concept for which we no longer have even an unambiguous name is perhaps even more difficult. It is a task which in this case has to be achieved in the face of the contrary teaching of the dominant school of jurisprudence. I will try briefly to state the essential characteristics of laws in this specific narrow sense of the term before I turn to the institutional arrangements which would secure that the task of making such laws be really separated from the task of governing.

A good way is to consider the peculiar properties which judge-made law possesses of necessity, while they belong to the products of legislatures in general only in so far as these have endeavoured to emulate judge-made law. It is no accident that this concept of law has been preserved much longer in the common law countries whereas it was rarely understood in countries which relied wholly on statute law.

This law consists essentially of what used to be known as 'lawyer's law'—which is and can be applied by courts of justice and to which the agencies of government are as much subject as are private persons. Since this judge-made law arises out of the settlement of disputes, it relates solely to the relations of acting persons towards one another and does not control an individual's actions which do not affect others. It defines the protected domains of each person with which others are prohibited from interfering. The aim is to prevent conflicts between people who do not act under central direction but on their own initiative, pursuing their own ends on the basis of their own knowledge.

These rules must thus apply in circumstances which nobody can foresee and must therefore be designed to cover an uncertain number of future instances. This determines what is commonly but not very helpfully described as their 'abstract' character, by which is meant that they are intended to apply in the same manner to all situations in which certain generic factors are present and not only to particular designated persons, groups, places, times, etc. They do not prescribe to the individuals specific tasks or ends of their actions, but they are essentially prohibitions which aim at making it possible for them so mutually to adjust their plans that each will have a good chance of achieving his aims. The delimitations of the personal domains which achieve this purpose are of course determined chiefly by the law of property, contract, and torts, and the penal laws which protect 'life, liberty and property'.

An individual who is bound to obey only such rules of just conduct as I have called these rules of law in this narrow meaning is free in the sense that he is not legally subject to anybody's commands, that within known limits he can choose the means and ends of his activities. But where everybody is free in this sense each is thrown into a process which nobody controls and the outcome of which for each is in large measure unpredictable. Freedom and risk are thus inseparable. Nor can it be claimed that the magnitude of each individual's share of the national income, dependent on so many circumstances which nobody knows, will be just. But neither can these shares meaningfully be described as unjust. We must be content if we can prevent them from being affected by unjust actions. We can of course in a free society provide a floor below which nobody need fall, by providing outside the market for all some insurance against misfortune. There is indeed much we can do to improve the framework within which the market will operate beneficially. But we cannot in such a society make the distribution of incomes correspond to some standard of social or distributive justice, and attempts to do so are likely to destroy the market order.[8]

But if, to preserve individual freedom, we must confine coercion to the enforcement of general rules of just conduct, how can we prevent legislatures from authorising coercion to secure particular benefits for particular groups— especially a legislature organised on party lines where the governing majority frequently will be a majority only because it promises such special benefits to some groups? The truth is of course that the so-called legislatures have *never* been confined to making laws in this narrow sense, although the theory of the separation of powers tacitly assumed that they were. And since it has come to be accepted that not only legislation but also the direction of current government activities should be in the hands of the representatives of the majority, the direction of government has become the chief task of the legislatures. This has had the effect not only of entirely obliterating the distinction between laws in the sense of general rules of just conduct and laws in the

---

[8] [The claim that the provision outside of the market of a guaranteed minimum income, designed to protect every member of society against severe deprivation, is consistent with the principles of a liberal social order is found in several places in Hayek's writings, including *The Road to Serfdom*, pp. 147–48, 156; *The Mirage of Social Justice*, p. 87; and *The Political Order of a Free People*, pp. 54–55.—Ed.]

sense of specific commands, but also of organising the legislatures not in the manner most suitable for making laws in the classical sense but in the manner required for efficient government, that is above all on party lines.[9]

Now, I believe we are right in wanting both legislation in the old sense and current government to be conducted democratically. But it seems to me it was a fatal error, though historically probably inevitable, to entrust these two distinct tasks to the same representative assembly. This makes the distinction between legislation and government, and thereby also the observance of the principles of the rule of law and of a government under the law, practically impossible. Though it may secure that every act of government has the approval of the representative assembly, it does not protect the citizens against discretionary coercion. Indeed, a representative assembly organised in the manner necessary for efficient government, and not restrained by some general laws it cannot alter, is bound to be driven to use its powers to satisfy the demands of sectional interests.

It is no accident that most of the classical theorists of representative government and of the separation of powers disliked the party system and hoped that a division of the legislature on party lines could be avoided. They did so because they conceived of the legislatures as concerned with the making of laws in the narrow sense, and believed that there could exist on the rules of just conduct a prevalent common opinion independent of particular interests. But it cannot be denied that democratic *government* requires the support of an organised body of representatives, which we call parties, committed to a programme of action, and a similarly organised opposition which offers an alternative government.

It would seem the obvious solution of this difficulty to have two distinct representative assemblies with different tasks, one a true legislative body and the other concerned with government proper, i.e. everything except the making of laws in the narrow sense. And it is at least not inconceivable that such a system might have developed in Britain if at the time when the House of Commons with the exclusive power over money bills achieved in effect sole control of government, the House of Lords, as the supreme court of justice, had obtained the sole right to develop the law in the narrow sense. But such a development was of course not possible so long as the House of Lords represented not the people at large but a class.

On reflection, however, one realises that little would be gained by merely having two representative assemblies instead of one if they were elected and organised on the same principles and therefore also had the same composition. They would be driven by the same circumstances which govern the

[9] [Hayek explores at greater length the issues raised in the remainder of this section, and in the next section, in *The Political Order of a Free People*, pp. 105–27.—Ed.]

decisions of modern parliaments and acting in collusion would probably produce the same sort of authorisation for whatever the government of the day
wished to do. Even if we assume that the legislative chamber (as distinguished
from the governmental one) were restricted by the constitution to passing
laws in the narrow sense of general rules of just conduct, and this restriction
were made effective through the control by a constitutional court, little would
probably be achieved so long as the legislative assembly were under the same
necessity of satisfying the demands of particular groups which force the hands
of the governing majorities in today's parliaments.

While for the governmental assemblies we should want something more
or less of the same kind as the existing parliaments, whose organisation and
manner of proceeding have indeed been shaped by the needs of governing
rather than the making of laws, something very different would be needed
for a truly legislative assembly. We should want an assembly not concerned
with the particular needs of particular groups but rather with the general
permanent principles on which the activities of the community were to be
ordered. Its members and its resolutions should represent not specific groups
and their particular desires but the prevailing opinion on what kind of conduct was just and what kind was not. In laying down rules to be valid for long
periods ahead this assembly should be 'representative of', or reproduce a sort
of cross-section of, the prevailing opinions on right and wrong; its members
should not be the spokesmen of particular interests, or express the 'will' of
any particular section of the population on any specific measure of government. They should be men and women trusted and respected for the traits of
character they had shown in the ordinary business of life, and not dependent
on the approval by particular groups of electors. And they should be wholly
exempt from the party discipline necessary to keep a governing team together,
but evidently undesirable in the body which lays down the rules that limit the
powers of government.

Such a legislative assembly could be achieved if, first, its members were
elected for long periods, second, they were not eligible for re-election after the
end of the period, and, third, to secure a continuous renewal of the body in
accord with gradually changing opinions among the electorate, its members
were not all elected at the same time but a constant fraction of their number
replaced every year as their mandate expired; or, in other words, if they were
elected, for instance, for 15 years and one-fifteenth of their number replaced
every year. It would further seem to me expedient to provide that at each election the representatives should be chosen by and from only one age group so
that every citizen would vote only once in his life, say in his forty-fifth year, for
a representative chosen from his age group.

The result would be an assembly composed of persons between their forty-
fifth and their sixtieth year, elected after they had opportunity to prove their

ability in ordinary life (and, incidentally, of an average age somewhat below that of contemporary parliaments). It would probably be desirable to disqualify those who had occupied positions in the governmental assembly or other party-political organisations and it would also be necessary to assure to those elected for the period after their retirement some dignified, paid and pensionable position, such as lay judge or the like.

The advantage of an election by age groups, and at an age at which the individuals could have proved themselves in ordinary life, would be that in general a person's contemporaries are the best judges of his character and ability; and that among the relatively small numbers participating in each election the candidates would be more likely to be personally known to the voters and chosen according to the personal esteem in which they were held by the voters—especially if, as would seem likely and deserve encouragement, the anticipation of this common task led to the formation of clubs of the age groups for the discussion of public affairs.

5 Advantages of Legislative Separation

The purpose of all this would of course be to create a legislature which was not subservient to government and did not produce whatever laws government wanted for the achievement of its momentary purposes, but rather which with the law laid down the permanent limits to the coercive powers of government—limits within which government had to move and which even the democratically elected governmental assembly could not overstep. While the latter assembly would be entirely free in determining the organisation of government, the use to be made of the means placed at the disposal of government and the character of the services to be rendered by government, it would itself possess no coercive powers over the individual citizens. Such powers, including the power to raise by taxation the means for financing the services rendered by government, would extend only to the enforcement of the rules of just conduct laid down by the legislative assembly. Against any overstepping of these limits by government (or the governmental assembly) there would be open an appeal to a constitutional court which would be competent in the case of conflict between the legislature proper and the governmental bodies.

A further desirable effect of such an arrangement would be that the legislature would for once have enough time for its proper tasks. This is important because in modern times legislatures frequently have left the regulation of matters which might have been effected by general rules of law to administrative orders and even administrative discretion simply because they were so busy with their governmental tasks that they had neither time for nor interest in making law proper. It is also a task which requires expert knowledge which a long-serving representative might acquire but is not likely to be possessed by a busy politician anxious for results which he can show his constituents before the next election. It is a curious consequence of giving the representative assembly unlimited power that it has largely ceased to be the chief determining agent in shaping the law proper, but has left this task more and more to the bureaucracy.

I must, however, not make you impatient by pursuing further the details of this Utopia—though I must confess that I have found fascinating and instructive the exploration of the new opportunities offered by contemplating the possibility of separating the truly legislative assembly from the governmental body. You will rightly ask what the purpose of such a Utopian construction can be if by calling it thus I admit that I do not believe it can be realised in the foreseeable future. I can answer in the words of David Hume in his essay on "The Idea of a Perfect Commonwealth", that

> In all cases, it must be advantageous to know what is the most perfect in the kind, that we may be able to bring any real constitution or form of government as near it as possible, by such gentle alterations and innovations as may not give too great disturbance to society.[10]

---

[10] [David Hume, "Idea of a Perfect Commonwealth", in D. Hume, *Essays: Moral, Political, and Literary* [1777], ed. Eugene F. Miller (Indianapolis, IN: Liberty Fund, 1987), pp. 513–14.—Ed.]

TWENTY-FIVE

THE CAMPAIGN AGAINST KEYNESIAN INFLATION[1]

As I explain in one of the following papers (p. 219),[2] I had largely withdrawn from the debate on monetary policy when I found that most of my professional colleagues had started to speak a language and to discuss problems which seemed to me uninteresting.[3] By the summer of 1974, however, the problem of inflation had become so alarming that I felt it to be my duty once again to speak out. After an article in the English daily press (which had been preceded by a somewhat similar one in the German *Frankfurter Allgemeine Zeitung* of 19 August 1974), which is reprinted below as the first of a group, I devoted a large part of my Nobel Memorial Lecture in December to it. However, as this lecture is primarily devoted to problems of the philosophy of science, it is reprinted earlier on in this volume as chapter 2.[4] The next opportunity offered when I was asked to speak at the Accademia dei Lincei at Rome at a celebration of the hundredth birthday of Luigi Einaudi, a lecture now reprinted on pp. 197–209 below.[5] During the second quarter of 1975, at various places in the USA, I lectured on more or less the same lines and included, as the occasions suggested, discussions of various additional topics which I have now added as a sort of supplement on pp. 209–18. A lec-

[1] [This essay was first published as chapter 13 of F. A. Hayek, *New Studies in Philosophy, Politics, Economics and the History of Ideas* (London and Henley: Routledge & Kegan Paul, 1978.—Ed.]

[2] [Now see pp. 369–70 below.—Ed.]

[3] A collection of my occasional comments and observations on inflation has been edited by Sudha Shenoy for the Institute of Economic Affairs and published by the latter as Hobart Paperback 4 under the title *A Tiger by the Tail*, London, 1972. [F. A. Hayek, *A Tiger by the Tail: The Keynesian Legacy of Inflation* (London: Institute of Economic Affairs, 1972).—Ed.]

[4] [The article in German to which Hayek refers is F. A. Hayek, "Zwölf Thesen zur Inflationsbekämpfung", *Frankfurter Allgemeine Zeitung*, August 19, 1974, p. 9. Hayek also refers to F. A. Hayek, "The Pretence of Knowledge" [1975], reprinted as chapter 2 of *New Studies*. It has now also been reprinted as chapter 16 of F. A. Hayek, *The Market and Other Orders*, ed. B. Caldwell, vol. 15 (2014) of *The Collected Works of F. A. Hayek* (Chicago: The University of Chicago Press; London: Routledge).—Ed.]

[5] [Hayek directs the reader to the section entitled "Inflation, the misdirection of labour, and unemployment", which can now be found on pp. 347–59 below. Luigi Einaudi (1874–1961) was an Italian economist and statesman. He served as President of the Italian Republic from 1948 until 1955.—Ed.]

ture I gave to a conference at Geneva in the following September is reprinted on pp. 218–29. The suggestion it contains about future monetary institutions has now been expounded at greater length in a paper *Denationalisation of Money*, published by the Institute of Economic Affairs, London, 1976, of which a much enlarged edition is due shortly.[6]

I Inflation's path to unemployment[7]

1

The responsibility for current world-wide inflation, I am sorry to say, rests wholly and squarely with the economists, or at least with that great majority of my fellow economists who have embraced the teachings of Lord Keynes.[8]

What we are experiencing are simply the economic consequences of Lord Keynes. It was on the advice and even urging of his pupils that governments everywhere have financed increasing parts of their expenditure by creating money on a scale which every reputable economist before Keynes would have predicted would cause precisely the sort of inflation we have got. They did this in the erroneous belief that this was both a necessary and a lastingly effective method of securing full employment.

The seductive doctrine that a government deficit, as long as unemployment existed, was not only innocuous but even meritorious was of course most welcome to politicians. The advocates of this policy have long maintained that an increase of total expenditure which still led to an increase of employment could not be regarded as inflation at all. And now, when the steadily accelerating rise of prices has rather discredited this view, the general excuse is still that

---

[6] [Hayek refers the reader to the sections headed "Further considerations on the same topic" and "Choice in currency: a way to stop inflation" below. He also refers to F. A. Hayek, *Denationalisation of Money: An Analysis of the Theory and Practice of Competing Currencies* (London: The Institute of Economic Affairs, 1976), and F. A. Hayek, *Denationalisation of Money—The Argument Refined: An Analysis of the Theory and Practice of Competing Currencies* (London: The Institute of Economic Affairs, 1978). Now also see Hayek, "The Denationalization of Money: An Analysis of the Theory and Practice of Concurrent Currencies" [1978], reprinted as chapter 4 of F. A. Hayek, *Good Money, Part II: The Standard*, ed. S. Kresge, vol. 6 (1999) of *The Collected Works of F. A. Hayek.*—Ed.]

[7] From the *Daily Telegraph* (London), 15 and 16 October 1974. [See F. A. Hayek, "Inflation's Path to Unemployment", *Daily Telegraph*, October 15, 1974, p. 18, and F. A. Hayek, "What Living Standards Can We Afford?," *Daily Telegraph*, October 16, 1974, p. 18.—Ed.]

[8] [British economist John Maynard Keynes (1883–1946) argued that unemployment was a result of insufficient aggregate demand in *The General Theory of Employment, Interest, and Money* [1936], reprinted as vol. 7 (1973) of *The Collected Writings of John Maynard Keynes* (London: Macmillan for the Royal Economic Society). For more on Hayek's views on Keynes's economics, and on Keynes the man, see F. A. Hayek, *Contra Keynes and Cambridge: Essays, Correspondence*, ed. B. Caldwell, vol. 9 (1995) of *The Collected Works of F. A. Hayek.*—Ed.]

a moderate inflation is a small price to pay for full employment: "rather 5 per cent inflation than 5 per cent unemployment", as it has recently been put by the German Chancellor.[9] This persuades most people who do not see the grave harm which inflation does. It might seem—and even some economists have maintained—that all inflation does is bring about some redistribution of incomes, so that what some lose others will gain, while unemployment necessarily means a reduction of aggregate real income.

This, however, disregards the chief harm which inflation causes, namely that it gives the whole structure of the economy a distorted, lopsided character which sooner or later makes a more extensive unemployment inevitable than that which that policy was intended to prevent. It does so by drawing more and more workers into kinds of jobs which depend on continuing or even accelerating inflation. The result is a situation of rising instability in which an ever-increasing part of current employment is dependent on continuing and perhaps accelerating inflation and in which every attempt to slow down inflation will at once lead to so much unemployment that the authorities will rapidly abandon it and resume inflation.[10]

We are already familiar with the concept of 'stagflation' to describe that state in which the accepted rate of inflation no longer suffices to produce satisfactory employment. Politicians in that position have now little choice but to speed up inflation.

But this process cannot go on for ever, as an accelerating inflation soon leads to a complete disorganisation of all economic activity. Nor can this end be avoided by any effort to control prices and wages while the increase of the quantity of money continues: the particular jobs inflation has created depend on a continued rise of prices and will disappear as soon as that stops. A 'repressed' inflation, besides causing a still worse disorganisation of economic activity than an open one, has not even the advantage of maintaining that employment which the preceding open inflation has created.

We have in fact been led into a frightful position. All politicians promise that they will stop inflation *and* preserve full employment. But they *cannot* do this. And the longer they succeed in keeping up employment by continuing infla-

---

[9] [In July 1972, German politician Helmut Schmidt (1918–2015), who was at the time Minister of Finance and Economic Affairs, and who later became German Chancellor (1974–82), stated that, "It seems to me that the German population—pointedly expressed—can rather bear 5 per cent inflation than 5 per cent unemployment". See G. Kirchgässner, *Homo Oeconomicus: The Economic Model of Behaviour and Its Applications in Economics and Other Social Sciences* (New York: Springer-Verlag, 2008), pp. 76–77.—Ed.]

[10] [Here, and in much of what follows, Hayek draws on his theory of the business cycle, as set out in more detail in F. A. Hayek, *Business Cycles, Part I*, ed. H. Klausinger, vol. 7 (2012) of *The Collected Works of F. A. Hayek.*—Ed.]

tion, the greater will be the unemployment when the inflation finally comes to an end. There is no magic trick by which we can extricate ourselves from this position which we have created.

This does not mean that we need go through another period of unemployment as we did in the 1930s. That was due to the failure to prevent an actual shrinkage of the total demand for which there was no justification. But we must face the fact that in the present situation merely to stop the inflation or even to slow down its rate will produce substantial unemployment. Certainly nobody wishes this, but we can no longer avoid it and all attempts to postpone it will only increase its ultimate size.

The only alternative we have, and which, unfortunately, is a not unlikely outcome, is a command economy in which everyone is assigned his job; and though such an economy might avoid outright worklessness, the position of the great majority of workers in it would certainly be much worse than it would be even during a period of unemployment.

It is not the market economy (or 'the capitalist system') which is responsible for this calamity but our own mistaken monetary and financial policy. What we have done is to repeat on a colossal scale what in the past produced the recurring cycles of booms and depressions: to allow a long inflationary boom to bring about a misdirection of labour and other resources into employments in which they can be maintained only so long as inflation exceeds expectations. But while in the past the mechanism of the international monetary system brought such an inflation to a stop after a few years, we have managed to design a new system which allowed it to run on for two decades.

As long as we try to maintain this situation we are only making things worse in the long run. We can prevent a greater reaction than is necessary only by giving up the illusion that the boom can be prolonged indefinitely, and by facing now the task of mitigating the suffering and preventing the reaction from degenerating into a deflationary spiral. It will chiefly be a task not of preserving existing jobs but of facilitating the opening of (temporary and permanent) new jobs for those who will inevitably lose their present ones.

We can no longer hope to avoid this necessity, and closing our eyes to the problem will not make it go away. It may well be true that, because people have been taught that government can always prevent unemployment, its failure to do so will cause grave social disturbances. But if this is so, we probably have it no longer in our power to prevent it.

2

In order to see clearly the causes of our troubles it is necessary to understand the chief fault of the theory which has been guiding monetary and financial policy during the last twenty-five years and which was based on the belief that all important unemployment is due to an insufficiency of aggregate demand and can be cured by an increase of that demand. This is the more readily believed as it is true that some unemployment is due to that cause and that an increase in aggregate demand will in most circumstances lead to a temporary increase of employment. But not all unemployment is due to an insufficiency of total demand or would disappear if total demand were higher. And, worse, much of the employment which an increase of demand at first produces cannot be maintained by demand remaining at that higher level but only by a continued rise of demand.

This sort of unemployment which we temporarily 'cure' by inflation, but in the long run are making worse by it, is due to the misdirection of resources which inflation causes. It can be prevented only by a movement of workers from the jobs where there is an excess supply to those where there is a shortage. In other words, a continuous adjustment of the various kinds of labour to the changing demand requires a real labour market in which the wages of the different kinds of labour are determined by demand and supply.

Without a functioning labour market there can be no meaningful cost calculation and no efficient use of resources. Such a market can exist even with fairly strong trade unions so long as the unions bear the responsibility for any unemployment excessive wage demands will cause. But it disappears once government relieves the unions of this responsibility by promising maintenance of full employment at any level of wages.

This, incidentally, also answers the very confusing dispute about the role of the unions in causing inflation. There is, strictly speaking, no such thing as a cost-push inflation: all inflation is caused by excessive demand. To this extent the 'monetarists' led by Professor Milton Friedman are perfectly right. But unions can force a government committed to a Keynesian full employment policy to inflate in order to prevent the unemployment which their actions could otherwise cause; indeed, if it is believed that the government will prevent a rise of wages from leading to unemployment, there is no limit to the magnitude of wage demands—and indeed even little reason for the employers to resist them.[11]

There is a little more reason to question Professor Friedman's recommenda-

[11] [For Nobel Laureate in Economics Milton Friedman's (1912–2006) rejection of cost-push theories of inflation, see for example M. Friedman, "What Price Guideposts?" in *Guidelines, Informal Controls, and the Market Place: Policy Choices in a Full Employment Economy*, ed. G. Shultz and R. Aliber (Chicago: University of Chicago Press, 1966), pp. 21–25. For discussions of the differences between Hayek and Friedman on the role of the unions in causing inflation, see P. Jay, "Do Trade Unions Matter?", in *Inflation: Causes, Consequences, Cures* (London: Institute of Economic Affairs, 1974), and pp. 838–40 of B. Jackson, "Currents of Neo-liberalism: British Political Ideologies and the New Right, c. 1955–1979", *English Historical Review*, vol. 131, 2016, pp. 823–50.—Ed.]

tion of indexing as a means to combat the current inflation. No doubt index-ing could do a lot to mitigate the harm inflation does to such groups as pen-sioners or those who have retired on their savings. And it might even cure at the root such inflations as are due to the inability of a government to keep up revenue to cover current expenditure.[12]

But it is not likely to remedy the present inflation which is due to all people together trying to buy more than there is on the market and insisting that they be given enough money to enable them to buy at current prices what they expect to get. In this they must always be disappointed by a new rise of prices caused by their demand, and the vicious circle can be broken only by people contenting themselves with a somewhat lower real buying power than that which they have been vainly chasing for so long. This effect, however, a general adoption of indexing would prevent. It might even make a continu-ous inflation inevitable.

But at present it is not chiefly wage demands that drive us into accelerating inflation—though they are part of the mechanism that does so. But people will learn before long that the increase of money wages is self-defeating. What is likely to drive us further on the perilous road will be the panicky reactions of politicians every time a slowing down of inflation leads to a substantial rise of unemployment. They are likely to react to it by resuming inflation and will find that every time it needs a larger dose of inflation to restore employ-ment until in the end this medicine will altogether fail to work. It is this pro-cess which we must avoid at any price. It can be tolerated only by those who wish to destroy the market order and to replace it by a Communist or some other totalitarian system.

The first requirement, if we are to avoid this fate, is that we face the facts, and make people at large understand that, after the mistakes we have made, it simply is no longer in our power to maintain uninterrupted full employ-ment. No economist who has lived through the experience of the 1930s will doubt that extensive and prolonged unemployment is one of the worst disas-ters which can befall a country. But all we can hope now is to prevent it from becoming too extensive and too prolonged and that it will be no more than an unavoidable period of transition to a state in which we can again hope to achieve the reasonable goal of a high and stable level of employment.

What the public must learn to understand if a rational policy is to be pos-sible is that, whatever may be the fault of past governments, in the present

---

[12] [Friedman's arguments for the indexation of taxation and government securities, and of private-sector wage and price contracts, can be found in M. Friedman, *Monetary Correction: A Pro-posal for Escalator Clauses to Reduce the Costs of Ending Inflation*, IEA Occasional Paper 41 (London: Institute of Economic Affairs, 1974), and M. Friedman, "Inflation, Taxation, Indexation", pub-lished as chapter 5 of *Inflation: Causes, Consequences, Cures.*—Ed.]

position it is simply no longer in the power of government to maintain full employment and a tolerable productive organisation of the economy.

It will need great courage—and almost more understanding than one dares to hope for—on the part of the government to make people understand what the position is. We are probably approaching a critical test of democracy about the outcome of which one must feel apprehensive. One of the prime requirements of its successfully weathering this crisis is that the people are in time undeceived about the fateful illusion that there is a cheap and easy means of at the same time securing full employment and a continuous rapid rise of real wages. This can be achieved only by that steady restructuring of the use of all resources in adaptation to changing real conditions which the debauching of the monetary medium prevents and only a properly functioning market can bring about.

II Inflation, the misdirection of labour, and unemployment[13]

1

After a unique 25-year period of great prosperity the economy of the Western world has arrived at a critical juncture. I expect that the experience of these years will enter history under the name of the Great Prosperity as the 1930s are known as the Great Depression. We have indeed succeeded, by eliminating all the automatic brakes which operated in the past, such as the gold standard and fixed rates of exchange, in maintaining the full and even excessive employment which was created by an expansion of credit, and in the end by open inflation, for a much longer time than I should have thought possible. But the inevitable end is now near if it has not already arrived.

I find myself in this connection in the unpleasant position that, after I had preached for 40 years that the time to prevent the coming of a depression is the boom, and while during the boom nobody listened to me, people now again turn to me and ask how the consequence of a policy can be avoided of which I had constantly warned. I must witness heads of the governments of all the Western industrial countries promising their people that they will stop the inflation *and* preserve full employment knowing that they *cannot* do this.

---

[13] A lecture delivered at Rome on 8 February 1975 at the Convegno Internazionale, 'Il Problema Della Moneta Oggi', indetto nel Centenario della Nascita di Luigi Einaudi, Accademia Nazionale dei Lincei, Atti Convegni Lincei 12 (Roma, 1976). A version carefully revised by the editor and perhaps easier to read will be found in Occasional Paper 45, published under the title *Full Employment at Any Price?*, by the Institute of Economic Affairs, London, 1975. [F. A. Hayek, *Full Employment at Any Price?* IEA Occasional Paper 45 (London: Institute of Economic Affairs, 1975).—Ed.]

But I fear even that such attempts, as President Ford has just announced, to postpone the inevitable crisis by a new inflationary push, may temporarily succeed and make the eventual breakdown even worse.[14]

The disquieting but unalterable fact is that a false monetary and credit policy, through almost the whole time since the last war, has placed the economic systems of all the Western industrial countries in a highly unstable position in which anything we can do now will produce most unpleasant consequences. We have a choice only between three possibilities: to allow a rapidly accelerating open inflation to continue until it has brought about a complete disorganisation of all economic activity; to impose controls of wages and prices which will for a time conceal the effects of a continued inflation but would inevitably lead to a centrally directed and totalitarian economic system; and, finally, a determined termination of the increase of the quantity of money which would soon, through the appearance of substantial unemployment, make manifest all those misdirections of labour which the inflation of the past years has brought about and which the two other procedures would further increase.

To understand why the whole Western world allowed itself to be led into this frightful dilemma, it is necessary to glance briefly back at developments during the two decades between the great wars which have largely determined the views which have governed the policy of the post-war years. I want first to mention a lesson which has unfortunately been forgotten. In Austria and Germany the experience of the great inflation had of course directed our attention to the connection between changes of the quantity of money and changes of the degree of employment, and had especially shown to us that the employment created by inflation at once diminished as the inflation slowed down and that the termination of the inflation always produced what came to be called a 'stabilisation crisis' with substantial unemployment. It was the insight into this connection which made me and some of my contemporaries from the outside reject and oppose the kind of full employment policy propagated by Lord Keynes and his followers.

I do not want to leave this recollection of the great inflation without mentioning that I have probably learnt at least as much as, if not more than, I learnt from observing the actual facts of the great inflation by being taught to see—largely by my teacher, the late Ludwig von Mises—the utter stupidity of the arguments which were then, especially in Germany, propounded to explain and justify the increases in the quantity of money. Most of these arguments I am now encountering again in countries which then seemed econom-

---

[14] [Gerald Ford (1913–2006) was the 38th President of the United States (1974–77). In his State of the Union Address of January 1975, Ford proposed significant cuts in taxation, which were passed into law in March of the same year.—Ed.]

ically more sophisticated and whose economists rather looked down at the foolishness of the German economists. None of these apologists of the inflationary policy was able to propose or apply measures which made it possible to terminate the inflation, which was finally done by a man who believed in a crude and primitive version of the quantity theory, Hjalmar Schacht. But that only by the way.[15]

The policy of the recent decades, or the theory which underlies it, had its origin, however, in the specific experiences of Great Britain during the 1920s and 1930s. Great Britain in 1925, as you know, after what must seem to us the very modest inflation of the First World War, had, in my opinion very sensibly, returned to the gold standard, but unfortunately, very honestly but unreasonably, at the former parity. This had in no way been required by classical doctrine: David Ricardo had in 1821 written to a friend that he "should never advise a government to restore a currency, which had been depreciated 30 per cent, to par".[16] I ask myself often how different the economic history of the world might have been if in the discussion of the years preceding 1925 one English economist had remembered and pointed out this long-before published passage in one of Ricardo's letters.

In the event, the unfortunate decision taken in 1925 made a prolonged process of deflation inevitable, a process which might have been successful in maintaining the gold standard if it had been continued until a large part of the prevailing money wages had been reduced. I believe this attempt was near success when in the world crisis of 1931 England abandoned it together with the gold standard—which this event finally discredited.

It was during this period of most extensive unemployment in Great Britain, which preceded the world-wide economic crisis of 1929–31, that John Maynard Keynes developed his basic ideas. It is important to notice that this happened in a very exceptional and almost unique position of his country: at

[15] [Austrian economist Ludwig von Mises (1881–1973) was Hayek's mentor and, in his *Theorie des Geldes und der Umlaufsmittel* (Munich and Leipzig: Duncker & Humblot, 1912), gave an account of the business cycle in which expansions and contractions of credit played a central role. For more on Mises, see F. A. Hayek, "The Transmission of the Ideals of Economic Freedom" [1951], reprinted as chapter 2 of this volume, p. 42 n. 1. Hjalmar Schacht (1877–1970) was a German banker who achieved international renown whilst working in the German finance ministry in the 1920s by helping to devise the policies that halted hyperinflation in the Weimar Republic.—Ed.]

[16] David Ricardo to John Wheatley, 18 September 1821, reprinted in *The Works of David Ricardo*, ed. Piero Sraffa, Cambridge University Press, 1952, vol. IX, p. 73. [The letter by English stockbroker and economist David Ricardo (1772–1823) to which Hayek refers can be found on p. 73 of D. Ricardo, *Letters July 1821–1823*, ed. P. Sraffa with the collaboration of M. Dobb, vol. 9 of *The Works and Correspondence of David Ricardo* (Cambridge: Cambridge University Press for the Royal Economic Society, 1952). Ricardo wrote about a currency which "was depreciated 30 per cent", not "had been".—Ed.]

a time when as a result of the great appreciation of the international value of the pound sterling the real wages of practically all British workers had been substantially increased compared with the rest of the world, and British exporters had in consequence in a great measure become unable to compete successfully in the world markets. In order to give employment to the unemployed it would at that juncture therefore have been necessary either to lower all wages or to raise the sterling prices of most commodities.

In the development of Keynes' thought it is possible to distinguish three distinct phases: he began with the recognition that it was necessary to lower real wages, came to the conclusion that this was politically impossible, and finally convinced himself that it would be vain and even harmful. In this way the Keynes of 1919, who had still understood that

> There is no subtler, no surer means of overturning the existing basis of society than to debauch the currency. The process engages all the hidden forces of economic law on the side of destruction, and does it in a manner which not one man in a million is able to diagnose[17]

became the inflationist or at least rabid anti-deflationist of the 1930s. I have, however, strong reason to believe that he would have disapproved of what his pupils did in the post-war period and that, if he had not died so soon, he would have become one of the leaders in the fight against inflation.

It was in the course of that unfortunate episode in English monetary history that he became the intellectual leader who gained acceptance for the fatal idea that unemployment is predominantly due to an insufficiency of aggregate demand compared with the total of wages which would have to be paid if all workers were to be employed at current wages. This formula of employment as a direct function to total demand proved so extraordinarily effective because it seemed to be confirmed in some degree by the results of quantitative empirical data, while the alternative explanations of unemployment which I regard as correct could make no such claims. Eight weeks ago I made the dangerous effects which the scientistic prejudice has had in this connection the subject of my Nobel lecture at Stockholm and will consider it here only briefly.[18]

What we find here is the curious situation that the theory which is comparatively best confirmed by statistics, because it is the only one which *can* be tested statistically, is nevertheless false and has been widely accepted only because

[17] *The Economic Consequences of the Peace* (1919), reprinted in *The Collected Writings of John Maynard Keynes*, Macmillan for the Royal Economic Society, 1971, vol. II, p. 149. [See J. M. Keynes, *The Economic Consequences of the Peace* [1919], reprinted as vol. 2 (1971) of *The Collected Writings of John Maynard Keynes*, p. 149.—Ed.]

[18] [On what follows, now see Hayek, "The Pretence of Knowledge", pp. 362–68.—Ed.]

the explanation which had earlier been regarded as true, and which I still regard as true, by its very nature cannot be tested in this manner.[19]

The older, and to me convincing, explanation of extensive unemployment ascribes it to a discrepancy between the distribution of labour (and the other factors of production) between the different industries (and localities) and the distribution of demand among their products. This discrepancy is caused by a distortion of the system of relative prices and wages and can be corrected only by a change in these relations, that is, by the establishment of such relative prices and wages that in each sector of the economy supply will equal demand.

The cause of unemployment, in other words, is a deviation of prices and wages from their equilibrium position which would establish itself with a free market and stable money. But we can never know at what system of relative prices and wages such an equilibrium would establish itself. We are therefore unable to measure the deviation of the existing prices from that equilibrium position which is the cause of the impossibility of selling part of the labour supply; and we are therefore equally unable to demonstrate a statistical correlation between the distortion of relative prices and the volume of unemployment. Causes may, however, be very effective although not measurable, and the current superstition that only the measurable can be important has done much to mislead us.

Probably even more important, however, than those fashionable prejudices concerning scientific methods which made the new theory attractive to the professional economists, were the temptations it offered to the politicians. It offered to them not only a cheap and quick method of removing a chief source of real suffering; it promised them also release from the most restricting fetters which had impeded them in their striving for popularity. Spending more money and budget deficits were suddenly represented as virtues and it was even persuasively argued that increased government expenditure was wholly meritorious since it led to the utilisation of hitherto unused resources and this cost nothing to the community but brought it only a net gain.

These beliefs led in particular to the gradual removal of all effective barriers against an increase in the quantity of money by the monetary authorities. Already the Bretton Woods agreement had by its endeavour to place the burden of international adjustment exclusively on the surplus countries, i.e. to require them to expand but not to require the deficit countries to contract, laid the foundation for a world inflation. But this was at least done in the laud-

---

[19] [In the version of this essay published in *New Studies*, the final clause of this sentence read, "but by its very nature cannot be tested in this manner". The word 'but' has been removed from the version presented here, on the grounds that its presence is superfluous and indeed obscures the meaning Hayek was trying to convey.—Ed.]

able endeavour to secure fixed rates of exchange. Yet when the criticism of the inflationistically minded majority of the economists succeeded in removing this last obstacle to national inflation, there was no effective brake left.

It is, I believe, undeniable that the demand for flexible rates of exchange originated wholly from countries whose economists wanted a wider margin for credit expansion (called full employment policy). They have, unfortunately, later received support also from other economists who were not inspired by the desire for inflation. These men seem to me to have overlooked the strongest argument in favour of fixed rates of exchange, namely that they constitute the practically irreplaceable curb which we need to *compel* the politicians and the monetary authorities responsible to politicians to maintain a stable currency.

The maintenance of the value of money and the avoidance of inflation demand all the time from the politician highly unpopular measures which he can justify towards those who are unfavourably affected by them only by showing that he was compelled to take them. So long as the preservation of the external value of the national currency is regarded as an undisputable necessity, he can resist the constant demands for cheaper credits, avoidance of a rise in interest rates, more expenditure on public works and so on. But while a fall in the foreign value of the currency or an outflow of gold or foreign exchange acted as a signal requiring prompt reaction, the effect on the internal price level is much too slow—and usually preceded by a welcome increase in employment—to be generally recognised or to be charged to those ultimately responsible for it.

I understand, therefore, very well that, in the hope thereby to restrain the countries all too inclined towards inflation, countries like Germany and Switzerland, even while they were already noticeably suffering from imported inflation, hesitated to destroy altogether the system of fixed rates of exchange so long as it seemed that it might restrain the tendencies in other countries further to speed up the inflation. Now, of course, when the system of fixed rates of exchange appears to have definitely collapsed and there seems scarcely any hope that by observing discipline themselves they might induce other countries to restrain themselves, there is little reason left why they should adhere to a system which is no longer effective. And in retrospect one may well ask whether, out of a mistaken hope, the German Bundesbank or the Swiss National Bank have not waited too long and even then raised the value of their currency too little. But from a long-term point of view I do not believe that we shall regain a system of international stability without returning to a system of fixed rates of exchange which imposes upon the national central banks that compulsion which they need if they are to resist the pressure of the inflationistically minded forces of their country—usually including the ministers of finance.

2

But why all this fear of inflation? Should we not try to learn to live with it, as some South American countries seem to have done, particularly if, as some believe, this is the necessary price of securing full employment? If this were true and the harm done by inflation were only that which many people emphasise, we would have to consider this possibility seriously.

However, the answer is, first, that such inflation, in order to achieve the goal aimed at, would have constantly to accelerate and that such accelerating inflation would sooner or later reach a degree which makes all effective order of a market economy impossible; and, second and most important, that in the long run such inflation makes much greater unemployment inevitable than that which it was originally intended to prevent.

The argument often advanced that inflation produces merely a redistribution of the social product while unemployment reduces it and for this reason represents a greater evil is thus false, because inflation becomes the cause of increased unemployment.

I certainly do not wish to underestimate the other harmful effects of inflation. They are much worse than anyone can conceive who has not himself lived through a great inflation—and I count my first eight months in a job during which my salary rose to 200 times the initial amount as such an experience. I am indeed convinced that such a mismanagement of the currency is tolerated by the people only because, while such an inflation proceeds, nobody has the time or energy to organise a popular rising. What I want to say is merely that even these effects, which every citizen experiences, are not the worst effects of inflation. These are usually not understood because they become visible only when the inflation is past. This must particularly be said to those who like to point to the South American countries which have had inflations lasting through several generations and which seem to have learnt to live with them. But in these predominantly agrarian countries the important effects of inflation are chiefly limited to those I have just mentioned, while the chief effects of an inflation produced in industrial countries by an effort to create employment thereby are in these conditions of minor importance.

I have no time to discuss here the attempts made in some of these countries, in particular in Brazil, to deal with the problems of inflation by some method of indexing which can at best remedy some of the consequences but certainly not the chief causes of inflation, or its most harmful effects. They certainly would not prevent the worst damage which inflation causes, that is that misdirection of labour which I have already mentioned as its effect but which I must now consider more fully.

Inflation makes certain jobs attractive which will disappear when it stops or even when it ceases to accelerate at a sufficient rate in consequence of

(a) the changes in the proportional distribution of the money stream between the different sectors and stages of the process of production, and

(b) the effects of the expectations of a further future rise of prices which it causes.

The defenders of a monetary full employment policy often represent the position as if a single increase of total demand were sufficient to secure full employment for an indefinite but fairly long period. This argument overlooks the inevitable effects of such a policy on the wage policy of the trade unions.

As soon as government assumes the responsibility to maintain full employment at whatever wages the trade unions succeed in obtaining, these unions no longer have any reason to take account of the unemployment which their wage demands may cause. In this situation every increase of wages which exceeds the increase of productivity of the kind of labour concerned will make necessary an increase in total demand if unemployment is not to ensue. The increase in the quantity of money made necessary by the upward movement of wages thus released becomes a continuous process involving a constant influx of additional quantities of money which in turn must lead to changes in the relative strength of demand for the different kinds of goods and services. This in turn must lead to changes in relative prices and consequent changes in the direction of production and the allocation of the factors of production (including labour). I must leave aside here all the other reasons why the prices of the different goods—and the quantities of them that will be produced—will react differently to changes in the demand.

The chief point I want to bring out is that the longer the inflation lasts, the greater will be the number of the workers whose jobs depend on a continuation of the inflation, often even on a continuing acceleration of the rate of inflation—not because they would not have found employment without the inflation, but because they were drawn by the inflation into temporarily attractive jobs which after a slowing down or cessation of the inflation will again disappear.

We ought to have no illusion that we can escape the consequences of the mistakes we have made. Any attempt to preserve the particular jobs which have been made profitable by inflation would lead to a complete destruction of the market order. *We have once again missed the opportunity to forestall a depression while it was still in our power to do so.* We have in fact used our newly gained freedom from institutional compulsion in order to act more stupidly than we have ever done before.

But if we cannot escape the reappearance of substantial unemployment, this is not the effect of a failure of 'capitalism', or the market economy, but exclusively of our own errors which past experience and already available knowledge ought to have enabled us to avoid. It is unfortunately only too true that the disappointment of expectations which we have created may lead to serious social disturbances. But this does not mean that we can avoid this effect. The most serious danger now is certainly that attempts, so attractive for the politicians, to postpone the evil day and thereby make things in the long run even worse, may still succeed. I must confess that I have been wishing for some time that the inescapable crisis may come soon, and that I hope that any attempts that may be made at once to restart the process of monetary expansion will not succeed but that we shall be forced to face now the problem of choosing a new policy.

Let me, however, emphasise at once that, although I regard a period of some months, perhaps even more than a year, of considerable unemployment as unavoidable, this does not mean that we must expect another long period of mass unemployment comparable with the Great Depression of the 1930s if we do not commit very bad mistakes of policy. Such a development can be prevented by a sensible policy which does not repeat those errors which were responsible for the long duration of the Great Depression.

But before I turn to the question of what ought to be our future policy, I want emphatically to reject a misrepresentation of my argument which I have already experienced. I certainly do not recommend bringing about unemployment as a *means* in order to combat inflation, but have to advise in a situation in which the choice open to us is solely between some unemployment in the near future, and greater unemployment at a later date; and what I above all fear is the *après nous le déluge* attitude of the politicians who in their concern about the next elections are likely to choose the second alternative. Unfortunately even some experts, such as the writers of the English weekly *The Economist*, argue in a similar manner and call already for 'reflation' when the increase in the quantity of money is still lustily continuing.

The first necessity now is to stop the increase of the quantity of money, or at least to reduce it to the rate of real growth of production—and this cannot happen soon enough. I can see no advantage in a gradual deceleration, although for purely technical reasons it may prove necessary in some measure. This does, however, not mean that we should not endeavour to stop a real deflation when it should threaten to set in. Although I do not regard deflation as the original cause of a decline in business activity, such a reaction has unquestionably the tendency to induce a process of deflation—to cause what more than 40 years ago I called a 'secondary deflation'[20]—the effects of which may be worse, and in the 1930s certainly were worse than what the

[20] I recollect that this phrase was frequently used in the London School of Economics seminar during the 1930s. [On the notion of 'secondary deflation', now see F. A. Hayek, *Business Cycles, Part II*, ed. H. Klausinger, vol. 8 (2012) of *The Collected Works of F. A. Hayek*, pp. 176–77. For a helpful discussion, see H. Klausinger, "Introduction", in *Business Cycles, Part II*, pp. 5–15.—Ed.]

original cause of the reaction made necessary, and which have no steering function to perform.

I have to confess that 40 years ago I argued differently and that I have since altered my opinion—not about the theoretical explanation of the events but about the practical possibility of removing the obstacles to the functioning of the system in a particular way.

I did then believe that a short process of deflation might break that rigidity of money wages, that is what economists have since come to call their 'rigidity downwards' or the resistance against the reduction of some particular money wages, and that in this way we could restore a determination of relative wages by the market. This seems to me still an indispensable condition if the market mechanism is to function satisfactorily. But I no longer believe that it is practically possible to achieve this in this manner; and I probably should have seen then that the last chance was gone after the British government in 1931 abandoned the attempt to bring costs down by deflation just as it seemed near success.

If I were today responsible for the monetary policy of a country I would certainly endeavour to prevent a threatening actual deflation, that is an absolute decrease of the stream of incomes, with all suitable means, and would announce that I intend to do so. This alone would probably be sufficient to prevent a degeneration of the recession into a long-lasting depression. The re-establishment of a properly functioning market would, however, still require a restructuring of the whole system of relative prices and wages and a readjustment to the expectation of stable prices, which presupposes a much greater flexibility than exists now; what chance we have to achieve it and how long it may take I dare not predict.[21]

From a longer point of view it is obvious that, once we have got over the immediate difficulties, we must not avail ourselves again of the seemingly cheap and easy method of achieving full employment by aiming at the maximum of employment which can be brought about in the short run by monetary pressure.

The Keynesian dream is gone even if its ghost continues to plague politics for decades. It were to be wished that the words 'full employment' themselves, which have become so closely associated with the inflationist policy, should be

---

[21] [For analyses of the shift in Hayek's opinion on policy, away from the view (which he held in the 1930s) that there was little if any role for reflationary policies in combatting unemployment, and towards the position (expressed both in the main text above and on pp. 360–62 below) that there might be a role for monetary policy in countering "a 'secondary depression' caused by an induced deflation", see L. White, "Did Hayek and Robbins Deepen the Great Depression?", *Journal of Money, Credit and Banking*, vol. 40, 2008, pp. 751–68, and A. Magliulo, "Hayek and the Great Depression of 1929: Did He Really Change His Mind?", *European Journal of the History of Economic Thought*, vol. 23, 2016, pp. 31–58.—Ed.]

abandoned—or that we should at least remember the sense in which this was the aim of classical economists long before Keynes: John Stuart Mill reports in his autobiography how "full employment with high wages"[22] appeared to him in his youth as the chief desideratum of economic policy. What we must now be clear about is that our aim must not be that maximum of employment which can be achieved in the short run, but a "high and stable level of employment", as one of the post-war British White Papers on employment policy still phrased it.[23] This, however, we can achieve only through the re-establishment of a properly functioning market which, by the free play of prices and wages, secures in each sector a correspondence of supply and demand. Though it must remain one of the chief tasks of monetary policy to prevent great fluctuations of the quantity of money or the volume of the income stream, the effect on employment must not be the dominating consideration guiding it. The primary aim must again become the stability of the value of money and the currency authorities must again be effectively protected against that political pressure which today forces them so often to take measures which are politically advantageous in the short run but harmful in the long run.

I wish I could share the confidence of my friend Milton Friedman who thinks that one could deprive the monetary authorities, in order to prevent the abuse of their powers for political purposes, of all discretionary powers by prescribing the amount of money which they may (and have to) add to circulation in any one year.[24] It seems to me that he regards this as practicable because he has got used to drawing for statistical purposes a sharp distinction between what is to be regarded as money and what is not, which in fact does not exist. I believe that in order to ensure the convertibility of all kinds of near-money into real money, which is necessary if we are to avoid severe liquidity crises or panics, the monetary authorities must be given some discretion. But I do agree with him that we will have to try and get back to some more or less automatic system for regulating the quantity of money.

---

[22] *Autobiography and Other Writings*, ed. J. Stillinger, Boston, 1969. [See J. S. Mill, *Autobiography and Other Writings*, ed. J. Stillinger (Boston: Houghton Mifflin Co., 1969), p. 64; Mill actually writes "at high wages". For more on Hayek's views about John Stuart Mill (1806–73), see F. A. Hayek, "Liberalism" [1978], reprinted as chapter 1 of this volume, p. 18.—Ed.]

[23] *Employment Policy*, Cmd. 6527, HMSO, May 1944, Foreword. [In the version of this essay that appeared in *New Studies*, Hayek misquoted slightly the opening line of the Foreword to the 1944 White Paper, writing "label" instead of "level". That error has been corrected here. The complete sentence is as follows: "The Government accept as one of their primary aims and responsibilities the maintenance of a high and stable level of employment after the war". See *Employment Policy*, Cmd. 6527 (London: His Majesty's Stationary Office, 1944), p. 3.—Ed.]

[24] [See, for example, M. Friedman, *A Program for Monetary Stability* (New York: Fordham University Press, 1960), and M. Friedman, "The Role of Monetary Policy", *American Economic Review*, vol. 58, 1968, pp. 1–17.]

And although I am not as optimistic as the Chief Editor of the London *Times*, who some time ago in a sensational article[25] and now in a book has proposed a return to the gold standard,[26] it does make me feel somewhat more optimistic when I see such a proposal coming from so influential a quarter. I would even agree that among the *practicable* monetary systems the international gold standard is the best, if I did regard it as practicable, that is if I could believe that, if it were re-established, the most important countries could be trusted to obey those rules of the game which are necessary for its preservation. But this seems to me exceedingly unlikely, and no single country can have an effective gold standard: it is by its nature an international system and can function only as an international system.

It is, however, already a great step in the direction of a return to reason when at the end of this book Mr. Rees-Mogg argues that[27]

> We should be tearing up the full employment commitment of the 1944 White Paper, a great political and economic revolution.

This would until very recently have seemed a high price to pay; now it is no great price at all. There is little or no prospect of maintaining full employment with the present inflation, in Britain or in the world. The full employment standard became a commitment to inflation, but the inflation has now accelerated past the point at which it is compatible with full employment.

Equally encouraging is a statement of the British Chancellor of the Exchequer who is reported to have said that "It is far better that more people should be in work—even if that means lower wages on average—than that those lucky enough to keep their jobs should scrape the pool while millions are living on the dole."[28]

[25] 'Crisis of paper currencies: has the time come for Britain to return to the gold standard?' *The Times*, 1 May 1974. [William Rees-Mogg (1928–2012) was editor of *The Times* from 1967 until 1981. Hayek refers to W. Rees-Mogg, "Crisis of Paper Currencies: Has the Time Come for Britain to Return to the Gold Standard?" *The Times*, May 1, 1974, p. 16.—Ed.]

[26] William Rees-Mogg, *The Reigning Error. The Crisis of World Inflation*, London, 1974. [W. Rees-Mogg, *The Reigning Error: The Crisis of World Inflation* (London: Hamish Hamilton, 1974).—Ed.]

[27] *Ibid.*, p. 112. [Rees-Mogg, *The Reigning Error*, p. 112.—Ed.]

[28] Speech at the East Leeds Labour Club reported in *The Times*, 11 January 1975. [Hayek refers to a speech given by Labour Party politician Denis Healey (1917–2015), Chancellor of the Exchequer (1974–79), whose words—as reported in *The Times*—were actually as follows: "It is far better that more people should be in work, even if that means accepting lower wages on average, than that those lucky enough to keep their jobs should scoop the pool while millions are living on the dole. That is what the social contract is all about". See M. Brown, "State and Industry Closer on Curbing Inflation", *The Times*, January 11, 1975, p. 1. The final sentence of the quotation, which Hayek does not mention, ought to have tempered any encouragement he took from Healy's remarks, for it refers to an agreement between the recently-elected Labour government and the trade unions that saw the latter pledge to moderate their wage claims in

It would almost seem as if in the country in which the harmful doctrines originated a reversal of opinion were now under way. Let us hope that it will rapidly spread over the world.

III Further considerations on the same topic[29]

It seems to me that the primary duty today of any economist who deserves the name is to repeat on every occasion that the present unemployment is the direct and inevitable consequence of the so-called full employment policies pursued for the last 25 years. Most people still believe mistakenly that an increase in aggregate demand will remove the cause of unemployment. Nothing, therefore, short of the realisation that this remedy, though usually effective in the short run, produces much more unemployment later, will prevent the public from exerting irresistible pressure to resume inflation as soon as unemployment substantially increases.

To understand this basic truth is to recognise that the majority of economists whose advice governments have been following in Britain and the rest of the Western world during this period have thoroughly discredited themselves and ought to do penance in sackcloth and ashes. What was almost unquestioned orthodoxy for close on 30 years has been thoroughly discredited. And the present economic crisis also marks a severe setback in the authority of economics—or at least the long overdue collapse of the Keynesian bubble of the fashionable doctrine that has dominated opinion for a generation. I am fully convinced that before we can return to reasonable stability, not to mention lasting prosperity, we must exorcise the Keynesian incubus. By this I mean

---

return for the implementation of various policies designed to improve workers' welfare, including price controls and higher pensions. For more on this, see p. 483 n. 41 of F. A. Hayek, "Letters to *The Times*, 1931–1981", reprinted as chapter 31 of this volume.—Ed.]

[29] What follows are merely elaborations of particular points made in the preceding lecture while I spoke on the same general topic to various audiences in the USA in the course of the second quarter of 1975. A shorter collection of these supplementary observations was already added to the original text when, with the preceding chapters and the second section of this chapter, it was reprinted by the Institute of Economic Affairs in its Occasional Paper 45 under the title *Full Employment at Any Price?* London, 1975. Some further passages have now been included from addresses published in the *First Chicago Report* issued by the First National Bank of Chicago in May 1975, and a brochure entitled *A Discussion with Friedrich A. von Hayek* issued by the American Enterprise Institute for Public Policy Research, Washington DC, 1975. [Hayek refers to: Hayek, *Full Employment at Any Price?*; F. A. Hayek, "World Inflationary Recession", paper presented to the International Conference on World Economic Stabilisation, co-sponsored by the First National Bank of Chicago and the University of Chicago, April 17–18, 1975; and F. A. Hayek, *A Discussion with Friedrich von Hayek: Held at the American Enterprise Institute*, AEI Domestic Affairs Studies 39 (Washington, DC: American Enterprise Institute for Public Policy Research, 1975).—Ed.]

less what John Maynard Keynes himself thought—because you can find in Keynes, as in Marx, almost everything—than the teaching of those Keynesians who, as Professor Joan Robinson recently told us, "sometimes had trouble in getting Maynard to see what the point of his revolution really was".[30]

The conquest of opinion by Keynesian economics is mainly due to the fact that its argument conformed with the age-old belief of the shopkeeper that his prosperity depended on consumers' demand for his wares. The plausible but erroneous conclusion derived from this individual experience in business that general prosperity could be maintained by keeping general demand high, against which economic theory had been arguing for generations, was suddenly again made respectable by Keynes. And since the 1930s it has been embraced as obvious good sense by a whole generation of economists brought up on the teaching of his school. It has had the effect that for a quarter of a century we have systematically employed all available methods of increasing money expenditure, which in the short run creates additional employment but at the same time leads to misdirections of labour that must ultimately result in unemployment.

This fundamental connection between inflation and unemployment is obscured because, although insufficient general demand is normally not the primary source of unemployment (except during an actual deflation, i.e. a decrease in the quantity of money), unemployment may itself become the cause of an absolute shrinkage of aggregate demand which in turn may bring about a further increase of unemployment and thus lead to a cumulative process of contraction in which unemployment feeds on unemployment. Such a 'secondary depression' caused by an induced deflation should of course be prevented by appropriate monetary counter-measures. Though I am sometimes accused of having represented the deflationary cause of the business cycles as part of the curative process, I do not think that was ever what I argued. What I did believe at one time was that a deflation might be necessary

---

[30] Joan Robinson, 'What has become of the Keynesian revolution?', in Milo Keynes (ed.), *Essays on John Maynard Keynes*, Cambridge, 1975, p. 125. See also note on p. 229. [British economist Joan Robinson (1903–83) taught at Cambridge University from 1931 until 1971 and was in the 1930s part of the 'Cambridge Circus'—the group of young economists who helped Keynes first of all to develop and then to promote the ideas expressed in his *General Theory*. For a brief discussion of the Circus, and Robinson's role in it, see B. Caldwell, "Introduction", in Hayek, *Contra Keynes and Cambridge*, pp. 23–4, 35. It is the activities of that group to which Robinson refers in the remark slightly misquoted by Hayek: "there were moments when we had some trouble in getting Maynard to see what the point of his revolution really was, but when he came to sum it up after the book was published he got it into focus". See J. Robinson, "What Has Become of the Keynesian Revolution?", in *Essays on John Maynard Keynes*, ed. M. Keynes (Cambridge: Cambridge University Press, 1975), p. 125. The summary to which Robinson alludes is J. M. Keynes, "The General Theory of Employment", *Quarterly Journal of Economics*, vol. 51, 1937, pp. 209–23. The note to which Hayek refers now begins on p. 378 below.—Ed.]

to break the developing downward rigidity of all particular wages which has of course become one of the main causes of inflation. I no longer think that this is a politically possible method and we shall have to find other means to restore the flexibility of the wage structure than the present method of raising all wages except those which must fall relatively to all others. Nor did I ever doubt that in most situations employment could be temporarily increased by increasing money expenditure. There was one classical occasion when I even admitted that this might be politically necessary, whatever the long run economic harm it did.

The occasion was the situation in Germany in, I believe, 1930 when the depression was beginning to get quite serious and a political commission—the Braun Committee—had proposed to combat it by reflation (though that term had not yet been coined), i.e. a rapid expansion of credit. One of the members of the committee, in fact the main author of the report, was my late friend, Professor Wilhelm Röpke. I thought that in the circumstances the proposal was wrong and wrote an article criticising it.[31] I did not send it to a journal, however, but to Professor Röpke with a covering letter in which I made the following point:

> Apart from political considerations I feel you ought not—not yet at least—to start expanding credit. But if the political situation is so serious that continuing unemployment would lead to a political revolution, please do not publish my article. That is a political consideration, however, the merits of which I cannot judge from outside Germany but which you will be able to judge.

Röpke's reaction was not to publish the article, because he was convinced that at that time the political danger of increasing unemployment was so great that

---

[31] [See Hayek, *Business Cycles, Part II*, p. 250 n. 64: "There may be desperate situations in which it may indeed be necessary to increase employment at all costs, even if it be only for a short period—perhaps the situation in which Dr. Brüning found himself in Germany in 1932 was a situation in which desperate means would have been justified". The relevant passage is quoted in full at the outset of part 2 of section IV below. German statesman Heinrich Brüning (1885–1970) was chancellor and foreign minister of Germany between March 1930 and May 1932. Confronted with the need to make reparations payments during the Great Depression, he pursued a deflationary policy that led to rising unemployment and falling living standards. German economist Wilhelm Röpke (1899–1966) was a prominent classical liberal critic of Brüning's approach. The report of the Brauns-Kommission (not "Braun"), of which Röpke was a member and to which Hayek refers below, advocated an expansion of credit with a view to encouraging investment as the appropriate policy response. See W. Röpke, "Praktische Konjunkturpolitik. Die Arbeit der Brauns-Kommission", *Weltwirtschaftliches Archiv*, vol. 34, 1931, pp. 423–64, and pp. 429–31 of W. Röpke, "Trends in German Business Cycle Policy", *Economic Journal*, vol. 43, 1933, pp. 427–41. For more on Röpke, see Hayek, "The Transmission of the Ideals of Economic Freedom", p. 53 n. 19.—Ed.]

he would risk the danger of causing further misdirections by more inflation in the hope of postponing the crisis; at that particular moment this seemed to him politically necessary and I consequently withdrew my article.

To return, however, to the specific problem of preventing what I have called the secondary depression caused by the deflation which a crisis is likely to induce. Although it is clear that such a deflation, which does no good and only harm, ought to be prevented, it is not easy to see how this can be done without producing further misdirections of labour. In general it is probably true to say that an equilibrium position will be most effectively approached if consumers' demand is prevented from falling substantially by providing employment through public works at relatively low wages so that workers will wish to move as soon as they can to other and better paid occupations, and not by directly stimulating particular kinds of investment or similar kinds of public expenditure which will draw labour into jobs they will expect to be permanent but which must cease as the source of the expenditure dries up.

At the present moment, however, our problem is not yet to prevent any such deflation, and the cry for reflation is actually raised at a time when the increase of the quantity of money is everywhere still lustily proceeding. Our chief duty is, therefore, still to prevent attempts to combat the unemployment made inevitable through misdirections of labour by a renewed spurt of inflation, which would only increase those misdirections and thus in the long run make matters worse.

A short exposition cannot do justice to the complexity of the facts in another important respect. There is one special difficulty about accounting for the present situation. In the misdirection of labour and the distortion of the structure of production during past business cycles, it was fairly easy to point to the places where the excessive expansion had occurred because it was, on the whole, confined to the capital goods industries. The whole thing was due to an over-expansion of credit for investment purposes, and it was therefore possible to regard the industries producing capital equipment as those which had been over-expanded.

In contrast, the present expansion of money, which has been brought about partly by means of bank credit expansion and partly through budget deficits, has been the result of a deliberate policy, and has gone through somewhat different channels. The additional expenditure has been much more widely dispersed. In the earlier cases I had no difficulty in pointing to particular instances of over-expansion; now I am somewhat embarrassed when I am asked the question, because I would have to know the particular situation in a particular country, where these additional money flows went in the first place, etc. I would also have to trace the successive movements of prices which indicate these flows. In consequence, I have no general answer to the question.

I do not doubt that in a sense we have today the same kind of phenomenon, but the over-expansion, the undue increase of labour employed in particular occupations, is not confined to a single, clearly defined block such as the capital-goods industries. It is now spread much more widely, and the distribution is much more difficult to describe. It is a field I would wish some statistically minded economist would investigate in order to show how the process operated in particular countries. I am by no means sure where such an investigation would find the most important over-developments. The places where the misplaced, and in consequence now *dis*placed, workers can find lasting employment can be discovered only by letting the market operate freely.

We must certainly expect the recovery to come from a revival of industrial investment. But we want investment of the kind which will prove profitable and can be continued when a new position of fair stability and a high level of employment has been achieved. Neither a subsidisation of investment nor artificially low interest rates are likely to bring about this position. And least of all is the desirable (i.e. stable) form of investment to be brought about by stimulating consumers' demand.

The belief that, in order to make new investment profitable, consumers' demand must increase is part of the same widespread fallacy to which the businessman is especially prone. It is true only of investment designed to increase output by using the *same* techniques as hitherto employed, but not of the only sort of investment which can increase productivity per head of worker by equipping a given labour force with *more* capital equipment. Such intensification of capital use is indeed encouraged by relatively *low* product (consumer good) prices (which makes it necessary to save on labour costs) and discouraged by high ones. This is one of the elementary connections between wages and investment wholly overlooked in Keynesian economics.

I not only think that the belief that by pushing up monetary demand we can maintain full employment is entirely mistaken, but am also convinced that if this belief prevails among the public it becomes wholly impossible for a government which has any discretion in these matters to pursue a sensible policy. What current discussion leaves out of account is that governments and monetary authorities are very far from being free to act in the manner which they regard as wise and expedient in the long run. Their problem is chiefly one of finding an excuse for resisting the ever present demand for providing more and cheaper money. This has been a tradition of our civilisation for centuries and one that we had brought under control by certain institutions which were perhaps not particularly efficient or particularly wise, but which put a restraint upon governments to which they could appeal if they were asked to create more money in order to create employment. Central banks and ministers of finance would say, 'We cannot do it because it would drive us off the gold standard or because it would lower our rate of exchange'.

It was the ability to appeal to these institutional restraints which alone made it possible for governments to keep at least near a reasonable course. It was certainly not an ideal policy, nor what they would have done if they had been free to do what they regarded as wise, but it was the best course possible in the existing political set-up. A great many of the most intelligent economists of our time, including most of my personal friends, have contributed to the destruction of the gold standard and the régime of fixed rates of exchange. They instituted something like the Bretton Woods system in which the whole responsibility for adjusting international balances was placed on the creditor countries, and the debtor countries were released of all responsibility. There was even concern created about providing sufficient international liquidity at a time when we were already in the midst of serious inflation. Finally, the last restraints were removed when we left this system of fixed parities for one of flexible parities.

The importance of fixed parities is that they impose upon the monetary authorities a much needed discipline. What I strongly object to is the demand for flexible parities on the ground, which guided this demand on the part of the Anglo-Saxon countries, that it facilitated credit expansion. It was of course a different matter when finally, in resignation, some countries abandoned fixed exchanges in order to protect themselves against the importation of the inflation from the rest of the world. Germany and Switzerland were probably right when they finally and after long hesitation, perhaps too long hesitation, concluded that if fixed exchanges had already ceased to be effective checks on excessive expansion, they at least would not allow fixed rates to force them to participate in the international inflation, and therefore also adopted flexible exchanges. I have no way of reading the mind of the German Bundesbank or the Swiss National Bank, but they had long been guided by the consideration that it was more important to brake the inflationary tendencies in the Western countries than to exclude the effects of these policies on their own countries. In Germany they resigned themselves eventually— perhaps even too late—to the fact that, as the check on others had already become ineffective and fixed exchange rates no longer served their main purpose, they had better adopt floating rates as a protection against inflation.

In this sense, I believe, we ought as economists to think much more about the political significance of institutions which place a restraint on monetary policy and can shelter governments against political pressure, than about the ideal correctness of the policy which might be conducted. Central banks and ministers of finance will never be able to implement what the economist would regard as the wise policy. They will always have to act under political pressure, and all we can hope to do is to protect them against this political pressure as well as possible.

The contention that a general rise of prices such as we in the Western world have experienced in recent years is wholly due to, and made possible by, an excessive increase of the quantity of money, and that, therefore, governmental monetary policy is wholly responsible for it, is today usually described as the 'monetarist' position. It seems to me in this general form incontrovertible, even though it is also true that what has led governments to such a policy was chiefly the activity of trade unions and similar activities by other monopolistic organisations (such as the oil cartel). But in a narrower sense 'monetarist' is today frequently used to describe the expositors of a somewhat mechanical form of the quantity theory of the value of money which in my opinion oversimplifies the theoretical connections.

My chief objection against this theory is that, as what is called a 'macrotheory', it pays attention only to the effects of changes in the quantity of money on the general price level and not to the effects on the structure of relative prices. In consequence, it tends to disregard what seems to me the most harmful effects of inflation: the misdirection of resources it causes and the unemployment which ultimately results from it.

Nevertheless, for most practical purposes I regard this simple form of the quantity theory as a decidedly helpful guide and agree that we should not forget that the great inflations of the past, particularly those in Germany in the early 1920s and the late 1940s, were stopped by men who acted on this somewhat crude form of the quantity theory. But, though this over-simplified explanation of events seems to me inadequate to account for some of the deleterious effects of changes in the quantity of money, I emphasised nearly 45 years ago, when I attempted to remedy these defects, that "it would be one of the worst things that could befall us if the general public should ever again cease to believe in the elementary propositions of the quantity theory" (then represented chiefly by the economists Irving Fisher and Gustav Cassel).[32] But exactly this has happened as the result of the persuasive powers of Lord

---

[32] *Prices and Production,* London, 1931, p. 3. E. von Böhm-Bawerk used to speak of "the indestructible core of truth in the quantity theory". [Now see Hayek, *Business Cycles, Part I,* p. 195. In the original version of the sentence, Hayek wrote "which would" rather than "that could". American economist Irving Fisher (1867–1947) set out the transactions version of the quantity theory of money in I. Fisher, *The Purchasing Power of Money* (New York: Macmillan, 1911). Eugen von Böhm-Bawerk (1851–1914) was an Austrian economist and sometime Austrian finance minister, best known for his theory of capital and interest. For more on the remark quoted by Hayek, see G. Schumpeter, *Ten Great Economists: From Marx to Keynes* (London: George Allen & Unwin, 1952), pp. 161–62. Swedish economist Karl Gustav Cassel (1866–1945) relied on a version of the quantity theory of money in his work on general economic equilibrium and on purchasing power parity. See, for example, G. Cassel, *Money and Foreign Exchange after 1914* (New York: Macmillan Co., 1922), and G. Cassel, *The Theory of Social Economy,* trans. S. Barron, 2 vols. (London: Ernest Benn, 1932).—Ed.]

Keynes to whose proposals for combating the depression of the 1930s the traditional views had been an obstacle.

The defects of what became the traditional quantity theory approach had indeed been pointed out 200 years earlier when Richard Cantillon had argued against John Locke's similar mechanical quantity theory that[33]

> he realised well that the abundance of money makes everything dear, but he did not analyse how that takes place. The great difficulty of that analysis consists in the discovery by what path and in what proportion the increase on money raises the prices of things.

This analysis of Cantillon (and David Hume's similar efforts) were the first to attempt to trace the course through which an inflow of additional money alters the *relative* demand for different commodities and services. It led to an explanation of how inflation results in a misdirection of resources and particularly of labour which, in the jobs to which it has been attracted, becomes 'redundant' as soon as inflation slows down or even merely ceases to accelerate. But this promising stream of thought was smothered by the Keynesian flood which threw economists back to a state of knowledge that had been surpassed long before, and re-opened the gates to errors of government policy of which our grandparents would have been ashamed.

The present inflation has been deliberately brought about by governments on the advice of economists. The British Labour Party planned it that way as early as 1957, although it got a little out of hand, as it always will once you start playing with it: in its proposals for a National Pension Fund it dealt with the problem of future price movements by the assumption that prices would double between 1960 and 1980[34]—then an alarming prospect but now of

---

[33] Richard Cantillon, *An Essay on the Nature of Commerce in General*, ed. Henry Higgs, London, 1931, part I, chapter 6. [Richard Cantillon (c. 1680–1734) was an Irish economist and banker whose *Essai* was written around 1730–34 but published first in French in 1755. Hayek quotes, not entirely faithfully, from p. 161 of R. Cantillon, *Essai sur La Nature du Commerce en Général*, ed. with an English translation by H. Higgs (London: Macmillan & Co., for the Royal Economic Society, 1931), where the actual text reads as follows: "he has clearly seen that the abundance of money makes everything dear, but he has not considered how it does so. The great difficulty of this question consists in knowing in what way and in what proportion the increase of money raises prices". For more on Cantillon, see F. A. Hayek, "Economics" [1950], reprinted as chapter 11 of this volume, p. 160 n. 5.—Ed.]

[34] *National Superannuation. Labour's Policy for Security in Old Age,* published by the Labour Party, London, 1957, pp. 104 and 109. [The report cited by Hayek considers three scenarios: the first is one in which the price level and productivity are assumed to remain unchanged between 1960 and 1980; the second, upon which Hayek focuses, is based on the assumption that the price level doubles but productivity remains unchanged; while the third assumes that productivity doubles

course already far surpassed. And as long ago as 1948 a highly influential textbook of economics[35] could plead that a 5 per cent per annum increase of prices was innocuous (if that had occurred since 1948 prices would now be just about four times as high as they were then!). What these and other economists overlooked was, moreover, that the purpose which they approved required an accelerating inflation, and that any accelerating inflation sooner or later becomes unbearable. Inflation at a constant rate soon comes to be anticipated in ordinary business transactions, and then merely harms the recipients of fixed contractual incomes but does no good.

Much confusion is caused in current discussion by a constant misuse of the term 'inflation'. Its original and proper meaning is an excessive increase in the quantity of money which will normally lead to an increase of prices. But even a general rise of prices, for instance one caused by a shortage of food because of bad harvests, is not necessarily inflation. Nor could a general rise of prices caused by the shortage of oil and other sources of energy that led to an absolute reduction of consumption be properly called inflation—if this shortage had not been made the excuse for a further increase in the quantity of money. There may also be considerable inflation that seriously interferes with the working of the market without any rise of prices—if this effect is prevented by controls. Indeed, if there is anything worse than open inflation it is what the Germans learned to call 'repressed inflation', and the so-called attempts to combat inflation by imposing price controls are only likely to make matters worse because it disorganises all economic activity even more than open inflation. Moreover it has no beneficial effect whatever, even in the short run (except for the receivers of the additional money), and leads straight to a centrally directed economy.

Let me repeat in conclusion that inflation has of course many other bad effects, much more painful than most people understand who have not lived through one; but that the most serious and at the same time the least understood is that in the long run it inevitably produces extensive unemployment. It is simply not true, as some economists have suggested, that so long as unemployment exists, an increase in aggregate demand does only good and no harm. That may be true in the short run but not in the long run. We do not

---

with constant prices. See The Labour Party, *National Superannuation: Labour's Policy for Security in Old Age* (London: The Labour Party, 1957), pp. 103–15.—Ed.]

[35] Paul A. Samuelson, *Economics: An Introductory Analysis,* New York, 1948, p. 282: "If price increases could be held down to, say, less than 5 per cent per year, such a mild steady inflation need not cause too great concern". [American Nobel Laureate Paul Samuelson (1915–2009) was the author of many scholarly works, including the best-selling undergraduate textbook *Economics: An Introductory Analysis* (New York: McGraw-Hill, 1948), from p. 282 of which Hayek quotes.—Ed.]

have the choice between inflation and unemployment. It is like over-eating and indigestion: though over-eating may be very pleasant while it proceeds, the indigestion will invariably follow.

IV Choice in currency: a way to stop inflation[36]

1

The chief root of our present monetary troubles is, of course, the sanction of scientific authority which Lord Keynes and his disciples have given to the age-old superstition that by increasing the aggregate of money expenditure we can lastingly ensure prosperity and full employment. It is a superstition against which economists before Keynes had struggled with some success for at least two centuries.[37] It had governed most of earlier history. This history, indeed, has been largely a history of inflation; significantly, it was only during the rise of the prosperous modern industrial systems and during the rule of the gold standard that over a period of about two hundred years (in Britain from about 1714 to 1914, and in the United States from about 1749 to 1939) prices were at the end about where they had been at the beginning. During this unique period of monetary stability the gold standard had imposed upon monetary authorities a discipline which prevented them from abusing their powers, as they have done at nearly all other times. Experience in other parts of the world does not seem to have been very different: I have been told that a Chinese law attempted to prohibit paper money for all times (of course, ineffectively), long before the Europeans ever invented it!

It was John Maynard Keynes, a man of great intellect but limited knowledge of economic theory, who ultimately succeeded in rehabilitating a view long the preserve of cranks with whom he openly sympathised. He had attempted by a succession of new theories to justify the same, superficially persuasive, intuitive belief that had been held by many practical men before, but that will not withstand rigorous analysis of the price mechanism: just as there cannot be a uniform price for all kinds of labour, an equality of demand and supply for labour in general cannot be secured by managing *aggregate* demand. The volume of employment depends on the correspondence of demand and

---

[36] Based on an address entitled 'International Money' delivered to the Geneva Gold and Monetary Conference on 25 September 1975 at Lausanne, Switzerland, and published as a brochure with this title by the Institute of Economic Affairs, London, 1976. [The address was in fact published as F. A. Hayek, *Choice in Currency: A Way to Stop Inflation* (London: Institute of Economic Affairs, 1976). It was subsequently reprinted as chapter 3 of Hayek, *Good Money, Part II.*—Ed.]

[37] See note at the end of this chapter, p. 229. [Now see p. 378 below.—Ed.]

supply *in each sector* of the economy, and therefore on the wage structure and the distribution of demand between the sectors. The consequence is that over a longer period the Keynesian remedy does not cure unemployment but makes it worse.

The claim of an eminent public figure and brilliant polemicist to provide a cheap and easy means of permanently preventing serious unemployment conquered public opinion and, after his death, professional opinion too. Sir John Hicks has even proposed that we call the third quarter of this century, 1950 to 1975, the age of Keynes, as the second quarter was the age of Hitler.[38] I do not feel that the harm Keynes did is really so great as to justify *that* description. But it is true that, so long as his prescriptions seemed to work, they operated as an orthodoxy which it appeared useless to oppose.

I have often blamed myself for having given up the struggle after I had spent much time and energy criticising the first version of Keynes's theoretical framework. Only after the second part of my critique had appeared did he tell me he had changed his mind and no longer believed what he had said in the *Treatise on Money* of 1930 (somewhat unjustly towards himself, as it seems to me, since I still believe that volume II of the *Treatise* contains some of the best work he ever did). At any rate, I felt it then to be useless to return to the charge, because he seemed so likely to change his views again.[39] When it proved that this new version—the *General Theory* of 1936—conquered most of the professional opinion, and when in the end even some of the colleagues I most respected supported the wholly Keynesian Bretton Woods agreement, I largely withdrew from the debate, since to proclaim my dissent from the near-unanimous views of the orthodox phalanx would merely have deprived me of a hearing on other matters about which I was more concerned at the time. (I believe, however, that, so far as some of the best British economists were concerned, their support of Bretton Woods was determined more by a misguided patriotism—the hope that it would benefit Britain in her post-war

---

[38] John Hicks, *The Crisis in Keynesian Economics*, Oxford [Basil Blackwell], 1974, p. 1. [For more on English economist Sir John Hicks (1904–89), see Hayek, "Economics", p. 170 n. 18.—Ed.]

[39] [Hayek refers to J. M. Keynes, *A Treatise on Money*, 2 vols. [1930], reprinted as vols. 5 and 6 (1971) of *The Collected Writings of John Maynard Keynes*. For Hayek's two-part review of that book, see F. A. Hayek, "Reflections on the Pure Theory of Money of Mr. J. M. Keynes" [1931], and F. A. Hayek, "Reflections on the Pure Theory of Money of Mr. J. M. Keynes (continued)" [1932], reprinted as chapters 3 and 6 respectively of Hayek, *Contra Keynes and Cambridge*. Chapters 4–5 and 7–9 of that volume contain additional material pertaining to the debate between them, including the letter in which Keynes informs Hayek that he was "trying to re-shape and improve my central position". See J. M. Keynes to F. A. Hayek, March 29, 1932, now published on pp. 172–73 of the Addendum to F. A. Hayek, "A Rejoinder to Mr. Keynes" [1931], reprinted as chapter 5 of *Contra Keynes and Cambridge*. For an overview of the Hayek-Keynes debate, as well as a discussion of why Hayek chose not to review Keynes's *General Theory*, see Caldwell, "Introduction", in *Contra Keynes and Cambridge*.—Ed.]

difficulties—than by a belief that it would provide a satisfactory international monetary order.)

2

I wrote 36 years ago on the crucial point of difference:

> It may perhaps he pointed out here that it has, of course, never been denied that employment can be rapidly increased, and a position of 'full employment' achieved in the shortest possible time, by means of monetary expansion—least of all by those economists whose outlook has been influenced by the experience of a major inflation. All that has been contended is that the kind of full employment which can be created in this way is inherently unstable, and that to create employment by these means is to perpetuate fluctuations. There may be desperate situations in which it may indeed be necessary to increase employment at all costs, even if it be only for a short period—perhaps the situation in which Dr Brüning found himself in Germany in 1932 was such a situation in which desperate means would have been justified. But the economist should not conceal the fact that to aim at the maximum of employment which can be achieved in the short run by means of monetary policy is essentially the policy of the desperado who has nothing to lose and everything to gain from a short breathing space.[40]

To this I would now like to add, in reply to the constant deliberate misrepresentation of my views by politicians, who like to picture me as a sort of bogey whose influence makes conservative parties dangerous, what I regularly emphasise and stated nine months ago in my Nobel Memorial Prize Lecture at Stockholm in the following words:

> The truth is that by a mistaken theoretical view we have been led into a precarious position in which we cannot prevent substantial unemployment from re-appearing: not because, as my view is sometimes misrepresented, this unemployment is deliberately brought about as a means to combat inflation, but because it is now bound to appear as a deeply regrettable but *inescapable* consequence of the mistaken policies of the past as soon as inflation ceases to accelerate.[41]

---

[40] F. A. Hayek, *Profits, Interest and Investment,* London, 1939, p. 63n. [Now see F. A. Hayek, "Profits, Interest and Investment" [1939], reprinted as chapter 8 of *Business Cycles, Part II,* p. 250 n. 64. Also see p. 361 n. 31 above.—Ed.]

[41] F. A. Hayek, "The Pretence of Knowledge", Nobel Memorial Prize Lecture 1974, reprinted above, pp. 23–34. [Hayek quotes, with very minor changes and newly added italics, from

This manufacture of unemployment by what are called 'full employment policies' is a complex process. In essence it operates by temporary changes in the distribution of demand, drawing both unemployed and already employed workers into jobs which will disappear with the end of inflation. In the periodically recurrent crises of the pre-1914 years the expansion of credit during the preceding boom served largely to finance industrial investment, and the over-development and subsequent unemployment occurred mainly in the industries producing capital equipment. In the engineered inflation of the last decades things were more complex.

What will happen during a major inflation is illustrated by an observation from the early 1920s which many of my Viennese contemporaries will confirm: in the city many of the famous coffee houses were driven from the best corner sites by new bank offices and returned after the 'stabilisation crisis', when the banks had contracted or collapsed and thousands of bank clerks swelled the ranks of the unemployed.

The whole theory underlying the full employment policies has by now of course been thoroughly discredited by the experience of the last few years. In consequence the economists are also beginning to discover its fatal intellectual defects which they ought to have seen all along. Yet I fear the theory will still give us a lot of trouble: it has left us with a lost generation of economists who have learnt nothing else. One of our chief problems will be to protect our money against those economists who will continue to offer their quack remedies, the short-term effectiveness of which will continue to ensure them popularity. It will survive among blind doctrinaires who have always been convinced that they have the key to salvation.

In consequence, though the rapid descent of Keynesian doctrine from intellectual respectability can be denied no longer, it still gravely threatens the chances of a sensible monetary policy. Nor have people yet fully realised how much irreparable damage it has already done, particularly in Britain, the country of its origin. The sense of financial respectability which once guided British monetary policy has rapidly disappeared. From a model to be imitated Britain has in a few years descended to be a warning example for the rest of the world. This decay was recently brought home to me by a curious incident: I found in a drawer of my desk a British penny dated 1863 which a short 12 years ago, that is, when it was exactly a hundred years old, I had received as change from a London bus conductor and had taken back to Germany to show to my students what long-run monetary stability meant. I believe they were duly impressed. But they would laugh in my face if I now mentioned Britain as an instance of monetary stability.

---

pp. 29–30 of *New Studies*. Now also see p. 368 of the version of "The Pretence of Knowledge" reprinted in *The Market and Other Orders*.—Ed.]

3

A wise man should perhaps have foreseen that less than 30 years after the nationalisation of the Bank of England the purchasing power of the pound sterling would have been reduced to less than one-quarter of what it had been at that date. As has sooner or later happened everywhere, government control of the quantity of money has once again proved fatal. I do not want to question that a very intelligent and wholly independent national or international monetary authority *might* do better than an international gold standard, or any other sort of automatic system. But I see not the slightest hope that any government, or any institution subject to political pressure, will ever be able to act in such a manner.

I never had much illusion in this respect, but I must confess that in the course of a long life my opinion of governments has steadily worsened: the more intelligently they try to act (as distinguished from simply following an established rule), the more harm they seem to do—because once they are known to aim at particular goals (rather than merely maintaining a self-correcting spontaneous order) the less they can avoid serving sectional interests. And the demands of all organised group interests are almost invariably harmful—except when they protest against restrictions imposed upon them for the benefit of other group interests. I am by no means reassured by the fact that, at least in some countries, the civil servants who run affairs are mostly intelligent, well-meaning, and honest men. The point is that, if governments are to remain in office in the prevailing political order, they have no choice but to use their powers for the benefit of particular groups—and one strong interest is always to get additional money for extra expenditure. However harmful inflation is in general seen to be, there are always substantial groups of people, including some for whose support collectivist-inclined governments primarily look, which in the short run greatly gain by it—even if only by staving off for some time the loss of an income which it is human nature to believe will be only temporary if they can tide over the emergency.

The pressure for more and cheaper money is an ever-present political force which monetary authorities have never been able to resist, unless they were in a position credibly to point to an absolute obstacle which made it impossible for them to meet such demands. And it will become even more irresistible when these interests can appeal to an increasingly unrecognisable image of St. Maynard. There will be no more urgent need than to erect new defences against the onslaughts of popular forms of Keynesianism, that is, to replace or restore those restraints which, under the influence of his theory, have been systematically dismantled. It was the main function of the gold standard, of balanced budgets, of the necessity for deficit countries to contract their circulation, and of the limitation of the supply of 'international liquidity', to make it impossible for the monetary authorities to capitulate to the pressure for more money. And it was exactly for that reason that all these safeguards against inflation, which had made it possible for representative governments to resist the demands of powerful pressure groups for more money, have been removed at the instigation of economists who imagined that, if governments were released from the shackles of mechanical rules, they would be able to act wisely for the general benefit.

I do not believe we can now remedy this position by *constructing* some new international monetary order, whether a new international monetary authority or institution, or even an international agreement to adopt a particular mechanism or system of policy, such as the classical gold standard. I am fairly convinced that any attempt now to reinstate the gold standard by international agreement would break down within a short time and merely discredit the ideal of an international gold standard for even longer. Without the conviction of the public at large that certain immediately painful measures are occasionally necessary to preserve reasonable stability, we cannot hope that any authority which has power to determine the quantity of money will long resist the pressure for, or the seduction of, cheap money.

The politician, acting on a modified Keynesian maxim that in the long run we are all out of office, does not care if his successful cure of unemployment is bound to produce more unemployment in the future. The politicians who will be blamed for it will not be those who created the inflation but those who stopped it. No worse trap could have been set for a democratic system in which the government is forced to act on the beliefs that the people think to be true. Our only hope for a stable money is indeed now to find a way to protect money from politics.

With the exception only of the 200-year period of the gold standard, practically all governments of history have used their exclusive power to issue money in order to defraud and plunder the people. There is less ground than ever for hoping that, so long as the people have no choice but to use the money their government provides, governments will become more trustworthy. Under the prevailing systems of government, which are supposed to be guided by the opinion of the majority but under which in practice any sizeable group may create a 'political necessity' for the government by threatening to withhold the votes it needs to claim majority support, we cannot entrust dangerous instruments to it. Fortunately we need not yet fear, I hope, that governments will start a war to please some indispensable group of supporters, but money is certainly too dangerous an instrument to leave to the fortuitous expediency of politicians—or, it seems, economists.

What is so dangerous and ought to be done away with is not governments' right to issue money but the *exclusive* right to do so and their power to force people to use it and to accept it at a particular price. This monopoly of government, like the postal monopoly, has its origin not in any benefit it secures for the people but solely in the desire to enhance the coercive powers of government. I doubt whether it has ever done any good except to the rulers and their favourites. All history contradicts the belief that governments have given us a safer money than we would have had without their claiming an exclusive right to issue it.

4

But why should we not let people choose freely what money they want to use? By 'people' I mean the individuals who ought to have the right to decide whether they want to buy or sell for francs, pounds, dollars, D-marks, or ounces of gold. I have no objection to governments issuing money, but I believe their claim to a *monopoly*, or their power to *limit* the kinds of money in which contracts may be concluded within their territory, or to determine the *rates* at which monies can be exchanged, to be wholly harmful.

At this moment it seems that the best thing we could wish governments to do is for, say, all the members of the European Economic Community, or, better still, all the governments of the Atlantic Community, to bind themselves mutually not to place any restrictions on the free use within their territories of one another's—or any other—currencies, including their purchase and sale at any price the parties decide upon, or on their use as accounting units in which to keep books. This, and not a Utopian European Monetary Unit, seems to me now both the practicable and the desirable arrangement to aim at. To make the scheme effective it would be important, for reasons I shall state later, also to provide that banks in one country be free to establish branches in any of the others.

This suggestion may at first seem absurd to all brought up on the concept of 'legal tender'. Is it not essential that the law designate one kind of money as the legal money? This is, however, true only to the extent that, *if* the government does issue money, it must also say what must be accepted in discharge of debts incurred in that money. And it must also determine in what manner certain non-contractual legal obligations, such as taxes or liabilities for damage or torts, are to be discharged. But there is no reason whatever why people should not be free to make contracts, including ordinary purchases and sales, in any kind of money they choose, or why they should be obliged to sell against any particular kind of money.

There could be no more effective check against the abuse of money by the government than if people were free to refuse any money they distrusted and to prefer money in which they had confidence. Nor could there be a stronger inducement to governments to ensure the stability of their money than the knowledge that, so long as they kept the supply below the demand for it, that demand would tend to grow. Therefore, let us deprive governments (or their monetary authorities) of all power to protect their money against competition:

if they can no longer conceal that their money is becoming bad, they will have to restrict the issue.

The first reaction of many readers may be to ask whether the effect of such a system would not according to an old rule be that the bad money would drive out the good. But this would be a misunderstanding of what is called Gresham's Law. This indeed is one of the oldest insights into the mechanism of money, so old that 2,400 years ago Aristophanes, in one of his comedies, could say that it was with politicians as it is with coins, because the bad ones drive out the good.[42] But the truth which apparently even today is not generally understood is that Gresham's Law operates *only* if the two kinds of money have to be accepted at a prescribed rate of exchange. Exactly the opposite will happen when people are free to exchange the different kinds of money at whatever rate they can agree upon. This was observed many times during the great inflations when even the most severe penalties threatened by governments could not prevent people from using other kinds of money—even commodities like cigarettes and bottles of brandy rather than the government money—which clearly meant that the good money was driving out the bad.[43]

Make it merely legal and people will be very quick indeed to refuse to use the national currency once it depreciates noticeably, and they will make their dealings in a currency they trust. Employers, in particular, would find it in their interest to offer, in collective agreements, not wages anticipating a foreseen rise of prices but wages in a currency they trusted and could make the basis of rational calculation. This would deprive government of the power

[42] Aristophanes, *Frogs,* 891–8, in Frere's translation:
Oftentimes we have reflected on a similar abuse
In the choice of men for office, and of coins for common use,
For our old and standard pieces, valued and approved and tried,
Here among the Grecian nations, and in all the world besides,
Recognised in every realm for trusty stamp and pure assay,
Are rejected and abandoned for the trash of yesterday,
For a vile adulterated issue, drossy, counterfeit and base,
Which the traffic of the city passes current in their place.
About the same time, the philosopher Diogenes called money 'the legislators' game of dice'!
[The lines from Frere's translation of Aristophanes, to which Hayek has made very minor changes, can be found on pp. 41–42 of *The Frogs and Three Other Plays of Aristophanes*, trans. J. Frere, W. Hickie, T. Mitchell and R. Cumberland (London: J. M. Dent & Sons, 1911). Diogenes of Sinope (c. 404–323 BC)—the Cynic—was a Greek philosopher whose father was a money-changer exiled for having adulterated the coinage. He is said to have made it his life's mission to 'debase the currency' of life by seeking to undermine conventional moral standards and values. In his ideal state, dice would be used as money, the better to reveal the arbitrary value of currency. See D. Doyle, *Cities of the Gods: Communist Utopias in Greek Thought* (New York: Oxford University Press, 1992), pp. 180–81.—Ed.]
[43] During the German inflation after the First World War, when people began to use dollars and other solid currencies in the place of marks, a Dutch financier (if I rightly remember, Mr Vissering) asserted that Gresham's Law was false and the opposite true. [Gerard Vissering (1865–1937) was President of the Bank of the Netherlands from 1912 until 1932.—Ed.]

to counteract excessive wage increases, and the unemployment they would cause, by depreciating their currency. It would also prevent employers from conceding such wages in the expectation that the national monetary authority would bail them out if they promised more than they could pay.

There is no reason to be concerned about the effects of such an arrangement on ordinary men who know neither how to handle nor how to obtain strange kinds of money. So long as the shopkeepers knew that they could turn it instantly at the current rate of exchange into whatever money they preferred, they would be only too ready to sell their wares at an appropriate price for any currency. But the malpractices of government would show themselves much more rapidly if prices rose only in terms of the money issued by it, and people would soon learn to hold the government responsible for the value of the money in which they were paid. Electronic calculators, which in seconds would give the equivalent of any price in any currency at the current rate, would soon be used everywhere. But, unless the national government all too badly mismanaged the currency it issued, it would probably continue to be used in everyday retail transactions. What would be affected mostly would be not so much the use of money in daily payments as the willingness to *hold* different kinds of money. It would mainly be the tendency of all business and capital transactions rapidly to switch to a more reliable standard (and to base calculations and accounting on it) which would keep national monetary policy on the right path.

5

The upshot would probably be that the currencies of those countries trusted to pursue a responsible monetary policy would tend to displace gradually those of a less reliable character. The reputation of financial righteousness would become a jealously guarded asset of all issuers of money, since they would know that even the slightest deviation from the path of honesty would reduce the demand for their product.

I do not believe there is any reason to fear that in such a competition for the most general acceptance of a currency there would arise a tendency to deflation or an increasing value of money. People will be quite as reluctant to borrow or incur debts in a currency expected to appreciate as they will hesitate to lend in a currency expected to depreciate. The convenience of use is decidedly in favour of a currency which can be expected to retain an approximately stable value. If governments and other issuers of money have to compete in inducing people to *hold* their money, and make long-term contracts in it, they will have to create confidence in its long-run stability.

Where I am not sure is whether in such a competition for reliability any government-issued currency would prevail, or whether the predominant preference would not be in favour of some such units as ounces of gold. It seems not unlikely that gold would ultimately re-assert its place as "the universal prize in all countries, in all cultures, in all ages", as Jacob Bronowski has recently called it in his brilliant book on *The Ascent of Man*,[44] if people were given complete freedom to decide what to use as their standard and general medium of exchange—more likely, at any rate, than as the result of any organised attempt to restore the gold standard.

The reason why, in order to be fully effective, the free international market in currencies should extend also to the services of banks is, of course, that bank deposits subject to cheque represent today much the largest part of the liquid assets of most people. Even during the last hundred years or so of the gold standard this circumstance increasingly prevented it from operating as a fully international currency, because any flow in or out of a country required a proportionate expansion or contraction of the much larger superstructure of the national credit money, the effect of which falls indiscriminately on the whole economy instead of merely increasing or decreasing the demand for the particular goods which was required to bring about a new balance between imports and exports. With a truly international banking system money could be transferred directly without producing the harmful process of secondary contractions or expansions of the credit structure.

It would probably also impose the most effective discipline on governments if they felt immediately the effects of their policies on the attractiveness of investment in their country. I have just read in an English Whig tract more than 250 years old: "Who would establish a Bank in an arbitrary country, or trust his money constantly there?"[45] The tract, incidentally, tells us that yet another 50 years earlier a great French banker, Jean Baptiste Tavernier, invested all the riches he had amassed in his long rambles over the world in what the authors described as "the barren rocks of Switzerland"; when asked why by Louis XIV, he had the courage to tell him that "he was willing to have something which he could call his own"! Switzerland, apparently, laid the foundations of her prosperity earlier than most people realise.

I prefer the freeing of all dealings in money to any sort of monetary union also because the latter would demand an international monetary authority which I believe is neither practicable nor even desirable—and hardly to be

[44] Jacob Bronowski, *The Ascent of Man*, London, 1973. [J. Bronowski, *The Ascent of Man* (London: British Broadcasting Corporation, 1973), p. 134.—Ed.]

[45] Thomas Gordon and John Trenchard, *The Cato Letters*, letters dated 12 May 1722 and 3 February 1721 respectively, published in collected editions, London, 1724, and later. [The date of the second letter to which Hayek refers is February 3, 1722, not 1721. Now see J. Trenchard and T. Gordon, *Cato's Letters: Or, Essays on Liberty, Civil and Religious, and Other Important Subjects* [1724], ed. R. Hamowy, 4 vols. in 2 (Indianapolis: Liberty Fund 1995), vol. 3: *March 10, 1722 to December 1, 1722*, letter 76 for the first quotation and vol. 2: *June 24, 1721 to March 3, 1722*, letter 64 for the second and third quotations that appear later in this paragraph.—Ed.]

more trusted than a national authority. It seems to me that there is a very sound element in the widespread disinclination to confer sovereign powers, or at least powers to command, on any international authority. What we need are not international authorities possessing powers of direction, but merely international bodies (or, rather, international treaties which are effectively enforced) which can prohibit certain actions of governments that will harm other people. Effectively to prohibit all restrictions on dealings in (and the possession of) different kinds of money (or claims for money) would at last make it possible that the absence of tariffs, or other obstacles to the movement of goods and men, will secure a genuine free trade area or common market—and do more than anything else to create confidence in the countries committing themselves to it. It is now urgently needed to counter that monetary nationalism which I first criticised almost 40 years ago[46] and which is becoming even more dangerous when, as a consequence of the close kinship between the two views, it is turning into monetary socialism. I hope it will not be too long before complete freedom to deal in any money one likes will be regarded as the essential mark of a free country.[47]

You may feel that my proposal amounts to no less than the abolition of monetary policy; and you would not be quite wrong. As in other connections, I have come to the conclusion that the best the state can do with respect to money is to provide a framework of legal rules within which the people can develop the monetary institutions that best suit them. It seems to me that if we could prevent governments from meddling with money, we would do more good than any government has ever done in this regard. And private enterprise would probably have done better than the best they have ever done.

NOTE to page 368[48] Lord Keynes has always appeared to me a kind of new John Law. Law, like Keynes, had been a financial genius who made some

---

[46] *Monetary Nationalism and International Stability*, London, 1937. [Now see F. A. Hayek, "Monetary Nationalism and International Stability" [1937], reprinted as chapter 1 of Hayek, *Good Money, Part II.*—Ed.]

[47] It may at first seem as if this suggestion were in conflict with my general support of fixed exchange rates under the present system. But this is not so. Fixed exchange rates seem to me to be necessary so long as national governments have a monopoly of issuing money in their territory in order to place them under a very necessary discipline. But this is of course no longer necessary when they have to submit to the discipline of competition with other issuers of money equally current within their territory.

[48] [This Note appeared on pp. 23–24 of the version of *Choice in Currency* published by the Institute of Economic Affairs, under the heading, 'A Comment on Keynes, Beveridge, and Keynesian Economics'. Hayek edited it for publication in *New Studies*, most notably by replacing the original heading, adding material to what is now the penultimate paragraph, and including a new final paragraph.—Ed.]

real contributions to the theory of money. (Apart from an interesting and original discussion of the factors determining the value of money, Law gave the first satisfactory account of the cumulative growth of acceptability once a commodity was widely used as a medium of exchange.) And like Law Keynes could never free himself from the false popular belief that, as Law expressed it, "as this addition to the money will employ the people that are now idle, and those now employed to more advantage, so the product will be increased, and manufacture advanced".[49]

It was against the sort of view represented by Law that Richard Cantillon and David Hume began the development of modern monetary theory. Hume in particular put the central point at issue by saying that, in the process of inflation, "it is only in this interval or intermediate situation, between the acquisition of money and rise of prices, that the increasing quantity of gold and silver is favourable to industry".[50] It is this work we shall have to do again after the Keynesian flood.

In one sense, however, it would be somewhat unfair to blame Lord Keynes too much for the developments after his death. I am certain he would have been—whatever he had said earlier—a leader in the fight against inflation. But developments, at least in Britain, were also mainly determined by the version of Keynesianism published under the name of Lord Beveridge for which (since he himself understood no economics whatever) his scientific advisers must bear the responsibility. Perhaps, so far as the influence on British policy is

---

[49] John Law, *Money and Trade Considered with a Proposal for Supplying the Nation with Money* (1705), in *A Collection of Scarce and Valuable Tracts*, Somers Collection, vol. XIII, London, 1815, p. 821. [The quotation is to be found on p. 812, not p. 821, of *A Collection of Scarce and Valuable Tracts on the Most Entertaining Subjects: But chiefly such as relate to the History and Constitution of these Kingdoms. Selected from an infinite number in print and manuscript in the Royal, Cotton, Sion and other public as well as private libraries, particularly that of the Late Lord Somers*, 2nd edn., vol. 13 (London: T. Cadell and W. Davies, 1815). Now also see J. Law, *Money and Trade Considered: with a Proposal for Supplying the Nation with Money* [1705] (New York: Augustus M. Kelley, 1966), p. 105. John Law (1671–1729) was a Scottish banker and monetary reformer whose more theoretical contributions anticipated many aspects both of later accounts of the development of money as a spontaneous phenomenon and also of modern subjective value theory. Hayek discusses Law's ideas at greater length in F. A. Hayek, "First Paper Money in 18th-Century France" [1929], published as chapter 10 of F. A. Hayek, *The Trend of Economic Thinking: Essays on Political Economists and Economic History*, ed. W. W. Bartley III and S. Kresge, vol. 3 (1991) of *The Collected Works of F. A. Hayek*, where he also considers some of Law's more practical proposals, such as for the replacement of metallic coinage with paper money.—Ed.]

[50] David Hume, 'On money', *Essays*, III, ed. T. H. Green and T. H. Grose, London, 1875. [The words written by Scottish philosopher, historian and economist David Hume (1711–76) can be found in an essay entitled "Of Money" (not, as Hayek writes, "On Money"). See D. Hume, "Of Money", in *Essays: Moral, Political, and Literary*, 2 vols., ed. T. H. Green and T. H. Grose (London: Longmans, Green & Co., 1875), vol. 1, p. 313.—Ed.]

concerned, I ought to have spoken of the Kaldorian rather than the Keynesian inflation.[51]

Since I have been censured for charging Keynes in an earlier version of this with a limited knowledge of economic theory, I must become more specific. I believe that his inadequate knowledge of the theory of international trade or of the theory of capital is fairly widely recognised. His deficiencies in the theory of money which I had in mind were by no means his unfamiliarity with the discussion of the relation between money and interest by Swedish and Austrian scholars—that would until the 1930s have been true of most English and U.S. economists—though it was rather a misfortune that the chief works of Wicksell and Mises in this field were reviewed in the *Economic Journal* by Pigou and Keynes, neither of whom understood enough German really to be able to follow the argument.[52] What I had in mind concerning Keynes were

[51] [Hayek refers to British economist, social reformer and Liberal Party politician Sir William Beveridge (1879–1963), 1st Baron Beveridge, who was Director of the London School of Economics from 1919 until 1937 and whose *Full Employment in a Free Society* (London: George Allen & Unwin, 1944) provided the blueprint for a full employment policy within the context of the British welfare state. The report contained an appendix on "The Quantitative Aspects of the Full Employment Problem in Britain", written by Hungarian-born British economist Nicholas Kaldor (1908–86). Hayek claimed elsewhere that Kaldor's contribution extended well beyond the appendix: "He wrote Beveridge's book on employment . . . What economics is there is purely Kaldor's . . . In that book there was an essay which was admittedly by Kaldor, but the whole thing is by him". Hence the Keynesian revolution "probably should be called a Kaldorian revolution [because] . . . what spread it was really Lord Beveridge's book on full employment, and that was written by Kaldor and not by Beveridge, because Lord Beveridge never understood any economics". See F. A. Hayek, *Hayek on Hayek: An Autobiographical Dialogue*, ed. S. Kresge and L. Wenar (Chicago: University of Chicago Press, 1994), pp. 86, 88. Hayek's contemporaneous review of Beveridge's book can now be found as the "Addendum: Hayek on Beveridge" to chapter 10 of *Contra Keynes and Cambridge*. For more on Kaldor, see Hayek, "The Transmission of the Ideals of Economic Freedom", p. 44 n. 5.—Ed.]

[52] [Swedish economist Knut Wicksell (1851–1926) was one of the major architects of early twentieth-century work on capital, money and business cycles. The German translation of Wicksell's *Lectures on Political Economy*, which had first been published in Swedish, was reviewed by Cambridge economist Arthur Cecil Pigou (1877–1959), who concluded, "The somewhat laborious character of the exposition, coupled with the general familiarity of the ground covered, makes it unlikely that this new text-book will find many English readers—unless, indeed, an English as well as a German translation is produced". See A. C. Pigou, "*Vorlesungen über Nationalökonomie auf Grundlage des Marginalprinzipes*. By Professor Knut Wicksell. (Jena. 1913. Pp. 290.)", *Economic Journal*, vol. 23, 1913, pp. 605–6. For more on Wicksell, see Hayek, "Economics", p. 168 n. 16. Keynes reviewed Mises's *Theory of Money* the next year, writing that while the book "avoids all the usual pitfalls", it does so only "by pointing them out and turning back rather than by surmounting them": "One closes the book, therefore, with a feeling of disappointment that an author so intelligent, so candid, and so widely read should, after all, help one so little to a clear and constructive understanding of the fundamentals of his subject". See J. M. Keynes, "*Theorie des Geldes und der Umlaufsmittel*. By Ludwig von Mises. (Munich: Duncker and Humblot, 1912. Pp. xi + 476. M. 10.)", *Economic Journal*, vol. 24, 1914, pp. 417–19.—Ed.]

the surprising gaps in his knowledge of nineteenth-century English economic theory (and economic history). I had to tell him of the passage by Ricardo quoted earlier in this volume (p. 349) which, if he had known it, might well have helped him to win the battle against the return to gold at the old parity, and of John Stuart Mill's claim to have regarded in his youth "full employment at high wages" as the chief goal of economic policy (see p. 357 above). Apart from the Bullion Report and Ricardo's essays provoked by it, so far as I could discover Keynes was wholly unaware of the extensive discussions of that period and particularly of the great work of Henry Thornton, as well as of those later decisive contributions by English writers to the theory of the value of money such as W. N. Senior and J. E. Cairnes.[53] Nor did he appear to have ever heard of the long row of English inflationist writers of the last century who might possibly have inspired but more likely would have deterred him: I believe he would have rapidly spotted in their writings the elementary fallacy of believing that employment was a simple function of aggregate demand, and would not have wasted his energies on refinements of the explanation of the mechanism through which changes in the quantity of money would affect aggregate demand.[54]

[53] [The Bullion Report of 1810 was a contribution to debates, known as the 'Bullionist Controversy', that took place between 1797 and 1821 over the suspension by the Bank of England of the convertibility of its notes into specie during that period. Now see *The Paper Pound of 1797–1821: A Reprint of The Bullion Report*, ed. with an introduction by E. Cannan, 2nd edn. (London: P. S. King, 1925). Hayek discusses in detail Ricardo's contributions to debates over the Bullion Report in F. A. Hayek, "The Period of Restrictions, 1797–1821, and the Bullion Debate in England" [1929], published as chapter 11 of Hayek, *The Trend of Economic Thinking*. The same essay also contains a discussion of the contributions made to monetary theory by English banker, economist and philanthropist Henry Thornton (1760–1815), one of the authors of the Bullion Report. Hayek explores Thornton's work in more detail in his "Henry Thornton (1760–1815)" [1939], reprinted as chapter 14 of *The Trend of Economic Thinking*.

Hayek describes English lawyer and classical economist Nassau Senior (1790–1864) as having made "an absolutely first-rate contribution to monetary science . . . [in] a series of lectures on monetary theory . . . held . . . in 1828–9", most notably by "showing the weaknesses of the oversimplified mechanistic quantity theory of money". See F. A. Hayek, "The Dispute between the Currency School and the Banking School, 1821–1848" [1929], published as chapter 12 of *The Trend of Economic Thinking*, p. 223. For more on Senior, also see Hayek, "Economics", p. 165 n. 11. John Elliott Cairnes (1823–75) has often been described as the last of the classical economists. Elsewhere, Hayek states that Cairnes provided "probably the most noteworthy refinement of the argument of Hume and Cantillon" about the chain of cause and effect linking money and prices "before it was finally incorporated into more modern explanations based upon the subjective theories of value". See p. 199 of Hayek, *Business Cycles, Part I*, pp. 197–206 of which also discuss many of the authors mentioned by Hayek in this Note.—Ed.]

[54] [Perhaps the most notable representative of the "long row of English inflationist writers of the last century" was banker and politician Thomas Attwood (1783–1856). Attwood was the founder of the Birmingham Political Union for the Protection of Public Rights, which made an important contribution to persuading the British government to expand the franchise through

I hope somebody will some day write a history of inflationism from John Law to John Keynes. It would show how the uncritical acceptance of the belief of such a simple relation between aggregate demand and employment has throughout the last 150 years again and again caused much waste of ingenious intellectual effort.

---

the passage of the Great Reform Act of 1832, and leader of the so-called 'Birmingham School' of economics. An opponent of classical monetary theory, and advocate of the view that unemployment could be caused by under-consumption, Attwood consistently argued that the maintenance of full employment required the replacement of metallic monetary standards by a nonconvertible paper currency that would make it possible to use monetary expansion to increase employment. Hayek briefly refers to Attwood's opposition to Ricardo on pp. 222–23 of "The Dispute between the Currency School and the Banking School, 1821–1848". For more on Attwood and his fellow precursors to Keynes, see S. Checkland, "The Birmingham Economists, 1815–1850", *The Economic History Review*, 2nd series, vol. 1, 1948, pp. 1–19.—Ed.]

TWENTY-SIX

THE NEW CONFUSION
ABOUT 'PLANNING'[1]

I

It is a regrettable but undeniable fact that economics, more than other scientific disciplines, is liable to recurrent fashions and fads, the periodic re-intrusion into professional discussion of popular superstitions which earlier generations of economists had successfully driven back into the circles of cranks and demagogues. Inflationism is one of these irrepressible themes which again and again attract some half-trained economists, and the advocacy of collectivist economic planning has become another since it first became popular under this name through its use by the Russian communists. The conception, originally developed by some of the organisers of the German war economy during World War I, was thoroughly discussed by economists in the 1920s and 1930s; and all those familiar with that discussion will agree that it greatly contributed to the clarification of concepts and that one ought today to be entitled to assume that no competent economist who lived through that discussion would ever again talk about the issue in terms of the vague and confused concepts initially bandied about.[2]

[1] Reprinted from *The Morgan Guaranty Survey*, New York, January 1976. [The essay was first published as F. A. Hayek, "The New Confusion about 'Planning'", in *The Morgan Guaranty Survey*, January 1976, pp. 4–13. It was subsequently reprinted as chapter 14 of F. A. Hayek, *New Studies in Philosophy, Politics, Economics and the History of Ideas* (London and Henley: Routledge & Kegan Paul, 1978).—Ed.]

[2] [One of the organisers of the German economy during World War I was Austrian philosopher, sociologist, and political economist Otto Neurath (1882–1945). Neurath argued that the experience of running the 'war economy' during the 1914–18 conflict demonstrated the feasibility of central planning. See O. Neurath, *Durch die Kriegswirtschaft zur Naturalwirtschaft* (Munich: Georg D. W. Callwey, 1919). For more on Neurath, see F. A. Hayek, "Socialism and Science" [1976], reprinted as chapter 29 of this volume, p. 434 n. 13. The most prominent response to Neurath's argument was developed by Austrian economist Ludwig von Mises (1881–1973), who argued that because collectivist economic planning involves the abolition of private property, planned economies of the kind advocated by Neurath lack a market for capital goods. Absent such a market, there are no prices for capital goods, which leaves planners bereft of any means of identifying the relative scarcities of the various resources at their disposal, so that they are unable to act in a rational way. See L. von Mises, "Economic Calculation in the Socialist Com-

Nobody is of course bound to accept what seemed then the conclusions of those discussions, which were very unfavorable to central planning: in any scientific discipline the discovery of new facts or new considerations may lead to the revision of conclusions arrived at in the past. But what one must expect from a professional economist of recognised standing is that he not talk as if those past discussions had never taken place, and that he not use expressions in the ambiguous and misleading senses which had been painfully eliminated in the course of the earlier discussion.

It is in this respect that the pronouncements of Professor Wassily Leontief, recently of Harvard University, in the course of the reopened debate on the subject are so bitterly disappointing. That a senior economist of international reputation should again use the term 'planning' in all the ambiguity in which one would expect it to be used these days only by less responsible persons as a propaganda catchword, and that he should simply disregard the essential, if perhaps provisional, conclusions that emerged first from the discussion of central economic planning in the 1920s and 1930s and then from the no less intensive discussion of 'indicative planning' more recently, is wholly inexcusable. Although the statements with which I shall deal in this paper have been issued mostly on behalf of an 'Initiative Committee for National Economic Planning', it would seem that for the economic argument embodied in those statements Professor Leontief must bear the principal responsibility. He is the visible prime mover of the Committee and he clearly is the economist among its spokesmen who has the most relevant background of professional work. His Co-Chairman, Mr Leonard Woodcock, President of the United Auto Workers, is not, of course, a professional economist and has publicly acknowledged that he did not start to think seriously about economic planning on the part of government until the oil embargo. Indeed, some of the comments he has made rather suggest that he has not thought much about it even now.[3]

monwealth" [1920], in *Collectivist Economic Planning*, ed. F. A. Hayek (London: Routledge and Kegan Paul, 1935). Mises's essay set in train a debate over the possibility of collectivist economic planning, participants in which included economists Henry Douglas Dickinson (1899–1969), Evan Durbin (1906–48), Oskar Lange (1904–65), Abba P. Lerner (1903–82), and Frederick M. Taylor (1855–1932), as well as Hayek himself. Hayek discusses various aspects of this 'socialist calculation debate', as it came to be known, in Hayek, "Socialism and Science", and in F. A. Hayek, "Two Pages of Fiction" [1982], reprinted as chapter 30 of this volume, in which essays the interested reader can learn more about the economists just listed. Many of Hayek's other writings on the possibility of socialism are collected in F. A. Hayek, *Socialism and War: Essays, Documents, Reviews*, ed. B. Caldwell, vol. 10 (1997) of *The Collected Works of F. A. Hayek* (Chicago: The University of Chicago Press; London: Routledge). Useful overviews of the debate are provided by D. Lavoie, *Rivalry and Central Planning: The Socialist Calculation Debate Reconsidered* (Cambridge: Cambridge University Press, 1985), and by B. Caldwell, "Introduction", in Hayek, *Socialism and War.*—Ed.]

[3] [The 'Initiative Committee for National Economic Planning' was formed on October 14, 1974, with the goal of "promoting the widest possible public discussion on the need for economic and social planning in the United States, and the drafting of legislation to put such plan-

II

The worst confusion by which the new American agitation for 'planning' is permeated, not excluding the various statements by Professor Leontief himself, was most naively expressed in the first sentence of a lead editorial in the 23 February 1975 issue of *The New York Times*. It asked 'Why is planning considered a good thing for individuals and businesses but a bad thing for the national economy?'[4]

It is almost unbelievable that at this date an honest seeker after truth should innocently become the victim of the equivocal use of the word planning and believe that the discussion about economic planning refers to the question of whether people should plan their affairs and not to the question of *who* should plan their affairs. In reply to this I can only repeat what more than

---

ning into effect". See p. 51 of The Initiative Committee for National Economic Planning, "For a National Economic Planning System", *Challenge*, vol. 18, March–April 1975, pp. 51–53. As Hayek notes, the Co-chairmen of the Initiative Committee were Wassily Leontief and Leonard Woodcock. Wassily Leontief (1906–99) was a Russian-born economist who taught at Harvard University (1932–75) and New York University (1975–99), and who won the Nobel Prize for economics in 1973. He is best known for developing input-output analysis, which models the interdependence between the various parts of the economy by considering how the outputs produced by each sector are used not only for final consumption but also as inputs for the productive activities of the other sectors. Leontief believed that once this model of the structural relationships between the different sectors of the economy had been operationalised using statistical data, it could then be used to inform efforts to forecast and plan the future behaviour of the economy in ways that took into account the complex interdependencies between its parts. More specifically, Leontief argued that, after a number of detailed possible future growth paths had been identified using input-output analysis, the ultimate choice between these future scenarios would subsequently be made through a political process. See W. Leontief, *The Structure of American Economy 1919–1929: An Empirical Application of Equilibrium Analysis* (Cambridge, MA: Harvard University Press, 1941); W. Leontief, *Input-Output Economics* (New York: Oxford University Press, 1966); W. Leontief, "For a National Economic Planning Board", *The New York Times*, March 14, 1974, p. 37; and W. Leontief, "The Case for National Economic Planning", *Journal of Business Strategy*, vol. 1, 1981, pp. 3–7. Leonard Woodcock (1911–2001) was an American trade unionist, President of the United Automobile Workers Union from 1970 until 1977, and U.S. Ambassador to China from 1979 to 1981.

In addition to Leontief and Woodcock, the Initiative Committee had the following members: Anne Carter (1925–), an American academic economist and expert in input-output analysis who had worked for many years with Leontief at Harvard; Abram Chayes (1922–2000), a Professor of Law at Harvard Law School who served as legal advisor to the U.S. State Department during the Presidency of John F. Kennedy; Harvard economist and author John Kenneth Galbraith (1908–2006); American economist and historian of economic thought Robert Heilbroner (1919–2005); American socialist economist Robert Lekachman (1920–89); Robert R. Nathan (1908–2001), an economist who had helped to plan U.S. industrial production during World War Two; American economist, U.S. Treasury official, and investment banker Robert V. Roosa (1939–93); author and publisher Myron E. Sharpe (1928–), who was editor of *Challenge* when it published the Initiative Committee's letter; and Nat Weinberg (1914–85), then chief economist of the United Automobile Workers Union.—Ed.]

[4]["The Need to Plan . . .", *New York Times*, February 23, 1975, p. E12.—Ed.]

30 years ago I had, as I even then believed at unnecessary length, explained in a popular book:[5]

'Planning' owes its popularity largely to the fact that everybody desires, of course, that we should handle our common problems as rationally as possible and that, in so doing, we should use as much foresight as we can command. In this sense everybody who is not a complete fatalist is a planner, every political act is (or ought to be) an act of planning, and there can be differences only between good and bad, between wise and foresighted and foolish and shortsighted planning. An economist, whose whole task is the study of how men actually do and how they might plan their affairs, is the last person who could object to planning in this general sense. But it is not in this sense that our enthusiasts for a planned society now employ this term, nor merely in this sense that we must plan if we want the distribution of income or wealth to conform to some particular standard. According to the modern planners, and for their purposes, it is not sufficient to design the most rational permanent framework within which the various activities would be conducted by different persons according to their individual plans. This liberal plan, according to them, is no plan—and it is, indeed, not a plan designed to satisfy particular views about who should have what. What our planners demand is a central direction of all economic activity according to a single plan, laying down how the resources of society should be 'consciously directed' to serve particular ends in a definite way.

The dispute between the modern planners and their opponents is, therefore, *not* a dispute on whether we ought to choose intelligently between the various possible organisations of society; it is not a dispute on whether we ought to employ foresight and systematic thinking in planning our common affairs. It is a dispute about what is the best way of so doing. The question is whether for this purpose it is better that the holder of coercive power should confine himself in general to creating conditions under which the knowledge and initiative of individuals are given the best scope so that *they* can plan most successfully; or whether a rational utilisation of our resources requires *central* direction and organisation of all our activities according to some consciously constructed 'blueprint'. The socialists of all parties have appropriated the term 'planning' for planning of the latter type, and it is now generally accepted in this sense. But though this is meant to suggest that this is the only rational way of handling our affairs, it does not, of course, prove this. It remains the point on which the planners and the liberals disagree.

[5] In chapter III of *The Road to Serfdom*, Chicago, Ill., 1944, pp. 34ff. [Now see F. A. Hayek, *The Road to Serfdom: Text and Documents*, ed. B. Caldwell, vol. 2 (2007) of *The Collected Works of F. A. Hayek*, p. 85.—Ed.]

(The term 'liberal' is of course used here and also in an earlier part of the quote in the classical English, not in the modern American, sense.)[6] I should, perhaps, explain that this was written in a book concerned with the moral and political consequences of economic planning, written 10 years after the great discussion of the question of its economic efficiency or inefficiency to which I shall now have to turn. And I might, perhaps, also add that J. A. Schumpeter then accused me with respect to that book of "politeness to a fault" because I "hardly ever attributed to opponents anything beyond intellectual error".[7] I mention this as an apology in case that, on encountering the same empty phrases more than 30 years later, I should not be able to command quite the same patience and forbearance.

III

The great debate of the 1920s and 1930s turned mainly on the question of the justification of the socialist hopes of increasing productivity by substituting central planning for marketplace competition as the instrument for guiding economic activity. I don't think it can now be gainsaid by anybody who has studied these discussions that those hopes were shattered and that it came to be recognised that an attempt at centralised collectivist planning of a large economic system was on the contrary bound greatly to decrease productivity.[8] Even the communist countries have to various degrees felt compelled

---

[6] [For more on Hayek's views on liberalism, see F. A. Hayek, "Liberalism" [1978], reprinted as chapter 1 of this volume.—Ed.]

[7] J. A. Schumpeter, *The Journal of Political Economy*, vol. 54, 1946, p. 269. [Austrian economist and sociologist Joseph Alois Schumpeter (1883–1950) opens his review of Hayek's *Road to Serfdom* as follows: "This is a political book, so Hayek—setting an excellent example—frankly tells us in his Preface. It is, moreover, a courageous book: sincerity that scorns camouflage and never minces matters is its outstanding feature from beginning to end. Finally, it is also a polite book that hardly ever attributes to opponents anything beyond intellectual error. In fact, the author is polite to a fault; for not all relevant points can be made without more plain speaking about group interests than he is willing to resort to. In this respect—perhaps also in others—he might have learned a useful lesson from Karl Marx". See p. 269 of J. A. Schumpeter, "*The Road to Serfdom*. By FRIEDRICH A. HAYEK", *Journal of Political Economy*, vol. 54, 1946, pp. 269–70. Hayek assesses Schumpeter's own views on the possibility of socialism in Hayek, "Two Pages of Fiction".—Ed.]

[8] [At the time at which this essay was written, Hayek's views may have been overly optimistic. In the late 1970s, the consensus within the literature on comparative economic systems was that market socialists such Oskar Lange had developed an effective response to Mises's and Hayek's critique of central planning, thereby emerging victorious from the socialist calculation debate. See D. Lavoie, "A Critique of the Standard Account of the Socialist Calculation Debate", *Journal of Libertarian Studies*, vol. 5, 1981, pp. 41–87. The reason was that most subsequent observers of the debate viewed the Austrians' arguments through the same neoclassical conceptual lens

to reintroduce competition in order to provide both incentives and a set of meaningful prices to guide resource use. We can deal with those older ideals of centralised planning fairly briefly since even the proponents of the schemes under discussion today disclaim that they aim at a system of planning of the kind in which a central authority commands what the individual enterprise is to do—although it must remain doubtful whether what they aim at can be achieved without this sort of regimentation.

We shall therefore content ourselves, so far as the efficiency argument for central direction is concerned, with stating very briefly why such an argument is erroneous.

The chief reason why we cannot hope by central direction to achieve anything like the efficiency in the use of resources which the market makes possible is that the economic order of any large society rests on a utilisation of the knowledge of particular circumstances widely dispersed among thousands or millions of individuals. Of course, there always are many facts which the individual conductor of a business ought to know in order to be able to make the right decisions but which he can never know directly. But among the alternative possibilities for coping with these difficulties—either conveying to a central directing authority all the relevant information possessed by the different individuals, or communicating to the separate individuals as much as possible of the information relevant for their decisions—we have discovered a solution for the second task only: the market and the competitive determination of prices have provided a procedure by which it is possible to convey to the individual managers of productive units as much information in condensed form as they need in order to fit their plans into the order of the rest of the system.[9] The alternative of having all the individual managers of businesses convey to a central planning authority the knowledge of particular facts which they possess is clearly impossible—simply because they never can know beforehand which of the many concrete circumstances about which

---

used by the market socialists to make the case for planning, relying in particular on the static notion of general economic equilibrium and the view of competition as a state of 'perfect competition' in which nobody can affect market prices. This left them unable to understand and appreciate the merits of the Austrians' case against planning, which was based on a different vision of the market as a dynamic process of rivalrous competition between price-setting firms. Arguably, it was only after the publication in the 1980s of alternative, revisionist histories of the debate that the balance of opinion within the profession shifted towards the view that it was in fact the Austrian case that had prevailed. See K. Vaughn, "Economic Calculation under Socialism: The Austrian Contribution", *Economic Inquiry*, vol. 18, 1980, pp. 535–54, and Lavoie, *Rivalry and Central Planning.*—Ed.]

[9] [On this, see in particular F. A. Hayek, "The Use of Knowledge in Society" [1945], reprinted as chapter 3 of F. A. Hayek, *The Market and Other Orders*, ed. Bruce Caldwell, vol. 15 (2014) of *The Collected Works of F. A. Hayek.*—Ed.]

they have knowledge or could find out might be of importance to the central planning authority. We have come to understand that the market and the price mechanism provide in this sense a sort of discovery procedure which both makes the utilisation of more facts possible than any other known system, and which provides the incentive for constant discovery of new facts which improve adaptation to the ever-changing circumstances of the world in which we live.[10] Of course this adaptation is never as perfect as the mathematical models of market equilibrium suggest; but it is certainly much better than any which we know how to bring about by any other means. I believe there is substantive agreement on these points among serious students of these matters.

IV

But, curiously, one recently has begun to hear more and more frequently a new argument which inverts the historical role that the market and the price mechanism have played in maximising order and efficiency in individual economies and in the world economy at large. It is contended that the market may have been an adequate mechanism of coordination under earlier, simpler conditions, but that in modern times economic systems have become so complex that we no longer can rely on the spontaneous forces of the market for the ordering of economic priorities but must resort instead to central planning or direction. Such an argument carries some superficial plausibility, but, on examination, turns out to be particularly silly. In fact, of course, the very complexity which the structure of modern economic systems has assumed provides the strongest argument against central planning. It is becoming progressively less and less imaginable that any one mind or planning authority could picture or survey the millions of connections between the ever more numerous interlocking separate activities which have become indispensable for the efficient use of modern technology and even the maintenance of the standard of life Western man has achieved.

That we have been able to achieve a reasonably high degree of order in our economic lives despite modern complexities is *only* because our affairs have been guided, not by central direction, but by the operations of the market and competition in securing the mutual adjustment of separate efforts. The market system functions because it is able to take account of millions of separate facts and desires, because it reaches with thousands of sensitive feelers into

---

[10] [Hayek alludes here to the ideas set out in F. A. Hayek, "Competition as a Discovery Procedure" [1968], reprinted as chapter 12 of Hayek, *The Market and Other Orders.*—Ed.]

every nook and cranny of the economic world and feeds back the information acquired in coded form to a 'public information board'. What the market-place and its prices give most particularly is a continuing updating of the ever changing relative scarcities of different commodities and services. In other words, the complexity of the structure required to produce the real income we are now able to provide for the masses of the Western world—which exceeds anything we can survey or picture in detail—could develop *only* because we did *not* attempt to plan it or subject it to any central direction, but left it to be guided by a spontaneous ordering mechanism, or a self-generating order, as modern cybernetics calls it.[11]

V

Apart from such occasional flare-ups of old misunderstandings in lay circles, the efficiency argument for central economic planning has almost universally been abandoned. If central direction of all economic activity is still sometimes demanded by serious students, this is on the different and logical argument that only in this manner could the distribution of income and wealth between individuals and groups be made to conform to some preconceived moral stan-dard. Apparently a good many idealist socialists would be prepared to toler-ate a substantial sacrifice of material welfare if thereby what they regard as greater distributive or social justice could be achieved.

The objections to this demand for greater social justice, of course, must be and are of an entirely different character from those against the presumed greater efficiency of a planned system. There are two different fundamen-tal objections to these demands, each of which seems to me to be decisive. The first is that no agreement exists (or appears even conceivable) about the kind of distribution that is desirable or morally demanded; the second is that whatever particular distributive scheme were to be aimed at could in fact be realised only in a strictly totalitarian order in which individuals would not be allowed to use their own knowledge for their own purposes but would have to work under orders on jobs assigned to them for purposes determined by gov-ernment authority.[12]

---

[11] [Hayek argues at length that the increasing complexity of the economic system can be sus-tained only through a greater reliance on spontaneous market forces in F. A. Hayek, *Rules and Order*, vol. 1 (1973) of *Law, Legislation and Liberty* (Chicago: University of Chicago Press; Lon-don: Routledge, 1973–1979), pp. 29–71. Hayek's account of 'complexity' can be found in F. A. Hayek, "The Theory of Complex Phenomena" [1964], reprinted as chapter 9 of Hayek, *The Market and Other Orders*. For more on his views on cybernetics, see F. A. Hayek, "The Confusion of Language in Political Thought" [1968], reprinted as chapter 23 of this volume, p. 303 n. 7.—Ed.]

[12] [Hayek sets out these objections at length in *The Road to Serfdom*, pp. 134–56.—Ed.]

Freedom in the choice of activity as we know it is possible only if the reward to be expected from any job undertaken corresponds to the value the products will have to those fellow men to whom they actually are supplied. But this value often will unavoidably bear no relation whatever to the deserts, needs, or other claims of the producer. The belief in a society in which the remuneration of individuals is made to correspond to something called 'social justice' is a chimera which is threatening to seduce modern democracy to accept a system that would involve a disastrous loss of personal freedom. George Orwell and others ought by now to have taught even the layman what to expect from a system of such kind.[13]

VI

The new American advocates of planning will claim, however, that they know all this and that they never have advocated a system of central direction of individual economic activities and even have said so. Yet it is very doubtful whether what they do advocate would not in fact lead that way. They leave a great deal obscure and it is precisely this state of muddle which is the sure way to hell. To be sure, the statement of the Initiative Committee for National Economic Planning (*The Case for Planning*) says that:

It should be clear that the Planning Office would not set specific goals for General Motors, General Electric, General Foods, or any other individual firm. But it would indicate the number of cars, the number of generators, and the quantity of frozen foods we are likely to require in, say, five years, and it would try to induce the relevant industries to act accordingly.

But one cannot help wondering how that 'inducement' of an 'industry' would work if, as the Initiative Committee's statement at another point makes clear, the "means of influencing" the decisions of industry would include "selective

---

[13] [For more on the issues raised in this paragraph, see F. A. Hayek, *The Constitution of Liberty*, ed. Ronald Hamowy, vol. 17 (2011) of *The Collected Works of F. A. Hayek*, pp. 148–65; F. A. Hayek, *The Mirage of Social Justice*, vol. 2 (1976) of *Law, Legislation and Liberty*, pp. 62–106; F. A. Hayek, "The Moral Element in Free Enterprise" [1962], reprinted as chapter 20 of this volume, pp. 268–69; and F. A. Hayek, "The Atavism of Social Justice" [1978], reprinted as chapter 27 of this volume. George Orwell, the pseudonym of Eric Arthur Blair (1903–50), was an English novelist, essayist, and critic, whose most famous critiques of collectivism and totalitarianism are G. Orwell, *Animal Farm: A Fairy Story* (London: Secker and Warburg, 1945), and G. Orwell, *Nineteen Eighty-Four: A Novel* (London: Secker and Warburg, 1949). For Orwell's review of *The Road to Serfdom*, see G. Orwell, "Review: *The Road to Serfdom* by F. A. Hayek, and *The Mirror of the Past*, by Konni Zilliacus" [1944], in *The Collected Essays, Journalism, and Letters of George Orwell*, ed. S. Orwell and I. Angus (New York: Harcourt, Brace and World, 1968), vol. 3, pp. 117–19.—Ed.]

credit controls, guidance of basic capital flows, limits to the use of air, water and land, and *mandatory resource allocation* [italics added]."[14]

Indeed, as one reads on, it becomes increasingly difficult to find out what precisely the authors of the statement mean by National Economic Planning. Nor, in spite of its magniloquent language, is the text of the proposed Balanced Growth and Economic Planning Act of 1975, inspired by the Committee and introduced in the Senate by Senators Humphrey, Jackson, Javits, McGovern and others, in this respect more revealing. While the bill is loquacious on the organisation of a proposed Economic Planning Board, it is remarkably reticent on the methods and powers by which this body is to secure the execution of the 'balanced economic growth plan' which it is to draw up. About the elaborateness of the proposed machinery there can be no doubt. But what it is to do, and even more important what good it is to do, is difficult to discover.[15]

Underlying some of these arguments for central economic planning appears to be the curious conception that it would be an advantage, enhancing orderliness and predictability, if the gross outline, a sort of skeleton, of the future distribution of resources between industries and firms could be laid down for a fairly long period. In other words, what is today one of the chief tasks of business, namely to guess as correctly as possible future developments in its particular concerns, would be handled in advance by government decision; only the details within this general framework would be handled by busi-

[14] [The first, indented passage quoted by Hayek is taken from The Initiative Committee for National Economic Planning, "For a National Economic Planning System", pp. 52–53. The words quoted in the remaining sentences of the paragraph come from p. 52 of the same article. The insertion in square brackets is Hayek's.—Ed.]

[15] [The Balanced Growth and Economic Planning Act (S. 1795) was introduced in the Senate in May 1975 and sought to establish an Economic Planning Board in the Executive Office of the President of the United States, with the aim of developing a plan for balanced economic growth based on an appraisal of the nation's needs, resources, and economic goals. The Act was sponsored by Hubert H. Humphrey (1911–78), a Democratic Senator for Minnesota (1949–64, 1969–78) and former Vice-President of the United States (1965–69). The Act's co-sponsors included Jacob K. Javits (1904–86), a Republican Senator from New York (1957–81), Henry M. Jackson (1912–83), a Democratic Senator from Washington State (1953–83), and George McGovern (1922–2012), a Democratic Senator from South Dakota (1963–81) who was the unsuccessful Democratic Party nominee for President of the United States in 1972. The bill did not pass through Congress. It was subsequently replaced by the Full Employment and Balanced Growth Act of 1976, commonly known as the Hawkins-Humphrey Act after its main sponsor, Augustus F. Hawkins (1907–2007), a Democratic Senator from California (1963–1991), and Hubert Humphrey. This Act supported a milder form of planning than its predecessor, advocating the use of numerical targets for unemployment and inflation but not the creation of any new planning machinery beyond the existing government departments and agencies. A watered-down version of this Act was passed by Congress in 1978.—Ed.]

ness. The hope apparently is thereby to increase the opportunity for managers of individual firms to make correct forecasts concerning the facts which will directly affect their activities. But the exact opposite would be the result of such planning: the uncertainty for managers would be greatly increased since the opportunity they would have to adapt to changes in their immediate environments (i.e. the quantities they would have to buy or sell and the prices at which they could do so) would depend on the "mandatory resource allocation", the "guidance of basic capital flows", etc., of the government planning office. For the manager of an individual firm, that halfway house between a completely planned system and a free market would indeed be the worst of all possible worlds, since his ability to make changes would become critically dependent on the red tape, delay, and unpredictability that are characteristic of bureaucratic decisions.

Implied in the argument for government planning of industrial and commercial activity is the belief that government (with an appropriately increased bureaucracy, of course) would be in a better position to predict the future needs of consumer goods, materials, and productive equipment than the individual firms. But is it really seriously contended that some government office (or, worse, some politically sensitive plan-making committee) would be more likely to foresee correctly the effects of future changes in tastes, the success of some new device or other technical innovation, changes in the scarcity of different raw materials, etc., on the amounts of some commodity that ought to be produced some years hence, than the producers or professional dealers of those things? Is it really likely that a National Planning Office would have a better judgement of "the number of cars, the number of generators, and the quantities of frozen foods we are likely to require in, say, five years", than Ford or General Motors, etc., and, even more important, would it even be desirable that various companies in an industry all act on the same guess? Is it not the very rationale of the method of competition that we allow those who have shown the greatest skill in forecasting to make preparations for the future?

VII

In some sections of the statements made by the new advocates of 'planning' it becomes clear, however, that they are thinking mainly of another kind of planning, one which also has been thoroughly examined in the past in a discussion of which its present protagonists show as little awareness as of any other of the earlier scientific examinations of the problem. They show indeed a curious tendency to reject with disdain any suggestion that other peoples' experiences are relevant and insist, in Professor Leontief's words, that "America cannot import a planning system from abroad. Countries differ in their planning methods because the countries themselves differ. We should want and expect a distinctive American style."[16]

The earlier extensive discussion of these problems, from which the American proponents of that other sort of planning ought to have profited, took place chiefly in France in the early 1960s under the heading of 'indicative planning'. This conception had for a short while attracted much attention until it was decently buried after a thorough discussion at the Congress of French Speaking Economists in 1964 had revealed all the confusion and contradictions involved in it.[17] There is no excuse whatever for ignorance of the upshot of these discussions which are clearly expounded in an excellent book in English by the late Dr Vera Lutz.[18]

The whole idea of 'indicative planning', it turned out, rests on a curious combination, or rather confusion, of actions: making a prediction and setting a target. It was conceived that somehow a forecast of the quantities of the different commodities and services that will be produced would assist in determining the respective quantities which ought to be produced. The plan is conceived as a forecast by government at the achievement of which industry is to aim.

This sort of self-fulfilling prophecy may at first appear plausible, but on reflection it turns out, at least so far as a market economy based on competition

---

[16] Quoted by Jack Friedman in *The New York Times* of 18 May 1975. [See p. 11 of J. Friedman, "A Planned Economy in the U.S.?", *The New York Times*, May 18, 1975, section 3, pp. 1, 11.—Ed.]

[17] See particularly the contributions of Daniel Villey and Maurice Allais to the *Congrès des économistes de langue Française*, May 1964. [French liberal economist Daniel Villey (1911–68) served as Acting President of the Mont Pèlerin Society from 1967 until his death in 1968. French economist Maurice Allais (1911–2010) was awarded the Nobel Prize for Economics in 1988. Hayek refers to M. Allais, "Sur la Planification", and D. Villey, "Marché et plan. L'option de système", both in *Marché et Plan, Travaux du Congrès des Economistes de Langue Française*, ed. J. De Bandt, P. Bauchet and D. Villey (Paris: Editions Cujas, 1965). For more on Allais and Villey's connections to the French liberal tradition, see pp. 221–223, 226 of S. Audier, "Is There a French Neoliberalism?", in *French Liberalism from Montesquieu to the Present Day*, ed. R. Geenens and H. Rosenblatt (Cambridge: Cambridge University Press, 2012).—Ed.]

[18] Vera Lutz, *Central Planning for the Market Economy. An Analysis of the French Theory and Experience*, London, 1969. There is also a brief earlier statement by Dr Lutz, *French Planning*, Washington DC, 1965. [Vera Lutz (1912–76), née Smith, was an English economist who wrote her doctoral dissertation under Hayek's supervision at the London School of Economics in the 1930s. She is perhaps best known for the book based on her dissertation, and published under her maiden name, namely V. Smith, *The Rationale of Central Banking* (London: P. S. King and Son, 1936), in which she reviews the history of free banking in the nineteenth century and considers its merits and demerits. Hayek refers to V. Lutz, *French Planning* (Washington, DC.: American Enterprise Institute for Public Policy Research, 1965), and V. Lutz, *Central Planning for the Market Economy: An Analysis of the French Theory and Experience* (London: Longmans, Green and Co., 1969).—Ed.]

is concerned, to be an absurdity. There is absolutely no reason at all to assume that announcement of a target will make it likely that the aggregates of output named in it will actually be realised by the efforts of a number of producers acting in competition. Nor is there any reason to think that the government, or anybody else, is in a better position than are individual managers acting as they now do to determine beforehand appropriate quantities of different outputs of different industries so that supplies and demands will match.

It is at this point that it becomes clear that the present revival of the planning idea in the United States is inspired by the input–output representations developed by Professor Leontief, and rests entirely, I am sorry to say, on a colossal overestimation by its author of what this technique can achieve. Before the Joint Economic Committee,[19] Professor Leontief is reported to have explained that: "First of all, getting information is a passive activity. It does not tell anybody what to do. Presenting a picture of how good a situation could be if everything is geared nicely is not a dictation".

What Professor Leontief has in mind is clearly the technique of input-output tables which he himself has developed and which show in an instructive manner how, during some period in the past, various quantities of the products of different main branches of productive activity were used up by other branches. How the production of the tens of thousands of different things which are needed to produce a much smaller but still very large number of final products is determined by the market process is a matter of infinite complexity; and how order is brought about by a spontaneous mechanism which we do not fully understand is best illustrated by the very fact that we needed a Professor Leontief to give us even a very rough outline of the gross categories of commodities that in the past have passed from certain main groups of industries to others. One can understand that Professor Leontief wishes to refine and extend that technique and to construct input-output tables not for a few dozen but for a few thousand main classes of products. But the idea that such broad-outline information about what has happened in the past should be of significant help in deciding what ought to happen in the future is absurd. Even if we could get and organise information about the tens of thousands of different commodities actually produced in a specific past period, it would tell us about just one of an infinite number of possible input combinations that could produce a particular array of final products. It would tell us nothing at all about whether that specific combination of inputs or any other combination would be economical under changed conditions.

The source of belief in the value of input-output representations is the

---

[19] *Notes from the Joint Economic Committee,* Congress of the United States, vol. I, no. 19, 1 July 1975, p. 10.

wholly wrong idea that the efficient use of resources is determined mainly by technological and not by economic considerations.[20] That belief is evident in the fact that the advocates of planning visualise a team of a few thousand technical experts (perhaps 500 of them, as we learn from one of their spokesmen, at the cost of fifty million dollars a year)[21]—most of them scientists and engineers rather than economists—working on planning for either the White House or Congress.[22]

VIII

This, I am afraid, betrays a complete lack of understanding of how in the complex order of a great society the efficient use of resources can alone be determined. There is no need, to take a very simple example, to command a particular quantity of a particular raw material in order to make a particular quantity of tarpaulins. In a situation in which the buyers of tarpaulins are indifferent to the raw material from which they are made, output can be maximised by choosing among hemp, flax, jute, cotton, nylon, etc., that material which costs least—that is, that which we can obtain for this purpose at the least sacrifice of other desirable products. That we can substitute one material for another in this and thousands of other cases (most of which in practice involve much greater complexities) is due to the circumstance that in a competitive market the relative prices of materials will enable us to determine readily how much more of one material than of another can be acquired at any given expenditure level.

There is, therefore, without a knowledge of prices, no possibility for determining from statistics of the past how much of different materials will be wanted in the future. And statistics of the past help us little to predict what prices will be and therefore what quantities will be needed of different commodities. It is therefore difficult to see what possible purpose would be served

[20] [Hayek elaborates at length on the distinction between economic and technological problems in F. A. Hayek, "The Nature and History of the Problem" [1935], reprinted as chapter 1 of Hayek, *Socialism and War*, pp. 54–57, and in F. A. Hayek, "A New Look at Economic Theory" [1961], first published as Appendix A of Hayek, *The Market and Other Orders*, pp. 402–7, writing in the latter that: "The basic distinction seems to me that technology informs us of the different ways in which any given result can be produced, while the economic considerations tell us which of these ways to select in view of the other needs which in the particular situation compete for the same means" (p. 404).—Ed.]

[21] *Challenge*, May–June 1975, p. 6. [See p. 6 of M. E. Sharpe, "From the Editor: The Planning Bill", *Challenge*, vol. 18, May–June 1975, pp. 3–8.—Ed.]

[22] *The New York Times*, 28 February 1975, "Diverse Group Advocates Economic Planning for U.S." [See Unnamed author, "Diverse Group Advocates Economic Planning for U.S.", *The New York Times*, February 28, 1975, pp. 43, 48.—Ed.]

if it were announced beforehand what quantities of the different main classes of goods ought to be produced during a certain period of the future.[23] Even if it were possible, however, to say beforehand for every kind of commodity (or variety of a commodity) how much of it ought to be produced some years hence, it is difficult to see how this should lead the individual enterprises to produce just those amounts which together correspond to the desired quota—except, indeed, on the assumption that it is desired that the different firms should conspire together to produce an output of a certain size (presumably that must be profitable to them). This, in fact, is the ideal which clearly guided the French advocates of 'indicative planning'. And one cannot help feeling sometimes that the new American advocates of planning have become the innocent dupes of some aspiring cartelists.

The whole idea of 'guiding' private industry by announcing beforehand what quantities of different goods firms ought to produce over a long period of the future is a muddle from beginning to end, wholly ineffective and misleading if left without sanctions constraining industry to do what it is predicted that it will do, destructive of the competitive market and free enterprise, and leading by its inherent logic straight to a socialist system. It seems to have attracted all those who since the era of the New Deal have hankered for a revival of President Franklin D. Roosevelt's National Resources Planning Board. Indeed, Professor Leontief has specifically couched his proposal in that way,[24] thereby apparently hoping to give it an aura of progressiveness.

---

[23] [Hayek's argument here is an instance of his oft-repeated criticism of central planning, namely that in the absence of a rivalrous market process, the information required by the planners if they are to formulate plans that have a chance of being brought to fruition simply does not exist. See Hayek, "Two Pages of Fiction". For an extended 'Hayekian' critique of Leontief's arguments in favour of planning, see D. Lavoie (1985), *National Economic Planning: What Is Left?* (Cambridge, MA: Ballinger Publishing Co., 1985), pp. 93–124.—Ed.]

[24] W. Leontief, "For a National Economic Planning Board", *The New York Times*, 14 March 1974. Indeed the most familiar figures among the signatories of the statement of the Initiative Committee for National Economic Planning—Chester Bowles, John K. Galbraith, L. H. Keyserling, Gunnar Myrdal, Robert R. Nathan, and Arthur Schlesinger, Jr.—seem to be men who long for a new N.R.A. and who in any other country would be called socialists, but in the U.S. call themselves liberals. [See W. Leontief, "For a National Economic Planning Board", *The New York Times*, March 14, 1974, p. 37, where Leontief argues that because technical advances had greatly increased the scope for gathering and processing information about the state of the economy, it was time to revive Roosevelt's National Resource Planning Board. The latter, originally known as the National Planning Board, was established in 1933 in order to assist in the preparation of a comprehensive programme of public works and represented the first significant experiment in peacetime economic planning in the United States. It was abolished in 1943.

While the names of Democratic politician and diplomat Chester Bowles (1901–86), Harvard economist John Kenneth Galbraith, Swedish Nobel Prize-winning economist Gunnar Myrdal (1898–1987), American economist Robert R. Nathan, and American historian and public official Arthur Schlesinger, Jr. (1917–2007), all appear on the list of those who had endorsed the Initiative Committee's statement, one name that does not appear is that of Leon H. Keyserling

Yet, to the economist aware of the serious discussions of these problems during the last 40 years these, far from being progressive, are antiquated ideas, completely out of date and in conflict with all that we have learned about the problems involved.

IX

There is, however, yet another undercurrent discernible in the present demands for planning which indeed expresses a very legitimate dissatisfaction with prominent features of our economic life. This involves the hope for a kind of planning which would be highly desirable but which is not only wholly impossible politically in present conditions but also in direct conflict with the other demands for planning. The hope is for government to plan its own activities ahead for long periods, announce and commit itself to the execution of these plans, and thereby make government action more predictable. It would indeed be a great boon for industry if it could know a few years in advance what the government is likely to do. But this is, of course, wholly irreconcilable with the established use of economic measures for vote-catching purposes. Such an idea is even more irreconcilable with demands that government interfere with the activities of private enterprise to make them conform more closely to some plan government has made. The current agitation in the United States for a broad new planning initiative explicitly includes, in most of its variants, an indictment of government for its failure to think out its policies for the longer future. But the legitimacy of that indictment is not a justifi-

---

(1908–87), an American 'old' institutionalist economist, lawyer and public official who helped to draft various pieces of New Deal legislation such as the National Industrial Recovery Act and who served as Chair of the Council of Economic Advisors from 1950 to 1953. See The Initiative Committee for National Economic Planning, "For a National Economic Planning System", p. 51, along with p. 64 of the same issue of *Challenge* magazine. Keyserling was, however, the draftsman of the 1978 Full Employment and Balanced Growth Act, which is discussed in n. 15 of this chapter. See W. Brazelton, "The Economics of Leon Hirsch Keyserling", *Journal of Economic Perspectives*, vol. 11, 1997, pp. 189–97.

The National Recovery Administration or N.R.A. was a U.S. government agency established in 1933 as part of President Franklin D. Roosevelt's 'New Deal'. Its goal was to establish codes of 'fair' competition governing price- and wage-setting. These would, it was hoped, promote cooperation between businesses and thereby help the U.S. economy to recover from the Great Depression. While the N.R.A. ceased operations in 1935 after the National Industrial Recovery Act through which it was established was declared unconstitutional by the U.S. Supreme Court, many of its provisions were included in subsequent legislation. For more on the N.R.A., see D. Winch, *Economics and Policy: A Historical Study* (London: Hodder and Stoughton, 1969), pp. 227–32, while Hayek discusses one of its principal architects, American economist Rexford Tugwell, on pp. 58–59 of F. A. Hayek, "The Prospects of Freedom" [1946], reprinted as chapter 3 of the current volume.—Ed.]

cation for the demand that the same government which so notoriously fails to plan its own affairs should be entrusted with the planning of business.

X

The Balanced Growth and Economic Planning Act of 1975—popularly known after its chief sponsors as the Humphrey-Javits bill—is a decidedly curious product, both as to parentage and other matters. The so-called Coordinator of the Initiative Committee for National Economic Planning— Myron Sharpe, editor of *Challenge*—claims that the bill was originally drafted by members of the Initiative Committee and that the final draft is the "joint product of the Initiative Committee and the original Senate sponsors".[25] Senator Javits, however, is on record as wanting to make it clear that the sponsors of the bill "aren't an instrument for the Committee for National Economic Planning" and that the Committee's definitive statement "isn't applicable to our bill".[26] Senator Humphrey, for his part, has offered reassurance that no coerciveness would be involved. "I can categorically state", he has said, "that it is not the intent of the authors of this bill or of the bill itself, and there is not a single word or phrase in this bill which could be used to expand the Government's control over the economy".[27] Indeed the much touted National Planning Bill turns out to be an instrument for an undisclosed purpose. It proposes to create an enormous bureaucratic machinery for planning, but its chief sponsor, while constantly using the magic word planning, admittedly has no idea of what he means by it: Senator Humphrey explained the purpose of the Joint Economic Committee's Hearings on the bill last June by saying: "This is advisory and consultative and hopefully out of this dialogue and discussion . . . we will come down to a much more clear and precise understanding of exactly what we are talking about and what we mean".[28]

It is difficult for an outsider to understand how, after introducing so ill-considered and irresponsible a piece of legislation—which promises merely an empty machinery with no stated purpose, which will perhaps give us input-output tables for a few hundred commodities that will be of no conceivable

---

[25] *Challenge*, May–June 1975, p. 3. [See Sharpe, "From the Editor: The Planning Bill", p. 3.—Ed.]

[26] *Daily Report for Executives*, published by The Bureau of National Affairs, Inc., 11 June 1975, p. A 11.

[27] *Notes from the Joint Economic Committee*, U.S. Congress, vol. I, no. 19, p. 19. [See *National Economic Planning, Balanced Growth, and Full Employment: Hearings before the Joint Economic Committee, Congress of the United States, Ninety-Fourth Congress, First Session, June 11 and 12, 1975* (Washington, DC: U.S. Government Printing Office, 1976), p. 105.—Ed.]

[28] *Ibid*, p. 2. [*National Economic Planning, Balanced Growth, and Full Employment*, p. 151.—Ed.]

use to anybody except some future economic historian, but which may incidentally be used to enforce the disclosure of various sorts of information that would be exceedingly useful to a future authoritarian government—Senator Humphrey should be able to boast that it is his "single most important piece of legislation".[29] Somebody as innocent of American politics as this writer might suspect that the Senator from Minnesota is the unwitting tool of some other, presumably collectivist, wire pullers who want to use the machinery thus created for aims they prefer not to disclose. But when one re-reads the accounts of how the campaign for national planning has evolved in the articles of the editor of the magazine *Challenge*, whose hand one seems to recognise also in several of the other statements supporting the plan, one feels reassured that nothing more sinister than sheer intellectual muddle is at work.[30]

[29] 'Planning Economic Policy', *Challenge*, March–April 1975, p. 21. [See p. 21 of "Interview: Hubert H. Humphrey. *Planning Economic Policy*", *Challenge*, vol. 18, March–April 1975, pp. 21–7. Also see *Hearings before the Subcommittee on Economic Growth of the Joint Economic Committee, Congress of the United States, Ninety-Third Congress, Second Session, May 8 and 9, June 11, 12, and 26, 1974* (Washington, DC: U.S. Government Printing Office, 1974), p. 26.—Ed.]

[30] [See, in addition to the article mentioned in footnote 21 above, M. E. Sharpe, "From the Editor: The Fear of Planning", *Challenge*, vol. 18, March–April 1975, pp. 3–5, and M. E. Sharpe, "From the Editor: Reply to a Critic of Planning", *Challenge*, vol. 18, July–August 1975, pp. 3–5.—Ed.]

TWENTY-SEVEN

THE ATAVISM OF SOCIAL JUSTICE[1]

I

To discover the meaning of what is called 'social justice' has been one of my chief preoccupations for more than 10 years. I have failed in this endeavour— or, rather, have reached the conclusion that, with reference to a society of free men, the phrase has no meaning whatever. The search for the reason why the word has nevertheless for something like a century dominated political discussion, and has everywhere been successfully used to advance claims of particular groups for a larger share in the good things of life, remains, however, a very interesting one. It is this question with which I shall here chiefly concern myself.

But I must at first briefly explain, as I attempt to demonstrate at length in volume 2 of my *Law, Legislation and Liberty*, about to be published, why I have come to regard 'social justice' as nothing more than an empty formula, conventionally used to assert that a particular claim is justified without giving any reason. Indeed that volume, which bears the sub-title *The Mirage of Social Justice*, is mainly intended to convince intellectuals that the concept of 'social justice', which they are so fond of using, is intellectually disreputable.[2] Some of course have already tumbled to this; but with the unfortunate result that, since 'social' justice is the only kind of justice they have ever thought of, they have been led to the conclusion that all uses of the term justice have no meaningful content. I have therefore been forced to show in the same book that rules

---

[1] The 9th R. C. Mills Memorial Lecture delivered at the University of Sydney on 6 October 1976. [This essay was first published as chapter 5 of F. A. Hayek, *New Studies in Philosophy, Politics, Economics and the History of Ideas* (London and Henley: Routledge & Kegan Paul, 1978), the version used here. It was reprinted as chapter 1 of F. A. Hayek, *Social Justice, Socialism & Democracy: 3 Australian Lectures by F. A. Hayek*, CIS Occasional Papers 2 (Turramura: The Centre for Independent Studies, 1979). Richard Charles Mills (1886–1952) was an Australian economist and educational administrator who, having obtained his doctorate at the London School of Economics (1912–15), taught for many years in the University of Sydney, serving as Professor of Economics from 1922 to 1945. The university inaugurated the R. C. Mills lectures in his honour in 1957.—Ed.]

[2] [Hayek refers to F. A. Hayek, *The Mirage of Social Justice*, vol. 2 (1976) of *Law, Legislation and Liberty* (Chicago: University of Chicago Press; London: Routledge, 1973–79).—Ed.]

of just individual conduct are as indispensable to the preservation of a peaceful society of free men as endeavours to realise 'social' justice are incompatible with it.

The term 'social justice' is today generally used as a synonym of what used to be called 'distributive justice'. The latter term perhaps gives a somewhat better idea of what can be meant by it, and at the same time shows why it can have no application to the results of a market economy: there can be no distributive justice where no one distributes. Justice has meaning only as a rule of human conduct, and no conceivable rules for the conduct of individuals supplying each other with goods and services in a market economy would produce a distribution which could be meaningfully described as just or unjust. Individuals might conduct themselves as justly as possible, but as the results for separate individuals would be neither intended nor foreseeable by others, the resulting state of affairs could neither be called just nor unjust.

The complete emptiness of the phrase 'social justice' shows itself in the fact that no agreement exists about what social justice requires in particular instances; also that there is no known test by which to decide who is right if people differ, and that no preconceived scheme of distribution could be effectively devised in a society whose individuals are free, in the sense of being allowed to use their own knowledge for their own purposes. Indeed, individual moral responsibility for one's actions is incompatible with the realisation of any such desired overall pattern of distribution.

A little inquiry shows that, though a great many people are dissatisfied with the existing pattern of distribution, none of them has really any clear idea of what pattern he would regard as just. All that we find are intuitive assessments of individual cases as unjust. No one has yet found even a single general rule from which we could derive what is 'socially just' in all particular instances that would fall under it—except the rule of 'equal pay for equal work'. Free competition, precluding all that regard for merit or need and the like, on which demands for social justice are based, tends to enforce the equal pay rule.

II

The reason why most people continue firmly to believe in 'social justice', even after they discover that they do not really know what the phrase means, is that they think if almost everyone else believes in it, there must be something in the phrase. The ground for this almost universal acceptance of a belief, the significance of which people do not understand, is that we have all inherited from an earlier different type of society, in which man existed very much longer than in the present one, some now deeply ingrained instincts which are inapplicable to our present civilisation. In fact, man emerged from primitive society when in certain conditions increasing numbers succeeded by disregarding those very principles which had held the old groups together.[3] We must not forget that before the last 10,000 years, during which man has developed agriculture, towns and ultimately the 'Great Society', he existed for at least a hundred times as long in small food-sharing hunting bands of 50 or so, with a strict order of dominance within the defended common territory of the band. The needs of this ancient primitive kind of society determined much of the moral feelings which still govern us, and which we approve in others. It was a grouping in which, at least for all males, the common pursuit of a perceived physical common object under the direction of the alpha male was as much a condition of its continued existence as the assignment of different shares in the prey to the different members according to their importance for the survival of the band. It is more than probable that many of the moral feelings then acquired have not merely been culturally transmitted by teaching or imitation, but have become innate or genetically determined.[4]

But not all that is natural to us in this sense is therefore necessarily in different circumstances good or beneficial for the propagation of the species. In its primitive form the little band indeed did possess what is still attractive to so many people: a unitary purpose, or a common hierarchy of ends, and a deliberate sharing of means according to a common view of individual merits. These foundations of its coherence, however, also imposed limits on the possible development of this form of society. The events to which the group could adapt itself, and the opportunities it could take advantage of, were only those of which its members were directly aware. Even worse, the individual could do little of which others did not approve. It is a delusion to think of the individual in primitive society as free. There was no natural liberty for a social animal, while freedom is an artifact of civilisation. The individual had in the group no recognised domain of independent action; even the head of the band could expect obedience, support and understanding of his signals only

---

[3] [Hayek explores these issues in more detail in *The Mirage of Social Justice*, pp. 133–52, and in the Epilogue to F. A. Hayek, *The Political Order of a Free People*, vol. 3 (1979) of *Law, Legislation and Liberty*, especially pp. 155–69.—Ed.]

[4] [Hayek expands on the issues raised in this paragraph elsewhere in his writings, remarking in the course of a discussion of cultural evolution that "culturally transmitted patterns [of action] may in turn contribute to determine the selection of genetic properties". See F. A. Hayek, "Nature vs. Nurture Once Again" [1971], reprinted as chapter 15 of F. A. Hayek, *The Market and Other Orders*, ed. Bruce Caldwell, vol. 15 (2014) of *The Collected Works of F. A. Hayek* (Chicago: University of Chicago Press; London: Routledge), p. 359. A similar comment can be found in F. A. Hayek, "Notes on the Evolution of Systems of Rules of Conduct" [1967], reprinted as chapter 10 of *The Market and Other Orders*, p. 283.—Ed.]

for conventional activities. So long as each must serve that common order of rank for all needs, which present-day socialists dream of, there can be no free experimentation by the individual.

III

The great advance which made possible the development of civilisation and ultimately of the Open Society was the gradual substitution of abstract rules of conduct for specific obligatory ends, and with it the playing of a game for acting in concert under common indicators, thus fostering a spontaneous order. The great gain attained by this was that it made possible a procedure through which all relevant information widely dispersed was made available to ever-increasing numbers of men in the form of the symbols which we call market prices. But it also meant that the incidence of the results on different persons and groups no longer satisfied the age-old instincts.[5]

It has been suggested more than once that the theory explaining the working of the market be called catallactics from the classical Greek word for bartering or exchanging—*katalattein*. I have fallen somewhat in love with this word since discovering that in ancient Greek, in addition to 'exchanging', it also meant 'to admit into the community' and 'to change from enemy into friend'. I have therefore proposed that we call the game of the market, by which we can induce the stranger to welcome and serve us, the 'game of catallaxy'.[6]

The market process indeed corresponds fully to the definition of a game which we find in *The Oxford English Dictionary*. It is "a contest played according to rules and decided by superior skill, strength or good fortune". It is in this respect both a game of skill as well as a game of chance. Above all, it is a game which serves to elicit from each player the highest worthwhile contribution to the common pool from which each will win an uncertain share.

The game was probably started by men who had left the shelter and obligations of their own tribe to gain from serving the needs of others they did not know personally. When the early neolithic traders took boatloads of flint axes from Britain across the Channel to barter them against amber and probably also, even then, jars of wine, their aim was no longer to serve the needs

---

[5] [On what follows, in this section and the next, see Hayek, *The Mirage of Social Justice*, pp. 107–52, and Hayek, *The Political Order of a Free People*, pp. 159–73. For a detailed discussion of the informational role of market prices, see F. A. Hayek, "The Use of Knowledge in Society" [1945], reprinted as chapter 3 of *The Market and Other Orders*.—Ed.]

[6] [For more on the notion of catallaxy, see F. A. Hayek, "The Principles of a Liberal Social Order" [1966], reprinted as chapter 21 of the current volume, p. 278 n. 10, and F. A. Hayek, "The Confusion of Language in Political Thought" [1968], reprinted as chapter 23 of the current volume, p. 320 n. 29.—Ed.]

of known people, but to make the largest gain. Precisely because they were interested only in who would offer the best price for their products, they reached persons wholly unknown to them, whose standard of life they thereby enhanced much more than they could have that of their neighbours by handing the axes to those who no doubt could also have made good use of them.

IV

As the abstract signal-price thus took the place of the needs of known fellows as the goal towards which men's efforts were directed, entirely new possibilities for the utilisation of resources opened up—but this also required wholly different moral attitudes to encourage their exploitation. The change occurred largely at the new urban centres of trade and handicrafts, which grew up at ports or the cross-roads of trade routes, where men who had escaped from the discipline of tribal morals established commercial communities and gradually developed the new rules of the game of catallaxy.

The necessity to be brief forces me here somewhat to over-simplify and to employ familiar terms where they are not quite appropriate. When I pass from the morals of the hunting band in which man spent most of his history, to the morals which made possible the market order of the open society, I am jumping over a long intermediate stage, much shorter than man's life in the small band, but still of much greater length than the urban and commercial society has enjoyed yet, and important because from it date those codifications of ethics which became embodied in the teaching of the monotheistic religions. It is the period of man's life in tribal society. In many ways it represents a transitional stage between the concrete order of the primitive face-to-face society, in which all the members knew each other and served common particular ends, and the open and abstract society, in which an order results from individuals observing the same abstract rules of the game while using their own knowledge in the pursuit of their own ends.[7]

While our emotions are still governed by the instincts appropriate to the success of the small hunting band, our verbal tradition is dominated by duties to the 'neighbour', the fellow member of the tribe, and still regarding the alien largely as beyond the pale of moral obligation.

In a society in which individual aims were necessarily different, based on specialised knowledge, and efforts came to be directed towards future exchange of products with yet unknown partners, common rules of conduct increasingly

---

[7] [The distinction between an 'Open Society' and a 'closed' or 'tribal' society is taken from the work of philosopher Sir Karl Popper (1902–94). See K. Popper, *The Open Society and Its Enemies*, vol. I: *The Spell of Plato* (London: George Routledge, 1945), pp. 1, 151–55.—Ed.]

took the place of particular common ends as the foundations of social order and peace. The interaction of individuals became a game, because what was required from each individual was observation of the rules, not concern for a particular result, other than to win support for himself and his family. The rules which gradually developed, because they made this game most effective, were essentially those of the law of property and contract. These rules in turn made possible the progressive division of labour, and that mutual adjustment of independent efforts, which a functioning division of labour demands.

V

The full significance of this division of labour is often not appreciated, because most people think of it—partly because of the classical illustration given by Adam Smith—as a designed intra-mural arrangement in which different individuals contribute the successive steps in a planned process for shaping certain products.[8] In fact, however, co-ordination by the market of the endeavours of different enterprises in supplying the raw materials, tools and semi-finished products which the turning out of the final commodity requires, is probably much more important than the organised collaboration of numerous specialist workers.

It is in a great measure this inter-firm division of labour, or specialisation, on which the achievement of the competitive market depends, and which that market makes possible. Prices the producer finds on the market at once tell him what to produce and what means to use in producing it. From such market signals he knows that he can expect to sell at prices covering his outlays, and that he will not use up more resources than are necessary for the purpose. His selfish striving for gain makes him do, and enables him to do, precisely what he ought to do in order to improve the chances of any member of his society, taken at random, as much as possible—*but only if* the prices he can get are determined solely by market forces and not by the coercive powers of government. Only prices determined on the free market will bring it about that demand equals supply. But not only this. Free market prices also ensure that all of a society's dispersed knowledge will be taken into account and used.

The game of the market led to the growth and prosperity of communities who played it because it improved the chances for all. This was made possible because remuneration for the services of individuals depended on objec-

---

[8] [See Adam Smith, *An Enquiry into the Nature and Causes of the Wealth of Nations*, ed. W. B. Todd, vol. 2 of *The Glasgow Edition of the Works and Correspondence of Adam Smith* (Oxford: Oxford University Press, 1976; reprinted, Indianapolis, IN: Liberty Fund, 1981), book 1, chapter 1, paragraphs 1–11.—Ed.].

tive facts, all of which no one could know, and not on someone's opinions about what they ought to have. But it also meant that while skill and industry would improve each individual's chances, they could not guarantee him a specified income; and that the impersonal process which used all that dispersed knowledge set the signals of prices so as to tell people what to do, but without regard to needs or merits. Yet the ordering and productivity enhancing function of prices, and particularly the prices of services, depends on their informing people where they will find their most effective place in the overall pattern of activities—the place in which they are likely to make the greatest contribution to aggregate output. If, therefore, we regard *that* rule of remuneration as just which contributes as much as possible to increasing the chances of any member of the community picked out at random, we ought to regard the remunerations determined by a free market as the just ones.[9]

VI

But they are inevitably very different from the relative remunerations which assisted the organisation of the different type of society in which our species lived so much longer, and which therefore still governs the feelings which guide us. This point has become exceedingly important since prices ceased to be accepted as due to unknown circumstances, and governments came to believe they could determine prices with beneficial effects. When governments started to falsify the market price signals, whose appropriateness they had no means of judging (governments as little as anyone else possessing all the information precipitated in prices), in the hope of thereby giving benefits to groups claimed to be particularly deserving, things inevitably started to go wrong. Not only the efficient use of resources, but, what is worse, also the prospects of being able to buy or sell as expected through demand equalling supply were thereby greatly diminished.

It may be difficult to understand, but I believe there can be no doubt about it, that we are led to utilise more relevant information when our remuneration is made to depend indirectly on circumstances we do not know. It is thus that, in the language of modern cybernetics, the feedback mechanism secures the maintenance of a self-generating order. It was this which Adam Smith saw and described as the operation of the 'invisible hand'—to be ridiculed for 200 years by uncomprehending scoffers.[10] It is indeed *because* the

---

[9] [For more on these issues, see Hayek, *Rules and Order*, pp. 106–110, and Hayek, *The Mirage of Social Justice*, pp. 31–61.—Ed.]

[10] [Smith uses the term "invisible hand" only twice in his writings: once in *An Enquiry into the Nature and Causes of the Wealth of Nations*, book IV, chapter 2, paragraph 9; and once in Adam Smith, *The Theory of Moral Sentiments*, ed. D. D. Raphael and A. L. Macfie, vol. 1 of *The Glasgow*

game of catallaxy disregards human conceptions of what is due to each, and rewards according to success in playing the game under the same formal rules, that it produces a more efficient allocation of resources than any design could achieve. I feel that in any game that is played because it improves the prospects of all beyond those which we know how to provide by any other arrangements, the result must be accepted as fair, so long as all obey the same rules and no one cheats. If they accept their winnings from the game, it is cheating for individuals or groups to invoke the powers of government to divert the flow of good things in their favour—whatever we may do outside this game of the market to provide a decent minimum for those for whom the game did not supply it. It is not a valid objection to such a game, the outcome of which depends partly on skill and particular individual circumstances and partly on pure chance, that the initial prospects for different individuals, although they are all improved by playing that game, are very far from being the same. The answer to such an objection is precisely that one of the purposes of the game is to make the fullest possible use of the inevitably different skills, knowledge and environment of different individuals. Among the greatest assets which a society can use in this manner for increasing the pool from which the earnings of individuals are drawn, are the different moral, intellectual and material gifts parents can pass on to their children—and often will acquire, create or preserve only in order to be able to pass them on to their children.

VII

The result of this game of catallaxy, therefore, will necessarily be that many have much more than their fellows think they deserve, and even more will have much less than their fellows think they ought to have. It is not surprising that many people should wish to correct this by some authoritative act of redistribution. The trouble is that the aggregate product which they think is available for distribution exists only *because* returns for the different efforts are held out by the market with little regard to deserts or needs, and are needed to attract the owners of particular information, material means and personal skills to the points where at each moment they can make the greatest contribution. Those who prefer the quiet of an assured contractual income to the necessity of taking risks to exploit ever-changing opportunities feel at a disad-

---

Edition of the Works and Correspondence of Adam Smith (Oxford: Oxford University Press, 1976; reprinted, Indianapolis, IN: Liberty Fund, 1982), part IV, chapter 1, paragraph 10. For more on Hayek's views on Smith, see F. A. Hayek, "Adam Smith (1723–1790): His Message in Today's Language" [1976], reprinted as chapter 8 of F. A. Hayek, *The Trend of Economic Thinking: Essays on Political Economists and Economic History*, ed. W. W. Bartley III and S. Kresge, vol. 3 (1991) of *The Collected Works of F. A. Hayek.*—Ed.]

vantage compared with possessors of large incomes, which result from continual redisposition of resources.

High actual gains of the successful ones, whether this success is deserved or accidental, are an essential element for guiding resources to where they will make the largest contribution to the pool from which all draw their share. We should not have as much to share if *that* income of an individual were not treated as *just*, the prospects of which induced him to make the largest contribution to the pool. Incredibly high incomes may thus sometimes be just. What is more important, scope for achieving such incomes may be the necessary condition for the less enterprising, lucky, or clever to get the regular income on which they count.

The inequality, which so many people resent, however, has not only been the underlying condition for producing the relatively high incomes which most people in the West now enjoy. Some people seem to believe that a lowering of this general level of incomes—or at least a slowing down of its rate of increase—would not be too high a price for what they feel would be a juster distribution. But there is an even greater obstacle to such ambitions today. As a result of playing the game of catallaxy, which pays so little attention to justice but does so much to increase output, the population of the world has been able to increase so much, without the income of most people increasing very much, that we can maintain it, and the further increases in population which are irrevocably on the way, only if we make the fullest possible use of that game which elicits the highest contributions to productivity.

VIII

If people in general do not appreciate what they owe to catallaxy and how far they are even dependent on it for their very existence, and if they often bitterly resent what they regard as its injustice, this is so because they have never designed it and therefore do not understand it. The game rests on a method of providing benefits for others in which the individual will accomplish most if, within the conventional rules, he pursues solely his own interests—which need not be selfish in the ordinary sense of the word, but are in any case his own.[11]

The moral attitude which this order demands not only of the entrepreneur but of all those, curiously called 'self-employed', who have constantly to

---

[11] [Hayek discusses at length the idea that people are not narrowly selfish, and that economic theory need not assume them to be so, in F. A. Hayek, "Individualism: True and False" [1946], reprinted as the Prelude to F. A. Hayek, *Studies on the Abuse and Decline of Reason: Text and Documents*, ed. Bruce Caldwell, vol. 13 (2010) of *The Collected Works of F. A. Hayek*, pp. 57–60.—Ed.]

choose the directions of their efforts, if they are to confer the greatest benefit on their fellows, is that they compete honestly according to the rules of the game, guided only by the abstract signals of prices and giving no preferences because of their sympathies or views on the merits or needs of those with whom they deal. It would mean not merely a personal loss, but a failure in their duty to the public, to employ a less efficient instead of a more efficient person, to spare an incompetent competitor, or to favour particular users of their product.

The gradually spreading new liberal morals, which the Open or Great Society demanded, required above all that the same rules of conduct should apply to one's relation to all other members of society—except for natural ties to the members of one's family. This extension of old moral rules to wider circles, most people, and particularly the intellectuals, welcome as moral progress. But they apparently did not realise, and violently resented when they discovered it, that the equality of rules applicable to one's relationship to all other men necessarily implied not only that new obligations were extended to people who formerly had no such claims, but also that old obligations which were recognised to some people but could not be extended to all others had to disappear.

It was this unavoidable attenuation of the content of our obligations, which necessarily accompanied their extension, that people with strongly ingrained moral emotions resented. Yet these are kinds of obligations which are essential to the cohesion of the small group but which are irreconcilable with the order, the productivity, and the peace of a great society of free men. They are all those demands which under the name of 'social justice' assert a moral claim on government that it give us what it can take by force from those who in the game of catallaxy have been more successful than we have been. Such an artificial alteration of the relative attractiveness of the different directions of productive efforts can only be counter-productive.

If expected remunerations no longer tell people where their endeavours will make the greatest contribution to the total product, an efficient use of resources becomes impossible. Where the size of the social product, and no longer their contributions to it, gives individuals and groups a moral claim to a certain share of that product, the claims of what deserve really to be described as 'free riders' become an unbearable drag on the economy.

IX

I am told that there are still communities in Africa in which able young men, anxious to adopt modern commercial methods, find it impossible thereby to improve their position, because tribal customs demand that they share the products of their greater industry, skill or luck with all their kin. An increased income of such a man would merely mean that he had to share it with an ever-increasing number of claimants. He can, therefore, never rise substantially above the average level of his tribe.

The chief adverse effect of 'social justice' in our society is that it prevents individuals from achieving what they could achieve—through the means for further investment being taken from them. It is also the application of an incongruous principle to a civilisation whose productivity is high, *because* incomes are very unequally divided and thereby the use of scarce resources is directed and limited to where they bring the highest return. Thanks to this unequal distribution the poor get in a competitive market economy more than they would get in a centrally directed system.

All this is the outcome of the, as yet merely imperfect, victory of the obligatory abstract rule of individual conduct over the common particular end as the method of social co-ordination—the development which has made both the open society and individual freedom possible, but which the socialists now want to reverse. Socialists have the support of inherited instincts, while maintenance of the new wealth which creates the new ambitions requires an acquired discipline which the non-domesticated barbarians in our midst, who call themselves 'alienated', refuse to accept although they still claim all its benefits.

X

Let me, before I conclude, briefly meet an objection which is bound to be raised because it rests on a very widespread misunderstanding. My argument, that in a process of cultural selection we have built better than we understood, and that what we call our intelligence has been shaped concurrently with our institutions by a process of trial and error, is certain to be met by an outcry of 'social Darwinism'.[12] But such a cheap way of disposing of my argument by labelling it would rest on an error. It is true that during the latter part of the last century some social scientists, under the influence of Darwin, placed an excessive stress on the importance of natural selection of the most able individuals in free competition. I do not wish to underrate the importance of this, but it is not the main benefit we derive from competitive selection. This is the competitive selection of cultural institutions, for the discovery of which we did not need Darwin, but the growing understanding of which in fields like law and language rather helped Darwin to his biological theories.

[12] [For one such critique of Hayek, see J. Viner, "Hayek on Freedom and Coercion", *Southern Economic Journal*, vol. 27, 1961, pp. 230–36, in particular p. 235.—Ed.]

My problem is not genetic evolution of innate qualities, but cultural evolution through learning—which indeed leads sometimes to conflicts with near-animal natural instincts. Nevertheless, it is still true that civilisation grew not by the prevailing of that which man thought would be most successful, but by the growth of that which turned out to be so, and which, precisely because he did not understand it, led man beyond what he could ever have conceived.[13]

[13] [For Hayek's critique of 'social Darwinism', see F. A. Hayek, *The Constitution of Liberty*, ed. Ronald Hamowy, vol. 17 (2011) of *The Collected Works of F. A. Hayek*, pp. 116–18; Hayek, *Rules and Order*, pp. 22–24; and Hayek, *The Political Order of a Free People*, pp. 153–55. Hayek elaborates on his theory of cultural evolution via group selection in "Notes on the Evolution of Systems of Rules of Conduct". The development of Hayek's views on cultural evolution is discussed in detail in B. Caldwell, "The Emergence of Hayek's Ideas on Cultural Evolution", *Review of Austrian Economics*, vol. 13, 2000, pp. 5–22.—Ed.]

TWENTY-EIGHT

WHITHER DEMOCRACY?[1]

I

The concept of democracy has one meaning—I believe the true and original meaning—for which I hold it a high value well worth fighting for. Democracy has not proved to be a certain protection against tyranny and oppression, as once it was hoped. Nevertheless, as a convention which enables any majority to rid itself of a government it does not like, democracy is of inestimable value.

For this reason I am more and more disquieted by the growing loss of faith in democracy among thinking people.[2] This can no longer be overlooked. It is becoming serious just as—and perhaps partly because—the magic word democracy has become so all-powerful that all the inherited limitations on governmental power are breaking down before it. Sometimes it seems as if the sum of demands which are now everywhere advanced in the name of democracy have so alarmed even just and reasonable people that a serious reaction against democracy, as such, is a real danger. Yet it is not the basic conception of democracy, but additional connotations which have in the course of time been added to the original meaning of a particular kind of decision-making

---

[1] A lecture delivered to the Institute of Public Affairs, New South Wales, at Sydney, 8 October 1976. [The lecture was first published as chapter 10 of F. A. Hayek, *New Studies in Philosophy, Politics, Economics and the History of Ideas* (London and Henley: Routledge & Kegan Paul, 1978), which version is used here. It was subsequently reprinted with the same title as chapter 3 of F. A. Hayek, *Social Justice, Socialism & Democracy: 3 Australian Lectures by F. A. Hayek*, CIS Occasional Papers 2 (Turramura: The Centre for Independent Studies, 1979).—Ed].

[2] [Hayek lists several works expressing this lack of faith in F. A. Hayek, *The Political Order of a Free People*, vol. 3 (1979) of *Law, Legislation and Liberty* (Chicago: University of Chicago Press; London: Routledge, 1973–79), pp. 2, 177 n. 1. Other notable examples, in addition to those listed by Hayek, include S. Brittan, "The Economic Contradictions of Democracy", *British Journal of Political Science*, vol. 5, 1975, pp. 129–59; M. Crozier, S. Huntington and J. Watanuki, *The Crisis of Democracy: Report on the Governability of Democracies to the Trilateral Commission* (New York: New York University Press, 1975); and S. Huntington, "The Democratic Distemper", *The Public Interest*, vol. 41, 1975, pp. 9–38.—Ed.]

procedure, which now endanger the belief in a democracy so enlarged in content. What is happening is indeed precisely that which some had apprehended concerning democracy in the nineteenth century.[3] A wholesome method of arriving at widely acceptable political decisions has become the pretext for enforcing substantially egalitarian aims.

The advent of democracy in the last century brought a decisive change in the range of governmental powers. For centuries efforts had been directed towards limiting the powers of government; and the gradual development of constitutions served no other purpose than this. Suddenly it was believed that the control of government by elected representatives of the majority made any other checks on the powers of government unnecessary, so that all the various constitutional safeguards which had been developed in the course of time could be dispensed with.

Thus arose unlimited democracy—and it is unlimited democracy, not just democracy, which is the problem of today. All democracy that we know today in the West is more or less unlimited democracy. It is important to remember that, if the peculiar institutions of the unlimited democracy we have today should ultimately prove a failure, this need not mean that democracy itself was a mistake, but only that we tried it in the wrong way. While personally I believe that democratic decision on all issues on which there is general agreement that some government action is necessary is an indispensable method of peaceful change, I also feel that a form of government in which any temporary majority can decide that any matter it likes should be regarded as 'common affairs' subject to its control is an abomination.

II

The greatest and most important limitation upon the powers of democracy, which was swept away by the rise of an omnipotent representative assembly, was the principle of the 'separation of powers'. We shall see that the root of the trouble is that so-called 'legislatures', which the early theorists of representative government (and particularly John Locke) conceived to be limited to making laws in a very specific narrow sense of that word, have become omnipotent governmental bodies. The old ideal of the 'Rule of Law', or of 'Government under the Law', has thereby been destroyed. The 'sovereign'

[3] [Hayek alludes here to Alexis de Tocqueville's *Democracy in America*, 2 vols., trans. H. Reeve (New York: George Dearborn & Co, 1835 and 1840), and to John Stuart Mill's *Considerations on Representative Government* [1861], reprinted in J. S. Mill, *Essays on Politics and Society*, part 2, vol. 19 (1977) of the *Collected Works of John Stuart Mill*, ed. J. M. Robson (Toronto: Toronto University Press; reprinted, Indianapolis: Liberty Fund, 2006).—Ed.]

Parliament can do whatever the representatives of the majority find expedient to do in order to retain majority support.[4]

But to call 'law' everything that the elected representatives of the majority resolve, and to describe as 'Government under the Law' all the directives issued by them—however discriminating in favour of, or to the detriment of, some groups of individuals—is a very bad joke. It is in truth lawless government. It is a mere play on words to maintain that, so long as a majority approves of acts of government, the rule of law is preserved. The rule of law was regarded as a safeguard of individual freedom, because it meant that coercion was permissible only to enforce obedience to general rules of individual conduct equally applicable to all, in an unknown number of future instances. Arbitrary oppression—that is coercion undefined by any rule by the representatives of the majority—is no better than arbitrary action by any other ruler. Whether it requires that some hated person should be boiled and quartered, or that his property should be taken from him, comes in this respect to the same thing. Although there is good reason for preferring limited democratic government to a non-democratic one, I must confess to preferring non-democratic government under the law to unlimited (and therefore essentially lawless) democratic government. Government under the law seems to me to be the higher value, which it was once hoped that democratic watchdogs would preserve.

I believe indeed that the suggestion of a reform, to which my critique of the present institutions of democracy will lead, would result in a truer realisation of the common *opinion* of the majority of citizens than the present arrangements for the gratification of the *will* of the separate interest groups which add up to a majority.[5]

It is not suggested that the democratic claim of the elected representatives of the people to have a decisive word in the direction of government is any less strong than their claim to determine what the law shall be. The great

---

[4] [Hayek's account of how the assumption by the same representative assembly both of the task of 'legislation' (that is, of establishing universally-binding rules of just conduct), and also of 'government' (involving the power to direct resources for particular purposes, associated with the satisfaction of common needs the market was thought unlikely to meet), has led to the gradual erosion of constitutional restraints on government activity, and a concomitant decline of individual freedom, can be found in Hayek, *The Political Order of a Free People*, pp. 1–40, 98–107. Also see F. A. Hayek, "The Constitution of a Liberal State" [1967], reprinted as chapter 22 of the present volume, and Hayek, *Rules and Order*, vol. 1 (1973) of *Law, Legislation and Liberty*, pp. 89–91, 124–44.—Ed.]

[5] [Hayek outlines the concepts of 'will' and 'opinion' in more detail in F. A. Hayek, "The Confusion of Language in Political Thought" [1968], reprinted as chapter 23 of the current volume, pp. 311–17, and in F. A. Hayek, *The Mirage of Social Justice*, vol. 2 (1976) of *Law, Legislation and Liberty*, pp. 12–14.—Ed.]

tragedy of the historical development is that these two distinct powers were placed in the hands of one and the same assembly, and that government consequently ceased to be subject to law. The triumphant claim of the British Parliament to have become sovereign, and so able to govern subject to no law, may prove to have been the death-knell of both individual freedom and democracy.

III

This development may have been historically unavoidable. Certainly, it is not logically cogent. It is not difficult to imagine how development could have taken place along different lines. When in the eighteenth century the House of Commons successfully claimed exclusive power over the public purse, in effect it thereby gained exclusive control of government. If at this time the House of Lords had been in a position to concede this only on condition that the development of *the* law (that is, the private and criminal law which limits the powers of all government) should be exclusively *its* concern—a development not unnatural with the House of Lords being the highest court of law—such a division between a governmental and a legislative assembly might have been achieved and a restraint of government by law preserved. Politically, however, it was impossible to confer such legislative power on the representatives of a privileged class.

Prevailing forms of democracy, in which the sovereign representative assembly at one and the same time makes law and directs government, owe their authority to a delusion. This is the pious belief that such a democratic government will carry out the will of the people. It may be true of democratically elected legislatures in the strict sense of makers of law, in the original sense of the term. That is, it may be true of elected assemblies whose power is limited to laying down universal rules of just conduct, designed to delimit against each other the domains of control over individuals, and intended to apply to an unknown number of future instances. About such rules governing individual conduct, which prevent conflicts most people may find themselves in at either end, a community is likely to form a predominant *opinion,* and agreement is likely to exist among the representatives of a majority. An assembly with such a definite limited task is therefore likely to reflect the *opinion* of the majority—and, being concerned only with general rules, has little occasion to reflect the *will* of particular interests on specific matters.[6]

[6] [Hayek deploys the concepts of 'will' and 'opinion' in order to criticise the "pernicious principle of parliamentary sovereignty" in *The Political Order of a Free People*, pp. 3–5, 33–35, and in *Rules and Order*, pp. 91–93.—Ed.]

But the giving of *laws* in this classic sense of the word is the least part of the tasks of the assemblies which we still call 'legislatures'. Their main concern is government. For "lawyers' law", as an acute observer of the British Parliament wrote more than seventy years ago, "Parliament has neither time nor taste".[7] So much indeed are activities, character and procedures of representative assemblies everywhere determined by their governmental tasks that their name 'legislature' no longer derives from their making laws. The relation has rather been reversed. We now call practically every resolution of these assemblies laws, solely because they derive from a legislature—however little they may have that character of a commitment to a general rule of just conduct, to the enforcement of which the coercive powers of government were supposed to be limited in a free society.

IV

But as every resolution of this sovereign governmental authority has 'the force of law', its governmental actions are also not limited by law. Nor can they, and this is even more serious, still claim to be authorised by the opinion of a majority of the people. In fact, grounds for supporting members of an omnipotent majority are wholly different from those for supporting a majority on which the actions of a true legislature rest. Voting for a limited legislator is choosing between alternative ways of securing an overall order resulting from the decisions of free individuals. Voting for a member of a body with power to confer special benefits, without being itself bound by general rules, is something entirely different. In such a democratically elected assembly with unlimited power to confer special benefits and impose special burdens on particular groups, a majority can be formed only by buying the support of numerous special interests, through granting them such benefits at the expense of a minority.

It is easy to threaten to withhold support even of general laws one approves of unless one's votes are paid for by special concessions to one's group. In an omnipotent assembly, decisions therefore rest on a sanctioned process of blackmail and corruption. This has long been a recognised part of the system, from which even the best cannot escape.

Such decisions on favours for particular groups have little to do with any agreement by the majority about the substance of governmental action, since in most respects the members of the majority will know little more than that

---

[7] [The words are those of sometime Clerk of the House of Commons and Parliamentary Counsel to the Treasury Sir Courtenay Ilbert (1841–1924). They can be found on p. 213 of his *Legislative Methods and Forms* (Oxford: Clarendon Press, 1901).—Ed.]

they have conferred on some agency ill-defined powers to achieve some ill-defined objective. With regard to most measures, the majority of voters will have no reason to be for or against them, except that they know that in return for supporting those who advocate them, they are promised the satisfaction of some wishes of their own. It is the result of this bargaining process which is dignified as the 'will of the majority'.

What we call 'legislatures' are in fact bodies continually deciding on particular measures, and are authorising coercion for their execution, on which no genuine agreement among a majority exists, but for which the support of a majority has been obtained by *deals*. In an omnipotent assembly which is concerned mainly with particulars and not with principles, majorities are therefore not based on agreement of opinions, but are formed by aggregations of special interests mutually assisting each other.

The apparently paradoxical fact is that a nominally all-powerful assembly—whose authority is not limited to, or rests on its committing itself to, general rules—is necessarily exceedingly weak and wholly dependent on the support of those splinter groups which are bound to hold out for gifts which are at the government's command. The picture of the majority of such an assembly united by common moral convictions evaluating the merits of the claims of particular groups is of course a fantasy. It is a majority only because it has pledged itself not to a principle but to satisfying particular claims. The sovereign assembly is anything but sovereign in the use of its unlimited powers. It is rather quaint that the fact that 'all modern democracies' have found this or that necessary is sometimes quoted as proof of the desirability or equity of some measure. Most members of the majority often knew that a measure was stupid and unfair, but they had to consent to it, in order to remain members of a majority.

V

An unlimited legislature which is not prevented by convention or constitutional provisions from decreeing aimed and discriminatory measures of coercion, such as tariffs or taxes or subsidies, cannot avoid acting in such an unprincipled manner. Although attempts are inevitably made to disguise this purchase of support as beneficial assistance to the deserving, the moral pretence can hardly be taken seriously. Agreement of a majority on how to distribute the spoils it can extort from a dissenting minority can hardly claim any moral sanction for its proceedings—even if it invokes the figment of 'social justice' to defend it. What happens is that *political necessity created by the existing institutional set-up produces non-viable or even destructive moral beliefs.*

Agreement by the majority on sharing the booty gained by overwhelming a minority of fellow citizens, or deciding how much is to be taken from them, is not democracy. At least it is not that ideal of democracy which has any moral justification. Democracy itself is not egalitarianism. But unlimited democracy is bound to become egalitarian.

With regard to the fundamental immorality of all egalitarianism I will here point only to the fact that all our morals rest on the different esteem in which we hold people according to the manner in which they conduct themselves. While equality before the law—the treatment of all by government according to the same rules—appears to me to be an essential condition of individual freedom, that different treatment which is necessary in order to place people who are individually very different into the same material position seems to me not only incompatible with personal freedom, but highly immoral. But this is the kind of immorality towards which unlimited democracy is moving.

To repeat, it is not democracy but unlimited democracy which I regard as no better than any other unlimited government. The fatal error which gave the elected representative assembly unlimited powers is the superstition that a supreme authority must in its very nature be unlimited, because any limitation would presuppose another will above it, in which case it would not be a supreme power. But this is a misunderstanding deriving from the totalitarian-positivist conceptions of Francis Bacon and Thomas Hobbes, or the constructivism of Cartesian Rationalism, which fortunately in the Anglo-Saxon world was at least for a long time held back by the deeper understanding of Sir Edward Coke, Matthew Hale, John Locke and the Old Whigs.[8]

[8] [Hayek draws here on his oft-made distinction between the British or evolutionary and the Continental or constructivist rationalist traditions of social, legal, and political thought. Constructivist rationalism is the idea that all useful institutions are, and should be, the deliberate creation of conscious reason. Hayek contends that the modern influence of this tradition stems from the writings of French philosopher René Descartes (1596–1650); English philosopher, and sometime Lord Chancellor of England, Francis Bacon (1561–1626); English philosopher, social contract theorist, and legal positivist Thomas Hobbes (1588–1679); and philosopher James Mill (1773–1836). It is exemplified by Hobbes's view of human institutions as being invented by an antecedently-existing human reason via a social contract. In stark contrast, the evolutionary tradition suggests that many of the institutions essential for human civilization developed spontaneously (that is, as the unintended result of the separate actions of many people, without the overall guidance of a directing mind). On this view, the origin of many important institutions lies, not in conscious design, but in the survival of those institutions which proved most successful in supporting human society. The fact that, taken together, people's individual, freely-chosen actions can produce outcomes superior to those attainable through conscious direction implies for Hayek the importance of individual liberty.

In the main text, Hayek mentions or alludes to several thinkers in the evolutionary tradition. The English philosopher John Locke (1632–1704) argued in *Two Treatises of Government* (London: Awnsham Churchill, 1690) that legitimate governments are those that are established with the consent of the people and that act under the rule of law (that is, under laws that are general, certain, and applied by an independent judiciary). Locke contended that such laws, by establishing a sphere in which people can act independent of the arbitrary will of others, create—rather than inhibit—freedom: "[F]reedom of men under government is, to have a standing rule to live by, common to every one of that society, and made by the legislative power erected in it; a liberty to follow my own will in all things, where the rule prescribes not; and not to be subject to the inconstant, uncertain, unknown, arbitrary will of another man". See Locke, *Two Treatises*, bk. 2, chap. IV, sec. 22.

English lawyer, judge, and politician Sir Edward Coke (1552–1634) was a professional rival of Francis Bacon and, according to Hayek, "the great fountain of Whig principles". See F. A. Hayek, *The Constitution of Liberty*, ed. Ronald Hamowy, vol. 17 (2011) of *The Collected Works of F. A. Hayek* (Chicago: University of Chicago Press; London: Routledge), p. 248. Coke was a champion of the common law, arguing that judges find law rather than create it *ex nihilo*, and that the law embodies an 'artificial reason', reflecting the accumulated and refined wisdom of many generations, which no individual mind can match. He also contributed significantly to the creation of the modern notion of the rule of law, contending, for example, that laws apply only prospectively, not retrospectively. Coke's actions as a statesman and decisions as a judge helped to establish the independence of the law in England from the power of the crown and state, thereby helping to safeguard the freedom of individual citizens against abuses of power by the monarch or Parliament. His ruling in *Bonham's case* (1610) that judges can strike down unjust statutes laid the foundations for the judicial review of legislation and is commonly regarded as a forerunner of *Marbury v. Madison* (1803), which asserted the U.S. Supreme Court's right to invalidate federal laws that are in conflict with the Constitution. See Sir Edward Coke, *The Selected Writings and Speeches of Sir Edward Coke*, ed. S. Sheppard (Indianapolis: Liberty Fund, 2003). For more on Hayek's views on Coke, especially in comparison to Bacon, see F. A. Hayek, "Francis Bacon: Progenitor of Scientism (1561–1626)" [1960], reprinted as chapter 5 of *The Trend of Economic Thinking: Essays on Political Economists and Economic History*, ed. W. W. Bartley III and S. Kresge, vol. 3 (1991) of *The Collected Works of F. A. Hayek*.

The work of judge, politician, and writer Sir Matthew Hale (1609–76) was also rooted in the jurisprudence of the common law and, in particular, in the idea that the law is the outcome of an ongoing process whereby society adapts to new legal problems as they emerge over time. In his "Reflections by the Lrd. Cheife Justice Hale on Mr. Hobbes his Dialogue of the Lawe", reprinted as an appendix to W. Holdsworth, *A History of English Law*, vol. 5 (London: Macmillan, 1924), Hale defended Coke's views about the importance of legal custom and precedent as the repository of greater wisdom than any one man can possess against Hobbes's claim that the law should be based on abstract reason and deduction from first principles. Hale also contended, contra Hobbes's belief that law was created by the unbridled will of the sovereign, that the law should prevent all arbitrary exercises of power, including those of the monarch.

The "Old Whigs" to whom Hayek refers include the Irish statesman and political philosopher Edmund Burke (1729–97), who in his *Reflections on the Revolution in France* (London: J. Dodsley, 1790) argued in favour of appeals to tradition and past practice rather than to abstract principles when discussing constitutional matters, and who, in his "Speech on the Motion Made in the House of Commons, 7th of February, 1771, Relative to the Middlesex Election", in *The Works of the Right Honourable Edmund Burke*, vol. 7 (London: John C. Nimmo, 1887), emphasised that the scope of legitimate parliamentary action "ought to be defined by the fixed rule of law, what Lord Coke calls the golden metwand of the law, and not by the crooked cord of discretion" (pp. 66–67); the Scottish philosopher David Hume (1711–76), one of the central themes in whose work was the evolution of England from a government of will to a government of law; theologian and moralist William Paley (1743–1805), whose *Principles of Moral and Political Philosophy* [1785] (Indianapolis: Liberty Fund, 2002) Hayek regarded as providing the first complete statement of the doctrine of the rule of law; English politician, essayist, and historian Thomas Babington Macaulay (1800–1859), Baron Macaulay of Rothley, whose *History of England from the Accession of James II*, 5 vols. (London: Longman, Brown, Green & Longmans, 1849–61), celebrated the rise of constitutionally-protected individual liberty after the Glorious Revolution of 1688; English

In this respect the ancients were indeed often wiser than modern constructivistic thinking. A highest power need not be an unlimited power but may
owe its authority to its commitment to general rules approved by public opinion. The judge-king of early times was not selected in order that whatever he
said was to be right, but because, and so long as, what he pronounced was
generally felt to be right. He was not the source but merely the interpreter
of a law which rested on a diffused opinion, but which could lead to action
only if articulated by the approved authority. And if the supreme authority alone could order action, it extended only so far as it had the support of
the general assent to the principles on which it acted. The only and highest
authority entitled to take decisions on common action might well be a limited
authority—limited to decisions by which it committed itself to a general rule
of which public opinion approved.

The secret of decent government is precisely that the supreme power must
be limited power—a power that can lay down rules limiting all other power—
and which thus can restrain but not command the private citizen. All other
authority rests thus on its commitment to rules which its subjects recognise:
what makes a community is the common recognition of the same rules.

Thus the elected supreme body need not have any other power than that of
making laws in the classical sense of general rules guiding individual conduct.
Nor need there be any power of coercing private citizens other than that of
enforcing obedience to the rules of conduct thus laid down. Other branches
of government, including an elected governmental assembly, should be bound
and limited by the laws of the assembly confined to true legislation. These are
the requirements that would secure genuine government under the law.

VI

Solution of the problem, as I have already suggested, seems to be to divide the
truly legislative from the governmental tasks between distinct legislative and

---

historian and politician John Emerich Edward Dalberg-Acton, First Baron Acton (1834–1902),
whose writings on the 'history of liberty' emphasised, amongst other things, the need for constitutional restraints on the power of democratic majorities to impose their will on minorities; and
French historian and political scientist Alexis Charles Henri Clérel de Tocqueville (1805–59),
whose concerns about the potential for democracy to unleash a new kind of despotism ('the tyranny of the majority') led him to argue for the introduction of constitutional bulwarks against
the abuse of majority power, including judicial review of decisions made by the state.

Hayek elaborates on these points in more detail in *The Constitution of Liberty*, pp. 107–32, 232–
36, 246–60. Also see the discussion of these and related issues in F. A. Hayek, "The Results of
Human Action but Not of Human Design" [1967], and in F. A. Hayek, "The Errors of Constructivism" [1970], reprinted as chapters 11 and 14 respectively of F. A. Hayek, *The Market and
Other Orders*, ed. Bruce Caldwell, vol. 15 (2014) of *The Collected Works of F. A. Hayek.—*Ed.]

governmental assemblies. Naturally, little would be gained by merely having two such assemblies of essentially the present character, and merely charged with different tasks. Not only would two assemblies of essentially the same composition inevitably act in collusion, and thereby produce much the same sort of results as the existing assemblies. The character, procedures and composition of these have also been determined so completely by their predominant governmental tasks as to make them little suited for legislation proper.

Nothing is more illuminating in this respect than that the eighteenth-century theorists of representative government almost unanimously condemned an organisation of what they conceived as the legislature on party lines. They usually spoke of 'factions'.[9] But their predominant concern with governmental matters made their organisation on party lines universally necessary. A government, to perform its tasks successfully, needs the support of an organised majority committed to a programme of action. And to give the people an option, there must be a similarly organised opposition capable of forming an alternative government.

For their strictly governmental functions, existing 'legislatures' appear to have become fairly well adapted and might well be allowed to continue in their present form, if their power over the private citizen were limited by a law laid down by another democratic assembly, which the former could not alter. It would, in effect, administer the material and personal resources placed at the disposal of government to enable it to render various services to the citizens at large. It might also determine the aggregate amount of revenue to be raised from the citizens each year to finance those services. But the determination of the share each citizen would be compelled to contribute to this total would have to be made by a true law; that is, the sort of obligatory and uniform rule of individual conduct which only the legislative assembly could lay down. It is difficult to conceive of a more salutary control of expenditure than such a system in which every member of the governmental assembly would know that to every expenditure he supported he and his constituents would have to contribute at a rate he could not alter!

The critical issue then becomes the composition of the legislative assembly. How can we at the same time make it truly representative of general opinion about what is right, and yet make it immune from any pressure of special

---

[9] [Hayek refers here to thinkers such as James Madison (1751–1836), one of the founders of modern representative government and the fourth President of the United States, who in *Federalist* No. 10 wrote of the danger posed to the public good by the involvement of rival factions or political parties in the legislative process. Madison argues in *Federalist* No. 51 that the baleful effects of factions may be ameliorated by a separation of powers between the executive, legislative, and judicial arms of government, each of which would act as a check upon the others. See A. Hamilton, J. Jay and J. Madison, *The Federalist*, ed. G. Carey and J. McClellan (Washington: J. Gideon, 1818; reprinted, Indianapolis, IN: Liberty Fund, 2001).—Ed.]

interests? The legislative assembly constitutionally would be limited to passing general laws, so that any specific or discriminating order it issued would be invalid. It would owe its authority to its commitment to general rules. The constitution would define the properties such a rule must possess to be valid law, such as applicability to an unknown number of future instances, uniformity, generality, and so on. A constitutional court would gradually have to elaborate that definition as well as decide any conflict of competence between the two assemblies.[10]

But this limitation to passing genuine laws would hardly suffice to prevent collusion of the legislative with a similarly composed governmental assembly, for which it would be likely to provide the laws which that assembly needed for its particular purposes, with results little different from those of the present system. What we want in the legislative assembly is clearly a body representing general opinion, and not particular interests; and it should therefore be composed of individuals who, once entrusted with this task, are independent from the support of any particular group. It should also consist of men and women who could take a long-term view, and would not be swayed by the temporary passions and fashions of a fickle multitude which they had to please.

VII

This would seem to require, in the first instance, independence of parties, and this could be secured by the second, independently necessary condition—namely, not being influenced by the desire for re-election. I imagine for this reason a body of men and women who, after having gained reputation and trust in the ordinary pursuits of life, were elected for a single long period of something like 15 years. To assure that they had gained sufficient experience and respect, and that they did not have to be concerned about securing a livelihood for the period after the end of their tenure, I would fix the age of election comparatively high, say at 45 years, and assure them for another 10 years after expiry of their mandate at 60 of some dignified posts as lay-judges or the like. The average age of the member of such an assembly would, at less than 53 years, still be lower than that of most comparable assemblies today.

The assembly would of course not be elected as a whole at one date, but every year those who had served their 15 years' period would be replaced by 45-year-olds. I would favour these annual elections of one-fifteenth of the membership to be made by their contemporaries, so that every citizen

---

[10] [For more on what follows, in this section and the next, see Hayek, *The Political Order of a Free People*, pp. 107–27, and F. A. Hayek, "Economic Freedom and Representative Government" [1973], reprinted as chapter 24 of this volume.—Ed.]

would vote only once in his life, in his forty-fifth year, for one of his contemporaries to become a legislator. This seems to me desirable not only because of old experience in military and similar organisations that contemporaries are usually the best judges of a man's character and abilities, but also because it would probably become the occasion of the growth of such institutions as local age clubs which would make elections on the basis of personal knowledge possible.

Since there would be no parties, there would of course be no nonsense about proportional representation. Contemporaries of a region would confer the distinction as a sort of prize for the most admired member of the class. There are many other fascinating questions which an arrangement of this sort raises, such as whether for this purpose some sort of indirect election might not be preferable (with the local clubs vying for the honour of one of their delegates being elected representative), but which it would not be appropriate to consider in an exposition of the general principle.

VIII

I do not think experienced politicians will find my description of the procedure in our present legislatures very wrong, though they will probably regard as inevitable and beneficial what to me seems avoidable and harmful. But they ought not to be offended by hearing it described as institutionalised blackmail and corruption, because it is we who maintain institutions which make it necessary for them thus to act if they are to be able to do any good.

To a certain extent the bargaining I have described is probably in fact inevitable in democratic *government*.

What I object to is that the prevailing institutions carry this into that supreme body which ought to make the rules of the game and restrain government. The misfortune is not that those kinds of things happen—in local administration they can probably not be avoided—but that they happen in that supreme body that has to make our laws, which are supposed to protect us against oppression and arbitrariness.

One further important and very desirable effect of separating the legislative from the governmental power would be that it would eliminate the chief cause of the accelerating centralisation and concentration of power. This is today the result of the fact that, as a consequence of the fusion of the legislative and the governmental power in the same assembly, it possesses powers which in a free society no authority should possess. Of course, more and more governmental tasks are pushed up to that body which can meet particular demands by making special laws for the purpose. If the powers of the central government were no greater than those of the regional or local governments, only those matters where a uniform national regulation would seem advantageous to all would be handled by the central government, and much that is now so handled would be devolved to lower units.

Once it is generally recognised that government under the law and unlimited powers of the representatives of the majority are irreconcilable, and all government is equally placed under the law, little more than external relations need to be entrusted to central *government*—as distinct from legislation— and the regional and local governments, limited by the same uniform laws with regard to the manner in which they could make their individual inhabitants contribute to their revenue, would develop into business-like corporations competing with each other for citizens who could vote with their feet for that corporation which offered them the highest benefits compared with the price charged.[11]

In this manner we may still be able to preserve democracy and at the same time stop the drift towards what has been called 'totalitarian democracy', which to many people already appears irresistible.[12]

---

[11] [The classic economic analysis of this issue is C. Tiebout, "A Pure Theory of Local Expenditures", *Journal of Political Economy*, vol. 64, 1956, pp. 416–25.—Ed.]

[12] [Hayek refers to the work of political scientist and historian Jacob Talmon (1916–80), in particular *The Origins of Totalitarian Democracy* (London: Secker and Warburg, 1952).—Ed.]

TWENTY-NINE

SOCIALISM AND SCIENCE[1]

I

Socialism is related to Science in various ways. Probably the least interesting relation today is that from which Marxism lays claim to the name of 'scientific socialism', and according to which by an inner necessity, and without men doing anything about it, capitalism develops into socialism. This may still impress some novices, but it is hardly any longer taken seriously by competent thinkers in either camp. Socialists certainly do not act as if they believed that the transition from capitalism to socialism will be brought about by an ineluctable law of social evolution. Few people now believe in the existence of any 'historical laws'.

Experience has certainly refuted the predictions Marx made concerning the particular developments of capitalism.

There is, secondly, the undeniable propensity of minds trained in the physical sciences, as well as of engineers, to prefer a deliberately created orderly arrangement to the results of spontaneous growth—an influential and common attitude, which frequently attracts intellectuals to socialist schemes. This is a widespread and important phenomenon which has had a profound effect on the development of political thought. However, I have already on several occasions discussed the significance of these attitudes, calling them 'scientism' and 'constructivism' respectively, so that it is unnecessary to revert to these questions.[2]

[1] A lecture delivered on 19 October 1976 to the Canberra Branch of the Economic Society of Australia and New Zealand. [The lecture was first published as "Socialism and Science", *Institute of Public Affairs Review,* vol. 30, 1976, pp. 87–96. It was republished with minor stylistic changes as chapter 20 of F. A. Hayek, *New Studies in Philosophy, Politics, Economics and the History of Ideas* (London and Henley: Routledge & Kegan Paul, 1978), the version used here, and then as chapter 2 of F. A. Hayek, *Social Justice, Socialism & Democracy: 3 Australian Lectures by F. A. Hayek,* CIS Occasional Papers 2 (Turramura: Centre for Independent Studies, 1979).—Ed].

[2] [Hayek's account of the nature, origins, and shortcomings of 'scientism'—that is, the slavish and inappropriate imitation by those investigating the social world of the methods and language of the natural sciences—can be found in F. A. Hayek, *Studies on the Abuse and Decline of Reason: Text and Documents,* ed. Bruce Caldwell, vol. 13 (2010) of *The Collected Works of F. A. Hayek* (Chicago:

II

What I want to examine today is rather the peculiar manner in which most socialists attempt to shield their doctrines against scientific criticism, by claiming that differences from opponents are of a nature which precludes scientific refutation. Indeed, they frequently succeed in conveying the impression that any use of science to criticise socialist proposals is *ipso facto* proof of political prejudice, because the differences are wholly based on different value judgments, which the rules of scientific procedure prohibit, so that it is even indecent to introduce them into scientific discussions.

Two experiences have long made me impatient with these contentions. One is that not only I, but I believe also the majority of my contemporary libertarian fellow-economists, were originally led to economics by the more or less strong socialist beliefs—or at least dissatisfaction with existing society—which we felt in our youth, and the study of economics turned us into radical anti-socialists. The other experience is that my concrete differences with socialist fellow-economists on particular issues of social policy turn inevitably, not on differences of value, but on differences as to the effects particular measures will have.

It is true that in such discussions we frequently end up with differences about the probable magnitude of certain effects of the alternative policies. With regard to this both parties must often honestly admit that they have no conclusive proof. Probably I also ought to admit that my conviction that ordinary common sense clearly supports my position is often matched by an equally strong conviction of my opponents that ordinary common sense supports theirs.

III

Yet, when we survey the history of the results of the application of scientific analysis to socialist proposals, it seems abundantly clear that not only has it

University of Chicago Press; London: Routledge), pp. 75–304. As used by Hayek, the term 'constructivism' denotes the idea that all useful institutions are, and should be, the deliberate creation of conscious human reason. Hayek discusses the idea at length in "Kinds of Rationalism" [1965], "The Results of Human Action but Not of Human Design" [1967], and "The Errors of Constructivism" [1970], which are reprinted as the Prologue and chapters 11 and 14 respectively of F. A. Hayek, *The Market and Other Orders*, ed. Bruce Caldwell, vol. 15 (2014) of *The Collected Works of F. A. Hayek*. Hayek responded to the many natural scientists who in the 1930s advocated comprehensive central planning of the economy in F. A. Hayek, "Planning, Science, and Freedom" [1941], reprinted as chapter 10 of F. A. Hayek, *Socialism and War: Essays, Documents, Reviews*, ed. B. Caldwell, vol. 10 (1997) of *The Collected Works of F. A. Hayek.*—Ed.]

been shown that the methods advocated by socialists can never achieve what they promise, but also that the different values they hope or claim to serve cannot by *any* possible procedure be all realised at the same time, because they are mutually contradictory.

I will begin by considering the second of these questions which, in the present state of the discussion, appears to be the more interesting one—chiefly because it makes it necessary to clear up certain prevailing confusions concerning the inadmissibility of value judgments in scientific discussions. These are often used to represent scientific arguments against socialism as illegitimate or scientifically suspect. Such an examination raises important and interesting questions as to the possibility of the scientific treatment of moral beliefs, which have been unduly neglected. Economists, whose daily bread is the analysis of those conflicts of value which all economic activity has constantly to solve, have fought shy of frankly and systematically facing the task. It is as if they feared to soil their scientific purity by going beyond questions of cause and effect and *critically* evaluating the desirability of certain popular measures. They usually maintain that they can merely 'postulate' values without examining their validity. (So long as measures for the benefit of some supposedly 'underprivileged' groups are tacitly assumed to be good, such limitations are, however, usually forgotten.)[3]

It is indeed necessary in this connection to be very careful, and even pedantic, with regard to the expressions one chooses, because there exists a real danger of inadvertently slipping value judgments in an illegitimate manner into a scientific discussion, and also because those defending their socialist ideals are now mostly trained to use 'freedom from value judgments' as a sort of paradoxical defence mechanism for their creed, and are constantly on the look-out to catch their critics out in some incautious formulations. What play has not been made with occasional passages in the work of the greatest scientific critic of socialism, Ludwig von Mises, in which he described socialism as 'impossible'; Mises obviously meant that the proposed methods of socialism could not achieve what they were supposed to do![4] We can, of course, try any course of action, but what is questioned is whether any such course of action will produce the effects claimed to follow from it. This undoubtedly *is* a scientific question.[5]

---

[3] [Also see F. A. Hayek, "On Being an Economist" [1944], first published as chapter 2 of F. A. Hayek, *The Trend of Economic Thinking: Essays on Political Economists and Economic History*, ed. W. W. Bartley III and S. Kresge, vol. 3 (1991) of *The Collected Works of F. A. Hayek*, p. 44.—Ed.]

[4] [For more on this point, see F. A. Hayek, "The Present State of the Debate" [1935], reprinted as chapter 2 of *Socialism and War*, pp. 90–91.—Ed.]

[5] [Ludwig von Mises (1881–1973) was an Austrian economist who argued that rational economic calculation is impossible under socialism in the sense that, under that regime, there is no basis for the rational appraisal of alternative courses of action. The reason is that the com-

IV

So let me for a moment be pedantic and try to state precisely the kinds of value judgments which are admissible in a scientific discussion and the kinds that are not. Our starting point must be the logical truism that from premises containing *only* statements about cause and effect, we can derive no conclusions about what *ought* to be. No consequences whatever for action follow from such a statement, so long as we do not know (or agree) which consequences are desirable and which are undesirable. But once we include among our accepted premises *any* statement about the importance or harmfulness of different ends or consequences of action, all manner of different norms of action can be derived from it. Meaningful discussion about public affairs is clearly possible only with persons with whom we share at least some values. I doubt if we could even fully understand what someone says if we had no values whatever in common with him. This means, however, that in practically any discussion it will be in principle possible to show that some of the policies one person advocates are inconsistent or irreconcilable with some other beliefs he holds.

This brings me to a fundamental difference in the general attitudes to moral problems which seems to be characteristic of the now common political positions. The conservative is generally happy to cling to his belief in absolute values. While I envy him, I cannot share his beliefs.[6] It is the fate of the economist continually to encounter true conflicts of value; indeed, to analyse the manner in which such conflicts can be resolved is his professional task. The conflicts I have in mind here are not so much the obvious conflicts between the values held by different persons, or the gaps between their individual systems of values, but the conflicts and gaps within the system of values of any

_____

mon ownership of the means of production that is the hallmark of socialism precludes the existence of a market in which the prices of capital goods can be established. Consequently, people have no way of ascertaining the relative scarcity of different kinds of resource. They are therefore deprived of the information required to judge which of the many technically feasible projects they might pursue is in fact the most efficient way of achieving their goals, leaving them unable to act in a rational fashion. See L. von Mises, "Economic Calculation in the Socialist Commonwealth" [1920], in *Collectivist Economic Planning*, ed. F. A. Hayek (London: Routledge and Kegan Paul, 1935). Mises advances in that essay an immanent critique of socialism, of the kind described by Hayek in his 1933 inaugural lecture at the London School of Economics: "In criticising proposals for improvement, [economists] accepted the ethical postulates on which such proposals were based and tried to demonstrate that these were not conducive to the desired end and that, very often, policies of a radically different nature would bring about the desired result". See F. A. Hayek, "The Trend of Economic Thinking" [1933], reprinted as chapter 1 of Hayek, *The Trend of Economic Thinking*, p. 20.—Ed.]

[6] [For more on Hayek's views on conservatism, see F. A. Hayek, "Why I Am Not a Conservative" [1960], published as the Postscript to F. A. Hayek, *The Constitution of Liberty*, ed. Ronald Hamowy, vol. 17 (2011) of *The Collected Works of F. A. Hayek.*—Ed.]

one person. However much we dislike it, we are again and again forced to recognise that there are no truly absolute values whatever. Not even human life itself. This again and again we are prepared to sacrifice, and must sacrifice, for some other higher values, even if it be only one life to save a large number of other lives.

(I cannot here consider the interesting point that, though we may never feel entitled to sacrifice a particular known human life, we constantly take decisions which we know will cause the death of some unknown person.)

But the libertarians or true liberals—not those pink socialists who, as Josef Schumpeter said, "as a supreme but unintended compliment . . . have thought it wise to appropriate this label"—therefore do not fall into the opposite extreme of believing, like the socialists, that they can hedonistically construct some other new system of morals which they like, because they think that it will most increase human happiness, but who in fact merely hark back to the primitive instincts inherited from the tribal society.[7] Though the liberal must claim the right critically to examine every single value or moral rule of his society, he knows that he can and must do this while accepting as given for that purpose most of the other moral values of this society, and examine that about which he has doubts in terms of its compatibility with the rest of the dominant system of values.

Our moral task must indeed be a constant struggle to resolve moral conflict, or to fill gaps in our moral code—a responsibility we can discharge only if we learn to understand that order of peace and mutually adjusted efforts, which is the ultimate value that our moral conduct enhances. Our moral rules must be constantly tested against, and if necessary adjusted to, each other, in order to eliminate direct conflicts between the different rules, and also so as to make them serve the same functioning order of human actions.[8]

---

[7] [Having defined 'economic liberalism' as "the theory that the best way of promoting economic development and general welfare is to remove fetters from the private-enterprise economy and to leave it alone", Austrian economist and sociologist Joseph Alois Schumpeter (1883–1950) notes that "the term has acquired a different—in fact almost the opposite—meaning since about 1900 and especially since about 1930: as a supreme, if unintended, compliment, the enemies of the system of private enterprise have thought it wise to appropriate its label". See J. A. Schumpeter, *History of Economic Analysis* (London: Allen & Unwin, 1954), p. 394. For Hayek's views on the transformation of the meaning of the term 'liberalism', see F. A. Hayek, "Liberalism" [1978], reprinted as chapter 1 of the current volume. Hayek considers Schumpeter's own views on the possibility of socialism in particular in "Two Pages of Fiction" [1982], reprinted as chapter 30 of this volume, while he appraises Schumpeter's contributions more generally in F. A. Hayek, "Joseph Schumpeter (1883–1950)" [1980], reprinted as chapter 5 of F. A. Hayek, *The Fortunes of Liberalism: Essays on Austrian Economics and the Ideal of Freedom*, ed. Peter G. Klein, vol. 4 (1992) of *The Collected Works of F. A. Hayek.*—Ed.]

[8] [According to Hayek, the notion of justice, properly understood, requires people to act in accordance with a system of rules that underwrites an abstract "order of human actions" (that is, a pattern or structure of voluntary cooperation in which people's freely-chosen plans are

V

Moral tasks are individual tasks, and moral advance by some groups results from their members adopting rules which are more conducive to the preservation and welfare of the group.[9] Moral progress demands the possibility of individual experimentation; in particular, that within a limited framework of compulsory abstract rules the individual is free to use his own knowledge for his own purposes. The growth of what we call civilisation is due to this principle of a person's responsibility for his own actions and their consequences, and the freedom to pursue his own ends without having to obey the leader of the band to which he belongs. It is true that our moral beliefs are still somewhat schizophrenic, as I tried to show on an earlier occasion, divided between instincts inherited from the primitive band, and the rules of just conduct which have made the open society possible.[10] The morality of individual responsibility of the able adult for the welfare of himself and his family is still the basis for most moral judgments of action. Thus it is the indispensable framework for the peaceful working of any complex society.

Call it science or not, no objective analysis of those basic beliefs on which our existing morals rest, and without the acceptance of which any commu-

---

mutually coordinated and which therefore facilitates the successful pursuit of a myriad of concrete individual objectives). It is the maintenance of this abstract order, rather than the promotion of any particular concrete goal, that is the aim of the legal system (or, as Hayek also puts it, the value served by that system). Hayek argues moreover that under the common law, rules that conflict with one another, and which therefore lead people to devise incompatible plans, will gradually be eliminated through the efforts of judges to settle legal disputes. Hayek believes that, through this evolutionary process, the prevailing system of rules will gradually come to serve more effectively its goal of sustaining the abstract order of actions (i.e. of achieving justice, in his sense). See F. A. Hayek, *Rules and Order*, vol. 1 (1973) of *Law, Legislation and Liberty* (Chicago: University of Chicago Press; London: Routledge, 1973–79), pp. 85–89, 94–123, and F. A. Hayek, *The Mirage of Social Justice*, vol. 2 (1976) of *Law, Legislation and Liberty*, pp. 31–61. For an overview, see E. Mack, "Hayek on Justice and the Order of Actions", in *The Cambridge Companion to Hayek*, ed. E. Feser (Cambridge: Cambridge University Press, 2006).—Ed.]

[9] [Hayek's theory of cultural evolution via group selection is set out in Hayek, *The Constitution of Liberty*, pp. 73–99, 107–32; in F. A. Hayek, "Notes on the Evolution of Systems of Rules of Conduct" [1967], reprinted as chapter 10 of Hayek, *The Market and Other Orders*; and in F. A. Hayek, *The Political Order of a Free People*, vol. 3 (1979) of *Law, Legislation and Liberty*, pp. 155–63. For a summary, see pp. 1178–86 of P. A. Lewis, "Notions of Order and Process in Hayek: The Significance of Emergence", *Cambridge Journal of Economics*, vol. 39, 2015, pp. 1167–90.—Ed.]

[10] [Hayek explained the nature and significance of the distinction between those moral beliefs that reflect people's ingrained instincts and those that stem from people's commitment to abstract rules of just conduct of the kind that facilitate order in modern industrial economies earlier in his Australian lecture tour, in his R. C. Mills Memorial Lecture at the University of Sydney. See F. A. Hayek, "The Atavism of Social Justice" [1978], reprinted as chapter 27 of this volume. More extended treatments can be found in Hayek, *The Mirage of Social Justice*, pp. 133–52, and in Hayek, *The Political Order of a Free People*, pp. 159–69.—Ed.]

nication on moral issues becomes impossible—namely, recognition of the responsibility of the individual and of the general grounds on which we esteem the actions of others—can leave any doubt that they are irreconcilable with the socialist demand for a forcible redistribution of incomes by authority. Such an assignment of a particular share according to the views of some authority as to the merits or needs of the different persons is immoral; not simply because I say so, but because it is in conflict with certain basic moral values which those who advocate it also share. The mere fact that commonly accepted ethics have no generally recognised solutions to the conflicts of values which undeniably arise in this sphere is, of course, of the greatest significance for the political problems which arise here, and for the moral evaluation of the use of coercion in enforcing any particular solution.

VI

That collectivist economic planning, which used earlier to be thought to require the nationalisation of the means of 'production, distribution and exchange', leads inevitably to totalitarian tyranny has come to be fairly generally recognised in the West since I analysed the process in some detail in *The Road to Serfdom* more than 40 years ago.[11] I do not know if it was partly for this reason, or because socialists increasingly recognised the incurable economic inefficiency of central planning, about which I shall have to say a few words

---

[11] [See F. A. Hayek, *The Road to Serfdom: Text and Documents*, ed. B. Caldwell, vol. 2 (2007) of *The Collected Works of F. A. Hayek*, in particular pp. 91–170. It is far from clear that Hayek's claim that "collectivist economic planning . . . leads inevitably to totalitarian tyranny" either was at the time of writing of this paper, or currently is, "fairly generally recognised". On the contrary, this 'inevitability thesis', or 'slippery slope' argument as it is also known, was and remains the subject of considerable controversy. To take one notable example, American Nobel Prize-winning economist Paul Samuelson (1915–2009) wrote of *The Road to Serfdom* that, "For years libertarians have been challenged to explain what appears to most observers to be the greater political freedoms and tolerances that prevail in Scandinavia than in America . . . I was told that none of this would last, active government economic policy had to result in loss of civil liberties and personal freedoms . . . One still waits". See P. A. Samuelson, "Personal Freedoms and Economic Freedoms in the Mixed Economy", in *The Business Environment*, ed. E. F. Cheit (New York: Wiley, 1964), pp. 226–27.

Samuelson expressed similar views elsewhere. For example, see P. A. Samuelson, *Economics*, 10th edn. (New York: McGraw-Hill, 1976), pp. 868, 885–86, and p. 3 of P. A. Samuelson, "A Few Remembrances of Friedrich von Hayek (1899–1992)", *Journal of Economic Behavior and Organization*, vol. 69, 2009, pp. 1–4. Also see A. Farrant and E. McPhail, "Hayek, Samuelson, and the Logic of the Mixed Economy?", *Journal of Economic Behavior and Organization*, vol. 69, 2009, pp. 5–16, which contains an account of the correspondence between Hayek and Samuelson about the inevitability thesis.—Ed.]

later, or whether they simply discovered that redistribution through taxation and aimed financial benefits was an easier and quicker method of achieving their aims; but, in any event, socialist parties in the West have almost all for the time being abandoned the most obviously dangerous demands for a centrally planned economy. Left wing doctrinaires in some countries, and the communist parties, still press for it, and may of course sooner or later gain power. But the supposedly moderate leaders, who at present guide most of the socialist parties of the free world, claim—or have it claimed by the media on their behalf—that as good democrats they can be trusted to prevent any such developments.

But can they? I do not mean to question their good faith. Nevertheless, I greatly doubt their capacity to combine their aim of a thorough governmental redistribution of wealth with the preservation, in the long run, of a modicum of personal freedom, even if they succeed in preserving the forms of democracy. It is true that the substitution of cold socialism has much slowed down the process which I had predicted hot socialism would bring about. But can it lastingly avoid the same effects? There are strong reasons for doubting that cold socialism can avoid them.

Governments, to be successful, would at the same time have to preserve functioning markets, on which depends the possibility of competition so determining prices of all products and factors of production in such a way as to serve as reliable guides to production, *and* also somehow so to influence at least the prices of labour (obviously including those of the farmer and other 'self-employed') as to satisfy demands for just or equitable remuneration. To satisfy both of these requirements in full is impossible. Governments can aim at best at some kind of compromise, and refrain from many interventions in the market which would be necessary if they were even approximately to satisfy the most pressing demands. But governments bowing to the inevitabilities of the market, after commencing to manipulate the results of the market to favour some groups, would clearly be embarking on a political impossibility. Once claims for interference with the market in favour of particular groups have come to be frequently recognised, a democratic government cannot refuse to comply with similar demands of any groups on whose votes it depends. Though the process may be gradual, a government which begins to control prices to secure popular conceptions of justice is bound to be driven step by step towards the control of all prices; and, since this must destroy the functioning of the market, to a central direction of the economy. Even if governments try not to use such central planning as an instrument, if they persist in the endeavour to create a just distribution they will be driven to use central direction as the only instrument by which it is possible to determine the overall distribution of remunerations (without thereby making it just)—and thus be driven to establish an essentially totalitarian system.

VII

It took a long time to convince socialists that central planning is inefficient. Practical men were probably convinced not by argument but only by the warning example of the Russian system; contemporary theoreticians, however, retreated only slowly from the position laid down by the founders of Marxism and generally maintained by their leading theoreticians until 50 years ago. Somehow, however, they nevertheless managed, as they gave up successive positions and attempted new solutions of the problem, to convey the impression that they had victoriously beaten off the onslaughts of hostile critics.

The founders of socialism, including Marx and Engels, did not even understand that any central direction of the machinery of production owned by society required, if resources were to be effectively used, calculations in terms of value. As Friedrich Engels put it, the social plan of production "will be settled very simply without the intervention of the famous 'value'".[12] Even when discussion of the problem was seriously started, immediately after the First World War, it was caused by the social science expert among the Vienna school of logical positivists claiming that all calculations of the efficiency of social production could be carried out *in natura*—that is, without relying on any variable rates of conversion between the different physical units used. It was against this position that Ludwig von Mises and some of his contemporaries (including Max Weber) developed the first decisive critique of the socialist position.[13]

[12] [F. Engels, *Herr Eugen Dühring's Revolution in Science (Anti-Dühring)* [1877–78] (New York: International Publishers, 1935), p. 338. German philosopher Frederick Engels (1820–95) was Karl Marx's closest collaborator. *Anti-Dühring* was a polemic against the ideas of rival German socialist Eugen Karl Dühring (1833–1921). Commenting on how production would be planned under socialism, Engels wrote on the page in question that, "People will be able to manage everything very simply, without the intervention of the famous 'value'".—Ed.]

[13] [The "social science expert among the Vienna school of logical positivists" was Austrian philosopher, sociologist, and political economist Otto Neurath (1882–1945). Before the First World War, Neurath wrote articles on the subject of 'war economy'—that is, on how to run an economy under conditions of modern warfare—in which he argued that the continued use of a peacetime market economy would hinder the pursuit of military objectives and that a successful war effort required central control of the economy. Neurath later maintained that the wartime experience had demonstrated the feasibility of central planning, arguing moreover that considerations of justice demanded that such planning be put into practice. Neurath himself served as President of the Central Planning Office of the short-lived Bavarian Soviet Republic in 1919, the same year in which he published a collection of his articles. See O. Neurath, *Durch die Kriegswirtschaft zur Naturalwirtschaft* (Munich: Georg D. W. Callwey, 1919). According to Hayek, it was this collection that "provoked" Mises into developing his ideas about the difficulties of economic calculation under socialism. See F. A. Hayek, "Ludwig von Mises (1881–1973)", in Hayek, *The Fortunes of Liberalism*, p. 139. Translations of some of Neurath's papers on economics can be

The crucial point here—which, it must be admitted, even the leading classical economists down to John Stuart Mill did not understand—is the universal significance of changing rates of substitution between different commodities. This simple insight, which helped us at last to understand the role of differences and variability of the prices of different commodities, began slowly to develop with the recognition—I will not say the discovery, since of course every simple peasant knew the facts if not their theoretical significance—of decreasing returns from successive applications of labour and capital to land. It was next found to govern, under the name of decreasing marginal utility, the rates of marginal substitution between different consumers' goods. And it was finally discovered to be the universal relation prevailing between all useful resources, determining at once if they are economically the same or different, and if they are scarce or not. Only when it was understood that changing supplies of the different factors of production (or means of satisfaction) determines their variable marginal rate of substitution, was the indispensability of known rates of equivalence (or rates of marginal substitution) for any efficient calculation fully understood. Only when it was at last seen that through market prices this rate of equivalence in all their different uses, mostly known only to a few of the many persons who would like to use them, could be made equal to the rates at which any pair of commodities could be substituted in any of its countless uses, was the indispensable function of prices in a complex economy fully understood.[14]

Variable 'marginal rates of substitution' for different commodities, to which I have previously referred, naturally mean their temporary rates of equivalence determined by the situation at the moment, and at which these things must be substitutable at the margin in all their possible uses—if we are to get their full capacity out of them.

---

found in O. Neurath, *Empiricism and Sociology*, ed. M. Neurath and R. S. Cohen (Dordrecht: D. Reidel, 1973), especially chapter 5, and in O. Neurath, *Economic Writings: Selections 1904–1945*, ed. T. E. Uebel and R. S. Cohen (Dordrecht: Kluwer Academic Publishers, 2004). For more on Neurath, see B. Caldwell, "Introduction", in Hayek, *Socialism and War*, pp. 4–10.

German sociologist and political economist Max Weber (1864–1920) wrote extensively on the nature of capitalism, the methodology of the social sciences, and the sociology of religion. Weber's critique of Neurath's claim that the central planning bureau's calculations about what to produce, and how to produce it, need not be carried out in monetary terms but could rather be made simply in terms of the physical quantities of goods (i.e. *in natura*) can be found in M. Weber, *Economy and Society: An Outline of Interpretive Sociology*, ed. G. Roth and C. Wittich (Berkeley: University of California Press, 1968), vol. 1, pp. 100–13. Hayek considers Weber's work on socialism in more detail in F. A. Hayek, "The Nature and History of the Problem" [1935], reprinted as chapter 1 of Hayek, *Socialism and War*, pp. 74–76.—Ed.]

[14] [Hayek elaborates on the informational roles of prices in F. A. Hayek, "The Use of Knowledge in Society" [1945], and in F. A. Hayek, "Competition as a Discovery Procedure" [1968], reprinted as chapters 3 and 12 respectively of Hayek, *The Market and Other Orders*.—Ed.]

It was both the understanding of the function of changing rates of equivalence between physically defined objects as the basis of calculation, and the communication function of prices which combined into a single signal all the information on these circumstances dispersed among large numbers of people, which at last made it fully clear to every person who could follow the argument that rational calculation in a complex economy is possible only in terms of values or prices, and that these values will be adequate guides only if they are the joint efforts, such as the values formed on the market, of all the knowledge of potential suppliers or consumers about their possible uses and availability.

The first reaction of the socialist theoreticians, once they could no longer refuse to admit this fact, was to suggest that their socialist planning boards should determine prices by the same system of simultaneous equations by which mathematical economists had attempted to explain market prices in equilibrium. They even tried to suggest that Wieser, Pareto and Barone had long ago pointed out the possibility of this.[15] In fact, these three scholars had pointed out what a socialist planning board *would have to try to do* in order to equal the efficiency of the market—not, as the socialist theoreticians incorrectly suggested, how such an impossible result could be achieved. Pareto, in particular, had made clear that the system of simultaneous equations, development of which made him famous, was intended to show only the general pattern (as we would today express this), but could never be used to determine particular prices, because any central authority could never know all the cir-

---

[15] [Austrian economist Friedrich von Wieser (1851–1926), Italian economist and sociologist Vilfredo Pareto (1848–1923), and Italian economist Enrico Barone (1859–1924) argued that capitalism and socialism are formally similar to one another in the sense that both kinds of economy can be represented by the same system of simultaneous equations. See F. Wieser, *Natural Value*, ed. W. Smart, trans. C. Malloch (London and New York: Macmillan, 1893), pp. 60ff; V. Pareto, *Cours d'Economie Politique*, vol. 2 (Lausanne: Librairie de l'Université, 1897), pp. 364ff.; and E. Barone, "The Ministry of Production in the Collectivist State" [1908], reprinted as Appendix A of Hayek, *Collectivist Economic Planning*. The "socialist theoreticians" to whom Hayek refers include American economist Frederick M. Taylor (1855–1932) and English academic economist Henry Douglas Dickinson (1899–1969), who attempted to develop a practical method of planning on the basis of the formal similarity identified by Wieser, Pareto, and Barone. They did so by arguing that the planners could quite literally formulate the set of equations that described the economy and then solve them mathematically by means of a trial-and-error approach, thereby ultimately identifying the equilibrium allocation of resources. See F. M. Taylor, "The Guidance of Production in a Socialist State", *American Economic Review*, vol. 19, 1929, pp. 1–8, and H. D. Dickinson, "Price Formation in a Socialist Economy", *Economic Journal*, vol. 43, 1933, pp. 237–50. An early critique of these proposals can be found in Hayek, "The Present State of the Debate", pp. 93–97. For useful overviews of this first stage of the debate between Hayek and the supporters of socialist planning, see D. Lavoie, *Rivalry and Central Planning: The Socialist Calculation Debate Reconsidered* (Cambridge: Cambridge University Press, 1985), pp. 79–93, and Caldwell, "Introduction", in Hayek, *Socialism and War*, pp. 12–19.—Ed.]

cumstances of time and place which guide the actions of individuals, such actions being the information fed into the communication machine which we call the market.[16]

So the first attempt by the socialists to answer the critique by Mises and others soon collapsed. The next step, by which particularly Oskar Lange, but also others, are supposed to have refuted Mises, consisted of various attempts to reduce more or less the role of central planning and to re-introduce some market features under the name of 'socialist competition'. I will not dwell here on how great an intellectual reversal this meant for all those who for so long had emphasised the great superiority of central direction over the so-called 'chaos of competition'.[17] This self-contradictory approach raised new prob-

[16] [Pareto expresses his doubts about the possibility of planning on p. 171 of V. Pareto, *Manual of Political Economy*, trans. A. S. Schwier, ed. A. S. Schwier and A. N. Page (New York: Augustus M. Kelley, 1971). For details, see F. A. Hayek, "Two Pages of Fiction" [1982], reprinted as chapter 30 of this volume, pp. 452–53. Arguably, both Wieser and Barone were also sceptical about the ability of the planning authorities actually to solve the equations. See F. Wieser, *Social Economics*, trans. A. Ford Hinrichs (London: Allen and Unwin, 1927), pp. 396–97, and Barone, "The Ministry of Production in the Collectivist State", pp. 286–90.—Ed.]

[17] [The second stage of the socialist calculation debate was initiated by the publication in 1936 by Polish economist Oskar Lange (1904–65) of a classic article outlining the principles of so-called *market socialism*. Starting, like Dickinson and Taylor, from the formal similarity of the sets of equations used to describe capitalist and socialist economies, Lange argued that the planning authorities could identify the equilibrium allocation of resources, not by solving the equations mathematically themselves, but rather by using a trial-and-error process that mimicked the operation of the market. Under the scheme proposed by Lange, instead of prices being bid up and down via rivalrous market competition, the planners would announce 'accounting prices' specifying the terms on which goods were to be offered, on the basis of which the managers of publicly-owned firms would report back how much of each good they proposed to produce and how much of each input they intended to use. Having thus elicited information about the total demand for, and supply of, each good, the planners would increase or decrease 'prices' depending on whether there was excess demand for or supply of the good in question. In this way, Lange argued, the planner could use a trial-and-error process to find the equilibrium set of prices. See O. Lange, "On the Economic Theory of Socialism", *Review of Economic Studies*, vol. 4, no. 1, 1936, pp. 53–71, and vol. 4, no. 2, 1937, pp. 123–42.

Similar arguments were advanced by others, perhaps most notably Abba Lerner, Evan Durbin, and H. D. Dickinson. Abba P. Lerner (1903–82) was a Russian-born economist who studied at the London School of Economics. Lerner's contributions to the socialist calculation debate were made in a series of articles published in the 1930s and in his treatise on welfare economics published in 1944. See, for example, A. P. Lerner, "Economic Theory and Socialist Economy", *Review of Economic* Studies, vol. 2, 1934, pp. 51–61; A. P. Lerner, "Theory and Practice in Socialist Economics", *Review of Economic* Studies, vol. 6, 1938, pp. 71–5; and A. P. Lerner, *The Economics of Control: Principles of Welfare Economics* (New York: Macmillan Co., 1944). British academic economist and politician Evan Durbin (1906–48) was a colleague of Hayek's at the LSE, where he taught in the 1930s a course on democratic socialist planning that vied for students' attention with Hayek's own lectures on the problems of collectivist planning, and later a Labour Member of Parliament (1945–48). See E. Durbin, "Economic Calculus in a Planned Economy" [1936], reprinted in E. Durbin, *Problems of Economic Planning: Papers on Planning and*

lems of an altogether new kind. However, it could in no way overcome two crucial difficulties. First, the socialist authority could not, as long as all the industrial equipment and other capital belonged to 'society' (that is, the government), let competition or the market decide how much capital each enterprise was to have, or what risks the manager would be allowed to run—both decisive points if a market is to operate properly. Second, if the government were otherwise to let the market operate freely, it could do nothing to secure that the remuneration the market gave to each participant would correspond to what the government regarded as socially just. Yet to achieve such a so-called 'just' remuneration was, after all, the whole intended purpose of the socialist revolution!

VIII

The answers to the three questions we have been discussing do not depend on particular value judgments, except the answer to the first question, in which certain values (such as personal liberty and responsibility) were taken for granted. It can be assumed that such values would be shared by all persons with whom one cared to discuss such problems. The fundamental problem was always whether socialism could achieve what it promised. This is a purely scientific problem, even if the answer may in part depend on points on which we cannot strictly demonstrate the correctness of our answer. Yet, the answers at which we have arrived on all three counts are purely negative. On the moral side, socialism cannot but destroy the basis of all morals, personal freedom and responsibility. On the political side, it leads sooner or later to totalitarian government. On the material side it will greatly impede the production of wealth, if it does not actually cause impoverishment. All

---

Economics (London: Routledge & Kegan Paul, 1949). For more on Durbin's debates with Hayek, which later concerned Hayek's book *The Road to Serfdom*, see B. Caldwell, "Introduction", in Hayek, *The Road to Serfdom*, pp. 8, 24–28. H. D. Dickinson advocated a form of market socialism in his *Economics of Socialism* (London: Oxford University Press, 1939).

Hayek's response to the work of Lange and his fellow market socialists centred on his claim that their assumption that the relevant knowledge of consumers' tastes, of the availability of resources and methods of production, and of the costs of producing different levels of output was known by, or 'given' to, the plant managers independently of the market process was mistaken. For Hayek, such knowledge simply would not exist without the rivalrous process of market competition between firms. An early statement of this critique is F. A. Hayek, "Socialist Calculation: The Competitive 'Solution'" [1940], reprinted as chapter 3 of Hayek, *Socialism and War*. A later exposition, directed at Lange's essay in particular, can be found in Hayek, "Two Pages of Fiction". Fuller accounts of this second stage of the debate can be found in Lavoie, *Rivalry and Central Planning*, pp. 118–78, and Caldwell, "Introduction", in Hayek, *Socialism and War*, pp. 19–30.—Ed.]

these objections to socialism were raised a long time ago on purely intellectual grounds, which in the course of time have been elaborated and refined. There have been no serious attempts to refute these objections to socialism rationally. Indeed, the most surprising thing about the treatment of these problems by the majority of professional economists is how little they have made them the central point of their discussions. One would think that nothing could be of more concern for economists than the relative efficiency and conduciveness to general welfare of alternative orders of economic affairs. Instead they have fought shy of the topic, as if fearing to soil their hands by concerning themselves with 'political' topics. They have left the discussion to specialists in 'economic systems' who in their textbooks provide stale accounts of discussions of long ago, carefully avoiding taking sides. It is as if the circumstance that that issue had become the subject of political dispute were a cause for the silence of the scientists who knew they could definitely refute at least some of the arguments of one side. This kind of neutrality seems to me not discretion but cowardice. Surely it is high time for us to cry from the house-tops that the intellectual foundations of socialism have all collapsed.

I have to admit that, after vainly waiting for upwards of 40 years to find a respectably intellectual defence against objections raised to socialist proposals, I am becoming a little impatient. Since I have always acknowledged that the socialist camp includes many people of good will, I have tried to deal with their doctrines gently. But the time is overdue to proclaim loudly that intellectually the foundations of socialism are as hollow as can be, and that opposition to socialism is based, not on different values or on prejudice, but on unrefuted logical argument. This must be openly said, especially in view of the tactics so frequently employed by most advocates and defenders of socialism. Instead of reasoning logically to meet the substantial objections they have to answer, socialists impugn the motives and throw suspicion on the good faith of defenders of what they choose to call 'capitalism'. Such crude efforts to turn discussion from whether a belief is true to why it is being held seems to me itself an outgrowth of the weakness of the intellectual position of the socialists. Quite generally, the socialist counter-critique seems often to be more concerned to discredit the author than to refute his arguments. The favourite tactics of the counter-critiques is to warn the young against taking the author or his book seriously. This technique indeed has been developed to a certain mastership. What young man will bother with such a book as my *Constitution of Liberty* which, he is told by a 'progressive' British political science don, is one of those "dinosaurs that still occasionally stalk on the scene, apparently impervious to natural selection"?[18] The principle seems generally: if you can't

[18] [Leaving aside the question of how legitimate the concerns expressed by Hayek here are in general, it is unclear that he chose an apt illustration of his point. The phrase quoted by Hayek

refute the argument, defame the author. That the argument against them may be genuine, honest and perhaps true, these left-wing intellectuals do not seem prepared to consider even as a possibility, since it might mean that they themselves are entirely wrong.

Certainly, political differences are frequently based on differences of ultimate values, on which science has little or nothing to say. But the crucial differences which exist today at least between the socialist intellectuals, who, after all, invented socialism, and their opponents are not of this kind. They are intellectual differences which between people not irredeemably wed to a muddled dream can be sorted out and decided by logical reasoning. I have never belonged to any political party. Long ago I shocked many of my friends by explaining why I cannot be a conservative. Insight into the nature of the economic problems of society turned me into a radical anti-socialist, I can honestly say. Moreover, it convinced me that as an economist I can do more for my fellow-men by explaining the reasons for opposing socialism than in any other manner. Anti-socialism means here opposition to *all* direct government interference with the market, no matter in whose interest such interference may be exercised.

It is not correct to describe this as a *laissez faire* attitude—another of the smear-words so frequently substituted for argument—because a functioning market requires a framework of appropriate rules within which the market

---

is taken from the introduction to a set of readings on contemporary political philosophy edited in 1967 by Oxford philosopher Anthony Quinton (1925–2010). Far from being a "progressive", Quinton was broadly conservative in outlook and acted as an advisor to British Prime Minister Margaret Thatcher, who made him a life peer in 1982. Moreover, an examination of the passage in which the words in question appear suggests that its meaning is not as clear-cut as Hayek suggests. Quinton's remark comes in the course of a discussion of the "great tradition of large-scale reflection about politics", as exemplified by books such as Aristotle's *Politics*, Hobbes's *Leviathan*, Locke's *Treatises on Civil Government*, Hegel's *The Philosophy of Right*, and Mill's *On Liberty*. Quinton avers that these are works whose "all-inclusiveness has not been much imitated in recent years", the reason being that a "great increase in methodological self-consciousness among recent philosophers . . . has led them to accept a more limited conception of their powers and, in consequence, of their responsibilities". He elaborates as follows: "A sign of this change in the way the subject is concerned has been the apparent petering out of the great tradition. Surveys of the history of political thought either come to an end with Marx and Mill in the mid-nineteenth century or they wind up with apologetic chapters on the major ideological components of the most recent period and on the highly engaged, rhetorical and practical thinking of the more articulate political leaders. But an occasional magnificent dinosaur stills stalks on to the scene, such as Hayek's *Constitution of Liberty*, seemingly impervious to natural selection". Quinton's observation that the wide-ranging nature of Hayek's book is out of keeping with the narrower focus characteristic of political philosophy in the late 1960s does not necessarily imply an attitude of disapproval towards the work. Indeed, by assimilating *The Constitution of Liberty* to the great tradition of wide-ranging work in political thought, Quinton might quite reasonably be read as complimenting Hayek. See A. Quinton, "Introduction", in *Political Philosophy*, ed. A. Quinton (Oxford: Oxford University Press, 1967), pp. 1–2.—Ed.]

will operate smoothly. Strong reasons also exist for wishing government to render *outside the market* various services, which for one reason or another the market cannot supply. But the state certainly ought never to have the *monopoly* of any such service, especially not of postal services, broadcasting, or the issue of money.[19]

Some signs are appearing of a return to sanity. But I do not really feel hopeful about prospects for the future. There is much talk about countries becoming 'ungovernable',[20] but little realisation that attempts to govern too much are at the root of the trouble, and even less awareness of how deeply the evil has already become entrenched in prevailing institutions. For progress towards its aims, socialism needs government with unlimited powers, and has already got this. In such a system various groups must be given, not what a majority thinks they deserve, but what those groups themselves think they are entitled to. Granting these groups what they think they deserve therefore becomes the price that must be paid so that some groups may become a majority. Omnipotent democracy indeed leads of necessity to a kind of socialism, but to a socialism which nobody foresaw or probably wanted: a position in which the individual elected representative as well as the governing majority must work to redress every imagined grievance which it has power to redress, however little justified the claim may be. It is not the assessment of the merits of persons or groups by a majority, but the power of those persons or groups to extort special benefits from the government, which now determines the distribution of incomes.

The paradox is that the all-powerful government which socialism needs, must, if it is to be democratic, aim at remedying all such dissatisfaction, and to remove all dissatisfaction means that it must reward groups at their own estimates of their deserts. But no viable society can reward everyone at his own valuation. A society in which a few can use power to extort what they feel they are entitled to may be highly unpleasant for the others, but would at least be viable. A society in which everyone is organised as a member of some groups to force government to help him get what he wants is self-destructive.

---

[19] [For details of the reasons to which Hayek alludes, see Hayek, *The Constitution of Liberty*, pp. 332–34; Hayek, *The Political Order of a Free People*, pp. 41–64; and F. A. Hayek, "The Denationalization of Money: An Analysis of the Theory and Practice of Concurrent Currencies" [1978], reprinted as chapter 4 of F. A. Hayek, *Good Money, Part II: The Standard*, ed. S. Kresge, vol. 6 (1999) of *The Collected Works of F. A. Hayek.—Ed.*]

[20] [See, for example, S. Brittan, "The Economic Contradictions of Democracy", *British Journal of Political Science*, vol. 5, 1975, pp. 129–59; M. Crozier, S. Huntington and J. Watanuki, *The Crisis of Democracy: Report on the Governability of Democracies to the Trilateral Commission* (New York: New York University Press, 1975); A. King, "Overload: Problems of Governing in the 1970s", *Political Studies*, vol. 23, 1975, pp. 284–96; and J. Douglas, "Review Article: The Overloaded Crown", *British Journal of Political Science*, vol. 6, 1976, pp. 483–505. Also see F. A. Hayek, "Whither Democracy?" [1978], reprinted as chapter 28 of this volume, p. 413 n. 2.—Ed.]

There is no way of preventing some from feeling that they have been treated unjustly—that is bound to be widespread in any social order—but arrangements which enable groups of disgruntled people to extort satisfaction of their claims—or the recognition of an 'entitlement', to use this new-fangled phrase—make any society unmanageable.

There is no limit to the wishes of the people which an unlimited democratic government is obliged to try to satisfy. We have indeed the considered opinion of a leading British Labour politician that he regards it as his task to remedy all dissatisfaction![21] It would be unfair, however, to blame the politicians too much for being unable to say 'no'. Under prevailing arrangements perhaps an established leader could afford occasionally to do so, but the ordinary representative cannot say 'no' to any large number of his constituents, however unjust their demands, and still hope to retain his seat.

In a society whose wealth rests on prompt adaptation to constantly changing circumstances, the individual can be left free to choose the directions of his efforts only if rewards fluctuate with the value of the services he can contribute to the society's common pool of resources. If his income is politically

[21] [Elsewhere, Hayek identifies the politician in question as C. A. R. Crosland, referencing p. 205 of C. A. R Crosland, *The Future of Socialism* (London: Jonathan Cape, 1956). See Hayek, *The Constitution of Liberty*, p. 155, and Hayek, *Rules and Order*, pp. 144, 180 n. 36. Anthony Crosland (1918–77) was a British Labour politician and writer who served as Secretary of State for Education and Science (1965–67) and as Secretary of State for Foreign Affairs (1976–77). His 1956 book *The Future of Socialism* became the touchstone of the so-called 'revisionist' strand of social democratic thinking in Britain during the first twenty-five years after World War Two. In it, Crosland argued that the triumph of Keynesian economics, the advent of the welfare state, and the rise of managerial capitalism (in which a separation of ownership and control reduced the role of the profit motive in economic life) meant that the ultimate socialist goal of greater equality could be achieved within an economy that retained private property. Common ownership of the means of production, distribution and exchange was now best thought of by socialists, not as an essential prerequisite for achieving social justice, but rather as an eminently dispensable means to that end. An examination of p. 205 of *The Future of Socialism* reveals that Hayek may not have been entirely accurate in the views he attributed to Crosland. Crosland writes there as follows: "[T]he ethical basis for the first argument for greater equality is that it will increase social contentment and diminish social resentment . . . It is justified, first, by the ethical premiss that a contented society is better than a discontented one, and secondly by the judgment that the contentment of the community is an increasing function of the contentment of individuals. It then rests on the hypothesis . . . that some at least of our collective discontents can be traced to social inequality, and would be diminished if inequality were less: and on the further hypothesis that the consequent gain in contentment would outweigh the diminution in contentment of the present privileged classes". It is not obvious that this implies that the aim of politics should be to remove all sources of discontent. Indeed, while clearly in favour of greater equality, Crosland states later in the same chapter that, "I am sure that a definite limit exists to the degree of equality which is desirable. We do not want complete equality of incomes, since extra responsibility and exceptional talent require and deserve a differential reward". See Crosland, *The Future of Socialism*, p. 217.—Ed.]

determined, he loses not merely the incentive but also the possibility of deciding what he ought to do in the general interest. And if he cannot know himself what he must do to make his services valuable to his fellows, he must be commanded to do what is required. To suffer disappointment, adversity and hardship is a discipline to which in any society most must submit, and it is a discipline by which it is desirable that all able persons ought to have to submit. What mitigates these hardships in a free society is that no arbitrary human will imposes them, but that their incidence is determined by an impersonal process and unforeseeable chance.

I believe that, after a little socialism, people generally recognise that it is preferable for one's well-being and relative status to depend on the outcome of the game of the market than on the will of a superior, to whom one is assigned by authority. Present trends, however, make it seem likely that, before such an insight spreads widely enough, existing political institutions will break down under stresses which they cannot bear. Unless people learn to accept that many of their grievances are unjustified, and give them no claims on others, and that in this world government cannot effectively assume responsibility for how well off particular groups of people are to be, it will be impossible to build a decent society. Indeed, the most idealistic among the socialists will be forced to destroy democracy to serve their idealistic socialist vision of the future. What present trends point to is the emergence of ever larger numbers, for whose welfare and status government has assumed a responsibility it cannot discharge, and whose revolt when they are not paid enough, or asked to do more work than they like, will have to be subdued with the knout and the machine-gun: this, too, by the very people who genuinely intended to grant all their wishes.

THIRTY

TWO PAGES OF FICTION

The Impossibility of Socialist Calculation[1]

I

There is endless repetition of the claim that Professor Oskar Lange in 1936 refuted the contention advanced in 1921 by Ludwig von Mises that "economic calculation is impossible in a socialist society". The claim rests wholly on theoretical argument by Oskar Lange in little more than two pages, 59 to 61, in the most widely known reprint of his original essay, with Fred M. Taylor, *On the Economic Theory of Socialism* (ed. B. E. Lippincott, University of Minnesota Press, 1938).[2] It will be timely to analyse this argument clause

---

[1] [This essay was first published as F. A. Hayek, "Two Pages of Fiction: The Impossibility of Socialist Calculation", *The Journal of Economic Affairs*, vol. 2, 1982, pp. 135–42. The journal in question bore the title just mentioned from 1980 to 1983, subsequently being known simply as *Economic Affairs*. Earlier drafts of the essay had slightly different titles, including, "Socialist Planning: Comic Fiction?" and "Two Pages of Fiction Which Swayed Political Opinion: Oskar Lange and the Possibility of Socialist Calculation". See Hayek Collection, box 61, folder 1, and box 110, folder 14, Hoover Institution Archives, respectively.—Ed.]

[2] [Austrian economist Ludwig von Mises (1881–1973) argued that rational economic calculation is impossible under socialism. According to Mises, common ownership of the means of production precludes the existence of a market in which the prices of capital goods can be established. The absence of those monetary prices implies that people have no way of ascertaining the relative scarcity of different kinds of resource and, therefore, no grounds for judging which of the many technically feasible projects open to them constitutes the most efficient means of pursuing their goals. Mises concludes that under socialism, there is no basis for the rational appraisal of alternative courses of action: "Without economic calculation there can be no economy. Hence, in a socialist state wherein the pursuit of economic calculation is impossible, there can be—in our sense of the term—no economy whatsoever". See L. von Mises, "Economic Calculation in the Socialist Commonwealth" [1920], in *Collectivist Economic Planning*, ed. F. A. Hayek (London: Routledge and Kegan Paul, 1935), p. 105. Mises's article was first published, not in 1921, as Hayek states, but in 1920. See L. von Mises, "Die Wirtschaftsrechnung im sozialistischen Gemeinwesen", *Archiv für Sozialwissenschaft*, vol. 47, 1920, pp. 86–121.

Polish economist Oskar Lange (1904–65) was a leading proponent of market socialism, an approach which purported to reconcile the efficiency of a competitive market process with the redistributive goals of socialism. The essay by Lange to which Hayek refers presents one of the most famous blueprints for a market socialist system and is entitled "On the Economic Theory of Socialism". It was first published as a two-part article with the same title in the *Review of Eco-*

by clause. We shall here indent Lange's successive assertions with the crucial terms in italics, and examine their validity and bearing one by one. The theoretical argument commences as follows:

> Professor Mises' contention that a socialist economy cannot solve the problem of rational allocation of its resources is based on a confusion concerning the nature of prices. As Wicksteed has pointed out, the term 'price' has two meanings. It may mean either price in the ordinary sense, i.e., the exchange ratio of two commodities on a market, or it may have the generalized meaning of 'terms on which alternatives are offered'. Wicksteed says, "'Price', then, in the narrower sense of 'the money for which a material thing, a service, or a privilege can be obtained', is simply a special case of 'price' in the wider sense of 'the terms on which alternatives are offered to us'". [P. H. Wicksteed, *The Common Sense* of *Political Economy*, 2nd ed., London, 1933, p. 28]. It is only prices in the generalized sense which are indispensable to solving the problem of allocation of resources.[3]

------

nomic Studies, vol. 4, no. 1, 1936, pp. 53–71, and vol. 4, no. 2, 1937, pp. 123–42. As Hayek notes, it was subsequently reprinted with some additions and changes in *On the Economic Theory of Socialism*, ed. B. E. Lippincott (Minneapolis: University of Minnesota Press, 1938), pp. 57–143. The words quoted by Hayek in the first sentence of this essay come from p. 58 of the reprinted version of Lange's article, to which all subsequent references to Lange's article will also be made.

Frederick M. Taylor (1855–1932) was an American economist based at the University of Michigan and best known for his work on market socialism. The essay to which Hayek alludes is F. M. Taylor, "The Guidance of Production in a Socialist State", *American Economic Review*, vol. 19, 1929, pp. 1–8; reprinted as pp. 41–54 of the Lippincott volume.

Hayek's first attempt to engage with Lange's argument can be found in F. A. Hayek, "Socialist Calculation: The Competitive 'Solution'" [1940], reprinted as chapter 3 of F. A. Hayek, *Socialism and War: Essays, Documents, Reviews*, ed. B. Caldwell, vol. 10 (1997) of *The Collected Works of F. A. Hayek* (Chicago: University of Chicago Press; London: Routledge). That volume also contains many of Hayek's other writings on the possibility of socialism, as well as a useful overview of his involvement in debates on that topic. See B. Caldwell, "Introduction", in Hayek, *Socialism and War.*—Ed.]

[3] [See Lange, "On the Economic Theory of Socialism", pp. 59–60. Philip Wicksteed (1844–1927) was an English Unitarian minister who wrote on classics, literature, and theology, as well as economics. As befits a follower of William Stanley Jevons, Wicksteed was an exponent of marginalist economics. His first work in that field, published in the journal *To-day* in October 1884, was a marginalist critique of Marx's labour theory of value, entitled, "*Das Capital*: A Criticism", that is widely credited with turning Fabian socialists such as George Bernard Shaw away from Marx. Wicksteed developed in *An Essay on the Co-ordination of the Laws of Distribution* (London: Macmillan & Co., 1894) a marginal productivity theory of distribution, while he advanced in his *The Common Sense of Political Economy* a consistently subjectivist theory of choice. The passage cited by Lange comes from P. Wicksteed, *The Common Sense of Political Economy* [1910], 2nd edn., vol. 1, ed. L. Robbins (London: Routledge and Kegan Paul, 1933), p. 28. The bracketed reference in the main text is Hayek's and sees him insert into the main text Lange's reference to Wicksteed's book, which originally appeared as a footnote in Lange's article.—Ed.]

Wicksteed's honest warning that for the purposes of analysis he would use the term 'price' in a wider sense in no way indicates that those quasi-prices can generally operate as substitutes for the money prices where they are not known. Within his range of knowledge the individual will certainly often have to balance alternatives between which he must choose, but the problem is precisely how he can do so where he does not know the particular concrete facts determining this necessity. That the "alternatives [which] are offered to us" become known to us in most instances only as *money* prices is Mises' chief argument. To turn this against him is an inexcusable legerdemain of which a thinker not prejudiced by political preconceptions should be incapable.

Lange continues:

> The economic problem is a problem of choice between alternatives. To solve the problem three *data* are needed; (1) a preference scale which guides the acts of choice; (2) knowledge of the 'terms on which alternatives are offered'; and (3) knowledge of the amount of resources available. Those three *data* being *given*, the problem of choice is soluble.[4]

The illiterate expression 'given data' constantly recurs in Lange. It appears to have an irresistible attraction to mathematical economists because it doubly assures them that they know what they do not know. It seems to bewitch them into making assertions about the real world for which they have no empirical justification whatever. On the confusion supported by this pleonasm the whole of Lange's 'refutation' of Mises' argument (and most of the theory of resource allocation descending from it) is based. Note the following:

> . . . it is obvious that a socialist economy *may regard the data* under 1 and 3 as *given*, at least *in as great a degree* as they are given in a market economy.[5]

One is bound to ask: known (which I presume is the meaning of 'given') to whom? These circumstances are in a market economy known to some thousands of different individuals, but this of course in no way implies that they can be known to the central planning authority of a socialist economy. Yet Lange continues:

---

[4] [See Lange, "On the Economic Theory of Socialism", p. 60. The italics were added by Hayek, who also removed Lange's italics from the word "choice".—Ed.]

[5] [See Lange, "On the Economic Theory of Socialism", p. 60. The italics are Hayek's. Lange's original article refers to a "capitalist" rather than a "market" economy.—Ed.]

The *data* under 1 may be either *given* by the demand schedules of the individuals or be established by the judgement of the authorities administering the economic system. The question remains whether the *data* under 2 are accessible to the administrators of a socialist economy. Professor Mises denies this. However, a careful study of price *theory* and of the theory of production convinces us that, the *data* under 1 and under 3 being given, the 'terms on which alternatives are offered' *are determined* ultimately by the *technical possibilities* of transformation of one commodity into another, i.e. by the production functions [the relationships between input and output—ED.].[6]

It will be noticed that the assurance that these 'data' are being 'given' in no way explains *how* in day-to-day practice they become known to the socialist planning agency.

Before we go on to Lange's extraordinary answer to this question we ought first, perhaps, more carefully distinguish between the two senses in which the expression 'data' can be meaningfully employed. It can be used legitimately either for the assumption, necessarily made hypothetically by the theorist, that certain facts exist which are not known to him, or for the assumption that particular facts will be known to specified persons and will have certain effects on their actions. But it is an impermissible falsification of the sequence of cause and effect to claim that the 'data' presumed (though not known) by the theorist are also known to some agency without his showing the process by which they will become known to it. And when he claims that some further events are 'determined' by either kind of data, this does not show that these results are known to any particular person.[7]

Now to Lange's most extraordinary 'solution' of this problem. He asserts that

---

[6] [See Lange, "On the Economic Theory of Socialism", pp. 60–61. The italics are Hayek's. The words in the square brackets appear to have been added by the editor of the *Journal of Economic Affairs* for the benefit of readers unfamiliar with economics.—Ed.]

[7] [Hayek's discussion of the notion of 'given data' draws on his earlier analysis of that idea, found in F. A. Hayek, "Economics and Knowledge" [1937], reprinted as chapter 1 of F. A. Hayek, *The Market and Other Orders*, ed. Bruce Caldwell, vol. 15 (2014) of *The Collected Works of F. A. Hayek*, pp. 62–64. Hayek's reflections on the issue of to whom the data in question are given led him to the insight that the economic problem facing society is best described as that of utilising knowledge the totality of which is not given to any one individual: "The economic problem of society is thus not merely a problem of how to allocate 'given' resources—if 'given' is taken to mean given to a single mind which deliberately solves the problem set by these 'data'. It is rather a problem of how to secure the best use of resources known to any of the members of society, for ends whose relative importance only these individuals know. Or, to put it briefly, it is a problem of the utilisation of knowledge which is not given to anyone in its totality". See F. A. Hayek, "The Use of Knowledge in Society" [1945], reprinted as chapter 3 of *The Market and Other Orders*, pp. 93–94.—Ed.]

The administrators of a socialist economy will have exactly the same knowledge, or lack of knowledge, of the production functions as the capitalist entrepreneurs have.[8]

This brazen assertion is crucial for Lange's refutation of Mises' argument, but he offers no evidence or justification for it, even in this limited form confined to production functions. Yet it has been expanded by Lange's pupils into the even more fantastic assertion that a central planning board "would receive exactly the same information from a socialist economic system as did the entrepreneurs under the market system". (Thus Robert L. Heilbroner, *Between Capitalism and Socialism*, New York, 1970, p. 88.)[9]

II *The flaw in socialist planning*

I am afraid this is a blatant untruth, an assertion so absurd that it is difficult to understand how an intelligent person could ever honestly make it. It asserts a sheer impossibility which only a miracle could realise. In the first instance: most of the information which the capitalist entrepreneurs have consists of prices determined on a competitive market. This knowledge would *not* be available to anyone in a socialist economy where prices are not provided by the market. So far as the particular case of the production function is concerned, the relevant production functions which guide the competitive market

---

[8] [See Lange, "On the Economic Theory of Socialism", p. 61.—Ed.]

[9] [Robert Heilbroner (1919–2005) was an American economist and historian of economic thought, based at the New School for Social Research and best known for his celebrated introduction to the history of economics, *The Worldly Philosophers: The Lives, Times and Ideas of the Great Economic Thinkers* (New York: Simon and Schuster, 1953). Heilbroner was for most of his career an advocate of socialism who believed that "the effort of Ludwig von Mises and Friedrich Hayek to destroy the credibility of socialism as a desirable social order . . . did not fare very well. In the mid-1930s it was effectively demolished by Oskar Lange, the brilliant Polish economist then at Harvard. Lange demonstrated in two incisive articles that Mises had failed to see that a Central Planning Board could indeed plan rationally for the simple reason that it would receive exactly the same information from a socialized economic system as did entrepreneurs under a market system". See R. Heilbroner, *Between Capitalism and Socialism: Essays in Political Economics* (New York: Random House, 1970), p. 88. Towards the end of his life, however, Heilbroner expressed rather different views about the merits of socialism, declaring in 1989 that "Less than 75 years after it officially began, the contest between capitalism and socialism is over: capitalism has won . . . Capitalism organises the material affairs of humankind more satisfactorily than socialism". See R. Heilbroner, "The Triumph of Capitalism", *The New Yorker*, January 23, 1989, p. 98. The following year, writing after the collapse of the Soviet Union, Heilbroner argued that the socialist calculation debate ought to be re-examined in the light of recent events, acknowledging, "It turns out, of course, that Mises was right". See R. Heilbroner, "Reflections after Communism", *The New Yorker*, September 10, 1990, pp. 91–92.—Ed.]

are, of course, not (as the theoretical models simplifyingly assume) relations between general, generic categories of commodities, but very *specific* relations showing how, in a particular plant under the specific local conditions, changes in the combinations of the particular goods and services employed will affect the size of the output.[10]

The individual entrepreneur will not possess or require knowledge of general production functions, but he will currently learn from experience how at any given time variations in the qualities or the relative quantities of the different factors of production he uses will affect his output. The information relevant for and possessed by each entrepreneur will be very different from that possessed by others. To speak of the aggregate of such information dispersed among hundreds of different individuals as being available to the planning authority is pure fiction. What the planning authority would have to know would not be the mere totals but the distinct, peculiar conditions prevailing *in each enterprise* which affect the information about *values* transmitted through market prices but would be completely lost in any statistical information about *quantities* that might reach the authority from time to time.

Even if this purely technological information about the range of available physical possibilities could with reasonable promptness be communicated to the planning authority, it would by no means put it in command of all the information which capitalist entrepreneurs can and must use if they are to be successful. The production functions about which Lange is concerned indi-

---

[10] [Hayek argues elsewhere along similar lines that other kinds of knowledge—concerning, for example, the types of goods and services that people want and the lowest cost at which those goods and services can be produced—are also discovered only through rivalrous market competition and so do not exist in the absence of that process. See F. A. Hayek, "The Present State of the Debate" [1935], reprinted as chapter 2 of *Socialism and War*, p. 95; F. A. Hayek, "Socialist Calculation: The Competitive 'Solution'", p. 130; and F. A. Hayek, "The Meaning of Competition" [1948], reprinted as chapter 4 of *The Market and Other Orders*, pp. 106, 108, 112. A summary statement of Hayek's position on this issue, which relates back to his earlier discussion of 'given knowledge', can be found in F. A. Hayek, "Competition as a Discovery Procedure" [1968], reprinted as chapter 12 of *The Market and Other Orders*, pp. 306–7: "[E]conomic theory sometimes appears at the outset to bar its way to a true appreciation of the character of the process of competition, because it starts from the assumption of a 'given' supply of scarce goods. But which goods are scarce goods, or which things are goods, and how scarce or valuable they are—these are precisely the things which competition has to discover. Provisional results from the market process at each stage alone tell the individuals what to look for . . . Prices direct their attention to what is worth finding out about market offers for various things and services. This means that the, in some respects always unique, combinations of individual knowledge and skills, which the market enables them to use, will not merely, or even in the first instance, be such knowledge of facts as they could list and communicate if some authority asked them to do so. The knowledge of which I speak consists rather of a capacity to find out particular circumstances, which becomes effective only if possessors of this kind of knowledge are informed by the market which kinds of things or services are wanted, and how urgently they are wanted".—Ed.]

cate only the range of possibilities from which the individual producer has to choose. But the particular points on the curves by which the functions can be represented that they must choose to produce economically, depend on the relative scarcities of all the different factors of production. Entrepreneurs are informed about these scarcities solely by market prices. The planning authority would have no 'data' whatever. Lange appears to have been so confused between the knowledge possessed in day-to-day economic life by the individuals whose actions economics attempts to explain and the knowledge which the economist must pretend to possess in order to be able to do so, that he represents the latter as if it were something obviously perceivable to any observer of the economy. How the market brings about an adaptation to a multitude of circumstances which in their totality are not known to anyone is precisely the process which the science of economics has to explain. Yet Lange has the audacity to blame Mises for the very mistake he himself is committing.

> . . . Professor Mises seems to have confused prices in the narrower sense, i.e., the exchange ratios of commodities on a market, with prices in the wider sense of 'terms on which alternatives are offered'. As, in consequence of public ownership of the means of production, there is in a socialist economy no market on which capital goods are actually exchanged, there are obviously no prices of capital goods in the sense of exchange ratios on a market. And, hence, Professor Mises argues, there is no '*index* of alternatives' available in the sphere of capital goods. But this conclusion is based on a confusion of 'price' in the narrower sense with 'price' in the wider sense of an *index* of alternatives. It is only in the latter sense that 'prices' are indispensible for the allocation of resources, and *on the basis of the technical possibilities of transformation of one commodity into another* they are also *given* in a socialist economy.[11]

Now, if in this argument 'index' means, as it must for the conclusions to follow, a sign or indicator visible to anyone who cares to look for it, it is, of course, simply false. That 'price' can also measure 'terms on which alternatives are offered' does not mean that these terms are generally known or readily discoverable. The whole of Mises' argument is precisely that, though the theoretician will recognise that the increase of the output of some good will usually be possible only 'at the price' of the reduction of the output of some other goods, without market prices nobody will know how large that 'price' is. As we have seen, even if all the technical possibilities of transformation of one commodity to another could be known to the planning authorities (which, inter-

---

[11] [See Lange, "On the Economic Theory of Socialism", p. 61. The italics were added by Hayek.—Ed.]

preted as particular local and temporal possibilities, is of course not the case), this would be far from sufficient to allow the planning authority rationally to decide which of these possibilities to use.

The muddle involved in this is the same as that which makes so many contemporary socialist writers allege that, even before Mises, Vilfredo Pareto and Enrico Barone had shown that the problem of socialist calculation was soluble. It is perfectly true that these two authors had shown which information a socialist planning authority would have to possess in order to perform its task. But to know which kind of information would be required to solve a problem does not imply that it can be solved if the information is dispersed among millions of people.[12]

III Dispersed market knowledge cannot be mobilised centrally

I feel I should perhaps make it clear that I have never conceded, as is often alleged, that Lange had provided the theoretical solution of the problem, and I did not thereafter withdraw to pointing out practical difficulties. What I *did* say (in *Individualism and Economic Order*, p. 187) was merely that from the factually false hypothesis that the central planning board could command all the necessary information, it could *logically* follow that the problem was in principle soluble. To deduce from this observation the 'admission' that the real problem can be solved in theory is a rather scandalous misrepresentation.

[12] [Drawing on the general equilibrium analysis of Italian economist and sociologist Vilfredo Pareto (1848–1923), Italian economist Enrico Barone (1859–1924) argued that both capitalist and socialist economies can be represented mathematically by the same system of simultaneous equations. The difference between the two kinds of economy, Barone argued, consisted in how those equations are to be 'solved': within a capitalist system, they are solved through market competition; under socialism, the solution is to be found by the planning authorities, via an experimental or trial-and-error process. See E. Barone, "Il Ministro della Produzione nello Stato Collettivista", *Giornale degli Economisti*, vol. 37, 1908, pp. 267–93, 391–414. An English translation, entitled "The Ministry of Production in the Collectivist State", was published as Appendix A of Hayek's 1935 edited volume on *Collectivist Economic Planning*. As Hayek notes below, both Pareto and Barone were in fact highly sceptical about the ability of the planning authorities actually to solve the equations. Nevertheless, Barone's demonstration of the formal equivalence of the market and socialist systems led early advocates of market socialism such as English academic economist and Fabian socialist Henry Douglas Dickinson (1899–1969) to conclude that there was no difference between the two systems and that planners could solve the economic problem facing society via a trail-and-error method whereby prices were raised in markets where there was a shortage and reduced where there was a glut. See H. D. Dickinson, "Price Formation in a Socialist Economy", *Economic Journal*, vol. 43, 1933, pp. 237–50. Hayek's initial response to Dickinson's paper can be found in Hayek, "The Present State of the Debate", pp. 93–97.—Ed.]

Nobody can, of course, transfer to another all the knowledge he has, and certainly not the information he could discover only *if* market prices told him what was worth looking for.[13]

Neither Pareto nor Barone ever claimed that he knew how this knowledge could ever be obtained. Indeed, Pareto, on the contrary, explicitly denied it. After describing in his celebrated *Manuel d'économie politique* (2nd ed., 1971, pp. 233–34) all the information that would have to be taken into account to determine a market equilibrium, he continued: ". . . this determination has by no means the purpose to arrive at a numerical calculation of prices. Let us make the most favourable assumption for such a calculation, let us assume that we have triumphed over all the difficulties of finding the data of the problem and that we know the *ophélimités* [utility] of all the different commodities for each individual, and all the conditions of production of all the commodities, etc. *This is already an absurd hypothesis to make.* Yet it is not sufficient to make the solution of the problem possible. We have seen that in the case of 100 persons and 700 commodities there will be 70,699 conditions. [Actually, a great number of circumstances we have so far neglected] will further increase the number: we shall therefore have to solve a system of 70,699 equations. This exceeds practically the power of algebraic analysis, and this is even more true if one contemplates the fabulous number of equations which one obtains for a population of forty millions and several thousand commodities. In this case the roles would be changed; it would not be mathematics which would assist political economy, but political economy which would assist mathematics. In other words, if one really could know all these equations, the only means to solve them which is available to human powers is *to observe the practical solution given by the market*" (my italics).[14]

[13] [Hayek refers to his essay "Socialist Calculation: The Competitive 'Solution'". This essay was originally published in the journal *Economica*, vol. 7, 1940, pp. 125–49, and was later republished as chapter 9 of F. A. Hayek, *Individualism and Economic Order* (Chicago: University of Chicago Press, 1948). It can now be found as chapter 3 of *Socialism and War*. The passage to which Hayek refers can be found on pp. 122–23 of that *Collected Works* volume where, commenting on the trial-and-error process proposed by Dickinson and Lange, Hayek writes: "There is of course no *logical impossibility* of conceiving a directing organ of the collective economy which is not only 'omnipresent and omniscient', as Dickinson conceives it, but also omnipotent and which therefore would be in a position to change without delay every price by just the amount that is required. When, however, one proceeds to consider the actual apparatus by which this sort of adjustment is to be brought about, one begins to wonder whether anyone should really be prepared to suggest that, within the domain of practical possibility, such a system will ever even distantly approach the efficiency of a system where the required changes are brought about by the spontaneous action of the persons immediately concerned". The words quoted by Hayek come from H. D. Dickinson, *Economics of Socialism* (London: Oxford University Press), p. 191.—Ed.]

[14] [The words in square brackets, as well as the italics, were added by Hayek. The passage on which Hayek draws can be found on pp. 233–34 of the French edition of Pareto's work, which

Even today the solution of 100,000 equations is still an unachieved ambition of the constructors of computers. And it is regrettable that the mathematical difficulties Pareto introduced to illustrate further what he had called the 'absurdity' of the assumption have gained most attention. For the real problem is the impossibility of concentrating all the information required in the hands of any single agency. Apparently it was J. A. Schumpeter who gave currency to the myth that Pareto and Barone had solved the problem. At any rate, it was Schumpeter who in particularly drastic form tacitly re-introduced this assumption in his celebrated *Capitalism, Socialism and Democracy* (1942, pp. 172–77), as one of the "general logic of choice" where it is "possible to derive, from the data and from the rules of rational behaviour, uniquely determined solutions". This assumes that the planning authority knows all these 'data'.[15]

A 'logic of choice' can say something only about the consequences to be drawn from a set of statements known to some one mind, and in this sense it can account for the behaviour of one individual. But, as I showed about 45 years ago (*Individualism and Economic Order,* pp. 35–45), the step from this logic of choice to an empirical science which tells us anything about what can

---

was published in 1927. See V. Pareto, *Manuel d'économie politique,* 2nd edn. (Paris: M. Giard, 1927), pp. 233–34. The words quoted by Hayek are presumably his own translation of the French edition of Pareto's book (which was, of course, originally published in Italian). An English translation of the French edition was published in 1971. See V. Pareto, *Manual of Political Economy,* trans. A. S. Schwier, ed. A. S. Schwier and A. N. Page (New York: Augustus M. Kelley, 1971). The passage to which Hayek refers, the translation of which differs somewhat from Hayek's own rendering, can be found on p. 171 of that volume.

Barone expresses grave doubts about the capacity of planners to solve the system of equations that represents equilibrium resource allocation in the economy in "The Ministry of Production in the Collectivist State", pp. 286–90.—Ed.]

[15] [Joseph Alois Schumpeter (1883–1950) was an economist and sociologist best known for his analyses of capitalist development and business cycles. The phrases to which Hayek refers in this section of his paper are all taken from chapter 16 of J. A. Schumpeter, *Capitalism, Socialism, and Democracy* (New York: Harper, 1942). Schumpeter opens that chapter by posing the following question: "given a socialist system of the kind envisaged, is it possible to derive, from its data and from the rules of rational behaviour, uniquely determined decisions as to what and how to produce or, to put the same thing into the slogan of exact economics, do these data and rules, under the circumstances of a socialist economy, yield equations which are independent, compatible—i.e., free from contradiction—and sufficient in number to determine uniquely the unknowns of the problem before the central board or ministry of production?" It is from this passage, which appears on p. 172 of Schumpeter's book, that the words reported, somewhat imperfectly, by Hayek are drawn. Schumpeter continues immediately below the passage just quoted by stating his own response to the question he has just posed: "The answer is in the affirmative. There is nothing wrong with the pure logic of socialism". He goes on to note on p. 173 that, "The economist who settled the question in a manner that left little to do except elaboration and the clearing up of points of secondary importance, was Enrico Barone". The phrase "general logic of choice" can be found in n. 5 of p. 176, and on p. 182, of the same work.—Ed.]

happen in the real world requires additional knowledge about the process by which information is transmitted or communicated.[16] Like so many mathematical economists Schumpeter appears to have been seduced by the habitual assumption of 'given data' to believe that the relevant facts that for his construction the theorist must assume to exist are actually known to any one mind. This becomes evident in Schumpeter's most startling assertion that the possibility of "economic rationality", being attained in a planned system, follows for the theorist "from the elementary proposition that consumers in evaluating ('demanding') consumers' goods *ipso facto* also evaluate the means of production which enter into the production of those goods".[17] This is a meaningful statement only in the context of a system or equation in which not only all the technical possibilities of production but also their relative scarcities are assumed to be known. As an assertion about what happens in the real world it is sheer nonsense. Even if we had full information about what Pareto called "the *ophélimités* of all the different commodities for each individual", or even the prices they would be prepared to pay for each of any possible collection of commodities, we could not derive from them alone the prices of the different factors or intermediate products.

Schumpeter's attempt to prove his assertion to the layman characteristically begins by assuming that "means of production are present in given and, for the moment, unalterable quantities". He does not explain to *whom* these quantities are 'given', that is, known, nor how much about their various attributes and potentialities anybody knows. Yet the central planning board will allocate "productive resources—all of which are under its control—to these industrial managements according to certain rules". The first of these is that "they must produce as economically as possible".[18]

IV Schumpeter's equivocations

But if there are no market prices how do they know what is more and what is less economical? Apparently from "stated 'prices'"—presumably fixed by the

---

[16] [Hayek refers to his paper "Economics and Knowledge", which was first published in *Economica*, vol. 4, 1937, pp. 33–54, and subsequently reprinted as chapter 2 of Hayek, *Individualism and Economic Order*. It can now to be found as chapter 1 of *The Market and Other Orders*, in which volume the sections referred to by Hayek are on pp. 60–68.—Ed.]

[17] [Schumpeter defines 'economic rationality' as "a maximum of consumers' satisfaction". This definition, and the words quoted by Hayek, can be found on p. 175 of *Capitalism, Socialism, and Democracy*.—Ed.]

[18] [All of the quotations in this paragraph are taken from Schumpeter, *Capitalism, Socialism, and Democracy*, p. 175.—Ed.]

board. But from which sources does the board know which prices represent the relative scarcities of these resources? All we get in reply is one equivocation after another, but no real explanation. This is surely not worthy of a distinguished thinker. I should perhaps add that it is mostly based on the result of a German doctoral thesis done some years earlier under Schumpeter's supervision, though no more satisfactory on the crucial issues than Schumpeter's own statements (K. Tisch, *Wirtschaftsrechnung und Verteilung im zentralistisch organisierten sozialistischen Gemeinwesen,* doctoral thesis, University of Bonn, Wuppertal-Elberfeld, 1932).[19]

It was probably the influence of Schumpeter's teaching more than the direct influence of Oskar Lange that has given rise to the growth of an extensive literature of mathematical studies of 'resource allocation processes' (most recently summarised in K. J. Arrow and L. Hurwitz, *Studies in Resource Allocation Processes,* Cambridge University Press, 1977). As far as I can see they deal as irresponsibly with sets of fictitious 'data' which are in no way connected with what the acting individuals can learn as any of Lange's.[20]

[19] [Schumpeter uses the phrase "stated 'prices'" on p. 175 of *Capitalism, Socialism, and Democracy,* while the reference to Tisch's dissertation can be found in n. 2 on p. 173 of the same work. Klära—or Clära—Tisch (1907–41?) was a German economist who completed a PhD entitled "Economic Calculation and Distribution in the Centrally Organised Socialist Community" under Schumpeter's supervision in 1931. Her work, which was based on a version of Walrasian general equilibrium theory, was a precursor of the market socialism of Dickinson and Lange. See H. Hagemann, "Clära Tisch (1907–?41)", in *A Biographical Dictionary of Women Economists,* ed. R. W. Dimand, M. A. Dimand and E. L. Forget (Cheltenham: Edward Elgar, 2000), pp. 426–29.—Ed.]

[20] [Kenneth J. Arrow (1921–2017) was an American Nobel Prize-winning economist who made fundamental contributions to many areas of economics, most notably social choice theory, general equilibrium theory, and the economics of information. Leonid Hurwicz (1917–2008) was a Russian-born, American economist who won the 2007 Nobel Prize in economics for his pioneering work in the field of mechanism design (a field of research, often described as the 'engineering branch' of economics, that examines how the design of institutions, or 'resource allocation mechanisms' as they are also termed, affects the outcomes generated by people's behaviour, given that individuals act strategically and possess private information relevant to the decision at hand). The volume to which Hayek refers contains seminal papers in the history of work on mechanism design. See, for example, L. Hurwicz, "Optimality and Informational Efficiency in Resource Allocation Processes" [1960], and L. Hurwicz, "On Informationally Decentralised Systems" [1972], reprinted as pp. 393–412 and pp. 425–459 respectively of *Studies in Resource Allocation Processes,* ed. K. Arrow and L. Hurwicz (Cambridge: Cambridge University Press, 1977). As Arrow and Hurwicz's fellow Nobel Laureate, the American economist Eric Maskin (1950–), has noted, Hurwicz's work was directly inspired by the socialist calculation debate. See E. Maskin, "Friedrich von Hayek and Mechanism Design", *Review of Austrian Economics,* vol. 28, 2015, pp. 247–52. Also see Hurwicz, "On Informationally Decentralised Systems", p. 438, and L. Hurwicz, "The Design of Resource Allocation Mechanisms" [1973], in *Studies in Resource Allocation Processes,* pp. 7–8. Maskin (pp. 247, 251) describes Hayek's work as "an important precursor to the modern theory of mechanism design" and remarks that "Hayek had a

V From calculation to accountability

In the later parts of Lange's exposition, and increasingly in the more recent literature, the claim that in a socialist order economic *calculation* is possible is replaced by the assertion that economic *accounting* is possible without market prices.[21] If by this is meant that the managers of the socialist plants can be held responsible for not defrauding or misusing the resources entrusted to them, nobody will deny this. Any sort of recording in terms of physical quantities or any other magnitude will do this. But it has nothing to do with the original issue of rational allocation of resources. It does not answer any objection ever seriously raised against the capacity of a socialist order to fulfill the promises of its advocates. It is another symptom of the negligence and carelessness with which words have been used throughout this whole, long discussion. The mere idea that the planning authority could ever possess a complete inventory of the amounts and qualities of all the different materials and instruments of production of which the manager of a particular plant will know or be able to find out makes the whole proposal a somewhat comic fiction. Once this is recognised it becomes obvious that what prices ought to be can never be determined without relying on competitive markets. The suggestion that the planning authority could enable the managers of particular plants to make use of their specific knowledge by fixing uniform prices for certain classes of goods that will then have to remain in force until the planning authority learns whether at these prices inventories generally increase or decrease is just the crowning foolery of the whole farce.

A reconsideration of the discussion in which I took an active part more than 40 years ago has left me with a rather depressing view of the somewhat shameful state of what has become an established part of economic science, the subject of 'economic systems'. It appears to me that in this subject political attractiveness has been preserved by the flimsiest of arguments. The kindest thing one can say is that some well-meaning people have allowed themselves

---

remarkable intuitive understanding of some major propositions in mechanism design—and the assumptions they rest on—long before their precise formulation".

Hayek's remarks in the main text suggest, however, a certain scepticism about whether the literature on mechanism design did justice to his 'intuitions'. In particular, as Hayek states, while models such as those developed by Hurwicz treat information as being dispersed amongst the inhabitants of the economy, they nevertheless assume that it is known by, or given to, the individuals who possess it independent of the market process. However, as noted in footnote 10 above, it is precisely this assumption, that knowledge exists outside of the rivalrous process of market competition, that Hayek calls into question. Hayek's concerns about mechanism design theory are developed at greater length by D. Lavoie, "The Market as a Procedure for the Discovery and Conveyance of Inarticulate Knowledge", *Comparative Economic Studies*, vol. 28, 1986, pp. 1–19.—Ed.]

[21] [See Lange, "On the Economic Theory of Socialism", pp. 81–82, 86–98.—Ed.]

to be deceived by the vague and thoughtless language commonly used by specialists in the theory of these issues.[22]

---

[22] [An insightful assessment of the state of opinion prevailing in the field of comparative economic systems about the outcome of the socialist calculation debate is provided by D. Lavoie, *Rivalry and Central Planning: The Socialist Calculation Debate Reconsidered* (Cambridge: Cambridge University Press, 1985). Lavoie argues that while the consensus within the literature on comparative systems in the 1970s and early 1980s was that market socialists such Lange had developed an effective response to Mises's and Hayek's argument, thereby winning the debate, this standard interpretation was based on an erroneous reading of the Austrian case against planning. Most commentators interpreted the Austrian critique using the same neoclassical concepts that Lange and his fellow market socialists employed to express their arguments in favour of planning, most notably the static notion of general economic equilibrium and the view of competition as a state of affairs in which nobody has the power to affect market prices ('perfect competition'). This left them unable fully to appreciate the merits of the Austrians' case against planning, which was based on a vision of the market as an ongoing process of rivalrous competition between price-setting firms that generates the knowledge required to ensure orderly outcomes. Lavoie's book was instrumental in shifting the balance of opinion within the profession towards the view that it was in fact the Austrian side of the debate that had prevailed.—Ed.]

THIRTY-ONE

LETTERS TO *THE TIMES*, 1931–1981

Preface[1]

The first of this series of letters to *The Times* extending over a period of fifty years was written on November 25, 1931, a few weeks after taking up my professorship at the London School of Economics. It is the only one here reprinted which never appeared and I hardly expected that it would be printed. But to my surprise I received in early April 1932 proofs for corrections. Naively I returned them with the request that the letter should be printed with the original date, thereby provoking the inevitable reply in a letter from the editor dated April 10, 1932 saying that "the Editor quite appreciates that you may feel that the timeliness of your letter has now passed, and for that reason may wish to withdraw it", and that "it would be against the invariable rule, and also against our experience of our correspondents' wishes, if an old date was retained as you suggest, when the letter is published". All the other letters here reprinted did appear on the dates indicated, except No. 2 of which only part was printed under "Points from Letters".

I ought to explain why I deliberately refrained from including in this collection the one letter bearing also my signature which has been more frequently mentioned in discussions than any here reprinted and which appeared on October 19th, 1932 over the signatures of my colleagues Theodore A. G. Gregory, Arnold Plant, and Lionel Robbins (as they then were) as well as mine. That letter was wholly drafted by these colleagues and though, when I was invited to sign it I at first suggested some modifications (not intended to soften its argument!) my colleagues rightly persuaded me that fine theoretical points were not suitable for a letter to the press.[2]

---

[1] [This Preface, and the first hitherto unpublished letter to which Hayek refers in the opening paragraph, can be found in the Friedrich Hayek Papers, box 63, folder 4, Hoover Institution Archives.—Ed.]

[2] [Hayek refers to Sir Theodore Gregory (1870–1970), who at the time of the letter was Cassel Professor of Economics, Sir Arnold Plant (1898–1978), who was then Professor of Commerce and Head of the Department of Social Administration, and Lionel Robbins (1898–1984), Lord Robbins of Clare Market, who was Professor of Economics and Head of the Department of

I have felt it appropriate to include with all my letters to *The Times* a few which appeared in *The Times Literary Supplement* and *The Sunday Times* as well as some which had grown so long that they were printed as articles. The headings are those given by the editors and the date given is that of publication. The long gap in the 1950s is due to the fact that I was then resident in the United States where I saw English newspapers only very rarely.

The letters are not all about economics.

June 1981   F. A. Hayek

Contents

Economics. See T. Gregory, F. Hayek, A. Plant and L. Robbins, "Spending and Saving: Public Works from Rates", *The Times*, October 19, 1932, p. 10, where it was argued that a revival of investment, as distinct from consumption, was especially desirable as a means of extracting the economy from the slump in which it was then trapped; that it was very unwise for the government to do anything to deter private saving; and that increased public expenditure was particularly unwelcome because, by raising interest rates, it would deter private investment and thereby hinder the recovery. The letter was a response to one published two days earlier, in which a group of economists including John Maynard Keynes argued that reduced spending by private individuals and local government would exacerbate, rather than cure, the problem of unemployment. See D. H. MacGregor, A. C. Pigou, J. M. Keynes, W. Layton, A. Salter and J. C. Stamp, "Private Spending: Money for Productive Investment: A Comment by Economists", *The Times*, October 17, 1932, p. 13.—Ed.]

18. September 9, 1977, "Well-researched" (*Times Literary Supplement*)
19. September 12, 1977, "Defining Economic Terms"
20. February 11, 1978, "The Politics of Race and Immigration"
21. March 1, 1978, "Origins of Racialism"
22. March 9, 1978, "Integrating Immigrants"
23. June 11, 1978, "Can We Trust Money to Government?" (*Sunday Times*)
24. June 13, 1978, "Dispute in the Tory Party"
25. July 11, 1978, "The Dangers to Personal Liberty"
26. August 2, 1978, "Measuring Inflation"
27. August 3, 1978, "Freedom of Choice"
28. October 10, 1978, "The Powerful Reasons for Curbing Union Powers" (article)
29. November 16, 1979, "A Blessing for Britain?"
30. January 12, 1980, "Freeing the Hostages in Tehran"
31. March 5, 1980, "Monetarism and Hyper-inflation"
32. March 27, 1980, "How to Deal with Inflation" (article)
33. March 29, 1980, "Seeing the Budget in Perspective"
34. May 31, 1980, "Testing Time for Monetarism"
35. June 13, 1980, "A Testing Time for Monetarism"
36. January 9, 1981, "The Flaws in the Brandt Report" (article)
37. February 21, 1981, "Interpreting the Economic Trends"
38. March 16, 1981, "Advice and Consent"
39. April 4, 1981, "Beating Inflation Key to Recovery"

1

"England and the Gold Standard"

Unpublished, written November 25, 1931

For several weeks after the suspension of the gold standard there seemed to exist in England so complete an agreement on the cause of this occurrence that it would have been of little effect to point out that to most foreign observers the true explanation seemed to be exactly the reverse.[3] Recently, however, doubts concerning the correctness of this theory seem to have grown stronger, and the report of the opinions expressed by the well-known American economist Dr. B. M. Anderson and by Mr. F. C. Goodenough, chairman of Barclays Bank, which have appeared in your columns, will certainly lead many to

[3] [Britain left the gold standard on September 21, 1931, six years after the country had returned to it at pre-war parity.—Ed.]

reconsider the whole question.[4] It might be useful, therefore, at this point to put before the English public a short statement of the view held by a considerable number of foreign observers whose general attitude to this country cannot be described as unsympathetic.[5]

1. There is no evidence that the United States or France have not 'played the game of the gold standard according to its rules' but that they have 'sterilized' incoming gold.[6] While France, it is true, profiting from the experience of other Continental countries, has not permitted her circulation to expand after stabilisation as quickly as would have been possible, and has in this way avoided the serious stabilisation crisis which took place in other countries, she has not 'buried' any of the incoming gold but has increased her circulation constantly by more than the amount of gold which came in. In the United States, however, during this period an almost unprecedented credit expansion has taken place.

2. But, while no accusation of this order can be levied against the other Great Powers, it is true that Great Britain did not control her circulation (meaning by this not only bank notes, but also bank deposits and all other media of exchange) as gold was flowing out, and during the period 1927–29,

[4] [Hayek refers to American economist Benjamin Anderson (1886–1949), who at the time of Hayek's letter worked for Chase National Bank, and British banker Frederick Goodenough (1886–1934), who was chairman of Barclay's Bank from 1917 until 1934. The column in which Anderson's views are reported is unsigned and entitled "British Gold Policy: American Economist's Criticisms," *The Times*, November 19, 1931, p. 19. The two unsigned columns in which Goodenough's views are discussed are "Currency Problems: Macmillan Report Criticized: Mr. F. C. Goodenough's Address", *The Times*, November 24, 1931, p. 22, and "City Notes: Mr. Goodenough on Currency", *The Times*, November 24, 1931, p. 21.—Ed.]

[5] [A longer account of Hayek's views on the matters discussed below can be found in F. A. Hayek, "The Fate of the Gold Standard" [1932], reprinted as chapter 3 of *Good Money, Part I: The New World*, ed. S. Kresge, vol. 5 (1999) of *The Collected Works of F. A. Hayek* (Chicago: University of Chicago Press).—Ed.]

[6] [None of the words placed in quotation marks by Hayek in this letter appear in the columns to which Hayek refers. The expression "violation of gold standard rules" is used in the column discussing Anderson's views, having been taken from p. 10 of B. Anderson, "The Gold Standard and the American Gold Tradition", *Chase Economic Bulletin*, vol. 11, 1931, pp. 3–18, where he argues that the "collapse of the gold standard in England was absolutely unnecessary. It was the product of a prolonged violation of gold standard rules". The words "the rules of the gold standard game", which Hayek writes in the final sentence of his letter, were used by Keynes in his discussion of the gold standard. See J. M. Keynes, "The Economic Consequences of Mr Churchill" [1925], reprinted as chapter 5 of part III of J. M. Keynes, *Essays in Persuasion*, vol. 9 (1972) of *The Collected Writings of John Maynard Keynes* (London: Macmillan for the Royal Economic Society), p. 220. The phrase 'rules of the game' was also used in the discussion of the working of the gold standard found in paragraphs 46–47 of the Macmillan report, which had been issued in July 1931 and which was discussed in the address by Goodenough reported in *The Times*. See Committee on Finance and Industry, *Report* (Cmd. 3897) (London: His Majesty's Stationary Office, 1931).—Ed.]

although her exchange was continually in difficulties, no step was taken to contract credit—i.e. Great Britain did not (and was the only important country which did not) 'play the game according to its rules'. In addition to the figures quoted in Mr. Goodenough's address one need, as proof of this contention, only mention the fact that Great Britain went off the gold standard with a Bank Rate of 4½ per cent. This is surely the most astounding and unexpected phenomenon of recent monetary history.

3. It was mainly this fact—that the Bank of England carried on an easy money policy at a time when, according to all traditional rules, a high Bank Rate would have been required—coupled with the desire on the side of the American banking authorities not to make the position for the Bank of England more difficult, which made possible an unprecedented expansion of credit in America; moreover, it made it possible in 1927, when a reaction in America was imminent, to speed up this credit expansion to such a degree that the crisis was postponed for another two years, only to assume then the enormous proportions of the present depression.

4. All this means that there has not been too little but too much cooperation between the central banks, and that not the gold standard but efforts aimed at making the gold standard inoperative are the cause of the present monetary troubles.

5. Since the present gold supply has been sufficient to support in the United States one of the most colossal credit expansions which has ever taken place in a country on the gold standard, it is most unlikely that two years later a scarcity of gold should be the cause of the price slump. This price slump can easily be explained by a reaction from the preceding excessive—and artificially prolonged—boom. In fact, if one looks at the statistical data it becomes evident that in the recent past there was only one important country in the world where a scarcity of gold actually existed—namely, Great Britain: and here the scarcity was probably due to essentially the same cause as occasions a shortage of money in the case of a private individual—namely, spending more than is earned.

6. The fact that Great Britain has gone off the gold standard has made it easier and not more difficult for the other Great Powers to remain on gold, because it means that the demand for gold has decreased.

7. Besides this, the others have little interest to see Britain soon return to gold, since a long period of fluctuations of sterling is the one thing which can help them to gain a great part of the financial business which Great Britain has hitherto enjoyed.

8. Great Britain, therefore, is not in a position to exact conditions for returning to the gold standard. And I am bound to add that, to foreign observers, it seems that at the present time most of the demands which are commonly put forward as conditions for your returning to the gold standard mean simply that Great Britain will consent to go back to gold only if the other Powers will

help her to remain on gold even if she continues to infringe the rules of the gold standard game.

2

"Control of Armaments"

The Times, December 28, 1933, p. 6[7]

It is probably safe to say that Germany will never submit to a scheme of control of armaments which appears specially designed to allay the suspicions entertained against her by some of her neighbours. And it must be admitted that any scheme that is to be effective and that is drawn up at the present time with a view to immediate application to Germany, even if intended to apply in the same way to all other nations, is liable to be interpreted in this way. But why not, once we know that full success will not be achieved immediately and that we shall have to work for a more distant goal, begin with putting a detailed scheme of mutual control in operation between some other great Powers between whom no such suspicions exist? This would not only give an opportunity to test its efficacy and to make it more effective where it is found wanting, but also remove the main difficulty to later general application. Surely Germany could not refuse to accept a scheme of mutual control to which, say, France and Great Britain had voluntarily submitted and which had for some time been in operation between these and, perhaps, some other great Powers.

PROFESSOR F. A. Hayek
15, Turner Close, Hampstead, N.W. 11

3

"Gold: Relationship of Stock and Output"

The Times, June 22, 1937, p. 12

TO THE EDITOR OF THE TIMES

Sir,—Your readers may be interested in the preliminary results of an investigation which partly supports and partly supplements the information pro-

---

[7] [This letter has already been reprinted on p. 161 of F. A. Hayek, *Socialism and War: Essays, Documents, Reviews*, ed. B. Caldwell, vol. 10 (1997) of *The Collected Works of F. A. Hayek*.—Ed.]

vided in Mr. R. H. Brand's articles.[8] As Mr. Brand points out, under modern conditions practically all the monetary gold is used as reserve against central bank liabilities and paper money issues, and consequently the significance of changes in the stock of monetary gold and in the annual output of gold can only be judged by comparing them with the aggregate value of central bank liabilities and paper money circulation in the world. Yet since Mr. Loveday, seven or eight years ago, supplied such figures to the Gold Delegation of the League of Nations, no further information on this relationship seems to have become available.[9] The figures given below are the results of an investigation similar to Mr. Loveday's which is being undertaken by the Economic Research Division of the London School of Economics.[10] The first of the two columns gives the size of the stock of monetary gold in the world for the years since 1931 as a percentage (computed at current values) of the total of sight deposits of all central banks plus paper money circulation for practically all countries of the world, while the second column gives the value of the annual production of gold as a percentage of the same figure.

It will be seen that while the increase in these percentages is very considerable, it is hardly such that with a reasonable distribution of gold it would have to be regarded as very alarming. A substantial further increase in the yearly output of gold might, however, materially alter the situation. In such circumstances, if the price of gold were to be maintained, the avoidance of a dangerous credit inflation might well impose on the monetary authorities a burden which under present arrangements might prove very difficult to carry.

The general impression of a much greater abundance of gold than that suggested by the above figures is, of course, due to the concentration of gold in a few countries, particularly the United States and Great Britain. For pur-

---

[8] [British public servant and merchant banker Robert Brand, 1st Baron Brand (1878–1963), was at the time of Hayek's letter managing director of the banking firm Lazard Brothers and a director of The Times Publishing Company. Hayek refers to a series of three articles published in *The Times* on June 16–18, 1937, in which Brand describes the 'gold problem'—that is, the potential difficulties caused by large increases in central bank reserves of gold in the 1930s, especially in the United States and Britain—and the state of gold production and distribution at that time. See The Hon. R. H. Brand, "Gold: A World Economic Problem. I.—Present Stocks and Hoards", *The Times*, June 16, 1937, pp. 17–18; "Gold: II.—A Choice of Solvents", *The Times*, June 17, 1937, pp. 17–18; and "Gold: III.—Two Main Aims", *The Times*, June 18, 1937, pp. 17–18.—Ed.]

[9] [British economist Alexander Loveday (1888–1962) worked for the League of Nations from 1919 until 1946, becoming Director of the Financial Section and Economic Intelligence Service in 1931. Hayek refers to League of Nations, *Interim Report of the Gold Delegation of the Financial Committee* (Geneva: League of Nations, 1930).—Ed.]

[10] [Now see F. A. Hayek, "The Gold Problem" [1937], published as chapter 4 of *Good Money, Part I*.—Ed.]

	I	II
End of —	Per cent.	Per cent.
1931	53.5	1.97
1932	55.6	2.12
1933	62.4	2.39
1934	70.1	2.76
1935	66.6	2.81
1936	73.5	3.31

poses of comparison it might be mentioned that for these two countries alone the proportion of their stock of gold to the sight liabilities of their central banks, &c., amounted at the end of 1936 to approximately 95.5 per cent., while the net inflow of gold into these two countries during 1936 was in the neighbourhood of 14 per cent. of the same figure.

Yours, &c.,
F. A. HAYEK
The London School of Economics and Political
Science (University of London)
Houghton Street, Aldwych, W.C.2

4

"Good and Bad Unemployment Policies"

Sunday Times, April 30, 1944, p. 4 (article)[11]

One of the obstacles to a successful employment policy is, paradoxically enough, that it is so comparatively easy quickly to reduce unemployment, or even almost to extinguish it, for the time being. There is always ready at hand a way of rapidly bringing large numbers of people back to the kind of employment they are used to, at no greater immediate cost than the printing and spending of a few extra millions. In countries with a disturbed monetary history this has long been known, but it has not made the remedy much more popular. In England the recent discovery of this drug has produced a some-

[11] [The article was reprinted as part of F. A. Hayek, *A Tiger by the Tail?* 3rd edn. (London: Institute of Economic Affairs, 2009), pp. 138–42.—Ed.]

what intoxicating effect; and the present tendency to place exclusive reliance on its use is not without danger.

Though monetary expansion can afford quick relief, it can produce a lasting cure only to a limited extent. Few people will deny that monetary policy can successfully counteract the deflationary spiral into which every minor decline of activity tends to degenerate. This does not mean, however, that it is desirable that we should normally strain the instrument of monetary expansion to create the maximum amount of employment which it can produce in the short run. The trouble with such a policy is that it would be almost certain to aggravate the more fundamental or structural causes of unemployment and leave us in the end in a position worse than that from which we started.[12]

MALADJUSTMENTS

The main cause of this kind of unemployment is undoubtedly the disproportion between the distribution of labour among the different industries and the rates at which the output of these industries could be continuously absorbed. At the end of this war we shall, of course, be faced with a particularly difficult problem of this character. In the past the best known disproportion of this kind and, because of its connection with periodical slumps the most important, was the chronic over-development of all the industries making equipment for use in further production.

It is more than likely that these industries, because of the intermittent way in which they operated, have always had a larger labour force than they could *continuously* employ. And while it is not difficult to create by means of monetary expansion in those industries another burst of feverish activity which will create temporarily conditions of 'full employment', and even draw still more people into those industries, we are thereby making more difficult the task of maintaining even employment. A monetary policy aiming at a stable long-run position would indeed deliberately have to stop expansion *before* 'full employment' in those industries had been reached, in order to avoid a new maldirection of resources.

Though this is the most important single instance of structural maladjustments responsible for unemployment, the recurrent depression constitutes only part of our problem. The hard core of persistent unemployment is an even greater menace and is due largely to maldistributions of a different kind which monetary policy can do even less to cure. We must here face the fact that the problem of unemployment is in the last resort a wage problem—a

---

[12] [Hayek draws here, and in several later letters, on his theory of the business cycle, as now set out in F. A. Hayek, *Business Cycles, Part I*, ed. H. Klausinger, vol. 7 (2012) of *The Collected Works of F. A. Hayek.*—Ed.]

fact which used to be well understood but which a conspiracy of silence has recently relegated into oblivion.

WAGES AND MOBILITY

Demand shifts constantly to new articles and industries, and the more rapidly we advance the more frequent such changes become. Though the increased speed of change will necessarily swell the numbers temporarily out of work while looking for a new job, it need not cause an increase of lasting unemployment, or a reduction in the demand for labour as a whole. If movement into the advancing industries were free, they should readily absorb those laid off elsewhere. The new development which more and more prevents this, and which has become the most serious cause of protracted unemployment, is the tendency of those established in the progressing industries to exclude newcomers. If the increase in demand in those industries leads, not to an increase of employment and output, but merely to an increase of the wages and profits of those already established, there will indeed be no new demand for labour to offset the decrease. If every gain of an industry is treated as the preserve of a closed group, to be taken out almost entirely in higher wages and profits, every shift of demand must add to the lasting unemployment.

The very special and almost unique experience of this country in the years after the pound was artificially raised to its former gold value has produced a fallacious preoccupation with the general wage level. Where such an artificial increase of the national wage level is the cause of unemployment, monetary manipulation is indeed the simplest way to cure it. Such a situation, however, is altogether exceptional and not likely to occur, except in consequence of currency fluctuations.

In normal times employment depends much more on the relation between wages in the different industries—or, rather, on the degree of mobility which the wage structure allows. There is little that monetary policy can positively achieve in this connection. Indeed, if Lord Keynes is right in emphasising that workers attach more importance to the nominal figure of their money wages than to real wages, any attempt to meet the problems of wage rigidity by monetary expansion can only increase the immobility which is the real trouble: if money wages are maintained in declining industries the workers will become even more hesitant to leave them in order to break the protective walls sheltering the privileged groups in the advancing industries.[13]

The struggle against unemployment is in the last resort the same as the struggle against monopoly. Need it be added that on this fundamental issue we

---

[13] [A more detailed discussion of this point can be found in F. A. Hayek, "Inflation Resulting from the Downward Inflexibility of Wages" [1958], reprinted as chapter 15 of this volume.—Ed.]

are *not* moving in the right direction? Or that it would be a poor service to the community to pretend that there is an easy way out which makes it unnecessary to face the basic difficulties?

DANGERS AHEAD

It is easy to see how much more serious our problems must become if the present fashion should prevail and if it should become the accepted doctrine that it is the task of monetary policy to make good any harm done by monopolistic wage policies. Even apart from the effect on those responsible for wage policy, who are thus excused the responsibility for the effect of their action on employment, the one-sided emphasis on monetary policy may not only deprive our efforts of full results, but also produce effects as unlooked for as they are undesirable.

While it is true that an intelligent monetary policy is a *sine qua non* of the prevention of large-scale unemployment, it is equally certain that it is not enough. Short of universal compulsion we shall never lastingly conquer unemployment until we succeed in breaking the rigidities of our economic system which we have allowed the monopolies of capitalists and labour to create. To forget this and to trust solely to monetary policy is the more dangerous as it may succeed long enough to make it impossible to try anything else: the more we are induced to delay the more difficult adjustments, because for the time being we seem to be able to keep things going, the greater the sector of our economic system will grow which can be kept going only by the artificial stimulus of credit expansion and ever-increasing Government investment.

It is a path which would force us into progressively increasing Government control of all economic life, and eventually into the totalitarian state.[14]

5

"South Tirol"

The Times, December 22, 1945, p. 5

TO THE EDITOR OF *THE TIMES*

Sir,—Many of your readers must have been dismayed by the dispatch of your Rome Correspondent suggesting that it has been decided to hand the South

---

[14] [Hayek had published a book-length treatment of these issues in the same year as this article was published. See F. A. Hayek, *The Road to Serfdom: Text and Documents*, ed. B. Caldwell, vol. 2 (2007) of *The Collected Works of F. A. Hayek.*—Ed.]

Tirol back to Italy.[15] I trust it is not too late once more to state the reasons why such a decision would be both unwise and unjust. The Tirol has for hundreds of years been one of the most closely knit communities of Europe, with its own tradition of a free peasantry, known in few other German-speaking regions. The severance of the South Tirol not only tore out its natural centre of gravity but left the rest of the Tirol as two unconnected parts, thus inevitably creating further centrifugal tendencies. The demand for reunion is based not on nationalistic grounds but on much more intimate ties, and it has been pressed with rare persistence throughout the years of Italian control of the southern parts. The treatment of the South Tirolese by the Italians, even before the advent of Fascism worse than anything known until then in modern times in any part of Western or Central Europe, has made the population more unwilling than ever to endure it further.[16]

[15] [Hayek refers to a brief news item entitled "Return of Italian Territory", *The Times*, December 13, 1945, p. 4, in which the newspaper's anonymous Rome correspondent wrote that according to an announcement made by the Allied Military Government then in charge of Italy, various occupied territories were shortly to be returned to Italian administration, including the South Tirol.—Ed.]

[16] [The South Tyrol, as it is more commonly written in English, was part of the Austrian Empire under the Hapsburgs but in 1915 was allotted to Italy under the terms of the Treaty of London, as part of efforts made by Britain, France and Russia to entice that country to enter World War I on their side. That decision was subsequently endorsed by U.S. President Woodrow Wilson (1856–1924), contrary to the principle of self-determination to which Wilson ostensibly committed, and agreed on as part of the Treaty of Saint-Germain in 1919. While the Italians had promised to respect the distinctive culture of the region's predominantly German-speaking inhabitants, the rise of Fascism saw significant efforts to 'Italianise' the South Tyrol, involving measures—such as Italian being made the official language of the courts and government, as well as the mode of instruction in schools, the dismissal of German officials, and the encouragement of Italian immigration—designed to erode the cultural identity of the South Tyroleans. Hayek, who often spent his holidays in the South Tyrol, became involved with the 'Committee on Justice for the South Tyrol', a group whose other members included Hayek's friend the economic historian Sir John Clapham (1873–1946) and whose goal was the return of the area to Austria after World War II. Hayek wrote two brief essays on their behalf: "The Economic Position of the South Tyrol", in *Justice for the South Tirol!* (London: Justice for the South Tyrol Committee, 1944), whose subject-matter is readily apparent from its title; and F. A. Hayek, *The Case of the Tyrol* (unpublished pamphlet, 1944, located in the London School of Economics Archives, JC/E32). In this second essay, Hayek sketches the distinctive history of the South Tyrol, gives an account of the process of Italianisation, and describes its current population and economy. He argues on strategic, cultural and economic grounds for a return of the region to Austrian control. In handwritten notes inside the front cover, Hayek states that while he wrote the pamphlet for the South Tyrol Committee, "as it was first printed while I was absent from London and could not revise the draft or the proofs, I did not allow it to appear under my name". Notwithstanding the efforts of Hayek and the other members of the Committee, it was decided after World War Two that the region should remain part of Italy, with the South Tyrolese being afforded little scope for running their own affairs and protecting their own culture and

The specious strategic argument on which the Italian demands are based is entirely fallacious. The highest chain of the Alps in these parts happens to be that which can be most easily crossed, while the real barriers are formed by the hard outer shell of rugged limestone mountains within which the community of the Tirol has grown up. "The two ranges of mountains that go from the Stelvio Pass and the Dobbiaco Pass toward the Salorno gap", which, to quote the distinguished Italian historian Professor Gaetano Salvemini, "would have been an almost perfect line of division between Germans and Italians", are also the strongest strategical frontier. Professor Salvemini (in an article in *Foreign Affairs* for 1944) even went so far as to argue that "if things were today what they were in 1939 there would be no doubt in [his] mind that the South Tirol should be severed from Italy". We know now that the attempted transfer of population has not been carried so far as seemed probable when Professor Salvemini wrote and the uncertainty on this score made him "doubtful what would be a fair solution of this problem".[17]

There are not many errors of the treaties of 1919 which have been openly recognised by both President Wilson and Mr. Lloyd George.[18] The cession of the South Tirol to Italy is one of the few exceptions. It would be an evil augury for the new order we are trying to create if it refused to correct a mistake so candidly admitted by those who made it, and so universally condemned by all impartial observers when the consequences became known.

Yours, &c.,
F. A. HAYEK
8, Turner Close, N.W. 11

identity. See T. Parks, "Tyrol: Retreat to Reality", *The New York Review of Books*, vol. 51, May 27, 2004.—Ed.]

[17] [Gaetano Salvemini (1873–1957) was an Italian politician, historian and writer who, at the time of Hayek's letter, was teaching at Harvard University. Hayek refers to G. Salvemini, "The Frontiers of Italy", *Foreign Affairs*, vol. 23, 1944, pp. 57–65, quoting with a few very minor changes from p. 65. The addition in square brackets is Hayek's.—Ed.]

[18] [Woodrow Wilson's biographer reports him as viewing the cession of South Tyrol as "an action which he subsequently regarded as a great mistake and deeply regretted". See R, Baker, *Woodrow Wilson and World Settlement*, vol. 2 (Garden City, NY: Doubleday, Page & Co., 1922), p. 146. In a similar vein, British Prime Minister David Lloyd George (1863–1945) subsequently wrote that, "It must be admitted that the hacking of essentially Tyrolean villages and valleys from the rest of the Tyrol was incompatible with the principles of self-determination implicitly embodied in the original war aims of Allied Statesmanship". See D. Lloyd George, *Memoirs of the Peace Conference*, vol. 1 (New Haven: Yale University Press, 1939), p. 10.—Ed.]

6

"Portraits of J. S. Mill,"

Times Literary Supplement, November 11, 1949, p. 733[19]

Sir,—John Stuart Mill's appearance is generally known only from portraits taken very late in his life. The only known early portraits are the Daguerreotype reproduced as frontispiece to Volume 1, and the cameo or medaillon reproduced opposite page 233 of H. S. R. Elliot's edition of the *Letters of John Stuart Mill* (1910).[20] The latter is undoubtedly the earlier and almost certainly identical with, or at least derived from, a portrait of Mill done by an artist named Cunningham in Falmouth in April, 1840, when Mill was in his thirty-fourth year. It is mentioned in Caroline Fox's *Memories of Old Friends*, and referred to as a medaillon in an unpublished letter by John Sterling to Mill of the same year.[21]

The present whereabouts of the originals of both these portraits are unknown. They were almost certainly in the possession of the late Miss Mary Taylor, the granddaughter of Mrs. J. S. Mill, who died in 1918, but no portrait of Mill described as such can be traced among the effects which were sold after her death. It is to be feared that they were not recognised as portraits of Mill, and are lost, but it may not yet be too late to recover them for some national collection where they clearly belong. At the moment I am anxious to trace the medaillon for reproduction in an edition of the correspondence between Mill and Harriet Taylor, which is almost ready to go to press.[22]

---

[19] [This letter has already been republished as chapter 17 of F. A. Hayek, *Hayek on Mill: The Mill-Taylor Friendship and Related Writings*, ed. S. Peart, vol. 16 (2015) of *The Collected Works of F. A. Hayek*. For more on English philosopher, political economist, and social reformer John Stuart Mill (1806–73), see F. A. Hayek, "Liberalism" [1978], reprinted as chapter 1 of this volume, p. 18 n. 24.—Ed.]

[20] [The Daguerreotype is reproduced as the frontispiece of volume 1 of Mill's *Letters*, while the cameo or medaillon appears opposite p. 233 of the second volume. See *The Letters of John Stuart Mill*, 2 vols., ed. H. S. R. Elliot (London: Longman, Green and Co., 1910).—Ed.]

[21] [Cornish diarist Caroline Fox (1819–71) wrote in her diary entry for April 10, 1840, that, "Cunningham showed us his portrait of J. S. Mill, which is very beautiful; quite an ideal head, so expanded with patient thought, and a face of such exquisite refinement". See C. Fox, *Memories of Old Friends, Being Extracts from the Journals and Letters of Caroline Fox, of Penjerrick, Cornwall, From 1835 to 1871*, 2nd edn., ed. H. N. Pym (London: Smith, Elder and Co., 1882), vol. 1, p. 168. Elsewhere, Hayek records that the letter written to Mill by Scottish writer and poet John Sterling (1806–44) can be found in the Library of King's College, Cambridge, and that in the letter Sterling refers to the portrait as a 'medaillon', a word which Hayek uses here in place of the more common term 'medallion'. See Hayek, *Hayek on Mill*, p. 28 n. 31.—Ed.]

[22] [See F. A. Hayek, *John Stuart Mill and Harriet Taylor: Their Correspondence and Subsequent Marriage* (Chicago: University of Chicago Press, 1951), now republished—with the amended subtitle,

I should be most grateful to any of your readers who might be able to help me in this or in identifying the artist.

F. A. HAYEK
London School of Economics
Houghton Street, W.C.2

7

"Incidents in S. Tirol: Harsh Treatment by Police"

The Times, August 3, 1961, p. 9

TO THE EDITOR OF *THE TIMES*

Sir,—Yesterday I had an opportunity in one of the more remote valleys of the Italian Tirol to speak at length to two native men who a few days before had been subject to examination by the *carabinieri*. The men were produced at my request by an old friend in the locality whom I know to be absolutely reliable.

They were both quiet, solid men in their late thirties, married and with families, member of their parish council (*municipalità*) and highly respected in their community—the least likely type of men to engage in any violent activity. They had been arrested at their work, refused permission to inform their families or even to get a coat, taken in their shirts to the local *carabinieri* station and kept there *incomunicado* for three and a half days.

The arrest was evidently solely for the purpose of obtaining information, as no definite charges were brought against the two men, who were merely asked about the activities of others about which they were supposed to know. Before they were examined they were kept standing at attention for 10 and over 20 hours respectively and beaten with hands and fists in face and body whenever they ever so slightly relaxed their position.

They were also left without food or drink for 36 hours after their arrest. Both men were medically examined two days after their release and I have seen the certificates issued by the local Medical Officer of Health. Besides bruises and other signs of heavy beating shown by both men, one had suffered a broken jaw, confirmed by X-rays. The police examination—in Italian, which both men understood only imperfectly, and without any assistance—followed the treatment described with every intimation that the latter would

Their Friendship and Subsequent Marriage—as Part I of *Hayek on Mill.* A reproduction of the medaillon can now be found on p. 145 of *Hayek on Mill.*—Ed.]

be resumed if the men did not tell all they knew. They were ultimately released with the threat that they would soon be fetched again.

Both men were so frightened by this experience that they could be induced to talk about it only by the firm promise that I would not mention their names. From my knowledge of the people of the district I have not the slightest doubt that their account of what happened to them is true in every particular.

In these two cases, I am assured by my local friends, the treatment was comparatively mild because it was obvious that the two men could not possibly have any direct connexion with the acts of violence.[23] One of my friends, a Merano lawyer, told me of two other men, his clients, not available at the moment, who at the *carabinieri* station had been made to stand on the tips of their toes up to 24 hours, been beaten on the soft parts of their necks till these had swollen to twice their normal size, and then examined for hours with two strong lights playing on their eyes.

All this refers to a quiet region at some distance from the scene of the bomb outrages. Very much uglier stories are told and believed by responsible people, including the parish priest of one of the most disturbed regions, about what has been happening farther south. They include in particular the assertion that suspects have been forced during their examination to drink some turbid liquid and that, if they refused, their mouths were opened with tools and the liquid poured down their throats.

The nature of the confessions published has much strengthened the widely held belief that drugs have been used to obtain them. The phrase current among the local people is that the methods employed by the police are indistinguishable from those employed in Hungary after the rising.

Particular indignation has been caused by the report of a reply supposed to have been given by Signori Scelba to a delegation of South Tirolese members of the Italian Chamber of Deputies who waited upon him to protest against the procedure of the police and to whom he is said to have suggested that those were the methods of the police in the whole world. The memory of the South Tirolese is long enough to know that this is not true.[24]

[23] [After World War Two, frustration on the part of the South Tyrolese at the Italian government's refusal to grant them sufficient autonomy ultimately led to violence, with a campaign of bombing that targeted Italian infrastructure beginning in 1956 and culminating with the destruction of thirty-seven electricity pylons on the night of June 11, 1961 (an event that is likely to be the "bomb outrages" to which Hayek refers in the next paragraph of this letter). The level of violence escalated later in the 1960s, with the targeting of Italian security forces leading to several deaths. The conflict came to an end only in 1972, after the signing of an agreement under which the South Tyrol was granted significant autonomy and the rights of its German-speaking inhabitants protected. See Parks, "Tyrol: Retreat to Reality."—Ed.]

[24] [Italian politician Mario Scelba (1901–91) was a former Prime Minister of Italy who in the early 1960s became Minister for the Interior. He was infamous for the ruthless tactics he deployed in discharging his duties, and under his leadership complaints about the inhumane

There can be no doubt that recent events have persuaded many of them who after 1946 had fully resigned themselves into the inevitability of the incorporation of their country into Italy, that Italian rule is intolerable.

Yours faithfully,
F. A. HAYEK
(University of Chicago)
Obergurgl, Tirol, Austria
July 30

8

"Indonesia: The Generals"

Sunday Times, November 5, 1967, p. 10

Arriving at Rome Airport from Djakarta early on Sunday morning, it was good to be met by the Sunday Times with Henry Brandon's sensible article on Indonesia. It needs to be supplemented, however.[25]

First, the 'generals' who now govern Indonesia are mostly not what we would regard as military men. They are in many instances men coming from other professions who in the fight for independence have risen in rank and remained in the army to ward off communism.

Secondly, nobody could be more aware of the extent of corruption than the generals. Under Sukarno the number of civil servants was increased to several times the country's needs and the Government is unable to pay them a salary on which they can live.

---

treatment of prisoners by the police were common in the South Tyrol. See R. Steininger, *South Tyrol: A Minority Conflict of the Twentieth Century* (London and New York: Routledge, 2003), p. 125.—Ed.]

[25] [Hayek refers to H. Brandon, "Suharto Has a Problem His Guru Can't Solve", *The Sunday Times*, October 29, 1967, p. 7. Brandon reports concerns amongst Indonesians about the increasing influence of the army, and about widespread corruption in the military, but also describes how some Indonesians regarded military rule as the only means of reforming the economy and keeping order in the face of a Communist insurgency. The country had been governed since 1949 by Indonesian politician Sukarno (1901–70), who led the country's independence movement and became its first President (1949–67), establishing an increasingly authoritarian, anti-market regime. At the time of Brandon's article, Sukarno had just been deposed by the army under General Suharto (1921–2008), who was President from 1967 until 1998. Suharto's military regime, which reduced government intervention in the economy and encouraged foreign investment, oversaw high rates of economic growth as well as significant corruption, the restriction of civil liberties and the suppression of dissent until he was forced to resign in 1998.—Ed.]

On the other hand it would be politically fatal to dismiss a large number as they would create an intellectual proletariat which would acutely endanger the political stability.

Rome

F A Hayek

9

"'Literarism' versus 'Scientism'"

Times Literary Supplement, May 21, 1970, p. 564[26]

Sir,—As I appear to be partly responsible for the current vogue of the term 'scientism' I would like to protest against its constant use in such a vague sense as to deprive it of any precise meaning. In *Economica* in 1942 I proposed that

> wherever we are concerned, not with the general spirit of disinterested inquiry but with slavish imitation of the method and language of Science [the capital 'S' indicating that I was speaking of natural science]—we should speak of 'scientism' or the 'scientistic prejudice'. Although these terms are not completely unknown in English, they are actually borrowed from the French, where in recent years they have come to be generally used in very much the same sense in which they will be used here. It should be noted that,

---

[26] [Hayek's letter was one of several written in response to an article published in *The Times Literary Supplement* by English literary critic F. R. Leavis (1895–1978). In "'Literarism' Versus 'Scientism': The Misconception and the Menace", *Times Literary Supplement*, April 23, 1970, pp. 441–44, Leavis inveighs against scientism, a notion he attributes not to Hayek but to British scientist and writer C. P. Snow (1905–80) and to English novelist and critic Aldous Huxley (1894–1963). For Leavis, scientism involves an emphasis on the over-riding importance of science in education, leading to a dismissal of the great creative writers of the nineteenth century and after on the grounds that they have few insights into the modern technological age. But this view is mistaken, Leavis argues, because there is more to modern life than science can comprehend; scientific analysis excludes human creativity and therefore cannot do justice to all the attributes of a good life in the way that great literature can. Leavis's essay culminates in an assault on what he describes as the technologico-utilitarian conception of the university as a factory that ought to be run to full capacity throughout the year, a view he ascribes to—amongst others—Hayek's close friend Lionel Robbins, whose 1963 review of British higher education recommended a significant increase in student numbers. See Committee on Higher Education, *Higher Education: Report of the Committee appointed by the Prime Minister under the Chairmanship of Lord Robbins* (London: Her Majesty's Stationary Office, 1963). Responses to Leavis' essay appeared in the April 30, May 7, 14, 21, and July 16 and 23 issues of the *Times Literary Supplement*, but none discussed Hayek's ideas.—Ed.]

in the sense in which will shall use these terms, they describe, of course, an attitude which is decidedly unscientific in the true sense of the word, since it involves a mechanical and uncritical application of habits of thought to fields different from those in which they have been formed. The scientistic as distinguished from the scientific view is not an unprejudiced but a very prejudiced approach which, before it has considered its subject, claims to know what is the most appropriate way of investigating it.[27]

The target of my criticism then was not the natural scientists, but the majority of the sociologists. After all I have since learnt on the true character of scientific method (and its misunderstanding by many of the scientists themselves), chiefly from Sir Karl Popper, I would wish to put my argument in many ways differently than I did then.[28] The characteristic feature of scientism now seems to me that it insists on applying the techniques that were developed for the explanation of essentially simple phenomena to the explanation of essentially complex phenomena. There are wide fields in which explanation cannot successfully be accomplished by relying on 'laws' which represent a magnitude as a function of at most two or three others, as physics has so successfully done for many phenomena which for this reason are regarded as 'physical' or 'mechanical'. There exist in the world essentially complex phenomena in the sense that they occur only when a great multiplicity of different events interact—events which are yet not numerous enough to make them accessible to statistical treatment. It is in the scientific treatment of these "problems of organised complexity", as Dr Warren Weaver has called them, that the prejudice of scientism has done so much harm.[29]

F. A. HAYEK
Firmianstrasse 17a, Salzburg

---

[27] [Hayek quotes, with a few very minor alterations and the addition of the words in square brackets, a passage found on p. 269 of F. A. Hayek, "Scientism and the Study of Society", *Economica*, vol. 9, 1942, pp. 267–91. Now also see F. A. Hayek, *Studies on the Abuse and Decline of Reason: Text and Documents*, ed. Bruce Caldwell, vol. 13 (2010) of *The Collected Works of F. A. Hayek*, p. 80.—Ed.]

[28] [See F. A. Hayek, "Degrees of Explanation" [1955] and F. A. Hayek, "The Theory of Complex Phenomena" [1964], reprinted as chapters 6 and 9 respectively of F. A. Hayek, *The Market and Other Orders*, ed. B. Caldwell, vol. 15 (2014) of *The Collected Works of F. A. Hayek*.—Ed.]

[29] [Warren Weaver (1894–1978) was an American mathematician who distinguished between problems of simplicity, disorganised complexity, and organised complexity in W. Weaver, "Science and Complexity", *American Scientist*, vol. 36, 1948, pp. 536–44. The words quoted by Hayek appear on p. 539 of Weaver's article. Weaver's influence on Hayek's account of the nature of science, along with that of philosopher Karl Popper (1902–94), is discussed on pp. 14–15 of B. Caldwell, "Introduction", in Hayek, *The Market and Other Orders*.—Ed.]

10

"Wittgenstein"

Times Literary Supplement, February 8, 1974, p. 134

Sir,—As I have not preserved the correspondence which would provide the proof I should not wish to enter into controversy with Professor Anscombe (January 18). But as Professor Bartley's statement (January 11) is based on information I have given him long ago, I must defend him. It is indeed not only my distinct recollection at present, but is confirmed by a note I wrote soon after the event, that I abandoned my plan to complete a longish biographical sketch of Ludwig Wittgenstein because Professor Anscombe, on behalf of Wittgenstein's literary executors, refused me permission to reprint, until they themselves had published them, those letters of Wittgenstein to Bertrand Russell around which I had written most of the early part of my draft.[30]

F. A. HAYEK
Firmianstrasse 17A, A5020
Salzburg, Austria

[30] [The events leading up to the publication of this letter began with the publication by American philosopher and sometime general editor of Hayek's *Collected Works,* William Warren Bartley III (1934–1990), of a biography of Austrian philosopher Ludwig Wittgenstein (1889–1951). The book received considerable attention, not least because of its portrayal of Wittgenstein as "a homosexual given to bouts of extravagant and almost uncontrollable promiscuity". See W. W. Bartley III, *Wittgenstein* (Philadelphia and New York: Lippincott, 1973), p. 33. This claim caused considerable controversy. The philosopher Elizabeth Anscombe (1919–2001), who had been one of Wittgenstein's most devoted students, wrote to the *Times Literary Supplement* to enquire about the evidence upon which Bartley's claims were based. In his response, Bartley stated that the information in his book was based on unnamed sources who were intimately familiar with this aspect of Wittgenstein's life. See G. E. M. Anscombe, "Wittgenstein", *Times Literary Supplement,* November 16, 1973, p. 1401, and W. W. Bartley III, "Wittgenstein", *Times Literary Supplement,* January 11, 1974, p. 32.

In his letter, Bartley also referred to what he described as Anscombe's long-standing opposition to biographical research on Wittgenstein, citing as an example the refusal of Wittgenstein's literary executors—of whom she was one, along with the philosophers Georg Henrik von Wright (1916–2003) and Rush Rees (1905–89)—to permit Hayek to publish some of Wittgenstein's letters before they themselves had done so. One consequence of this, Bartley indicated, was that Hayek had abandoned a biography of Wittgenstein that he had begun to write. Anscombe subsequently denied that Wittgenstein's literary executors had refused Hayek permission to publish the letters in question. See G. E. M. Anscombe, "Wittgenstein", *Times Literary Supplement,* January 18, 1974, p. 55. It was this letter that precipitated the one from Hayek reprinted here. Further correspondence relating to Bartley's book was published in the *Times Literary Supplement* on February 22, 1974, but it did not touch upon issues in which Hayek was involved. A summary and assessment of the controversy created by the publication of Bartley's book can

11

"Keynesian Kaleidics"

Times Literary Supplement, October 4, 1974, p. 1078

Sir,—One can hardly be more ignorant of the Austrian economists than must be your reviewer of G. L. S. Shackle's *Keynesian Kaleidics* (September 20) when he represents them as thinking in terms of a timeless general equilibrium definable in mathematical concepts.[31] Of the post-classical schools of economic theory they were the only ones who eschewed such techniques and argued in terms of a process analysis. If some of the younger adherents of that tradition, including myself, sometimes operated with the equilibrium con-

---

be found in R. Monk, *Ludwig Wittgenstein: The Duty of Genius* (London: Jonathan Cape, 1990), pp. 581–86.

Hayek was a distant cousin of Wittgenstein, and while he did not know the philosopher well, he was familiar with his background and many of his friends, and so viewed himself as well placed to write a biography. Hayek began work in 1953, producing three drafts during that year. However, one of Wittgenstein's sisters raised objections to the project, which contributed to a decision by Wittgenstein's literary executors to ask Hayek to postpone publication until after they had published Wittgenstein's letters to Bertrand Russell, upon which much of Hayek's manuscript was based. He complied with their request, abandoning the project. Nearly a quarter of a century later, Hayek did publish a short reminiscence of Wittgenstein. It focused on their few meetings and made little use of the wider material Hayek had collected. See F. A. Hayek, "Remembering My Cousin Ludwig Wittgenstein (1889–1951)" [1977], reprinted as the Coda to chapter 7 of F. A. Hayek, *The Fortunes of Liberalism: Essays on Austrian Economics and the Ideal of Freedom*, ed. P. Klein, vol. 4 (1992) of *The Collected Works of F. A. Hayek*. However, the third draft of Hayek's manuscript has now been published. See F. A. Hayek, "Unfinished Draft of a Sketch of a Biography of Ludwig Wittgenstein", in *Friedrich August von Hayek's Draft Biography of Ludwig Wittgenstein: The Text and Its History*, ed. C. Erbacher (Leiden: Brill, 2019). The editor's introduction to that volume provides more details about the history of Hayek's manuscript, including the circumstances in which he ceased working on it. See C. Erbacher, "The First Wittgenstein Biography and Why It Has Never Been Published", in *Friedrich August von Hayek's Draft Biography of Ludwig Wittgenstein.*—Ed.]

[31] [English economist George Shackle (1903–92) was Hayek's doctoral student at the LSE in the 1930s. Hayek refers to G. L. S. Shackle, *Keynesian Kaleidics: The Evolution of a General Political Economy* (Edinburgh: Edinburgh University Press, 1974), the anonymous review of which was entitled, "Marshalling Keynes. *Keynesian Kaleidics: The Evolution of a General Political Economy* by Shackle, G.L.S., Professor (author)", *Times Literary Supplement*, September 20, 1974, p. 1022. In the passage to which Hayek takes exception, the reviewer refers to the predominant place in the discipline of economics held by static general equilibrium theory and describes the latter as having Austrian origins.—Ed.]

cept, it was because we had learned it from Walras and Marshall but not from our Austrian masters.

F. A. HAYEK
Firmianstrasse 17A, A-5020
Salzburg

12

"The German Economy"

The Times, December 21, 1976, p. 13

From Professor F. A. Hayek

Sir, You report in your issue of December 18 that Mr Roy Jenkins is concerned about the solution of the fundamental problems of the unbalance caused by Germany being in a position quite different from that of France, Britain and Italy.[32] The solution is the simplest, most obvious possible. That the latter three countries abandon their socialist policies, and they will in a few years be where Germany has arrived now by this method.

Yours sincerely,
F. A. HAYEK
Salzburg, Austria

---

[32] [Roy Jenkins (1920–2003), Baron Jenkins of Hillhead, was a British politician and author. At the time of Hayek's letter, Jenkins was President-elect of the European Commission, having just completed a two-year stint as Home Secretary in the Labour Government led by Prime Minister Harold Wilson (1916–95). The report to which Hayek refers is anonymous and entitled "Jenkins Warning over German Dominance", *The Times*, December 18, 1976, p. 1.—Ed.]

13

"The German Economy"

The Times, December 31, 1976, p. 15

From Professor F. A. Hayek

Sir, For Lord Kaldor (in your issue of December 24) to describe a country that for 27 years has known no nationalization, no price controls, no exchange controls, no investment controls and whose now governing "social democratic" party has publicly committed itself to a market economy as "much ahead in 'socialist policies' of either France, Britain or Italy" suggests an ignorance of the policies he himself has been advising which is somewhat astounding.[33]

It is unfortunately true that Ludwig Erhard's decision of 1949 to scrap all price controls, which made socialist planning impossible and laid the foundation of Germany's prosperity, has recently been somewhat watered down by his successors—with what result, we shall see.[34]

Yours, etc.,
F. A. HAYEK
A-5020 Salzburg
Firmianstrasse 17A

[33] [In his letter, economist Nicholas Kaldor (1908–86), who was a student and teacher at the London School of Economics before moving to Cambridge University, also described West Germany as "the only country in Europe which introduced joint control of workers and shareholders . . . in enterprises of more than 2,000 employees" and as having "(apart from Sweden) the highest and the most comprehensive scheme of social security benefits for old age, sickness and unemployment". See N. Kaldor, "The German Economy", *The Times*, December 24, 1976, p. 13.—Ed.]

[34] [Ludwig Erhard (1897–1977) was economics minister in West Germany from 1949 until 1963 and is widely seen, not least by Hayek, as the main architect of that country's postwar economic recovery. See Hayek, "Liberalism", p. 20.—Ed.]

14

"Liberal Pact with Labour"

The Times, March 31, 1977, p. 15

From Professor F. A. Hayek, FBA

Sir, May one who has devoted a large part of his life to the study of the history and the principles of liberalism point out that a party that keeps a socialist government in power clearly has lost all title to the name 'Liberal'.[35] Certainly, no liberal can in future vote 'Liberal'.

Yours faithfully,
F. A. HAYEK
D-78 Freiburg i Brg,
Urachstrasse 27

15

"Trade Union Immunity under the Law"

The Times, July 21, 1977, p. 15

From Professor F. A. Hayek, FBA

Sir, When will the British public at last learn to understand that there is no salvation for Britain until the special privileges granted to the trade unions by the Trade Disputes Act of 1906 are revoked? Mr Robert Moss is probably right when in his recent book he writes that "the Liberals who blithely passed a Bill drawn up by the first generation of Labour MPs in keeping of an electoral promise quite literally had no idea what they were doing".[36]

But they were soon unmistakably told. A. V. Dicey presently spoke of the Act of 1906 as having conferred "upon a trade union a freedom from civil liability for the commission of even the most heinous wrong by the union or its servant, and in short conferred upon every trade union a privilege and pro-

---

[35] [From March 1977 until July 1978 the Liberal Party participated in the so-called 'Lib-Lab Pact', whereby Liberal MPs supported a minority Labour government led by Prime Minister James Callaghan (1912–2005) in votes in the House of Commons in return for some influence over policy.—Ed.]

[36] [R. Moss, *The Collapse of Democracy* (London: Temple Smith, 1975), p. 102.—Ed.]

tection not possessed by any other person or body of persons, whether corporate or incorporate. The law makes a trade union a privileged body exempted from the ordinary law of the land".[37]

And in 1925 another great jurist, Sir Paul Vinogradoff, again emphasised that "the Trades Disputes Act of 1906 conferred upon the unions an immunity from prosecution on the ground of tortious acts of their agents: the immunity stands in flagrant disagreement with the law of agency and the law as to companies represented by their officers in accordance with the Statutory Order of 1883".[38]

In 1942 a foreign economist intimately familiar with British affairs, the late Professor Joseph Schumpeter, looking back on developments, wrote that "it is difficult, at the present time, to realise how this measure must have struck people who still believed in a state and in a legal system that centred in the institution of private property. For in relaxing the law of conspiracy in respect to peaceful picketing—which practically amounted to legalisation of trade union action implying the threat of force—and in exempting trade union funds from liability in action for damages *for torts*—which practically amounted to enacting that trade unions could do no wrong—this measure in fact resigned to the trade unions part of the authority of the state and granted to them a position of privilege which the formal extension of the exemption to employers' unions was powerless to affect".[39]

[37] [Hayek slightly misquotes a passage from the work of English jurist Albert Venn Dicey (1835–1922). The actual passage states that the 1906 Trade Disputes Act "confers upon a trade union a freedom from civil liability for the commission of even the most heinous wrong by the union or its servants, and in short confers upon every trade union a privilege and protection not possessed by any other person or body of persons, whether corporate or unincorporate, throughout the United Kingdom. This is assuredly a very extraordinary state of the law; it points towards indirect results which have not yet been fully apprehended by the English Public. 1. It makes a trade union a privileged body exempted from the ordinary law of the land. No such privileged body has ever before been deliberately created by an English Parliament". See A. V. Dicey, *Lectures on the Relation between Law & Public Opinion in England* [1917], 2nd edn. (Indianapolis: Liberty Fund, 2008), p. 373. The 1906 Trades Disputes Act afforded British trade unions immunity from liability for damages arising from strike action. It contributed to Britain having for much of the twentieth century a 'voluntarist' system of industrial relations, whereby employers and unions were afforded significant scope to govern the employment relationship unencumbered by formal legal regulation (so-called 'free collective bargaining'). See R. Taylor, "Industrial Relations", in *The Ideas That Shaped Post-war Britain*, ed. D. Marquand and A. Seldon (London: Fontana Press, 1996), and pp. 70–71 of W. Brown, S. Deakin and P. Ryan, "The Effects of British Industrial Relations Legislation 1979–97", *National Institute Economic Review*, vol. 161, 1997, pp. 69–83.—Ed.]

[38] [The Anglo-Russian legal scholar and medievalist Sir Paul Vinogradoff (1854–1925) wrote the words reproduced, with very minor alterations, by Hayek on p. 10 of his *Custom and Right* (Oslo: H. Aschehoug, 1925).—Ed.]

[39] [Hayek refers to Austrian economist and sociologist Joseph Alois Schumpeter (1883–1950), quoting from his *Capitalism, Socialism, and Democracy* (New York: Harper and Brothers, 1942), p. 321 n. 4.—Ed.]

And only twenty years ago Lord MacDermott reiterated that, in short, the act "put trade unionism in the same privileged position which the Crown enjoyed until ten years ago in respect of wrongful acts committed on its behalf".[40]

Yet still, when the fatal effects of this are before everybody's eyes, nobody dares to consider removing the source of all that misfortune.

There can indeed be little doubt to a detached observer that the privileges then granted to the trade unions have become the chief source of Britain's economic decline. It is an illusion to believe that a Labour government is in a better position to deal with the unions. It is no use suggesting to them moderation when they do all that harm by exercising their chartered rights.

A Labour government cannot touch the sacred charter which is the authorisation of all this license. The public hardly yet understands that the power of the trade unions to destroy the economy has been conferred on them as a special privilege by an irresponsible government buying a few more years of power.[41] That fatal mistake must be undone if Britain is to recover. No government can pull the country out of the mire unless it obtains at the elections an explicit mandate to revoke the unique privileges which the trade unions have

---

[40] [John Clarke MacDermott, Baron MacDermott (1896–1979), was Lord Chief Justice of Northern Ireland from 1951 until 1971. Hayek quotes from MacDermott's *Protection from Power under English Law* (London: Stevens & Sons, 1957), p. 174.—Ed.]

[41] [In the early 1970s a Conservative government led by Edward Heath (1916–2005), Prime Minister from 1970 until 1974, attempted to engineer a shift away from voluntarism by introducing a greater role for the law in the conduct of industrial relations. Through the 1971 Industrial Relations Act, Heath sought to impose compulsory 'cooling off' periods and to require that unions ballot their members before going on strike. Financial sanctions would be imposed on unions whose members took industrial action without following the prescribed procedures. In this way, Heath attempted to reduce the scope for strikes and thereby curb the power of the unions, with the ultimate goal of making the labour market more competitive and controlling wage pressure. However, the Act provided a focal point for union resistance and was met by a policy of non-compliance, rendering it ineffective. When in 1974 Heath responded to the prospect of industrial action by mineworkers by calling a general election centring on the issue 'Who governs Britain?', he was defeated, with a Labour Party led by Harold Wilson assuming power. One of the central elements of the Wilson government's policies was the so-called 'Social Contract', an agreement between the unions and the government whereby union leaders pledged to restrict their claims for higher wages in return for the government implementing a range of policies designed to improve the lot of workers, such as price controls, higher pensions, and new rights for maternity leave and sick pay. See W. Brown, "Industrial Relations and the Economy", in *The Cambridge Economic History of Modern Britain*, vol. 3: *Structural Change and Growth, 1939–2000*, ed. R. Floud and P. Johnson (Cambridge: Cambridge University Press, 2004), pp. 410–14, and D. Sandbrook, *Seasons in the Sun: The Battle for Britain, 1974–1979* (London: Penguin Books, 2013), pp. 7–13, 42–46. Hayek would probably have viewed the Social Contract as being like the Trade Disputes Act in the sense that in both cases unions were granted "a special privilege by an irresponsible government buying a few more years of power".—Ed.]

enjoyed too long. Only such a power can enable a Conservative government to reverse the trend towards abject poverty.

I am, etc.,
F. A. HAYEK
Urachstrasse 27
D-78 Freiburg i Brg,
July 14

16

"Trade Union Privileges"

The Times, August 2, 1977, p. 11

From Professor F. A. Hayek, FBA

Sir, It is precisely because I have lived since before the trade unions were granted special legal privileges and much of the time in England, and because I am now living in a country in which the closed shop is constitutionally inadmissible that I have come to the conclusions which Mr Peter Wallington finds incredible (July 27).[42]

What is at issue is not union membership but compulsory union membership and not the right to strike but the right to compel others to strike. There is no need for any other explanation of why the British economy is decaying and the German highly prosperous.

The trade unions, being politically sacrosanct, have been allowed to destroy the British economy, and since even somebody as sympathetic to labour as Lady Wootton has told us that "it is in fact the business of a union to be antisocial", it is high time that somebody had the courage to eradicate that cancer of the British economy.[43]

That in its present structure the British economy is not viable should be

---

[42] [In a letter published under the heading "Stand against Excessive Pay Claims", *The Times*, July 27, 1977, p. 17, Peter Wallington argued that because the British working class became industrially organised before it was politically enfranchised, because the emerging trade union movement faced an openly hostile legal system, and because the law was biased in favour of organised capital over organised labour, the immunities afforded the unions were in fact warranted and ought to be preserved.—Ed.]

[43] [Barbara Wootton, Baroness Wootton of Abinger (1897–1988), was a British sociologist and criminologist. The statement quoted by Hayek can be found in B. Wootton, *Freedom under Planning* (London: George Allen & Unwin, 1945), p. 97.—Ed.]

clear for all to see. There is no reason to despair and accept it as an incurable deadly disease and there is little else than the elimination of these special privileges which Britain needs to be prosperous again. But one must indeed emancipate oneself from the prejudices which have governed "the unfolding saga of industrial relations in Britain over the last six years"[44] and look at the long-run causes of the decline of the British economy if one is to understand how it can be helped to recover.

Yours faithfully,
F. A. HAYEK
Obergurgl
Tyrol,
July 28.

17

"Trade Union Privileges"

The Times, August 20, 1977, p. 13

From Professor F. A. Hayek, FBA

Sir, Mr Arthur Palmer (August 10) surely has so far forgotten old English traditions which have made this country great that he confuses obeying a law which everybody has to obey with obeying dictates of the state. The trouble is that British trade unions refuse to accept the law which applies to everybody else.[45]

Since some people still seem to feel doubts that this is the chief cause of the British economic decline it might be helpful if, as an impartial test, the House of Commons invited the leaders of some of the great corporations which attempt to conduct similar enterprises in Britain and other European countries to give evidence on their experience in the respective countries. I suspect that for instance Mr Henry Ford II might have much useful information to give on why his German firm has just quintupled its profits over last

---

[44] [Hayek quotes from Wallington's letter.—Ed.]

[45] [Arthur Palmer (1912–94) was a Labour Party MP who, responding to Hayek's letter of August 2, described him as contrasting British trade unions' refusal to obey the dictates of the state with the willingness of the German trade unions to do so. Palmer went on to suggest that this difference reflected the histories of the British and German people, in particular their respective contributions to the cause of freedom. See A. Palmer, "Trade Union Privileges", *The Times*, August 10, 1977, p. 15.—Ed.]

year while one understands that his British firm has been a constant source of worry to him.

Yours faithfully,
F. A. HAYEK
Obergurgl, Tyrol, Austria
August 10

18

"Well-researched"

Times Literary Supplement, September 9, 1977, p. 1080

Sir,—Is it too late to protest against the monstrosity of the 'well-researched book' which now appears more and more frequently even in the *TLS*? One can do research 'into', 'after' or 'for' a subject and this subject may possibly be a book which is supposed to exist, and the result of such research may be a book, but in that case it cannot have been researched for. It is possible to describe the object one has frequently or intensively searched for in a book, but that does not make such a book a legitimate grammatical direct object of the verb 'research'.

It is perhaps a usage introduced to dignify the work of the backroom girls of the 'media' who look through card indexes and encyclopedias to assemble the information the editorial writer needs. But to call the work of a scholar or scientist 'well researched' is offensive. Shall we next read that Newton's *Principia* or Einstein's general theory of relativity were 'well researched'? Even a well-researched biography is an absurdity. If the term were intended to ridicule pretensions of scholarship or pseudo-scientific make-belief one might tolerate its jocular use. But any reputable scholar or scientist ought to reject with disdain such left-handed praise and at least reviewers of books ought to master the English language sufficiently not to become inadvertently offensive.

F. A. HAYEK.
Hotel Edelweiss, Obergurgl, Tirol.

19

"Defining Economic Terms"

The Times, September 12, 1977, p. 13

From Professor F. A. Hayek, FBA

Sir, With 'reflation' appearing again a couple of times on the front page of yesterday's edition of *The Times*, Lady Wootton's pertinent question about the meaning of the term in her letter of a few days earlier, deserves a plain answer.[46] In the present circumstances 'reflation' does and can mean only one thing which those who call for it do not dare to describe by its proper name, *viz*, accelerating the inflation.

Yours faithfully,
F. A. HAYEK,
Obergurgl, Tyrol, Austria,
September 6.

20

"The Politics of Race and Immigration,"

The Times, February 11, 1978, p. 15

From Professor F. A. Hayek, FBA

Sir, Nobody who has lived through the rise of the violent anti-semitism which led to Hitler can refuse Mrs Thatcher admiration for her courageous and out-spoken warning.[47] When I grew up in Vienna before World War I the estab-lished Jewish families were a generally respected group progressively merging with the rest of the population and all decent people would frown upon the occasional anti-Jewish outbursts of a few popular politicians. In fact the only

[46] [See Lady Wootton of Abinger, "The Meaning of Reflation", *The Times*, August 30, 1977, p. 11.—Ed.]
[47] [In a television interview broadcast on January 30, 1978, Margaret Thatcher (1925–2013), who was at the time the leader of the opposition Conservative Party, remarked that people in Britain "are really rather afraid that this country might be rather swamped by people with a different culture". See unnamed author, "Mrs Thatcher Fears People Might Become Hostile If Immigrant Flow Is Not Cut", *The Times*, January 31, 1978, p. 2.—Ed.]

serious nationalistic agitation I can remember from that time was directed against the Czechs who had been streaming into Vienna in large numbers and were beginning to create their own schools.

It was the sudden influx of large numbers of Galician and Polish Jews, fleeing before the invading Russians, which in a short period changed the attitude through a large part of society. They were too visibly different to be readily absorbed in what was still a fairly homogeneous population. I was shocked on my visits to Vienna in the early 1930s to find people who had not long before regarded as indecent any anti-semitic remark (including a good many people of Jewish descent) arguing that, though they detested Hitler, they had to agree with his anti-semitic policies—which, of course, had not yet revealed their most dreadful forms.

It was those recollections, confirmed by much that I observed later elsewhere, which made me write some 10 or 12 years ago without yet being aware of the acuteness of the problem in Britain, what I would like to be permitted to repeat here:

"While I look forward, as an ultimate ideal, to a state of affairs in which national boundaries have ceased to be obstacles to the free movement of men, I believe that within any period with which we can now be concerned, any attempt to realise it would lead to a revival of strong nationalist sentiments and a retreat from positions already achieved.

"However far modern man accepts in principle the ideal that the same rules should apply to all men, in fact he does concede it only to those whom he regards as similar to himself, and only slowly learns to extend the range of those he does accept as his likes. There is little legislation can do to speed up this process and much it may do to reverse it by re-awakening sentiments that are already on the wane".[48]

Whether we can undo the mistakes we have made in the past is another matter. But to be sensible in the future, we must first recognise that they were mistakes.

I am, etc.

F. A. HAYEK,
Urachstrasse 27
D-7800 Freiburg (Breisgau).

---

[48] [These words can be found in F. A. Hayek, *The Mirage of Social Justice*, vol. 2 (1976) of *Law, Legislation and Liberty* (Chicago: University of Chicago Press; London: Routledge, 1973–1979), p. 58.—Ed.]

21

"Origins of Racialism"

The Times, March 1, 1978, p. 13

From Professor F. A. Hayek, FBA

Sir, I certainly must protest against Mr Bernard Levin's interpretation (February 14) of what I said in the letter you were good enough to print on February 11.[49] I never suggested that "racialism is really all the fault of the victims, who only have to remain sufficiently few, sufficiently inconspicuous and sufficiently unsuccessful, for it to go away". What I argued was that experience has shown, regrettably, that ordinary man only slowly reconciles himself to a large increase of foreigners among his neighbours, even if they differ only in language and manners, and that therefore the wise statesman, to prevent an unpleasant reawakening of primitive instincts, ought to aim at keeping the rate of influx low.[50]

Concerning the letter of Mr Willi Frischauer in the same issue of *The Times*,[51] in which he suggests that I am either deceived by my memory or ignorant of Austrian political and social history, I will here only say that, though he may have gained that impression from history books, it was definitely not that of the generation who lived through and much discussed the consequences of the developments in the second decade of the century during the third and fourth.

Yours faithfully,
F. A. HAYEK,
Urachstrasse 27, D-78 Freiburg, Breisgau.

---

[49] [Bernard Levin (1928–2004) was educated at the LSE, where he was mentored by Harold Laski and Karl Popper, and became one of the most famous and controversial British journalists of the second half of the twentieth century. The article to which Hayek refers is B. Levin, "What Mrs Thatcher Might Have Said", *The Times*, February 14, 1978, p. 14.—Ed.]

[50] [For more on Hayek's views on "primitive instincts", see F. A. Hayek, "The Atavism of Social Justice" [1978], reprinted as chapter 27 of this volume.—Ed.]

[51] [Willi Frischauer (1906–78) was an Austrian journalist and author. See W. Frischauer, "Austrian Anti-Semitism", *The Times*, February 14, 1978, p. 15.—Ed.]

22

"Integrating Immigrants"

The Times, March 9, 1978, p. 17

From Professor F. A. Hayek, FBA

Sir, I have been puzzled before why the indignant protests about my letter of February 11 which you printed and the more abusive letters I received at home should insist to treat as a problem of race what I had been at pains to show was a problem of acculturation.[52] But since you yourself now publish a further letter from me (March 1) under the heading "Origins of racialism", you will perhaps permit me to make more precise what has evidently been misunderstood.

I had in my first letter deliberately dragged in the example of Czech immigration into Vienna before 1914, when probably something like a quarter of Vienna's population was of Czech descent, but which led to street riots as soon as a large number of new immigrants attempted to establish their Czech Komensky schools. Nothing like these riots demanding discriminatory government action had in recent history there been directed against the Jews until the flood of (differently dressed!) refugees from Galicia arrived.

The point is that acculturation is of necessity a slow process and may almost stop when the new immigrants are numerous enough to form their own communities. This, regrettably, is almost universally resented by an indigenous population.

Yours faithfully,
F. A. Hayek,
Urachstrasse 27, D-7800 Freiburg (Breisgau).
March 3.

[52] [The letters to which Hayek refers include G. Fink, "The Politics of Race and Immigration", *The Times*, February 15, 1978, p. 11; R. Glass, "The Politics of Race and Immigration", *The Times*, February 16, 1978, p. 13; and N. Kaldor, "The Rise of Hitler", *The Times*, February 15, 1978, p. 11. Kaldor's main claim was that "Professor Hayek (February 11) seems to forget that the main factor responsible for the rise of Hitler to power was not the immigration of Jews into Germany (which was negligible) but the increase of unemployment from one million in 1928 to seven million in the summer of 1932", the blame for which "lies with the 'monetarist' policies of the German Chancellor, Dr Brüning and his resolute refusal . . . to take any positive steps to reflate the economy". The conclusion Kaldor drew was that, "Mrs Thatcher would do well to ponder whether effective action for increasing employment would not be far more important and effective than further tightening of immigration as a means of preserving democracy in Britain."—Ed.]

23

"Can We Trust Money to Government?"

Sunday Times, June 11, 1978, p. 14

All concerned about the fatal course of monetary policy in most of the world must be profoundly grateful for the revelations about how monetary policy is made in the recent series of articles by Stephen Fay and Hugo Young (Review Front).[53]

Before I comment on the wider significance of the developments they describe, I hope you will allow me to point out a basic misconception which suggests that they tacitly accept the decisive error apparently shared by most participants in the controversy.

Probably the most frequently occurring technical term was 'deflation'. There was in fact no occasion ever to mention it. None of the parties involved in the dispute ever advocated deflation in the only meaningful sense of that term. The difference was entirely between groups who wanted more and others who wanted less inflation. But apparently nobody dared to suggest that inflation be stopped altogether.

It is true, of course, that to reduce the rate of inflation, or even to slow down its rate of increase below that which has come to be expected, produces effects somewhat similar to those of deflation. But this must happen sooner or later once a country has embarked on a course of inflation, since to maintain the stimulating effect which it has only as long as it turns out to be faster than was foreseen would lead to the sort of hyper-inflation which completely destroys any economic order.

[53] [Hayek refers to three articles by S. Fay and H. Young: "How the Hard Money Men Took over Britain. The Day the £ Nearly Died: Part I", The Sunday Times, May 14, 1978, pp. 33–35; "The Callaghan Offensive. The Day the £ Nearly Died: Part 2", *The Sunday Times*, May 21, 1978, pp. 33–35; and "How the Cabinet Embraced the IMF. The Day the £ Nearly Died: Part 3", *The Sunday Times*, May 28, 1978, pp. 33–34. Fay and Young recount how, faced with rapidly diminishing reserves of foreign currency with which to support the pound, whose value on the foreign exchanges had fallen well below two dollars, the British government was forced in late 1976 to seek a loan from the International Monetary Fund designed to restore faith in sterling. Conditions included cuts in public expenditure and reductions in the rate of growth of the money supply. The advent of monetary targeting did not, however, indicate a thoroughgoing conversion to monetarism; the Callaghan government continued to rely upon incomes polices to control inflation, reflecting a continued commitment to cost-push theories of inflation. The advent of full-blooded monetarism would have to wait until the election of Mrs Thatcher as Prime Minister in 1979. See pp. 283–87 of P. Hall, "Policy Paradigms, Social Learning, and the State: The Case of Economic Policy-Making in Britain", *Comparative Politics*, vol. 25, 1993, pp. 275–296, and Sandbrook, *Seasons in the Sun*, pp. 467–504.—Ed.]

The bitter necessity of causing such a 'stabilisation crisis' becomes inescapable once an expansionist policy has been pursued for any length of time. But the responsibility for the inevitability of such painful measures rests wholly with those who have in the first instance recommended an expansionist monetary policy as a palliative.

But the chief significance of your reporters' description of how governments determine monetary policy seems to me to be that it should, in any thinking persons, destroy all hope that we can ever again get from governments even tolerably good money.

Governments were prevented from grossly abusing their monopoly of the issue of money only as long as public opinion imposed upon them the discipline of the Gold Standard. This beneficial discipline, based on a quasi-religious belief, I am afraid cannot be restored. But no democratic government freed from this discipline can resist the pressure of those groups which it can temporarily help out of some difficulty by manufacturing a little more money.

Yet the necessity of governments possessing a monopoly to issue a distinctive national currency seems natural or inevitable only because this has always existed. Governments have always enforced it to secure power and sources of finance. But it could never be argued, and has never been shown, that this was necessary or even beneficial to the smooth flow of economic activities.

Competing private issuers, offering distinctive monies under different names, could stay in this profitable business only by offering the public good money—that is one it preferred to hold—making contracts, keeping accounts and calculating in. The public would soon show which kind of standard it preferred and only issuers who kept the value of the money they issued strictly to that standard could hope to stay in the business.[54]

Only when free enterprise is allowed to equip itself with the kind of money it needs to function properly can we now hope ever again to get decent money.

F A Hayek
University of Freiburg

[54] [Hayek elaborates on the argument sketched here in F. A. Hayek, "The Campaign against Keynesian Inflation" [1978], reprinted as chapter 25 of this volume.—Ed.]

24

"Dispute in the Tory Party"

The Times, June 13, 1978, p. 19

From Professor F. A. Hayek, FBA

Sir, Watching from a distance I find it surprising that the dispute in the Tory party in the face of an impending election should puzzle so many British commentators. It seems to me inevitable that at this stage genuine differences should appear within the party.

I have no way of knowing Mrs Thatcher's mind. But from her public statements it seems to me clear that Mrs Thatcher takes the statesmanlike view that it is more important to be placed in a position in which she can save Britain from accelerating economic decline than to win the next election. There can be little doubt that her high aim would require decisions as Prime Minster of which we still do not know whether the general public would yet be prepared to support them.[55]

The majority of the prospective Tory candidates are naturally and understandably primarily concerned about winning a seat in the coming election and feel that their chances may be reduced by what I have seen described as Mrs Thatcher's 'extremism'. There may be some foundation for this. But nothing could damage the long-run prospects of the Tory party more than being elected with a large majority without the authority of throwing round the rudder of policy.

If the country is not yet prepared for this, a statesman and patriot should prefer being defeated in the election to being charged with a task in which he has not the support of the public. This is perhaps not a view one can expect the run of members of Parliament to take. But I still hope that the British

---

[55] [An indication of Hayek's motivation for writing this letter may perhaps be found in private correspondence with William Rees-Mogg (1928–2012), editor of *The Times* from 1967 until 1981, in which, having referred to "a division within the Conservative Party as between the expediency of short term tactics and the desirable strategy" of challenging the legal privileges enjoyed by the unions, Hayek described Mrs Thatcher as being "on the right side needing support". The letter reproduced here was no doubt intended to help provide such support. See F. A. Hayek to W. Rees-Mogg, October 8, 1977, Friedrich Hayek Papers, box 101, folder 29. Hayek also suggested that, were she to announce the revocation of the unions' privileges, "Mrs. Thatcher, though she might risk winning the election, would get considerable credit even from the rank and file (though certainly not the leaderships) of the trade unions". This was indeed a perceptive observation, as one of the reasons why Mrs Thatcher won the 1979 general election was a widespread belief even amongst trade unionists that the unions had become too powerful.—Ed.]

people will honour Mrs Thatcher for putting the long-run interests of the nation above the short-run prospects of her party. The country will not be saved by the Tories being elected, but it may be saved by what they can do, but not a party dependent on the trade union leaders who owe their power to the very privileges which the law has granted them but which must be revoked. To hope for the necessary change from the negotiations with the trade union leaders is a phantasma. But the mandate for the necessary action may be obtained by appealing over their heads to the workers at large. The world belongs to the courageous and not to the timid.

Yours faithfully,
F. A. HAYEK,
Urachstrasse 27, D7800 Freiburg (Breisgau), Germany.

25

"The Dangers to Personal Liberty"

The Times, July 11, 1978, p. 15

From Professor F. A. Hayek, FBA

Sir, It is perhaps not surprising that the prop which has upheld a minority socialist government should be anxious to deny the conception that the prime danger to personal liberty today comes from the left. But Mr Steel (July 3) must be contradicted when he resorts to misrepresentations. If Conservatives are really "more forthright about the indissoluble link they proclaim between liberty and private enterprise than about the central link between liberty and democracy", they are surely right to stress what Mr Steel apparently does not understand and to be less emphatic about a phrase which is constantly abused.[56]

---

[56] [Hayek refers to D. Steel, "A Plea for Non-selective Liberty", *The Times,* July 3, 1978, p. 14. David Steel (1938–) was leader of the Liberal Party from 1976 until 1988. It was under his leadership that the Liberal Party participated in the 'Lib-Lab Pact'. In his article, Steel argued that by conceptualising liberty primarily in economic terms, Mrs Thatcher had adopted an impoverished conception of freedom that failed to do justice to the importance of political and civil liberties. Steel cited as an example of the dangers to which such an approach might give rise the case of Chile, where a democratically-elected socialist government led by Salvador Allende (1908–73) was overthrown in 1973 and replaced by a military dictatorship led by General Augusto Pinochet (1915–2006). In that case, Steel observed, the restoration of economic free-

A limited democracy might indeed be the best protector of individual liberty and be better than any other form of limited government, but an unlimited democracy is probably worse than any other form of limited government, because its government loses the power even to do what it thinks right if any group on which its majority depends thinks otherwise. If Mrs Thatcher said that free choice is to be exercised more in the market place than in the ballot box, she has merely uttered the truism that the first is indispensable for individual freedom while the second is not: free choice can at least exist under a dictatorship that can limit itself but not under the government of an unlimited democracy which cannot.[57]

It is simply not true that a free society *requires* "social justice and an equitable distribution of wealth and power, which in turn require a degree of active government intervention", or that "we have not yet [. . .] created the conditions of liberty for all our citizens". The other boons may also be desirable, but it is simply an abuse of language to represent them as part of liberty with which in fact the striving for them may come into conflict. Mr Steel indeed confirms the old saying that with a little massage 'liberty' can be made to mean anything.

May I finally suggest that in his political pronouncement Mr Steel ought to mind his language. Even penalties for obscene publications would not mean "censorship". I wonder whether he can explain to me what "support for action on sex discrimination" means in English. And in his last paragraph, I hope unwittingly, he has made a major contribution to the debasement of political discussion. When he writes that "some professed defenders of liberty in Britain, on this definition, are guilty of criminal intent", and the only expression preceding it which in any sense may be called a definition is the last but one sentence preceding it about "the narrow 'freedom' for the privileged few which right-wing economists somehow consider worthy of the name", this can logically mean only that people who think as I do "are guilty of criminal intent".[58]

---

dom had been accompanied by the abolition of political liberty and serious abuses of human rights. Steel also argued that the Conservative Party under Mrs Thatcher was paying insufficient attention to the need for a measure of social and economic justice if all citizens were to enjoy genuine freedom.—Ed.]

[57] [For more on Hayek's views on democracy, see F. A. Hayek, "Whither Democracy?" [1978], reprinted as chapter 28 of this volume.—Ed.]

[58] [The quotations in this paragraph come from Steel, "A Plea for Non-selective Liberty". A brief response from Steel to Hayek's letter was published as D. Steel, "Personal Liberty in a Market Economy", *The Times*, July 15, 1978, p. 13, in which he took issue with Hayek's claim that freedom of choice can persist under dictatorship and argued that the downtrodden condition of the poorest in society prevented them from making effective use of their putative liberty.—Ed.]

I will concede him the *Narrenfreiheit* so to designate me, but he must not be surprised if I regret to see the leadership of a once great Liberal party in the hands of a man with such opinions.

Yours faithfully,
F. A. HAYEK
Urachstrasse 27, D-7800 Freiburg, Breisgau, West Germany
July 4

26

"Measuring Inflation"

The Times, August 2, 1978, p. 15

From Professor F. A. Hayek, FBA

Sir, One is used to politicians deliberately using deceptive language. But sometimes one wonders whether they are not deceiving themselves by using language which they do not understand.

When the Prime Minister prides himself in Parliament (July 25) that "inflation was *increasing* at half the rate it was" when his party assumed power, is he aware that he was referring not simply to the rate of inflation but to the rate at which the rate of inflation increased?[59] And would he really claim, if e.g., the rate of inflation had four years ago increased from 1 per cent per annum to 2 per cent, i.e., by 100 per cent, and now was increasing from 10 per cent to 18 per cent per annum, i.e. by 'only' 80 per cent, this was a great achievement? Such a claim would of course be entirely compatible with the rate of inflation having increased all the time!

Yours faithfully,
F. A. HAYEK
Urachstrasse 27, D-7800 Freiburg (Breisgau), West Germany
July 27

[59] [Hayek refers to James Callaghan, who was Prime Minister of the United Kingdom from 1976 until 1979. Callaghan made the claim reported by Hayek in a speech on the economy delivered in the House of Commons on July 25, 1978. See unnamed author, "Mr Callaghan's Pay Policy Test: Not How Many Pounds in the Pocket but How Much They Buy", *The Times*, July 26, 1978, p. 8. The italics in the quotation were added by Hayek.—Ed.]

27

"Freedom of Choice"

The Times, August 3, 1978, p. 15

Sir, Though I can scarcely expect you to find space in your columns for the instruction Mr. William Wallace (July 24) evidently needs, I shall appreciate it if you can do so for a brief reply.[60]

I have certainly never contended that generally authoritarian governments are more likely to secure individual liberty than democratic ones, but rather the contrary. This does not mean, however, that in some historical circumstances personal liberty may not have been better protected under an authoritarian than under a democratic government. This has occasionally been true since the beginning of democracy in ancient Athens, where the liberty of the subjects was undoubtedly safer under the 'thirty tyrants' than under the democracy which killed Socrates and sent dozens of its best men into exile by arbitrary decrees.

In modern times there have of course been many instances of authoritarian governments under which personal liberty was safer than under many democracies. I have never heard of anything to the contrary of the early years of Dr Salazar's early government in Portugal and I doubt whether there is today in any democracy in Eastern Europe or on the continents of Africa, South America or Asia (with the exception of Israel, Singapore and Hongkong), personal liberty as well secured as it was then in Portugal.[61]

More recently I have not been able to find a single person even in much maligned Chile who did not agree that personal freedom was much greater under Pinochet than it had been under Allende.[62] Nor have I heard any sen-

[60] [In a response to Hayek's letter of July 11, Wallace challenged Hayek to offer an example of an authoritarian government that defended freedom better than did a democracy. See W. Wallace, "Defending Freedom", *The Times*, July 24, 1978, p. 13.—Ed.]

[61] [António de Oliveira Salazar (1889–1970) was Prime Minister of Portugal from 1932 to 1968, establishing an authoritarian regime that persisted until 1974. Individual freedom was in fact significantly curtailed from the outset of Salazar's *Estado Novo*: freedom of association was restricted by the abolition of trade unions and all but one political party; and freedom of expression was reduced through censorship and the activities of a secret police force. See, for example, T. Gallagher, "Controlled Repression in Salazar's Portugal", *Journal of Contemporary History*, vol. 14, 1979, pp. 385–402.—Ed.]

[62] [One correspondent wrote in response to this claim of his incredulity at Hayek's failure to appreciate that the absence of dissenting voices reflected the way that critics of the Pinochet regime had been imprisoned, exiled, murdered or intimated into silence. See R. Cohen, "Freedom of Choice", *The Times*, August 7, 1978, p. 13. Equally caustic criticisms were made by Nicholas Kaldor who, having noted that "Chile is a dictatorship equipped with secret police,

sible person claim that in the principalities of Monaco or Lichtenstein, which I am told are not precisely democratic, personal liberty is smaller than anywhere else!

That a limited democracy is probably the best possible known form of government does not mean that we can have it everywhere, or even that it is itself a supreme value rather than the best means to secure peace, a *defensor pacis* or instrument of peaceful change of government. Indeed our doctrinaire democrats clearly ought to take more seriously the question when democracy is possible.

Perhaps they can be induced to reflect on this by pointing to the truism that, except in the direct democracy based on an assembly of all citizens, a democracy can never create itself, but must always be the product of the authoritarian decision of a few—and be this only the decisions about the questions to be asked and the procedure to be followed in a plebiscite. After all, some democracies have been made possible only by the military power of some generals.[63] And my old doubts whether a democracy can be maintained in a country which has not by different institutions been taught the tradition of the rule of law has certainly been only confirmed by recent history.

Yours faithfully,
F. A. HAYEK
Urachstrasse 27
D-7800 Freiburg (Breisgau)
West Germany
July 26

---

detention camps, etc.", went on to argue that "if we take Professor Hayek literally, a fascist dictatorship of some kind should be regarded as the necessary pre-condition (along with monetarism) of a 'free society'". See N. Kaldor, "Chicago Boys in Chile," *The Times*, October 18, 1978, p. 17. Even Mrs Thatcher baulked at some aspects of Hayek's views on Chile, writing in the early 1980s that while the transition from the socialist policies pursued by Allende to a more market-oriented approach under Pinochet constituted "a striking example of economic reform from which we can learn many lessons", it was also true that "in Britain with our democratic institutions and the need for a high degree of consent, some of the measures adopted in Chile are quite unacceptable". See M. Thatcher to F. A. Hayek, February 17, 1982, Friedrich Hayek Papers, box 101, folder 26. Hayek had in fact been informed about concerns about human rights abuses in Chile under Pinochet by one of his former doctoral students. See R. Raico to F. A. Hayek, June 13, 1977, Friedrich Hayek Papers, box 14, folder 20. For additional details, see pp. 345–46 of A. Farrant and E. McPhail, "Can a Dictator Turn a Constitution into a Can-opener? F. A. Hayek and the Alchemy of Transitional Dictatorship in Chile", *Review of Political Economy*, vol. 26, 2014, pp. 331–48.—Ed.]

[63] [For examples of who Hayek has in mind, and a summary and assessment of his argument, see pp. 520–29 of A. Farrant, E. McPhail and S. Berger, "Preventing the 'Abuses' of Democracy: Hayek, the 'Military Usurper' and Transitional Dictatorship in Chile?", *American Journal of Economics and Sociology*, vol. 71, 2012, pp. 513–38. Also see F. A. Hayek, "New Nations and the Problem of Power", *The Listener*, vol. 64, no. 1650, 1960, pp. 819–21.—Ed.]

28

"The Powerful Reasons for Curbing Union Powers"

The Times, October 10, 1978, p. 12 (article)[64]

Sometimes one is forced to doubt whether it is still honest stupidity rather than sinister intention that leads politicians to invert the truth. One of the most glaring recent examples was the attempt to represent the present British trade unions as free institutions. They were when they fought for freedom of association and thereby gained the support of all believers in liberty. They unfortunately retained the support of some naïve pseudo-Liberals after they had become the only privileged institution licensed to use coercion without law.

The coercion on which their present power rests is the coercion of other workers who are deterred by the threat of violence from offering their labour on their own terms. The coercion of enterprise is always secondary and operates through depriving other workers of their opportunities.[65]

The unions have of course now become the open enemies of the ideal of freedom of association by which they once gained the sympathy of the true Liberals. Freedom of association means the freedom to decide whether one wants to join an association or not. Such freedom no longer exists for most workers. The present unions offer to a skilled worker only the choice between joining and starving, and it is solely by keeping non-members out of jobs that they can raise the wages of particular groups of workers above the level they would reach in a free market.

There are certainly many useful tasks unions can perform with respect to the internal organisations of enterprises—questions on which the arrangements of large organisations depend. But they cease to operate beneficially when they are conceded the power of keeping non-members out of a job, or refuse to work with others who prefer different contracts from those which they obtain for their members. The higher wages the unions can thus obtain for those who can be employed at their terms are gained at the expense of those who cannot be thus employed.

Like all other monopolistic control of prices its main effect is to suspend the process which brings about the balancing of demand and supply in the

---

[64] [A slightly amended version of this article was published as part V of F. A. Hayek, *1980s Unemployment and the Unions: The Distortion of Relative Prices by Monopoly in the Labour Market*, 2nd edn. (London: Institute of Economic Affairs, 1984). That pamphlet provides a useful overview of Hayek's views about the unions in the early 1980s.—Ed.]

[65] [For more on this issue, see F. A. Hayek, *The Constitution of Liberty*, ed. R. Hamowy, vol. 17 (2011) of *The Collected Works of F. A. Hayek*, pp. 388–94, 397–98, and Hayek, *1980s Unemployment and the Unions*, pp. 51–53.—Ed.]

different sectors of economic activity. It is in this way that the licensed use of force by the trade unions to determine a structure of relative wages which the individual unions or smaller groups of workers regard as attainable has become the chief obstacle to a high and stable level of employment.

It is a complete inversion of the truth to represent the unions as improving the prospect of employment at high wages. They have become in Britain the chief cause of unemployment and the falling standard of living of the working class.

I prefer to believe that it is doctrinaire blindness rather than a devious attempt to destroy the existing order which can make a politician deny this obvious truth. For a country depending for its livelihood on international trade the endeavour to shelter relative wages against the forces of the international market can have no other effect than growing unemployment at falling real wages. Britain has been led into a position in which it has become impossible to know how its labour force can be deployed most productively.

It was the most extraordinary part of Mr Michael Foot's recent outburst that he represented unions as simultaneously a part of free institutions and the restriction of their coercive powers as a cause of unemployment.[66] The reason why I believe that the license to use coercion conceded to unions some 70 years ago should be withdrawn is precisely that their actions have become the chief cause of unemployment. They bring this about in two ways. The first is the obvious one of an increased demand for some product being absorbed by an increase of the wages of the workers already employed in it rather than by an influx of additional workers, leaving out in the cold those in the industries from which demand has turned.

The second way is less understood but even more serious because it is more permanent. At wages higher than those which would prevail on a free market, employers must, in order to be able to pay them, use the limited amount of capital that is available in a manner which will require fewer workers for a given output. It is true that higher wages can enforce 'rationalisation': they bring this about by making it necessary to use the available capital for equipping a smaller number of workers with more capital per head, leaving correspondingly less for the rest.

All this had been well understood long ago, and it was initially only his despair about the political impossibility of making wages again flexible which led J. M. Keynes to resort to the palliative of temporarily reducing real wages

---

[66] [Michael Foot (1913–2010) was a politician, journalist and writer who served as Secretary of State for Employment (1974–76) and Leader of the House of Commons (1976–79), before becoming leader of the Labour Party (1980–83). Whilst employment secretary, he repealed the 1971 Industrial Relations Act, thereby restoring the legal immunities enjoyed by the trade unions, and played a key role in the negotiations that led to the establishment of the Social Contract. It has proven impossible to identify the precise "outburst" to which Hayek refers.—Ed.]

by inflation.[67] But one may thus for a time evade the difficulties caused by a rigid wage *level*, but not those caused by an artificially fixed structure of relative wages. This is what apparently even some of the more experienced trade union leaders are beginning to understand, but what the illusionists and demagogues of the Labour Party refuse to recognise.

In an ever changing world there is as little chance of the market for labour ever being cleared with rigid relative wages based on some traditional standards as there would be for the different commodities at rigid relative prices. And the power to stop the whole supply of an essential element of production is, of course, the power to kill enterprise. Since there will usually exist some reserves which can sustain life for a time even after an enterprise has been mortally wounded, the demagogues who do not think beyond tomorrow can continue for a time to suck its blood. However, I fear in many instances the process of capital shrinkage is merely temporarily concealed by inflation but will manifest itself as soon as inflation stops, as it must sooner or later.

It will then be vain to ask Government to preserve the existing jobs. The Government can do nothing to force the world to buy British goods. Indeed, the present pressure on it to secure particular jobs is the most certain means progressively to reduce the productivity of the British worker and their earning power in international exchange.

Britain can scarcely hope to be self-sufficient even on a level of great general prosperity; but she can certainly not be a wealthy country without that constant redirection of efforts which in recent times has been so lamentably impeded by the political necessity of enabling people to carry on as before by providing the means out of the pockets of others. The greater we allow the number of those to grow who are maintained in their present employment while producing what the world market will not buy at prices adequate to maintain them at their present level, the greater will be the ultimate catastrophe when the fools' paradise collapses.

There is no hope of Great Britain maintaining her position in international trade—and for her people that means no hope of maintaining their already reduced standard of living—unless the unions are deprived of their coercive powers. So long as they possess them, even the wisest union leaders can, as we see every day, be forced by little groups to exercise them.[68] This is killing

---

[67] [For more on this, see Hayek, "Inflation Resulting from the Downward Inflexibility of Wages."—Ed.]

[68] [One of the defining features of the British system of industrial relations in the first three decades after World War Two was the rise of workplace bargaining, whereby employers increasingly subverted the formal system of industry-level agreements with the unions by engaging in informal bargaining over pay and working practices with groups of workers in individual enterprises. This led to an erosion of the authority of the trade union leadership that culminated in a rash of unofficial strikes during the so-called 'Winter of Discontent' (1978–79), a series of events

enterprise after enterprise and causing a continuous dissipation of capital, the full effect of which we have not yet experienced. As a result of a mistake of legislation in the past they have Britain by the throat and are not intelligent enough to understand that they are killing the hen which lays the golden eggs.[69]

I am not qualified to judge what is today politically possible. That depends on prevalent opinion. All that I can say with conviction is that so long as general opinion makes it politically impossible to deprive the trade unions of their coercive powers, an economic recovery of Great Britain is also impossible.[70]

It is sufficiently alarming when one watches developments in Britain from the inside. But one is reduced to complete despair when one observes what is happening in the rest of the world while Britain remains paralysed by the consequences of the privileges irresponsibly conceded to the trade unions by law. I am writing in the Far East and when one watches here how even Japan is now being beaten in ever more fields by South Korea and other newcomers who have discovered the benefits of free markets, one cannot but shudder when one asks how in a few years' time Britain is to get the food to feed her people.

---

that contributed much to the downfall of the Callaghan government in the 1979 general election. See Taylor, "Industrial Relations", pp. 102–10, and Brown, "Industrial Relations and the Economy", pp. 405–15.—Ed.]

[69] [For an assessment of the empirical basis for Hayek's claims about the significance of the unions in causing unemployment and contributing to Britain's relative economic decline, see R. Richardson, "Hayek on Trade Unions: Social Philosopher or Propagandist?", in *Hayek: Economist and Social Philosopher*, ed. S. Frowen (Basingstoke: Macmillan, 1997). The political significance of Hayek's writings on trade unions is discussed by B. Jackson, "Neo-Liberalism and the Trade Unions, c. 1930–79", in *Classes, Cultures, and Politics: Essays on British History for Ross Mckibbin*, ed. C. Griffiths, J. Nott and W. Whyte (Oxford: Oxford University Press, 2011), pp. 274–77.—Ed.]

[70] [The Thatcher government that came into power in 1979, and was re-elected in 1983 and 1987, gradually introduced legislation designed to remove many of the privileges enjoyed by the unions and thereby curtail their power. The law was changed both to reduce the scope of the immunities enjoyed by the unions, so that it became unlawful to engage in secondary industrial action, secondary picketing, and action in defence of the closed shop, and also to impose various procedural requirements relating to the conduct of industrial action. See Brown *et al.*, "The Effects of British Industrial Relations Legislation," pp. 71–81, and Brown, "Industrial Relations and the Economy," pp. 415–22, for summaries of the legislation and assessments of its significance. The pragmatic approach to the enactment of this legislation, which was introduced on a step-by-step basis, reflected a concern to avoid the kind of problems that had befallen the earlier Conservative government led by Edward Heath, whose 1971 Industrial Relations Act had provided a focus for opposition on the part of the unions and had been decisively rebuffed. A desire to avoid a similar fate led the Thatcher governments to introduce anti-union legislation more gradually in order to avoid confrontation with the unions until the government was confident it could triumph.—Ed.]

This is not merely a question of whether Britain can do without Japanese or Korean cars or other products. It is a question of how other people can be made to buy British ships, or shoes, or steel, or textiles, or chemicals when not only Japanese and Korean factories and shipyards produce them more efficiently and cheaply, but more and more other people surpass Britain in an astounding versatility—and when not only British scientists and engineers but increasingly also skilled British workers find that they can do better in countries whose business structure has not been ossified by trade union restrictions. A drastic change may still provide an outlet, but after another decade during which nobody dares to touch the sacred cow, it will certainly be too late.

29

"A Blessing for Britain?"

The Times, November 16, 1979, p. 13

From Professor F. A. Hayek, FBA

Sir, Congratulations on "The sparks" (leading article, November 13). If *The Times* has learnt all that and will persist teaching it, its calamities may prove a blessing for Britain.[71]

Yours faithfully,
F. A. Hayek
Urachstrasse 27
D=7800 Freiburg (Breisgau)
West Germany
November 14

---

[71] [November 13, 1979, was the first day for almost a year on which *The Times* had been published, the hiatus having been caused by an industrial dispute over the introduction of new technology and manning levels. The article praised by Hayek argued that increases in productivity of the kind those changes were intended to produce were sorely needed throughout British industry. However, the introduction of new, productivity-enhancing technology and working practices was being impeded by the erosion of free labour markets by trade unions. The solution to these problems lay in curbing the unions' power through the withdrawal of their legal immunities, coupled with a campaign to educate the public of the damage caused by the unions and thereby shift public opinion behind the requisite reforms. See Unnamed author, "The Sparks Are Falling on the Gunpowder", *The Times*, November 13, 1979, p. 17.—Ed.]

30

"Freeing the Hostages in Tehran"

The Times, January 12, 1980, p. 13

From Professor F. A. Hayek, FBA

Sir, I am genuinely puzzled by the restraint shown by the United States in the recent emergency and would be grateful to be instructed what the moral or political arguments are against the kinds of steps which in the past any of the great powers would have taken in such a situation.[72]

It seems to me that the future of peaceful international relations and the safety of persons in foreign countries would have been much better served if, after the Iranian Government placed itself outside the community of nations by approving the holding captive of the personnel of the United States embassy, the United States Government had at once sent an ultimatum saying that, unless every single member of the embassy staff were within 48 hours handed over unharmed to representatives of the United States Government at some place outside Iran, bombs would be falling at an increasing rate at the seat of the Iranian Government.

Assuming it to be true that a military operation to free the hostages was impracticable and would probably have led to their being killed, the Iranian Government have created a position in which violence governs. In such a situation, in which the future principles of the relations between nations are at issue, the lives of 50 employees of government cannot count more than those of 50 soldiers in another war situation.

Nobody would hesitate to risk the lives of 50 naval personnel if pirates had placed themselves in command of a modern warship and begun preying upon trade, nor doubt that even the lives of private citizens threatened for blackmail in a foreign country must not be allowed to force government to do anything contrary to the basic laws of the country. I believe that in the long run not only many lives would have been saved but peaceful intercourse between nations been better secured if a government with the power to punish international evil-doers had promptly done so. Is it not yet understood

---

[72] [In November 1979, sixty-six American citizens were taken hostage by Iranian militants who had stormed the U.S. Embassy in Tehran. The crisis ended with the release of the captives in January 1981.—Ed.]

that the new international organisations do not yet possess this indispensable power?

Yours faithfully,
F. A. HAYEK
Urachstrasse 27
D-7800 Freiburg (Breisgau)
West Germany

31

"Monetarism and Hyper-inflation"

The Times, March 5, 1980, p. 17

From Professor F. A. Hayek, FBA

Sir, The newfangled word monetarism means of course no more than the good old name 'quantity theory of money', as it was formulated in modern times by the late Professor Irving Fisher and reformulated by Professor Milton Friedman.[73] Of course I said nearly 50 years ago in the first lecture I delivered in this country that "from a practical point of view, it would be one of the worst things which could befall us if the general public should ever again cease to believe in the elementary propositions of the quantity theory".[74] This was, however, unfortunately brought about by the seductive theories of Lord Keynes. I then said that it was in many respects a crude over-simplification, but the irrefutable chief content is still that inflation is always and everywhere the effect of an excessive supply of money and that it can be cured only by a restriction of its supply. The problem is that in its crude form it provides no adequate measure of what is the supply of money and that not only the supply of all kinds of money but also the demand for them determines its value. This, however, does not alter the fact that its value can be controlled and can be

---

[73] [American economist Irving Fisher (1867–1947) set out the so-called transactions version of the quantity theory of money in I. Fisher, *The Purchasing Power of Money* (New York: Macmillan, 1911). Nobel Laureate Milton Friedman (1912–2006) reformulated the theory as an account of the demand for money in M. Friedman, "The Quantity Theory of Money: A Restatement", in *Studies in the Quantity Theory of Money*, ed. M. Friedman (Chicago: University of Chicago Press, 1956).—Ed.]

[74] [F. A. Hayek, *Business Cycles, Part I*, p. 195. In quoting his own work in this letter, Hayek replaced the phrase "would befall" used in the original text with "could befall".—Ed.]

adequately restricted only by limiting the basic cash, supplied under the existing system by the central bank. Since this is a government institution, all inflation is made by government and nobody else can do anything about it. It does, however, make impracticable the Friedmanite plan of fixing by law the rate at which the quantity of money may and should increase. This would probably produce the greatest financial panic of history.[75]

I trust nobody doubts today that inflation must be stopped. The chief issue is how far this can and ought to be done. On this, I am afraid, my difference from Friedman makes me take an even more radical view than he and most of my friends take. The reason is that the artificial stimulus which inflation gives to business and employment lasts only so long as it accelerates, that is so long as prices turn out to be generally higher than expected. It clearly cannot accelerate indefinitely. But as soon as it ceases to accelerate all the windfalls which kept unprofitable businesses and employments going disappear. Every slowdown of inflation must produce temporary conditions of extensive failure and unemployment. No inflation has yet been terminated without a 'stabilisation crisis'. To believe that it can be slowed down gradually over a period of years means accepting a prolonged misery. No government could stand such a course of prolonged depression.[76] If we want to stop inflation we must do it here and now. It can be done. After World War One the United States brought prices down in six months (August, 1920–February, 1921) by one third! The suffering was great but another six months later a new boom was under way! There is no question now of bringing prices actually down, but merely of stopping all further rise. If this is not done by a determined

[75] [Friedman advocated a fixed money supply rule in M. Friedman, *A Program for Monetary Stability* (New York: Fordham University Press, 1960), and M. Friedman, "The Role of Monetary Policy", *American Economic Review*, vol. 58, 1968, pp. 1–17.]

[76] [The Thatcher governments did not share Hayek's view, expressed here and in other letters published in this chapter, that inflation ought to be reduced rapidly, preferring a more gradual approach. This took the form of the so-called 'Medium Term Financial Strategy' (MTFS), which involved the government setting steadily declining targets for the public sector borrowing requirement and rate of growth of particular measures of the money supply. In Mrs Thatcher's estimation, a more rapid disinflation of the kind advocated by Hayek "would have caused too much social and economic disruption in the short run for it to have been feasible". See M. Thatcher to F. A. Hayek, May 13, 1980, Friedrich Hayek Papers, box 101, folder 26. Hayek expressed his disappointment in an interview published in *The Times* later the same year, lamenting what he saw as Mrs Thatcher's decision to adopt a Friedmanite approach whereby the rate of growth of the money supply would be reduced only gradually and arguing that this would lead to a prolonged period of high unemployment that would prove politically unsustainable. See I. Bradley, "The Hayek Cure: Bigger and Better Bankruptcies", *The Times*, November 21, 1980, p. 12. In fact, notwithstanding a prolonged period of high unemployment in the early 1980s, the Conservative Party did succeed both in reducing inflation and in retaining power.—Ed.]

Government like the present it will not be done before, after a vain attempt of concealing inflation by price controls, the pound finally collapses entirely.

Yours faithfully,
F. A. HAYEK
Urachstrasse 27
D-7800 Freiburg (Breisgau)
Federal Republic of Germany
February 26

32

"How to Deal with Inflation"

The Times, March 27, 1980, p. 16 (article)

That inflation *can* be stopped at any time, and can be stopped *only* by cutting down increases in the quantity of money, I have no doubt whatsoever. What I said nearly 40 years ago in the very first lecture I was ever allowed to give in this country appears to me as true as ever: that "it would be one of the worst things which could ever befall us (but which John Maynard Keynes has unfortunately brought about) if the general public should ever again cease to believe in the elementary propositions of the quantity theory".[77]

I will admit that in its classic form, as now revived by my friend, Milton Friedman, this theory grossly over-simplifies things by making it all an issue of statistical aggregates and averages. Unfortunately the quantity of money is not a measurable homogenous magnitude but consists of a wide range of mutually more or less substitutable things of varying degrees of liquidity.

Secondly, the value of money does not depend simply on the total quantity of it being available, but also on the variable demand for it. And thirdly, the harmful effects of an excessive supply of money consist not merely in the changes of the average price level but quite as much in the distortion of the whole structure of relative prices and the consequent misdirection of productive effort which it causes.

Nevertheless, I have no doubt that inflation is caused solely by an undue increase in the quantity of money and that it can and must be prevented under the prevailing arrangements only by the restriction of the basic money supplied by the central bank. There is no such thing as cost-push inflation; all

---

[77] [Hayek roughly summarises remarks made in Hayek, *Business Cycles, Part I*, p. 195.—Ed.]

inflation is brought about by what that agency of government is made to do. Nobody else can do anything about it.[78]

The chief practical issue today is how fast inflation can be and ought to be stopped. On this, I am afraid, my difference from Friedman makes me take an even more radical position. The reason is that I believe that the artificial stimulus which inflation gives to business and employment lasts only so long as inflation accelerates, that is, as long as prices turn out to be higher than expected.

Inflation clearly cannot accelerate indefinitely, but as soon as it ceases to accelerate, all the windfalls due to prices turning out higher than expected, which kept unprofitable businesses and employment going, disappear. Every slowing down of inflation must therefore produce temporary conditions of extensive failures and unemployment.

No inflation has yet been terminated without a 'stabilization crisis'. To advocate that inflation should be slowed down gradually over a period of years is to advocate a long period of protracted misery. No government could stand such a course.

If we want to stop inflation we must do it here and now. It can be done, after the First World War the United States brought prices down by a third in six months (August 1920–February 1921). The suffering was great, but another six months later a new boom was under way.

There is no question now of bringing prices *down*, but merely of stopping any further rise. If this is not done by a determined government like the present, it will not be done before—after a vain attempt to conceal inflation by price controls (called an 'incomes policy')—the pound finally collapses entirely.

The practical difficulties are due to the fact that, because of the alleged beneficial effect on employment, we have been led into the practice of increasingly financing government expenditure by borrowing—and that at

---

[78] [The diagnosis of inflation as a purely monetary phenomenon afforded the Conservatives significant political benefits once they returned to government in 1979. By suggesting that inflation could be controlled by monetary policy alone, monetarism implied that incomes policies were no longer needed, releasing the Thatcher government from the need to engage in the kind of bargaining with the unions that had proven to be so difficult for Heath and Callaghan. Monetarism thus offered the Conservative Party a way of reasserting its authority after its humiliation under Heath. See J. Bulpitt, "The Discipline of the New Democracy: Mrs Thatcher's Domestic Statecraft", *Political Studies*, vol. 34, 1986, pp. 19–39.—Ed.]

the moment we just do not know how to maintain the existing apparatus of government without continuing to inflate.[79]

F. A. Hayek

This article is an extract from a lecture to the Monday Club last night.

33

"Seeing the Budget in Perspective"

The Times, March 29, 1980, p. 13

From Professor F. A. Hayek, FBA

Sir, May I express my concern to find today (March 27) even a leading article in *The Times* speaking of deflation (or "deflationary policies") when what is meant is a reduction of inflation.[80] I do not deflate a bladder or balloon by blowing a little less strongly into it. Conceptual clarity is important in this connection, just because it is true that the *effects* of reducing the rate of inflation are very similar to the effects of deflation. This will be understood only if it is clearly stated and it is most important that it is generally recognised that in the state into which we have got, an interval of fairly severe depression is inescapable. Yet once this is seen, nobody can believe that it is politically possible to drag out the process over five years. So far as the crucial supply of money is concerned, there can be no doubt that its excessive increase can be terminated in the course of weeks or months. And if this is the only politically pos-

---

[79] [In practice, increasing innovation in UK financial markets led to instability in the demand for money, which in turn meant that relationships between particular measures of the money supply and the rate of inflation were too unreliable to support monetary targeting of the kind that was so central to the MTFS. As a result, by the mid-1980s policy had shifted away from monetary targeting towards a more pragmatic approach that emphasised the exchange rate as an indicator of domestic monetary conditions. See C. Goodhart, "The Conduct of Monetary Policy," *Economic Journal*, vol. 99, 1989, pp. 293–346, and S. Howson, "Money and Monetary Policy since 1945", in *The Cambridge Economic History of Modern Britain.*—Ed]

[80] [Hayek refers to unnamed author, "5 Per Cent Inflation by 1985", *The Times*, March 27, 1980, p. 17.—Ed.]

sible way of stopping inflation, government will have to put its financial house in order over some such period, however painful the process may be.

Yours faithfully,
F. A. HAYEK
Reform Club
Pall Mall, SW 1.

34

"Testing Time for Monetarism"

The Times, May 31, 1980, p. 13

From Professor F. A. Hayek, FBA

Sir, There is no such contradiction between Mr Rees-Mogg's simplified formula about the relation between changes of the quantity of money and changes of the price level and recent events as Mr Godley (May 24) suggests. It is an experience as old as inflation itself that when it accelerates prices begin to rise faster than the quantity of money.[81]

This is readily explained by the circumstance that as further increases of prices come to be generally expected, people try to reduce their cash holdings and the consequent increase of the 'velocity of circulation' magnifies the effect on prices.

But we probably have indeed reached the point where even a further increase of inflation cannot prevent the depression which we have made inevi-

---

[81] [In an article published in 1976, British journalist and editor of *The Times* William Rees-Mogg had argued that monetarism's predictions about the relationship between the money supply and prices were borne out by the British experience between 1965 and 1975. See W. Rees-Mogg, "How a 9.4% Excess Money Supply Gave Britain 9.4% Inflation", *The Times*, July 13, 1976, p. 14. In his letter, British economist Wynne Godley (1926–2010), who was at the time based at the Department of Applied Economics, Cambridge University, argued that the correlation between the rate of growth of the money supply and the rate of inflation had broken down during the period from 1975 to 1980, indicating that "monetarism is failing in a very big way to pass the scientific test set for it by Mr Rees-Mogg". See W. Godley, "Testing Time for Monetarism", *The Times*, May 24, 1980, p. 15.—Ed.]

table by past inflation. It is bound to last as long as we reduce the rate of infla-tion and the only thing we can do about it is to get it over as fast as possible.

Yours faithfully,
F. A. HAYEK
Urachstrasse 27
D-7800 Freiburg
Breisgau
West Germany

35

"A Testing Time for Monetarism"

The Times, June 13, 1980, p. 15

From Professor F. A. Hayek, FBA

Sir, The question which Professor Pearce (June 5) raises is at the same time so important and so complex that it is hardly possible even to sketch an ade-quate answer within the same frame.[82] I am still convinced that, as far as eco-nomic causation is concerned, the value of money is wholly determined by the magnitude of the supply of money in relation to the demand for hold-ing it. In this sense I agree with Professor Milton Friedman that there is no such thing as cost-push inflation. But politically it is unfortunately true that by pushing up wages the trade unions can make it 'politically necessary' to increase the quantity of money, i.e., create a condition in which government believes it must do so.[83]

[82] [Ivor Pearce (1916–2001) was Professor of Economics at Southampton University. In the letter to which Hayek refers, which was written in response to Hayek's letter of May 31, Pearce argued that in the United Kingdom in the 1970s increases in the money supply had been caused by wages increases, rather than being the cause of them, as firms sought to meet wage demands by using money newly created by banks. See I. Pearce, "A Testing Time for Monetarism", *The Times*, June 5, 1980, p. 19.—Ed.]

[83] [Friedman rejected cost-push theories of inflation, famously stating that, "Inflation is always and everywhere a monetary phenomenon, resulting from and accompanied by a rise in the quantity of money relative to output". See M. Friedman, "What Price Guideposts?" in *Guide-lines, Informal Controls, and the Market Place: Policy Choices in a Full Employment Economy*, ed. G. Shultz and R. Aliber (Chicago: University of Chicago Press, 1966), p. 18 (also see pp. 21–25). The cor-ollary is that, as Friedman wrote in a letter to *The Economist* following a visit to Britain in 1974, while unions do considerable harm, they do not cause inflation. See M. Friedman, "Economic Policy", *The Economist*, September 28, 1974, p. 4. Hayek further compares his and Friedman's

For this reason I am even convinced that trade union reform must *precede* monetary reform. It is this which makes the former so exceedingly urgent and is the chief reason why in both fields gradualism cannot help. If, as I believe to be true, with the present power of the trade unions no government that has the power over the supply of money can politically resist the pressure for more money, the urgently needed termination of inflation cannot succeed before the power of the trade unions is curbed. But time is becoming short and it will soon be necessary to proceed on a timetable if the necessary operation is to be completed.

The theoretician must always, and particularly if he lives abroad, hesitate to give advice on what must be a political decision. But if this Government, within its limited life, is to achieve the salvation of Britain, a radical procedure will soon be essential. As I see it, within the time available what is required can be achieved only if the Government, in the near future, obtains through a referendum popular instruction at once to rescind all the special privileges which have been granted to the trade unions by law, and is then ready immediately afterwards to terminate inflation instantly. Only this can make it possible for the beneficial effects of such a policy to manifest itself some time before the term of the present Government runs out.[84]

From the technical point of view there is no serious difficulty about stopping inflation. As the former chairman of the Federal Reserve Board, Arthur Burns, has recently confirmed in a much noticed lecture, the monetary authority can always stop inflation "with little delay".[85] The difficulties are not economic but political and especially problems of government finance. Ending inflation demands that government is deprived of the recourse to the printing

---

views on the role of the unions in inflation in Hayek, "The Campaign against Keynesian Inflation", p. 345.—Ed.]

[84] [Hayek also wrote privately to Prime Minister Margaret Thatcher shortly before the publication of this letter to *The Times*, arguing that "a referendum authorising Parliament to deprive the trade unions of all special privileges" was an essential precursor to a rapid cut in the rate of growth of the money supply in order to control inflation. Thatcher responded in a noncommittal fashion, writing that "we are passing legislation this summer to reduce the privileges of the unions; but we may well need to do more". In response to a subsequent letter from Hayek advocating a referendum, the Secretary of State for Employment, Norman Tebbit (1931–), wrote that, "I have to say that a step so radical as that which you propose, whilst it would galvanise the economy, would I fear be so controversial that it would be frustrated in this over-conservative nation!" See F. A. Hayek to M. Thatcher, April 24, 1980, Margaret Thatcher to F. A. Hayek, May 13, 1980, Friedrich Hayek Papers, box 101, folder 26, and N. Tebbit to F. A. Hayek, September 29, 1981, Friedrich Hayek Papers, box 101, folder 25.—Ed.]

[85] [American economist Arthur F. Burns (1904–87) was chairman of the Board of Governors of the Federal Reserve System from 1970 until 1978. The words quoted by Hayek can be found in A. Burns, *The Anguish of Central Banking: The 1979 Per Jacobsson Lecture* (Belgrade: Per Jacobsson Foundation, 1979), p. 15.—Ed.]

press for financing its expenditure. Government must balance its budget and I admit that it is not humanly possible to do so overnight.

The central problem thus becomes how government can be offered a period up to two years or so during which it can reduce its expenditure so that it will be covered by revenue. But all borrowing in sterling at present would be likely to cause further inflation and impose an unbearable burden.

The only escape I can see is that government obtain the funds which will give it a period during which it can balance its budget by issuing a, chiefly internal, loan in terms of an indexed unit called, say, 'solids'. Large amounts could probably be raised cheaply, at perhaps three or even 2½ per cent, if a public which no longer knows what to do with its savings were offered such an opportunity. It seems to me that the British Government, perhaps undeservedly, enjoys in the world still a reputation for honesty which may make a first experiment of this sort a great success. The 'solids', in terms of which the loan would be issued would have to be defined as, and be redeemable with, so much of a bundle of other currencies as would at the time be required to buy on the world market a 'basket' of a wide range of standard internationally traded raw materials in precisely stated quantitative combinations. Ultimately this unit might become, if necessary, the basis of a new British currency.[86]

Slowness of procedure might at the time destroy all chances. If the present rightly directed efforts fail because of delay, it may be the loss of the last chance of a British recovery for generations. It is not too late yet, but it may be soon.

Yours faithfully,
F. A. HAYEK
Urachstrasse 27
D-7800 Freiburg (Breisgau)
Federal Republic of Germany
June 7

---

[86] [Hayek explores this proposal in greater detail in F. A. Hayek, "The Future Unit of Value" [1981], reprinted as chapter 6 of F. A. Hayek, *Good Money, Part II: The Standard*, ed. S. Kresge, vol. 6 (1999) of *The Collected Works of F. A. Hayek.—*Ed.]

36

"The Flaws in the Brandt Report"

The Times, January 9, 1981, p. 10 (article)

We are constantly being told that a dangerous gap is opening as a result of the richer countries getting richer and the poorer countries getting poorer all the time. There is a certain tautological truth in this in so far as those countries whose wealth is growing rapidly tend to get richer than those where it grows little or not at all. But this does not mean that wealth is growing faster in those countries which were richest a generation or two ago, while those which were the poor are now all getting absolutely or relatively poorer.

Some of the countries which show now the most spectacular growth of wealth started from a very low level of wealth indeed: South Korea, Hong-kong, Taiwan, Singapore, Malaysia, Mexico, Venezuela and, most recently and impressively, Chile, not to speak of the proverbial 'economic miracles' of West Germany and Japan.

On the other hand, countries which 50 years ago were envied as among the wealthiest, like Great Britain, Argentina, or Czechoslovakia, have experienced a sad relative or absolute decline.

The obvious fact is simply that there are conspicuously rising countries and that these are the ones that have developed an effective market economy; and there are countries which have become increasingly socialist and have during this period suffered a relative or absolute decline in their standard of living and their prospects. This is the 'increasing gap', carried by the policies pursued by these countries and by nobody else. We need compare merely West and East Germany, which 30 years ago started equally poor.

The extraordinary feature of the present positions is that the governments who bear the responsibility claim that the socialist principles which have ruined the economies of their countries should be applied internationally to enable them to continue.

I am not questioning that, in the general interest, larger amounts of capital should flow from the wealthy to the poorer countries. That is how in the past economic progress spread. What I am questioning is whether this capital should go to the governments of these countries to enable them to continue with their socialist experiments. I am convinced that by providing the means in this form we harm rather than benefit the people of those countries.

The Western world seems to have been led to its present policies by a silly kind of competition with Russia for the sympathy of those countries. But it is not from the goodwill of the intellectual elites whose misguided doctrines now govern so much of the third world, but from the growing welfare of the masses that we must hope in the long run to derive their friendship. Since the majority of the people of the Western world rightly believe that they owe their wealth to the market economy which they maintain, it would only be reasonable if they confined their assistance to the countries in which they could expect that the people at large would benefit from the investment of capital.

Let the Russians assist those governments which wish to organise their economies on the Russian model and let the 'capitalist' countries confine their help to those where they can believe that what they do will really benefit the people at large.

It is deeply to be regretted that a former Conservative British Prime Minister has joined the former socialist Prime Ministers of Germany, Sweden and elsewhere in the notorious *North-South* report to support the traditional fallacy that poverty can be cured by a massive transfer of wealth.[87] This is not the place in which the basic error of this can be conclusively refuted. I can here only implore all readers who have been moved by the specious plausibility of the Brandt report to study the full analyses which British experts in the field have during the past few months published in various journals, such as Professor P. D. Henderson in *The World Economy* (June), Professors P. T. Bauer and B. S. Yamey in *Commentary* (September) and several others in the current issue of *Encounter*.[88]

They do not argue that no help should be given to the third world but merely that the methods now practised or recommended in the Brandt Report are not only ineffective but would in several ways produce effects opposite to those desired. Personally, I still believe that the alternative I suggested 27 years ago with respect to American help to Europe would equally apply to all Western help to the third world. There seems to me, I then argued, "a strong case for a division of functions between American business and government.

"Let American Government, while withdrawing entirely from direct lend-

---

[87] [*North-South: A Programme for Survival* (London: Macmillan, 1980), widely known as 'Brandt Report', was produced by the Independent Commission on International Development Issues, which was chaired by former Chancellor of West Germany Willy Brandt (1913–92) and whose members included the former Prime Ministers of Britain, Edward Heath, and Sweden, Olof Palme (1927–86). The report sought to outline ways of reducing income disparities between the North and the South, one of which involved an increase in the transfer of resources from the former to the latter.—Ed.]

[88] [Hayek refers to P. D. Henderson, "Survival, Development and the Report of the Brandt Commission", *The World Economy*, vol. 3, 1980, pp. 87–118, and P. Bauer and B. Yamey, "East-West/North-South: Peace and Prosperity?" *Commentary*, vol. 70, 1980, pp. 57–63. He also alludes to "What's Wrong with the Brandt Report?", *Encounter*, December 1980, which contains the following short articles: P. D. Henderson, "Economics Askew", pp. 12–17; K. Minogue, "Between Rhetoric and Fantasy", pp. 17–23; W. Letwin, "The Real Poverty of Nations", pp. 23–27; J.-F. Revel, "A View from Paris", pp. 24–25; and E. Kedourie, "The Politics of Self-Deception", pp. 27–30.—Ed.]

ing, at the same time assume, for a limited period of transition, the role of guarantor against political risks, of private loans to private foreign borrowers, and especially against the risk of the non-transferability of the proceeds of such investments. The economic risk of the particular investment—of the borrower paying interest, or dividends, and repaying the capital in his own country—would still remain entirely with the investor. The United States Government would merely guarantee that any money thus paid to his credit on the borrowing country would become available in free dollars.

"Such a guarantee should of course be given only on loans and other investments made while the borrower's country abided by the undertaking on which the arrangement was based. The appropriate foundation would be an agreement between the United States and the country concerned, in which the latter undertook to refrain from imposing any obstacles to the transfer of returns from such investments, from levying discriminatory taxation, and from acts of expropriation or confiscation affecting such investment. The country concerned would, in addition, agree to assume full responsibility for any debts on which, through its failure to live up to its obligations, the guarantee of the United States Government became effective."[89]

37

"Interpreting the Economic Trends"

The Times, February 21, 1981, p. 13

From Professor F. A. Hayek, FBA

Sir, I take it you would not head an article: 'Withdrawal symptoms increasing despite increasing reduction of drug intake'. Why, then, do you allow your front page to be opened (February 14) by the headline, "Recession deepening despite sharp fall in inflation rate", which makes quite as much sense?[90]

Yours faithfully,
F. A. HAYEK
Urachstrasse 27
D-7800 Freiburg (Breisgau)

[89] [Hayek here reproduces, with a few very minor changes, sentences from p. 483 of F. A. Hayek, "Substitute for Foreign Aid", *The Freeman*, April 6, 1953, pp. 482–84.—Ed.]
[90] [Unnamed author, "Recession Deepening despite Sharp Fall in Inflation Rate", *The Times*, February 14, 1981, p. 1.—Ed.]

38

"Advice and Consent"

The Times, March 16, 1981, p. 13

From Professor F. A. Hayek, FBA

Sir, Since you describe me as one "of Mrs Margaret Thatcher's economic advisers" (March 10)[91] I may be allowed to say that, while I have the greatest admiration for her principles and [am] proud when told that they resemble mine, I am too much aware of my limited knowledge of political possibilities to presume to advise her on particular decisions.

Yours faithfully,
F. A. HAYEK
Urachstrasse 27
D-7800 Freiburg (Breisgau)
March 12

39

"Beating Inflation Key to Recovery"

The Times, April 4, 1981, p. 13

From Professor F. A. Hayek, FBA

Sir, It should surprise no one that the lost generation of British economists who had succumbed to the teaching of Lord Keynes should form a panicky mob when a reversal of the policies they had inspired reveals the damage they have done. They significantly can only refer to, but cannot specify, the "other methods" by which their professed aim can be achieved. (Letter from 364 economists to Mrs. Thatcher.)[92]

[91] [Unnamed author, "Economists Criticize Government", *The Times*, March 10, 1981, p. 2.—Ed.]
[92] [Hayek refers to an open letter criticising the Thatcher government's macroeconomic policies, which was written in the aftermath of a March 1981 budget that saw fiscal policy tightened through increases in taxation even though the British economy was in the midst of the deepest recession since the 1930s. The letter was drafted by Frank Hahn (1925–2013) and Robert Neild (1924–2018), both Professors of Economics at Cambridge University, and signed by 364 econo-

Following their advice has induced a structure of employment that can be maintained only by accelerating inflation but will collapse only when it becomes a gallop and destroys any possibility of a rational use of resources. Nobody has ever claimed that so long as it is necessary to reduce inflation to get out of this vicious circle the effect can be anything but to destroy the particular employments created by past inflation.

Only after inflation has been brought to a full stop can the market be expected to guide workers to jobs which can be maintained without accelerating inflation. All those who plead for 'mild' inflation and oppose 'too much' inflation are merely preparing the ground for a later depression.

If the present Government, I don't believe its head, can be blamed for anything, it is for going too slowly about the job. As I have stressed more than once in these pages, even a very high unemployment will be borne for a short period if it leads in a few months to a condition of monetary stability in which a new recovery can start, in the course of which workers are drawn into employment that will continue without new inflation. All employment which can be maintained only by (even moderate) inflation is a waste of resources for which we shall have to pay later by renewed growth of unemployment.

Lest the readers be unduly impressed by the sheer numbers of the signers of the statement I may perhaps add that, so far as I can see, less than a quarter of the economists who are Fellows of the British Academy have signed that statement.

F. A. HAYEK
Urachstrasse
7800 Freiburg
West Germany
April 1

---

mists based at British universities. Its text was reproduced in a front-page article in *The Times*, namely D. Blake, "Monetarism Attacked by Top Economists", *The Times*, March 30, 1981, pp. 1, 15. While the words placed in inverted commas by Hayek do not appear in the letter, it does refer to "alternative policies".—Ed.]

NAME INDEX

SUBJECT INDEX

"Introduction" in L. Rougier, *The Genius of the West* (Hayek), 86n12
investment: employment and the magnitude of, 212; final demand and, 218; union monopolies as deterrent to, 221–22
'invisible hand,' 304n7, 407
Iranian hostage crisis, 504–5
IS-LM model, 170n18
Italy, South Tirol and, 468–70, 472–74

John Stuart Mill and Harriet Taylor (Hayek), 471n22
"Joseph Schumpeter (1883–1950)" (Hayek), 430n7
judicial review, 14n18
justice: abstract order and, 430n8; to be discovered, not an act of authoritative will, 279; distribution, inapplicability to, 259–60, 283–88 (*see also* distributive justice; social justice); judging a person's actions, criterion for, liii, 268–69 (*see also* remuneration); liberal conception of, liv, 28–29, 279–82 (*see also* rules of just conduct); as a moral value essential for free society, lii–liii, 268; private property and, 281; undermined as an ethical notion by the term 'social,' li, 259–60
just price: Aquinas's support for the notion of, 158n2; Aristotle's notion of, 158n2; concept of, 284
just remuneration/distribution of incomes, 284–86

"Keynesian Kaleidics" (Hayek), 478–79
'Keynesian Revolution,' 210–11
"Kinds of Rationalism" (Hayek), xxxviiin68, lin92, lxiiin120, 274n4, 301n3, 427n2
knowledge: complexity of society and, l–li, 256–57; of data by socialist planners, 446–54; derived from freedom of opinion and of action, 36–37;

dispersed, abstract and general rules make possible the use of, l; dispersed, the market mechanism and, 288, 451–54; limits to individual human, 300–301; market competition as the source of (*see* competition); of men and the world, 193–94; rules and the dissemination/use of, xxxvii–xxxviii; specialisation of (*see* specialisation); tacit, evolved social rules as repositories of, li; utilisation of as the economic problem facing society, 447n7; utilisation of in a self-generating order, xv, 25–26, 300–301; utilised in a spontaneous (*cosmos*) order distinguished from that utilised in a made organisation (*taxis*), 304–5

labour: changing employment as the only safeguard against the power of employers, 234; corporate goals and, 234–35; distribution of, employment and, 205–6; distribution of, monetary expansion and, 203–4; division of, 406; establishing wages compatible with stable money, problem of, 213; mobility of, general demand and, 204–5; monopolistic practices of, 290–91; profit sharing by, 225, 228–29; reduced mobility of, rent control and, 149–50; supply of, impact of rent control on the wage level via the, 152. *See also* employment; unemployment
Labour Party: Galbraith's ideas informing the, xlviii, 250; inflation planned by, 366n34
labour/trade unions: British politics of the 1970s and, 483n41; coercive powers exercised by, 216; competitive order and, 99–100; corporations and the power of, 230; curbing the powers of, 499–503, 512; development of liberal opinion regarding, 99; failure to apply liberal principles to, 34–35; as monopolies, 221–22; new demands of, eco-

nomic context for, 216–19; political power of, monetary policy and, 214; push for higher wages, inflation and, 216–17, 220–21, 345, 354; special privileges granted to, 481–86; syndicalism implied by UAW demands, 228–30; the Thatcher government and, 502n70, 512n84; UAW demands, long-run implications for the economy of, 220–31; in the United States, 215, 219–31; 'Winter of Discontent' for, 501n68

laissez-faire: extreme version of by Cobden and Bright, 17; Hayek's departure from, xlvii, 440–41; the ordo-liberals' departure from, xxi; over-emphasis on, xvii–xviii; "paleo-liberals" who remained committed to, xxin24; Smith's exceptions to, 162

land: conceptions of property become problematic in reference to, 96; development charges and (see development charges in the Town and Country Planning Act of 1947); indispensability in industrial activity, 128–29; market value of, town planning and significance of, 137–38; nationalization of, 139; planning, broader implications of, 140–41

"Land Planning Law in a Free Society" by Charles M. Haar (reviewed by Hayek and Dunham), 134–43

language: confusions about institutions based on, lviii–lix, 301–2; deceptive, politicians and, 496; 'deflation' not the same as reducing inflation, 509–10; 'democracy,' confusion surrounding, 322–27; 'economy' and 'catallaxy,' distinction between, 319–21 (see also catallaxy); 'end' and 'value' as terms for the aims of 'will' and 'opinion,' 315–16; 'nomocracy' and 'teleocracy,' distinction between, 317–18; 'order' as an indispensable term, 303; social orders that are made (taxis) distin-

guished from those that are spontaneous (cosmos), terminology for, lix, 302–6; universal rules of just conduct (nomos) distinguished from rules applicable to particular people or ends (thesis), terminology for, 306–9; "well-researched" in a book review, objection to, 486; 'will' and 'opinion,' distinction between, 311–17

law: all legislative action misunderstood as, liv–lviii, 283, 292–93, 309, 335, 415–17 (see also legal positivism); based on opinion, not will, 293; commands and, distinction between, 293; competitive order and, 95–99 (see also contract[s]; property); conceptions of, older distinguished from today's, 332, 335; of corporations, 98–99; discovered, not created/legislated, lvii, 28–29, 279, 295–96 (see also rules of just conduct); equality before/impartiality of the, xxxii–xxxiv, 119–23; liberal conception of, 23–24, 279–82; public distinguished from private and criminal, lvi, 282–83, 285, 308–9; spontaneous growth of, 275n5; as universal, non-instrumental rules of just conduct, 335–36, lvn103 (see also rules of just conduct). See also rules

Law, Legislation and Liberty (Hayek), xl–xlin74, liii–liv, lxxi–lxxii, 301n4, 401

laws of nature: Continental conception of in the Middle Ages, 9; European theorists of, discussion of economic topics by, 160; liberalism and, 28–29; Stoic conception of, 8

"Legal and Political Philosophy of David Hume (1711–1776), The" (Hayek), 4n2

legal positivism, lvii, 28, 279, 293, 308, 331

legislation: law, distinguished from, lvn103; organisation and conduct of government through, 295–96